UNITED STATES TARIFF COMMISSION

WASHINGTON

RECIPROCITY AND COMMERCIAL TREATIES

GREENWOOD PRESS, PUBLISHERS

WESTPORT, CONNECTICUT

Library of Congress Cataloging in Publication Data

United States. Tariff Commission.
  Reciprocity and commercial treaties.

    Reprint of the 1919 ed. published by the Govt. Print.
Off., Washington.
    Includes index.
    1. Reciprocity. 2. United States--Commercial
treaties. 3. Favored nation clause. 4. Tariff--
Europe. I. Title.
HF1731.U57 1976   382'.9   75-35367
ISBN 0-8371-8598-X

UNITED STATES TARIFF COMMISSION.

Office: 1322 New York Avenue, Washington, D. C.

COMMISSIONERS.

F. W. TAUSSIG, *Chairman.*
THOMAS WALKER PAGE, *Vice Chairman.*
DAVID J. LEWIS.
WILLIAM KENT.
WILLIAM S. CULBERTSON.
EDWARD P. COSTIGAN.

WILLIAM M. STEUART, *Secretary.*

Originally published in 1919 by Government Printing Office,
Washington

Reprinted in 1976 by Greenwood Press,
a division of Williamhouse-Regency Inc.

Library of Congress Catalog Card Number 75-35367

ISBN 0-8371-8598-X

Printed in the United States of America

LETTER OF TRANSMITTAL.

UNITED STATES TARIFF COMMISSION,
Washington, December, 4, 1918.

To the CONGRESS OF THE UNITED STATES:

I have the honor to transmit herewith a report on reciprocity and commercial treaties, prepared by this commission in pursuance of section 704 of Title VII of the act of September 8, 1916.

Very respectfully,

F. W. TAUSSIG,
Chairman.

3

FOREWORD.

The body of the report is preceded by the conclusions and recommendations of the Commission and an introduction and a summary which explain the purposes and scope of the report and summarize concisely its contents.

The body of the report is divided into three sections as follows:

(1) A study of the reciprocity and tariff agreements of the United States, covering the reciprocity treaty with Canada of 1854; with Hawaii of 1875; the agreements concluded under the tariff act of 1890; the agreements concluded and the treaties negotiated, but not ratified, under the tariff act of 1897; the bargaining features of the tariff acts of 1909 and 1913; the Brazilian preferential treatment of American products since 1904; the reciprocity treaty with Cuba of 1902; the attempt of 1910–11 to establish a reciprocity arrangement with Canada; and finally some minor episodes in the commercial relations of the United States with other countries.

Most of the foregoing studies include careful statistical examinations of the commercial effects of the agreements upon the trade of the United States.

(2) A study of the most-favored-nation clause with particular reference to the negotiation and application of reciprocity agreements, the differing theories and practices governing the use of the clause, and possible developments in the near future.

(3) An examination of the tariff systems and commercial policies of European States, including historical surveys of the recent policies and experiences, in relation to tariffs and tariff treaties, of Germany, France, and Russia, and a classification and description of the tariff systems of the important European countries.

Each section is preceded by a table of contents.

The Commission has had the services, among others, of Stanley K. Hornbeck, Jacob Viner, Clive Day, and Walter B. Palmer, in the preparation of this report.

CONTENTS.

CONCLUSIONS AND RECOMMENDATIONS.

The Commission begs to submit to the Congress the following conclusions and recommendations:

Absence of a continuous policy in the past.—The survey of the reciprocity experiences and commercial arrangements of the United States which is made in this report shows that the country has not in the past followed a consistent and continuous policy. It is true that there has been a steady current of opinion in favor of the principle of securing for ourselves and of extending to others equality of treatment. Early American statesmen believed that the offer of equality of opportunity of access to American markets, in return for the removal of the discriminatory barriers which then prevailed in other countries, together with denial of equal treatment to those countries which persisted in discrimination against the trade of the United States, would bring about a general régime of liberal and equal treatment. The method to be employed, however, was that of individual negotiation. Hence arose the special form and interpretation given by the United States to the clause in commercial agreements by which nations engage to extend to each other the most-favored-nation treatment, a clause to whose history and significance detailed consideration is given in Part II of the report.[1] The practice of individual bargaining, which followed inevitably in view of the national circumstances and international situation of the United States through the larger part of its history, has led to special arrangements and has stood in the way of the adoption of a general policy.

To the early liberal attitude of the United States, the States of Europe did not on the whole respond. In the course of time, therefore, as separate and independent commercial arrangements were entered into, the treatment accorded by the United States to different countries became not infrequently unequal. Special agreements and provisions were made in separate cases as they arose. Having begun with the intention to offer equality of treatment, and with the hope of securing such equality in return, the United States has nevertheless been led into commercial relations with individual nations of which the effect was inequality.

During the period before 1890 two isolated agreements were made, those with Canada and with the Hawaiian Islands. Others were negotiated during this period, but were not consummated. Both those projected and those carried out were determined by the particular circumstances of time and conditions. The reciprocity agreements made, subsequently, under the acts of 1890 and 1897, were intended, it is true, to conform to the principles of a fixed general policy. But in operation even these acquired the character of special agreements. Both the policy and the agreements have since been given up.

---

[1] See also in the Summary, *infra*, p. 39.

An opportunist attitude was natural so long as the United States kept aloof from foreign complications and was intent upon avoiding them. Now, however, the situation is completely altered. The United States has become committed to far-reaching participation in world politics. The American Government can no longer shape its commercial negotiations solely with reference to the results of each particular arrangement. It must consider the world at large and must shape its commercial policy in conformity with the political and humanitarian principles which govern its general attitude in the international sphere.

So far as commercial policy and commercial negotiations are concerned, the evidence presented in the present report indicates that a policy of special arrangements, such as the United States has followed in recent decades, leads to troublesome complications. Whether as regards our reciprocity treaties or as regards our interpretation of the most-favored-nation clause, the separate and individual treatment of each case tends to create misunderstanding and friction with countries which, though supposed to be not concerned, yet are in reality much concerned. When each country with which we negotiate is treated by itself, and separate arrangements are made with the expectation that they shall be applicable individually, claims are none the less made by other States with whom such arrangements have not been made. Concessions are asked; they are sometimes refused; counter concessions are proposed; reprisal and retaliation are suggested; unpleasant controversies and sometimes international friction result.

A clear and simple policy needed for the future—Equality of treatment.—A great gain would be secured, now that the United States is committed to wide participation in world politics, if a clear and simple policy could be adopted and followed. The guiding principle might well be that of equality of treatment—a principle in accord with American ideals of the past and of the present. Equality of treatment should mean that the United States treat all countries on the same terms, and in turn require equal treatment from every other country. So far as concerns general industrial policy and general tariff legislation, each country—the United States as well as others—should be left free to enact such measures as it deems expedient for its own welfare. But the measures adopted, whatever they be, should be carried out with the same terms and the same treatment for all nations.

Possible exceptions to the principle of equal treatment.—In the application of any general principle of this kind, there may be occasion for qualifications or exceptions. Some allowance for exceptional treatment, not inconsistent, under certain circumstances, with the principle of equality of treatment, has been made by almost all countries in connection with discussions and negotiations with reference to the most-favored-nation clause. Special treatment, or the concession of special rates of duty, has been regarded as admissible, particularly in two sets of cases. First, it has been on occasions recognized that where one country has a long frontier line in common with another country, the unique ties of geographical connection give ground for exceptional arrangements. Considerations and exceptions of this kind are exemplified in the relations between Spain and Portugal, and those between Canada and the United States. Second, special political ties and political responsibilities have led to commercial relations also of a special character. Such were the relations that existed for a considerable time between the United States and Hawaii, and such are now the relations between the United States and Cuba. But these cases of exception, whether they are universally admitted to rest upon valid grounds or are debatable, do not make it impossible to carry out, with reference to the great mass of international relations and negotiations, the principle of equality of treatment.

It must be further admitted that, just as special political ties may lead to exceptional treatment, so also the severance of normal international relations may be followed by exceptional treatment. It remains to be seen what conditions of peace will be established and what commercial relations will ensue on the termination of the war. The nature of the settlement must affect the commercial arrangements also. Political and perhaps military considerations may compel modification of a policy which nevertheless should aim in general at reciprocal equality of commercial treatment.

So far as concerns existing commercial treaties and arrangements, the international relations of the United States, as they have been gradually shaped since the opening of the present century, are in conformity with the principle of equality of treatment, when interpreted and qualified with regard to special political affiliations and special geographical ties. The treaty between the United States and Cuba, providing for special remissions of duty on both sides, is to be judged in the light of the special political relations between the two countries. The act which stands upon our statute book, making possible a reciprocity arrangement with Canada, also rests upon grounds of its own, being influenced by the exceptional geographical relations. Only one commercial arrangement of the United States now in effect can be said to be inconsistent with the general principle, namely, that with Brazil. And this rests, not upon a treaty to which the United States is formally a party, but upon legislative and administrative measures of Brazil.

Methods of enforcing equality of treatment.—If, however, the principle of equality of treatment is to be adopted, something more than a bare declaration of policy is needed. In view of the divergent attitudes and demands of different countries, and of the undeniable possibility that other countries may not follow, in their own dealings with the United States, the principle of equality of treatment, some method of enforcement is indispensable.

As matters now stand, the United States has no way of bringing pressure to bear, or rather, none that is immediately available. If not accorded equality of treatment by other countries, this country is almost helpless. There has been provided no authorization for action on the part of the Executive. If the United States wishes to exercise pressure upon another country for the purpose of bringing that country's measures into conformity with demands of the United States for equality of treatment, the slow-moving process of legislative enactment alone is now available.

Measures for the purpose of securing just treatment by other countries may take one of two forms. The first of these is that of concessions, or of concessional arrangements, by which reductions of duty may be conceded to countries which grant the United States equality of treatment. The second is that of additional duties, in the nature of penalty or retaliatory duties, made applicable to countries which fail to give the United States satisfactory treatment. Each of these methods has its advantages and its disadvantages.

The method of concessions.—The main advantage of the concessional method—that of reductions of duty—is that it appears more conciliatory. To offer a concession is less irritating than to impose a penalty. But it must be borne in mind that if the granting of a concession be carried out with full effect and in full accord with the principle of equality of treatment, the concession must be extended alike to all countries which conform to the principle. Only a few countries are then left unaffected, and, as regards its effect upon these, a concessional method becomes the equivalent of a penalizing method.

A disadvantage of the concessional method, when the concessional schedule includes a considerable number of items, is that it causes the effective tariff schedules of the country in respect to those items for which concessional rates are provided to consist largely or mainly of the concessional or reduced rates of duty. It involves, if carried out fully and with the desired effect, a lowering of what is declared to be the general tariff. This brings it about that the general tariff becomes nominal; it contains rates higher than those which are expected actually to go into effect. This leads in turn to some uncertainty, at the time when the general rates are fixed, as to the extent to which they will be modified by the concessional arrangements. The outcome is likely to be virtually a maximum-and-minimum tariff, with possible uncertainty as to the extent to which the minimum rates shall be applied.

As regards economic effect, reductions of duty under the concessional method have different consequences under varying conditions of supply as regards the article affected. Where a reduction of duty affects only a fraction of the imports of a particular article, and the major portion of the imports of that article is still left subject to the main, or non-concessional duty, the result is not only a loss of revenue to the Treasury, because of the lower rates of duty, but absence of any gain to consumers. The reduction of duty redounds only to the advantage of the foreign producer. This situation was exemplified by our experience with Hawaii, as detailed in this report, under the reciprocity treaty of 1875.[1] That experience was not indeed part of a general concessional policy; but it, nevertheless, supplies an example of the working of a limited concession. If, on the other hand, virtually the entire imported supply of a given article is admitted at the lowered concessional rates, the effect is that of a general reduction of duty. Such a result ensued, at least in the more recent years of the operation of the reciprocity treaty with Cuba, as a consequence of our concession of a reduced duty upon Cuban sugar. As shown in the discussion of Cuban relations,[2] this concession resulted in a gain to the Cuban sugar producer during the first years after the reciprocity arrangement went into effect, but had come to redound, during the years immediately preceding the European war, mainly to the advantage of the domestic consumer.

---

[1] See page 129, *infra.*   [2] See page 330, *infra.*

The method of additional duties.—The other method—that of the imposition of additional duties on articles coming from countries which discriminate against the United States—has also its advantages and disadvantages. The main disadvantage is that, employing something in the nature of a threat, it seems combative in principle, unfriendly in appearance, and therefore irritating. In this respect it is in its outward aspect the reverse of the concessional method. But it should be borne in mind that when the additional duties are put into effect solely for the purpose of securing equality of treatment, and are therefore subject to termination as soon as such treatment has been attained, they can hardly give reasonable ground for complaint.

A distinct advantage of this method is that it does not affect the general tariff rates of the country which uses it. It is directed against those countries only which do not themselves apply the principle of equality of treatment. The probabilities are great—so great as almost to amount to a certainty—that it will not be applied to any considerable number of countries or articles. Administered with discretion, and with due regard to the character of the trade with different sources of supply, it leads to no substantial change in the general tariff system, and therefore leaves this to be determined solely with regard to the country's domestic needs and wishes.

As regards economic effect, additional duties, like the concessional, have different consequences according to their range of application. If a country to which such duties are applied sends to the United States only a fraction of the imports of a given article, the effect is simply that this fraction is excluded from the domestic market and is displaced by additional imports of the same commodity from elsewhere. Only in very rare cases would the domestic consumer be affected by the imposition of an additional duty on such fractional imports. If, indeed, a very large portion of the supply of a given article comes from the penalized country, the situation is different; still more is it different if the entire supply comes from that one country. In such cases additional duties are likely to entail a burden on the domestic consumer.

It follows that there is special need of care in the application of additional duties. They are most effective if there be competing countries, each desirous of sending to the United States the same or like goods, as is usually the case when applied to countries which send us manufactured products. For such, the conditions of production and the control of products are not determined by physical or climatic causes, and there is not likely to be found anything in the nature of exclusive control of a partcular article by any single country. Additional duties then establish a preference of one foreign producer over another, but the pressure on the offending foreign country does not affect injuriously the domestic consumer.

Under the existing tariff system of the United States—that embodied in the tariff act of 1913—the method of additional duties would seem the only one that could be put at once into operation. For the time being it may be presumed that no concessions below the rates of the act of 1913 are likely to be proposed by the Executive or considered by Congress. Congress could provide for additional duties, the design being, not to bring about any substantial changes in the general tariff rates, and certainly not to entail increased prices to consumers, but to secure fair reciprocal treatment from foreign countries.

Possible problems of the future.—Looking to the more distant future, the choice between the additional and the concessional methods must be influenced by the international relations which may develop as a result of the war. The latter method may then seem as effective a method as the former for securing equality of treatment from other countries. More particularly may this be the case if the concessions— in the form of lowered rates, within limits set by Congress—be arranged with the intent and with the effect of their being applicable to almost all countries, the higher non-concessional rates being designed for application, if at all, to a few recalcitrant countries only. Thus applied, the concessional method, as has already been said, is virtually a more conciliatory form of the additional method. It still has the disadvantage that it does not clearly and unequivocally leave the country free in the independent determination of its own tariff policy. It is less satisfactorily adapted to the single-tariff system, which the United States has generally used in the settlement of its own internal problems.

Conclusion as to methods.—To conclude, the method of additional duties is that which can be put into effect by the United States at once, without disturbance of its general tariff policy, and without committing the country definitively as regards the permanent commercial arrangements which may be evolved as part of the coming international settlement. The necessary flexibility can be secured by leaving the actual imposition of additional duties to the discretion of the President, who shall act always in conformity with a stated general principle and subject to general limitations defined by statute. Indeed, either system, the concessional or the additional, can be safely applied only when there is a provision for elasticity in its application and administration. It would seem indispensable that a considerable degree of freedom be left to the executive department. The restrictions within which that freedom shall be exercised must be prescribed according to the judgment of Congress. They may take the form of limiting the additions or penalties to stated ad valorem supplements to the existing duties, or to stated ad valorem duties (or equivalent specific duties) on articles appearing upon the general free list. The early enactment of legislation authorizing the imposition of additional duties at the discretion of the President is accordingly recommended by the Tariff Commission.

Concerning the position which the United States should take with regard to the most-favored-nation clause the Commission now makes no recommendation. There has been shown in the body of the report sharp diversity between the usage of the United States and that of most other countries in the interpretation of that clause; and there is also diversity of opinion as to its present and future value. An attentive, even exhaustive, consideration of its form and interpretation, and of its substantive effect, will be necessary in the course of the coming international readjustments. The extent to which the clause may be embodied henceforth in commercial and tariff agreements will depend largely on the general character of those adjustments. The other policies which the Commission recommends for immediate consideration may be adopted consistently with the use of either of the two main forms of the most-favored-nation clause. It seems to the Commission premature for the United States to commit itself at this moment either to the maintenance without modification of the country's traditional most-favored-nation policy or to the advocacy or adoption of a different policy.

Finally, it can not be too much emphasized that any policy adopted by the United States should have for its object, on the one hand, the prevention of discrimination and the securing of equality of treatment for American commerce and for American citizens, and, on the other hand, the frank offer of the same equality of treatment to all countries that reciprocate in the same spirit and to the same effect. The United States should ask no special favors and should grant no special favors. It should exercise its powers and should impose its penalties, not for the purpose of securing discrimination in its favor, but to prevent discrimination to its disadvantage.

Respectfully submitted.

F. W. TAUSSIG, *Chairman.*
THOMAS WALKER PAGE, *Vice Chairman.*
DAVID J. LEWIS.
WILLIAM KENT.
WILLIAM S. CULBERTSON.
EDWARD P. COSTIGAN.

RECIPROCITY AND COMMERCIAL TREATIES.

INTRODUCTION TO THE REPORT.

Subject and scope of this report.—The present report is concerned primarily with the reciprocity experiences of the United States, and, in connection with and in relation thereto, the American theory and practice of most-favored-nation treatment. It gives also somewhat extensive attention to the tariff systems and commercial treaty practices of other, and especially of European, countries.

Commercial treaties.—Modern commercial treaties cover a wide variety of subjects. They relate to the treatment to be accorded to persons, to vehicles of communication and transportation, and to commerce in all its phases. Within them there appear provisions as to admission of diplomatic and consular officials, and their rights and activities; immigration and emigration; police protection and civil rights; conditions of travel, residence, and trade; exemptions from extraordinary levies, forced loans, and military service; navigation, quarantine, and harbor regulations and dues; conditions for importation, exportation, transit, transfer, warehousing; tariffs and customs laws; protection to patents, copyrights, and trade-marks. In a tariff study those provisions are of chief concern which have to do with trade and with customs laws and regulations.

Reciprocity agreements.—In the adoption of a commercial policy and in the making of arrangements connected therewith, every State has a twofold object—it seeks to gain and to preserve for itself advantages, and to escape, avoid, and guard against disadvantages. This being the case, the making of a commercial treaty becomes a form of concluding a bargain.

Where each of the parties to a treaty makes special concessions to the other with the intention that the transaction shall be looked upon as a particular bargain and with the understanding that its benefits are not to be extended automatically, generally, and freely to other States, the agreement is called a "reciprocity" agreement.

The most-favored-nation clause.—In the making of commercial treaties a State may or may not seek a special and privileged position, but it has been a matter of especial concern to each State to be assured that it shall receive treatment at the hands of other States at least as favorable as that which the latter accord to any others. Each State desires that such concessions and guarantees as have been made to other States shall be extended to it; also that all which may in the future be granted to other States shall equally be granted to it.

In order to safeguard against oversight at the moment of making a treaty, and to reduce the necessity for repetitions, an instrument was devised which should automatically assure or offer to newly contracting States the benefit of concessions made, previously or afterwards, to third States. That instrument was the "most-favored-nation clause." It is neither the purpose nor the effect of the most-favored-nation clause to establish a "most-favored nation;" on the contrary, its use implies the intention that the maximum of advan-

17

tages which either of the parties to a treaty has extended or shall
extend to any third State—for the moment the "most-favored "—
shall be given or be made accessible to the other party; thus in practice to prevent the establishing of distinctions or discrimination in
the extending of concessions and guarantees.

**Conditional and unconditional forms of the most-favored-nation
clause.**—Up to the time of the American Revolution the most-
favored-nation provision appeared in but one form: the pledge was
not qualified; no limitations were laid down as to the circumstances
under which concessions granted to other States should be extended as
between the contracting parties. But in the first American treaty,
that made by the American Confederation with France on February
6, 1778, the clause was given a new phraseology. In this treaty there
appeared the usual pledge that advantages which either of the contracting parties had granted or might grant to a third State should
be granted to the other, but there was attached a qualifying conditional provision, " *\ * * freely, if the concession (to the third
State) was freely made, or on allowing the same compensation, if
the concession was conditional." From that time forward the most-
favored-nation clause has been used sometimes with the qualifying
stipulation and sometimes without it. Where no such stipulation is
attached, it is customary to speak of the clause as being "unconditional;" when it is specified that there shall be compensation, the
clause is described as "conditional."

European and American practice.—From the time when its representatives first subscribed to the conditional form of the clause, the
United States, when pledging itself to favored-nation treatment,
has employed that form almost without exception. The States of
Europe, which had previously used the unconditional form only,
have since employed sometimes the one and sometimes the other of
the two forms—up to 1850 very frequently the conditional, after
1860 almost exclusively the unconditional. At the same time, in the
negotiation of their earlier treaties the European States had been
governed strictly by the principle of making concessions only in return for concessions sought: they had been in the habit of making
treaty bargains with those States only from which they wished at a
particular time to secure particular concessions. The American Government adopted the policy of offering favorable treatment to all
who would reciprocate; it was frankly seeking to secure equality
of opportunity in foreign markets, and it offered equality of opportunity to all countries seeking American markets on the basis of
mutual concessions.

The willingness to treat with all nations equally and to offer the
same concessions to all in return for compensatory concessions by
each was essentially a step forward. It was no part, however, of the
American policy to give to some States "freely" such concessions as
were given to others in consideration of reciprocal concessions. The
earliest American statesmen adopted the "special bargain " principle,
and the American Government has acted ever since in conformity with
the conception that commercial concessions are to be given for specific compensation, and that most-favored-nation treatment implies
and requires nothing more than the granting of opportunity to
purchase, on the basis of reciprocal give and take, treatment identical with, or similar to, that accorded other States.

Changes in European practice—Tariff schedules by negotiations.— European States have long since altered their commercial policies: they have experimented with various tariff systems; or they have adopted new theories and practices in regard to commercial treaties and treaty bargaining. The commercial liberalism which met with favor in the leading States of Europe after the middle of the nineteenth century emphasized the theory and practice of generalizing concessions—that is, of extending, without condition, to all nations entitled to most-favored-nation treatment, the benefit of concessions made to any. Thus the use of the unconditional form of the most-favored-nation clause, together with the application of the unconditional interpretation, became the common European practice. Notwithstanding later changes in their commercial policies and tariff systems, European States have found it still convenient to generalize the concessions which they make, and such being the case, their most-favored-nation practice has remained, and is, "unconditional."

Many of these States now devise the rates in their statutory tariff schedules with distinct and particular reference to bargaining possibilities; they expect to make reductions, on the basis of concession for concession, by negotiation with other States individually, and then to extend the benefit of all their reductions, generalizing them, to all the States with which they have most-favored-nation agreements.

Practice of the United States—Single-tariff system.—These practices the United States has not adopted. Throughout the tariff history of the United States there has been an unbroken line of tariff laws in which it has been the uniform practice, except for the slight deviation in 1909, to employ a single list of fixed duties intended for general application to imports from all countries alike. It has not been the policy of the United States to modify its schedule of duties by granting concessions to various nations with the intention that all the concessions shall be grouped into a supplementary tariff schedule and be extended to all.

As a result of the continuity of its tariff policy in this respect, the commercial treaty pledges to which the United States has subscribed exhibit less variation in intent and wording than appears in European treaties. There has been a continuity in the American conception and construction of these pledges, particularly of the most-favored-nation clause, which has not been paralleled in the course of the European conception and interpretation.

While the United States has not practiced the type of commercial treaty bargaining now prevalent in Europe, it has, however, had no little experience with tariff treaties in the pursuance of "reciprocity." The American conception of a commercial treaty as an agreement based on the principle of bargaining has made it possible for the United States to enter in good faith into "reciprocity" agreements with individual countries, giving and receiving special concessions. By means of reciprocity treaties, the United States has granted various concessions to certain countries, for compensation, and has accepted concessions from them. This has involved in each case particular reductions from the rates established in the general tariff. In most cases the determination to enter into such agreement has come as a result of unusual circumstances, such as a peculiar geographical factor or peculiar political relations. Having made concessions under special circumstances, or for special compensation, the United States has not considered it obligatory or even just to extend the same favors to third states " freely."

Differences in principles and practices.—The principle which has consistently guided the practice of the United States in respect to treaty bargaining is thus different from that which has prevailed in Europe in recent decades. The American and the European conceptions of reciprocity and of the proper function of the most-favored-nation clause have differed. Proper appraisement of either requires an understanding of the commercial theories and policies and of the tariff systems and practices with which it is associated and of which it is made an instrument. To make possible such an appraisement, the Tariff Commission has made the studies which constitute the basis of this report.

SUMMARY OF THE REPORT.

I. RECIPROCITY AND TARIFF AGREEMENTS OF THE UNITED STATES.

The reciprocity experiences of the United States.—Reciprocity treaties, in the specialized sense indicated above, have been an increasingly important factor in the commercial policies of the United States. Before 1890 seven such treaties had been negotiated; but of these only two, those made with Canada in 1854 and with Hawaii in 1875, became effective. A commercial agreement of minor importance was concluded with Spain—for Cuba and Porto Rico—in 1883, which agreement remained in effect until 1892.

In accordance with section 3 of the tariff act of 1890, reciprocity agreements of a more generalized type were made with six American countries, and with Austria-Hungary, Germany, Great Britain (for the West Indies) and Spain (for Cuba and Porto Rico). These were terminated when the tariff act of 1894 went into effect.

Under the provision of section 4 of the tariff act of 1897, treaties, also of a more generalized type, were negotiated with Great Britain (for certain colonies), Denmark (for the Danish West Indies), Nicaragua, Ecuador, the Argentine, and France. These were, however, never ratified. Agreements more restricted in scope were concluded under section 3 of this act with France, Portugal, Germany, Italy, Switzerland, Spain, Bulgaria, Great Britain, and the Netherlands. These were terminated by the act of 1909.

Since 1904 special treatment for United States imports into Brazil has been established by a special arrangement. In 1903 a treaty, independent of general tariff legislation, was made with Cuba. This treaty is still in effect. In 1909–1911 President Taft arranged with representatives of the Canadian Government for a reciprocity agreement between Canada and the United States, but this failed of ratification by Canada.

1. THE CANADIAN RECIPROCITY TREATY OF 1854.

The arrangement which the Canadian people rejected in 1911 was but the latest of a long series of attempts which have been made to bring Canada and the United States, by the removal of commercial restrictions, into closer commercial relations. Only once has such an attempt been successful. A reciprocity treaty negotiated in 1854 was ratified, was put into force in 1855, and remained in force for eleven years. The great revolution in colonial and commercial policy which was carried through by the British Government in and after 1846 had thrown the British North American Provinces very much upon their own resources economically. Among policies possible at the moment, the most promising was that of close commercial relations with the United States, and to this the Canadian Government committed itself.

Tentative negotiations looking to reciprocity were begun in 1846. It was agreed in 1848 that reciprocity should be secured by concurrent legislation. The necessary legislation was passed by the Canadian Parliament and by the House of Representatives in the United States, but it never came to a vote in the Senate. The British Government next proposed that there should be a reciprocity treaty, but President Tyler objected to this on constitutional grounds. In 1852 the fisheries question assumed very serious aspects, and the British Government refused to discuss the diplomatic points therein involved if the discussion of reciprocity were excluded. Concerned over the political consequences much more than over the trade relations of the Canadian Provinces, the British Government finally pushed negotiations to a successful conclusion in Washington in 1854. A treaty was signed and ratified which provided that the United States and Canada should enjoy mutually the Atlantic coast fisheries and the canal systems of both countries and which provided also for the use by Americans of the St. Lawrence River and by British subjects of Lake Michigan. With respect to commerce, it virtually established free trade in natural products between the United States and the British North American Provinces. The legislation necessary to make the treaty effective was passed on both sides, and the treaty was put into effect by proclamation of President Pierce on March 16, 1855. It was to run for ten years, and thereafter subject to two years' notice for termination.

The operation of the treaty.—The treaty achieved the main purpose for which it was negotiated—relief of the tension over the fisheries controversy; but it did not have the effect of stimulating the American fishing industry. The opening of the St. Lawrence River and the Canadian canals to American shipping did not result in an increase in American traffic on those highways, but it did afford a choice of routes, which relieved congestion and insured reasonable railway rates to the Atlantic seaboard.

In any attempt to estimate the effect of the tariff changes on the trade between Canada and the United States, cognizance must be taken of a number of factors which complicated the situation and of facts which make calculations difficult. The investment in Canada of great sums of English capital, the Crimean War, the opening of new settlement areas in the West, increase in population, improvement of transportation facilities, speculation, a commercial crisis in both countries in 1857, financial difficulties leading to a fundamental change in Canadian fiscal policy, and, finally, the Civil War—all these influenced the course of developments both within each country and between the two, making it impossible to determine conclusively with regard to various increases and decreases whether they were or were not consequences of the treaty. The trade statistics of the period, also, both Canadian and American, are by no means satisfactory for the purpose of making accurate calculations.

There resulted from the treaty increased trade with Canada, which was more marked in regard to imports from Canada than in regard to exports to Canada. During the treaty period, the relative share of the United States in Canada's import trade increased; after the termination of the treaty, it decreased. While the treaty actually benefited some American producers and injured none save fishing, lumber, and possibly coal interests—and these in small degree—it was, on the whole, of greater benefit to the export trade of Canada than to that of the United States. It was anticipated when the treaty was concluded that such would be the case, but it was expected that the United States would be compensated for this by the opening of the Canadian coast fisheries and waterways and by the benefits to American railways and commission houses. These expectations were fulfilled in a considerable measure until the revision of fiscal policy in Canada and the conditions of the Civil War in the United States altered the situation. During the eleven years of the reciprocity period, the total trade between the two countries increased approximately threefold, and, for the United States, the trade with Canada became second in importance only to that with Great Britain. How much of this was due to the improvement in general relations between the two countries and how much to the reciprocity provisions of the treaty can not be determined. But it may safely be asserted that, in its several features the reciprocity arrangement contributed largely to the very considerable growth of trade and that both countries were benefited by it.

Abrogation of the treaty.—The main causes which brought about the abrogation of the treaty were the adoption of protectionist principles and practices in Canada, the resentment aroused in the United States by the attitude of Canada during the Civil War, and the need of increased revenue in both countries. To these may be added the dissatisfaction of the fish, lumber, and coal interests in the United States.

The denunciation of the treaty came from the side of the United States. In the winter of 1863–64, a bill calling for abrogation was passed in Congress, and on March 17 the President gave the required year's notice for termination.

Effects of the abrogation.—The termination of the treaty involved the termination of the arrangements which had relieved the political tension in Canadian-American relations. It offered the possibility of serious political consequences. The action of the United States and the hostile attitude of the American people, of which it was an evidence, were prominent among the factors which brought about, in 1867, the uniting of the Canadian Provinces into the Dominion of Canada.

The commercial effects of the abrogation were less than had been expected. In so far as trade was affected at all, it was the United States rather than Canada that suffered. The chief direct effects on the United States seem to have been to lay the burden of certain duties on the American consumer and to divert from American railways and merchants a part of the business of transporting, handling, and reexporting Canadian produce. The chief indirect result was to establish among the Canadian people a sense of grievance which affected trade to some extent and which undoubtedly contributed in no small measure later to Canada's rejection of reciprocity when the United States finally proposed it.

Efforts to restore reciprocity.—For thirty years after the termination of the treaty, Canadians continued to express a desire for reciprocity, and they made overtures several times to that end.

The treaty of Washington of 1871, disposing, among other things, of the fisheries and the waterways controversies, was a bitter disappointment to the people of Canada. They felt that the British Government had thrown away the most effective lever for opening the American market. When the Liberals entered office in 1874, they sent Mr. George Brown to the United States to negotiate for reciprocity. Mr. Brown offered reciprocity, not only in reference to natural products, but also on a long list of manufactures. A treaty was drafted, but with the provision that everything made free by Canada to the United States should also be made free to Great Britain, and the Senate rejected the draft. The Conservative party in Canada thereafter urged a policy of consistent retaliation against the United States, and they secured an overwhelming victory at the polls in 1878. In the ensuing tariff act of 1879 the Canadian free list was materially abbreviated. In 1887 Canadian commissioners offered to negotiate a treaty combining a settlement of the fisheries question with reciprocity, but this proposal was rejected by Secretary of State Bayard. The hostility which had characterized the relations of the two countries for twenty years was by this time rapidly decreasing and official attitudes became more conciliatory. In the spring of 1888 the House Committee on Foreign Affairs recommended that a commission be appointed to meet with Canadian commissioners and prepare a plan for commercial union, and at the next session a bill to that end was passed in the House, but was not acted upon in the Senate.

In 1890 a reciprocity treaty with Newfoundland was drafted at Washington, but this was withheld by the British foreign office at the instance of Canada.

Between 1890 and 1892 the Conservative Government in Canada made another effort to secure reciprocity, but the terms which it proposed were not acceptable to Mr. Blaine, nor were his proposals acceptable to the British and Canadian representatives. This was the last effort of the Conservatives on behalf of reciprocity. Thereafter Canadian public sentiment even among the Liberals swung strongly toward the " National," self-sufficiency policy, and from 1891 to 1910 the reciprocity question ceased to be a live issue.

2. THE HAWAIIAN RECIPROCITY TREATY OF 1875.

The reciprocity treaty concluded between Hawaii and the United States in 1875, which was in operation for twenty-five years, was a product of political rather than of economic considerations.

The location, resources, and political weakness of Hawaii made the islands, from the early part of the nineteenth century, attractive to several strong powers. Their strategic position made it inevitable that the United States should view with uneasiness and dissatisfaction their being brought under the control of any other power.

Several times before the middle of the nineteenth century, European States had made attempts upon the political integrity of Hawaii. In 1851 the King of Hawaii actually prepared to place his Kingdom under the protection of the United States in order to escape the aggression of a European power. In the years which followed, it became evident that protection by the United States was necessary, and the choice of methods lay between reciprocity and annexation. An annexation treaty was negotiated in 1854, but was not concluded. In the next year a reciprocity treaty was negotiated, but this failed of ratification. In 1867, for the second time, a reciprocity treaty was negotiated, but the attention of Congress was very much taken up with other matters, problems of reconstruction were imperative, and the treaty did not secure ratification. In 1874 the question was brought up under peculiarly favorable circumstances, and in the next year a reciprocity treaty was negotiated and ratified. Congress thereafter passed the legislation necessary for putting it into effect, and it went into force on September 9, 1876.

In the treaty there were no political concessions other than the pledge that while the treaty remained in force Hawaii would not lease territory or grant special privileges to any other power, or make any treaty by which any other powers should obtain the same privileges which were assured by the treaty to the United States. The commercial provisions involved the admission by each country of a considerable number of products of the other, free of duty. Claims of right to the benefit of the commercial concessions were soon advanced by certain nations, on the basis of the most-favored-nation clause. The United States combatted these claims, on the score both of the conditional interpretation of the most-favored-nation clause and of the special and peculiar circumstances governing the relations between Hawaii and the United States, and the American contention was ultimately accepted.

The question of the renewal of the treaty came up in 1882. A convention to extend its term was negotiated in 1884. It was recognized that the operation of the treaty was more advantageous commercially to Hawaii than to the United States, but, even more than in 1875, political considerations weighed in the minds of American statesmen. There was incorporated in the convention which was to extend the treaty, a provision for the cession of Pearl River Harbor to the United States as a naval base. This became an item in the bargain. The convention was finally ratified, after its adoption had been strongly urged by President Cleveland, in 1887. It extended the duration of the original treaty, without any alteration in the commercial reciprocity provision, for a period of seven years from the moment of ratification, and thereafter subject to one year's notice.

Effects of the treaty.—The most important articles of Hawaiian export in the reciprocity group were brown sugar, molasses, fruits and nuts, and rice. These comprised at all times more than three-fourths of the aggregate exports of the islands. Sugar was first in importance, in a class by itself. The chief consideration which Hawaii received was the admission into the United States, duty free, of the specified products originating in the islands, while similar commodities, when coming from other sources were subjected to substantial rates of duty. The special preference, not the free admission, was the significant feature so far as the effect on Hawaiian exports was concerned.

Even before the establishment of reciprocity, the bulk of the Hawaiian exports had gone to the United States. Under reciprocity the percentage increased, and after annexation the United States absorbed practically the whole of the Hawaiian exports.

Reciprocity was more conspicuously effective in increasing the absolute amount of Hawaiian exports to the United States than in increasing the share which these formed of the total Hawaiian exports. The exports multiplied to many times the maximum figure which they had reached previously. The one commodity signally affected was sugar, the Hawaiian production and export of which increased enormously, beyond all expectation and imagination. The remission of duty on this sugar was not followed by a reduction in price to the American consumer; the gain went to the sugar producers. Under this stimulus the cultivation of sugar in the islands became highly intensified.

The effects of the United States tariff act of 1890 emphasized among Hawaiian commercial interests the insecurity of a position dependent on reciprocity alone, and the question of annexation came again strongly to the fore. Dissatisfaction with the government of the islands, together with actual political disturbances, strengthened the desire, as well as the case, of those who favored putting the islands under the control of the United States. The political disturbances ended in a revolution in 1893, and the temporary government which came into control asked immediately for annexation, but this the United States refused. A permanent government of republican form was thereupon organized in Hawaii. With the passage in the United States of the tariff act of 1894, which once more put Hawaiian sugar in a favored position, economic conditions in the Islands improved. But the failure of reciprocity to assure constantly favorable conditions was remembered, and in 1897 the agitation for annexation was renewed. In the course of the next year, in view of the fact that the United States was at war, annexation appeared highly desirable, and the administration resorted to the procedure of a joint resolution of both Houses. Such a resolution was passed in the summer of 1898, and the President of Hawaii surrendered the sovereignty of the islands on August 12, 1898. The tariff arrangements of the treaty continued in effect until June 15, 1900, when the Organic Act providing for the political reorganization of the islands became operative.

The prosperity and greatly increased purchasing power which reciprocity had brought Hawaii under the influence of the tariff preference to Hawaiian producers had resulted in an increase of imports into Hawaii from the United States. This was not, however, comparable in volume to the increase of imports from Hawaii into the United States. The commercial development of Hawaii had led also to increased demand for the services of American shipping, banking, insurance, and the like. But when all the various factors have been taken into account, the conclusion is inevitable that the reciprocity relationship with Hawaii was economically unprofitable to the United States. However, in a comprehensive estimate, the fact must not be overlooked that in entering into the reciprocity arrangement Congress had not been actuated primarily by economic considerations.

3. NEGOTIATIONS, 1882–1890.

In the decade following 1880, repeated efforts were made to develop closer trade relations with Latin America, and several treaties were negotiated, but these did not secure the ratification of the United States Senate.

4. TREATIES AND AGREEMENTS UNDER THE TARIFF ACT OF 1890.

The legislative record.—The provision in the tariff act of 1890 for the imposition of penalty duties upon imports from countries which discriminated in their tariff treatment against goods from the United States may be considered the first authorization ever given by Congress for a comprehensive program of tariff bargaining.

Early in 1890, with the Republican party in power, the McKinley tariff bill was introduced. It provided for several changes in the tariff schedules, important among them being the free admission of sugar and molasses; but it contained no reciprocity provision, in spite of the strong recommendation of Mr. Blaine, Secretary of State, that such a provision be incorporated in the bill. The bill passed the House on May 21.

In the Senate an amendment was offered which would have practically established, through negotiation, free trade between the United States and the Latin-American countries. This never came to a vote. The Finance Committee finally recommended an amendment which would leave coffee, tea, hides, sugar, and molasses on the free list, but at the same time would provide that the President might suspend, by proclamation, their free admission from countries imposing unequal or unreasonable duties on products of the United States, and instead might impose thereon a stated list of penalty duties. The bill, so amended, was passed by the Senate, and, after going to conference without receiving any modification of its bargaining features, became law on October 1, 1890. Congress aimed by this act to secure more favorable trade relations with other countries by penalizing such countries as did not treat American products favorably, rather than by following the method which had been favored by the administration—that of remitting or lowering duties on the products of countries which in return would make similar tariff concessions. The act gave the President, within prescribed limits, a free hand in negotiations. The articles upon which penalty duties could be imposed, especially sugar, were particularly adapted to bargaining with South and Central American countries and also with the great beet-sugar producing States of Europe.

Under the terms of this act, Secretary Blaine began the negotiation of a series of agreements. Between January 31, 1891, and May 26, 1892, ten reciprocity arrangements were concluded, all but two of them being with countries of the Western Hemisphere. In each of these agreements the United States undertook to admit free of duty, when coming from the other country, the five articles—coffee, tea, hides, sugar, and molasses—enumerated in the penalizing provision of the act. In most cases the other contracting party agreed to admit free or at substantially reduced tariff rates the bulk of its imports from the United States.

The penalty duties were imposed only on Colombia, Venezuela, and Haiti, after these States had been asked to negotiate and had failed satisfactorily to respond. Several other countries, producers of the specified articles, conspicuously the Argentine and Mexico, failed to conclude agreements, but the penalty duties were not imposed on them; and this led to protests by Colombia and Venezuela against what they considered to be unfair discrimination.

Effect of the treaties on the trade of the United States.—An analysis of imports and exports during the period covered by these reciprocity treaties indicates that the penalty duties were moderately effective both as a measure of retaliation and as a means of securing tariff favors. There was a marked decrease in the imports from the penalized countries. The conditions of the sugar industry made it possible to secure liberal tariff concessions in return for a free market for sugar in the United States, while at the same time the imposition of the penalty duties did not prevent the consumer from profiting through the fall in the price of sugar in the American market.

Exports from the United States to the reciprocity States, favored by special reductions of duty, showed a substantial increase, in spite of the handicap of severe industrial depression and revolutionary disturbances existing in many of these States, while at the same time there were decreases in the aggregate exports to all other countries.

The termination of the reciprocity agreements.—In 1894, under a Democratic administration, a new tariff act was passed which did away with the reciprocity provision. It imposed a duty on raw sugar, raised that on refined sugar, and repealed the bounty on the domestic product. It further provided that treaties not inconsistent with this new provision might remain in force; but the reimposition of the duty on raw sugar acted almost automatically to annul the agreements made under the act of 1890, and was so interpreted by the State Department. Protests were made against the reimposition of the duty on sugar and against the abrupt termination of the agreements of the act of 1890 by several of the countries concerned. Considerable resentment was shown, and measures of retaliation followed in certain cases.

The termination of these agreements left only the treaty with Hawaii in operation.

5. TREATIES AND AGREEMENTS UNDER THE TARIFF ACT OF 1897.

In the congressional elections of 1896 the Republican Party once more came into power. Reciprocity, as a means of securing fairness of treatment for the expanding export trade of the United States in Europe, had been made a plank in the platform upon which the election was carried.

The passing of the tariff act of 1897.—At a special session of Congress, called on March 18, 1897, the Dingley tariff bill was introduced. This provided, in section 3, for tariff bargaining by two methods. The first part of the section contained a provision empowering the President to reduce duties on a specified list of articles (including argols, wines, and sugar) when coming from countries making equivalent concessions to the products of the United States. The second part consisted of a penalizing provision, also to be used at the discretion of the President, imposing an additional duty on coffee, tea, and hides when coming from countries deemed to be subjecting products of the United States to unequal or unreasonable treatment.

Less than two weeks after its introduction, and with very little attention to the reciprocity provisions, the bill was passed in the House. In the Senate the question of reciprocity was given careful consideration. An amendment was inserted, as a substitute for section 3 of the House bill, giving the President the right to negotiate commercial treaties, and, in return for concessions to the United States, to grant reciprocal reductions on the products of the treaty countries. The opposition to this amendment contended emphatically that the conferring of this power on the President and the Senate would take from the House its constitutional right to levy revenue taxes, but both the amendment and the bill were passed by the Senate.

The conference committee restored the original House measure as section 3, but from the list of articles upon which penalty duties could be imposed they removed sugar, hides, skins, and certain other items of less importance and substituted in their place tonka and vanilla beans, articles of little commercial importance. The committee retained the Senate amendment as section 4, but with a provision requiring that treaties negotiated under it must be submitted for approval to Congress, instead of merely for ratification to the Senate. Thus altered, the bill was accepted and passed by both Houses, and it became law on July 24, 1897.

Provision for negotiation of agreements.—President McKinley appointed John A. Kasson, of Iowa, as special commissioner, to be assisted by a " reciprocity commission," for the negotiation of agreements under the new tariff act.

The " argol agreements," negotiated under section 3 of the act of 1897.—In conformity with the provisions of the first part of section 3, two series of agreements, known from the first article specified on the list as " argol agreements," were concluded. The first series, agreements with France, Portugal, Germany, and Italy, was negotiated by Mr. Kasson during the McKinley administration. The concessions obtained by the United States, in return for a few and small reductions of duty, were of some importance. In general this series of agreements was received with satisfaction by the American public.

An indirect result of the conclusion of these agreements was that Switzerland, through the unconditional most-favored-nation clause of her treaty of 1850 with the United States, claimed and was given, without compensation, the benefit of the concessions extended by treaty to France. The most-favored-nation treaty provision upon which Switzerland based her claim was promptly denounced by the United States Government with due notice, and in March, 1900, ceased to be operative.

During President Roosevelt's administration, the United States negotiated a second series of " argol agreements." In this, new agreements similar to those of the first series were made with Spain and Bulgaria, and, of a more limited character, with Great Britain and the Netherlands; the treaties with France, Portugal, Germany, and Italy were supplemented or extended; sparkling wines were added to the list of articles upon which concessions were granted by the United States; and Switzerland and the United States once more resumed reciprocal commercial relations, although without the negotiation of a formal agreement.

Commercial treaties concluded (but not ratified) under section 4 of the tariff act of 1897.—Section 4 of the tariff act of 1897 authorized the President to negotiate treaties providing for the reduction by not more than 20 per cent of the duties on any articles imported into the United States in return for equivalent concessions by the other party. Accordingly, Mr. Kasson negotiated a series of treaties, all of which made provision for tariff reductions of considerable importance.

Of these treaties the first to be agreed upon, and the one which aroused the most interest, was that with France, in 1899. After lengthy negotiations, the French conceded the rates of their minimum schedule on all but a few articles. In return the United States was to admit a long list of French products at reductions of from 5 to 20 per cent from the rates of the tariff of 1897.

Other treaties negotiated under this section of the act promised also to prove of considerable importance. They were all with or on behalf of American countries—the Argentine, Ecuador, Nicaragua, the Dominican Republic, Denmark (for St. Croix), and Great Britain (for various American colonies). The concessions made to the United States by these countries were numerous and varied; coal was one thing in particular for which favorable terms were secured. Important items upon which the United States agreed to make concessions were sugar, molasses, hides, and wool.

An attempt was made to conclude an agreement with Russia, but the imposition of a countervailing duty on Russian sugar in 1901 caused the breaking off of negotiations and was followed by retaliatory measures on Russia's part. Not until 1905, when Russia withdrew her retaliatory duties, were satisfactory commercial relations between the two countries reestablished.

The treaties submitted for ratification.—In December, 1899, the Kasson treaties were presented to the Senate for ratification, and early in 1900 the Committee on Foreign Relations took up their study. Popular interest was keen and much attention was given to the discussion, especially to that of the treaty with France. Two groups of interests finally stood in opposition—on the one side the representatives of American industries which were on an export basis, such as the iron and steel and the agricultural implement trades; on the other, both domestic producers who feared foreign competition and those persons who saw in the treaties an undesirable infringement of the principle of protection. Mr. Kasson strongly urged ratification of the treaties; President McKinley was in favor of them. No action was taken in 1900 and 1901, however, other than to extend the time during which ratifications might be secured.

Disheartened by his failure to secure ratification, Mr. Kasson resigned in March, 1901. The administration still supported the ratification of the treaties, and, in his last speech, at Buffalo, President McKinley expressed himself more strongly than ever in favor of the policy of reciprocity.

On November 19, 1901, the Manufacturers' Reciprocity Convention met in Washington and declared itself for protection and favorable to reciprocity only when the latter could be secured without injury to any of the domestic interests of manufacturing, commerce, or farming. Although President Roosevelt adhered to the views of his predecessor with regard to reciprocity, he likewise found it impossible to secure for the treaties the necessary approval of the Senate.

Finally, in 1903, action on the treaties was considered to have been abandoned; no mention of reciprocity was made in the President's message of 1904; and the treaties remained pigeonholed, without further action, in the Senate Committee on Foreign Relations.

Termination of the argol agreements by the act of 1909.—Six years later, the tariff act of 1909 provided for giving to all countries other than Cuba notice of termination of their reciprocity agreements with the United States.

Effect of the argol agreements upon trade.—The articles upon which the United States had made reductions of duty in the argol agreements were few, and, although some of these articles were imported in quantities and to values not inconsiderable, the reductions of duty were often small, and they were not exclusive, but were shared by most of the important countries. As regards imports, the influence of reciprocity was to be seen most clearly in increased imports of argols and sparkling wines from the reciprocity countries. As regards exports, the result appeared in a number of instances in increased shipments of articles upon which reductions of duty had been made. In most cases, however, the terms secured for the United States were merely a continuance of the most-favored-nation treatment, to which the United States had already been entitled under treaties in existence previous to the conclusion of the agreements. The only general conclusion derivable is negative. When reductions obtained by agreement are few and small, and are shared by all or most of the competing countries, the agreements will have very limited influence on the amount or the direction of trade.

6. TWO-SCHEDULE PROVISION OF THE TARIFF ACT OF 1909.

The movement for reciprocity gradually lost vigor. When, in 1909, the Republican Party began the revision of the tariff, provision was made in the bill introduced in the House for a two-schedule system, the minimum to be the general rates and the maximum the penalizing rates, the latter to be applied, at the discretion of the Treasury Department, to products from countries discriminating against the United States. All existing reciprocity treaties other than the one with Cuba were, after due notice, to be terminated.

The bill was amended in the Senate to provide that the free list and the rates in the general schedule of the House bill should constitute the minimum rates, while the maximum schedule should be made up by adding to the minimum 25 per cent of the values of the articles; the maximum schedule should be the general tariff, applicable to all countries, but the President should be authorized to extend the benefit of the minimum schedule to all countries found not discriminating against the United States.

The act, as passed August 5, 1909, followed the plan of the Senate amendment for making the maximum the general schedule. It marked a distinct departure from the policy of seeking special favors by granting reciprocal concessions. Though in form the policy was that of the concession of a minimum tariff, virtually it amounted to a provision to impose maximum rates by way of penalty against unequal treatment of American products.

France was the only country that protested, the protest being on the score that, on account of the wording of her 1908 agreement, the notice given her was shorter than that to the other reciprocity countries.

Before the maximum tariff was applied to any country, the Tariff Board, which had been created for the purpose under authority of the act (sec. 2), made an investigation of the existing tariff treatment of products of the United States by other countries. Discrimination was discovered in the case of a number of countries, and negotiations with such countries were entered into. In consequence of the negotiations, there were issued prior to April 1, 1910, proclamations applying the minimum rates to the countries comprising the entire commercial world; in no case was the maximum rate applied. In certain important instances, however, notably those of Germany and France, full equality of treatment was not extended to imports from the United States, and it would appear therefore that the act of 1909 did not provide a penalty method effective for the total elimination of all discrimination against American products in European markets.

7. RECIPROCITY SECTION OF THE TARIFF ACT OF 1913.

In 1913 the Democratic Party gained control of both the executive and the legislative branches of the Government. They at once prepared to revise the tariff. The Underwood bill as first drafted contained no provision for maximum and minimum schedules, but included a section authorizing the President to negotiate reciprocity agreements with foreign countries, such agreements, however, to be submitted to Congress for ratification or rejection. In the House a proposed amendment that there should be added a provision for maximum and minimum duties was rejected. In the Senate the bill was amended to include a provision for penalty duties to be imposed by the President at his discretion upon imports from countries whose treatment of American products was not " reciprocal and equivalent." In conference the Senate amendment was withdrawn and the bill was passed on October 3, 1913, with the reciprocity provision left as it had stood in the original bill.

8. BRAZILIAN PREFERENTIAL ARRANGEMENT.

Brazil had been among the countries with which, as has already been mentioned, the United States made reciprocity agreements under the provisions of the tariff act of 1890. The Brazilian agreement was terminated with the others by the tariff act of 1894.

The chief items in the Brazilian export trade to the United States were coffee and rubber, and these had both been duty-free in the United States without a reciprocity agreement. The articles of the export trade from the United States to Brazil were, however, in the absence of a special arrangement, subject to very heavy import duties on entering Brazil.

Such were the conditions governing the trade between the two countries from 1894 to 1897. The United States tariff act of 1897 authorized the President to impose a penalty duty of 3 cents a pound on coffee from countries according unequal or unreasonable treatment to American products. For various reasons it was not attempted to make an arrangement with Brazil by treaty. In 1904, moved by the possibility that this duty might be imposed on its coffee, and by representations of the United States minister, the Brazilian Government was induced to plan considerable reductions in a number of its rates in favor of United States products, the most important of the articles thus provided for being wheat flour.

Much opposition to this measure, especially from the wheat and flour interests, developed in the Brazilian Congress and the reduction was effected only by an order of the President, under the authority of an old law which empowered him to reduce certain duties by as much as 20 per cent. The Brazilian Congress in the next year repealed the legislation which gave this authority, and from January 1, 1905, to July 1, 1906, the preference was not in effect. But on July 1, 1906, legislation restoring this authority to the President and adding a number of items to the original list became effective.

Upon the passage in the United States of the tariff act of 1909, the State·Department negotiated with Brazil for tariff reductions in return for which Brazil might be entitled to the minimum rates. This, it may be noted, was an attempt to use the bargaining provisions of the act of 1909 as a means of securing special treatment for American products in a foreign market. As a result, numerous articles were added to the Brazilian list of 1906, and later the President of Brazil was given authority to extend this list at his discretion. In 1911 the preference on American flour was raised to 30 per cent. In 1916 the stipulation was made that the imports given this preferential treatment must be the product of the United States, and not merely imported via that country. In 1917 and 1918 the preferential list was renewed without change.

Effect of the Brazilian preferential treatment on American exports.— The important article on the Brazilian preferential list was wheat flour, and an analysis of the figures indicates that the United States exports to Brazil of this product did not increase, though the preference undoubtedly tended to check a decrease which other factors were bringing about. Other preferred articles were less important, forming only a small fraction of the total American exports to Brazil; but the preference had more effect on them, producing an appreciable increase, both absolutely and in relation to the total of Brazilian imports from all sources. Certain lines of trade, as, for instance, pianos and cement, were practically established by the preference.

In addition to a growth in the trade in the preferred articles, there was an increase in the general trade, due in part to the aroused interest in the new field. It would appear that although preference did not secure the desired results with respect to the chief item, wheat flour, it was moderately sucessful in stimulating an expansion of American trade in general with Brazil.

9. THE CUBAN RECIPROCITY TREATY OF 1902.

The close political relations of the United States with Cuba after the conclusion of the Spanish-American War turned the attention of the Cubans to the United States as a possible friend, who might rescue them from the depressed economic condition into which the years of revolution and war had thrown the island. The American administration in Cuba and President Roosevelt in Washington were in favor of giving Cuban products special tariff privileges in the American market, but the attitude of Congress was at first adverse. Many members looked upon any reductions of duty as a possible starting point for others less desirable. They, together with the domestic beet-sugar and cane-sugar producers, were opposed to any action which would involve a lowering of the tariff.

Public opinion, however, developed favorably toward closer economic relations between the two countries, and when the Fifty-seventh Congress convened for the second time, in January, 1902, the question became the subject of extended hearings, followed by the introduction of a bill in the House on March 19, 1902. The bill provided for reciprocal reductions of duties of 20 per cent, upon condition that Cuba should first adopt immigration laws as fully restrictive as were the laws of the United States. The arguments in support of reciprocal relations with Cuba emphasized particularly the alleged moral obligations of the United States toward Cuba and made no great claims for the economic desirability of the arrangement. After long debate, the bill passed the House by a large majority, but Congress adjourned before it came to a vote in the Senate.

President Roosevelt next sought to attain the same end by the negotiation of a treaty. His efforts resulted in the signing, on December 11, 1902, of a convention providing for a reduction of 20 per cent from the American duties on Cuban imports and reductions of from 20 to 40 per cent from the Cuban rates on American products. The Senate advised ratification, and the Cuban Government signified its approval of the treaty. The treaty required, however, the approval of Congress. Early in November, 1903, it was submitted to the Fifty-eighth Congress for approval. In the debates the arguments were similar to those in the earlier discussions. The measure was finally passed by both Houses, and on December 17, 1903, it was formally proclaimed.

This treaty was independent of the reciprocal provisions of the act of 1897, and was in no way connected with the treaties negotiated under that act. It contained in Article VIII some unusual provisions, namely, that the reductions in duty specified should not be extended to any other country, that during the continuance of the treaty no Cuban sugar should be admitted to the United States at a rate of duty less by more than 20 per cent than the rate imposed by the tariff act of 1897, and that no sugar from countries other than Cuba should be admitted by treaty or convention into the United States at a rate of duty lower than that provided by the act of 1897. The agreement has been in force continuously since 1903, with the exception that a portion of Article VIII was abrogated by a provision in the United States tariff act of 1913.

Second treaty with Cuba.—In addition to this commercial arrangement, another treaty had been negotiated, signed May 22, 1903, which prescribed the conditions under which American military authority would be withdrawn from and those under which it might be reinstated in the island. The guaranty of public order which this second treaty insured to labor and capital contributed much to the great commercial development which has subsequently occurred in the island, and any estimate of the effects of the first treaty must take into consideration the influence of the second.

Effect of the treaty on trade.—The supporters of the treaty had placed but little emphasis upon its possible commercial results. The major portion of the Cuban exports already found their market in the United States, and it did not appear likely that great benefits would accrue from an increase in the share of the Cuban imports which was or would be contributed by the United States. The years immediately preceding the treaty had formed a period of gradual and halting recovery of Cuban industry. The first years under the treaty showed a decided increase for both American exports to and imports from Cuba. Following the depression of 1907, the growth showed a relative decrease, but after 1908 there was again a tendency toward increase in value in both the imports and the exports.

The imports into the United States from Cuba have reflected the influence of reciprocity in a less significant degree than have the exports from the United States to Cuba. The principal gains made by the imports have been due to the fact that several important staple articles of Cuban production, especially sugar and tobacco, have found a steady and growing market in the United States, a market which would probably have expanded in some measure without the extension of tariff preferences.

A comparison of the United States exports to Cuba with similar exports to a group of Caribbean countries, which in a general way resemble Cuba as regards location, climatic conditions, and economic development, shows that the exports to Cuba increased immediately after the conclusion of the treaty, whereas those to the other countries did not. But since 1907 the rates of growth of the two trades have not been substantially different.

When the articles of export are examined in groups according to the amount of tariff preference received, it appears that the increases in the American exports to Cuba for the several groups have varied directly with the amount of the preference. From another classification of Cuban imports—grouping selected articles in which the United States encountered competition from other countries—it again appears that the increases in the American exports have varied directly with the amount of the preference. The fact must not be overlooked, however, that these increases in trade with Cuba have been due not only to the treaty of 1902, but also in considerable part to the favorable influence upon Cuba of the reconstruction program carried out under the assurance of law and order guaranteed by the treaty of 1903. The close political relations between the United States and Cuba, the investment of American capital, the development in the United States of a large-scale export trade in manufactures, and the settlement in Cuba of Americans—these and other factors have operated along with the tariff preference to increase the trade between the two countries.

10. COMMERCIAL RELATIONS OF THE UNITED STATES WITH NEWFOUNDLAND.

Newfoundland was included with the Canadian Provinces in the operation of the reciprocity treaty of 1854. The treaty of Washington, of 1871, contained provisions for reciprocal free admission of products of the fisheries of the United States on the one hand and the British North American colonies on the other, but these ceased to operate in 1885. A treaty relating to Canadian and Newfoundland fisheries products was negotiated in 1888, which failed of ratification by the Senate of the United States. A convention for reciprocity between the United States and Newfoundland was negotiated in

1890, but in view of the objections of the Canadian Government, the British Government was not prepared to ratify this. A similar treaty was negotiated in 1902, but this was later so amended by the Senate Committee on Foreign Affairs that it became unacceptable to Newfoundland. Finally, in 1910, the fisheries question was settled by arbitration proceedings between the United States and Great Britain.

11. THE ATTEMPT TO ESTABLISH A RECIPROCITY ARRANGE-MENT WITH CANADA, 1910–1911.

Ever since the precipitate termination of the reciprocity treaty in 1865, there have been a number of obstacles operating to check the flow of trade between the United States and Canada, but not sufficing to discourage or to divert it. The United States tariff had always been something of a barrier. In Canada the Conservative Party framed a tariff (1879) intended especially to curtail the volume of importations from the United States, and when the Liberals came into power (1896) under Sir Wilfrid Laurier and adopted the "National Policy" of their opponents, they framed a tariff little less exclusive than that of the Conservatives.

The United States tariff act of 1897 contained a provision for increasing the import duties upon lumber by an amount equal to the export duties imposed by Canada upon logs. This threat was sufficient to cause Canada to remove her export duty, but several of the Canadian Provinces subsequently placed restrictions upon the exporting of timber, with the result that American capital went into the forests of those Provinces. The rates of the tariff of 1897 were almost prohibitive for certain Canadaian products. The influence of that fact was shown in the failure of the imports of these articles to increase in proportion to the growing ability of Canada to compete in the American market. On their side the Canadians had adopted the preferential tariff system and were turning their attention to developing better markets in the mother country and the other British colonies. Nevertheless, in spite of commercial policies, a number of factors—geographic, social, and industrial—tended to offset or nullify artificial restrictions upon the trade between the two countries.

The years at the end of the nineteenth century and the beginning of the twentieth were the most prosperous that Canada had ever experienced. This prosperity and the visions which it aroused of future development account, along with the influence of the tariff legislation of the United States, for the almost universal approval in Canada of the protective and preferential tariff policy. Yet the growth of Canadian manufactures and the establishing of protective duties, aimed principally at the wares of the United States, had remarkably little effect in reducing the imports from the latter country.

In operation, the preferential system, however it may have encouraged British-Canadian commerce, did not prevent American-Canadian commerce from growing rapidly. The United States has advantages in competition for the Canadian market which the measures actually adopted could not overcome,

When the Canadian Government revised the tariff in 1907, the most important feature of the revision was the adoption of an intermediate schedule of duties framed and intended for bargaining purposes. When in the United States the Republican Congress revised the tariff in 1909, it was no part of its purpose to weaken the principle of protection. Such reductions of duty as were made were chiefly in reference to foodstuffs and raw materials. The distinctive feature of the tariff act of 1909 was the approach to the two-schedule tariff system in the adoption of a general schedule and a maximum schedule, making it possible, without special negotiation, to invite favorable treatment of United States products and to penalize unfavorable treatment.

When the tariff act of 1909 went into effect, Canada was threatened with the maximum duties. Their imposition would probably have provoked a tariff war. To avert this, President Taft made advances to the Canadian Government which resulted finally in formal negotiations at Washington. An arrangement was agreed upon whereby Canada should give to certain specified imports from the United States the benefit of her intermediate instead of her general rates, and should in return be given the general, or minimum, rates of the American tariff. Slight though the Canadian concessions were, the arrangement was attacked by the Conservative Party in the Canadian Parliament.

The concluding conferences between the representatives of the two Governments were held in Washington in January, 1911. It was decided that a reciprocity arrangement should be framed, after which its provisions should be brought into effect by means of concurrent legislation rather than by treaty. The Canadians refused to grant the use of the inshore fisheries in return for the free admission of fish to the United States, but they consented to annul the license charges which had been required under the *modus vivendi* of 1887. It was found impossible to arrive at an agreement concerning pulp and paper duties, but it was agreed that the United States should admit free of duty Canadian wood pulp and paper upon which no export duty had been charged in Canada. This provision was later a part of the legislation passed by Congress and it became effective in spite of the defeat of the reciprocity measure in Canada. The proposed changes in the general tariff rates affected a considerable number of articles listed in four schedules. The arrangement was such that Canada was to obtain practically all the advantages that she had sought formerly in reciprocity proposals. while she was to concede little more than what she was already extending to most countries, but not to the United States, through the operation of her concessional tariff schedule.

Legislation to carry the arrangement into effect was introduced concurrently in the Congress of the United States and the Parliament of Canada on January 26, 1911. This legislation was passed by Congress. In Canada it became the subject of extended parliamentary debate and widespread and vigorous public discussion. The Conservative Party made the issue the basis of a concerted effort to drive the Liberals from power. Reasons of great variety were urged why the arrangement should not be approved. The past unconciliatory attitude of the United States and the allegation of sinister political designs—nothing less than a policy of annexation—were made use of as powerful arguments. The possibility of an injurious effect upon commerce within the Empire, with the consequent disadvantageous effect upon imperial relations, was strongly and effectively urged. Economic arguments of various types were presented. After several months' debate in the House of Commons, the Government appealed to the country. In the elections which followed, the Liberals were defeated and the Conservatives returned to power. The most potent among the causes which brought about the defeat of the Liberals appears to have been the argument that the adoption of the reciprocity policy would have as a consequence annexation. Other considerations, however, in no way connected with the reciprocity issue, contributed to the defeat.

The result of the Canadian election put an end to further consideration of the reciprocity measure. In 1913 a resolution was introduced in the House of Representatives in the United States, calling for the repeal of the reciprocity legislation of 1911, but this was rejected. The act providing for reciprocity with Canada still stands upon the statute books of the United States. The passage of a like act by the Canadian Parliament would put the arrangement, as negotiated in 1911, into effect.

II. THE MOST-FAVORED-NATION CLAUSE AND RECI-
PROCITY AGREEMENTS.

The most-favored-nation clause and the practice of reciprocity.—No single feature of modern commercial treaties has occasioned more or greater difficulty of interpretation than the presence therein of the most-favored-nation clause. Occurring almost universally, under widely differing conditions, in both the unconditional and the conditional forms, and in a veritable network of treaties, this clause has contributed at once to the solution of some and to the creation of other serious problems in commercial relations. Many such problems are bound to arise where and when some States do and some do not make reciprocity treaties.

As has already been mentioned, it has been the practice of the United States almost without exception to employ the conditional form of the most-favored-nation clause and to maintain the conditional construction. It is the practice of the European States to-day, though it has not always been, to employ the unconditional form and to maintain the unconditional construction.

The present European attitude is essentially a development of the past fifty years. The American position began with the making of the very first treaty of the United States, and from then until the present time the guiding principle in the commercial treaty-making policy of the United States has been that of bargaining between individual nations on the basis of reciprocal and progressive giving of favor for favor and concession for concession.

American statesmen have contended for equality of opportunity to bargain, but not for identity of treatment; for the removal and prevention of discriminations, but not for the same terms to all States at all times and in relation to all trade. A survey of the treaties to which the United States has been a party shows that this principle has been written expressly into nearly all of the most-favored-nation clauses. It further shows that since 1890 the United States has employed the favored-nation clause by no means as regularly as it did before that date; and that it has employed it in a less number of agreements, proportionately, than have some other States. In late years the United States has made various commercial agreements wherein most-favored-nation clauses have not been included; also, other types of commercial treaties and conventions wherein, because of previous difficulty over the interpretation of the most-favored-nation clause, it has apparently seemed advisable to both parties not to include the most-favored-nation provision specifically.

Theories and practices.—A survey of the United States practice in treaty construction shows that both the executive and the judicial departments of the American Government have consistently interpreted the favored-nation pledge as conditional and contingent upon the offering and acceptance of compensation. The leading commercial countries of Europe have moved first from the unconditional toward the conditional, and later back to the unconditional interpretation. British practice exhibits with greater regularity, with greater consistency, and with greater simplicity than does that of any other State the possibilities of unconditional most-favored-nation treatment. The Britsh attitude may be explained in part by reference to the fact of the free-trade policy and the peculiar commercial position of the United Kingdom, but it by no means follows that such circumstances are essential to the acceptance and maintenance of the unconditional favored-nation practice. The States of continental Europe, a few of them free trade, most of them protectionist, all practice unconditional favored-nation treatment. However, the views and practices of the European States have been subject to change and there are evidences that they may not hereafter continue what they have been in recent years.

Relation to the negotiation and application of reciprocity agreements.—In the controversy with Great Britain over the construction of the United States-Hawaiian treaty, both by the Hawaiian and by the United States Governments, the latter pointed out that "special privileges had been given in return for special, valuable considerations," and took the position that this was, because of geographical and political circumstances, a special and extraordinary case. Ultimately the logic of this position was accepted.

The application of the unconditional interpretation would have rendered of little effect the provisions of the United States tariff acts of 1890 and 1897, which authorized the negotiation of reciprocity agreements. To render the policy of special reciprocity effective, it is essential that the "American" interpretation of favored-nation obligations be applied. But the penalty-duties clause in the act of 1890 presented an issue which even the conditional interpretation would not properly meet. The principle of applying penalties on the basis of comparison of the relative heights of the tariff rates of the United States and those of the countries whose treatment of American goods laid them open to penalty is altogether different from that of bargaining with a view to securing and giving equality of treatment. It would leave it possible for some States, charging relatively low duties, to discriminate against the United States and yet escape the imposition of penalty duties; while other States not discriminating against the United States might nevertheless, because their general rates were higher than those of the United States, be subjected to the penalty duties. Penalty duties were actually thus applied to Colombia and Haiti, although those countries did not discriminate against the United States, while at the same time the benefit of the ordinary rates was extended to several countries which made no special concession to the United States.

In the course of a discussion which arose during the negotiation of reciprocity treaties under the tariff act of 1897, Mr. Sherman, Secretary of State, made a lengthy statement, thoroughly in conformity with views expressed by the long line of his predecessors, which succinctly sets forth the American conception of most-favored-nation obligations. Among other things, he said:

[The most-favored-nation clause] does not control the right of the nation adopting it to make exclusive compensatory agreements in just reciprocity with other nations * * *; the allowance of the same privileges and the same sacrifices of revenue duties, to a nation which makes no compensation, that has been conceded to another nation for an adequate compensation * * * destroys that equallty of market privileges which * * * the clause was intended to secure. * * * The right of other nations to enjoy the same special concessions depends on their ability to offer an equivalent compensation. * * * Such is the construction of the treaty clauses in question which the Government of the United States adopts in carrying out the late provisions of law for reciprocal conventions with other States.

The experience of the United States in meeting the claim of Switzerland in 1898 affords an excellent example of the impossibility of reconciling the practice of entering into reciprocity agreements with the giving of unconditional most-favored-nation pledges. It had to be admitted that, in the negotiation of the treaty of 1850 with Switzerland, the American plenipotentiary had pledged the United States to unconditional most-favored-nation treatment. The Government stood by the pledge. Switzerland was therefore given, without compensation, the benefit of concessions made to France in the special reciprocity treaty which had been concluded under the provisions of the act of 1897. Other States at once claimed the right to the same treatment, and it became necessary to denounce the favored-nation provision in the Swiss treaty.

Relations and discussions with Germany.—Not until the enactment of the bargaining provisions of the act of 1890 was the United States Government in a position to bargain effectively with Germany. Then, possessed of the necessary instruments, it did not undertake to enforce the claim of being entitled, without compensation, to the concessions which Germany made in her new treaties to European countries. Instead, in 1891, it entered into a bargain, which took form in the Saratoga convention, giving concessions for concessions.

In the course of the diplomatic controversies which arose and continued intermittently, and in which various claims were made by Germany on the basis of the treaty of 1828 between the United States and Prussia, the status of the treaty itself was finally brought into question. Although neither Government has ever officially declared the treaty not in force, it is possible to show that neither in theory nor in practice were its terms applied to German-American commercial relations after about 1890. The Saratoga convention of 1891 amounted to an admission on the part of each Government that it was not entitled automatically to concessions which the other had made to third nations. In 1900 the two countries negotiated a reciprocity convention whose terms were in conformity with the requirements of conditional most-favored-nation practice, but in 1903 Count Posadowsky declared, " The United States no longer enjoys most-favored-nation treatment in Germany." Nevertheless, when the reciprocity treaty was concluded between the United States and Cuba, the German Government contended that it should be given the opportunity to offer a concession through which to secure the benefit of the concessions made to Cuba. The circumstances being in several respects similar to those which had earlier attended Hawaiian-United States reciprocity relations, the United States did not in any way concede the German claim.

After the new German tariff law went into effect in 1906 a *modus vivendi* was arranged by which the United States secured the reduced rates made in the German treaties with European States, but this was not interpreted by Germany to include reductions subsequently made to other States.

Difficulty of reconciling reciprocity and most-favored-nation pledges.— The evidences show that the conclusion of reciprocity treaties is likely to lead to claims from States outside the agreement which, if granted, will defeat the purposes of the treaties, and which, if not granted, occasion the preferring of a charge of disloyalty to treaty obligations. The practice of making reciprocity treaties requires the conditional construction of the most-favored-nation clause. But the use by the United States of the conditional interpretation of the most-favored-nation clause has for half a century occasioned, and, if it is persisted in, will continue to occasion frequent controversies between the United States and European countries.

Possible developments.—So many have been the inconveniences and difficulties of most-favored-nation practice, it has frequently been suggested that the pledge be done away with. Any proposal entirely to eliminate it would call for very careful scrutiny of the arguments by which such proposal may be accompanied. The clause has performed, undoubtedly, very useful functions. The fact that it has had its inconveniences is not sufficient reason for abandoning it. Such a proposal, to merit consideration, should offer a substitute affording promise of more satisfactory performance.

On the other hand, if the clause is to be retained, it should be possible for the nations either to agree by common stipulation upon the meanings to be attached to each of the various forms and types of the clause or to adopt one standard form whose phraseology shall be unequivocal and whose function shall be clearly defined.

The effect, whether the conditional or the unconditional practice is followed, depends most of all upon the honesty, consistency, and rigidity or liberality with which the application is made to conform to the principle.

Whatever the relative advantages and whatever the difference in net results, the practice of " preference," " reciprocity," and conditional most-favored-nation treatment necessitate frequent and repeated special negotiations, constant bargaining, inevitable delays, actual inequality of treatment. There are without question circumstances in which special treatment is warranted; this is recognized in relation to certain circumstances in the favored-nation practices of all nations. But in the absence of special circumstances or special relations, special treatment inevitably creates unwarranted distinctions and tends to perpetuate discriminations.

When the peace settlement is being decided, it should be found possible to frame a model pledge or pledges intended to secure equality of treatment; also to devise machinery for the construction and enforcement of such, along with other international pledges.

III. BARGAINING TARIFFS AND COMMERCIAL TREATIES OF EUROPEAN STATES.

Tariff systems.—Practically every nation frames its tariff policy with the primary aim of promoting domestic industries. Most nations add to this primary object that of encouraging their export trade. To carry out its policy, each country chooses that system which appears to it best adapted to its circumstances and purposes. Various tariff systems may be distinguished according to the methods by which the lists of duties are made and by the numbers of lists employed. Thus there are statutory tariffs and conventional tariffs, single-schedule systems and multiple-schedule systems. Among multiple-schedule systems are the preferential, the maximum-and-minimum, and the general-and-conventional, and there are combinations of these. Of European States, five have single-schedule systems; the others have all adopted one or another of the multiple-schedule systems, most of them the general-and-conventional.

History of recent tariff and tariff treaty policies.—The most conspicuous single event in the commercial history of the nineteenth century was the conclusion of the Cobden treaty of 1860 between England and France, which marked the full acceptance by Great Britain of the principle of free trade. The contracting parties agreed to unconditional most-favored-nation treatment. Almost at once England generalized the concessions which she had made. There followed among European States a rapid succession of treaties, involving tariff reductions and including the unconditional most-favored-nation clause. The tendency of the period was toward free trade.

After 1875 protectionist sentiment began again to prevail, Germany taking the lead in a movement for the restoration and raising of rates of duty. New tariffs and new treaties superseded those which had been made after 1860.

In 1891 France adopted the maximum-and-minimum tariff system, and at about the same time Germany adopted the general and conventional system.

Thenceforth and until the beginning of the present war there might be distinguished in Europe three groups of States, representing three types of commercial policy and practice—a free trade, single-schedule tariff group; a protectionist, maximum-and-minimum tariff group; and a protectionist, general-and-conventional group. In the realm of treaty-making, all have retained the principle of most-favored-nation treatment, but the practical effect of the favored-nation pledge has been limited very decidedly by increased specialization of tariff schedules. The importance of the bargaining or bartering process has been constantly and considerably increased.

The commercial policy and tariff system of Germany.—Among the Central European States, commercial policy has been in no small measure made a means to political ends. First, Prussian policy was directed with a view to the unification of Germany; then, German policy was directed with a view to consolidating the interests of the Central European States. In 1871 Bismarck concluded with France the treaty of Frankfort, in which article XI provided for permanent, unconditional most-favored-nation treatment between Germany and France. This agreement has had, in operation, some advantages and some disadvantages for each of the contracting parties; it has operated, however, probably more than any other single treaty provision or other law, as a stabilizer of European commercial policy.

In 1879 Germany adopted a new tariff law whereby many protective duties were revived, duties on manufactured articles were increased, and the country was definitely committed to the policy of protection. In 1891 the Government presented to the Reichstag a new series of treaties, the Caprivi Treaties, which it had negotiated with neighboring countries, and these were soon confirmed almost without opposition. The characteristic feature of these treaties was that of tariff bargaining. The concessions made to each State were in the long run extended, by the operation of the most-favored-nation clause, to all the others of the treaty group and to some not in the group. The chief advantage which the treaties brought both to Germany and to the countries with which they were concluded lay in the fact that the duties in the conventional schedules could be counted on as fixed for a considerable and definite period. The effect upon German trade was far from decisive, but the treaties doubtless prevented certain undesirable developments which were imminent at the time when they were made.

Russia, following a tariff policy decidedly hostile to Germany, had raised the rates of her tariff, already high. Germany was provoked to retaliation, and there ensued a brief but bitter tariff war. In 1893 Russia adopted a maximum-and-minimum tariff, and subsequently each of the two countries raised its duties on the products which it imported from the other. So injurious were the effects on both that an agreement was effected and a new commercial treaty concluded between them in 1894, in which each made concessions to the other and most-favored-nation treatment was mutually pledged. There ensued a rapid revival of the trade which had suffered.

In 1892 Spain, the originator of the maximum-and-minimum system, though not the most conspicuous user, raised the rates of her schedules. This led to a tariff war between that country and Germany, which continued until, in 1906, each agreed to grant the other its lowest normal rates.

The adoption of the preferential system by Canada in 1897 led to strong representations by the German Government to the British Government, but to no actual disturbance of the commercial relations between Germany and the United Kingdom. Against Canada, Germany put into force the rates of her general tariff, and a tariff war ensued which lasted until a working arrangement was effected in 1910.

As between the United States and Germany, the trade was such that Germany was in no position to follow an aggressive tariff policy. An agreement was effected by the Saratoga convention of 1891, already mentioned, but it appears that during the years which followed nothing but the circumspection of the two Governments averted a tariff war. A convention was made in 1900 whereby Germany granted the United States the benefits of her conventional tariff and was given in return the rates which the United States had already extended on certain articles to France, Italy, and Portugal.

In 1897 the German Government appointed a commission which made extensive investigations by way of preparation for revision of the tariff and the making of new treaties. In 1901, in the face of bitter opposition from the agrarians, the Government introduced its proposals, involving the retention of the general-and-conventional system; a new 'tariff law was passed in 1902; new treaties were forthwith negotiated; and the new tariff and the new treaties went into effect in 1906.

The rates of the German tariff of 1906 evinced an inclination toward stricter application of the policy of protection. In the arrangement of schedules, though the general-and-conventional principle was retained, there was a partial adoption of features of the maximum-and-minimum system. The rates of the general schedule were specialized to an extent previously unknown. They were prepared with a view to negotiation, adjusted to the balancing of concession against concession with all the nicety of the most minute distinctions. The Government was authorized to employ penalty duties to enforce satisfactory treatment from States inclined to discriminate.

Treaties were concluded with eleven States, and from the concessions there was made up the conventional schedule, which was to be in force for twelve years from 1906. Though it may not be susceptible of conclusive proof, Germany appears on the whole to have bargained more successfully than the other parties to the treaties. She had had the advantage of superior organization and of patient and painstaking preparation for the negotiations.

In 1907 an agreement was made between the German and the American Governments whereby the United States was given the benefit of the German conventional rates. In 1909 the United States granted to Germany the minimum rates of the new tariff. After the passage of the United States tariff act of 1913, Germany attempted to negotiate a special agreement, but the response to her proposals was not favorable.

The commercial policy and tariff systems of France.—Although the Emperor, Napoleon III, had accepted the lead of England in making the Cobden treaty and others which followed, there remained in France strong opposition to the policy represented by these treaties. In 1875–76 the Government made an extensive investigation, from the returns of which it was evident that there was a preponderance of opinion favoring the multiple rather than the single-schedule tariff system.

In 1881 a new tariff law was passed, in which the rates on manufactured wares were increased, while raw materials and foodstuffs remained, as a rule, on the free list or were made subject to low rates. The general schedule was to be modified in operation by agreements with other powers. On the basis of this law, the Government negotiated treaties with seven European powers, in which rates were fixed, thereby establishing a new conventional schedule. With Great Britain, Germany, and Austria-Hungary there were framed simple conventions granting most favored-nation treatment.

In 1887 Italy promulgated a new tariff with sharp increases of rates, terminated her treaty with France, and demanded new and greater concessions. This led in 1888 to a tariff war, from which both countries suffered—Italy the more—and the two countries did not come to an agreement until 1898.

In 1892 France adopted a new tariff law which altered the whole basis of her commercial relations. She abandoned the general-and-conventional system in favor of an autonomous "maximum-and-minimum" system. The difference between the minimum and the maximum rates was approximately 25 per cent, and the law provided that the minimum rates should be applied to goods the produce of countries where French goods enjoyed equivalent concessions and were admitted at the lowest rates of duty. The Government was empowered to prolong the expiring commercial treaties, except in so far as they involved fixed rates of duty, and to apply the minimum rates to the wares of countries which would promise most-favored-nation treatment to France.

Several States were unwilling to make treaties on the basis of the concessions which France offered, and against such countries France put into effect the general tariff. Switzerland insisted upon modifications which the French Government refused to concede, and there resulted a tariff war which led to a considerable shrinkage in the trade between the two countries. Finally, in 1905, a convention was signed on the basis of a compromise on both sides. During the tariff war there had been a diversion of trade of both countries to other States, by which several of the latter, especially Germany and Belgium, profited.

A threatened tariff war with Spain was averted by an exchange of notes which did not involve changes of rates of duty. A short tariff war with Roumania was brought to an end by an agreement on the basis of most-favored-nation treatment.

Although France succeeded eventually in making agreements with all countries of commercial importance and in securing most-favored-nation pledges from most of these, she reached this end only after serious complications, which caused losses and left a permanent and somewhat adverse effect on her commercial relations. She did establish and maintain her autonomy in rate-making. The maximum tariff schedule stood essentially as a standardized warning. For the measure of autonomy which she gained, France paid by conceding a like measure to other countries, and she sacrificed guaranties of stability which the treaties of a former period had established.

When the time came for revision, the principles of autonomy and of the double schedule were accepted as established. The revision was confined to the rates. In the new law of 1910 the rates of both schedules were in general increased, though some were reduced. The disparity between the two was made almost systematically 50 per cent. The proposal of an intermediate tariff was rejected, but it was provided that the Government might under exceptional circumstances, and temporarily, apply the rates of the general tariff to products originating in countries where French products were not discriminated against, measures to carry out this provision to be submitted for ratification to the Parliament.

France had not, since 1892, extended her minimum rates in their entirety to the United States. A convention, signed in 1899, which would have given the United States most of the rates of the minimum tariff was not ratified by the American Government. Special provision for American trade was made in the French law of February 24, 1900, but all arrangements between the two countries were rendered void by the passage of the American tariff act of 1909, which terminated all reciprocity agreements.

On the day on which it enacted the tariff law of 1910, the French Parliament passed a law regulating commercial relations with the United States. This authorized the admission of certain products from the United States at the minimum rates and of certain other products at the rates of the old general tariff. More than two-thirds of the American imports into France were already entitled to enter free of duty. It was estimated that 29.3 per cent of the total imports would be admitted at the minimum rates, 0.4 per cent would be admitted at the old general rates, and 3.2 per cent of the total imports would be subjected to the new general rates.

The commercial policy and tariff system of Russia.—In Russia, as in the neighboring countries, the last quarter of the nineteenth century was marked by a movement toward higher rates of duty. The Russian Government was influenced, in addition to the usual motives, by a desire to make use of the tariff to control the balance of trade and to protect the national currency from an outflow of specie. Russia employed at that time the autonomous, single-schedule tariff system. In her treaties, she had in some cases the unconditional and in some the conditional most-favored-nation clause, but in her relations with Austria and Germany she had no claim for favored-nation treatment. In 1893 the Russian Government adopted the machinery both of the maximum-and-minimum and of the general-and-conventional tariff systems. The application of the maximum schedule to imports from Germany led to a tariff war, which was brought to an end by a commercial treaty whose conclusion marked the definite acceptance by Russia of the general-and-conventional tariff system. This was the product of political as well as economic considerations. Other treaties, on the model of the German treaty, followed with several countries.

Between 1901 and 1905 Russia applied penalty duties to various imports from the United States, in retaliation for the levying of countervailing duties on Russian sugar and petroleum. These punitive rates were withdrawn in 1905.

In 1903 Russia adopted a new general tariff designed for bargaining purposes, in which the rates were raised on many items, particularly manufactured wares, and the schedule was more sharply specialized than before. Commercial treaties followed with Germany, France, and several other States, and the new tariff went into effect in 1906. The system thus established was not materially altered until after the beginning of the European war.

Classification and characteristics of tariff systems.—Germany, Russia, Austria-Hungary, Bulgaria, Greece, Italy, Portugal, Roumania, Sweden, and Switzerland have adopted the general-and-conventional system and have made with their neighbors treaties involving reciprocal tariff concessions. Spain originated the maximum-and-minimum system and is still classed as a maximum-and-minimum country, but her practice has become essentially that of the general-and-conventional system.

France and Norway employ the maximum-and-minimum system. The theory of this system is that there shall be two schedules of rates, made autonomously, below the lower of which the treaty-making authorities may not make concessions. In practice, however, it has been found necessary to make concessions.

The preferential system requires at least two schedules and is autonomous, but its minimum schedule is intended, not for the most-favored nation, but for specially "preferred" nations. There is in Europe no State which employs a tariff which may properly be designated as "preferential"; but preferential practices in some form and degree are in force between several European countries and their colonies.

The countries of Europe which still adhere to the single schedule system are either "free-trade" countries with peculiar advantages, or countries of minor commercial importance. There has been a marked tendency toward the abandonment of a single-schedule system, especially among countries whose tariff policy has a "protective" feature.

As matters stood until 1914, it was the universal practice of European States to extend unconditional favored-nation treatment to each other. But the tendency in framing tariff schedules was toward detailed specifications, with the intent frequently and with the result that numerous concessions, apparently generalized, were in application particular and exclusive. As a consequence, it is by no means the case that the generalizing of concessions under the European construction of the most-favored-nation clause effects or maintains complete equality of treatment in a given market. One thing, however, tariff treaties do accomplish positively and effectively: they fix, or "bind," rates of duty for a specified term of years, thus creating an assurance that during that term these rates will not be increased.

As with constitutions, so with commercial policies and tariff systems—the advantages or disadvantages of a particular type or feature must be estimated from the point of view of the situation and circumstances, the needs and the possibilities of each individual country at a particular time.

PART I. RECIPROCITY AND TARIFF AGREEMENTS OF THE UNITED STATES.

PART I. RECIPROCITY AND TARIFF AGREEMENTS OF THE UNITED STATES.

RECIPROCITY AND TARIFF AGREEMENTS OF THE UNITED STATES.

"RECIPROCITY."

It is necessary to distinguish between the practice of making agreements on the basis of reciprocal concessions and that of making what may be designated in a strict sense as "reciprocity agreements." States may reciprocally agree to give each other the same treatment in respect to particular and identical matters; in such a transaction there is exchanged a mutual pledge. Or, they may agree that one shall concede certain things and the other shall reciprocate by conceding other things in return; here there are exchanged concessions considered equivalent. But the mere making of an agreement on the basis of such reciprocal giving and taking, whether of identical or of equivalent concessions, does not constitute the making of a "reciprocity agreement," in the specialized sense of the term. A "reciprocity agreement," in the specialized sense, is a treaty or convention in which the contracting States grant to each other particular concessions in return for particular concessions, without the intention or expectation that these concessions shall be generalized. This does not imply that the concessions need in all cases be exclusive, still less that the making of like concessions to some other countries is debarred by the absence of the expectation that they shall be generalized. In the present report, the terms "reciprocity," "reciprocity agreements," and "reciprocity experiences," are used in the specialized sense.

THE RECIPROCITY EXPERIENCES OF THE UNITED STATES.

Previous to 1890 the United States had negotiated tariff treaties with six countries: One each with the German Zollverein (1844), Canada (1854), Hawaii (1875), Spain—for Cuba and Porto Rico (1884), the Dominican Republic (1884), and two with Mexico (1856 and 1883). Two of these only, the treaties with Canada and Hawaii, became effective. The treaty with the Zollverein was not ratified by the Senate. The treaties with Spain and the Dominican Republic, which were negotiated during the administration of President Arthur, were withdrawn by President Cleveland before securing the ratification of the Senate. A treaty with Great Britain for the British West Indies had been in process of negotiation, but when the British Government heard of the fate of the Spanish treaty it withdrew from the negotiations. The first of the treaties with Mexico failed of ratification in the Senate; the second was ratified, but could not be put into effect because the legislation necessary was never enacted by Congress. There was also negotiated in 1884, with Spain for Cuba and Porto Rico, a commercial agreement of minor importance, providing for reciprocal abolition of certain discriminating

59

duties, which remained in effect until the negotiation of a new agreement in 1892 in conformity with the provisions of section 3 of the act of 1890.

With 1890 there began a period in which reciprocity agreements were made, not sporadically and independently, but according to a definite policy adopted and provided for by Congress. In accordance with the provisions of the tariff act of 1890 the United States made reciprocity agreements with six American countries and with Austria-Hungary, Germany, Great Britain—for the British West Indies, and Spain—for Cuba and Porto Rico. An informal arrangement was also made with France. A treaty which had been negotiated with Costa Rica was not ratified by the legislature of that country. In 1888 a treaty for the fisheries had been negotiated with Newfoundland, but it failed to secure ratification by the United States Senate. In 1890 a draft of a convention with Newfoundland was signed in Washington, but this was withdrawn by the British Foreign Office as a consequence of representations made by Canada. The treaties actually concluded in this period were terminated when the tariff act of 1894 went into effect.

A second period of systematic agreements began in 1897. Under the provisions of section 3 of the tariff act of 1897 a group of reciprocity treaties were negotiated: With the United Kingdom for Jamaica, Turks and Caicos Islands, Barbados, Bermuda, and British Guiana; with Denmark for the Danish West Indies; with the Dominican Republic; with Nicaragua; with Ecuador; with the Argentine; and with France; but the treaties of this group were not ratified. Agreements were negotiated with France, Portugal, Germany, Italy, Switzerland, Spain, Bulgaria, the United Kingdom, and the Netherlands; and these were ratified. Brazil established a special preferential arrangement. In 1902 a convention was negotiated with Newfoundland, but this was not ratified. In 1903 a special reciprocity treaty, independent of the tariff act, was made with Cuba.

After the enacting of the tariff act of 1909, a reciprocity arrangement was negotiated with Canada; the legislation necessary to put this into effect was passed by Congress, but the Canadian people rejected the plan at the polls and the arrangement did not receive the approval of the Canadian Parliament.

1. RECIPROCITY TREATY WITH CANADA, 1854.

RECIPROCITY TREATY WITH CANADA, 1854.

Special factors affecting commercial and political relations between Canada and the United States.—Canada and the United States are uniquely situated with regard to each other. Geographically they are contiguous across the whole of a broad continent; nowhere is the political separation emphasized by difficult physical barriers. The boundary is in fact throughout half of its extent a mere geometrical line. Socially the populations on both sides are possessed, generally speaking, of a striking similarity in race, language, laws, and institutions. Thus, both inherent and incidental factors would seem favorable to the growth of a reciprocal trade based upon considerations of mutual advantage. "Each several Province of the Dominion," Goldwin Smith once remarked, "is by nature wedded to a commercial partner on the south." The very closeness of the people and of their interests has tended, however, to emphasize such divergences of opinion as the political separation of the two peoples would naturally foster. As time has passed, it is true, these political sources of disagreement have been made to yield somewhat—by usage and by treaty—to economic considerations, but now and again the old issues have prominently reasserted themselves, and they remain even today among the decisive factors which can not be overlooked.

Attempts have been made several times to bring the two countries, by the removal of commercial restrictions, into closer economic relations. Although in some instances these efforts have been productive of positive results, they have more often failed, and in all cases they have been impeded by political, industrial, and territorial considerations. Commercial interests on one or both sides have been confused with, and sometimes obscured by, conflicting claims over fisheries and over lake and river navigation; by incompatible policies of railway and canal control; by boundary disputes; by dissimilarity of industrial conditions and developments; and by the fact of different relations, respectively, with other countries. On the Canadian side the question of possible political consequences has dominated all other considerations; even in the United States this question has sometimes influenced opinion. On both sides of the border unrestricted commerce has been regarded in some quarters as the only certain preventive of annexation, in others as a condition tending irresistibly to induce it.

ANTECEDENTS AND MAKING OF THE RECIPROCITY TREATY.

British colonial policy before 1850.—Until the year 1846 the British North American Provinces had not a commercial policy of their own. In their relations with other countries they were governed from England: British interests and policies, rather than Canadian, determined the form and the course of their relations with other countries. While this was the case, efforts of the United States to establish freer intercourse with the people of the Provinces proved futile. "The Government of the United States," wrote Henry Clay in 1826, "has always been anxious that the trade between them and the British colonies should be placed upon a liberal and equitable basis. There has not been a moment since the adoption of the present Constitution when they were not willing to apply to it the principles of a fair reciprocity and equal competition; there has not been a time during the same period when they have understood the British Government to be prepared to adopt that principle. The struggle on the side of Great Britain was to maintain her monopoly and on that of the United States to secure an equal participation in the trade and intercourse between them and the British colonies."[1] This applied to the British West Indian colonies as well as to the Canadian Provinces.

Changed conditions after 1850.—The great revolution in colonial and commercial policy which was carried through by the British Government in 1846 and the years immediately following made it at once possible and necessary for the North American Provinces to seek closer commercial relations with the United States. "Canada," which then consisted of the united Provinces of Upper and Lower Canada (later Ontario and Quebec), was hard hit by the repeal of the Corn Laws, under which grain from the Provinces had been admitted to Great Britain at generously preferential rates. The Maritime Provinces also suffered, though not in equal degree, in their shipbuilding and seafaring interests from the repeal of the Navigation Acts, and in their forest industry from the reduction of the preference in the British duties on lumber.

Influence of the new British policy upon Canada.—In 1850 the total population of these British North American Provinces was slightly less than two and one-half millions. Of them all, "Canada," with 1,852,265 inhabitants, was by far the most populous and progressive, but was at the same time the least advantageously circumstanced in respect to commercial opportunities. The only access of this Province to the outside world was either through the United States or by way of the St. Lawrence River—which was closed to navigation for five months in the year. There were no railways in Upper Canada, and in Lower Canada there had been built only fifty-five miles. The greater part of the trade, even of the western part of the Province, had to pass through Montreal and along the river. The canals and railways south of the border, which afforded an outlet safer, quicker, cheaper, and more regular than the river route, were first made available for the Provinces in 1850 by the passage in the United States of the bonding act, permitting Canadian imports to pass in bond without duty through the American customs houses. The importance of this act to the Province of Canada was shown in the following year, when nearly half of her imports crossed the American border. Hampered by her comparative isolation, Canada's commerce was further restricted by the limited variety of her products—which were derived almost wholly from agriculture and forestry, supplemented by milling and by a certain amount of shipbuilding at the river ports. Her staple exports were lumber, wheat, and flour, and for these England was her principal market.

---

[1] Clay to Vaughan, Oct. 11, 1826; quoted, Andrews Report, 1850. 31st Cong., 2d sess., Sen. Ex. Doc. No. 23, p. 6.

The withdrawal of the British preferences forced the colony to shift for itself and produced for the time being a most depressing effect upon its commerce. A select committee, appointed by the Canadian Parliament in 1858 to inquire into the course of trade, declared that the effect of the repeal "was to depreciate the value of all articles grown or produced in Canada 20 per cent under the value of like articles grown or produced in the United States, and this difference in value continued until 1854." By 1849, according to Lord Elgin, property in most of the Canadian towns had fallen 50 per cent in value. Three-fourths of the commercial men were bankrupt, and a large proportion of the exportable products of Canada were obliged to seek a market in the States. They paid at the frontier a duty of 20 per cent. "* * * If free navigation and reciprocal trade with the Union be not secured for us, the worst, I fear, will come, and that at no distant day."[1] Even before the preference was abolished, protests and petitions sent to England from the Provincial Parliament, from boards of trade, and from the Governor General and other prominent individuals, had met with the reply from Gladstone, then Secretary for the Colonies, that the policy of the Imperial Government would not be modified in Canada's interest.

Attempts to establish closer relations with the United States.—But the legislation of the Peel government, although it thus threw the Provinces upon their own resources, afforded to them by that very fact the opportunity to act for themselves. An amendment in 1846 to the British Possessions Act put it in their power thereafter to initiate and determine their own commercial policy. The Canadian Inspector General of Customs, speaking in Parliament in 1847, said: "The British Possessions Act leaves the Province [Canada] free to pass such enactments with regard to duties and trade as may be found best suited to her wants and position, and * * * to meet on terms of friendly reciprocity any advances which the neighboring Republic may be disposed to make for the mutual encouragement of industry and trade * * *."[2]

It became possible, then, for Canada to choose among three divergent policies. She might seek to subordinate foreign to domestic trade, by protection and bounties, and to secure her independence of American canals and railroads by building up a transportation system of her own. Or she might, going to the other extreme, cast in her lot with the neighboring Republic, and ask for annexation. Or, between these two extremes, she might seek the necessary outlet for her products in and through the United States, and yet retain her political connection with the mother country. Each of these possible policies had its advocates, and the situation was further complicated by internal dissensions arising from racial and religious antipathies. Of these possibilities, the course most promising at the moment was that offered by the compromise policy of close commercial relations with, but political independence of, the United States. To this plan the Canadian Government committed itself, with the hearty acquiescence, from the beginning, of Great Britain.

---

[1] Walrond, Letters and Journals of Lord Elgin, p. 70.   [2] Mirror of Parliament, Mar. 24, 1847.

Political complications.—Although the Canadian and the British Governments had chosen the policy indicated, the tardy methods of diplomacy and the indifference of the United States to all overtures reinforced the position of the advocates of the extreme policies. Business depressions and bitter domestic dissensions gave rise to an organized movement, short-lived but threatening, for annexation. Lord Elgin's letters to the Secretary for the Colonies show that the matter gave him no little anxiety. In 1849 he wrote: "A great deal of this talk (of annexation) is * * * bravado, and a great deal the mere product of thoughtlessness. Undoubtedly it is in some quarters the utterance of very serious conviction; and if England will not make the sacrifices which are absolutely necessary to put the colonists here in as good a position commercially as the citizens of the States * * * the end may be nearer than we wot of."[1] The movement seems to have culminated six months later with the publication in Toronto, Montreal, and Quebec of manifestoes in favor of annexation. After this there was no further organized effort to promote annexation; but the movement led to a widespread conviction on both sides of the border that the opening of the American market was vital to Canadian prosperity, and that Canada's failure to secure that market by other means would inevitably lead to her absorption into the United States. On the other hand there were those who considered that intimate and unrestricted commerce would be an entering wedge for political union. As early as 1846 the Quebec Board of Trade made this an argument against the repeal of the British preferential duties, asserting that it would "gradually, silently, and imperceptibly" wean Canada from allegiance to England and would foster closer connection with the United States.[2] In the United States, also, anticipation of such a political result was hinted at or voiced more than once in the Senate debates on reciprocity. Whatever the validity and bearing of the contention then and subsequently, there can be no question of the fact that the movement for annexation in 1849 strengthened the efforts of Lord Elgin and the Canadian Parliament to secure commercial reciprocity.

Beginnings of the protectionist movement in Canada.—The delay which occurred before success followed the efforts to secure reciprocity turned the thoughts of the Canadians toward other possibilities; sentiment grew among them favoring protection and Government aid to transportation and industry. Finance ministers and other cabinet officers of Canada came, in the formative years of that country's commercial policy, one after another to Washington with offers of reciprocity, assimilation of duties, and other measures looking toward freer commercial intercourse. Meeting with delays or rebuffs, they returned to Canada urging retaliation, protection to home industries, and development of national self-sufficiency. Within a decade Cayley and Galt were able to put through distinctly protectionist tariff acts; and Isaac Buchanan, earlier an ardent free trader, abandoned his former principles and became the Canadian apostle of protection.[3] So utterly dependent, however, was Canada on American markets and transportation facilities that no serious opposition was offered from any quarter to proposals for commercial reciprocity.

---

[1] Walrond, Letters and Journals of Lord Elgin, p. 100.
[2] Porritt, E., Sixty Years of Protection in Canada, 1846–1907, p. 54.
[3] Porritt, op. cit., p. 218.

Attitude of the United States.—In the United States, meanwhile, certain features of the situation were favorable to Canada's hopes. The Walker Tariff Act was passed in 1846, the year of the repeal of the British Corn Laws. From that date to the outbreak of the Civil War sentiment in the United States in favor of protection was probably weaker than it had been at any other time since 1815. Although the act of 1846 went no further than to reduce the amount of protection given in the previous tariff law, its author professed to be a free trader and was actively favorable to Canadian overtures. Here and there voices were raised predicting disaster; but the sentiment in Congress and in the country as a whole was favorable to a liberal commercial policy.

Obstacles to the removal of trade barriers.—But there were two obstacles in the way of reciprocity. One was that Canada had little to offer for which the United States cared to bargain. Outside of the border States little was known in the United States of Canada's possibilities. Imports into Canada were relatively small in amount and not much impeded by the tariff, which had now been reduced to an average of $7\frac{1}{2}$ per cent ad valorem. Previous to 1846 there had been but four years in which the total exports of the United States to all the British Provinces in North America had exceeded $6,000,000; and in no year had the imports therefrom reached $2,000,000.[1] A more important obstacle to adequate consideration of Canadian trade relations lay in the fact that the attention of the United States was taken up with the Mexican War. The prosecution of that war, the terms of peace, the organizing of the territory acquired, and the problem of extending or excluding slavery—all involving grave constitutional questions—occupied Congress so completely that there was left little time or interest for such a matter as Canadian commerce. These two groups of factors, rather than any positive opposition in the United States to reciprocity, delayed for eight years efforts to arrive at an agreement.

THE TREATY OF 1854.

Unsuccessful efforts toward concurrent legislation.—Despite the difficulties which stood in the way, sentiment in Canada was committed to the policy. As early as May, 1846, the Canadian Parliament had voted an address to the Queen, praying that if the Corn Laws were to be repealed, negotiations should be opened with the United States with a view to securing free admission of Canadian products. Accordingly Sir Richard Pakenham, the British minister in Washington, was instructed to take up the matter at the first favorable opportunity. Inasmuch as a general revision of the Canadian tariff was pending, Pakenham waited until December, and then approached Mr. Walker, Secretary of the Treasury, on the subject. He found Walker favorably disposed. In the following year, 1847, however, Pakenham left Washington, and no further action was taken at that time; but in order to show good will and to pave the way for reciprocity, Canada, by lowering the duties on American manufactures from $12\frac{1}{2}$ per cent to $7\frac{1}{2}$ per cent and raising the duties on British manufactures from $5\frac{1}{2}$ per cent to $7\frac{1}{2}$ per cent, repealed her differential duties and put her commerce with the United

---

[1] Report of Bureau of Statistics, 1894, and 53d Cong., 2d sess., Sen. Ex. Doc. No. 106, p. 2.

States on the same footing as that with Great Britain. In January, 1848, negotiations were resumed between the Secretary of the Treasury and the British chargé d'affaires, and it was agreed that the best way to effect reciprocity would be by concurrent legislation rather than by treaty. To that end a bill was drafted providing for the free admission to each country from the other of grain, breadstuffs, vegetables, fruits, seeds, animals, hides, wool, butter, cheese, tallow, horn, salt and fresh meat, ores of all metals, ashes, timber, staves, wood, and lumber. This schedule included almost everything that Canada then had to sell and but few items which she bought in other than insignificant quantities. But the arrangement was not so unequal as it appeared, for in the previous years Canada had repealed the British preference; her tariff was designed to afford a moderate revenue rather than protection, and it was hoped that the United States would be moved by this liberal policy to reciprocate.

Furthermore, it was expected that opposition to extension of the schedule—so as to include, for instance, manufactures—would come from the region south of the border, not from that north of it. According to a memorandum presented the following year by the Canadian Inspector of Customs: "It has been suggested that the same principle should be extended to the manufactures of the United States and Canada. To this Canada could have no objection; on the contrary, we feel persuaded that it would be to our advantage; but it was considered unwise even to propose it, because American manufacturers would feel apprehensive that British fabrics might be introduced by this means through Canada into the United States, at duties considerably lower than those imposed by the present American tariff."

In the United States the bill, as drawn, was favorably reported from the House Committee on Commerce. So little interest was shown that it passed the House without opposition or discussion. In the Senate it was brought in without any report, statistics, or explanation of details. But here it found a harder road. Although reported in July, 1848, it did not come up for discussion until January of the next year. Opposition at once developed. The obvious criticism was made that all the enumerated articles were exported from and few of them were imported into Canada. Furthermore, it was claimed by the opponents of reciprocity that under the most-favored-nation clause in other commercial treaties, the American market would be opened to the agricultural products of the world, and American farmers would be put on a free trade basis, while manufacturers would be left protected.[1] Even among Southern free traders there was objection to this as class discrimination. A further objection was that the measure would sacrifice the interests of the western agricultural sections to the interests of New York and New England, since it would enable the latter region to absorb the trade between Canada and foreign countries. Senator Hunter, of Virginia, remarked that the arguments favoring the bill seemed to contemplate annexation—which the South would have bitterly opposed as disturbing the balance of power in the Federal Government. These arguments were vigorously combated, however, by Gen. Dix, chairman of the Senate Committee on Commerce, who was the chief ad-

---

[1] See p. 383, infra.

vocate of the bill. He denied that any injury would come to the farmers, since the United States exported agricultural produce to the same foreign markets as Canada and in enormously greater quantities; he considered the suggestion of sectionalism baseless, for the benefits to northern railroads, shipping, commission merchants, and other commercial interests would not involve the sacrificing of other regions; and he refused to admit that political union was contemplated. Sentiment in the Senate appeared, on the whole, decidedly favorable to the bill, but a few determined men stood in the way of its passage and it did not come to a vote in that body.

In spite of this setback, the Canadian Parliament passed the measure in the following April, 1849, with the provision that it should take effect as soon as similar legislation should be secured in the United States.

New Proposals.—The proposals were subsequently given a new form. The repeal of the British navigation laws in 1849 and the reduction of preferential lumber duties in the United States threatened to injure the Maritime Provinces, as the repeal of the corn duties had injured all the Canadian Provinces. Meanwhile a new president, Tyler, and a new Congress had been installed at Washington. The whole reciprocity question was taken up anew. Under instructions from his Government the British chargé d'affaires proposed a treaty of reciprocity which should include all the British North American Provinces. The Governor General of Canada sent to Washington a special commissioner—a mission which appears to have been the first instance of any participation by Canada in negotiations with a foreign country. After an interval of several months, Mr. Clayton, Secretary of State, informed the British chargé that the President objected to the proposed treaty because "any measure affecting the revenue of the United States should be considered by the representatives of the people." [1]

Thus thrown back upon Congress, the supporters of reciprocity introduced in 1850 bills in both Houses. The Senate bill never received a hearing. The House bill, after an attempt had been made to include provision for the free navigation of the St. Lawrence, was dropped, this despite the promise of the British minister at Washington that if it were passed his Government would at once consent to open the river.

The Fisheries Incident.—In Canada the delay and frequent postponements had by this time aroused no little resentment. The Canadian Parliament threatened to reenact the differential duties and to close the Canadian canals to American traffic. [2] The Maritime Provinces began a more effective retaliation by stringently enforcing the inshore fishery restrictions. But Congress ignored these threats, and for more than a year "did nothing, said nothing, thought nothing on the subject." [3] The British minister renewed to Mr. Webster, who had succeeded Clayton as Secretary of State, proposals for a treaty, offering in return for reciprocity the free use of the coast fisheries and free navigation of the St. Lawrence. The President declined to negotiate, although in his annual message he asked the favorable attention of Congress to the correspondence.

---

[1] Clayton to Crampton, June 26, 1849.
[2] 32d Cong., 1st sess., Sen. Ex. Doc. No. 1, pt. 1, p. 87.
[3] Senator Seward, Cong. Globe, Aug. 14, 1852.

In the summer of 1852 a bill embracing the British proposals was again under discussion in the House when there occurred an interruption: the Maritime Provinces had undertaken to exclude American fishermen from provincial waters. The question of the inshore fisheries was a source of contention between the United States and the British North American Provinces throughout the nineteenth century. Up to the War of 1812 American fishermen had been subjected to no restrictions in respect to these waters; they had enjoyed their free use; but by the Convention of 1818 they were excluded from waters within the 3-mile limit except for refuge and repairs, and to take wood and water. According to the British interpretation, the 3-mile limit was to be measured from headland to headland, which meant the closing to Americans of the richest fishing grounds, the great bays. In 1852 the Maritime Provinces attempted rigidly to enforce the exclusion for the purpose, among others, of impressing upon the United States the desirability of reciprocity. They seized many American vessels, confiscated some, fined some, and held some until the close of the season. The Americans threatened to defend themselves by force, whereupon the Provinces appealed for help, and there were sent from England several armed vessels. This produced a sensation, and brought about immediate action in Washington. Commodore Perry was ordered to the fishing grounds to protect Americans in the exercise of their rights. A very delicate situation developed, but fortunately nothing untoward occurred, and the tension was somewhat eased by England's explanation of the character of the force sent over and the instructions given for its guidance. It was obvious, however, that a very real menace to peaceful relations existed while the fisheries disputes remained unsettled. The British Government refused to treat of the question apart from commercial reciprocity, and progress in diplomatic conferences was delayed on account of the necessity of referring every point and step of importance to London.

Increased interest in the United States.—The people of the United States began meanwhile to show more interest in the economic aspects of reciprocity. Petitions were sent to Washington from the chambers of commerce of New York and other cities and from the larger towns of the northern frontier; and articles commending reciprocity appeared throughout the country in many important journals and reviews. Accordingly, while conferences were still being held at the State Department, the House Committee on Commerce, under the chairmanship of Seymour of New York, brought in a new reciprocity bill with an enthusiastically favorable report. The schedule drafted in the earlier bill was lengthened to include agricultural implements, axes, fish of all kinds, burrstones, ground and unground gypsum; dyestuffs, rice, cotton, hemp, flax, unmanufactured tobacco, and unrefined sugar. The first two items were intended to conciliate the manufacturing interests; free fish was to be a compensation to the Provinces in return for American use of the St. Lawrence and the coast fisheries; grindstones and gypsum were products peculiar to Nova Scotia and in great demand in the United States; the other articles were inserted to gain the favorable attention of the South. But the opposition to free lumber, free manufactured gypsum, and some minor details, though it was not strenuous, was effective. Once more during the remainder of a short session "disputes over the Territories blocked the ordinary course of legislation," and a vote was not reached.

The situation was peculiar. The Canadian Provinces were clamoring for reciprocity, and to secure it, were offering the use of their canals, rivers, and the coast fisheries; in the United States, with the exception of the Maine lumbermen and some minor interests, the sentiment was almost universally favorable. Yet despite the obvious disadvantage to both countries of leaving outstanding problems in their relations unsettled, the American Government after seven years seemed still totally incapable of reaching a decision. The disturbed state of domestic affairs, manifestly growing worse, obscured the importance of everything else.

Negotiation of the treaty.—The British Government finally pushed the negotiations to a successful conclusion. Although but slightly interested in the trade relations of the Provinces with their neighbor, Great Britain was much concerned, as was later frankly stated,[1] over the political complications in which she was involved through protecting their claims. In order to relieve this situation, the Governor General, Lord Elgin, was directed to proceed to Washington, where, during the spring of 1854, he and Secretary Marcy drew up a treaty which covered the several matters then at issue. This was signed on June 5, it was ratified by the Senate on August 2, ratifications were exchanged on September 9, and it was proclaimed on September 11, 1854.

Provisions of the treaty.—The treaty provided for:

Articles I and II. The mutual enjoyment of the fisheries on the Atlantic coast north of the thirty-sixth parallel, north latitude.

Article III. The reciprocal admission by each country of articles the growth or produce of the other, as follows:

Grain, flour, and breadstuffs of all kinds.
Animals of all kinds.
Fresh, smoked, and salted meats.
Cotton, wool, seeds, and vegetables.
Undried fruits, dried fruits.
Fish of all kinds.
Products of fish and of all other creatures living in the water.
Poultry, eggs.
Hides, furs, skins, or tails undressed.
Stone or marble in its crude or unwrought state.
Slate.
Butter, cheese, tallow.
Lard, horns, manures.
Ores of metals of all kinds.
Coal.
Pitch, tar, turpentine, ashes.
Timber and lumber of all kinds, round, hewed, and sawed, unmanufactured in whole or in part.
Firewood.
Plants, shrubs, and trees.
Pelts, wool.
Fish oil.
Rice, broom corn, and bark.
Gypsum, ground and unground.
Hewn, or wrought, or unwrought burr of grindstones.
Dyestuffs.
Flax, hemp, and tow, unmanufactured.
Unmanufactured tobacco.
Rags.

---

[1] Gray, Confederation of Canada, p. 156.

Article IV. The reciprocal use of canals; the use by Americans of the St. Lawrence River; the use by British subjects of Lake Michigan; and freedom from duty on lumber cut on American territory, floated down the St. John River, and exported from the Province of New Brunswick to the United States.

The treaty put into effect.—The treaty was to take effect as soon as the laws required to put it in operation had been passed by the British Parliament, the Provincial Parliaments, and Congress. It was to remain in force for ten years, and thereafter subject to twelve months' notice by either party for termination.

Legislation was passed by Congress on August 5, 1854, authorizing the President, when he had sufficient evidence that the necessary laws had been passed on the other side, to put the treaty in force by proclamation. Pursuant to this provision, President Pierce issued a proclamation putting the treaty into effect on March 16, 1855.

At the expiration of the tenth year the United States Government gave notice of abrogation, so the treaty was in force for but eleven years.

ABROGATION OF THE TREATY.

Three main causes contributed to bring about the abrogation of the reciprocity treaty: the growth in Canada of opinion favorable to protection, the hostile sentiment aroused in the United States by Canada's attitude during the Civil War, and the need of increased revenue in both countries. To these may be added the dissatisfaction of the fish, coal, and lumber interests in the United States, opposed to the treaty from the first, but with whose opposition Congress and the country generally had not been in sympathy.

The development of protectionist opinion in Canada.—The idea of an independent national development for Canada had won increasing favor during the years of uncertainty immediately preceding the treaty. To achieve this, a protective tariff and Government assistance for the building of railways were deemed essential, and these measures continued to be strongly advocated, in spite of the increased prosperity, during the ensuing period. The Association for the Promotion of Industry used much the same form of reasoning in Canada as had been current among advocates of protection in the United States thirty years before, and pointed to the industrial growth across the border as proof of the soundness of its theories. But few of the members were willing wholly to sacrifice reciprocity for protection, and the most ardent of them urged a customs union with the United States and protection against the rest of the world. In the United States the proposal for a customs union was not seriously considered. It was urged on both sides of the border that a high tariff on Canada's part would run counter to "the spirit of the treaty."

Canada's revenue requirements.—The compelling need for increased revenues was seized upon by the protectionists in Canada to force the revision of the tariff to the disadvantage of the United States. Many public men and the boards of trade of the chief cities of Canada strongly opposed the new policy; but the very urgent necessity for more revenue enabled the protectionists to triumph. When to the new tariff was added a discriminatory canal policy, there arose in the United States complaints that could not be ignored. The railroads particularly resented a policy designed to afford a revenue to be spent upon public works and intended to divert business which had been theirs. Agents of the Treasury Department, detailed to investigate the operation of Canada's new legislation, reported in the spring of 1860,[1] but no action was taken by the Government.

Opposition to the treaty in the United States—Action of Congress.—In the spring of 1861 the New York Legislature requested Congress to appoint commissioners to negotiate for relief or by some other means to protect American citizens from the unjust and unequal operation of Canada's measures. Nothing effective came of this. A year and a half went by before, in December, 1863, threats of retaliation were heard in Congress. A joint resolution to abrogate the treaty was introduced in the House by Mr. Morrill, of Vermont; but for a time it was successfully opposed by Mr. Ward, chairman of the Committee on Commerce. Mr. Ward himself offered a bill for the appointment of commissioners to negotiate a new treaty. In the debate over the bill, in May, 1864, there developed a strong opposition to the continuance of the treaty. Most of the speeches against it were vague; they expressed the belief that Canada was deriving more benefit than the United States, but failed to show how any American interest was actually being damaged. A few speakers were more definite. Mr. Kellogg, of Michigan, thought the treaty injured the lumbermen and woolgrowers of his State. Mr. Pike, of Maine, commented at great length upon the hostile sentiment shown by Canadians after the war began. Mr. Morrill expressed a general belief that not a single interest in the United States was subserved by the treaty; that it was not needed to secure the use of Canadian railroads and canals, since these were dependent upon American patronage; and that it had completely reversed the "balance of trade." He offered an amendment providing that notice be given for the abrogation of the treaty. The majority of the House, however, were still opposed to abrogation, and the amendment was defeated by a vote of 82 to 74. Though the House showed a general approval of Mr. Ward's proposal for a commission, it postponed the vote on the bill as a whole until the following December. During the interim the ill feeling against Canada and Great Britain was greatly stimulated by the lawless acts along the Canadian border of sympathizers with the Confederacy, acts which had become so menacing that President Lincoln had deemed it necessary to address a note on the subject to the British Government.

The House votes to abrogate the treaty.—Profoundly exasperated by these "assaults and depredations," the House reversed its vote of the previous May and passed, on December 13, 1864, by a vote of 85 to 57, Mr. Morrill's joint resolution for unconditional notice of abrogation.

In the Senate the fight for abrogation was led by Sumner of Massachusetts, and Collamer of Vermont. Collamer objected to the treaty, first, because of the adverse "trade balance" which he claimed resulted from it, and, secondly, because of Canada's discriminatory tariff and canal policy. Sumner based his opposition to it upon the need of the United States for increased revenue. He admitted that the fisheries settlement was satisfactory and that commerce had grown during the existence of the treaty; but he

[1] 36th Cong., 1st sess., H. Ex. Doc. No. 96.

believed that most of this growth was due to increase of population and transportation facilities and would therefore not be affected by abrogation. His appeal to fiscal considerations was the most telling argument used in either House. In 1850 the customs receipts on imports from all the Provinces had been only half a million dollars.[1] By 1854 they had grown to $1,524,457, of which $1,243,403 was collected upon imports from Canada alone. But under the treaty the cost of collection exceeded the amount of the duties.[2] Sumner estimated that in ten years under the treaty, assuming that "trade had increased in the same ratio as before the treaty," the United States had by virtue of the treaty lost no less than $16,373,880 in customs revenue, while Canada had given up only $2,650,890. During that decade American goods imported by Canada had paid in duties $16,802,962, and Canadian goods imported by the United States had paid only $930,447, which are "vast disproportions." Furthermore, he continued, in spite of the great need for revenue, Congress had been unable to tax many articles which had to compete with free imports from Canada. Thus, on lumber alone a 5 per cent excise tax would have yielded $5,000,000, but this could not be imposed because Canadian lumber was duty free. Even as it was, he urged, the heavy internal taxes on agricultural implements, tools, etc., put American producers at a great disadvantage in competing with the untaxed produce of the Province.[3]

The chief friends of the treaty in the Senate were Hale of New Hampshire, and Howe of Wisconsin. In a long and able speech Senator Hale exposed the "balance of trade" fallacy, emphasized the political, social, and commercial benefits derived from the treaty, deprecated the influence of "passion and resentment," and urged the retention of the treaty at least until efforts should have been made to secure satisfactory amendments. Howe ridiculed Sumner's assumption that the marked growth of trade with the Provinces would have occurred without the treaty. Nevertheless, the friends of the treaty were unsuccessful.

The Senate votes to abrogate.—The resolution calling for abrogation came to a vote in the Senate on January 12, 1865, and was passed by 33 to 8. On the 17th of the following March the President gave the required year's notice, and the treaty thus became due to terminate on March 17, 1866.

Canada makes a new offer.—The Canadian Government had long been aware that the fate of the treaty was in the balance. As early as 1863 John A. Macdonald had interviewed Mr. Seward, Secretary of State, with regard to it and had been advised to send to Washington a "quasi-political" Canadian agent with whom the Secretary of State and the British minister might informally confer. Macdonald had endeavored to engage the well-known Liberal leader, George Brown, to undertake the task, but Brown declined to go. When at last an emissary was sent, Congress had already acted. A delegation from Canada, New Brunswick, and Nova Scotia, headed by Galt, visited Washington in January of 1866. The Secretary of the Treasury referred them to the House Committee on Ways and Means, but their

---

[1] Andrews Report, 32d Cong., 1st sess., Sen. Ex. Doc. No. 112.
[2] Hatch Report, 1860, 36th Cong., 1st sess., H. Ex. Doc. No. 96, p. 39.
[3] Cong. Globe, Jan. 12, 1865, pp. 206, 207.

negotiations with that body were brief. They asked for a renewal of reciprocity upon terms that would allow the United States to impose duties high enough to balance the internal taxes, professed willingness to add new articles to the provincial free list, and promised improvement of the Canadian canals. The delegation reported to the provincial governments that the committee would agree to admit free only gypsum, burrstones, rags, and firewood. On everything else the committee insisted upon duties "so much beyond what the delegates conceived to be the equivalent for the internal taxation of the United States, that they are reluctantly brought to the conclusion that the committee no longer desire the trade between the two countries to be carried on upon the principle of reciprocity."[1]

Congress refrains from further action.—The reluctant conclusion of the delegation was correct. In the following summer a Senate resolution was presented, requesting the President to furnish information "concerning the practicability of establishing equal reciprocal relations between the United States and the British Provinces of North America." The only result of this was the printing of several reports by special agents of the Treasury Department, upon which Congress took no action whatsoever.

EFFECTS OF THE ABROGATION.

Public sentiment in the two countries.—The treaty had provided not alone for commercial reciprocity; it had effected an adjustment of a number of difficulties between the two countries. The termination of the treaty involved the termination of the arrangements which had temporarily relaxed the tension. To this fact the United States was, however, indifferent. With an enormous army of trained and victorious soldiers, the United States was not inclined to fear that its rights would be imposed upon. Many American statesmen had been so incensed at the attitude of the British during the war of secession that they welcomed the rupture of reciprocity relations with Canada as a token of their resentment. Others believed the abrogation would make for a more permanent settlement of Canadian-American problems by reducing the Provinces to such straits that they would be compelled to ask for annexation.

In the Provinces, on the contrary, the possibility of serious political consequences from abrogation excited grave concern. War seemed at that time not beyond contemplation. There were still living many men who remembered the efforts of the United States to seize Canada during the War of 1812. All were aware of the hostile sentiment prevailing in the United States toward all things British, and many knew how narrowly an open breach had been averted at the time of the Trent affair. There were matters in dispute that might at any time precipitate trouble—the western boundary question, the inshore fisheries, the *Alabama* claims.

Formation of the Dominion of Canada, 1867.—In view of the circumstances, the Provinces exhibited tact and wisdom. Their first step was taken in 1867 when, with the approval of the British Government, three of the separate Provinces were united to form the Dominion of Canada. There is no doubt that the establishing of Canadian union in 1867 was due primarily to the action of the Amer-

---

[1] Gray, Confederation of Canada, p. 299.

ican Government on the matter of reciprocity, and the hostility which the people of the United States had so clearly exhibited. For some time the attitude of the Dominion toward the United States remained conciliatory. It is true that just before the confederation the Maritime Provinces had raised their duties in retaliation against the American tariff, but they still permitted access to the fisheries upon the payment by American vessels of a license fee of 50 cents a ton.[1] Canada continued the rates of canal tolls which had been in force under the treaty, continued the free admission of wheat, cotton, wool, and certain other raw materials, and reduced the average rate of customs duties by 25 per cent. These measures were intended, however, not so much to serve as a bid for favor in the United States, as to facilitate confederation with the Maritime Provinces, where protective duties had been employed to less extent; while free wheat and raw materials were calculated to increase the business of the railroads and to encourage manufacturing.

THE OPERATION OF THE TREATY OF 1854.

(Treaty effective from Mar. 16, 1855, to Mar. 17, 1866.)

The treaty contained three main provisions. It stipulated that American fishermen should be permitted to use the Atlantic coast fisheries north of the thirty-sixth parallel on equal terms with the fishermen of the Provinces; it made navigation on Lake Michigan, the St. Lawrence, and the Canadian canals open on equal terms to the inhabitants of both countries; it established reciprocal free trade in natural products between the United States and the British North American Provinces. Of these provisions the last proved to be by far the most important.

Effect of the Treaty on the American Fishing Industry.—The negotiation of the treaty of 1854 achieved its main purpose—to relieve the tension over the fisheries controversy; but the operation of the treaty failed to stimulate the American fishing industry. In spite of the fact that by the treaty American fishermen were granted equal privileges with the fishermen of the Provinces in the fishing grounds north of the thirty-sixth parallel, the tonnage engaged in both the cod and mackerel fisheries actually decreased.[2] Those engaged in the industry attributed the decline to the free admission, granted under the treaty, of fish from the Provinces. But between 1856 and 1865 the imports of pickled fish increased but little—from 240,595 barrels to 296,802; and the imports of dried and other fish fell from nearly 20,000,000 pounds to less than 4,000,000 pounds.[3] The decline of the industry in the early years of the reciprocity period resulted from the greater inducements offered to labor and capital in other occupations; during the later years the heavy war taxes on salt and other materials accelerated the downward tendency. This seems to have been generally understood, and the complaints of the fishermen received scant attention. Even Sumner, who led the fight for abrogation in the Senate in 1865, admitted that the settlement of the fisheries troubles was entirely satisfactory.[4]

[1] U. S. Foreign Relations, 1873, Vol. III, Pt. II, p. 286.
[2] Larned Report, Jan. 28, 1871, 41st Cong., 3d sess. H. Ex. Doc. No. 94.
[3] U. S. Commerce and Navigation. 53d Cong., 2d sess. Sen. Ex. Doc. No. 106, p. 32.
[4] Cong. Globe, Jan. 12, 1865, p. 206.

Effect of the St. Lawrence and canal concessions.—The opening of the St. Lawrence River and the Canadian canals to American shipping had much less effect than had been expected. The great growth of the railroads on both sides of the border, and especially to the south, during the decade from 1850 to 1860, was an important factor in causing a reduction in St. Lawrence River traffic. Even before the treaty period the extension of the Grand Trunk Railway to Portland by lease of the line from Quebec to that port and the grant to Canada of the privilege of shipping goods through the United States in bond, had diverted a large part even of Canadian trade from the St. Lawrence.

In 1859 the Canadian Legislature, at the solicitation of Galt, the Minister of Finance, passed a measure whereby 90 per cent of the tolls collected on shipping by way of the Welland Canal was returned in case the shipping passed down the St. Lawrence to a Canadian port. This measure established a preference in toll rates in favor of the Canadian route. Nevertheless, of the total shipments of grain from the American and Canadian west, the percentage which reached tidewater by the St. Lawrence was undergoing constant diminution.

TABLE I.—*Movement of American wheat and flour to tidewater by water routes, 1856–1862.*[1]

Year.	Total bushels.	Through Erie Canal.		Down the St. Lawrence.	
		Bushels.	Per cent of total.	Bushels.	Per cent of total.
1856	16,552,445	15,342,833	92.69	1,209,612	7.31
1857	12,531,812	10,601,532	84.59	1,930,280	15.41
1858	15,634,216	13,757,283	87.99	1,876,933	12.01
1859	12,360,725	10,371,966	83.91	1,988,759	16.09
1860	25,758,462	23,912,000	92.83	1,846,462	7.17
1861	37,530,953	34,427,800	91.73	3,103,153	8.27
1862	44,560,185	39,240,131	88.06	5,320,054	11.94

[1] 38th Cong., 1st sess. H. Ex. Doc. No. 32, p. 38.

TABLE II.—*Tonnage and nationality of vessels passing through the Canadian canals, 1854–1864.*[1]

Year.	Total tons.	Up.			
		Tons.	Per cent of total.	Tons.	Per cent of total.
		British.		*Foreign.*	
1854	1,290,982	805,838	62.42	485,144	37.58
1855	1,299,947	1,000,127	76.94	299,820	23.06
1856	1,537,341	1,096,670	71.34	440,671	28.66
				American.	
1857	1,217,137	822,737	67.60	394,400	32.40
1858	1,219,011	776,949	63.74	442,062	36.26
1859	1,227,098	929,003	75.71	298,095	24.29
1860	1,500,807	1,028,333	68.52	472,474	31.48
1861	1,602,997	1,116,424	69.65	486,573	30.35
1862	1,807,367	(2)	(2)	(2)	(2)
1863	1,806,277	1,354,007	74.96	452,270	25.04
1864	1,720,648	1,394,354	81.04	326,294	18.96

[1] From Canada Sessional Papers as compiled by Chalfant Robinson, A History of Two Reciprocity Treaties, p. 214.
[2] No data.

TABLE II.—*Tonnage and nationality of vessels passing through the Canadian canals, 1854–1864*—Continued.

Year.	Down.				
	Total tons.	Tons.	Per cent of total.	Tons.	Per cent of total.
		British.		*Foreign.*	
1854	1,476,148	963,385	65.27	512,763	34.73
1855	1,058,067	765,084	72.31	293,019	27.69
1856	1,135,745	753,648	66.36	382,097	33.64
				American.	
1857	1,098,757	690,233	62.82	408,524	37.18
1858	1,183,129	759,926	64.23	423,203	35.77
1859	1,227,923	899,360	73.24	328,543	26.76
1860	1,529,923	1,037,547	67.81	492,376	32.19
1861	1,704,914	1,219,257	71.51	485,657	28.49
1862	1,775,029	(1)	(1)	(1)	(1)
1863	1,767,636	1,316,170	74.46	451,466	25.54
1864	1,700,187	1,373,327	80.77	326,860	19.23

1 No data.

Table I gives the volumes of American shipments of wheat and flour via the Erie Canal and via the St. Lawrence River system and shows how small a proportion of the American water-borne freight used the St. Lawrence route. Large amounts of grain were shipped from the American Northwest to tidewater by rail only. The figures in Table II further confirm the indication that reciprocity did not lead to a substantially increased use of the Canadian canals by American shipping. But the opening of the Canadian canals to American vessels did afford a choice of routes which both relieved congestion and insured, by potential competition, reasonable railway rates to the Atlantic seaboard.

EFFECT OF THE TREATY ON TRADE BETWEEN THE TWO COUNTRIES.

The effect of the reciprocity arrangement on the trade between Canada and the United States has been a matter of dispute from the time of the ratification of the treaty to the present day. This has been due in part to the highly unsatisfactory character of the statistics of both the United States and the British North American Provinces during the period when the treaty was in force, and in part to the fact that there were in operation contemporaneously with the treaty a number of other factors which peculiarly affected the volume of trade between the two countries.

During the period immediately preceding and also during the first years of the reciprocity period, great sums of English capital were being invested in the construction of railways in Canada, and this involved large purchases of materials and supplies in the United States. The Crimean War, which lasted from 1853 to 1856, increased the demand for agricultural products and advanced their prices. This operated to increase the trade between the United States and the British North American Provinces by increasing the purchasing power of the latter, which facilitated their importation of manufactures. A considerable portion of the increased exports of foodstuffs to Europe was shipped from each of the two countries via the transportation systems of the other, and the apparent volume of trade between the two countries as recorded in their official statistics was thus expanded. Meanwhile, both in Canada and in the American Northwest, new lands were being opened to settlement, the population was increasing, and transportation facilities were being vastly improved. In both countries this was a period of expansion, development, and considerable speculation. A marked growth of commerce between the two would doubtless have occurred even had there been no treaty.

The crisis of 1857 and the Civil War.—In 1857 both countries experienced a commercial crisis which was followed by a short period of acute business depression. In Canada recovery was more gradual, because of the failure of the crops, and the crisis, which involved the Government in financial difficulties, was the main factor in bringing about a fundamental change in Canadian fiscal policy. Owing to the business depression and especially to the decline in transportation receipts, the Canadian revenue became insufficient to meet the interest and other necessary expenditures of the Government. Galt, the Canadian Minister of Finance, thereupon introduced into the Canadian Legislature a series of measures intended to relieve this situation.

Galt's first measure was to convert the tariff duties from a specific to an ad valorem basis, and to levy the duties according to the valuation of imports at the last port of shipment. This operated to increase the customs valuation of foreign products coming through the United States, and thus indirectly to make the level of duties higher on such products when imported via the United States than when directly imported. The measure further operated to reduce greatly the business of American jobbing and commission firms engaged in handling and transporting foreign goods in transit to Canada.

Galt's second measure was to increase the revenue by raising the tariff rates. The articles enumerated in the treaty could not be altered; but the rates on manufactures and on products from third countries via the United States were greatly increased. As a result of these measures, the Canadian tariff duties which had averaged, at the time when the treaty was negotiated, but 7½ per cent—too low materially to affect trade—now became a serious handicap to the importation of manufactures from the United States.

The influence of the treaty during its later years was much obscured by effects of the American Civil War. The export of American manufactures to Canada was checked as much by war conditions, high prices, taxation, and scarcity of labor in the United States as by the barrier of Galt's tariff. On the other hand, the producers of wheat and breadstuffs of the Northwest sought to recoup in Europe the loss of the market of the South, and in order to avoid danger from the Confederate cruisers they sent a considerable portion of their exports to Europe by way of Canada. The Civil War caused an increased demand in the United States for horses, meat, wool, lumber, fish, and some other articles which the Provinces were able to supply. The high war tariffs of the United States were, in operation, an encouragement rather than a deterrent to imports from Canada. The important Canadian products were free of duty by treaty, and the increased duties on similar articles when imported into the United States from other countries increased the amount of the tariff preference in favor of Canada.

Similarity between the products of the two countries.—Of the articles enumerated in the reciprocity treaty, the Provinces produced, with very few exceptions, more than they consumed. Of these exceptions corn was probably the most important. The Canadian climate was too severe for its production, and it was imported in increasing quantities from the United States to fatten hogs and to make whisky. The United States likewise normally produced a surplus of most of the enumerated articles, the important exceptions being gypsum, barley, the combing wool of Leicester and Cotswold sheep, and the soft pine of New Brunswick. Worsted spinning in the United States received an impetus from the free admission of wool. The immigration of Germans during this period, and the free admission of Canadian barley—which is peculiarly suitable for brewing—greatly stimulated the brewing industry. With these exceptions the trade in natural products between the two countries was in a large measure based upon the geographical distribution of products which, though common to both countries, were not common to all sections of either; it followed those channels which convenience and cheapness of transportation made most economical. In respect to products nominally the same, differences in quality and adaptability to different purposes also contributed in some degree to the development of trade between the two countries. These were factors which would have asserted themselves independently of the treaty, but the removal of duties facilitated their operation and added to the gross effect.

There follows herewith a statistical analysis of the trade between the two countries immediately preceding, during, and immediately following the reciprocity period.

The trade statistics of this period, both of the United States and of the British North American Provinces—and especially the statistics relating to exports—are of very questionable accuracy. The data which follow are of value for the light they throw on the tendencies appearing in the trade between the two countries during the period under investigation, but they do not afford a trustworthy measurement of the absolute changes in the amounts of trade.[1]

Imports into the United States under reciprocity.—Tables III to VI present the figures of imports into the United States from the British North American Provinces, as compiled from the official publications both of the United States and of the Provinces. The Canadian figures for the period prior to 1867 refer only to the "United Province of Canada," i. e., Ontario and Quebec.

---

[1] Wherever possible, use has been made of the official Canadian statistics in addition to the data from American sources. No satisfactory statistics of the Maritime Provinces are available. The American statistics of imports from and exports to the British North American Provinces therefore cover a arger volume of trade than the corresponding statistics of the Province of Canada [after Confederation, the Provinces of Ontario and Quebec].

TABLE III.—*Merchandise imports from the British North American Provinces into the United States, 1850–1870.*[1]

Year.	Value of imports from all countries.	From British North American Provinces.	
		Value.	Per cent of imports from all countries.
1850	$173,509,526	$5,179,500	3.00
1851	210,771,429	5,279,718	2.50
1852	207,440,398	5,469,445	2.64
1853	263,777,265	6,527,559	2.47
1854	297,803,794	8,784,412	2.95
1855	257,808,708	15,118,289	5.86
1856	310,432,310	21,276,614	6.85
1857	348,428,342	22,108,916	6.35
1858	263,338,654	15,784,836	5.99
1859	331,333,341	19,287,565	5.82
1860	353,616,119	23,572,796	6.67
1861	289,310,512	22,724,489	7.85
1862	189,356,677	18,511,025	9.78
1863	243,335,815	17,184,786	7.19
1864	316,447,283	29,608,736	9.36
1865	238,745,580	33,264,403	13.93
1866	434,812,066	48,528,628	11.16
1867	395,761,096	25,044,005	6.33
1868	357,436,440	26,261,379	7.35
1869	417,506,379	29,293,766	7.02
1870	435,958,408	36,265,328	8.32

[1] U. S. Statistical Abstract; and 53d Cong., 2d sess., Sen. Ex. Doc. No. 106, p. 2.

TABLE IV.—*Total merchandise imports from the British North American Provinces into the United States and imports of reciprocity articles, 1850–1866.*[1]

Year.	Value of total imports.	Reciprocity articles.	
		Value.	Per cent of total imports.
1850	$5,179,500	$3,375,546	65.17
1851	5,279,718	3,331,341	63.09
1852	5,469,445	3,109,972	56.86
1853	6,527,559	4,141,370	63.44
1854	8,784,412	6,107,053	69.52
1855	15,118,289	12,527,882	82.86
1856	21,276,614	19,407,086	91.21
1857	22,108,916	20,280,210	91.72
1858	15,784,836	14,752,255	93.45
1859	19,287,565	16,384,416	84.94
1860	23,572,796	20,446,586	86.73
1861	22,724,489	20,047,525	88.21
1862	18,511,025	17,152,552	92.66
1863	17,484,786	15,762,190	90.14
1864	29,608,736	27,031,130	91.36
1865	33,264,403	30,569,658	91.89
1866	48,528,628	39,582,505	81.56

[1] 38th Cong., 1st sess., H. Ex. Doc. No. 32, p. 7; and 53d Cong., 2d sess., Sen. Ex. Doc. No. 106, pp. 2 and 35.

In 1853 the United States Government granted to Canada the privilege of using Portland as the winter terminus of the Grand Trunk Railway and allowed Canadian exporters to ship their products to Europe through Portland without payment of duties. This was followed in 1854 by a considerable increase in the American imports from Canada (Table III). The first year of reciprocity, 1855, was marked by an increase of over 70 per cent in imports from Canada, and in the next year, 1856, there occurred a still further increase of 40 per cent over the 1855 figures. In the five years previous to reciprocity the imports averaged $6,200,000. In the first five years of the reciprocity period they averaged $18,700,000. This increase in imports from Canada was relatively much greater than the increase of total imports into the United States. The imports from Canada rose from 2.95 per cent of total imports in 1854 to 5.86 per cent in 1855—the first year of reciprocity. On the other hand, they fell from 13.93 per cent of all imports in 1865 to 6.33 per cent in 1867—during which year reciprocity was no longer effective.

In Table IV, the figures of total imports from the British North American Provinces are compared with the figures of imports of reciprocity articles from these Provinces. Although the imports of reciprocity articles more than doubled in 1855, the aggregate imports of all other articles from British North America were less in that year than in 1854. The reciprocity articles in 1854 already formed 69 per cent of all imports from the Provinces, but in 1856, the first full treaty year, they rose to over 91 per cent of the total imports from British North America and they averaged, during the treaty period, over 90 per cent.

TABLE V.—*Merchandise exports from the Province of Canada, 1853–1867;* [1] *from the Dominion of Canada, 1868–1870.* [2]

Year.	Value of total exports to all countries.	To the United States.		To Great Britain.	
		Value.	Per cent of total exports.	Value.	Per cent of total exports.
From the Province of Canada:					
1853	$15,606,686	$7,541,397	48.32	$6,847,780	43.88
1854	23,394,871	9,715,641	41.53	10,781,586	46.09
1855	22,849,267	10,183,688	44.59	10,859,871	47.53
1856	28,444,680	20,105,664	70.68	6,622,660	23.28
1857	34,310,243	21,561,782	62.84	11,128,391	32.43
1858	28,980,376	15,847,703	54.68	12,622,300	43.55
1859	21,285,925	11,930,094	56.04	8,154,971	38.31
1860	22,677,160	13,922,314	61.39	7,551,540	33.30
1861	31,522,964	18,427,918	58.45	12,000,623	38.07
1862	33,061,255	14,261,427	43.13	17,376,112	52.56
1863	33,511,620	(3)	....	14,056,992	41.95
1864	35,374,596	18,426,891	52.09	15,113,955	42.73
1865	35,996,134	21,340,350	55.29	12,755,284	35.44
1866	....	....	......	....	......
1867	39,471,028	22,859,084	57.91	12,435,466	31.51
From the Dominion of Canada:					
1868	45,543,177	22,387,846	49.16	17,905,808	39.32
1869	49,323,304	23,640,188	47.93	20,486,389	41.53
1870	56,081,192	27,398,930	48.86	22,512,991	40.14

[1] From Canada Sessional Papers, as compiled by Chalfant Robinson, A History of Two Reciprocity Treaties, p. 60, and 40th Cong., 2d sess., H. Ex. Doc. No. 240.
[2] From the Canada Year Book, 1908, p. 187.
[3] No data.

TABLE VI.—*Exports of natural products from the Province of Canada, 1853–1867,*[1] *and from the Dominion of Canada, 1868–1870.*[2]

Year.	Value of total exports.	To the United States.		To Great Britain.	
		Value.	Per cent of total exports.	Value	Per cent of total exports.
From the Province of Canada:					
1853	$15,385,113	$7,367,913	47.89	$6,821,731	44.34
1854	23,193,297	9,535,064	41.11	10,769,184	46.43
1855	23,305,481	10,103,472	43.35	10,854,374	46.57
1856	27,791,582	19,809,720	71.29	6,548,462	23.56
1857	33,813,835	21,338,308	63.11	10,975,286	32.46
1858	28,156,428	15,493,156	55.03	12,460,675	41.26
1859	20,842,011	11,656,769	55.91	8,080,530	38.76
1860	22,079,197	13,624,467	61.71	7,340,589	33.25
1861	30,883,687	18,095,399	58.59	11,716,863	37.94
1862	32,617,407	13,971,795	42.83	17,281,435	52.98
1863	32,854,291	14,535,359	44.25	14,001,612	42.62
1864	34,180,155	17,573,999	51.42	14,904,058	43.61
1865	34,561,578	20,566,718	59.51	12,257,727	35.47
1866 [3]					
1867	38,158,138	22,051,764	57.79	12,200,388	31.98
From the Dominion of Canada:					
1868	43,140,486	21,433,988	49.68	16,782,609	38.90
1869	46,560,186	22,621,228	48.58	19,085,944	40.99
1870	53,149,170	25,977,847	48.87	21,487,510	40.42

[1] From Canada Sessional Papers, as compiled by Chalfant Robinson, A History of Two Reciprocity Treaties, p. 220.
[2] From the Canada Year Book, 1908, pp. 180–185.
[3] No data.

The Canadian official figures throw further light on the course of trade between the two countries under reciprocity. The influence of reciprocity is to be seen throughout the treaty period in the greatly increased exports of Canadian merchandise to the United States as compared with similar exports to Great Britain and with all exports (Table V).

The increase in trade which resulted from reciprocity is reflected in even more marked manner in the figures, in Table VI, for exports of natural products from Canada. Of these increased imports, much was destined finally for Europe. The free admission of the chief Canadian products into the United States removed the necessity for bonding shipments in transit to Europe, and thus stimulated the use by Canadian exporters of the superior American transport facilities and export trade organization.

Exports from the United States under reciprocity.—The following tables present the figures of exports from the United States under reciprocity, and are compiled from the official publications of both countries. The United States figures are for exports to all the British North American Provinces. The Canadian figures, on the other hand, cover, until 1867, only the trade of the "United Province of Canada," i. e., Ontario and Quebec.

TABLE VII.—*Exports of domestic merchandise from the United States, 1850–1870.*[1]

Year.	Value of exports to all countries.	To British North American Provinces.	
		Value.	Per cent of exports to all countries.
1850	$134,900,233	$7,725,247	5.73
1851	178,620,138	9,050,357	5.07
1852	154,931,147	6,604,097	4.26
1853	189,869,162	7,301,327	3.85
1854	215,328,300	15,005,244	6.97
1855	192,751,135	15,746,642	8.17
1856	266,438,051	22,710,697	8.52
1857	278,906,713	19,820,113	7.10
1858	251,351,033	19,591,758	7.79
1859	278,392,080	21,724,947	7.80
1860	316,242,423	18,657,029	5.90
1861	204,899,616	18,814,615	9.18
1862	179,644,024	18,185,224	10.12
1863	186,003,912	24,967,894	13.42
1864	143,504,027	24,188,147	16.86
1865	136,940,248	27,045,024	19.75
1866	337,518,102	22,380,652	6.63
1867	279,786,809	17,295,837	6.18
1868	269,389,900	21,419,222	7.95
1869	275,166,697	20,085,805	7.30
1870	376,616,473	21,060,369	5.59

[1] U. S. Statistical Abstract; and 53d Cong., 2d sess., Sen. Ex. Doc. No. 106, p. 2.

TABLE VIII.—*Imports into the Province of Canada, 1853–1867,*[1] *and into the Dominion of Canada, 1868–1870.*[2]

Year.	Value of total imports.	From the United States.		From Great Britain.		From British North American colonies.		From other countries.	
		Value.	Per cent of total imports.	Value.	Per cent of total imports.	Value	Per cent of total imports.	Value.	Per cent of total imports.
Into the Province of Canada:									
1853	$38,377,707	$14,138,572	36.84	$22,186,944	57.81	$759,187	1.98	$1,293,004	3.37
1854	48,635,188	18,639,715	38.33	27,555,993	56.66	810,134	1.67	1,629,346	3.34
1855	43,303,401	24,994,411	57.72	15,964,152	36.87	1,039,180	2.40	1,305,658	3.02
1856	52,301,260	27,245,409	52.09	21,855,518	41.79	1,239,110	2.37	1,961,223	3.75
1857	46,316,715	24,269,577	52.40	21,070,828	45.50	902,265	1.95	74,045	.15
1858	29,078,527	15,635,565	53.77	12,287,053	42.25	423,826	1.46	732,083	2.52
1859	33,555,161	17,592,916	52.43	14,786,084	44.07	381,755	1.14	794,406	2.36
1860	34,447,935	17,273,029	50.15	15,859,980	46.04	393,864	1.14	921,062	2.67
1861	43,054,836	21,069,388	48.94	20,386,937	47.35	499,177	1.16	1,099,334	2.55
1862	48,600,633	25,173,157	51.79	21,179,312	43.58	535,469	1.10	1,712,695	3.53
1863	45,964,493	23,109,362	50.27	20,177,572	43.89	510,713	1.11	2,166,846	4.73
1864	49,753,467	22,555,519	45.33	23,884,696	48.00	523,295	1.05	2,789,957	5.62
1865	44,620,469	19,589,055	43.90	21,035,871	47.14	511,570	1.14	3,483,973	7.82
1866	53,802,319	20,424,692	37.96	28,994,530	53.89	857,922	1.59	3,525,175	6.56
1867	59,048,987	20,272,907	34.33	34,260,509	58.02	1,103,373	1.86	3,412,198	5.79
Into the Dominion of Canada:									
1868	67,090,159	22,660,132	33.77	37,617,325	56.07	....	......	6,812,702	10.16
1869	63,154,941	21,497,380	34.03	35,496,764	56.21	....	......	6,160,797	9.76
1870	66,902,074	21,697,237	32.43	37,537,095	56.11	....	......	7,667,742	11.46

[1] From Canada Sessional Papers, as compiled by Chalfant Robinson, A History of Two Reciprocity Treaties, p. 217. Includes coin and bullion.
[2] From the Canada Year Book, 1908, pp. 188–89, "Imports entered for consumption."

The influence of reciprocity showed itself much less conspicuously in the figures of exports to Canada (Table VII), The most important part of the United States exports to Canada consisted of manufactures, and the trade in these was checked during this period by the increase in duties established thereon by the Galt ministry. Nevertheless, the first years of reciprocity coincided with a considerable. increase of exports to Canada, both in absolute amount and in relation to total exports. After the termination of reciprocity early in 1866, although for United States exports as a whole this was a period of great expansion, the exports to British North America declined. Whereas in 1864 these exports formed over 16 per cent and in 1865 over 19 per cent of the total of United States exports, in 1866 they were only a little over 6 per cent and in subsequent years they fell to even lower levels.

The Canadian figures of imports into Canada (Table VIII) are more accurate than the American statistics of exports thereto. They indicate a more marked influence of reciprocity on American exports to Canada than is reflected in the American statistics. Imports from the United States formed in 1853 only 37 per cent of the total imports into the Province of Canada and in 1854 only 38 per cent, but rose in 1855—the first year of reciprocity—to 57 per cent and, with the exception of one year, they remained over 50 per cent until 1864, when they constituted 45 per cent of the total Canadian imports. In 1866, the year of the termination of reciprocity, they showed a further decline to 38 per cent of total imports, and in 1867 they had fallen to 34 per cent, a proportion below that of the original level prior to reciprocity. The reciprocity arrangement apparently operated to increase Canadian imports from the United States at the expense of imports from Great Britain, and its termination operated in exactly the counter direction. Much of the increased Canadian importation accredited as coming from the United States under reciprocity represented, however, merely increased imports from Europe via the United States.

TABLE IX.—*Exports of foreign merchandise from the United States, 1850–1870.*

Year.	Value of exports to all countries.[1]	To British North American Provinces.[2]	
		Value.	Per cent of exports to all countries.
1850	$9,475,493	$1,790,744	18.89
1851	10,295,121	2,719,735	26.41
1852	12,053,084	3,625,511	30.07
1853	13,620,120	5,131,270	37.67
1854	21,715,464	9,068,164	41.75
1855	26,158,368	11,995,166	45.85
1856	14,781,372	6,314,652	42.72
1857	14,917,047	4,318,369	28.94
1858	20,660,241	4,012,768	19.42
1859	14,509,971	6,384,547	44.00
1860	17,333,634	4,038,899	23.30
1861	14,654,217	3,861,898	26.35
1862	11,026,477	2,387,846	21.65
1863	17,960,535	2,651,920	14.76
1864	15,333,961	2,386,477	15.56
1865	29,089,055	1,784,378	6.13
1866	11,341,420	2,448,228	21.58
1867	14,719,332	3,724,465	25.30
1868	12,562,999	2,661,555	21.18
1869	10,951,000	3,295,666	30.09
1870	16,155,295	4,278,885	26.48

[1] U. S. Statistical Abstract.　　[2] 53d Cong., 2d sess., Sen. Ex. Doc. No. 106, p. 2.

Table IX shows the figures of exports of foreign merchandise from the United States to the British North American colonies. The drop, after 1860, in the amount of these exports may be accounted for in part by the Galt legislation of 1858 and 1859, establishing for Canada the ad valorem method of levying duties and requiring customs valuation of imports into Canada to be made on the basis of their value in the market where last purchased, and not on the basis of their original cost. But the Civil War was probably a 'more potent factor in reducing the amount of Canadian purchases of foreign products in the United States.

Trade between the two countries by commodities.—The effect of reciprocity was most clearly revealed in the case of wheat and coal. Both countries were exporters of wheat to Liverpool where, it was maintained, the prices of wheat were determined. Yet for seven years prior to the treaty wheat sold in Canada at a price 20 per cent less than it brought in the United States.[1] This was due primarily to the inferior Canadian transportation facilities, and perhaps in some degree to the less developed state of Canadian export business. The removal of the American duty on wheat, which at that time was 20 per cent ad valorem, enabled Canada to take advantage of the higher American price; and during the first five years of the treaty she sent to the United States six times as much wheat and flour as she sent to Great Britain.[2] But, at the same time, she lost the market of the Maritime Provinces, which produced no wheat, and which, under the treaty, could buy from the near-by States more cheaply than from Canada. Thus of the wheat which the Americans bought in the Canadian Northwest, a considerable portion was sold to the people of the Maritime Provinces; the balance they profitably exported to Europe in the form of flour. This exchange was highly advantageous to all concerned. So greatly did it benefit the Canadian farmers that traditions of the golden days of reciprocity survive among them to the present time.

The trade in coal was of the same reciprocal character. Neither Canada nor the New England States produced coal, while both Nova Scotia and the Middle States produced it for export. Owing to transportation costs, Nova Scotia could not supply coal to Canada at so low a price as did the operators of Pennsylvania and Ohio, but she could undersell them in New England. Indeed, even before the treaty, the Nova Scotian coal exports to the United States were valued at more than a quarter of a million dollars, in spite of the duty of 30 per cent.[3] As a result of reciprocity, therefore, the United States bought coal in the Northeast and sold it in the Northwest. But the relatively small Canadian demand was inadequate compensation to American coal operators for the loss of the New England market, and these interests became persistent opponents of the treaty. On the other hand, the industrial interests of New England became equally persistent in its support.

In the case of forest products and fish the treaty was more advantageous for the Provinces than for the United States. The

---

[1] Report of Select Committee Canadian Parliament to Inquire into the Course of Trade, 1858, Vol. XVI, p. 505.
[2] Hatch Report, 36th Cong., 1st sess., H. Ex. Doc. No. 96, p. 26.
[3] U. S. Commerce and Navigation, 1850–1854.

Provinces could supply these commodities more cheaply than could the United States, owing to lower wages and an abundance of available natural resources. The treaty could not, therefore, affect the Canadian importation, but by removing the American duties it made possible the extending of the market of the Provinces across the border. The Canadian output of these products was, of course, too small in comparison with that of the United States to lower prices appreciably. The value of the lumber produced in the United States in 1860 was about $96,000,000, while the imports from the Provinces did not exceed $3,800,000.[1] During the Civil War, however, the increased supplies from the Provinces probably contributed to the prevention of a more pronounced rise than that which actually occurred in the American prices of these commodities.

Of the other enumerated articles, the majority were affected in the same way as lumber and fish. The course of trade in such commodities as wool, gypsum, and ores could be but little affected by the application or removal of provincial duties, the American sale of these articles in the Provinces being merely local and incidental. In the United States all of the enumerated articles, except ores and unground gypsum (which were free before the treaty) and hides (which carried a duty of 10 per cent) had been dutiable at from 20 to 30 per cent. In respect to these articles the treaty, therefore, served merely to open the American market, but did not contribute in any appreciable way to the expansion of American exports to the Canadian market.

General conclusions as to the effect of the treaty.—While on the whole the treaty aided some American producers and injured none save the fishing and lumber interests, it was in its operation undoubtedly more favorable to provincial exports than to those of the United States. This disproportion in advantages, in so far as the export trade of the two countries was concerned, was well understood when the treaty was negotiated, but it was expected to be fully compensated for by the opening to America of the provincial waterways and coast fisheries, by the benefits to American railways and commission houses, and by the lowering of prices to the American consumer. These expectations were fulfilled in a large measure until Galt's financial legislation in Canada and war conditions in the United States changed the situation. The degree to which the trade between the two countries was indirectly favored by the improved political relations established by the treaty can not be estimated. The effect of the treaty in this respect was undoubtedly considerable. In the eleven years of reciprocity the aggregate trade between the two countries increased approximately threefold; 52 per cent of the trade of the Provinces was with the United States.[2] From being a matter of minor importance to the United States, the trade with British North America, under the treaty, became second, in order of importance, to the trade with Great Britain. To this growth, as has been pointed out, various factors contributed, but it is impossible to escape the conclusion that to the treaty must be attributed a large part of the growth, and that both countries benefited therefrom.

---

[1] Senator Howe, of Wisconsin, Cong. Globe, Jan. 12, 1865.
[2] 44th Cong., 1st sess., H. Rept. No. 9, p. 3.

EFFECTS OF THE ABROGATION UPON TRADE BETWEEN THE TWO COUNTRIES.

The commercial effects of abrogation were less than had been anticipated. Many of the concessions which the United States enjoyed under the treaty were not withdrawn by Canada after its termination. During the life of the treaty the average annual exports of the United States to the Provinces had amounted in value to somewhat less than twenty-five and a half millions of dollars; the imports from the Provinces had averaged not quite twenty-three millions. During the first five years after abrogation the average of the exports was almost the same, the average of the imports increased, the tendency was upward in both, and there was no great fluctuation.

American agents who investigated the effects of the abrogation were in general agreement that, so far as trade was affected at all, it was the United States and not Canada that was injured. One Treasury agent stated in 1867: "Our tariff and the reprisals to which it has led have done serious damage to our commerce." Another agent reported, in 1868, that prices in Canada of export articles formerly covered by the treaty had actually risen after its termination, and therefore, "up to this time the abrogation of the treaty has not affected Canadian interests injuriously." An expert, who had long been employed in connection with Canadian trade relations, said in 1869: "The commerce between the two countries has not been materially disturbed by the termination of the treaty," and this was confirmed in still another report in 1871.[1]

Canada less injured than the United States.—The potential blow to Canada was moderated by several factors. One of the most important was the improvement in American currency. Another was the reopening, after the war, of the market for fish, lumber, and other articles in the Southern States. Reconstruction in the United States and the establishing of more settled business conditions encouraged the demand for certain of Canada's products. Among the articles which Canada sent to the States, lumber and barley made up about one-third, in value, of the total; both were indispensable to American industries and they were now bought in increasing quantities, the duties falling on the consumers. In spite, however, of these mitigating factors, the Maritime Provinces felt severely the loss of a free market for their fish and coal. In the case of these products no other market could be substituted for that of the United States, and the exports were materially reduced. After Confederation the duties of these Provinces were replaced by the Canadian tariff, the rates of which, although they had been somewhat reduced to facilitate union, were much higher than those to which the Maritime Provinces had been accustomed. These Provinces were, however, reluctant to adopt a policy of protection, and they have continued to the present day to regard the free admission to the United States of their fish, coal, lumber, and vegetables as the greatest economic boon that could come to them. As late as the general election of 1911 they gave a majority for the Liberal Party on the issue of reciprocity.

---

[1] For above opinions, see, in order: E. H. Derby, 39th Cong., 2d sess., Sen. Ex. Doc. No. 30, p. 17; Geo. W. Brega, 40th Cong., 2d sess., H. Ex. Doc. No. 240, pp. 6, 7, 9; I. T. Hatch, 40th Cong., 3d sess., H. Ex. Doc. No. 36, p. 6; J. N. Larned, 41st Cong., 3d sess., H. Ex. Doc. No. 94.

The chief direct result of abrogation in the United States appears, therefore, to have been, on the one hand, to burden the American consumer with duties, as in the case of barley and pine lumber, and on the other to divert from American railways and merchants the business of transporting, handling, and reexporting Canadian produce.

Indirect results.—There was also an indirect result of great importance. The summary abrogation of the treaty by the United States and the rejection of all subsequent overtures hurt the pride of the Canadian people and gave them a sense of grievance which has never entirely disappeared. It is, of course, impossible to estimate with accuracy the commercial effect of this feeling. But it was clearly responsible for several retaliatory measures which interrupted the course of trade; it stimulated Canada to seek new markets and to restrict her own against American imports; and it was in large measure responsible for her rejection of reciprocity when the United States ultimately proposed it. According to the House Committee on Commerce in 1876, it drove Canadian trade away, and all investigators have testified that the United States was the principal loser.

REASONS FOR THE REJECTION OF RECIPROCITY BY THE UNITED STATES.

Although it was the United States that had served the notice terminating the treaty of 1854, and although Congress thereafter consistently rejected Canada's repeated proposals for a new reciprocity arrangement, it is not to be supposed, as may have been inferred from the above account, that the opinion and wishes of the people of the United States were unanimously averse to reciprocity with Canada. On the contrary, there was a considerable and not unimportant element, both in the country and in Congress, who favored liberal arrangements with the growing Commonwealth to the north. One of the most telling among the arguments for the abrogation of the treaty had been that a new and more satisfactory agreement could and would be negotiated. There were, however, several factors which account for the failure of Congress to welcome renewed efforts in that direction. Prominent among these was indifference. There were well-informed individuals in business organizations and in Congress who urged the benefits of reciprocity; they were opposed in Congress by an organized and determined group who were able to delay and to defeat the various proposals which came up for debate. A widespread popular demand could not be expected in the United States. While the Canadian-United States trade was a matter of vital concern for Canada, it was to the United States—in whose total foreign trade it amounted to but 6 per cent—comparatively unimportant. During the years from 1874 to 1893 the lowest percentage which this trade formed in the total trade of Canada was 38.15; the highest which it formed in the total trade of the United States was 6.59. The figures following show the highest and the lowest points reached by these percentages.

United States-Canadian trade.

Year.	Per cent of total United States trade.[1]	Per cent of total Canadian trade.[1]
1874	[2] 6. 59	40. 90
1880	[5] 4. 15	[3] 38. 15
1888	5. 55	[3] 46. 62
1893	4. 94	40. 12

[1] 53d Cong., 2d sess., Sen. Ex. Doc. No. 106, pp. 4–5.   [2] Highest.   [5] Lowest.

Furthermore, it was widely felt on the American side that the United States must in the nature of things hold a considerable share of the Canadian trade. For two years after 1878, Macdonald's protective tariff reduced the imports from the United States by about 20 per cent, but by 1881 the lost ground had been more than recovered. During the period from 1886 to 1890, Canada's imports from the United States increased; from 1890 to 1896 they continued to increase, being at the end of the period 25 per cent higher than they had been ten years before. During the same decade the imports from Great Britain decreased, the figure for 1896 being about 16 per cent lower than that of 1886.

Year.	Canadian imports from Great Britain.[1]	Canadian imports from the United States.[1]
1886	$39,033,006	$42,818,651
1890	43,277,009	51,365,661
1891	42,018,943	52,033,477
1896	32,824,505	53,529,390

[1] 62d Cong., 1st sess., Sen. Ex. Doc. No. 49.

Canada's protective legislation was intended primarily to affect American manufactures, but American producers had several advantages which went far to nullify its effect. Conditions and tastes in the two countries were similar; the implements, machinery, plumbing supplies, leather, wood, and metal manufactures produced in the United States were suited to Canadian as well as American needs. Proximity favored promptness of delivery and reduced the costs thereof. Some of the articles were produced only in the United States, and Canadian consumers preferred to purchase the American article, even with the price increased by the duties, rather than to take substitutes from elsewhere. As the market was limited, and as it was already to a large extent occupied by American products, the Canadian proposals for more liberal treatment did not command wide or insistent attention among American manufacturers.

Arguments used against reciprocity.—In the United States, during the first decade after the Civil War, fiscal considerations played an important part in the opposition to tariff reductions. The administration planned the removal of internal taxes and it conceived of and advocated a high tariff as both a revenue and a protective device. In subsequent years when there was a surplus in the Treasury the fiscal consideration was of less importance; but at the time when Canada was willing to make the greatest concessions it served as a substantial argument on the side of the opponents of reciprocity.

More enduring as an argument was reference to the "unfavorable balance of trade." For half a century not a speech in Congress, not a report presented in opposition to reciprocal arrangements, failed to mention the "balance against" the United States during the last years of the treaty of 1854. The belief could not be dispelled that the United States derived no benefit from trade with any country in the course of which it took from that country more in the way of imports than it sent to it as exports.

By many the possibility of any benefit at all to Canada was regarded as a conclusive objection to any arrangement. Resentment at British sympathy for the South died slowly after the Civil War. All arrangements with Canada had to be negotiated through England, and it was looked upon as highly improbable that a treaty might be concluded by which there would not be profit to England.

Against all reciprocity treaties there was the alleged constitutional objection that they deprived the House of Representatives of the control which it was intended that it should exercise over revenue measures. For the President and the Senate to make, without the consent or even the knowledge of the House, a treaty by which duties would be reduced and the revenues affected, was held to be a direct violation of the Constitution.[1]

It has often been asserted, especially in Canada, that the real explanation of the reluctance of the United States to enter into a reciprocity treaty was the expectation that the withholding of reciprocity would compel Canada to dissolve her connections with England and sue for admission to the Union. In 1880 the minority report of the Ways and Means Committee, while anticipating a political union, opposed rather than favored reciprocity, that Canada might develop "not only by force of her own elements of growth, but from our contiguity and example," and thus be more fit for admission to the Union. It does not appear, however, that there was at any time, except upon the part of scattered individuals, an active sentiment in favor of annexing Canada. There is no reason whatever to believe that since the Civil War period the commercial policy of the United States with regard to Canada has been influenced in the slightest degree by the question of annexation.

The fundamental obstacle.—The fundamental reason for the rejection of reciprocity by the United States was the belief that it would be a blow to the policy of protection. In the period before reciprocity ceased to be a practical issue, Canadian manufacturers could not, it is true, effectively compete with those of the United States, and protectionists might have been expected, therefore, to welcome an arrangement extending the market for American manufactures. But it was the common argument that free raw materials and low wages in Canada—and, after 1883, the Canadian bounty system— would tend, in the absence of duties, to encourage the transfer of American manufacturing industries across the border. It is quite possible that those in the United States who favored high duties

---

[1] On this subject see Chalfant Robinson, A History of Two Reciprocity Treaties, Part III, "The treaty-making power of the House of Representatives," p. 162.

might have been willing in spite of this to accept a complete commercial union; but such a measure, though much discussed in Canada and warmly advocated by the more extreme Liberals, was never embodied in any of the Canadian proposals for a treaty. The reciprocity generally contemplated by Canadians was limited to terms that would affect trade in "natural products" alone—which really meant fish, lumber, and agricultural produce. What Canada offered actually in return was the use of the fisheries and the canals, and when the United States secured these by other means, the retention of a reciprocity clause in successive Canadian tariff acts was nothing more than a campaign device.

The adverse attitude of certain American interests toward reciprocity was strongly influenced by the position taken by Canada; but perhaps a still more powerful factor was the necessity of conciliating the fishermen, lumbermen, and farmers. In New England the political influence of the fishing interests remained considerable long after the relative economic importance of the fisheries had waned. In Michigan and some other States the lumber interests played a similar rôle. The agricultural interests everywhere were powerful and in many States completely dominant. Although nearly all the duties upon farm products were without effect, there were a few important exceptions. Most prominent among these were the duties upon wool, which was always included in the proposed treaty lists. The woolgrowers were opposed to the free entry of wool, and through the woolgrowers the manufacturers secured political support among the farmers. Although few of the agricultural duties had any appreciable effect, many farmers, especially near the border, were by no means of that opinion; and to remove the duties by reciprocity was considered liable to demonstrate the futility of such duties and thereby cause dissatisfaction among the farmers.

The view which prevailed in the United States as to what might constitute a satisfactory reciprocity policy may be expressed somewhat as follows: Provide for removal of duties on such articles only as are not produced in the United States; and provide that, to whatever degree the importation of these articles shall be stimulated, there shall be free admission of an equal quantity of American exports to the countries from which they come. So long as the American Government was guided by this principle, the type of reciprocity desired and offered by Canada was out of the question.

EFFORTS TO RESTORE RECIPROCITY.

Attitude of Canadian political parties after 1866.—For thirty years after the termination of the treaty of 1854 Canadians continued to express, both officially and unofficially, a desire for the renewal of reciprocity, and to that end overtures were made several times. The Conservative Party had introduced the protective system, known in Canada as the "national policy." But for years the thought of ultimate national self-sufficiency was less attractive than that of immediate free trade with the United States, and the policy gained in strength only in proportion as the hope of reciprocity waned. During its long tenure of power the Conservative Party at no time ventured openly to oppose a renewal of reciprocal tariff reductions with the United States, but as the years passed its efforts on behalf of renewal were less and less forceful.   The Liberal Party, as long as it was in opposition, continued to advocate unrestricted reciprocity and to denounce protectionism.   But when the Liberals acceded to office in 1896 they took over the "national policy" almost unchanged; and until 1910 their efforts to secure reciprocity were as perfunctory as those of the Conservatives had been.   In fact, they terminated the standing offer of reciprocity that had been inserted in the Conservative tariff acts prior to 1896.

The Canadian tariff left practically unchanged.—In the negotiations regarding commerce between the two countries during the thirty years which followed 1866 Canada invariably took the initiative.   Her proposals throughout were moved by the desire to gain for her natural products access to the American market, and one proposal differed from another only in what it offered in exchange.

At first Canada's statesmen looked upon the attitude of the United States as transitory; they expected an early return of sentiment favorable to reciprocity.   Accordingly, the successive tariff acts of the Dominion retained the moderate level of duties introduced just before confederation; the free list continued to include most of the articles that had been free under the treaty, and there were added to it raw materials and partly manufactured goods that were essential to various manufactures, shipbuilding, and railroads.   One change was made, indeed, that was to play an important part in later negotiations—the imposition of an export duty upon pine, oak, and spruce logs to encourage sawmilling by offsetting the American duty upon lumber.   Meanwhile, scarcely a year was allowed to pass without an effort to reopen discussion with the American Government.

Rejection of Canadian proposals in 1869.—As early as 1869 circumstances seemed propitious.   It was known that Congress had instituted inquiries as to the effect of abrogating the treaty, and that the reports of the official agents agreed in declaring it detrimental to American interests.   Furthermore, it was believed that a great deterrent had been removed by the reduction of the American war taxes.   Therefore, the Minister of Finance, Mr. Rose, visited Washington in July, 1869, with proposals for a new treaty.   He offered— in return for the free admission of Canadian natural products—free access to the inshore fisheries, enlargement and use upon equal terms of the Canadian canals, free navigation of the St. Lawrence, partial assimilation of customs and excise duties, the concession of an import duty equal to the United States internal-revenue taxes, and the free admission to each country of certain manufactures of the other. But the American Government did not even give these proposals serious consideration.   Provoked by the rebuff, and finally despairing of success through conciliatory measures, the Canadian Government in the spring of 1870 made a tentative experiment in retaliation. Duties were put upon coal, salt, grain, flour, and hops, with the provision that the Governor General in council might suspend these "whenever it appears to his satisfaction that similar articles from Canada may be imported into the United States free of duty." [1]   The effect of this was unsatisfactory in Canada, and it influenced American policy not at all.   Accordingly, in the following year the Canadian Government repealed the duties.

---

[1] Larned Report, 1871, 41st Cong., 3d sess., H. Ex. Doc. No. 94, p. 9.

Pro-reciprocity sentiment in the United States.—Despite the persistence with which Congress rejected Canada's reciprocity proposals, there was an important and active element, both in the country generally and in Congress, that favored more liberal commercial arrangements with the growing market to the north. The chief commercial organizations of the country strongly favored the negotiation of a new treaty, petitions came to Congress from boards of trade and similar organizations in the largest and most important cities, various State legislatures passed resolutions to the same purport, and many of the leading papers advocated the cause. This body of opinion was not, however, of sufficient authority to command the necessary support in Congress.

Disappointment in Canada over the treaty of Washington.—In 1871 there was concluded between the United States and Great Britain the treaty of Washington. In the conference leading up to the treaty, the British high commissioners, among whom was Sir John Macdonald, the Canadian Premier, proposed a renewal of the Canadian reciprocity agreement of 1854; but the American commissioners objected to negotiating upon that basis. The British commissioners contended that the inshore fisheries were of great value, and that the most satisfactory method of providing for their use would be a reciprocal tariff arrangement and reciprocity in the coasting trade. The Americans replied that the value of the fisheries was overestimated, and that they could hold out no hope that Congress would give its assent to such a tariff arrangement as was proposed or to any extended plan for reciprocal free admission of the products of the two countries. It was finally agreed, however, that for the use of the fisheries the United States would concede free admission of fish and oil, and in further compensation would pay any sum fixed by a commission to be appointed later for the purpose. (Arts. XVIII–XXV.) The arrangement concerning the fisheries was to endure for ten years, and thereafter until the end of the second year following notice by either party of a desire to terminate it. (Art. XXXIII.) Reciprocal provisions were made for the use of national waters and waterways, and the American Government further engaged to urge upon the State governments to grant the same rights upon State canals. The treaty also provided for the transit of goods in bond free of duty through either country to the other.[1]

The treaty was a bitter disappointment to Canada, where it was felt that England, in disposing of the fisheries and waterways controversies, had thrown away the most effective lever for opening the American market. Macdonald had strenuously opposed it, but he had been voted down by the other British commissioners.

Negotiations initiated at the instance of the Liberal government.— The Conservative government found no excuse for further overtures to the United States, and until its defeat at the polls in 1874 it concentrated its efforts upon internal development. The Liberal government, which entered office in 1874, requested the Imperial Government to appoint George Brown as joint plenipotentiary to be associated with Thornton, then British minister at Washington. Upon his arrival in Washington, Brown found a remarkable misapprehension of Canadian conditions and ignorance of the value of her

---

[1] U. S. Foreign Relations, 1873, Pt. II, Vol. III, pp. 410–424.

trade. It was apparently the common impression in the United States that the abrogation of the reciprocity treaty had blighted Canada's progress, reduced her Government to its wits' end, and would soon compel her to sue for annexation. To dispel these erroneous ideas, Brown prepared a long and powerful memorandum and used his journalistic connections to secure the aid of the leading American papers. But the Canadian case had been weakened by the settlement, already effected, of the waterways and the fisheries questions. There was prevalent in the United States a strong sentiment that would brook no lowering of the tariff wall at any point. Although convinced that reciprocity applying only to natural products would benefit the United States, Brown was aware of the American belief that such an arrangement would be one-sided, and therefore he offered to accompany it with reciprocity in a long list of manufactures.

Treaty drafted and rejected.—The Canadian commissioners and the Department of State finally concluded a draft of a treaty wherein the free list not only contained the articles which had appeared in the treaty of 1854, but also, in addition, agricultural implements, boots, shoes, furniture, vehicles, print paper, woolen tweeds, and many manufactures of cotton, iron, steel, leather, and wool.[1] But there was included a provision whereby everything made free to the United States was also to be made free to Great Britain; therefore when President Grant sent the draft of the treaty to the Senate and asked for advice, it was returned with the opinion that it was inexpedient to proceed with the matter.

Influence of the crisis of 1873 upon trade and upon Canadian public opinion.—The rejection of Brown's proposals came in the midst of the business depression which followed the crisis of 1873. Hard times prevailed on both sides of the border, but owing to her less highly developed business organization Canada suffered less than the United States, and prices there were somewhat better maintained. This led to a preponderance of imports from, over exports to, the United States—a phenomenon which strongly influenced public opinion, since it was construed as a reversal of what had been previously, for Canada, a "favorable" balance of trade. Depression and low prices in the United States greatly stimulated American exports to the Dominion, and the subsequent change of trade currents was destined to be maintained, with a few exceptions, for over a decade. The result was to give more strength to the growing demand for protection in Canada. Fiscal conditions combined with those of a more general economic nature to promote a higher tariff policy. The decrease of Canadian imports from all countries, by diminishing the customs receipts, caused recurring deficits that greatly embarrassed the administration.

The movement toward protection and the act of 1879.—The Conservatives made the tariff the leading issue in the next election. The Liberals, having failed in their negotiations with the United States, had no further measures to suggest. The Conservatives proposed a policy of consistent retaliation, and made "reciprocity of trade or reciprocity of tariffs" their motto. Sir Charles Tupper solicited votes

---

[1] See Brown's speech in the Canadian senate, 1875, and in Alexander Mackenzie's "Life and Speeches of George Brown," pp. 351 ff.

for the Conservative Party upon the particular ground that since conciliatory methods had failed to win reciprocity, the only way to move the United States was by the adoption of a high retaliatory tariff. Throughout Canada the attitude of the United States was resented, and this fact went far to account for the overwheming Conservative victory at the polls in 1878. In office again, the Conservative party abundantly redeemed its pledges; it put the "national policy" into operation in the tariff act of 1879. In that act the free list was materially abbreviated, notably by the removal of coal, flour, and pig iron, and upon most articles commonly imported from the United States the new rates were made higher than the old by all the way from 20 to more than 100 per cent. In his speech introducing the bill, the Minister of Finance, Sir Leonard Tilley, stated that a special effort had been made to adjust the duties so that the heaviest burden would fall upon American goods. To give greater point to the retaliatory intent, Macdonald embodied in the act an offer of reciprocity in coal, lumber, and agricultural products at any time that the United States should express a desire for it—an offer 'which, with slight modification, remained a feature of Canadian tariff legislation for eighteen years.

The passage of this act by the Canadian Parliament was followed in the United States by several efforts to arouse the interest of Congress in reciprocity. Thus, in 1880 the House Committee on Foreign Relations took up the matter and in its majority report commented upon the retaliatory ·tariff legislation in Canada, and upon the unanimity of opinion among American commercial bodies in favor of reciprocity. The minority report vigorously opposed reciprocity, and no action was taken.

Circumstances compelling renewal of negotiations.—In 1884, after Canada's foreign trade had attained a remarkable growth, there began a depression from which it did not recover entirely until 1890. This encouraged the Liberal Party to renew the agitation for freer trade with the United States, while an active though unofficial group carried on a widespread and effective propaganda in favor of a complete commercial union. As it happened, the reopening of negotiations between the two countries was at this time practically forced by two circumstances—one was Canadian discrimination in transportation rates; the other, more important, was the abrogation by the United States of the fisheries clauses in the treaty of Washington.

The abolition of tolls on the Erie Canal in 1882, which enabled vessels thereafter to pass free on all American canals, diverted much traffic from the Canadian routes. On the Canadian canals the charges were 20 cents a ton, and to remove this disadvantage there was established in 1884 a drawback of 18 cents per ton upon shipments to Montreal, while upon cargoes going to American ports the full rate was maintained. Next the Canadian Pacific Railway (completed in 1885) offered transcontinental traffic rates too low for the American lines to meet.

Abrogation of the fisheries provisions.—The sense of injustice which these measures aroused in the United States was intensified by the treatment which Canada accorded to American fishermen. The disposition of the fisheries question made in the treaty of Washington and under the Halifax award had not been satisfactory to American fishermen; notice had been given by the United States in 1883 of a desire to terminate the fisheries provisions; and on July 1, 1885, these provisions ceased to be effective. The situation thus again reverted to the arrangement made in the treaty of 1818, by the terms of which American fishermen might enter Canadian waters for shelter, repairs, wood, and water, "and for no other purpose." The Dominion Government now undertook to enforce these terms literally and rigorously. The Canadian authorities seemed determined to use the fisheries as they had tried to do in 1852, as a means of securing a commercial treaty. Irritated by the severity of the Canadian measure and by the unfriendly methods by which it was enforced, Congress passed, by a practically unanimous vote in both Houses, a drastic non-intercourse act. Under this act, approved March 3, 1887, the President was authorized, whenever he was satisfied that American fisheries or fishermen were being unjustly vexed or harassed in Canadian waters, to deny to Canadian vessels entrance to American ports, and to prohibit the entry of fish or any other product of the Dominion or of any goods coming from the Dominion. It may readily be surmised that grave consequences to business and even to peace between the countries might have followed the enforcing of such an act. Fortunately the matter never came to that extreme, partly because of the good judgment of President Cleveland, partly because of the desire of the British Government to reestablish harmonious relations.

Negotiation and rejection of a new treaty, 1888.—After preliminary arrangements, during which the Dominion Government suspended its stringent restrictions, Mr. Joseph Chamberlain and Sir Charles Tupper were sent as high commissioners to join the British minister at Washington in the negotiating of a new treaty. These commissioners offered a settlement of the fisheries difficulty, "in consideration of a mutual arrangement providing for greater freedom of commercial intercourse." But the Secretary of State, Mr. Bayard, knowing the attitude of Congress, refused even to ask the President for authority to negotiate on the question of commercial reciprocity. A treaty to regulate the use of the North Atlantic fisheries was signed February 17, 1888, but when presented to the Senate it was rejected.

Subsequent improvement in relations.—This episode marks the climax of the ill feeling which had persisted from the time of the Civil War. Thereafter this feeling gradually gave way to a more friendly and conciliatory attitude. On the Canadian side, the subsequent years held in store an abundant prosperity; the vigor and forcefulness of the people, applied to the development of almost unlimited natural resources, assured for Canada the economic independence which Macdonald aimed to achieve, and the tariff policy of the United States ceased to occasion such general resentment. The most persistent cause of discord had been removed by the disposal of the long disputed fisheries question; a *modus vivendi* established while the treaty was under discussion in 1888 was extended from year to year, and in the course of time this arrangement came to be tacitly regarded as permanent.

Disposal of the canal tolls question.—There still remained open the matter of Canadian rail and canal discriminations. As a means of settling this, President Cleveland, who had wisely refrained from enforcing the non-intercourse act, requested in a special message of

August 23, 1888, the power to suspend free transit through the United States of goods shipped between Canada and foreign countries; but Congress failed to take action.   The situation was to some extent improved in 1889 through the entry of the Canadian Pacific Railway into the Transcontinental Rates Association.   By the act of July 26, 1892, the President was instructed to countervail discriminating rates on the Dominion canals by suspending the free passage of Canadian vessels using the Sault Ste. Marie Canal and imposing retaliatory tolls. Canada thereupon substituted for her former charges and drawback a uniform toll of 10 cents per ton, payable on both the Welland and (or) the St. Lawrence Canals.   This was a concession in form rather than in substance; but the American charges were removed and the retaliatory practices were discontinued.[1]

Sentiment in Congress favorable to reciprocity.—Secretary Bayard's absolute refusal to discuss Tupper's commercial proposals at the treaty conference in 1888, and the return to power of the Republican Party in the election of the same year, precluded the immediate re-opening of reciprocity negotiations.   But evidences were not lacking of the growth in the United States of a more liberal attitude toward Canada.   In 1888 the House Committee on Foreign Affairs recommended the appointment by the President of commissioners to meet Canadian commissioners and to prepare a plan for commercial union; and at the next session, March 1, 1889, a bill to that end was passed in the House.   In the next Congress a similar recommendation was made by the same committee, and in the Senate the trend of opinion seemed to be in this general direction.   It was significant of a change of attitude that some suggestions at this time contemplated not mere partial tariff reductions, but complete commercial union.   Such was, of course, no part of the general reciprocity policy which was urged by Blaine and a few other Republican leaders during the debate in 1890 on the McKinley tariff bill.   Nor did it appear in the proposed Newfoundland reciprocity treaty, drawn up in the same year between Blaine and Sir Julian Pauncefote, and pigeonholed by Lord Salisbury at the instance of Canada.[2]   In spite of the limited form of reciprocity provided for in the McKinley Act, all signs indicated a widespread change of sentiment among the American people and in Congress.

In Canada these signs were not overlooked.   They attracted all the more attention for the reason that the prosperity attending the earlier years of the régime of the "national policy" had waned.   Certain branches of manufacturing appear to have expanded, under the optimistic influence of that policy, beyond the capacity of the limited Canadian market to absorb their products.   Prices of farm products had fallen.   The exodus across the border had increased to such a degree that the population at the end of the decade was only 11.76 per cent greater than in 1880, while that of the United States had increased in the same period by 24.86 per cent.[3]   Favored by these circumstances, the Liberals once more made a leading issue of the Dominion's commercial relations with the United States.   In 1889 Sir Richard Cartwright offered a motion in the House of Commons, "that in the present condition of affairs and in view of the recent action of the House of Representatives of the United States, it is

---

[1] U. S. Foreign Relations, 1893, p. 330.
[2] See p. 360, infra.
[3] Skelton, O. D., Canada and its Provinces, Vol. IX, p. 152.

expedient that steps should be taken to ascertain on what terms and conditions arrangements can be effected with the United States for the purpose of securing full and unrestricted reciprocity of trade therewith."[1]

Canadian overtures.—Since "reciprocity" was still a term with which to conjure votes, the Conservatives were not willing to relinquish all credit for supporting the policy which it implies. Hence, in spite of the rejection of Tupper's offer in 1888, they came out for the "renewal of the Reciprocity Treaty of 1854, subject to such modifications as the altered circumstances of both countries require and to such extensions as the Commission may deem to be in the interests of the United States and Canada."[2] By these non-committal phrases they retained a claim to the reciprocity policy, and joined issue with the Liberals only as to the degree to which it should be carried. Asserting that Blaine had taken the initiative in proposing a renewal of negotiations, Macdonald sought support upon the ground that he would be able to secure the long-wished-for concessions. Mr. Blaine, in a report to President Harrison in 1892, gave an account of what had actually occurred. In point of fact, he declared, the initiative had been taken by the British minister. In the course of conferences which took place after the interval of more than a year, Blaine had taken the position that the United States could not agree to commercial reciprocity unless there was included in the schedule a list of manufactured articles, and that the United States desired that such an arrangement be exclusive in its application—other countries should not enjoy gratuitously the favors which the contracting parties received from each other for valuable considerations and at a large sacrifice of revenue. Into such a convention the Canadian commissioners declined to enter, on the grounds that, in the first place, the Dominion could not afford the loss of revenue involved in the free admission of a considerable list of manufactures, and, in the second place, the Government of the Dominion was not competent to enter into any commercial arrangement from the benefits of which Great Britain and her colonies should be excluded. "The announcement of these conclusions of the Canadian commissioners was accepted as a bar to further negotiations on this subject, and it was not again discussed except in connection with the fishing privileges on the Atlantic coast."[3]

Change of attitude.—This was the last action taken by the Conservative government with a view to securing commercial reciprocity. Even among the Liberals, converts to the "national policy" were appearing. Among these, Edward Blake, who preceded Sir Wilfrid Laurier as his party's leader, expressed the belief, in a letter written just after the election of 1891, that either unrestricted reciprocity or commercial union would undoubtedly lead to the political absorption of Canada by the United States. This letter exercised a wide influence upon public opinion at the time, and played an important part in the parliamentary debates on reciprocity twenty years later.[4]

---

[1] House of Commons Debates, 1889, p. 468.
[2] Canada Sessional Papers, 1891, No. 38, S. 4, p. 13, vol. 17.
[3] Mr. Blaine, Secretary of State, to President Harrison, Apr. 15, 1892; 52d Cong., 1st sess., Sen. Ex. Doc. No. 114, p. 5.
[4] See speech of R. L. Borden, House of Commons Debates, Feb. 2, 1911, p. 3021.

Loss of interest, in Canada.—From 1891 until 1911 reciprocity ceased to be a practical issue.   In Canada, where it had been a feature of political platforms for half a century, there was no formal disavowal; on the contrary the Canadian tariff, until 1897, continued to include an offer of reciprocity in natural products; but everyone knew that the provision was meaningless.   The Canadian public gradually lost interest in a policy which appeared to be impossible of realization, and efforts were concentrated upon fostering the means of domestic traffic and opening the necessary markets for Canadian exports in other parts of the world.   The matter of trade relations came up again in 1898, during the futile discussions of the Joint High Commission whose chief purpose was to settle the Alaska boundary dispute; but agreement upon the removal of commercial restrictions was not very ardently sought, and upon his return to Ottawa Mr. Laurier announced, "There will be no more pilgrimages to Washington.   We are turning our hopes to the old motherland."   Mr. Fielding, who was Minister of Finance in the Liberal cabinet, said in 1899, "Whatever our American friends may have intended by their trade policy, there is one thing they certainly have done; they have made Canadians more independent and self-reliant and have caused them to look more steadily than before to their home market and to their markets over the sea, where there is an open door.   *   *   *   Therefore the market of our friends to the south of us is much less important to us than it was a few years ago, and we are better able to do without reciprocity than we have been at any previous time in the history of Canada."[1]

---

[1] Quoted by James Arthurs, House of Commons Debates, July 18, 1911, p. 9842.

2. RECIPROCITY WITH HAWAII.

RECIPROCITY WITH HAWAII.

THE DIPLOMATIC AND LEGISLATIVE RECORD.

The second reciprocity experiment of the United States was that made with the Hawaiian Islands under the treaty of 1875. The history of United States-Hawaiian relations during fifty years previous to the negotiation of this reciprocity treaty, the character of the arguments which finally carried the day in favor of the treaty, and the nature of developments while it was in force, point to the conclusion that the entrance of the United States into this special arrangement was dictated by political and strategic considerations rather than by the thought and expectation of great economic gain.

Bound up with the political and strategic considerations, however, were economic considerations centering about the desire of the Hawaiian sugar planters to secure preference for their sugar in the American market and the determination of the domestic producers to prevent the establishment of such preference. Both sets of interests were possessed of considerable political influence and the part which they played in the history of the United States relations with Hawaii was always important.

Hawaii's foreign relations.—The location, the resources, and the political weakness of the islands rendered it practically inevitable that strong powers should compete for influence in the Hawaiian Kingdom. To the United States it was first a matter of concern that the region should not be brought under the control of any other power.

Four times before the middle of the nineteenth century, flags of European nations had been run up on Hawaiian soil in token of political authority—twice the British, once the Russian, once the French. The United States had been first among the nations to negotiate a treaty with the Hawaiians, but this treaty, drafted in 1826, had not been ratified. It remained for the British to conclude the first treaty with the Hawaiian Government, the negotiations being conducted under the guns of a man-of-war, in 1836. The French were next in treaty making, following the arrival of a 60-gun frigate and the presentation of excessive demands by its commander, in 1839. It was later asserted that it had been the intention of the commander to seize and retain the islands.[1] Shortly thereafter, the British consul at Honolulu, who had been in the islands for many years, returned to England to inform his Government that the influence of the United States in the islands was negligible.

In 1842 the Hawaiian Government appointed a commission of three persons—a British official, an American missionary, and a native chief—to visit the United States, Great Britain, and France, to make representations—including a request for recognition of the independence of the Hawaiian Kingdom.

---

[1] See U. S. Foreign Relations, 1894, Appendix II, p. 92.

Mr. Webster's declaration of the attitude of the United States, 1842.—In the United States, Mr. Webster, Secretary of State, promptly took up the matter. On December 19, 1842, he declared, in the name of the President, the United States' recognition of the independence of the Hawaiian Government. President Tyler sent a special message, of Webster's drafting, to Congress on December 30, in which he declared that the facts of the relative proximity of the islands to the American Continent, and the intercourse of American vessels with the islands, would—

"create dissatisfaction on the part of the United States at any attempt by another power * * * to take possession of the islands, colonize them, and subvert the native Government. The United States sought "no peculiar advantages, no exclusive control over the Hawaiian Government * * *. Its forbearance in this respect, under the circumstances of the very large intercourse of their citizens with the islands, would justify the Government * * * in making a decided remonstrance against the adoption of an opposite policy by any other power."[1]

Three months before, the French had proclaimed their protectorate over Tahiti, a move which led to civil disorders within Tahiti during the next ten years and ultimately to formal annexation by France in 1880. Also in 1842 the Marquesas Islands had been surrendered to the French.

British attempt on Hawaii, 1843.—In the next year, 1843, Lord George Paulet, commander of the British frigate *Carysport,* acting on the basis of representations made to him by the consul referred to above, proceeded to Honolulu and made a series of demands. Rather than accept the situation which would have resulted from yielding to these demands, the Hawaiian King and his council decided to cede the possession of the islands entire and to appeal to the Queen of England for restoration. Paulet accepted the cession, ran up the British flag, and took possession. Within the year the King of Hawaii appealed to the Queen of Great Britain and the President of the United States; Commodore Kearney, in command of the U. S. S. *Constellation,* arrived at Honolulu and, representing the views of his Government, protested against the cession and every act connected with it; Admiral Thomas, commander of the British naval forces in the Pacific, arrived and—representing instructions from his Government—restored the islands to the Hawaiian Government; the British Government disavowed Paulet's annexation, and the British minister at Washington made formal and positive announcement of the fact. During the diplomatic discussion Mr. Legaré, Acting Secretary of State at Washington, had written to Mr. Everett, American minister to Great Britain:

* * * there is something so entirely peculiar in the relations between this little commonwealth [the Hawaiian Kingdom] and ourselves that we might even feel justified, consistently with our own principles, in interfering by force to prevent its falling into the hands of one of the great powers of Europe.[2]

British-French agreement concerning Hawaii, 1843.—On November 28 (1843), the British and the French signed in London a declaration engaging "reciprocally, to consider the Sandwich Islands as an independent State, and never to take possession * * * of any part of the territory of which they are composed."[3] In the interval the United States had appointed a commissioner to the islands, and

---

[1] 27th Cong., 3d sess., H. Ex. Doc. No. 35; also, U. S. Foreign Relations, 1894, Appendix II, p. 39.
[2] U. S. Foreign Relations, 1894, Appendix II, p. 113,
[3] U. S. Foreign Relations, 1894, Appendix II, p. 64.

its first appointee to that post reached Honolulu in October. In receiving this, envoy, the Hawaiian King declared that citizens of the United States would always receive from him the privileges accorded those of the most favored nations.[1]

New Hawaiian treaties with England, France, and the United States, 1844-1857.—In 1844 and 1846, respectively, the British and the French secured new treaties with Hawaii, in which the terms of their earlier treaties were considerably modified. Instructed by his Government to secure a treaty, the then American commissioner began negotiations, but his attitude antagonized the Hawaiian authorities and delayed the conclusion. The admission of California to the Union, in 1848, quickened the interest of the American people in the possibilities of developments in the Pacific Ocean, negotiations with Hawaii were again taken up, and a satisfactory treaty was signed on December 20, 1849. This treaty, similar in its provisions to those made by the United States with other nations, remained in force during all the subsequent existence of the Hawaiian Government. It became the model, also, for treaties made by Great Britain and France in 1851 and 1857.

Hawaiian Government asks the protection of the United States.— While these negotiations for the American treaty were being concluded, a new French consul had arrived at Honolulu and had become involved in difficulties with the Hawaiian officials. In August, 1849, two French men-of-war had arrived, and the admiral sent to the King a group of arbitrary demands, followed by the landing of an armed force. Again the Hawaiian Government sent a special commission to Paris, London, and Washington, its particular object being to secure a tripartite agreement affirming Hawaiian neutrality. The French Government sent to Hawaii a special commissioner, in a war vessel, and this representative pressed the French demands so aggressively that the Hawaiian King decided to put his realm under the protection of the United States; he gave the American commissioner, in 1851, a signed and sealed proclamation—which had received the approval of the Hawaiian Parliament—declaring that, "all our islands, and all our rights as sovereign over them, are * * * placed under the protection and safeguard of the United States of America," this document to be opened and carried into effect if the French began hostilities. In the meantime, under instructions from Mr. Webster, the American minister in Paris intimated to the French Government that, having a paramount interest in the islands, the United States would allow no forcible occupation by any foreign power.[2]

Mr. Webster's statement of United States policy, 1851.—Mr. Webster had taken the position that it was the purpose of the United States to observe the principle of the independence of the Hawaiian Islands, and his Government would expect other nations to observe the same principle.

The Hawaiian Islands are ten times nearer to the United States than to any of the powers of Europe. Five-sixths of all their commercial intercourse is with the United States, and these considerations, together with others of a more general character, have fixed the course which the Government of the United States will pursue. * * * That policy is that while the Government of the United States, itself faithful to its original assurance, scrupulously regards the independence of the Hawaiian Islands,

[1] U. S. Foreign Relations, 1894; Appendix II, p. 64.
[2] Ibid., pp. 97-99, 103-105.

it can never consent to see those islands taken possession of by either of the great commercial powers of Europe, nor can it consent that demands, manifestly unjust and derogatory and inconsistent with a bona fide independence, shall be enforced against that Government.[1]

He also took pains to let it be understood that the Navy had been instructed to be in a state of strength in the Pacific and that he would favor the use of force in defense of the policy thus outlined if the action of France made it necessary. The effect of Webster's resolute attitude was the relaxation of the French pressure upon the Hawaiian Government, and the difficulty was settled without further aggression.

Possibilities in United States-Hawaiian relations.—Near together as the United States and Hawaii are, there were four possible courses which the development of their relations might take: The two countries might continue to stand resolutely and entirely apart and independent of one another, or the United States might establish a protectorate; they might agree to commercial reciprocity, or Hawaii might come under the jurisdiction of the United States. So long as the first of these conditions prevailed, the likelihood or possibility of Hawaii being interfered with by other States was at its maximum. An increasing commercial prosperity was to prove at once the instrument and the creator of decisive influence. From 1851 on there was a disposition, especially on the part of influential sections of Hawaiian population, to establish some closer bond; but in the United States it was recognized that protection without jurisdiction would bring many obligations with few compensations and this possible relationship seems to have been little considered.

Negotiation of a treaty of annexation, 1854.—Sentiment favorable to annexation having been expressed in Hawaii, and the idea being not unfavorably received by the leaders in the United States, in 1854 Mr. Marcy, Secretary of State, committed himself to the principle and a treaty of annexation was negotiated. Dissatisfaction over certain conditions—the provision for the immediate statehood of Hawaii and a too large annuity for the royal court of Hawaii—necessitated a revision; but before that could be accomplished the King of Hawaii died and was succeeded by a ruler whose opposition to annexation ended the matter for the time being.

Negotiation of a reciprocity treaty, 1855.—Reciprocity was looked upon as the practicable alternative to annexation. Under what appeared favorable conditions, there was negotiated and signed at Washington, on July 20, 1855, a reciprocity treaty which provided for the free admission of various Hawaiian products into the United States and of various United States products into Hawaii. This treaty was approved by the Senate Committee on Foreign Affairs; but it was opposed by the sugar-growing interests of the southern States, its terms were not financially attractive to the United States, and it failed of ratification in the Senate.

The period of the Civil War affected the Hawaiian question in three ways at least: It diverted the attention of the United States to problems of a more vital nature. It led to an investigation of the islands as a possible source of cotton by English commissioners and for a while British influence substantially supplanted American. And it brought business stagnation and debt to the

---

[1] U. S. Foreign Relations, 1894, Appendix II, p. 100.

Hawaiian Islands through the destruction of the American whaling fleet in the Pacific, thereby emphasizing the necessity of some special arrangements calculated to come to the rescue of business interests. When the Hawaiians proposed reconsideration of the reciprocity question, the American Government, in view of the probably adverse effect on the public revenue, declined to consider it.

Second negotiation of a reciprocity treaty, 1867.—Later, however, in 1867, the year of the Alaska purchase, there was negotiated, under instructions from Mr. Seward, Secretary of State, a new reciprocity treaty. This treaty provided somewhat more liberally than had that of 1855 for the admission of American products to Hawaii. It was ratified by the Hawaiian Government; but it had no chance of gaining the approval of Congress. The reciprocity treaty with Canada had just been abrogated; a congressional and presidential election was approaching; Congress was preoccupied with questions of reconstruction. As had been the case with the treaty negotiated in 1855, no assurance was offered that Hawaii, after being developed by American capital and at the expense of American interest, effort, and favor, would not pass at some future time under the control of some other power. President Johnson, in his annual message in 1868, urged that reciprocity was desirable; but the treaty was definitely rejected by the Senate a year and a half later, on June 1, 1870.

During the next few years there was no little concern both in the islands and in the United States as to the future of Hawaii. The prosperity of the islands continued to decline. As officials, planters, and merchants cast about for means and methods of improving conditions, reciprocity with or annexation to the United States were the only apparent remedies. Either conclusion promised economic advantage to Hawaii. In the United States the history of the *Alabama* raids was fresh in the public mind, pointing to the possibility that some hostile power might some day use the islands as a base. The United States did not wish to annex the islands; it was chiefly concerned that no other country should annex them. It was evident, however, from the experiences in 1855 and 1867, that simple commercial reciprocity was not likely to gain the approval of Congress. To Hawaii the markets of the United States were important; to the United States the market of Hawaii was of no great consequence. Hawaii had, in fact, little to offer commercially in bargaining for tariff concessions. The Hawaiian customs duties were already low, the population of the islands was less than 60,000, their purchasing power was small, and they produced most of their own foodstuffs and necessities. It was recognized, however, that there should be established some arrangement which would constitute an official evidence of the interest of the United States in the welfare and security of Hawaii.

Third negotiation and final conclusion of a reciprocity treaty, 1875.—In February, 1874, the death of the King of Hawaii left the succession to the throne in dispute, and American armed forces were landed to assist in preserving order. Under the protection of this force, the legislature elected a new king, who was at once recognized by the American, the British, and the French representatives. Most cordial sentiments prevailed between the American and the new Hawaiian Governments, and the King of Hawaii visited the United States.

One of the objects of his trip was to obtain a reciprocity treaty,[1] and in the next year, 1875, the long-considered question was again taken up, and a reciprocity treaty was negotiated and ratified— much to the gratification of the Hawaiian people.

Terms of the treaty.—The treaty of 1875, as negotiated and ratified, did not differ greatly from the former treaties which had been rejected by the Senate. Commercial reciprocity was agreed on as a matter of course, each of the countries admitting free of duty various articles the products of the other, and neither country charging export duties on any of the articles which the other admitted free.[2] It had been suggested in 1873 that the Hawaiians might offer a political consideration in the form of the cession of the mouth of the Pearl River and territory ten miles square surrounding it for the use of the United States.[3] In the treaty as actually framed, however, this suggestion was not followed up. The special consideration granted by Hawaii in favor of the United States was as follows:

ARTICLE IV. * * * His Hawaiian Majesty * * * so long as this treaty shall remain in force * * * will not lease or otherwise dispose of or create any lien upon any port, harbor, or other territory in his dominions, or grant any special privilege or rights of use therein, to any other power, State, or government, nor make any treaty by which any other nation shall obtain the same privileges, relative to the admission of any articles free of duty, hereby secured to the United States.

As in the previous reciprocity negotiations, it was on the Hawaiian side that consideration of the question had been urgently moved. There was in 1875 no immediate political reason for action on the part of the United States. Commercially the United States already controlled the carrying trade between San Francisco and Honolulu, sold to the Hawaiians most of what they imported, and was receiving a satisfactory revenue upon Hawaiian products imported in return.

There was, however, a particular factor which enabled the advocates of action to command attention at the moment: the Hawaiian planters claimed that they could dispose of their sugar to great advantage in the free-trade ports of Australia, and it was made to appear that they were preparing to send their sugar crop of 1875–76 to those ports. Should the sugar trade be diverted, the Hawaiians would no longer be bound by commercial ties to the United States, the trade of the islands would drift to English control, and the Hawaiian Government would come more and more under the influence of Great Britain.[4]

Legislation to put the treaty into effect, 1876.—The treaty was signed on January 30, 1875. It was promptly ratified by the Hawaiian Legislature. It was ratified by the United States Senate on March 18, by a vote of 51 to 12; ratifications were exchanged at Washington on June 3, and the treaty was proclaimed on June 30, 1875. But, inasmuch as the arrangement involved the abolishing of duties imposed by law in the United States, an act of Congress was necessary to carry it into effect; not only must the House of Representatives consent, but the bill to put the treaty into operation must, as a revenue bill, originate in the House. On January 16, 1876, such a bill was introduced. On February 24, the Committee on Ways

---

[1] Moore's Digest, I, p. 485; U. S. Foreign Relations, 1875, I, pp. 669–679.
[2] For further discussion of this feature, see p. 121 et seq., infra.
[3] Mr. Pierce to Mr. Fish, Feb. 10, 1873, and reports; U. S. Foreign Relations, 1894, Appendix II, p. 152 ff.
[4] Taken from Chalfant Robinson, A History of Two Reciprocity Treaties, p. 123; Morgan, 53d Cong., 2d sess., Sen. Doc. No. 231, vol. 8, pt. 8.

and Means returned a majority report (Mr. Wood) in favor of, and a minority report (Mr. Morrison) against the bill.   The majority rested their   case   on   political   considerations.   They   conceded   that the arrangement would not be advantageous from the point of view of revenue, that it would not secure the United States a great amount of new foreign trade, but they urged that it would insure against the occupation of Hawaii by any other power.   As the immediate occasion for the treaty, they referred to the fact that the trade of Hawaii was being attracted to the British colonies in the Pacific.

If the exports and imports were equal, as they probably will be, it would be an equal bargain.   *   *   *   But supposing that there were no reciprocity of commerce in this treaty, that the commerce and advantages were against us, and that we lose even $400,000 annual revenue, yet there are political reasons of sufficient magnitude to warrant us to make it.   This is their geographical position in relation to our Pacific coast, and to the countries adjacent to the Pacific Ocean.   This group is the key to the Pacific   *   *   *   [1]

The minority report went much more carefully than that of the majority into consideration of the commercial and fiscal advantages and disadvantages, contending that reciprocity would be, for the United States, a bad bargain.   It made the assertion, among other things, that, under the operation of the most-favored-nation clause, the sugar of other countries would be exempted, along with that of Hawaii, from duty,[2] which would mean a great loss in revenue.   It agreed with the view of the majority that it was necessary to prevent the islands from being occupied by a foreign power, but it denied that the provisions of the treaty were necessary or satisfactory to that end.   Our defense lay in our internal strength.   "We hold the power of peace with * * * all nations in doing justice to all * * *."[3]

In the debates it was contended against the treaty that the remission of duty would constitute a gift to the sugar producers of the Hawaiian Islands.   It was asserted that backers of the treaty were speculating in sugar lands —with the expectation of extensive development or profitable sale after reciprocity should be secured.   Mr. Morrison, against the treaty, declared:

There is no protection in this treaty, for there are no American interests to be protected.   There is no free trade in it, for there is but little trade of any kind, and that is to be made exclusive for one side.   There is no reciprocity in it, for much is given and nothing is received.[4]

American producers of sugar cane protested against the treaty on the ground that it would stimulate production of sugar in Hawaii, and would thus divert American capital from the cane and sugar-beet industries in the United States.

It was, however, on the basis mainly of other than economic considerations that the treaty had been signed and ratified; there was strong support by Americans interested in the Hawaiian sugar plantations; and, in spite of the representations that the arrangement would be a losing transaction financially, the House passed the bill to put it into effect.   The bill was then passed in the Senate on August 14, 1876, the vote being 29 for, 12 against.   (Six senators were paired and 24 were absent or did not vote.)

---

[1] 44th Cong., 1st sess., H. Rept. No. 116, p. 7.
[2] On this point see section on the Most-Favored-Nation Clause, p. 418, infra.
[3] 44th Cong., 1st sess., H. Rept. No. 116, pt. 2, p. 5.
[4] 44th Cong., 1st sess., Cong. Rec., vol. 4.

Protocol putting the treaty into operation.—The necessary legislation having been secured, the treaty was put into operation by special protocol on September 9, 1876, to remain in force for seven years, and thereafter subject to one year's notice for termination.[1]

Diplomatic difficulties—Claims of other nations for most-favored-nation treatment.—When the reciprocity treaty went into effect the British commissioner to Hawaii notified the Hawaiian Government that " * * * Her Majesty's Government can not allow of British goods imported into the Sandwich Islands being subjected to treatment other than that which is accorded to similar goods of American origin," and that British importers would claim under their treaty, for British products, equality with American products under the United States reciprocity treaty. This position was taken on the basis, of course, of the most-favored-nation clause in the British-Hawaiian treaty of 1851. The German Government also raised a question of most-favored-nation treatment, but Germany had no treaty with Hawaii upon which to base a claim. Over the British contention a long diplomatic correspondence followed, in the course of which the American minister to Hawaii was frequently consulted by the Hawaiian Government. The American minister uniformly insisted that it would be a violation of the treaty to allow to British or any other products the same privileges as those extended to the United States; and that it would be a violation of the sovereignty of Hawaii for Great Britain to assume to dictate what rate of customs duties the Hawaiian Government should levy upon British goods as compared with those of other countries.[2]

The American minister made the following representation to the Hawaiian Minister of Foreign Affairs:

No treaty in existence at the time this compact was entered into secured to any other nation the privileges as to the admission of certain articles free of duty, which have been guaranteed to the United States by this treaty. These privileges were secured, not through any general treaty rights or stipulations, but by giving certain valuable considerations in a special treaty of reciprocal covenants. The concession of these privileges to the United States can not, therefore, form any just basis for a claim to like privileges by any other nation, under the parity clause of the ordinary form of treaty. The uttermost that might be conceded under such parity clause would be the claim to purchase the same immunities through special treaty, upon like terms with those agreed upon between the United States and the Hawaiian Islands. But this is in the nature of the case impossible. Those concessions by the United States which are of the greatest value to the islands under this treaty would be of no value whatever from other powers, whose great distance from the best markets for island products would be as effectual a bar to the enjoyment of reciprocity as a prohibitory edict. The effect of such an arrangement would be, if attempted with other powers on the same basis, that the United States would remit some millions of duty on island products during the seven years, in order that other nations might not pay duty to His Hawaiian Majesty on goods brought here to compete with American products.

This is the precise thing the treaty does not intend. Its intention is to secure exclusive benefits to both contracting parties through special privileges granted by each to the other. To admit the claim of a third party to come in and enjoy all the benefits conceded by both principals, without any payment in equivalent special privileges to either, would be an unprecedented thing.[3]

Article III of the British-Hawaiian treaty of 1851 had provided that any favor or immunity whatever in matters of commerce and

---

[1] See Malloy, Treaties, Conventions, etc., p. 918, and U. S. Foreign Relations, 1877, p. 296.
[2] U. S. Foreign Relations, 1879-80, 1881, passim.
[3] U. S. Foreign Relations, 1879, p. 404.

navigation which either party granted to citizens of any other State should be extended to the other contracting party gratuitously if the concession to the third State was gratuitous, or in return for a compensation as nearly as possible of proportionate value and effect, to be adjusted by mutual agreement, if the concession was conditional.[1]

The Hawaiian Minister of Foreign Affairs pointed out to the British commissioner that the most-favored-nation provision in Article III of the treaty was conditional, and continued:

This article clearly acknowledges the right of either party to make reciprocal conventions, and clearly lays down the doctrine of compensation, and the liability of either party to be held to compensate if they claim like privileges.[2]

He cited in support of this position a communication, dated March 28, 1856, from one of the British negotiators of the treaty of 1851 to the other, in which appeared the following statement (under instructions from Lord Clarendon, Secretary of State for Foreign Affairs):

The fourth article of the treaty between Great Britain and the Sandwich Islands of the 10th of July, 1851, stipulates that no other or higher duties shall be charged on the importation into the Sandwich Islands of any article the growth, produce, or manufacture of the British dominions than are or shall be payable on the like articles the growth, produce, or manufacture of any other foreign country. If this were the only stipulation in the treaty bearing upon the subject, the claim of Great Britain to participate in the advantages conceded to the United States by the convention in question would be clear; but as the next preceding article (III) of the treaty of 1851 contains a stipulation that any favor which either party may grant to a third country shall be extended to the other party on corresponding terms, that is, either gratuitously or for an equivalent compensation, as the case may be, and as the advantages conceded to the United States by the Sandwich Islands are expressly stated to be given in consideration of, and as an equivalent for, certain reciprocal concessions on the part of the United States, Great Britain can not as a matter of right claim the same advantages for her trade under the strict letter of the treaty of 1851.[3]

As the British Government insisted upon its claim, the Hawaiian Government gave one year's notice of the termination of Articles IV, V, and VI of the Anglo-Hawaiian treaty of 1851, and sent Mr. Carter, its Minister of Foreign Affairs, as an envoy to Europe to negotiate with the British and the German Governments. Lord Derby proposed that England would drop the contention if Hawaii would withdraw the denunciation of the treaty articles in question and would agree that British products corresponding to articles on the free schedule of the American treaty would not be taxed more than 10 per cent. The Hawaiian Legislature had passed a tariff act in 1876 raising the duties on certain articles to 25 per cent ad valorem. Mr. Carter declined to promise the repeal of this act. The British Government finally agreed not to question the right of the Hawaiian Legislature to pass such a law, but made no formal surrender of the claim of right to enjoy privileges on a parity with the United States.

The Hawaiian representative succeeded in negotiating with Germany a treaty to which there was attached a provision that Germany would not claim the special advantages enjoyed by the United States under the treaty of 1875 in consideration of equivalent advantages reciprocally conceded.[4]

---

[1] U. S. Foreign Relations, 1878–79, p. 386.
[2] Ibid.
[3] Ibid., p. 388.
[4] See section on the Most-Favored-Nation Clause, p. 410, infra.

Upon the return of the Hawaiian representative to Honolulu the committee on foreign relations made a report to the Hawaiian Legislature. The majority, favoring the British contention regarding treaty rights, asked that the assembly approve the British claim, and that it repay all duties improperly levied on British goods and extend to Great Britain the treatment accorded to the United States under the treaty. This the legislature did not do. It amended the tariff law, however, substantially as had been suggested by Lord Derby, bringing most of the rates to 10 per cent ad valorem.

Still later, British firms demanded a refund of duties which they had paid, under protest, at the rates prescribed in the law of 1876. The controversy over this question continued for some time; the British Government seemed determined to press the claim diplomatically and the Hawaiian Government equally determined that it should be settled by the Hawaiian courts. This situation provoked a strong communication from Mr. Blaine, American Secretary of State.[1]

Mr. Blaine wrote to Mr. Comly, minister to Hawaii, on June 30, 1881, for communication to the Hawaiian Government:

* * * this Government can not permit any violation, direct or indirect, of the terms and conditions of the treaty of 1875.

The treaty was made at the continuous and urgent request of the Hawaiian Government. * * * it was expressly stipulated—"On the part of His Hawaiian Majesty that so long as this treaty shall remain in force, he will not make any treaty by which any other nation shall obtain the same privileges, relative to the admission of any articles free of duty, hereby secured to the United States." (Art. IV.)

* * * the extension of the privileges of this treaty to other nations under a "most-favored-nation clause" in existing treaties would be as flagrant a violation of the explicit stipulation as a specific treaty making the concession.

* * * the Government of the United States considers this stipulation as of the very essence of the treaty and can not consent to its abrogation or modification, directly or indirectly. * * * if any other power should deem it proper to employ undue influence upon the Hawaiian Government to persuade or compel action in derogation of this treaty, the Government of the United States will not be unobservant of its rights and interests and will be neither unwilling nor unprepared to support the Hawaiian Government in the faithful discharge of its treaty obligations.[2]

On August 29, 1881, the American minister wrote from Honolulu:

The British claims arising out of the reciprocity treaty are still held over the head of the Hawaiian Government * * * [3]

The United States construction prevails.—The controversy led to a change of ministry in Hawaii, and finally to acceptance of the position taken by the United States—that the privileges must be exclusive—and to the giving of a pledge that the treaty would be so interpreted.

Whatever may be said of the legality of this position or of its consistency or inconsistency with the American theory of favored-nation practice, the contention of the American Government was practical and logical, inasmuch as, unless the privileges were construed as exclusive, the United States would have been in the position of a country making very extensive commercial concessions and gaining, reciprocally, absolutely none.

Great Britain proposes a special arrangement, 1881.—In 1881 Great Britain attempted to make with Hawaii a treaty concerning the

---

[1] For basis of the above account, see U. S. Foreign Relations, 1878–79, 1881, passim; also U. S. Foreign Relations, 1894, Appendix II, pp. 20–21; also 45th Cong., 3d sess., Ex. Doc., No. 249, Vol. I.

[2] U. S. Foreign Relations, 1881, pp. 624–625.

[3] U. S. Foreign Relations, 1881, p. 629. For further reference to the question, in 1888, see p. 116, infra.

immigration of coolies from India, with a provision for a certain degree of extraterritoriality in connection with them. The Hawaiian Government was inclined to accede to this; the United States Government objected.

Mr. Blaine's statement of the policy of the United States.—Mr. Blaine wrote to the American minister at Honolulu on November 19:

* * * the Government of the United States * * * now repeats that, under no circumstances, will it permit the transfer of the territory or sovereignty of these islands to any of the great European powers. * * * the possession of these islands by a great maritime power * * * in case of international difficulty it would be a positive threat to interests too large and important to be lightly risked.

Neither can * * * the United States allow an arrangement which, by diplomatic finesse or legal technicality, substitutes for the native and legitimate constitutional Government of Hawaii, the controlling influence of a great foreign power.* * *[1]

Question of extension of the treaty.—As the seven-year period at the end of which the treaty might be terminated was drawing to a close, the question presented itself—should the term of the treaty be extended, or should the treaty be terminated; there was also some quiet reference to annexation.

In 1882 Mr. Comly, minister to Hawaii, wrote to Mr. Frelinghuysen, Secretary of State:

The native Hawaiians own scarcely any property, yet they control absolutely the rate of taxation and amount of expenditure. The enterprising foreign residents—largely American—who have brought their capital here and are developing the resources of the Kingdom, own nearly all the estates * * * and do nearly all the business. * * *

There is such a state of anxiety in the minds of foreign residents that a number of the most prominent planters and business men have pressed me earnestly for some assurance that the United States Government would protect American citizens against such native legislation as might amount to practical confiscation of a large share of their estates in these islands.[2]

The Hawaiian Government proposed the renewal of the term of the treaty. At the same time there were presented to Congress various petitions, especially from the sugar-raising sections of the United States, asking for its abrogation.

Questions which arose from the operation of the treaty were referred to various committees, and the matter was much discussed in Congress and by diplomatic correspondence. On January 16, 1883, the House Committee on Foreign Relations returned a majority report (by Mr. Kasson) in favor of the treaty.[3] The report of the minority dealt with the economic losses of the United States and alleged frauds under the treaty.[4]

The Senate Committee on Finance brought in a report (Senator Morrill) on February 27, 1883, dealing extensively with objections to the treaty, exhibiting statistics, declaring that the products of Hawaii must find their market in the United States, that it could be no concern of the United States who the rulers of the islands might be, that they require no naval outpost, and concluding, "The present reciprocity treaty * * * is so obviously adverse to the interests of the United States * * * that nothing less than its abrogation affords a sufficient remedy." The committee recommended the adoption of a resolution for termination of the treaty. The minority concurred with the report of the majority, but added to it three special objections to reciprocity treaties in general: That

[1] U. S. Foreign Relations, 1881, p. 634.
[2] U. S. Foreign Relations, 1882-83, pp. 342-343.
[3] 47th Cong., 2d sess., H. Doc. No. 1860, p. 2.
[4] 47th Cong., 2d sess., H. Doc. No. 1860, p. 4.

they are unconstitutional; that they make for difficulty with other nations over questions of most-favored-nation treatment; and that "experience shows, in every instance, where a reciprocity treaty has been tried, that immense American interests have been sacrificed." [1]

The resolution to terminate the treaty was referred to the Committee on Foreign Relations. This committee reported on January 24, 1884, recommending the indefinite postponement of the resolution. This report (Senator Morgan) addressed itself chiefly to the refutation of the arguments and conclusions of the Committee on Finance. It laid stress on the growth of American influence in the Pacific and close relations with the Government of Hawaii. It emphasized the importance of Hawaii as a base both in commercial and in naval strategy. It gave a sketch of the general consequences already ascribable to the operation of the treaty and then proceeded, on the basis of a report of the Secretary of the Treasury, with an exposition intended to show that the reciprocity arrangement was not unprofitable economically. It made the claim that much of the profits which appeared to accrue to Hawaii really went to American shippers and sugar merchants. In conclusion:

Whatever objections have so far been found to the workings or results of this treaty are greatly overbalanced by the advantages we have acquired in a national sense, and by the benefits to our people of a profitable trade with the Hawaiian people, and by the duty we owe the people of both countries to give certainty and permanence to the gratifying prosperity which this treaty has created.[2]

In disagreement with this, the minority submitted a report (Senator Sherman) on the same day, embodying the adverse report of the Committee on Finance and emphasizing the fiscal losses to the United States:

The loss of revenue entailed by the treaty seems * * * 'far greater than any benefit derived from it, and it is submitted that the better way is to terminate the treaty with a view to entering into such commercial relations with the Sandwich Islands as will be more nearly reciprocal than the provisions of the present treaty.[3]

The Senate was convinced that the existing treaty was not conferring reciprocal advantages, but it was undecided whether it was wiser to prolong the old arrangement or to abrogate it and negotiate a new treaty. It was possible to ask either that the list of articles admitted duty free from the United States into Hawaii be enlarged or that Hawaii make some special concession, such as that of a coaling station, to the United States, or both. Mr. Frelinghuysen, Secretary of State, favored "an arrangement for establishing a coaling station, or even a naval and repair station, under the flag of this Government (United States) at some available harbor in the Hawaiian Islands"; bu; it seemed to him "inexpedient to join such a provision to the commercial treaty." [4]

Negotiation of convention to extend the term of the treaty, 1884.— The Senate committee, to which had been referred the question of extending the duration of the treaty, reported, on June 19, 1884, a resolution favoring the extension for seven years and advising that

---

[1] 47th Cong., 2d sess., Sen. Rept. No. 1013; and 57th Cong., 2d sess., Sen. Doc., No. 206, pp. 5–10.
[2] 48th Cong., 1st sess., Sen. Rept. No. 76, p. 8; and 56th Cong., 2d sess., Sen. Doc., No. 231, pt. 8, p. 233.
[3] 56th Cong., 2d sess., Sen. Doc., No. 231, pt. 2, p. 240.
[4] Mr. Frelinghuysen to Mr. Miller, June 17, 1884; 56th Cong., 2d sess., 1900–1901, Sen. Doc., No. 231, pt. 8, pp. 242–243.

the President secure by negotiation "the privilege of establishing permanently a proper naval station for the United States in the vicinity of Honolulu, and also a revision and extension of the schedule of articles to be admitted free of duty from the United States into the Hawaiian Kingdom." [1] The provision for the extension of the schedule was subsequently dropped, and the resolution was passed. Negotiations with the Hawaiian Government were concluded and a supplementary convention was framed, which was passed by the Senate in executive session on December 6, 1884. This convention provided (Article I) that the duration of the treaty of 1875 be extended for a term of 7 years from the date of the exchange of ratifications, and beyond this period indefinitely subject to 12 months' notice for termination. In Article II—

His Majesty, the King of the Hawaiian Islands, grants to * * * the United States the exclusive right to enter the harbor of Pearl River * * * and to establish and maintain there a coaling and repair station for the use of the vessels of the United States, and to that end the United States may improve the entrance to said harbor and do all other things needful to the purpose aforesaid

The House Committee on Ways and Means made an exhaustive study of trade conditions for the period during which the treaty had been in force. The report (Mr. Mills) of the majority, brought in on April 20, 1886, took the view that the treaty had not been commercially successful. The United States had given a bounty out of the Public Treasury to the Hawaiian planters which had greatly stimulated the growth of population and wealth on the islands and had enhanced the growth of American export trade; but the remission of revenue had amounted to more than $23,000,000, while the total exports to the islands had amounted to a little over $22,000,000. The United States had paid dearly for what it gained.

It must be evident that we have gained nothing commercially by the treaty. * * * This larger bounty has gone into the pockets of the owners of the estates on the islands, while our people have been compelled to pay higher for their free sugar on the Pacific slope than their kinsmen have had to pay for their dutiable sugar on the Atlantic seaboard

The majority recommended a resolution to terminate the treaty. The minority were—

not prepared to say that the treaty * * * is commercially a good bargain, and they would be glad to see it modified; yet there are geographical and international reasons which are conclusive with them that the treaty ought not to be abrogated. They are not willing to surrender any advantage that may be given by that treaty to this Government to the possible future control of those islands.[2]

It was generally conceded throughout the discussion that the American consumer had not profited in the matter of prices. The benefit of the reduction in duties had gone into the pockets of the Hawaiian sugar producers.

A strong party had developed in the United States which was opposed in principle to all reciprocity involving one-sided concessions as did that of the Hawaiian arrangement. The view of this group was expressed by Senator Morrill in a resolution offered on January 7, 1885:

Resolved, That so-called reciprocity treaties having no possible basis of reciprocity with nations of inferior population and wealth involving the surrender of enormously

---

[1] 56th Cong., 2d sess., 1900-1901, Sen. Doc., No. 231, pt. 8, p. 242.
[2] 49th Cong., 1st sess., H. Rept., No. 1759, p. 37.

unequal sums of revenue, involving the surrender of immensely larger volumes of home trade than are offered to us in return, and involving constitutional questions of the gravest character, are untimely, and should everywhere be regarded with disfavor.[1]

Later Mr. Morrill remarked:

Such treaties are unrepublican in their origin and character, having been sternly and unanimously rejected by the earlier statesmen of our country, * * *.[2]

President Cleveland urges ratification.—The opinion has been expressed that the convention might not have reached the stage of ratification had not President Cleveland given it his personal support.[3] The President, though not in general in favor of reciprocity treaties, actually urged, in his message of December 7, 1886, that the treaty be extended.

I express my unhesitating conviction that the intimacy of our relations with Hawaii should be emphasized. As a result of the reciprocity treaty of 1875, those islands, on the highway of Oriental and Australasian traffic, are virtually an outpost of American commerce and a stepping-stone to the growing trade of the Pacific. * * * Our treaty * * * to abrogate it would be, in my judgment, most ill-advised. The paramount influence we have there acquired, once relinquished, could only with difficulty be regained, and a valuable ground of vantage for ourselves might be converted into a stronghold for our commercial competitors. I earnestly recommend that the existing treaty stipulations be extended for a further term of seven years * * *.[4]

Ratification and proclamation of the convention extending the treaty, 1887.—The convention was approved by the Senate on January 20, 1887, ratified by the Hawaiian King on October 20, and ratified by President Cleveland on November 7. Ratifications were exchanged at Washington, November 9, 1887, and the treaty was proclaimed on the same day.[5] Thus extended, the reciprocity arrangement of the treaty of 1875 continued and remained in force, unaffected by political changes which took place in the islands, until June 15, 1900.[6]

The remaining years of reciprocity.—In the following paragraphs the diplomatic and legislative narrative is carried to the moment of annexation.

As was to be expected, the cession of the harbor of Pearl River created some diplomatic difficulties. By Article II of the convention of 1884 the King of Hawaii had granted to the United States exclusive right to enter this harbor and to establish there a station, and to make needful improvements. The harbor in question was capable of being made one of the best harbors in the Pacific, of great value as a mid-sea stopping place and a naval outpost. Under instructions from his Government, the British commissioner in Hawaii protested against the arrangement and particularly requested the attention of the Hawaiian Government to Article II of the British-Hawaiian treaty of 1851, wherein the contracting parties had pledged mutually that the ships of war of each should have liberty to enter all the harbors, etc., of the other "to which the ships of war of other nations are or may be permitted to come * * *"[7]

---

[1] 48th Cong., 2d sess., Cong. Rec., p. 506.
[2] Ibid., p. 513.
[3] Laughlin and Willis, Reciprocity, p. 94.
[4] U. S. Foreign Relations, 1886, p. vi.
[5] 52d Cong., 2d Sess., Sen. Ex. Doc. No. 77, p. 166.
[6] The Organic Act was passed on Apr. 30 and went into effect on June 15, 1900.
[7] U. S. Foreign Relations, 1894, Appendix II, p. 25.

The Hawaiian Minister of Foreign Affairs replied, inter alia, that—

His Majesty's Government regards the question of preferential concessions in reciprocal treaties as one which has been thoroughly settled in favor of the right to grant such concessions in return for grants of similar value; indeed Article III of the treaty of 1851 (invoked) * * * distinctly recognizes that right.[1]

Various other questions arose from time to time tending to emphasize the peculiar interest of the United States in the affairs, both international and domestic, of the islands. In 1889, domestic political disturbances led to the landing of American forces at Honolulu for the restoration of order.

The McKinley Tariff Act.—In the next year, 1890, the McKinley Tariff Act was passed in the United States. When the bill was under discussion in the House of Representatives a question was raised as to whether it would or would not abrogate the Hawaiian reciprocity arrangement. To remove all doubt on this point a special bill was framed providing against that effect. Mr. McKinley introduced this bill on December 4, 1890. The Committee on Ways and Means, reporting favorably to this on January 30, 1891, said: "There are special reasons for the maintenance of the treaty at this time." The bill was passed on February 16, 1891.

The McKinley Act removed the duty in the United States on sugars not above No. 16 Dutch standard, thus putting Hawaiian sugar on the same level as that of other countries. Not only were the Hawaiian sugar interests hard hit by the American legislation; they were actually in fear, by this time, of hostile measures on the part of the Hawaiian Legislature. Attempts were made in 1891 to make some type of arrangement with the United States which would better the position of the islands, but these efforts came to nothing.

Revolution of 1893.—In 1891 Queen Liliuokalani came to the throne. Dissatisfaction with her government, adding to the general unrest due to the depression of the sugar industry—which resulted directly from the operation of the sugar-free provision of the McKinley Act, rendered increasingly emphatic the renewed agitation for annexation. When, in January, 1893, a contest between the Queen and the legislature reached a crisis, sailors and marines were landed from the U. S. S. *Boston*. A provisional government was formed and the monarchy was abrogated. The Queen, protesting, yielded her authority to the President of the United States and asked that she be reinstated.

Negotiation of treaty of annexation, 1893.—The new government concluded a treaty of annexation with the United States on February 14, 1893.[2] This was not acted upon at once by the Senate, and when Mr. Cleveland came to the presidential chair on March 4 he withdrew it. Congress, after a careful investigation, approved the recognition which the American minister had given the provisional government.

Organization of the Hawaiian Republic.—The provisional government abandoned the attempt at annexation and formed a permanent organization of republican form on July 4, 1894. At the outset it was somewhat embarrassed by the hostile attitude of the American administration and by a casual attempt at encroachment on the part of Great Britain.

---

[1] U. S. Foreign Relations, 1888, pt. I, p. 863.
[2] U. S. Foreign Relations, 1894, Appendix II, pp. 197 198.

The Wilson Tariff Act—Sugar interests urge annexation.—The passage of the Wilson Tariff Act in 1894 by reimposing a duty upon sugar—Hawaiian sugar remaining, under the treaty, free—restored to Hawaii the advantage which the islands had enjoyed before 1891 in the sugar market. The Hawaiian sugar interests had learned, however, especially from the recent experience, that their position, dependent upon a combination of favorable treaty terms and favorable legislation in the United States, was precarious. Annexation to the United States might not absolutely insure their prosperity—it would certainly give it much greater assurance than lay in the existing situation. Agitation for annexation became active; in this the planters of Hawaii were actively and cordially seconded by sugar-refining interests in the United States.

Negotiation of a treaty of annexation, 1897.—In 1896 the Hawaiian problem figured in the presidential campaign in the United States. Mr. McKinley was known to be favorably disposed to annexation. Soon after his election a new annexation treaty was negotiated, similar in terms to that of 1893 which President Cleveland had withdrawn from the Senate—except that it made no provision for indemnity or pension for the Hawaiian Court. This treaty became the subject of bitter debate in the Senate, where it was soon seen that it would not be given the two-thirds majority necessary for ratification.

Spanish-American War.—When the Spanish-American War made it necessary for the United States to send large forces across the Pacific the Hawaiian Government threw open its ports freely for American use, thus practically making itself the ally of the United States. This brought the question of annexation and the undisposed-of treaty again to the fore.

Joint resolution providing for annexation.—As it was known that the treaty would still be denied the two-thirds majority in the Senate, the administration decided to resort to a method of procedure which had been employed with regard to Texas under similar circumstances half a century before. A joint resolution for the annexation of Hawaii was introduced into the House, where it was passed by an overwhelming majority; it was bitterly opposed in the Senate, but was passed; and a few days later it was signed by the President. The transfer of Hawaiian sovereignty to the United States was made by President Dole of Hawaii on August 12, 1898.

The Organic Act of 1900 terminates the reciprocity treaty—As the Joint Resolution of July 7, 1898, had provided that the existing customs regulations of the Hawaiian Islands should remain unchanged until legislation should be enacted extending the customs laws and regulations of the United States to the islands, the commercial provisions of the reciprocity treaty continued in force after the annexation. They were effective until June 15, 1900, at which date the putting into force of the Organic Act of April 30—establishing a new government for the Territory of Hawaii—made the islands a customs district under and subject to the customs laws and regulations of the United States. Henceforth there were no customs duties, either import or export, between the two regions.

RÉSUMÉ.

From the earliest years of United States-Hawaiian relations the general policy of the United States had been founded on motives of good will; it was shaped by the desire to improve the conditions of the Hawaiians themselves and to discourage international aggression and disharmony in relation to and within the islands. In the pursuit of this policy it became necessary for the American Government to extend to Hawaii the benefit of an informal protection. It was finally deemed expedient to accept and assume the political control which would at once establish political and commercial stability in the islands and increase the security of the United States in the strategy of the Pacific.

The active intervention of European powers in Hawaii had first given occasion for alarm; later the tendency of some of these powers to extend their domains over all the small island realms in the Pacific, together with the constant injection of petty but ever irritating objections, claims, and protests into the otherwise little-troubled waters of American-Hawaiian relations, determined the bent and course of American diplomacy in reference to the islands. In a sense, European nations had driven Hawaii to ask special relations with the United States. Reciprocity was long favored by Hawaiians before the United States was persuaded to it. The political influence of the Hawaiian sugar planters was also a potent factor. Ultimately the weight of all these considerations prevailed upon Congress to accept reciprocity. Both in 1875 and in 1884–87 the most substantial opposition to the reciprocity arrangement came from the sugar growers of the United States and Cuba. At the end of the first seven years of the operation of the treaty it was fairly well demonstrated that reciprocity had not been commercially profitable to the United States. The renewal in 1887 was due to the fact that Congress considered the sum total of benefits, to which an addition was made by the convention of that year, sufficient to offset the fiscal losses.

There has always been more or less contention as to whether and how much it profited or cost the United States financially and what effect reciprocity had on trade. It will be the purpose of the following section to present and analyze figures from which to arrive at conclusions upon these points.

OPERATION OF THE UNITED STATES-HAWAIIAN RECIPROCITY TREATY.

PROVISIONS OF THE RECIPROCITY TREATY.

The commercial reciprocity which prevailed between the United States and Hawaii from 1876 to 1900 was based on Articles I, II, and IV of the treaty of 1875. Article I read:

For and in consideration of the rights and privileges granted by His Majesty the King of the Hawaiian Islands in the next succeeding article of this convention and as an equivalent therefor, the United States of America hereby agree to admit all the articles named in the following schedule, the same being the growth and manufacture or produce of the Hawaiian Islands, into all the ports of the United States free of duty.

In the schedule which followed, the most important articles were, bananas; hides and skins, undressed; rice; pulu; and "muscovado, brown, and all other unrefined sugar, meaning * * * the grades of sugar * * * now known in the markets of San Francisco and Portland as 'Sandwich Island sugar'; syrups of cane-sugar, melado, and molasses." Among these articles, rice and sugar were those conspicuously important; and sugar was many times the most important. The full list of articles comprised over 95 per cent of the total exports from Hawaii to the United States.

Article II read:

> For and in consideration of the rights and privileges granted by the United States of America in the preceding article of this convention, and as an equivalent therefor, His Majesty the King of the Hawaiian Islands hereby agrees to admit all the articles named in the following schedule, the same being the growth, manufacture, or produce of the United States of America, into all the ports of the Hawaiian Islands free of duty.

The most important items in this schedule were: agricultural implements; meat and breadstuffs; coal; cotton and manufactures thereof; hardware; iron and steel and manufactures thereof; machinery of all kinds; mineral oils; wool and manufactures thereof other than ready-made clothing; wood and manufactures thereof; manufactures of leather; naval stores.

The Hawaiian tariff was consistently a low tariff. Its rates were mostly 10 per cent ad valorem; several rates were 25 per cent, and a few were specific. There were also a number of important articles which were admitted free of duty under the Civil Code.

The treaty went into effect in both countries on September 9, 1876. In its commercial aspects it was not altered by the conclusion of the supplementary convention ratified and proclaimed in 1887. Between 1883 and 1887, and after 1894, it offered the assurance of its advantages for but one year from any moment, being terminable upon twelve months' notice.

TARIFF CHANGES AFTER ANNEXATION.

In the joint resolution for annexation, of 1898, it was provided that the existing customs regulations of the Hawaiian Islands should remain unchanged until legislation should be passed extending the customs laws and regulations of the United States to the islands. As a consequence, the commercial provisions of the reciprocity treaty continued in force for some time after the formal annexation; they were terminated by the Organic Act of April 30, 1900—effective June 15, 1900—which, among other things, made the islands a customs district of the United States. The term "annexation" as used in the following discussion refers to the legal changes which went into effect in June, 1900. Since that time there have been no duties between the two regions, and products entering the Hawaiian Islands from foreign countries have been subjected to the rates of the United States tariff.

Annexation brought no important direct change in the treatment of Hawaiian exports to the United States. All the important Hawaiian products had already been entering the United States free of duty by the provisions of the treaty or under the general tariff.

The free admission, after annexation, of Hawaiian products which under reciprocity had remained dutiable, may have stimulated their production, but such articles were so few and of so slight importance that there could not result from their free admission any appreciable change in the character or destination of Hawaiian exports. The chief importance of annexation to the islands lay, therefore, not in any further remission of United States duties, but in the assurance it gave to Hawaiian producers that the free admission of their chief products into their most important market—upon which free admission their prosperity seemed to them to be dependent—would no longer be contingent upon the shifting course of politics in the United States. Annexation established an added measure of stability and assurance for Hawaiian investment and brought an increase of capital investment and an expansion of industry relatively comparable with that which had earlier followed upon the establishment of reciprocity.

In regard to the tariff treatment of United States exports to Hawaii, the inclusion of Hawaii as a customs district of the United States meant more than that American products would enter Hawaii free of duty. It meant also that products of foreign origin would be required to pay in Hawaii the rates of the Dingley tariff instead of the much lower rates of the former Hawaiian tariff. Annexation, therefore, secured for American exports to Hawaii preference over exports from other countries, which was equal in amount to the rates of the Dingley tariff. For articles which had been admitted free under the treaty annexation brought an increase of the preference equal to the difference between the rates of the Dingley tariff and the lower rates of the former Hawaiian tariff.

COMMERCIAL EFFECTS OF THE RECIPROCITY TREATY.

Effect on imports from Hawaii into the United States.—To explain the commercial effects of the treaty it will be convenient to examine the influence of the treaty, first, on imports from Hawaii, and second, on exports to Hawaii.[1]

---

[1] Customs collectors were not required, after the inclusion of Hawaii as a United States customs district and prior to May, 1902, to furnish statements of shipments of merchandise to or from the non-contiguous possessions of the United States. As a consequence, there are no complete data of such shipments for the fiscal years 1900 and 1901, and in some of the following tables it has not been possible to include figures for these years. Hawaiian statistics for the year 1895 are also unavailable and are therefore absent from several of the tables. All figures not specifically attributed to Hawaiian sources are from United States Commerce and Navigation Reports, or Monthly Summaries, and are for fiscal years ending June 30. The data from Hawaiian sources are for calendar years.

TABLE I.—*Imports from Hawaii into the United States, 1871–1900.*[1]

Year.	Value of total imports	Selected reciprocity articles.[2]		Selected articles, free under general tariff.[3]		Selected dutiable nonreciprocity articles.[4]	
		Value.	Per cent of total imports.	Value.	Per cent of total imports.	Value.	Per cent of total imports.
1871	$1,143,244	$974,373	85.23	$88,752	7.76	$18,814	1.64
1872	1,280,833	989,783	77.27	89,406	6.98	111,351	8.69
1873	1,275,061	1,012,909	79.44	136,354	10.69	40,407	3.17
1874	1,016,952	801,097	78.77	129,496	12.73	24,863	2.45
1875	1,227,191	1,016,709	82.85	112,117	9.14	26,853	2.19
1876	1,373,681	1,154,348	84.03	101,943	7.41	1,992	.14
1877	2,550,335	2,274,271	89.18	83,923	3.29	227	.009
1878	2,678,830	2,513,077	93.82	105,497	3.94	22,970	.86
1879	3,257,938	3,110,086	95.46	103,938	3.19	12,498	.38
1880	4,606,444	4,464,005	96.91	81,005	1.76	35,462	.77
1881	5,533,000	5,374,257	97.13	118,516	2.14	6,970	.12
1882	7,646,294	7,470,601	97.70	102,518	1.34	22,651	.30
1883	8,238,461	8,027,374	97.44	121,841	1.48	20,182	.25
1884	7,925,965	7,753,126	97.82	113,761	1.44	16,831	.21
1885	8,857,497	8,679,897	97.99	103,858	1.17	100	
1886	9,805,707	9,589,723	97.80	104,973	1.07		
1887	9,922,075	9,698,289	97.74	128,658	1.30	11,968	.12
1888	11,060,379	10,886,283	98.43	93,469	.85		
1889	12,817,740	12,669,859	98.85	98,894	.76	5,291	.04
1890	12,313,908	12,166,911	98.80	93,426	.76	95	
1891	13,895,597	13,699,323	98.59	75,510	.54	22,453	.16
1892	8,075,882	7,937,299	98.28	73,776	.91	9,400	.12
1893	9,146,767	8,953,432	97.88	63,285	.69		
1894	10,065,317	9,838,452	97.75	60,655	.60		
1895	7,888,961	7,723,950	97.91	84,561	1.07		
1896	11,757,704	11,578,393	98.47	90,167	.77		
1897	13,687,799	13,461,790	98.35	140,191	1.02	17,366	.13
1898	17,187,380	16,897,803	98.31	216,679	1.26	746	.004
1899	17,831,463	17,476,420	98.01	234,722	1.32		
1900	20,707,903	20,462,227	98.81	166,220	.80	177	

Shipments to the United States from Hawaii, 1902 to 1906.

1902	$24,700,429	$24,008,535	97.20	$192,753	0.78	$42,285	0.17
1903	26,201,175	25,395,245	96.92	307,491	1.17	43,934	.17
1904	25,133,533	24,489,431	97.44	243,563	.96	22,406	.089
1905	34,069,109	34,225,063	94.89	257,722	.71	53,558	.148
1906	26,850,463	24,351,595	90.69	375,043	1.39	45,883	.17

[1] U. S. Monthly Summary Jan. to June, 1899, p. 1945.
[2] Brown sugar, molasses, fruits and nuts, and rice.
[3] Coffee, hides, and skins.
[4] Salt and raw wool.

Table I presents figures of imports from Hawaii into the United States which make possible a comparison between total imports and the imports of: First, the important reciprocity articles; second, a group of selected articles free under the general tariff; and third, a group of selected, dutiable, nonreciprocity articles. The articles included in the selected reciprocity group are brown sugar, molasses, fruits and nuts, and rice. These were the most important articles in the Hawaiian export trade with the United States, comprising at all times over three-fourths of the aggregate exports. Of this group, sugar was by far the most important. The articles included in the group free under the general tariff are coffee, and hides and skins,[1] and the articles in the dutiable group are salt, and raw wool,[2] of which wool was by far the more important. Imports into the United

[1] Free under the general tariff only from 1883 to 1897.
[2] Free under tariff act of 1894 (Aug. 27, 1894 to July 24, 1897).

States from Hawaii had been growing at a very slow rate or not at all in the years from 1871 to 1876, but immediately upon the establishment of reciprocity they increased very considerably. They almost doubled in 1877 over what they had been in the previous year, grew at a rapid rate until the period from 1891 to 1895—during which years the McKinley tariff with its free admission of raw sugar was effective—and after 1895 they increased more rapidly than ever. In 1896 they amounted to over $11,000,000, and in 1900 to over $20,000,000. Following the annexation of the islands by the United States, the shipments to the United States from Hawaii increased to even greater proportions, and in the year 1905—during which year, however, the sugar crop was exceptionally large—the shipments to the United States amounted to over $36,000,000.

The proportion of the imports from Hawaii which constituted the group of "selected reciprocity articles"—mainly sugar and rice—increased from about 84 per cent in 1876 to over 89 per cent in 1877 and to 97 per cent and over during the later years of the reciprocity period. After the annexation of the islands the free admission of Hawaiian products other than those mentioned in the reciprocity treaty resulted in an increase in the share which such products formed of the total shipments to the United States, and in a corresponding decrease in the proportion of the total shipments which consisted of the selected reciprocity articles.

The chief consideration which Hawaii received in the treaty was the admission into the United States, duty free, of sugar, rice, and other staple products of the islands, at the same time that similar commodities, when coming from other sources, were subjected to substantial rates of duty. The figures of imports from Hawaii in the period from 1891 to 1895 confirm the conjecture that it was the special preference created in favor of Hawaiian products by the treaty and not simply the free admission of these products into the United States which was the significant aspect of reciprocity in so far as its effect on Hawaiian exports was concerned. In these years, during which all raw sugar was admitted into the United States free of duty, and preference therefore ceased, there was a decline in the proportion which sugar formed of the total imports from Hawaii into the United States.

The imports into the United States of the articles which were free under the general tariff both prior to and during the treaty period not only showed no increase following the establishment of reciprocity, but on the contrary suffered a slight decrease in amount and a considerable decrease in the proportion which they formed of the total imports from Hawaii. They increased considerably in the late 90's and continued to increase after annexation.

The imports into the United States of wool and salt decreased after the establishment of reciprocity and practically disappeared after 1880. The free admission of Hawaiian wool into the United States after annexation resulted in some revival in the wool exports from Hawaii, but these did not attain any significant volume. Grazing land is limited in the islands, and the increase of population led to a transfer from grazing of sheep for their wool to grazing of cattle for meat and dairy products to supply the domestic demand.

Effect on exports from Hawaii to the United States.—The effects of the treaty on exports from Hawaii can be gauged by the following tables:

TABLE II–A.—*Total exports from Hawaii and imports from Hawaii into the United States, 1872–1899.*

Year.	Total exports from Hawaii to all countries (calendar years).[1]	Imports into the United States from Hawaii (fiscal years).[2]	Year.	Total exports from Hawaii to all countries (calendar years).[1]	Imports into the United States from Hawaii (fiscal years).[2]
1872	$1,607,522	$1,280,833	1886	$10,565,886	$9,805,707
1873	2,128,055	1,275,061	1887	9,707,047	9,922,075
1874	1,839,620	1,016,952	1888	11,707,599	11,060,379
1875	2,089,736	1,227,191	1889	13,874,341	12,847,740
1876	2,241,042	1,376,681	1890	13,142,829	12,313,908
1877	2,676,203	2,550,335	1891	10,258,788	13,895,597
1878	3,548,472	2,678,830	1892	8,060,087	8,075,882
1879	3,781,718	3,257,808	1893	10,818,158	9,146,767
1880	4,968,445	4,606,444	1894	9,140,795	10,065,317
1881	6,855,437	5,533,000	1895	8,474,138	7,888,961
1882	8,299,017	7,646,294	1896	15,515,230	11,757,704
1883	8,133,344	8,238,461	1897	16,021,775	13,687,799
1884	8,856,610	7,925,965	1898	17,346,745	17,187,380
1885	9,158,818	8,857,497	1899	22,628,742	17,831,463

[1] Hawaiian Annual Report of the Collector General of Customs, 1898, p. 7, and the U. S. Monthly Summary of Commerce and Finance, July, 1901, p. 22.
[2] U. S. Commerce and Navigation.

TABLE II–B.—*Exports from Hawaii to the United States and to all countries, 1896–1899,[1] and 1902–1906.[2]*

Year.	Value of exports to all countries.	Exports to the United States.		Year.	Value of exports to all countries.	Exports to the United States.	
		Total value.	Per cent of value of exports to all countries.			Total value.	Per cent of value of exports to all countries.
1896	$15,515,230	$15,460,097	99.64	1903	$26,275,438	$26,242,860	99.87
1897	16,021,775	15,962,029	99.62	1904	25,204,875	25,157,255	99.81
1898	17,346,745	17,256,084	99.48	1905	36,171,596	36,112,055	99.83
1899	22,628,742	22,517,759	99.51	1906	26,938,512	26,882,199	99.79
1902	24,793,607	24,730,060	99.74				

[1] Hawaiian Annual Report of the Collector General of Customs.
[2] U. S. Commerce and Navigation reports.

Even prior to the establishment of reciprocity, the bulk of the Hawaiian exports had gone to the United States. Under the operation of the treaty, the share going to the United States underwent even further increase, and the annexation of the islands resulted in the absorption by the United States of practically the whole of the Hawaiian exports. The figures in Table II–A, of total exports from Hawaii to all countries and of imports into the United States from Hawaii, although not strictly comparable, adequately indicate the extent of the increase under reciprocity in the share which shipments to the United States formed of the total exports from Hawaii. Table II–B shows that in each of the four years preceding the annexation of the islands, over 99 per cent of the exports from Hawaii went to the United States.

Reciprocity, therefore, was more conspicuously effective in increasing the absolute amount of Hawaiian exports to the United States than in increasing the share which these formed of the total Hawaiian exports. Under the stimulus of special free admission of its important products into the United States, Hawaiian industry increased and prospered, and the Hawaiian exports grew to many times the maximum amount which they had reached previous to the establishment of reciprocity. Table III gives in greater detail the effect of reciprocity on the Hawaiian export trade.

TABLE III.—*Total exports from Hawaii of important domestic products and exports to the United States, by quantities, 1872-1906.*[1]

Year.	Sugar.			Rice.			Coffee.		
	Total exports.	Exported to United States.		Total exports.	Exported to United States.		Total exports.	Exported to United States.	
		Quantity.	Per cent of total.		Quantity.	Per cent of total.		Quantity.	Per cent of total.
	S. tons.	*S. tons.*		*Pounds.*	*Pounds.*		*Pounds.*	*Pounds.*	
1872	8,497.7	7,203.8	84.77	455,121	422,821	92.90	39,276	34,730	88.43
1873	11,564.5	7,414.1	64.11	941,438	892,720	94.83	262,025	255,025	97.33
1874	12,283.3	9,096.6	74.06	1,187,986	885,646	74.55	75,496	67,286	89.13
1875	12,540.0	11,881.3	94.75	1,573,739	1,461,835	92.89	165,677	163,715	98.82
1876	13,036.2	12,500.6	95.80	2,259,324	2,191,708	97.01	153,667	144,066	93.75
1877	12,787.9	12,753.2	99.73	2,691,370	2,627,325	97.62	131,045	118,249	90.24
1878	19,215.7	19,199.9	99.92	2,767,798	2,751,698	99.42	127,963	120,185	93.92
1879	24,510.5	24,508.1	99.99	4,792,813	4,769,580	99.52	74,275	68,134	91.73
1880	31,713.9	31,708.0	99.98	6,469,840	6,454,740	99.76	99,508	75,222	75.59
1881	46,804.7	46,886.6	99.98	7,682,700	7,628,700	99.30	18,912	18,629	98.50
1882	57,088.9	57,087.1	100.00	12,169,475	12,135,074	99.72	8,131	7,981	98.16
1883	57,053.5	57,051.8	100.00	11,619,000	11,569,800	99.58	16,057	15,857	98.76
1884	71,327.4	71,318.7	99.99	9,493,000	9,478,900	99.84	4,231	4,181	98.82
1885	85,675.1	85,673.3	100.00	7,367,253	7,362,200	99.93	1,675	1,300	77.61
1886	108,111.8	108,105.5	99.99	7,338,615	7,331,350	99.90	5,931	4,256	71.76
1887	106,381.8	106,377.9	100.00	13,684,200	13,671,600	99.91	5,300	5,300	100.00
1888	117,944.1	117,939.9	100.00	12,878,600	12,865,100	89.90	7,130	5,980	83.87
1889	121,082.9	121,080.8	100.00	9,669,896	9,669,896	100.00	43,673	43,023	98.51
1890	129,899.2	129,893.5	100.00	10,579,000	10,579,000	100.00	88,593	88,491	99.89
1891	137,491.7	137,491.7	100.00	4,900,450	4,894,752	99.88	3,051	2,851	93.45
1892	131,828.3	131,324.9	99.62	7,800,972	7,304,509	93.40	13,568	13,568	100.00
1893	165,411.4	165,406.9	100.00	7,821,004	7,301,509	93.40	49,311	49,111	99.59
1894	153,342.4	153,332.9	99.99	5,994,087	5,994,087	76.81	189,150	147,159	77.80
1896	221,784.6	221,784.0	100.00	5,025,491	5,014,850	99.79	255,655	236,766	92.62
1897	260,268.5	260,266.0	100.00	5,499,499	5,448,700	99.06	337,158	288,228	85.49
1898	222,481.5	222,480.8	100.00	2,865,700	2,865,500	99.99	733,285	659,947	90.00
1899	272,690.1	272,690.1	100.00	946,100	946,100	100.00	824,864	716,779	86.90
1902	360,276.6	360,276.6	100.00	342,300	340,600	99.50	1,210,498	1,082,994	89.47
1903	387,412.7	387,412.7	100.00	234,980	234,930	99.98	1,930,804	1,852,212	95.93
1904	368,246.2	368,246.2	100.00	40,261	39,911	99.13	1,482,268	1,372,549	92.60
1905	416,860.6	416,830.6	100.00	2,774,100	2,771,083	99.89	1,543,426	1,437,117	93.11
1906	373,301.6	373,301.3	100.00	225,012	223,012	99.11	2,311,494	2,147,279	92.90

[1] 1872 to 1899, Hawaiian Annual Report of the Collector General of Customs; 1902 to 1906, U. S. Commerce and Navigation Reports; no data for the years 1895, 1900, and 1901.

TABLE III.—*Total exports from Hawaii of important domestic products and exports to the United States, by quantities, 1872–1906*—Continued.

Year.	Hides and skins.			Wool.			Bananas.		
	Total exports.	Exported to United States.		Total exports.	Exported to United States.		Total exports	Exported to United States.	
		Quantity.	Percent of total.		Quantity.	Percent of total.		Quantity.	Per cent of total.
	Pieces.	*Pieces.*		*Pounds.*	*Pounds.*		*Bunches*	*Bunches.*	
1872	80,622	74,943	92.97	288,526	288,526	100.00	4,520	4,508	99.73
1873	87,579	81,137	92.65	329,507	138,046	41.89	6,492	6,492	100.00
1874	94,575	85,128	90.01	399,926	399,926	100.00	6,494	6,494	100.00
1875	83,375	71,770	86.08	465,469	326,540	70.15	10,518	10,418	99.05
1876	56,370	51,085	90.63	405,542	244,696	60.34	14,982	14,971	99.93
1877	73,910	62,534	84.61	385,703	326,775	84.72	15,995	15,995	100.00
1878	90,485	67,951	75.10	522,757	366,199	70.05	13,431	13,431	100.00
1879	49,993	39,142	78.30	464,308	270,379	58.23	12,369	12,369	100.00
1880	54,038	54,038	100.00	381,316	381,316	100.00	19,164	19,164	100.00
1881	50,160	50,160	100.00	528,489	528,489	100.00	20,776	20,776	100.00
1882	49,479	49,479	100.00	528,913	528,913	100.00	28,848	28,848	100.00
1883	63,943	63,943	100.00	318,271	316,216	99.35	44,902	44,902	100.00
1884	49,306	49,306	100.00	407,623	300,369	73.69	58,040	58,040	100.00
1885	47,636	47,636	100.00	474,121	474,121	100.00	60,046	60,046	100.00
1886	52,485	52,485	100.00	418,784	305,902	73.05	45,862	45,862	100.00
1887	51,825	51,825	100.00	75,911	69,511	91.57	58,938	58,838	100.00
1888	47,764	47,764	100.00	562,289	562,289	100.00	71,335	71,335	100.00
1889	45,061	45,061	100.00	241,925	241,925	100.00	105,630	105,590	99.96
1890	44,422	44,422	100.00	374,724	374,724	100.00	97,204	97,204	100.00
1891	40,843	40,843	100.00	97,119	97,119	100.00	116,660	116,630	99.97
1892	30,429	30,429	100.00	288,969	186,696	64.61	105,375	105,370	99.99
1893	31,899	30,549	95.77	391,592	363,296	92.77	108,239	92,909	85.84
1894	34,834	29,352	84.26	261,337	120,106	45.96	123,004	113,118	91.96
1896		(¹)		462,819	336,931	72.80	126,413	120,659	95.45
1897	36,092	36,092	100.00	249,200	204,720	82.15	75,835	74,759	98.58
1898	47,890	47,836	99.89	3,731	3,731	100.00	80,643	79,482	98.56
1899	44,257	44,257	100.00	307,551	203,147	66.05	90,611	88,416	97.58
	Pounds.	*Pounds.*					*Dollars.*	*Dollars.*	
1902	850,786	850,786	100.00	151,418	151,418	100.00	66,161	² 65,732	99.35
1903	917,663	917,663	100.00	364,794	364,794	100.00	66,398	² 66,150	99.63
1904	970,381	970,381	100.00	169,928	169,928	100.00	91,990	² 91,292	99.24
1905	899,963	899,963	100.00	423,114	423,114	100.00	121,751	²120,580	99.04
1906	1,136,994	1,136,994	100.00	313,366	313,366	100.00	134,443	²131,417	97.75

¹ Not given.
² Includes all other green, ripe, or dried fruits.

The six commodities for which data are given in Table III together comprised from 98 to 99 per cent of the total exports from Hawaii. Other than these six commodities, there were in the years after the establishment of reciprocity and prior to 1900 no items of considerable importance.[1] It is to be noted that in the case of all of these commodities the bulk of the exports went, even prior to the treaty period, to the United States. After 1876, when reciprocity came into effect, the proportion which went to the United States increased in the case of sugar and of rice, both of which were reciprocity commodities; decreased in the case of coffee, which had been admitted free of duty since 1872; and also decreased in the case of hides, which was a reciprocity article. The exports of bananas went entirely to the United States prior to 1876, and reciprocity resulted in no change in the direction of this trade, although it led to a very considerable

[1] Since 1900 pineapples have become an important export product of the islands.

increase in its volume. The amount of exports of wool, as of hides, showed no tendency to increase after 1876. The greater profit to be derived from the production of those articles which received preferential treatment in the United States and which also were adapted to intensive cultivation led to a withdrawal of labor and capital from industries, such as cattle raising, which required an extensive use of land.

Effect on Hawaiian industry.—After the establishment of reciprocity, the Hawaiians turned, therefore, from the production of all such articles as were not specially favored by the United States under the treaty, or which were not adapted to intensive cultivation, to the production of those reciprocity articles—mainly sugar, rice, and bananas—in which the treaty gave them the greatest comparative advantage. The free admission of these Hawaiian products into the United States brought about an enormous expansion in the sugar industry and a considerable growth, although on a much smaller scale, in the rice and banana-growing industries. The conditions surrounding sugar production in Hawaii at that time, taken together with the situation in the sugar market in the United States, were such as to give, under the terms of the treaty, a tremendous impetus to sugar growing in Hawaii, and thereby to bring about, or at least to hasten, changes of economic and social importance to the people of the islands. Sugar had long been the most important product of the islands, but the especially favorable treatment of Hawaiian sugar by the United States under reciprocity so stimulated sugar growing that it attained unexpectedly great dimensions and dominated the industry of the islands.

Reciprocity and Hawaiian sugar.—At the time when the treaty went into effect the duty in the United States on the grade of sugar chiefly imported was from 2¼ to 2¾ cents per pound. The rate was changed several times during the continuance of the treaty, but except during the period from April 1, 1891, to August 27, 1894, when raw sugar was admitted free under the McKinley tariff, a substantial duty was maintained on all except Hawaiian sugar.[1]

---

[1] Act of Mar. 3, 1883: Sugar above No. 13 and not above No. 16 Dutch standard, 2¾ cents per pound. Act of Oct. 1, 1890 (McKinley): Provision for free admission of sugar not above No. 16 Dutch standard, effective Apr. 1, 1891. Bounty on domestic product. Act of Aug. 27, 1894 (Wilson): 40 per cent ad valorem. Act of July 24, 1897 (Dingley): 95° polariscope test, 1.65 cents per pound.

TABLE IV.—*Total imports of sugar into the United States and imports of sugar from Hawaii, in quantities and values, 1870-1916.*

Year.	Quantity of imports from—			Value of imports from—		
	All countries.	Hawaii.		All countries.	Hawaii.	
		Quantity.	Per cent of all countries.		Value.	Per cent of all countries.
	1,000 lbs.	*1,000 lbs.*				
1870	1,196,774	14,016	1.17	$56,923,745	$901,645	1.58
1871	1,277,474	15,018	1.18	64,621,239	935,909	1.44
1872	1,509,186	15,360	1.02	81,213,001	923,471	1.13
1873	1,568,305	15,805	1.01	82,716,955	936,738	1.14
1874	1,701,298	13,583	.80	81,887,463	741,047	.90
1875	1,797,509	17,909	1.00	73,330,556	939,418	1.28
1876	1,493,977	20,978	1.40	58,120,583	1,051,987	1.81
1877	1,654,557	32,785	1.98	84,978,185	2,233,537	2.62
1878	1,537,452	30,435	1.98	73,047,880	2,280,350	3.11
1879	1,834,366	41,697	2.27	72,078,688	2,807,675	3.89
1880	1,829,302	61,557	3.37	80,036,868	4,135,531	5.14
1881	1,946,745	76,907	3.95	86,659,977	4,927,021	5.68
1882	1,990,152	106,182	5.34	90,416,803	6,918,319	7.65
1883	2,137,668	114,113	5.35	91,626,937	7,340,033	8.01
1884	2,756,417	125,159	4.54	98,262,607	7,108,302	7.23
1885	2,717,885	169,653	6.24	72,519,514	8,198,164	11.30
1886	2,689,882	191,623	7.12	80,773,744	9,166,826	11.34
1887	3,136,443	218,291	6.96	78,411,224	9,255,351	11.80
1888	2,700,284	228,541	8.46	74,245,206	10,260,048	13.81
1889	2,762,203	243,325	8.81	88,543,971	12,078,518	13.64
1890	2,934,012	224,439	7.65	96,094,532	11,549,828	12.01
1891	3,483,477	312,255	8.96	105,728,216	13,152,724	12.43
1892	3,556,509	262,612	7.38	104,408,813	7,442,047	7.12
1893	3,766,445	289,554	7.69	116,255,784	8,502,226	7.31
1894	4,345,194	326,575	7.52	126,871,889	9,461,857	7.39
1895	3,574,510	274,385	7.68	76,462,836	7,403,658	9.68
1896	3,896,339	352,175	9.04	89,219,773	11,336,796	12.70
1897	4,918,906	431,217	8.77	99,066,181	13,165,084	13.28
1898	2,689,921	499,777	18.58	60,472,749	16,660,412	27.54
1899	3,980,251	462,424	11.62	94,964,120	17,292,723	18.20
1900	4,018,087	504,713	12.56	100,250,974	20,392,150	20.34
1901	4,808,661	690,880	14.38	122,506,589	27,094,095	22.11
1902	3,936,286	720,553	18.31	84,871,299	23,920,113	28.18
1903	5,217,077	774,825	14.85	104,867,236	25,310,684	24.13
1904	4,696,348	736,492	15.68	104,964,094	24,359,390	23.20
1905	4,784,974	832,721	17.42	144,683,151	35,112,127	24.26
1906	5,136,479	746,603	14.53	125,139,834	25,495,427	20.37
1907	5,621,005	821,015	14.61	135,269,604	27,692,997	20.47
1908	4,918,773	1,077,571	21.91	138,764,358	39,816,062	28.69
1909	5,700,738	1,022,864	17.94	152,618,490	37,632,742	24.65
1910	5,774,180	1,110,594	19.23	172,519,732	42,625,062	24.70
1911	5,595,029	1,011,216	18.07	157,874,911	36,704,656	23.24
1912	6,044,374	1,205,466	19.94	197,020,651	49,961,509	25.35
1913	6,590,824	1,085,362	16.47	166,866,801	36,607,820	21.93
1914	6,822,825	1,114,751	16.34	155,077,126	33,187,920	21.40
1915	7,290,588	1,280,684	17.57	254,220,139	52,949,697	20.82
1916	7,620,085	1,137,160	14.92	308,986,793	54,418,095	17.61
1917	7,472,729	1,162,605	15.56	347,674,625	62,741,164	18.05
1918	6,657,173	1,080,909	16.24	342,434,756	64,108,540	18.72

Before the reciprocity treaty was adopted, and while the "Sandwich Island sugar" still paid the full duty, the Hawaiian planters were building up a substantial trade with the United States, indicating that sugar could be produced in the islands at a cost sufficiently low to compete in the United States with other full-duty-paying sugar and with the protected domestic product. Imports of Hawaiian sugar, though greatly stimulated by the special remission of duty, prior to 1898 never amounted to as much as one-seventh of the total imports of sugar into the United States. The balance of the American imports was subjected to the full duties. But the Hawaiian sugar sold in the American market at as high a price as that

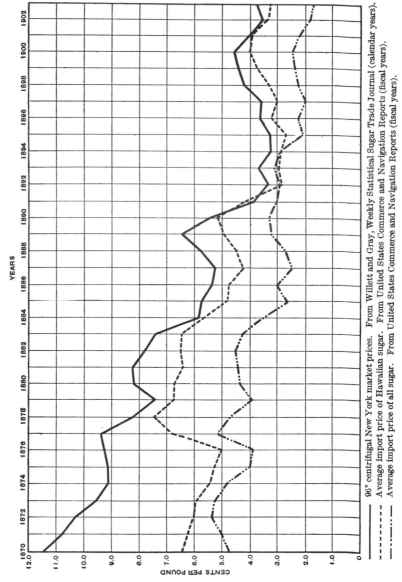

Average Yearly Sugar Prices in Hawaii and in the United States, 1870 to 1902.

——— 96° centrifugal New York market prices. From Willett and Gray, Weekly Statistical Sugar Trade Journal (calendar years).

– – – – Average import price of Hawaiian sugar. From United States Commerce and Navigation Reports (fiscal years).

–··–··– Average import price of all sugar. From United States Commerce and Navigation Reports (fiscal years).

of sugar which paid the full duty and of domestic sugar of the same grade. Reciprocity therefore put the Hawaiian planter in a position similar to that of a protected domestic producer.

Sugar prices in Hawaii and in the United States.—The Hawaiian producers, however, have not received, since shortly after the establishment of reciprocity, quite the full amount of the New York or of the San Francisco price of raw sugar. Hawaiian sugar, whether it went to San Francisco or to New York, has been sold to the refiners on a special form of contract, whereby in return for the assurance that all of their product would be taken as shipped, the Hawaiian producers have agreed to accept a price a fraction of a cent less than the ruling price on the New York market on the day on which the sugar arrives. Sugar arriving in San Francisco was subjected to a slightly greater reduction from the New York price than was sugar arriving at an Atlantic port. A more guarded contract is now in use, whereby the price received by the Hawaiian producers depends on the average quotations in the New York market during a stated period prior to the date of arrival of a cargo. This has eliminated the chance of substantial losses or gains depending upon the precise day or even hour of arrival, and has removed any incentive to delay shipments when approaching the harbor upon expectation that the New York quotations would rise on the following day or days. This arrangement has not been in any way dependent upon the maintenance of reciprocity and was continued throughout the years when under the act of 1890 no tariff preference was granted to Hawaiian sugar. To the Hawaiian producer the assurance that the supply would be taken immediately upon its arrival at an American port and the elimination of the necessity of establishing an expensive sales organization in the United States make it advantageous to concede the reduction from the New York quotation. To the refiners the reduction from the market price is compensation for the risk involved in guaranteeing the purchase of all shipments made.

The chart (facing this page) throws further light on the operation of Hawaiian reciprocity in respect to sugar. Significant features in the chart are: First, the sharp increase, immediately upon the establishment of reciprocity, in the "average import price" of Hawaiian sugar—i. e., the invoice price in Hawaii of sugar ready for shipment; and, second, the fluctuation in the amount of the margin between this "average import price" of Hawaiian sugar and the price of raw sugar in the New York market. The margin between the Hawaiian and the New York price of sugars of the same grade normally should cover the expenses of freight, insurance, commissions, importer's profit and import duties (if any). The elimination of one element in the margin, the duty on Hawaiian sugar, in 1876, was followed by a corresponding reduction in the size of the margin.

There were three ways in which the margin between the Hawaiian price and the New York price of sugar might be reduced: First, the New York price might fall by the amount of the remitted duty, which would indicate that the American consumer derived the full benefit of the remission of duty; or, second, the Hawaiian price might rise by the amount of the remitted duty, which would indicate that the remission of duty inured to the benefit of the Hawaiian producers only; or, third, there might be both a fall in the New York price, although not by the full amount of the duty, and a rise in the Hawaiian price, although not by the full amount of the duty, which would indicate that the gain had been divided between producer and consumer. The chart indicates that the reduction in the excess of the New York over the Hawaiian price which followed upon the establishment of reciprocity resulted from a rise in the Hawaiian price and not from a fall in the New York price. The remission of duty inured to the benefit of the Hawaiian producer. The American consumer derived no benefit therefrom.

Further indication that the remission of duties operated to increase the price received by the Hawaiian producer, and that it did not result in a reduction in price paid by the American consumer, is furnished by the evidence, exhibited in this chart, of the variations in the margin between the "average import price" of Hawaiian sugar and the "average import price" of all sugar.[1] The import price is the price at which the sugar is invoiced for export at the foreign ports. In 1877 the free admission of Hawaiian sugar resulted in an increase in the margin between the import price of Hawaiian sugar and the import price of all sugar, in favor of the first named. In 1877 and 1878, at the same time that the import price of all sugar was falling, the Hawaiian import price rose. The elimination of the preference to Hawaiian sugar in the years 1891–1894, by the free admission of all raw sugar into the United States under the tariff act of 1890, resulted in a disappearance of the former excess of the Hawaiian price over the price of all imported sugar. Whereas, in other producing markets which exported to the United States, the prices of sugar held their own after the enactment of the tariff act of 1890, in Hawaii the prices fell by approximately the amount of the former duty, $2\frac{1}{4}$ cents. The reestablishment of duties by the tariff act of 1894—i. e., the reestablishment of a preference on Hawaiian sugar—was followed by the reappearance of a margin between the Hawaiian import price and the import price of all sugar, in favor of the Hawaiian product. Duties on raw sugar under the tariff acts of 1894 and 1897 lower than those which had been in force from 1870 to 1890, and a steady diminution in ocean freights—and possibly also an improvement in the fineness of the Hawaiian sugar customarily imported—these together explain the reduction in the margin between the New York and the Hawaiian sugar prices after 1894.

Production of sugar in Hawaii.—Under such stimulus it is not surprising that the Hawaiian sugar industry prospered beyond all precedents. Those Hawaiian planters who were favorably situated gained by an amount equivalent to the full duty. It became profitable to cultivate the rich and advantageously situated soils more intensively and also to resort to soils of gradually decreasing productivity, down to a point where the last increment of product yielded a normal profit but secured to its owner no special advantage. There is a great difference in rainfall on different portions of the islands, and the cultivation of less advantageously situated soil in many cases took the form of extending plantations from the windward to the drier leeward side of the islands and the projecting and constructing of extensive irrigation works. Heavy applications of capital and labor in sugar operations thus became a regular practice.

---

[1] Owing to variations in the qualities of sugar usually imported from different sugar-producing regions these two prices are not altogether comparable, but they adequately serve the purpose of an approximate study.

Nowhere has organization become more complete, or science been more effectively applied to cane raising.

The prodigious growth of the industry under the stimulus of the tariff preference, and the effect of the tariff changes, in the act of 1890, in checking that growth, are indicated in Tables IV and V.

TABLE V.—*Production of sugar in Hawaii, 1870–1916.*[1]

[In long tons.]

1870–71	9,715	1886–87	95,000	1902–3	391,06[2]
1871–72	7,587	1887–88	100,000	1903–4	328,00[3]
1872–73	10,325	1888–89	120,000	1904–5	380,576
1873–74	10,967	1889–90	120,000	1905–6	383,225
1874–75	11,197	1890–91	125,000	1906–7	392,871
1875–76	11,639	1891–92	115,598	1907–8	465,288
1876–77	11,418	1892–93	140,000	1908–9	477,817
1877–78	17,157	1893–94	136,689	1909–10	462,613
1878–79	21,884	1894–95	131,698	1910–11	506,090
1879–80	28,386	1895–96	201,632	1911–12	531,480
1880–81	41,870	1896–97	224,218	1912–13	487,968
1881–82	50,972	1897–98	204,833	1913–14	546,429
1882–83	51,705	1898–99	252,507	1914–15	576,830
1883–84	63,948	1899–1900	258,521	1915–16	529,253
1884–85	76,496	1900–1	321,461		
1885–86	96,500	1901–2	317,509		

[2] From the Yearbook of the Department of Agriculture, 1912, pp. 650–651; 1916, p. 643.

In Table V are presented data of the annual production of sugar in Hawaii from the period dating from the crop year 1870–71 to the crop year 1915–16. The production of sugar in Hawaii increased from 11,197 tons in 1874–75 to 17,157 tons in 1877–78, 96,500 tons in 1885–86, and 125,000 tons in 1890–1891. From 1891 to 1895 it increased at a much slower rate, but after 1895 the increases were greater than ever, both relatively and in absolute amount. In 1896–97 the production of sugar was 224,218 tons, in 1902–3—or after annexation—it had mounted to 391,062 tons, and since 1906–7, it has risen steadily until in 1914–15 it reached the total of 576,830 tons.

Effect of remission of sugar duty in 1891.—The preference give to Hawaiian sugar by the United States during the period of the treaty was intermitted during the four years, 1891 to 1894, while the tariff act of 1890 was in force. Under this act all raw sugars were admitted free, and to compensate American producers for the loss of protection, a bounty of 2 cents per pound was granted to them. The Hawaiian producers were during this period not only at a disadvantage in relation to the domestic producers, because of the bounty paid the latter, but they also lost their preferential advantage over the producers of Cuba, Java, and the beet-sugar countries of Europe, as this advantage was contingent not alone upon the free admission of their sugar into the United States, but also upon their enjoying such free admission while other foreign producers paid duty.

The blow to the Hawaiian sugar interests was undoubtedly heavy. The average price of sugar in Hawaii, as shown by the following table, dropped appreciably, though not by the full amount of the duty; on occasions it was very low. Nevertheless, that it was not a blow to the maintenance of the industry is indicated by the fact that even during this period the output increased, although with some fluctuations in individual years. This period of lean years undoubtedly proved beneficial to the industry in the long run; the rigor of competition was stimulating and compulsive of improved methods of production—a result reflected in the rapidly increasing production during the succeeding four years when, under the Wilson and the Dingley tariffs, the advantage of the preference was in part restored.

Period.	Tariff law effective.	Average import price of Hawaiian sugar.	Average import price of all sugar.
		Cents per pound.	Cents per pound.
1887–1890	Act of 1883	4.72	2.92
1892–1894	Act of 1890 (McKinley tariff)	2.88	2.98
1896–97	Act of 1894 (Wilson tariff)	3.13	2.13
1898–99	Act of 1897 (Dingley tariff)	3.53	2.33

Table IV [1] furnishes further evidence of the growth of the Hawaiian sugar industry under the stimulus of reciprocity. Imports of sugar from Hawaii constituted a steadily and rapidly increasing percentage of total imports of sugar into the United States during the treaty period. In the years in which the McKinley tariff was effective there was no further increase in the relative share which the imports from Hawaii formed of total imports; but the tendency to increase resumed its course after the enactment of the Wilson tariff in 1894.

It must be pointed out, however, that undoubtedly some portion of the growth of the sugar industry in Hawaii was due to normal causes which would have been operative even in the absence of reciprocity. The chief market for Hawaiian sugar was in the Pacific States, and these were relatively undeveloped at the time when reciprocity came into effect. The natural advantages which Hawaiian sugar had in the Pacific market would by themselves have contributed to a considerable development of the Hawaiian exports as the Pacific market itself developed.

Influence of reciprocity on imports into the United States.—The foregoing analysis indicates in sufficient detail the significant aspects of the influence of reciprocity on the imports into the United States from Hawaii. Reciprocity may benefit a party thereto in respect to imports by effecting, through remissions or reductions of duty, reductions of price to the consumer. Where reduction in price does not follow remission of duty—including as "reduction" any instance of the price being lower than it would have been in the absence of reciprocity—the amount of duty remitted is a loss to the importing country. This loss may or may not be offset by a gain at some other point.

Special attention has been given to the sugar trade because sugar was the outstanding item in the export trade of Hawaii with the United States. But what was found to be true in the case of sugar would hold also for rice, hides, fruits, and the other Hawaiian products upon which remissions of duty were made by the treaty. The imports of these products from Hawaii were in no case sufficient in proportion to the total imports of such articles into the United States appreciably to affect the prices on the American market. The remission of duty on Hawaiian products by the reciprocity treaty consequently resulted in no significant benefit to the American consumer and entailed a substantial loss of revenue to the United States. In

---

[1] See p. 128, infra.

any effort to determine the favorable or unfavorable balance of economic profit resulting from the treaty, the amount of remission of duty must be set against any possible gains which may have accrued from an increase in the exports to Hawaii, or from other developments consequent upon reciprocity.

EFFECTS OF THE RECIPROCITY TREATY ON UNITED STATES EXPORTS TO HAWAII.

The prosperity and greatly increased purchasing power which reciprocity brought to Hawaii, together with the influence of the special tariff preference to American products, resulted in a great increase in the Hawaiian imports from the United States.

IMPORTS INTO HAWAII.

Table VI, which presents the figures of imports into Hawaii by countries, shows that after the conclusion of the reciprocity treaty imports from the United States increased more rapidly than did total imports.

TABLE VI.—*Imports into Hawaii, by countries, 1872–1899.*[1]

Year.	From all countries.	From the United States.		Per cent of imports from all countries.	From the United Kingdom.	From Germany.	From China and Japan.	From other countries.
		Value.						
Calendar years:								
1872	$1,746,179	$905,679		51.87	$177,741	$229,301	$29,879	$403,579
1873	1,437,611	786,514		54.71	59,513	195,136	31,497	369,049
1874	1,310,827	771,452		58.85	93,181	151,070	25,727	269,397
1875	1,682,471	947,260		56.30	180,922	180,029	36,575	337,685
1876	1,811,770	1,115,238		61.56	83,351	214,574	51,317	347,290
1877	2,554,356	1,762,806		69.01	291,706	202,149	32,119	265,576
1878	3,046,370	2,053,727		67.42	549,116	119,746	83,793	239,988
1879	3,742,978	2,294,252		61.29	841,945	190,744	125,903	290,134
1880	3,673,268	2,628,289		71.56	622,067	48,689	121,219	253,004
1881	4,547,979	3,171,853		69.74	871,855	123,713	77,083	303,475
1882	4,974,510	3,558,932		71.54	798,763	185,190	138,837	292,788
1883	5,624,240	4,058,487		72.16	939,295	216,332	70,093	340,033
1884[2]	4,637,514	3,367,586		72.62	769,005	225,544	179,162	96,217
1885	3,830,545	2,940,837		76.77	486,023	161,803	118,164	123,608
1886	4,877,730	4,001,924		82.04	369,740	94,463	266,203	145,409
1887	4,943,841	3,647,994		73.78	661,541	184,569	262,556	187,188
1888	4,540,887	3,329,512		73.32	652,172	183,125	199,706	176,372
1889	5,438,791	4,305,621		79.17	674,831	90,741	200,925	166,673
1890	6,962,201	5,259,154		75.54	1,104,022	148,288	277,607	173,130
1891	7,439,483	5,294,279		71.16	1,201,329	384,146	287,957	271,772
1892	4,684,207	3,838,360		81.94	380,080	99,114	214,701	151,952
1893	5,346,809	4,308,188		80.57	421,018	73,956	311,573	232,074
1894	5,713,181	4,354,290		76.21	465,480	140,233	414,138	339,040
1895	5,714,018	4,510,010		70.04	471,123	110,752	430,827	184,997
1896	7,164,561	5,464,208		76.27	755,801	147,527	375,555	221,475
1897	8,838,203	6,800,028		76.94	865,781	192,932	552,734	426,727
1898	11,650,890	8,695,592		74.63	1,287,727	352,044	683,177	677,348
1899	19,059,605	15,020,830		78.81	1,774,655	384,102	1,057,932	822,086
Fiscal years:								
1902		(3)			259,311	432,498	[4] 910,686	1,434,088
1903	13,929,679	[5] 10,787,666		77.44	507,350	387,470	[4] 971,741	1,267,452
1904	15,399,721	[5] 11,602,080		75.34	622,465	347,359	[4] 1,205,106	1,622,711
1905	14,658,483	[5] 11,643,519		79.43	305,879	544,534	[4] 967,070	1,197,481
1906	15,046,397	[5] 11,771,155		78.23	424,976	171,497	[4] 1,249,779	1,428,990
1907	18,276,085	[5] 14,124,376		77.28	483,341	348,667	1,561,570	2,758,131

[1] Hawaiian customhouse statistics.
[2] Previous to 1884 imports free by Civil Code not classified by countries.
[3] No data.
[4] Chiefly from Japan.
[5] Figures for the United States represent total shipments of domestic merchandise from the United States to Hawaii.

In the period from 1891 to 1895 the diminished prosperity of the islands, resulting from the general free admission to the United States of raw sugar, is reflected in a decrease both in total imports and in imports from the United States. It would be expected that annexation, which was followed by the free admission into Hawaii of all American products, including those previously dutiable, and which raised the rates on imports from other countries to the higher American level, would have been followed by a further increase in the proportion of the total Hawaiian imports which was supplied by the United States. No such relative increase occurred, however, although the imports from the United States were much greater in absolute amount, along with the total imports, after the annexation of the islands. The immigration into the islands of many Asiatics resulted in an increased demand for products which only China and Japan—chiefly the latter—were in a position to supply, and led to pronounced expansion of the imports from these countries. The growing need for fertilizer brought about substantially increased imports from Chile. There was also a greater degree of commercial intercourse with the British colonies of the Pacific and with British India, which resulted in a gain for these regions in the import trade of Hawaii. Whatever the explanation, the fact remains—there did not accrue to the United States after annexation a greater share in the Hawaiian imports.

In Table VII there is presented data for a comparison of the imports of all reciprocity articles with total imports into Hawaii, but only for the years within the reciprocity period.

TABLE VII.—*Imports into Hawaii from the United States, 1876–1899.*[1]

Year.	Value of total imports.	Reciprocity articles.		Articles free of duty under Civil Code.[2]		Dutiable articles.	
		Value.	Per cent of total.	Value.	Per cent of total.	Value.	Per cent of total.
1876	$1,115,238	[3] $343,831	30.83	....	....	$771,407	69.17
1877	1,762,806	1,100,643	62.44	....	....	662,163	37.56
1878[4]	2,046,903	1,619,988	79.14	....	....	426,915	20.86
1879	2,294,252	1,820,355	79.35	....	....	473,762	20.65
1880	2,628,289	2,026,558	77.11	....	....	601,731	22.89
1881	3,171,853	2,646,577	83.44	....	....	525,271	16.56
1882[4]	3,473,608	2,788,975	80.29	....	....	684,633	19.71
1883	4,058,487	3,169,416	78.09	....	....	889,071	21.91
1884[4]	3,344,773	2,619,512	78.32	$169,270	5.06	555,991	16.62
1885	2,940,837	2,293,693	77.99	97,881	3.33	549,263	18.68
1886[4]	3,717,158	2,829,159	76.11	109,925	2.96	778,073	20.93
1887	3,647,994	2,685,284	73.61	169,526	4.65	793,184	21.74
1888	3,329,512	2,442,539	73.36	212,955	6.40	674,018	20.24
1889	4,305,621	3,161,010	73.42	266,702	6.19	877,908	20.39
1890	5,259,154	3,972,125	75.53	289,109	5.50	997,921	18.97
1891	5,294,278	3,980,056	75.18	329,337	6.22	984,886	18.60
1892	3,838,360	2,328,578	60.67	870,525	22.68	639,257	16.65
1893	4,308,188	2,395,057	55.59	1,257,679	29.20	655,451	15.21
1894	4,354,290	2,737,714	62.87	986,043	22.65	630,533	14.48
1895	4,516,319	3,018,755	66.84	805,913	17.84	692,276	15.32
1896	5,464,208	3,225,660	59.03	1,532,526	28.05	706,023	12.92
1897	6,800,028	4,318,944	63.51	1,716,460	25.24	764,624	11.25
1898	8,695,594	5,720,171	65.78	2,085,186	23.98	890,235	10.24
1899	15,020,830	9,578,206	63.76	4,016,399	26.74	1,426,226	9.50

[1] Compiled from Hawaiian customhouse statistics. Figures for years 1892 to 1899 include importations of specie.
[2] Imports free by Civil Code first classified by countries in 1884.
[3] Only from Sept. 9 to Dec. 31, 1876.
[4] Figures for these years are exclusive of imports into island ports other than Honolulu.

Under the treaty most of the imports from the United States were admitted free of duty. In addition, there were considerable imports from the United States of articles which were admitted free of duty under the Hawaiian Civil Code. In the later years of the treaty period not more than 15 per cent of the American exports to Hawaii were subject to duty.

EXPORTS TO HAWAII.

Tables VIII–A and B present figures of exports to Hawaii from the United States of all articles as compared with selected dutiable non-reciprocity articles.

TABLE VIII–A.—*Exports to Hawaii of selected dutiable non-reciprocity articles* [1] *compared with total exports to Hawaii, 1871–1883.*

Year.	Value of total exports.	Selected nonreciprocity articles.		Year.	Value of total exports.	Selected nonreciprocity articles.	
		Value.	Percent of total.			Value.	Per cent of total.
1871	$814,885	$141,309	17.34	1878	$1,683,446	$177,368	10.55
1872	590,295	106,946	18.12	1879	2,288,178	287,057	12.56
1873	631,103	100,086	15.86	1880	1,985,506	206,868	10.42
1874	588,280	94,571	16.09	1881	2,694,583	253,645	9.42
1875	621,974	110,826	17.82	1882	3,272,172	285,252	8.72
1876	724,267	120,199	16.60	1883	3,683,460	412,511	11.20
1877	1,109,429	146,723	13.23				

[1] Beer, ale, and porter; billiard tables and apparatus; drugs, chemicals, and medicines; glass and glassware; jewelry and manufactures of gold and silver; hats, caps, and bonnets; paints and painters' colors; spirits from grain; wearing apparel; wines; household furniture.

TABLE VIII–B.—*Exports to Hawaii of selected dutiable non-reciprocity articles* [1] *compared with total exports to Hawaii, 1895–1899, 1903–1907.*

Year.	Value of total exports.	Selected nonreciprocity articles.		Year.	Value of total exports.	Selected nonreciprocity articles.	
		Value.	Percent of total.			Value.	Per cent of total.
1895	$3,648,472	$348,850	9.56	1903	$10,787,666	$1,170,328	10.84
1896	3,928,187	382,563	9.74	1904	11,602,080	1,140,794	9.83
1897	4,622,581	468,132	10.12	1905	11,643,519	1,167,730	10.03
1898	5,773,672	493,195	8.54	1906	11,771,155	1,094,203	9.29
1899	9,006,671	675,699	7.50	1907	14,124,376	1,386,797	9.82

[1] Chemicals, drugs, and dyes; fancy articles; flax, hemp, and manufactures of same; gunpowder and other explosives; glass and glassware; india rubber and gutta-percha and manufactures thereof; jewelry and manufactures of gold and silver; malt liquors; painters' pigments and colors; spirits; woolen wearing apparel. This group corresponds closely to the group in the first part of this table, but changes in classification and lack of continuity of statistics for certain of the items prevent complete uniformity.

The United States exports of the non-reciprocity articles increased after the conclusion of the reciprocity treaty—owing to the increased purchasing power of Hawaii—but did not expand as rapidly as did the total exports, which consisted mainly of reciprocity articles. Annexation was followed by the free admission of these non-reciprocity articles when coming from the United States. There resulted a considerable increase, both absolute and relative, in the amount of United States exports of these articles to Hawaii.

TOTAL EXPORTS TO HAWAII AND TOTAL DUTIES REMITTED UNDER RECIPROCITY.

In Table IX the amount of total exports of domestic merchandise from the United States to Hawaii during the treaty period is compared with the estimated amount of duties remitted under the treaty.

TABLE IX.—*Domestic exports to Hawaii from the United States and estimated amount of duty remitted on imports from Hawaii into the United States under reciprocity, 1877–1899.*[1]

Year.	Exports of domestic merchandise from the United States to Hawaii.	Estimated amount of duty remitted on imports from Hawaii to the United States under treaty.	Year.	Exports of domestic merchandise from the United States to Hawaii.	Estimated amount of duty remitted on imports from Hawaii to the United States under treaty.
1877	$1,109,429	$1,064,225	1890	$4,606,900	$5,046,146
1878	1,683,446	1,029,854	1891	4,935,911	5,721,061
1879	2,288,178	1,387,380	1892	3,662,018	168,518
1880	1,985,506	2,009,060	1893	2,717,338	169,476
1881	2,694,583	2,604,776	1894	3,217,713	182,309
1882	3,272,172	3,539,293	1895	3,648,472	77,161
1883	3,683,460	4,279,975	1896	3,928,187	4,600,710
1884	3,446,024	3,307,270	1897	4,622,581	5,354,513
1885	2,709,573	4,103,775	1898	5,773,672	13,171,833
1886	3,115,889	4,590,282	1899	9,006,671	12,903,980
1887	3,520,593	5,224,814			
1888	3,025,898	5,305,892	Total	81,990,254	91,294,685
1889	3,336,040	5,452,382			

[1] From U. S. Monthly Summary of Commerce and Finance, Nov., 1899, p. 1374.

The total exports to Hawaii during the reciprocity period amounted in value to approximately $82,000,000. A considerable proportion of this total would have been exported even in the absence of reciprocity. The total loss of revenue attributable to the operation of the treaty was estimated by the United States Bureau of Statistics at $91,000,000. The reciprocity treaty with Hawaii was to a substantial degree unprofitable in dollars and cents to the United States. But non-economic considerations were more important in determining policy, at least in so far as the United States was concerned, than were calculations of economic profit and loss. To judge the treaty merely in its economic phases would be to disregard the main considerations which led the American Government to accede first to reciprocity and finally to annexation.

3. RECIPROCITY NEGOTIATIONS, 1882 TO 1890.

RECIPROCITY NEGOTIATIONS, 1882 TO 1890.

After 1880 there developed in the United States considerable sentiment in favor of reciprocity treaties as a means of securing more favorable tariff treatment for American products in foreign markets. In Europe a reaction from the free-trade movement of the sixties was under way, and there seemed little likelihood that any of the important nations would consent to substantial reductions by treaties from their tariffs in return for such concessions as the United States could offer. Several successive administrations showed interest in the policy of securing special reciprocity agreements, and their attention was of necessity directed to American countries, especially to the Latin American countries and colonies.

NEGOTIATION OF TREATIES WITH LATIN AMERICAN COUNTRIES.

Negotiations with Mexico.—President Arthur in 1882 initiated the efforts to develop closer trade relations with Latin America. In pursuance of this policy he effected the negotiation of a reciprocity convention with Mexico in 1883. Inasmuch as this treaty provided for remission of duties by both countries on a long list of articles, it would have established, if it had been put in force, a considerable measure of free trade between the United States and Mexico. The treaty received the ratification of the Senate in 1884, but it could not go into effect until Congress had given its approval by passing legislation necessary to its operation.

Negotiations with Spain.—The United States had for some years been protesting against the difficulties placed by the Spanish Government in the way of commercial intercourse with Cuba. Under the Arthur administration repeated representations were made to the Spanish Government at Madrid by the American minister, John W. Foster, but nothing resulted therefrom. In his message to Congress of December 4, 1883, President Arthur referred to the injurious and vexatious restrictions suffered by American trade in the Spanish West Indies and expressed doubt as to the possibility of securing adequate relief for such unfair treatment merely by means of the negotiation of reciprocity treaties such as those with Hawaii and Mexico. "Is it not advisable," he asked, "to provide some measure of equitable retaliation in our relations with Governments which discriminate against our own?" [1]

Agreement with Spain, January 2–February 13, 1884.—On December 26 1883, the Spanish Government made a partial concession to American demands by revoking the decree of March 12, 1867, which excepted American products from the reduction of duties upon imports into Cuba which entered in vessels under the Spanish flag. Mr. Foster plainly indicated to the Spanish Government that this would not be considered by his Government an adequate solution of the difficulties in the way of commercial intercourse between the United States and Cuba. He brought to the attention of the Spanish Government the threatening note in the President's message of 1883, referred to above. As a result, he succeeded in negotiating an agreement, signed on January 2, 1884, which, among other provisions,

---

[1] U. S. Foreign Relations, 1883, p. ix.

granted to American products the benefit of the third column of the tariffs of Cuba and Porto Rico, thereby freeing them from the 30 to 60 per cent extra duty of the fourth column to which they had previously been subjected. In return for this and other concessions the American representative agreed to the removal of the extra duty, of 10 per cent *ad valorem* on cargoes brought from the Antilles under the Spanish flag, which had been imposed by the United States Government, under section 2501 of the tariff act of 1883, in retaliation for the Spanish differential flag duty. The agreement was to continue in force until superseded by a new treaty.

In the form in which it had originally been drafted the agreement required the ratification of the Spanish Cortes. In order to avoid the delay and trouble which this would have necessitated, the agreement was slightly modified and put into such form that the signature of the Spanish representative would make it binding for Spain. In its amended form the agreement was signed on February 13, 1884, and was proclaimed in both countries on February 16, to become effective on March 1.[1]

In operation this agreement proved unsatisfactory to the United States. The stipulations in regard to export duties and shipping taxes were subjected to conflicting interpretations in the islands, and the agreement left the duties on imports into Cuba from the United States so high, both absolutely and in relation to the duties on imports from Spain, as to be in many cases prohibitive. Furthermore, the concessions which were granted to the United States were also enjoyed by many other countries by virtue of their most-favored-nation agreements with Spain. Negotiations were therefore renewed at Madrid for a complete treaty aiming at a freer measure of commercial intercourse between the United States and the Spanish West Indies.

Further negotiations with Spain for Cuba and Porto Rico, 1884.— These efforts resulted, in 1884, in the conclusion of a treaty which, in addition to the recasting of the language and provisions of the treaty of 1795 with Spain, provided for reductions and remissions of the Cuban and Porto Rican duties on a considerable number of American agricultural and industrial products in return for, among other considerations, the admission into the United States of Cuban and Porto Rican sugar free of duty and of tobacco at a reduction of 50 per cent from the rates of the general tariff.[2]

Negotiations with the Dominican Republic.—Another treaty of much the same character was negotiated in the same year with the Dominican Republic.

President Cleveland withdraws the Spanish and the Dominican treaties.—These three treaties were submitted to the Senate by President Arthur, but before they could be acted upon his term of office expired and President Cleveland came to the White House. In March, 1885, President Cleveland withdrew the treaties from the Senate, for further consideration. They were never resubmitted to the Senate. Among the reasons which the President gave for his disapproval were the following: That the treaties contemplated the surrender by the United States of large revenues without adequate compensation; that embarrassing questions would arise under the

---

[1] U. S. Foreign Relations, 1884, pp. 471–493.
[2] Signed at Madrid on Nov. 18, 1884. The text of the treaty was printed in the Congressional Record for Dec. 10, 1884.

most-favored-nation pledges in treaties with other countries; and that tariff regulation by treaties involved a diminution of the independence of control over revenues "which is essential to the safety and welfare of any Government." More important, however, in explanation of his disapproval of these treaties were the facts that they affected only a limited portion of the commercial intercourse between the United States and the treaty countries, and that in his opinion the concessions of revenue involved in the tariff reductions made by the United States would not be offset by a compensating benefit to the American consumer. "Upon sugar alone duties were surrendered to an amount far exceeding all the advantages offered in exchange. Even were it intended to relieve our consumers, it was evident that so long as the exemption but partially covered our importation such relief would be illusory." [1]

Unsuccessful negotiations with Great Britain.—A treaty similar to that which had been signed with Spain was in process of negotiation with Great Britain on behalf of the British West Indies; but when the British Government became aware of the disinclination of the Cleveland administration to press for ratification of the Spanish treaty, it withdrew from the negotiations.

Failure of Congress to pass legislation to render Mexican treaty effective.—President Cleveland did not ask Congress to postpone consideration of the Mexican treaty; on the contrary, he strongly urged the passage of legislation necessary to put that treaty into effect. The Mexican treaty covered a greater proportion of the trade between the countries concerned and made more substantial reductions than did the treaties with Spain and the Dominican Republic. Moreover, the Mexican treaty did not involve so obviously, if at all, the remission of substantial revenue without benefit to the American consumer, which in Cleveland's opinion would result from the operation of the Spanish and the Dominican treaties. It appears, from his messages to Congress, that it was these considerations which led the President to regard with favor the Mexican treaty at the very moment when he was expressing his disapproval of the other treaties. The opposition to the Mexican treaty was, however, too strong; Congress failed to enact the necessary legislation; the period allowed for ratification expired on March 20, 1887; and the treaty never went into effect.

Commission to Latin America, 1884.—In support of President Arthur's policy of developing closer commercial relations with Latin America, Congress had added to the act of July 7, 1884— providing for the consular and diplomatic service—a provision authorizing the President, with a special appropriation, to appoint a commission whose duty it should be to make an investigation of the commercial relations of the United States with the countries of Central and South America. The commission was duly appointed; and after a series of hearings in the United States and a tour of Central and South America, submitted its findings to Congress in three reports, in February, 1885. The general tenor of its conclusions was that the fiscal systems of the countries investigated were so largely dependent upon the revenues obtained from customs duties, and their revenues so comparatively meager, that

---

[1] President Cleveland's message to Congress, Dec. 8, 1885. Messages and Papers of the Presidents, Vol. VIII, p. 337.

they would be little inclined to make reductions in their tariffs except in return for generous concessions by the United States.[1]

Most important among the imports into the United States from Central and South American countries were coffee, hides, and wool; the principal import from British Guiana and the British and Spanish West Indies was sugar. Coffee and hides had been on the free list since 1872, but sugar and wool were dutiable. Officials and other persons in the countries visited expressed to the commission the opinion that tariff concessions from these countries could be expected only on the basis of the admission by the United States of wool and sugar free or at considerably reduced rates. Chile and the Argentine, large producers of wool, considered that unless the United States made concessions in the admission of their wool, they would gain nothing by reciprocity arrangements such as were proposed. The commission had not been able to give these countries any assurance that the duties on sugar and wool would be remitted or reduced in order to secure reciprocity. In its final report the commission said:

In any convention we, on our part, must admit wool or sugar free of duty or at greatly reduced rates. Central America, including Mexico, can furnish sugar cheaper than we can possibly produce it at home and in large quantities. Peru, Chile, and La Plata Valley can supply us with wool at far less cost than it can be grown either in our new or old settlements. In any reciprocity treaty we must take one or the other of these articles as a basis of the concessions we are willing to grant. They are the peculiar products of those countries which they look to for revenue and which we do not admit free of duty. And they are precisely the two products we felt we had no authority to even consider in our negotiations with these people. Had we been at liberty to bring on a discussion as to them, we have no doubt the result in every case, except perhaps Chile, would have been a very favorable reciprocity treaty.

International American Conference in 1889.—The commission recommended that an international American conference be held in Washington to discuss reciprocity and other trade relations, and declared: "The States of Central and South America stand ready to respond heartily to our call for such a convention." A bill providing for such a conference was passed by Congress in 1888, and President Cleveland allowed it to become a law without his signature. The invitation was issued, and all of the independent American nations except the Dominican Republic sent representatives to the conference, which was held in Washington in 1889. The report of the Committee on Customs Union, which was adopted by the conference, contained the following summary of its conclusions:

* * * Although it is not easy, in the opinion of the committee, to reach at once unrestricted reciprocity, that end might be obtained gradually and partially. The first and most efficient step in that direction is the negotiation of partial reciprocity treaties among the American nations, whereby each may agree to remove or diminish their respective import duties on some of the natural or manufactured products of one or more of the other nations in exchange for similar and equivalent advantages, as, if the mutual concessions were no equivalent, the treaties would soon become odious, and could not last but for a limited time, and would discredit the system. . If, after this had been tried for some reasonable time a good result should follow, as it is to be expected, the number of articles on the free list might be enlarged in each case, from time to time, until they attain, through the development of the natural elements of wealth, other sources of revenue or an increase of the existing ones, which would allow the contracting nations to reach unrestricted reciprocity or a free trade among some or all of the American nations.[2]

[1] The reports appeared in 49th Cong., 1st sess., H. Ex. Doc. No. 50, and 48th Cong., 2d sess., H. Ex. Doc. No. 226.
[2] 51st Cong., 1st sess., Sen. Ex. Doc. No. 158, p. 11.

4. TREATIES AND AGREEMENTS UNDER THE TARIFF ACT OF 1890.

TREATIES AND AGREEMENTS UNDER THE TARIFF ACT OF 1890.

THE LEGISLATIVE RECORD.

THE TARIFF ACT OF 1890.

The introduction of the McKinley tariff bill, 1890.—In 1889 the Cleveland administration was succeeded by that of President Harrison, supported by a Republican majority in Congress. Early in 1890, William McKinley, of Ohio, introduced in the House of Representatives a new tariff bill. On February 10, while the bill was before the House Committee on Ways and Means, James G. Blaine, Secretary of State, appeared before the Republican members of the Committee to urge the expediency of incorporating in it a provision authorizing the President to make reciprocity agreements, but Mr. Blaine was unable to secure the adoption of his recommendation.[1] As reported by the committee on April 16, and passed by the House of Representatives on May 21, the bill provided for the continued admission free of duty of coffee, tea, and hides, and for the transfer to the free list of sugar and molasses; it provided also for a bounty on the domestic production of sugar, to compensate sugar growers for the removal of duty; but it contained no reciprocity provisions.

The bill in the Senate.—Largely through the influence of President Harrison and of Mr. Blaine, the Senate inserted in the bill provisions for reciprocity. In a letter to the President on June 4, Mr. Blaine called attention to the fact that the International American Conference (of 1889) had recommended "that the several Governments represented negotiate reciprocity treaties." The only delegates who had not concurred in the recommendations were those from Chile and the Argentine, from whose countries the chief article of export was wool. Those delegates had not concurred, Mr. Blaine said, "for the reason that the attitude of our Congress at that time was not such as to encourage them to expect favorable response from the United States in return for concessions which their Governments might offer." The lack of shipping facilities for reaching South American markets had been the chief obstacle, Mr. Blaine asserted, in the way of increased exports. He believed that the United States would be by far the greatest gainer from reciprocity with Latin American countries. Nearly all the articles exported to these countries were subjected to heavy customs duties, so heavy, in many cases, as to prohibit their consumption by the masses of the people. On the other hand, over 85 per cent of the American imports from the Latin American countries were admitted free. Of their important products, coffee, cocoa, India rubber, hides, cinchona bark, dye and cabinet woods, and some other articles entered free of duty. He suggested that, to escape the delay and uncertainty in making treaties, an amendment should be submitted to the pending

---

[1] Letter to Senator Frye, July 22; New York Tribune, July 26, 1890.

tariff bill, authorizing the President to declare the ports of the United States free to all the products of any nation of the American hemisphere, whenever such nation should admit to its ports free of all duties American foodstuffs, lumber, furniture and other wood products, manufactures of iron and steel, cottonseed oil, refined petroleum, and other articles in which an important trade with Latin America could be developed. He thought it would be impossible to negotiate any successful reciprocity treaties if Congress were to repeal the duty on sugar by direct legislation instead of allowing the same object to be attained through the machinery of reciprocity, which he suggested.

When the tariff bill was first reported to the Senate by the Committee on Finance, on June 18, it contained no reciprocity provision. On the next day, June 19, in a special message to Congress, President Harrison transmitted the letter from the Secretary of State to which reference has been made. Alluding to the statement that over 87 per cent of the imports from Latin America to the United States were admitted free, the President said:

If sugar is placed upon the free list, practically every important article exported from those States will be given untaxed access to our markets, except wool. The real difficulty in the way of negotiating profitable reciprocity treaties is that we have given freely so much that would have had value in the mutual concessions which such treaties imply.[1]

Amendment proposed by Senator Hale.—On the day on which the President transmitted this letter, Senator Hale, of Maine, offered the first reciprocity amendment proposed in either House. Mr. Hale later stated that this amendment "had been drawn in the State Department by the Secretary," and "presumably represented the administration and the Republican sentiment generally."[2] The amendment read as follows:

And the President of the United States is hereby authorized, without further legislation, to declare the ports of the United States free and open to all the products of any nation of the American hemisphere upon which no export duties are imposed whenever and so long as such nation shall admit to its ports, free of all national, provincial (state), municipal, and all other taxes, flour, corn meal, and other breadstuffs, preserved meats, fish, vegetables, and fruits, cottonseed oil, rice, and other provisions, including all articles of food, lumber, furniture, and all other articles of wood, agricultural implements and machinery, mining and mechanical machinery, structural steel and iron, steel rails, locomotives, railway cars and supplies, street cars, refined petroleum, or such products of the United States as may be agreed upon.

If the Hale amendment had been accepted and treaties concluded in conformity with its provisions, the result would have been practically the establishment—by negotiation and mutual concession— of free trade between the United States, on the one hand, and Canada, Mexico, and the Central and South American countries, on the other. If the United States had been willing to admit free of duty all the products of these countries, they in return would have admitted free all the important products of the United States. This would have meant the free importation into the United States not only of sugar and hides, which were already on the free list in the bill, but also of coal, lumber, and wool. The amendment which Senator Hale proposed did not reach a vote at the time, nor, again, when it was

---

[1] The message and letter appear in the Congressional Record, June 19, 1890; 51st Cong., 1st sess., Sen. Ex. Doc. No. 158, p. 1; Appleton's Annual Cyclopædia, 1890, p. 202.
[2] Speech in Senate, June 29, 1894.

reintroduced on September 2. It served, however, to arouse discussion not only in Congress, but throughout the country.

Secretary Blaine on reciprocity.—In a letter to Senator Frye of Maine, under date of July 22, 1890,[1] Secretary Blaine remarked with regard to the unratified treaties of 1883 with Mexico and of 1884 with Spain (for Cuba and Porto Rico), that both these treaties of reciprocity had failed to secure the approval of Congress for the express reason that both had provided for the free admission of sugar. He criticized the rapid change of opinion on the part of Congress, whereby it suddenly became willing to remove the duty on sugar, without even attempting to secure thereby advantageous tariff concessions from other countries.

In a speech delivered on August 29, 1890,[2] Mr. Blaine spoke in favor of "a system of reciprocity not in conflict with the protective tariff but supplementary thereto." He stated that in 1889 the exports from the United States to Europe, Asia, Africa, Australia, Canada, and Hawaii amounted to $658,000,000, and that the imports from those countries amounted to $529,000,000. This should have shown a balance of $129,000,000 "in favor" of the United States, but, when all the accounts were closed, the United States owed $13,000,000 to foreign countries. This, Mr. Blaine declared, was due to the fact that the United States had bought from the countries to the south of it more than it exported to them—e. g., from Mexico, an excess of $10,000,000; from Cuba, of $11,000,000; from Brazil, of $51,000,000. The trade of the United States with all countries in North, Central, and South America, Canada excepted, showed an excess of imports to the amount of $142,000,000, and Mr. Blaine said: "By no figure of speech can we flatter ourselves into the belief that our trade with our American neighbors is in a prosperous condition." It would be a great mistake, in his opinion, to repeal the duties (which had been in force from the time of the Civil War) on so large an amount of imports from Latin American countries, without an attempt to secure in return reciprocal arrangements which would stimulate American export trade with Latin America.

Provision for penalty duties.—The McKinley bill, as it had passed the House of Representatives, and as it was first reported to the Senate by the Committee on Finance, retained coffee, tea, and hides on the free list (as in the tariff acts of 1872 and 1883) and placed sugar and molasses, which formerly had been dutiable, also on that list. A new section, reported to the Senate by the Committee on Finance on September 9, further provided that the President could suspend by proclamation the free admission of these five commodities, products of any country, if he deemed the duties imposed by that country upon products of the United States to be "reciprocally unequal and unreasonable."

Several amendments were immediately submitted, based upon the principle of imposing penalty duties, but offering various methods of procedure. Senator Evarts, of New York, proposed that the President be required to obtain the approval of Congress before imposing penalty duties. Senator Gibson, of Louisiana, proposed that wool be added to the free list, with the provision that a duty of 10 cents a pound be imposed on wool imported from producing countries which did not make reciprocal concessions to the United States.

---

[1] New York Tribune, July 26, 1890. [2] At Waterville, Me.—New York Tribune, Aug. 30, 1890.

Senator Edmunds, of Vermont, offered an amendment based on the principle, which the administration favored, of levying duties and preparing to make reductions in return for concessions from other countries. His amendment provided that sugar, molasses, coffee, and tea should be dutiable and that the President should be authorized, when satisfied that any country producing any of these had abolished its duties on the principal agricultural products of the United States, to remit, by proclamation, the duties on any of these articles. This proposal was rejected by the narrow margin of 34 nays to 29 ayes. The other amendments offered were also rejected.

The passing of the act.—The tariff bill, with the amendment providing for penalty duties left as the Committee on Finance had reported it, was passed by the Senate on September 10, 1890, and then sent to a conference committee. The report of the conference committee—retaining in the bill the section providing for reciprocity—was agreed to by the House of Representatives on September 27, and by the Senate on September 30. The bill was approved by the President on October 1, 1890, and, with the exception of the provisions for the free admission of sugar and molasses and for the payment of a bounty on sugar of domestic production, went into effect at once. The provisions regarding sugar and molasses became effective on April 1, 1891.

Section 3 of the tariff act of 1890—"Reciprocity."—Section 3 of the tariff act of 1890 provided that penalty duties should be imposed on five commodities when imported from countries whose duties on American products were, in the opinion of the President, "unequal and unreasonable." It reads as follows:

SEC. 3. That with a view to secure reciprocal trade with countries producing the following articles, and for this purpose, on and after the first day of January, eighteen hundred and ninety-two, whenever, and so often as the President shall be satisfied that the Government of any country producing and exporting sugars, molasses, coffee, tea, and hides, raw and uncured, or any of such articles, imposes duties or other exactions upon the agricultural or other products of the United States, which in the view of the free introduction of such sugar, molasses, coffee, tea, and hides into the United States he may deem to be reciprocally unequal and unreasonable, he shall have the power and it shall be his duty to suspend, by proclamation to that effect, the provisions of this act relating to the free introduction of such sugar, molasses, coffee, tea, and hides, the production of such country, for such time as he shall deem just, and in such case and during such suspension duties shall be levied, collected, and paid upon sugar, molasses, coffee, tea, and hides, the product of or exported from such designated country, as follows, namely:

[The following is a paraphrase.]

Sugar.—Sugar of or below No. 13 Dutch standard in color, to pay duty according to polariscope tests: If not above 75°, seven-tenths of 1 cent per pound; for every additional degree, two-hundredths of 1 cent per pound. Sugar above No. 13 Dutch standard in color, classified by the Dutch standard of color: Between No. 13 and No. 16, to pay 1⅜ cents per pound; between No. 17 and No. 20, to pay 1⅝ cents per pound; above No. 20, to pay 2 cents per pound;

Molasses, if testing above 56°, to pay 4 cents per gallon;

Coffee, to pay 3 cents per pound;

Tea, to pay 10 cents per pound; and

Hides and skins, of various types, but excepting Angora goatskins and sheepskins with the wool on, to pay 1½ cents per pound.

Character of the reciprocity provision.—The "reciprocity" provision of the act of 1890 was, therefore, based on the principle of penalizing, not on that of inviting tariff reductions by offering corresponding reductions. The form in which the measure was adopted was thus quite different from that which Secretary Blaine and President Harrison had advocated: Mr. Blaine's letter of June 4 to President Harrison, and the President's message transmitting that letter to Congress on June 18, showed that, while both strongly favored reciprocity with Latin American countries, the method which they preferred adopting in the tariff act was that of retaining or establishing duties on the leading products of these countries and providing that these duties might be remitted in case reciprocity arrangements should be effected.[1]

Twelve years later Mr. Grosvenor, speaking in the House of Representatives on a bill to establish reciprocity with Cuba, made the following reference to the difference of opinion, in 1890, between Mr. McKinley, the House leader, on the one hand, and Secretary Blaine, on the other, regarding the form which a reciprocity provision should take:

It so happened that I myself heard in the State Department an almost acrimonious discussion between Mr. McKinley and Mr. Blaine upon this question, one side favoring a tariff on sugar, hides, etc., all put into the schedule, and then left competent for the President of the United States, in case of reciprocity, to take the tax off sugar.

The other great leaders of the party at the time took exactly the other view of it, and argued in favor of leaving the duty off or prescribing the amount that should be proclaimed by the President in case reciprocity should fail. And so it was that we ultimately placed sugar on the free list, providing that if there was no adequate or sufficient or satisfactory reciprocity granted by the foreign State, then the President of the United States might put sugar coming from such countries into the tariff schedule at a rate of duty which we prescribed in the law.[2]

The administrative feature.—Nowhere in the act of 1890 were specific instructions laid down as to the method by which negotiations should be conducted or agreements concluded, subject to the provisions of section 3. This was in conformity with the views and efforts of Secretary Blaine, who desired that the administration should adopt a vigorous reciprocity policy. The failure of the Mexican treaty was fresh in his mind, and he feared that reciprocity negotiations would repeatedly come to nothing if it were necessary for Congress to approve, or even for the Senate to ratify each treaty. To the President alone, therefore, was to be left the determination as to what concessions foreign countries must make to avoid being subjected to penalty duties and to secure arrangements guaranteeing for their specified products free admission to the United States. This left the President free to choose his own method of initiating and carrying to a conclusion the negotiations which should prove necessary or desirable if section 3 was to serve its intended purpose of establishing reciprocally advantageous commercial relations between the United States and other countries. Any agreements which the President might conclude in conformity with section 3 would require neither the ratification of the Senate nor the approval of Congress.

The "reciprocity" articles.—The five articles enumerated in section 3 were often spoken of as constituting a "tropical" list. All of them except tea were produced in the Central and South American countries with which reciprocity was especially desired. With the possible exception of wool, there were no other commodities whose

---

[1] 51st Cong., 1st sess., Sen. Ex. Doc. No. 158, pp. 1–6.
[2] Speech in House of Representatives, Apr. 10, 1902.

free admission into the United States would have offered as strong an inducement to these countries to enter into reciprocal relations with the United States. There were likewise no other important products of these countries which offered as little competition with domestic industries as did coffee, tea, hides, sugar, and molasses. Neither tea nor coffee were produced in the United States; hides were produced in large quantities, but the domestic supply was far from sufficient to meet the demand of the tanners and boot and shoe manufacturers; sugar was then produced only to the extent of about one-tenth of the quantity imported; and the production of molasses was also insufficient to satisfy the domestic demand.

The placing of sugar on the free list and its inclusion in the list of articles upon which the President could impose penalty duties paved the way to the negotiation of reciprocity agreements with the great sugar-producing countries of Europe. The European sugar industry at this time was in a very depressed condition, and prospects were even more unpromising for the immediate future. In practically all of the countries of Europe which produced beet sugar in large quantities, the industry had been greatly overstimulated by high import duties and by large export bounties. As a result, there had developed a great and long sustained overproduction, and prices for many years were at a very low level. The free admission of sugar by a country which was one of the greatest, if not the greatest, of sugar importers, was an advantage in return for which the sugar-producing countries might be expected to offer tariff concessions of considerable value to the American export trade.

Bargaining provisions in American tariff acts.—The act of 1890 was the first among the tariff acts of the United States to make systematic general provision for reciprocal negotiations relating to tariff rates by themselves, independent of navigation questions and the like; and it initiated a series of experiments in reciprocity which were continued in varying forms in the tariff acts of 1897 and 1909.

NEGOTIATION OF AGREEMENTS.

Notification to foreign representatives.—After the enactment of the tariff law of 1890, Mr. Blaine, as Secretary of State, wrote to the diplomatic representatives at Washington of countries which produced coffee, tea, hides, sugar, and molasses, to inform them that the law provided for the free admission of these five commodities, but that the President was authorized and directed to impose duties on such products when imported from countries which did not grant reciprocal treatment to the United States. The communications to the various foreign representatives were in substance the same. The character of these communications is indicated by the following communication to the minister from Brazil: [1]

DEPARTMENT OF STATE,
Washington, November 3, 1890.

SIR: The Congress of the United States of America, at its late session, enacted a new tariff law, in the third section of which provision was made for the admission into the ports of the United States, free of all duty, whether national, State, or municipal, of the following articles:

Sugars—all not above No. 16 Dutch standard in color, all tank bottoms, all sugar drainings and sugar sweepings, sirups of cane juice, melada, concentrated melada, and concrete and concentrated molasses.

---

[1] U. S. Foreign Relations, 1891, p. 43.

Molasses.

Coffee.

Hides—raw or uncured, whether dry, salted, or pickled. Angora goat-skins, raw, without the wool, unmanufactured. Asses' skins, raw or unmanufactured, and skins, except sheepskins with the wool on.

In the law providing for the free admission of the foregoing articles, Congress added a section declaring that these remissions of duty were made "with a view to secure reciprocal trade with countries producing those articles;" and that, whenever the President should become satisfied that reciprocal favors were not granted to the products of the United States in the countries referred to, it was made his duty to impose upon the articles above enumerated the rates of duty set forth in the section of the law above cited, of which I have heretofore transmitted you a copy.

The Government of the United States of America being desirous of maintaining with the United States of Brazil such trade relations as shall be reciprocally equal, I should be glad to receive from you an assurance that the Government of Brazil will meet the Government of the United States in a spirit of sincere friendship, and that it may prove to be the happy fortune of you, Mr. Minister, and myself to be instrumental in establishing commercial relations between the two Republics on a permanent basis of reciprocity, profitable alike to both.

To this end I should be glad if you could advise me of the changes which Brazil would be willing to make in her system of tariff, duties, in response to the changes proposed in the tariff of the United States which are favorable to your country.

In case the Government of Brazil should see proper to provide for the free admission into its ports of any of the products or manufactures of the United States, or at a specified reduction of the existing rates of duty, your Government may be assured that no export tax, whether national, State, or municipal, will be imposed upon such products and manufactures in the United States.

It may be further understood that while the Government of the United States of America would reserve the right to adopt such laws and regulations as should be found necessary to protect the revenue and prevent fraud in the declarations and proof that the articles herein enumerated, and whose free admission are provided for by the tariff law above cited, are the product or manufacture of Brazil, the laws and regulations to be adopted to that end would place no undue restrictions on the importer, nor impose any additional charges or fees upon the articles imported.

In the happy event of an agreement between the two Governments, the same can be notified to each other and to the world by an official announcement simultaneously issued by the executive departments of the United States of America and the United States of Brazil; and such an agreement can remain in force so long as neither Government shall definitely inform the other of its intention and decision to consider it at an end.

Accept, Mr. Minister, the renewed assurances of my highest consideration.

JAMES G. BLAINE.

Hon. SALVADOR DE MENDONÇA.

Envoy Extraordinary and Minister Plenipotentiary
of Brazil, on special mission.

The reply of the Minister from Brazil to the Secretary of State, dated January 31, 1891,[1] stated that Brazil, in due reciprocity for the free admission of the five specified commodities into the ports of the United States, had, by legal enactment, authorized the admission into the ports of Brazil of specified articles free of duty, and of other articles with a reduction of 25 per cent of the rates of duty prescribed in the tariff law of that country. In acknowledging the reply of the Minister, the Secretary of State wrote, on January 31, 1891:

I shall be pleased to meet you * * * to agree upon the time and manner of making public announcement of this commercial arrangement, which it is understood, shall remain in force so long as neither Government shall definitely, at least three months in advance, inform the other of its intention and decision to consider it at an end at the expiration of the time indicated; provided, however, that the termination of the commercial arrangement shall begin to take effect either on the 1st day of January or the 1st day of July.[2]

---

[1] U. S. Foreign Relations, 1891, p. 44.   [2] Ibid.

A proclamation by President Harrison, dated February 5, 1891, announced that, under the reciprocity agreement made with Brazil, that country, in return for the free admission by the United States of the articles enumerated in section 3 of the act of 1890, would admit, on and after April 1, 1891, certain articles free of duty and certain articles at a reduction of 25 per cent in the rates of duty.[1]

Further negotiations.—Reciprocity agreements were made with Spain—for Cuba and Porto Rico—with the Dominican Republic, and with most of the Central American countries; and these were put into effect in the United States by proclamation of the President.

Negotiations with Germany for reciprocity were carried on at Saratoga, New York, in August, 1891, between John W. Foster, special plenipotentiary of the United States, and Baron von Mumm, the German chargé d'affaires at Washington. In a note to Mr. Foster, Baron von Mumm stated that the Imperial German Government was prepared to grant to the United States "the same reductions in customs duties on agricultural products that have been granted by it (or still are so) to Austria-Hungary and other States during the negotiations for the conclusion of a treaty of commerce that are now being conducted by Germany." This was accepted by Mr. Foster, on behalf of the President, "as a due reciprocity" for the free admission of the articles enumerated in section 3 of the tariff act of 1890; on February 1, 1892, the President proclaimed reciprocity with Germany.[2]

Great Britain at first showed no inclination to enter into negotiations under the reciprocity provision of the tariff act of 1890 on behalf of its sugar and coffee producing colonies in America. But after the Brazilian, Dominican, German, and Cuban reciprocity arrangements had been concluded, the sugar planters of the British West Indies and British Guiana strongly urged upon the home Government the need of an agreement with the United States which would assure their sugar as favorable tariff treatment upon import into the United States as was given these other countries. The British representative at Washington thereupon entered into negotiations with the State Department which resulted in the conclusion, early in 1892, of two agreements, one on behalf of Jamaica and the other on behalf of other West Indian colonies and British Guiana. By the terms of these agreements the colonies were to give reductions or remissions of duty on a large number of American products, in return for the free admission into the United States of the articles specified in section 3. Of these articles sugar, molasses, and coffee were important products of these colonies.

To the minister from Austria-Hungary the Secretary of State wrote, on January 7, 1892, in part, as follows:

I am directed by the President to inform you that, in view of the free introduction into the United States of the articles named, the product of Austria-Hungary, he deems the duties imposed upon the agricultural and other products of the United States, on their introduction into Austria-Hungary, to be reciprocally unequal and unreasonable; and that, unless on or before the 15th day of March next some satisfactory commercial arrangement is entered upon between the Government of the United States and the Government of Austria-Hungary, or unless some action is taken by the latter Government whereby the unequal and unreasonable state of the trade relations between the two countries is removed, the President will, on the date last

---

[1] 51st Cong., 2d sess., Sen. Ex. Doc. No. 66, p. 2.
[2] 52d Cong., 1st sess., Sen. Ex. Doc. No. 119, pp. 110–111. A more detailed account of the negotiations with Germany is given in Part II of this Report, p. 422 seq.

named, issue his proclamation suspending the provisions of the tariff law cited relating to the free introduction of such sugar, molasses, coffee, tea, and hides, the production of Austria-Hungary, and during such suspension the duties set forth in section 3 of said law shall be levied, collected, and paid upon sugar, molasses, coffee, tea, and hides, the product of or exported from Austria-Hungary.

In asking you to transmit to your Government the foregoing information, I beg that you will also convey to it the assurance that the Government of the United States is earnestly desirous of maintaining with Austria-Hungary such trade relations as shall be reciprocally equal and mutually advantageous, and state that this Government entertains the hope that, before the time fixed in this note, you may be empowered to enter with me upon some equitable and satisfactory arrangement, based upon the concessions proposed in the law of the Congress of the United States.[1]

The Austro-Hungarian Government, in reply, offered to grant to the United States the rates of its conventional tariff as applied to countries enjoying most-favored-nation treatment, in return for the continued exemption of duty on the articles specified in section 3, and especially on sugar. This was accepted by the American Government as a reciprocal concession for the free admission of the specified products.[2]

On May 25, 1892, the decree according most-favored-nation treatment to the imports of the United States was published in Vienna, and on the following day President Harrison issued a proclamation assuring to Austria-Hungary the free admission into the United States of the articles specified in section 3.

Agreements concluded.—Between January 31, 1891, and May 26, 1892, ten reciprocity arrangements were concluded, as shown in the following table:

Reciprocity agreements under section 3 of the act of Oct. 1, 1890.

Country.	Concluded.	American concessions in effect.	Concessions of other country in effect.
Brazil	Jan. 31, 1891	Apr. 1, 1891–Aug. 27, 1894	Apr. 1, 1891–Jan. 1, 1895.
Dominican Republic	June 4, 1891	Aug. 1, 1891–Aug. 27, 1894	Sept. 1, 1891–Sept. 28, 1894.
Spain for Cuba and Porto Rico.	June 16, 1891	Aug. 1, 1891[1]–Aug. 27, 1894.	Sept. 1, 1891–Aug. 27, 1894.
Salvador	Dec. 30, 1891	Dec. 31, 1891–Aug. 27, 1894.	Feb. 1, 1892.[2,3]
German Empire	Jan. 30, 1892	Feb. 1, 1892–Aug. 27, 1894	Feb. 1, 1892.[4]
Great Britain, for West India Colonies,[5] including Jamaica, Barbados, Trinidad (and Tobago), Leeward Islands (including Virgin Islands), Windward Islands (excluding Grenada), and British Guiana.	Feb. 1, 1892	Feb. 1, 1892[6]–Aug. 27, 1894.	Feb. 1, 1892[6]–Aug. 27, 1894.
Nicaragua	Mar. 11, 1892	Mar. 12, 1892–Aug. 27, 1894	Apr. 15, 1892–Jan. 9, 1895.
Honduras	Apr. 29, 1892	Apr. 30, 1892–Aug. 27, 1894	May 25, 1892.[3]
Guatemala	Dec. 30, 1891	May 18, 1892–Aug. 27, 1894	May 30, 1892–Sept. 24, 1894.[7]
Austria-Hungary	May 25, 1892	May 26, 1892–Aug. 27, 1894	May 25, 1892.[4]

[1] Transitory schedule effective Sept. 1, 1891, superseded by permanent schedule, July 1, 1892.
[2] Provisional act, superseded by permanent act, Dec. 27, 1892.
[3] No information available.
[4] Concessions not withdrawn.
[5] Not including Bermuda and the Bahamas.
[6] Effective as to British Guiana, Apr. 1, 1892.
[7] See p. 162, infra.

Terms of the agreements.—All of these reciprocity agreements were alike in being based upon the free admission into the United States of the five articles specified in section 3 of the McKinley Act, namely: coffee, tea, hides, sugar, and molasses. They differed with respect

[1] 52d Cong., 1st sess., Sen. Ex. Doc. No. 110, pp. 110 and 111.
[2] Ibid.

to the specification of products of the United States which would be admitted into the various countries free of duty or at rates of duty lower than the ordinary. Many classes of commodities, both agricultural products and manufactured articles, were mentioned in the different agreements, no two of which were exactly the same. The articles specified were such as the countries were compelled to import either from the United States or from Europe, and in most cases they comprised the bulk of their imports from the United States. The concessions granted to the United States by Central and South American countries, and by Spain for her West Indian colonies, were not granted by those countries to any other country. For most of these countries the chief consideration for the granting of concessions to the United States was the free admission of sugar by the latter country. No such consideration could have been offered with any effect by European countries to sugar-producing countries in the West Indies, Central or South America, because the continental European countries themselves produced much more sugar than they could consume, and to most of these Latin-American countries the free admission by the United States of coffee and hides was also important.

The only countries outside of the Western Hemisphere with which reciprocity agreements on their own behalf were concluded at this time were Germany and Austria-Hungary. The concessions granted by Germany and Austria-Hungary were given, like those of the other States, mainly in consideration of the free admission of sugar by the United States. Both of these countries were large producers of beet-sugar, and had a surplus of that commodity, but neither exported to the United States any of the other articles specified in section 3 of the act of 1890, except skins of goats and other small animals.

Germany and Austria-Hungary each had in its tariff a general schedule and a conventional schedule. The conventional schedule was lower than the general, and, in treaties between themselves or with other countries, the rates of the conventional schedule were granted in whole or in part. By a treaty concluded in 1891, Germany and Austria-Hungary had granted conventional rates of duty to each other. This treaty was superseded by a new treaty, signed on January 25, 1892, under which new conventional rates of duty were granted on specified articles.[1]

The reciprocity agreement between Germany and the United States (Saratoga Convention) was concluded on January 30, 1892, only five days after the signing of the treaty between Germany and Austria-Hungary just mentioned. It granted to the United States on certain specified agricultural products the conventional rates which Germany had granted on the same classes of commodities imported from Austria-Hungary. The list of articles on which Germany granted concessions to Austria-Hungary was very comprehensive and included many manufactured articles, but the list on which concessions were granted to the United States included only a few agricultural products and no manufactures except flour and certain wood products.

The reciprocity agreement between the United States and Austria-Hungary, concluded on May 25, 1892, extended to the United States

---

the full benefit of the conventional rates of duty granted by Austria-Hungary to the most-favored nation, that is, every tariff concession granted to any other country.

Arrangement with France.—An informal commercial arrangement with France was concluded by an exchange of notes, March 10–April 12, 1892, between the American Minister to France (Whitelaw Reid) and the French Minister of Foreign Affairs, and was put into effect in France by the law of January 27, 1893. France had just adopted—in 1892—the two-schedule tariff system. In return for the assurance by the United States Government that the penalty duties provided for in section 3 of the tariff act of 1890 would not be imposed on French products, the French Government agreed to extend the minimum rates of her new tariff to a small number of American products, of which fresh and preserved fruits, certain wood products, canned meats, and lard were most important. While the minimum rates on these articles were appreciably lower than the maximum rates of the new tariff, they were in no case much lower and in several cases they were higher than the general rates of the old tariff. On July 7, 1893, the minimum rates on mineral oils also were applied to the American products.[1]

France did not withdraw these rates when the provisions of section 3 of the act of 1890 were abrogated by the tariff act of 1894. In 1898 another arrangement was concluded between the two countries whereby the continued application of these minimum rates to American products was assured to the United States.[2]

Unratified agreement with Costa Rica.—An agreement negotiated with Costa Rica was not ratified by the legislative body in that country.

Application of penalty duties.—Three countries, Colombia, Venezuela, and Haiti, which had not entered into reciprocity agreements with the United States, were warned, on January 7, 1892, by Mr. Blaine, that unless they made satisfactory arrangements by March 15, the privilege of free entry of their coffee, hides, sugar, and molasses, granted under the tariff act of 1890, would be denied to them, and the penalty duties provided for in section 3 of that act would be applied. The notes to the ministers of these countries were of practically the same tenor as the note to the minister of Austria-Hungary quoted above.[3]

The Colombian Government took no action upon the invitation to enter into negotiations for reciprocity with the United States. Mr. Blaine wrote to the Colombian minister at Washington: "It is deeply regretted by the President that his invitation to the Government of Colombia has not been responded to in the same conciliatory spirit." The minister from Colombia, in reply, while contending that under the most-favored-nation provision of the treaty of 1846 Colombia was entitled to all the privileges which the United States might concede to other nations,[4] promised that the President of Colombia would "use all the influence at his command to obtain from [the

---

[1] This arrangement has been overlooked in most American accounts of the act of 1890 and most of the information was obtainable only from French sources. For the text of the exchange of notes, Clercq. *Recueil des Traités de la France*, Vol. 19, pp. 434–435. For the laws applying the minimum rates, ibid., pp. 547, 567, 588. The arrangement is discussed in Arnauné, le Commerce Extérieur et les Tarifs de Douane. Paris, 1911, pp. 372–374.
[2] See p. 205, infra.
[3] The note to Venezuela appears in the Congressional Record for Jan. 11, 1892, p. 245.
[4] See Part II, p. 421, infra.

Colombian] congress at its next meeting such an extension of the list of nondutiable merchandise as will justify any action which the President [of the United States] may be pleased to take postponing the suspension of the free entry" of Colombian coffee and hides into the United States. Mr. Blaine thereupon requested a detailed statement of the changes in the tariff of Colombia which the President of that country had recommended, in order that the President of the United States might judge as to whether they involved concessions sufficient to compensate the United States for continuing the free admission of certain products of Colombia. The minister replied simply that he would forward the note to the Colombian Government. No further communication from that Government having been received, President Harrison issued a proclamation on March 15, 1892, which imposed duties on imports from Colombia, as provided in section 3 of the tariff act of 1890.

At the same time the President issued similar proclamations imposing the penalty duties on imports from Haiti and Venezuela. Haiti had made no response to the invitation. Mr. Blaine's letters on the subject to the Haitian minister at Washington and the communications of the United States minister at Port au Prince to the Haitian Government were acknowledged, but were never answered. The Government of Venezuela showed an inclination, when the subject was first proposed, to enter into a reciprocity arrangement, and the Venezuelan minister at Washington negotiated with the Department of State the terms of a convention which he forwarded to his government for its approval. The Venezuelan president transmitted the convention to the congress of Venezuela, which appointed a special commissioner to continue the negotiations. This commissioner did not carry out his instructions. No further progress having been made, President Harrison on March 15, 1892, suspended the free admission of the products specified in section 3 when coming from Venezuela.

Negotiations with the Argentine and Mexico.—Although the United States imported large amounts of coffee, hides, and sugar from certain other South American countries which did not respond to Secretary Blaine's invitation to them to enter into reciprocity negotiations, the penalty duties were not applied to any countries except Colombia, Venezuela, and Haiti. In a report on reciprocity and commercial treaties, presented by the House Committee on Ways and Means on June 6, 1896, there was included a statement upon trade with the Argentine, written by William C. Curtis, who had been secretary and later a member of the commission which visited South America in 1884 and 1885. In this statement there appears the following explanation:

No attempt was made to apply the retaliatory provision of the reciprocity section of the tariff act of 1890 to any other country except Colombia, Venezuela, and Haiti, for the reason that the President believed the duties imposed by them alone were onerous to American commerce and reciprocally unequal and unreasonable. There was some correspondence with the Argentine Republic. That Government contended that the duties it imposed upon our peculiar products, such as lumber, refined petroleum, agricultural implements, machinery, and other manufactures of iron and steel, were not unreasonable in view of the tax we imposed upon wool, which was its principal item of export to the United States. It was intimated at various times during the negotiation that if the United States would remove the duty from wool, the Argentine Government would make generous concessions in favor of our manufactures, but such an arrangement was not authorized by the law.[1]

---

[1] 54th Cong., 1st sess., H. Rept. No. 2263, sup. B.

The import of wool from the Argentine was considerable, but was not half as large as the import of hides from that country. The import of wool from Chile was small. From the other countries to the south which did not agree to reciprocity, and to which penalty duties were not applied, the imports of wool were still smaller and much less in quantity than the imports of reciprocity articles.

On April 20, 1892, the House Committee on Foreign Affairs reported favorably upon a resolution introduced by Mr. Stewart, of Texas, providing for the initiation of reciprocity negotiations with Mexico. The report urged that every consideration suggested by geographical location, similarity of institutions, and community of commercial interests, would seem to justify every reasonable effort to promote closer trade relations with Mexico. It declared that the removal of the American duty on lead ores would probably be of mutual advantage to the two countries, and it recommended the free admission of wool from Mexico, in return for equivalent concessions that might be made by that country.[1]

Accordingly the American minister to Mexico was charged with the negotiations on behalf of the United States, and the President of Mexico nominated a commissioner to represent the Mexican Government. But of the articles enumerated in section 3, none but coffee and hides were exported by Mexico to the United States in considerable quantities, and the prospect of their exemption from duty by the United States was not a sufficient inducement to persuade the Mexican Government to make reciprocal concessions. This was all the more the case since it was by no means certain that in the eventuality of the two countries failing to reach an agreement the United States would impose the penalty duties upon the products of Mexico. Furthermore, Mexico had uniformly followed the practice of having a "single tariff" with no discrimination between the imports from different countries and was reluctant to change its historical policy. The negotiations were, therefore, without result.

THE TERMINATION OF THE RECIPROCITY AGREEMENTS.

The passage of the tariff act of 1894.—In 1892 Grover Cleveland was elected for the second time President of the United States. To the House of Representatives there was returned a large Democratic majority, and the Senate became Democratic by a small majority. The tariff bill which the House Committee on Ways and Means introduced received consideration during a period of eight months, a period longer than that which Congress had ever before given to a tariff bill. The bill was introduced on December 19, 1893, and it was finally passed on August 13, 1894, after the House had receded from its attitude of opposition to the Senate amendments.

In its report accompanying the bill at the moment of introduction, the Committee on Ways and Means explained that it was the purpose of the tariff bill "to repeal in toto section 3 of the tariff act of October 1, 1890, commonly but erroneously called its reciprocity provision," and gave the following reasons:

This section has brought no appreciable advantage to American exporters; it is not in intention or effect a provision for reciprocity, but for retaliation. It inflicts penalties upon the American people by making them pay higher prices for these

---

[1] 52d Cong., 1st sess., H. Rept. No. 1145, p. 4.

articles if the fiscal necessities of other nations compel them to levy duties upon the products of the United States which, in the opinion of the President, are reciprocally unequal and unreasonable. Under the provisions of this section presidential proclamations have been issued imposing retaliatory duties upon the five above-mentioned articles (coffee, tea, hides, sugar, and molasses) when coming from certain countries. These proclamations have naturally led to ill feeling in the countries thus discriminated against, and to diplomatic correspondence, in which it has been claimed with apparent justice that such discriminations were in violation of our solemn treaty obligations * * *.

Moreover, we do not believe that Congress can rightly vest in the President of the United States any authority or power to impose or release taxes on our people by proclamation or otherwise, or to suspend or dispense with the operation of a law of Congress * * *.[1]

Further to insure the repeal of section 3 of the act of 1890, the House of Representatives passed on January 25, 1895, an amendment introduced by Mr. Wilson of West Virginia, chairman of the Committee on Ways and Means, which specifically provided for the repeal.

The Wilson tariff bill, as it was reported by the Committee on Ways and Means to the House of Representatives, provided that raw sugar should remain on the free list and that the duties on refined sugar should be reduced. It provided that coffee, tea, hides, and molasses should be admitted free, as under the act of 1890, and it put wool on the free list. It further provided that the bounty on the domestic production of sugar, established by the act of 1890, should be reduced one-eighth of a cent per pound, beginning July 1, 1895, and continuing until July 1, 1902, after which all sugar bounties should terminate. The House amended the bill so as to put refined sugar as well as raw sugar on the free list. By another amendment in the House, the bounty paid to domestic sugar producers was abolished.

The bill, as it was revised and reported by the Senate Committee on Finance and as it was passed by the Senate, was greatly altered. The amendments of greatest importance were those making raw sugar dutiable and increasing the duties on refined sugar. Some of the important changes made by the Senate were explained to the House by Mr. Wilson on July 19, as follows:

* * * the great difficulty in the pathway of an agreement has been the proper adjustment of the sugar schedule. This House voted for free sugar, raw and refined. It voted down the proposal of the Committee on Ways and Means for a gradual repeal of the bounty and a reduction by more than one-half of the duty upon refined sugar. The Senate has reintroduced into the proposed tariff bill a sugar schedule, which, whether truly or not, has been accepted by the country, by the press of the country, by the people of the country, as unduly favorable to the great sugar trust. It proposes a duty of 40 per cent *ad valorem* on all grades of sugar, a differential of one-eighth of a cent upon refined sugar in addition to a differential of one-tenth of a cent on sugar imported from countries that pay an export bounty upon their sugar.[2]

Mr. Payne, of New York, speaking in the House, on August 13, said:

The Republican Party, when it made sugar free in 1890, determined to get something for the surrender of the duty. We enacted a duty on coffee, tea, sugar, hides, and rubber against those countries which did not give us free-trade relations. With the aid of this clause we increased the trade with the South American Republics as well as with Cuba, and opened the ports of France and Germany and Spain to the American hog.

You surrender the duty on wool without any compensation whatever. You might extend your trade in the wool-producing countries of South America and Australia

---

[1] 53d Cong., 2d sess., H. Rept. 234, p. 11.   [2] Cong. Rec. July 19, 1894.

and New Zealand by imposing a duty on their wool until they gave us fair trade relations; but you go farther than this and strike down all the reciprocal trade relations established by the act of 1890.[1]

As the bill was finally passed, it provided for a duty on raw sugar and for higher duties on refined sugar than had been in force under the act of 1890. It also repealed entirely the bounty on the domestic production of sugar. The Senate, however, had agreed to the House provision for free wool.

The Senate had adopted on July 3, an amendment proposed by Senator Vest, of Missouri, which provided that existing reciprocity arrangements should not be affected unless they were inconsistent with the provisions of the act. The bill as finally enacted incorporated this amendment in section 71, as follows:

SEC. 71. That section three of an act approved October first, eighteen hundred and ninety, entitled "An act to reduce the revenue and equalize duties on imports, and for other purposes," is hereby repealed; but nothing herein contained shall be held to abrogate or in any way affect such reciprocal commercial arrangements as have been heretofore made and now exist between the United States and foreign countries, except where such arrangements are inconsistent with the provisions of this act. * * *

Effect of the act of 1894 on the agreements.—It might appear, therefore, that the existing reciprocity agreements would have been continued had it not been for the reimposition, by the act of 1894, of a duty on raw sugar. The free entry of raw sugar, which the act of 1890 had guaranteed to the countries which should make "reciprocal and equivalent" concessions to the United States, had been the principal inducement for the majority of them to make such agreements. But what now rendered the agreements unattractive to the reciprocity countries was not so much the reimposition of a duty on sugar as the repeal of the provision of the act of 1890 which had empowered the President to impose penalty duties against the five specified products of countries which refused to make such concessions. Under the new act the grant of special concessions to the United States could assure no concessions in return and the withdrawal of concessions could bring no penalties. Very little sugar was imported from the Central American reciprocity countries; nevertheless, these were as ready to terminate their agreements as were the sugar-producing countries.

The reciprocity arrangements made under section 3 of the act of 1890, although expressed in the form of a contract, constituted no sort of a guaranty that the United States, in view of the traditional American position that a statute repeals any stipulations of treaties of earlier date which are inconsistent with the terms of the statute, would refrain from reimposing duties on the articles whose free admission was assured in the agreements, or from terminating the agreements at will. Nevertheless, upon the passage of the tariff act of 1894, many of the reciprocity countries made protests, particularly against the imposition of duties on sugar, regarding this as a direct violation of their rights under the reciprocity agreements.

Protests against the abrogation of the agreements.—The Brazilian agreement alone had expressly included conditions for its own termination. In a letter by Mr. Blaine, Secretary of State, to Senhor Mendonça, the Brazilian representative, dated June 31, 1891, there occurs the following statement, adopting the terms and language of a

---

[1] Cong. Rec. Aug. 13, 1894.

previous letter of the Brazilian representative in answer to which it was written:

* * * this commercial arrangement * * * it is understood shall remain in force so long as neither Government shall definitely, at least three months in advance, inform the other of its intention and decision to consider it at an end, at the expiration of the time indicated: *Provided, however,* That the termination of the commercial arrangement shall begin to take effect either on the 1st day of January or the 1st day of July.[1]

On October 25, 1894, immediately prior to the passage of the new tariff act, the Secretary of State, Mr. Gresham, in answer to a protest of the Brazilian representative, against the impending imposition of duties on sugar as a violation of the reciprocity agreement of 1892, made the following statement:

I think that the reciprocity arrangement between Brazil and the United States was terminated by the going into force of our existing tariff law, and I do not think the executive department can act upon any other theory. This is the view of the Secretary of the Treasury. The so-called treaties or agreements that were entered into, based upon the third section of the McKinley bill, were not treaties binding upon the two Governments, and the present law is mandatory. Notice to your Government that the arrangement would terminate as provided by its terms would have no force, as the arrangement actually exists no longer.[2]

On September 24, 1894, Senhor Mendonça communicated to the United States the intention of Brazil to denounce the commercial agreement in the manner provided in the original interchange of notes, so that the termination of the Brazilian tariff concessions would take effect on January 1, 1895, on which date the rates of the old Brazilian tariff would again be imposed on American products. The Brazilian concessions, therefore, were continued for some months longer than the corresponding concessions on the part of the United States.

Germany also protested against the reimposition of duties on sugar and especially against the provision for countervailing duties on bounty-fed sugar, as a violation both of most-favored-nation obligations and of the reciprocity agreement of 1892. The American authorities took the same attitude in regard to the termination of the German reciprocity agreement as had been taken toward that with Brazil, claiming the right to terminate it at will.[3] Germany did not withdraw the tariff concessions which she had granted in 1892, but in retaliation for the imposition of duties on sugar, although not expressly so, the German Government promulgated orders similar to those which had been in effect prior to the negotiations of the agreement of 1892 establishing the prohibition of importation of American cattle into Germany.[4] The German protests against the method adopted by the American Government in terminating the agreement of 1892 were resumed even more vigorously in 1897, when the imposition of still higher countervailing duties on bounty-fed sugar emphasized the adverse effect upon Germany of the abrogation of the agreement. The American Government adhered to its position that the reciprocity agreements were not intended to restrict and did not restrict the power of Congress to make any changes in duties that seemed wise to it, and claimed that the mere change of the duties forming part of the consideration of the original agreement operated, without further notice, to terminate such agreement. The controversy between Germany and the United States was not settled

---

[1] U. S. Foreign Relations, 1891, pp. 43–44.   [3] Ibid, 1894, p. 239.
[2] Ibid, 1894, pp. 77–79.   [4] Ibid, 1896, p. 209.

until, by the reciprocity agreement of 1900, there was effected a temporary understanding in regard to the commercial relations of the two countries.

Austria-Hungary, by the agreement of 1892, had extended the minimum rates of her newly enacted tariff to all the products of the United States. Upon the termination of the agreement, Austria made no change in her tariff treatment of American products, but claimed that the provisions of her most-favored-nation treaty of 1829 with the United States [1] assured her the right of as favorable treatment of her products by the United States as was granted to any other country. [2] On October 12, 1894, Mr. Gresham, Secretary of State, in a report to the President upon the protests of Germany and of Austria, reaffirmed the right of the United States to terminate the reciprocity agreements at its pleasure.[3]

Modus vivendi with Spain.—The Spanish Government, after consultation with the American ambassador at Madrid, held the view that the commercial arrangement in regard to Cuba and Porto Rico terminated at the moment when the new American tariff law came into force and that the first column of the Spanish tariff (the maximum schedule) was applicable, in the absence of a new agreement, to American products.[4] As a result, the prohibitive duties of the Spanish maximum tariff were imposed on flour and other American products exported to the Spanish West Indies. A threat was made by the United States to exercise the authority of section 5 of the act of August 30, 1890,[5] against Spanish products, and especially sugar, if more favorable treatment were not extended to American products. Spain suggested a new commercial agreement as the only solution consistent with her tariff laws; but under the pressure of the Cuban sugar producers, who feared the retaliatory measures threatened by the United States, the absence of countervailing duties on Cuban sugar, which received no bounty, was considered a sufficient tariff favor to justify the extension to American products of the Spanish conventional tariff for Cuba and Porto Rico. This decision was arrived at in December, 1894. By an exchange of notes at Madrid on January 9–10, 1895, a *modus vivendi* was established, guaranteeing to the products and manufactures of the United States the benefit of the conventional rates of the tariff then in force in the islands of Cuba and Porto Rico, in exchange for which the United States was to apply its lowest tariff rates to the products of these islands. This was ratified by the Spanish Cortes on February 5, 1895. This *modus vivendi* was to continue in effect until the execution of a definite treaty between the two parties or until one of them should give notice three months in advance of the day upon which it was desired that it terminate.[6] It served to regulate the commercial relations of the United States and the West Indian colonies of Spain until Cuba gained its independence.

Official correspondence with other treaty countries.—On August 24, 1894, the British ambassador at Washington, Sir Julian Pauncefote,

---

[1] In this treaty clauses V and IX are identical with the similarly numbered clauses of the United States-Prussia treaty of 1828.
[2] U. S. Foreign Relations, 1897, p. 23.
[3] 53d Cong., 3d sess., Sen. Ex. Doc. No. 58, p. 19.
[4] U. S. Foreign Relations, 1894, p. 619.
[5] For the text of this section see Part II, p. 424, infra.
[6] U. S. Foreign Relations, 1894, pp. 625–633; 1895, pt. 2, p. 1185.

sent a note to the Secretary of State in which he pointed out that sections 182½–189 of the new tariff bill would, on coming into force, be assumed to cancel entirely the agreements made concerning the West Indies and British Guiana under the McKinley Act and that these agreements would not be continued in operation by the passage of an act admitting sugar free without regard to the country of its origin.   On August 25, Mr. Gresham confirmed this view of the effect which the tariff bill of 1894 would have, if enacted, upon the reciprocity agreements.[1]

In answer to an inquiry from the Guatemalan minister at Washington, Mr. Gresham stated that the commercial agreement of 1892 with that country had terminated upon the passage of the tariff act of October 27, 1894.   On September 24, 1894, the Guatemalan minister notified Mr. Gresham of the transmittal of this note to his government.[2]   The minister of Guatemala, in a written memorandum, and in personal interviews, later remonstrated against the abrogation of the reciprocity agreement, on the ground that, with a view to enjoying the benefits of the American market, large sums of money had been invested in plantations and in machinery for the production of sugar; that this large outlay would not have been incurred had it been supposed that the abandonment of the reciprocity policy by the United States and the reimposition of a tax on sugar would soon occur; that the ability of Guatemala to produce sugar had been demonstrated; and that financial ruin would befall the sugar producers should the bill become a law and a duty be imposed upon sugar imported from that country into the United States.[3]

The President of the Dominican Republic issued a decree on September 28, 1894, revoking the commercial agreement of 1891 and making American goods subject to the duties of the general tariff in force.[4]   On November 5, 1896, the Dominican Republic gave notice of its intention to renounce the treaty of friendship, commerce and navigation of February 5, 1867.   The notice was received at Washington on January 12, to become effective January 13, 1897.

The Nicaraguan Government gave notice on January 9, 1895, through its representative in Washington, that henceforth the reciprocity agreement of 1892 would be regarded as non-existent because of the passage of the new tariff act of 1894.[5]

No record has been found of any protest or communication from Salvador or Honduras in regard to the termination of their agreements.   But as neither of these were sugar-producing countries, the termination of the agreements affected them very slightly, if at all.

Reciprocity in the period, 1894–1897.—In the period between the passage of the act of 1894 and the moment when this act was superseded by the tariff act of 1897, the only reciprocity relations of the United States were those which continued under the treaties with Hawaii.   In 1897 the new tariff act again provided for reciprocity in a manner and with consequences to which attention will be given in a subsequent chapter.   In anticipation, it is pertinent to note

---

[1] U. S. Foreign Relations, 1894, p. 289.
[2] Ibid, 1894, p. 332.
[3] Report of the House Committee on Ways and Means concerning Reciprocity and Commercial Treaties, 54th Cong., 1st sess., H. Rept. No. 2263, p. 24.
[4] Republicana Dominicana, Tratados Internacionales, Tomo 1, 1915, p. 149.
[5] U. S. Foreign Relations, 1894, p. 448.

that, when the agreements which arose out of the legislation of 1897 were in their turn to be terminated by the enactment of a new law in 1909, much greater care was exercised than had been the case in 1894 in framing the provisions of the law so that they would conform to the conditions regarding termination which had been written into the agreements themselves.

There follows a statistical analysis of the effects exerted upon the trade of the United States by the penalizing provisions of the act of 1890 and consequent agreements.

EFFECTS ON AMERICAN TRADE.

Abnormal conditions during reciprocity period.—Because of the prevalence of abnormal business conditions during the reciprocity period, it is extremely difficult to estimate the effect of the reciprocity agreements upon the foreign trade of the United States. The year 1890 marked the beginning of a commercial crisis of world-wide extent. This began with the suspension, on November 15, 1890, of the great London banking firm of Baring Bros., which was deeply involved in South American affairs. The Baring failure precipitated a financial panic which spread throughout the world, but had its sharpest effect in the Latin-American countries. Revolutionary insurrections then in progress in South and Central America combined with the depression which followed the panic to check the commerce, paralyze the industry, and destroy the credit of Latin America. In Nicaragua, Honduras, Brazil, and Chile the depression was especially severe; foreign capital was withdrawn, and many banks, mercantile houses, and manufacturers were forced into insolvency. The depression came somewhat later in the United States than elsewhere, but by 1893 it was as marked in this country as in others.

The course of trade during this period was further disturbed by tariff revisions in France, Germany, and other countries; by the depreciation of the paper currencies of countries which at the same time were suffering from the financial and industrial depression; by the sugar-bounty competition among the beet-sugar-producing countries; and by the general decline in prices, which tended to minimize increases and to exaggerate decreases in the volume of imports and exports when expressed in terms of their value. Allowance for the influence of these factors must be made before the tendencies indicated by an analysis of the statistics of imports and exports can be attributed with any degree of confidence to the specific influence of tariff changes.

EFFECT UPON IMPORTS.

In examining the effects of the reciprocity provisions of 1890 and the consequent commercial agreements, separate consideration will be given to their influence upon imports into and upon exports from the United States. Taking the first of these, which is the simpler, it may at once be said that no great effect upon the imports into the United States can be traced directly to the reciprocity features of the act of 1890. Under the provisions of that act, the United States could not offer especially favorable treatment to countries which would grant special tariff concessions; it could only subject to especially unfavorable treatment such countries as refused to grant such concessions. In the absence of a discriminatory distinction between imports from reciprocity countries and those from non-penalized non-reciprocity countries, no changes in imports except those due to the imposition of penalty duties can be attributed directly to the reciprocity provisions. The penalized countries furnished only a small fraction of the reciprocity articles which were imported into the United States. Hence the influence of the reciprocity provisions on imports could be but slight. Nevertheless the evidence on the effect of penalizing discrimination is here presented, bearing as it does on the effectiveness and success of this form of international commercial negotiation.

The articles specified in section 3 of the act of 1890, namely, coffee, sugar, molasses, hides, and tea, were made free of duty except when coming from countries subject to penalty duties. Three of these articles—coffee, hides, and tea—had been admitted free prior to the act of 1890; the other two—sugar and molasses—had been subject to specific duties of which those on sugar averaged about 2 cents a pound. For the general range of imports the act of 1890 involved a considerable increase in duties. The imports of reciprocity articles might therefore be expected to show a more pronounced relative increase than the imports of other articles, and, because of the remission of duty, this increase might be expected to appear most clearly in the case of sugar.

IMPORTS INTO THE UNITED STATES UNDER RECIPROCITY.

Table I shows the imports of the reciprocity articles as compared with other imports. As no agreements were negotiated with tea-producing countries, tea is omitted from among the reciprocity articles considered in this inquiry.

TABLE I.—*Imports into the United States, by classes of articles, 1888–1897.*

Year.	Total imports.		Imports of reciprocity articles.			Import of nonreciprocity articles.		
	Value.	Per cent increase over 3-year average 1888-1890.[1]	Value.	Per cent increase over 3-year average 1888-1890.[1]	Per cent of total imports.	Value.	Per cent increase or decrease over 3-year average 1888-1890.[1]	Per cent of total imports.
1888.........	$723,957,114	....	$164,183,270	....	22.68	$559,773,844	....	77.32
1889.........	745,131,652	....	193,150,500	....	25.92	551,981,152	....	74.08
1890.........	789,310,409	4.85	201,412,645	8.14	25.52	587,897,764	3.77	74.48
1891.........	844,916,196	12.24	232,441,924	24.80	27.51	612,474,272	8.11	72.49
1892.........	827,402,462	9.91	262,178,705	40.77	31.69	565,223,757	.24	68.31
1893.........	866,400,922	15.09	227,081,572	21.92	26.21	639,319,350	12.84	73.79
1894.........	654,994,622	12.99	235,957,495	26.69	36.03	419,037,127	26.04	63.97
1895.........	731,969,965	2.77	200,011,641	7.39	27.33	531,958,324	6.11	72.67
1896.........	779,724,674	3.58	205,270,339	10.21	26.33	574,454,335	1.40	73.67
1897.........	764,730,412	1.58	209,060,104	12.25	27.34	555,670,308	1.92	72.66

[1] Decreases in italics.

TABLE I-A.—*Imports into the United States of reciprocity articles (tea omitted).*

Year.	Total reciprocity articles.			Coffee.			Sugar.		
	Value.	Per cent increase over 3-year average, 1888–1890.	Per cent of total imports.	Value.	Per cent increase over 3-year average, 1888–1890.	Per cent of total reciprocity imports.[1]	Value.	Per cent increase over 3-year average, 1888–1890.[1]	Per cent of total reciprocity imports.
1888..	$164,183,270	....	22.68	$60,507,630	....	36.85	$74,245,206	....	45.22
1889..	193,150,500	....	25.92	74,724,882	....	38.69	88,543,971	....	45.84
1890..	201,412,645	8.14	25.52	78,267,432	9.98	38.86	96,094,532	11.36	47.71
1891..	232,441,924	24.80	27.51	96,123,777	35.07	41.36	105,728,216	22.52	45.49
1892.	262,178,705	40.77	31.69	128,041,930	79.92	48.84	104,408,813	20.99	39.82
1893..	227,081,572	21.92	26.21	80,485,558	13.09	35.44	116,255,784	34.72	51.19
1894..	235,957,495	26.69	36.03	90,314,676	26.91	38.27	126,871,889	47.02	53.76
1895..	200,011,641	7.41	27.33	96,130,717	35.08	48.06	76,462,836	11.39	38.23
1896..	205,270,339	10.21	26.33	84,793,124	19.15	41.31	89,219,773	3.39	43.46
1897..	209,060,104	12.25	27.34	81,544,384	14.58	39.00	99,066,181	14.80	47.39

Year.	Molasses.			Hides.		
	Value.	Per cent increase over 3-year average, 1888–1890.	Per cent of total reciprocity imports.	Value.	Per cent increase over 3-year average, 1888–1890.[1]	Per cent of total reciprocity imports.
1888	$5,491,095	....	3.35	$23,939,339	....	14.58
1889	4,753,897	....	2.46	25,127,750	....	13.01
1890	5,168,795	.60	2.57	21,881,886	7.47	10.86
1891	2,659,172	48.24	1.14	27,930,759	18.10	12.01
1892	2,877,744	43.99	1.10	26,850,218	13.53	10.24
1893	1,992,334	61.22	.88	28,347,896	19.87	12.49
1894	1,984,778	61.37	.85	16,786,152	29.02	7.12
1895	1,295,146	74.79	.64	26,122,942	10.46	13.07
1896	737,265	85.65	.36	30,520,177	29.05	14.87
1897	586,513	88.58	.28	27,863,026	17.82	13.33

[1] Decreases in italics.

The figures for each year following the enactment of the new tariff show an increased volume of imports of reciprocity articles over that of the years just prior to reciprocity, as compared with either a smaller increase or a decrease, during the corresponding years, in the imports of other articles and in the total imports. The relative increase of imports of reciprocity articles in comparison with that of other imports was most marked in 1894: from 25 per cent of the total imports in 1890, 32 per cent in 1892, and 26 per cent in 1893, the imports of reciprocity articles increased to 36 per cent in 1894. This relative increase in the imports of reciprocity articles was undoubtedly due in part to the remission of duty on sugar and to the retention on the free list of coffee and hides, while the average of rates on other articles had been increased. The industrial depression of the period may also have contributed. "Hard times" would have less effect upon the importation and consumption of such staple consumers' goods as sugar and coffee than upon luxuries and materials for industry, the demands for which are always more sensitive to changes in industrial conditions. Between 1892 and 1894 the total imports increased less rapidly than the imports of the reciprocity articles. But after 1894, in which year a new tariff act was passed, putting an end to the reciprocity arrangements, the situation was reversed: total imports increased considerably, while imports of reciprocity articles fell from $235,000,000 in 1894 to $200,000,000 in 1895 and were but $209,000,000 in 1897.

As will appear from the analysis of imports by separate commodities, the decrease in amount after 1894 was due in most part to a reduction in the imports of sugar following the reimposition, in the tariff act of 1894, of a duty on sugar.

IMPORTS BY COMMODITIES.

Coffee.—The act of 1890 made no change in the tariff treatment of coffee, éxcept in its provision for penalty duties, which were applied only to a small fraction of the coffee imports. The imports of coffee showed a striking increase of about $50,000,000 between 1890 and 1892, and they decreased by a like sum in 1893.

TABLE II.—*Imports of coffee into the United States, 1888–1897.*

Year.	Imports.				New York average market price No. 7 standard Rio, per pound.	Domestic consumption per capita.
	Quantity.	Per cent increase in quantity over 3-year average, 1888–1890. [1]	Value.	Per cent increase in value over 3-year average, 1888–1890.		
	Pounds.				*Cents.*	*Pounds.*
1888	423,645,794	....	$60,507,630	....	13.4	6.8
1889	578,397,454	....	74,724,882	....	16.8	9.2
1890	499,159,120	0.25	78,267,432	9.98	18.0	7.8
1891	519,528,432	3.82	96,123,777	35.07	16.4	8.0
1892	640,210,788	27.94	128,041,930	79.92	14.4	9.6
1893	563,469,068	12.60	80,485,558	13.09	17.4	8.2
1894	550,934,337	10.10	90,314,676	26.91	16.4	8.3
1895	652,208,975	30.34	96,130,717	35.08	15.8	9.2
1896	580,597,915	16.03	84,793,124	19.15	12.1	8.0
1897	737,645,670	47.41	81,544,384	14.58	10.0	10.0

[1] Decrease in italics.

TABLE III-A.—*Price of coffee, by months, 1892 and 1893.*

Month.	Average import price per pound.	Month.	Average import price per pound as recorded.	Average import price per pound as corrected.	Average price at Rio de Janeiro per pound.
1892.	*Cents.*	*1892.*	*Cents.*	*Cents.*	*Cents.*
Jan	20.6	July	22.0	11.8	12.5
Feb	19.2	Aug	26.5	13.2	13.5
Mar	20.0	Sept	23.3	15.2	14.1
Apr	21.6	Oct	30.3	14.3	15.0
May	20.8	Nov	24.5	12.7	15.5
June	22.9	Dec	23.4	13.5	15.8

Month.	Average import price per pound as recorded.	Average import price per pound as corrected.	Average price at Rio de Janeiro per pound.	Month.	Average import price per pound.
1893.	*Cents.*	*Cents.*	*Cents.*	*1893.*	*Cents.*
Jan	26.5	13.4	15.8	July	16.3
Feb	24.6	14.4	17.0	Aug	17.0
Mar	25.4	15.6	17.0	Sept	14.7
Apr	26.3	15.2	16.0	Oct	16.3
May	24.6	16.0	15.1	Nov	16.5
June	27.3	14.9	15.7	Dec	17.0

TABLE III–B.—*Price of coffee, by years, 1890–1895.*

	1890	1891	1892	1893	1894	1895
	Cents.	*Cents.*	*Cents.*	*Cents.*	*Cents.*	*Cents.*
Average import price, per pound	16.0	18.5	20.0	{ 25.9 [1] 14.2 }	16.4	14.7
Average import price of Brazil coffee, per pound	14.7	18.9	21.1	28.7 { [1] 13.3 [2] 15.3 }	16.0	13.9
New York market price Brazil No. 7 standard, per pound	18.0	15.4	14.4	17.4	16.4	15.8

[1] Corrected figures.　　　　[2] Quotation at Rio de Janeiro of No. 7 standard.

But in examining the yearly changes in the coffee imports, the figures for quantities are much more significant and more trustworthy than are those for values. From 1892 to 1894 there was rescinded a requirement of the Treasury Department that, for imports which were free of duty or subject to a specific duty, the invoices from countries whose currencies were depreciated must have attached a currency certificate giving the gold values of the local currency at the time of export. Brazil possessed such a depreciated currency, and the values of coffee imports from Brazil were uncertainly expressed in these years, the return being in some instances in terms of paper money and in others in terms of gold. An attempt was made by the Treasury Department to correct the figures for 1893 by reducing the value of the coffee imports from Brazil by $60,000,000, which explains the much lower figure for the import value of that year.[1] But since the figures for 1892 were not thus corrected, the great increase in the reported value of imports for that year is to be accounted for principally by the valuation in the depreciated Brazilian currency. In 1892 the quantity of coffee imported into the United States (almost wholly from Brazil) increased considerably; a similar increase occurred in the same year in the imports of Brazilian coffee into France and Germany. In that year the New York price of Brazilian coffee reached an unusually low level. Apparently, then, the increased purchases of coffee by the United States in 1892 were mainly due to a fall in price resulting from an exceptionally heavy crop in Brazil. The conclusion is that the fluctuation in the imports of coffee was not an effect of the tariff; and that, with the exception of the moderate tendency to increase—which might be attributed in part to the maintenance of coffee on the free list, the tariff act of 1890 had no tangible effect upon the imports of coffee.

Sugar.—In Table IV are presented data relating to the imports of sugar during the period under investigation.

[1] Monthly Summary of Imports and Exports of the United States, 1894, pp. 3–7. This correction may have been somewhat too large, as will appear from an examination of the figures in Table III.

TABLE IV.—*Imports of sugar into the United States, 1888–1897.*

Year.	Quantity.	Per cent increase in quantity over 3-year average, 1888-1890.	Value.	Per cent increase in value over 3-year average, 1888-1890.[1]	Average import price.	Per cent of imports to total sugar consumed.[3]	Domestic consumption per capita.	Raw-sugar market price, New York.[2]
	Pounds.				*Cents.*		*Pounds.*	*Cents.*
1888	2,700,284,282	....	$74,245,206	....	2.75	83.6	56.7	5.93
1889	2,762,202,967	....	88,543,971	....	3.21	84.3	51.8	6.57
1890	2,934,011,560	4.83	96,094,532	11.36	3.28	85.1	52.8	5.57
1891	3,483,477,222	24.46	105,728,216	22.52	3.03	85.5	66.1	3.92
1892	3,556,509,165	27.07	104,408,813	20.99	2.93	86.1	63.5	3.32
1893	3,766,445,347	34.57	116,255,784	34.72	3.09	85.1	63.9	3.69
1894	4,345,193,881	55.25	126,871,889	47.02	2.92	84.4	66.0	3.24
1895	3,574,510,454	27.71	76,462,836	*11.39*	2.15	80.6	62.6	3.23
1896	3,896,338,557	39.21	89,219,773	3.39	2.29	85.2	61.6	3.62
1897	4,918,905,733	75.75	99,066,181	14.80	2.01	84.0	64.5	3.56

[1] Decrease in italics.
[2] Calendar years.
[3] From figures given in U. S. statistical abstract, 1897, p. 293.

The figures of imports by quantities, taken together with the average import prices, show that the effect of the remission of duty upon the value of imports was concealed by the sharp decline in the import price of sugar. If the quantity figures for sugar be compared with the similar figures for coffee presented in Table II, it will be seen that the imports of sugar increased more rapidly in quantity than did those of coffee.

At no time during these years did the domestic sugar industry in the United States provide more than one-fifth of the domestic consumption of sugar. Since only an insignificant fraction of the imports was subjected to penalty duties, the remission of duty must have caused the price of sugar to be lower in the United States than it would have been if the previous duties had been retained, and it was partly responsible therefore for the fall in price.[1] The lower price of sugar led to an increase in the imports. The reduced price of sugar resulted in an increase in the per capita consumption of sugar from an average of 52.8 pounds in 1890 to from 62 to 64 pounds per year during the reciprocity period. The reimposition of a duty on sugar by the act of 1894 checked the fall in price, and led to a considerable decline in the imports and in the per capita consumption in the fiscal years 1895 and 1896. The sharp increase in the fiscal year 1897 in both quantity and value of imports is to be explained in large degree by unusually large purchases by importers in anticipation of the heavier duties on sugar imposed by the tariff act of 1897.

Molasses.—In the case of molasses, the data for which are presented in Table V, the quantity of imports had been declining since 1887.

---

[1] See pp. 129 seq. and 331 seq., infra, where similar reasoning is applied to the experiences under Hawaiian and Cuban reciprocity.

TABLE V.—*Imports of molasses into the United States, 1888–1897.*

| Year. | Imports. | | | | | Domestic production. | Manufacture of sugar from imported molasses. |
	Quantity.	Per cent increase in quantity over 3-year average, 1888–1890.[1]	Value.	Per cent increase in value over 3-year average, 1888–1890.[1]	Average import price.		
	Gallons.				Cents.	Gallons.	Tons.
1888	35,582,539	....	$5,491,095	....	2.75	26,631,501	58,840
1889	27,024,551	....	4,753,897	....	3.21	18,484,462	43,715
1890	31,497,243	0.41	5,168,795	0.60	3.28	22,381,988	53,282
1891	20,604,463	*34.32*	2,659,172	*48.25*	3.03	29,200,000	31,320
1892	22,118,209	*28.44*	2,877,744	*43.99*	2.93	20,629,868	30,000
1893	15,490,679	*50.62*	1,992,334	*61.22*	3.09	21,525,997	20,000
1894	19,670,663	*37.29*	1,984,778	*61.37*	2.92	26,908,726	15,000
1895	15,075,879	*51.94*	1,295,146	*74.79*	2.15	37,617,074	15,000
1896	4,687,664	*85.06*	737,265	*85.65*	2.29	27,232,957	603
1897	3,702,471	*88.20*	586,513	*88.58*	2.01	27,707,057	....

[1] Decreases in italics.

The remission of duties in April, 1891, failed to check this decline, which was more marked for the first full reciprocity year than it had been in any previous year. The fall in quantity of imports prior to 1890 was accompanied by a rise in the price of molasses, with the result that from 1887 to 1890 the value of imports was fairly constant. But, following 1890, there was a fall both in quantities imported and in prices. The lessening of the demand for foreign molasses is partly to be explained, apparently, by the increase in the domestic production which occurred during this period. But the imported and the domestic molasses were used at that time for different purposes. In the United States better methods of manufacture made possible the removal of a much larger proportion of sugar from the molasses, and it paid to import Cuban molasses for the purpose of removing the sugar therefrom. Later, as modern methods were introduced into the Cuban sugar industry, Cuban molasses approached more and more to the quality of the American product and became both less suitable for table use and of insufficient crystallizable sugar content to make profitable the further removal of sugar therefrom. Its imports into the United States consequently became negligible. The reimposition of a duty on molasses in 1894 still further checked the imports, and by 1897 the importation of molasses had practically ceased.

Hides.—The act of 1890, except in its provision for penalty duties, did not disturb the free admission of hides. The imports during the period under discussion supplied only a minor portion of the domestic consumption. The decline in the imports of hides in the fiscal year 1894[1] is probably a phase of the industrial depression of 1893; it contrasts with an increase in the imports of coffee and sugar in the same year. Only a small fraction of the hides imported was subjected to the penalty duties. No effect of the reciprocity provisions of the act of 1890 on the imports of hides is discoverable. ·

[1] See Table I, p. 165, infra.

IMPORTS BY GROUPS OF COUNTRIES.

Tables VI A and B give statistics of imports of reciprocity articles by specified countries and groups of countries.

TABLE VI-A.—IMPORTS OF RECIPROCITY ARTICLES INTO THE UNITED STATES, BY GROUPS OF COUNTRIES, 1888–1897.

Year.	Total value of imports of reciprocity articles.	From American reciprocity countries.				From Germany.		
		Value of reciprocity articles.	Per cent of total imports of reciprocity articles.	Per cent of total imports of all articles from all American reciprocity countries.	Value.	Per cent of total imports of reciprocity articles from all countries.	Per cent of total imports of all articles from Germany.
1888	$164,183,270	$101,333,683	61.72	77.8	$2,485,638	1.51	3.2
1889	193,150,500	118,107,008	61.15	81.4	6,963,417	3.60	8.5
1890	201,412,645	113,216,214	56.21	78.3	18,732,021	9.30	19.0
1891	232,441,924	140,551,121	60.47	78.9	13,932,977	5.99	14.3
1892	262,178,705	189,725,158	72.37	83.6	6,283,870	2.40	7.6
1893	227,081,572	150,342,580	66.20	79.8	10,727,190	4.72	11.1
1894	235,957,495	156,161,947	66.18	84.0	13,246,831	5.61	21.9
1895	200,011,641	122,252,266	61.12	78.6	8,799,516	4.40	10.9
1896	205,270,339	101,575,202	49.48	74.5	14,123,609	6.88	15.0
1897	209,060,104	87,008,769	41.62	70.4	31,840,429	15.23	28.6

Year.	From Austria-Hungary.			From nonpenalized nonreciprocity countries.			From penalized countries.		
	Value.	Per cent of total imports of reciprocity articles from all countries.	Per cent of total imports of all articles from Austria.	Value.	Per cent of total imports of reciprocity articles from all countries.	Per cent of total imports of all articles from nonpenalized nonreciprocity countries.	Value.	Per cent of total imports of reciprocity articles from all countries.	Per cent of total imports of all articles from penalized countries.
1888	$45,850	0.03	0.5	$45,598,348	27.77	9.3	$14,719,751	8.97	84.8
1889	277,253	.14	3.6	51,834,372	26.84	10.5	15,968,450	8.27	86.7
1890	1,616,555	.80	17.3	53,593,118	26.60	10.3	14,254,737	7.09	84.0
1891	4,034,965	1.73	34.8	56,903,925	24.47	10.6	17,018,936	7.32	84.7
1892	1,891,189	.72	24.5	49,646,253	18.93	10.1	14,632,235	5.58	82.9
1893	1,339,293	.59	13.3	59,486,260	26.20	10.6	5,186,339	2.29	65.4
1894	1,790,321	.75	26.0	60,673,346	25.71	15.4	4,085,050	1.73	62.5
1895	490,717	.24	7.5	54,726,867	27.36	11.6	13,741,275	6.95	83.1
1896	1,428,656	.70	18.7	74,231,366	36.16	14.1	13,911,506	6.78	85.3
1897	2,325,229	1.03	26.2	74,556,330	35.67	14.7	13,519,347	6.47	85.9

TABLE VI-B.—IMPORTS OF RECIPROCITY ARTICLES FROM AMERICAN RECIPROCITY COUNTRIES, 1888-1897.

Year.	Total.			Brazil.		
	Value of reciprocity articles.	Per cent of total imports of reciprocity articles.	Per cent of total imports of all articles from all American reciprocity countries.	Value.	Per cent of total imports of reciprocity articles from all countries.	Per cent of total imports of all articles from Brazil.
1888	$101,333,683	61.72	77.8	$41,873,998	25.51	78.0
1889	118,107,008	61.15	81.4	51,961,951	26.90	86.0
1890	113,216,214	56.21	78.3	49,501,260	24.57	83.4
1891	140,551,121	60.47	78.9	60,678,489	29.98	83.7
1892	189,725,158	72.37	83.6	103,035,951	39.30	86.9
1893	150,342,580	66.20	79.8	62,257,685	27.41	81.7
1894	156,161,947	66.18	84.0	67,507,581	28.62	85.1
1895	122,252,266	61.12	78.6	64,635,169	32.31	82.0
1896	101,575,202	49.43	74.5	59,963,402	29.21	84.4
1897	87,008,769	41.62	70.4	56,674,266	27.11	82.1

Year.	Cuba.			British West Indies.			All other American reciprocity countries.		
	Value.	Per cent of total imports of reciprocity articles from all countries.	Per cent of total imports of all articles from Cuba.	Value.	Per cent of total imports of reciprocity articles from all countries.	Per cent of total imports of all articles from British West Indies.	Value.	Per cent of total imports of reciprocity articles from all countries.	Per cent of total imports of all articles from other American reciprocity countries.
1888	$38,866,478	23.67	78.8	$8,148,610	4.96	64.9	$12,444,597	7.58	84.6
1889	39,900,019	20.66	76.5	11,699,342	6.06	73.2	14,544,796	7.53	87.3
1890	39,384,417	19.55	73.2	9,758,645	4.85	65.6	14,571,892	7.24	87.3
1891	47,186,402	20.30	76.5	9,760,193	4.20	59.9	13,926,037	5.99	82.3
1892	62,918,599	24.00	80.7	8,138,946	3.10	65.4	15,631,662	5.96	86.7
1893	61,998,252	27.30	78.8	10,833,337	4.77	67.6	15,253,306	6.72	87.5
1894	64,430,421	27.31	85.1	8,413,610	3.57	64.6	15,810,335	6.70	87.6
1895	40,951,042	20.47	77.5	5,026,777	2.51	51.4	11,639,278	5.82	84.2
1896	24,416,959	11.89	61.0	5,426,369	2.64	50.2	11,768,472	5.72	81.6
1897	12,681,829	6.06	68.9	6,394,686	3.06	52.0	11,257,938	5.39	80.9

The bulk of imports into the United States from the American countries with which reciprocity was arranged consisted of reciprocity articles, these forming 78 per cent of the total imports from these countries in 1890 and 84 per cent in 1894. This explains the effectiveness of the penalty duties in securing important tariff concessions from these countries. The imports from the penalized countries also consisted mainly of reciprocity articles, but of the imports from the other American non-reciprocity countries these articles formed only a small fraction. The reciprocity countries secured a larger percentage of the trade in reciprocity articles during the period of operation of the act of 1890, their proportion increasing from 56 per cent in 1890 to 66 per cent in 1894. The share of the non-penalized non-reciprocity countries remained about the same. The whole gain of the reciprocity countries was therefore at the cost, first, of the penalized countries, whose share of the trade in reciprocity articles fell from 7 per cent in 1890 to less than 2 per cent in 1894; and, second, of

Germany, whose share fell from 9 per cent in 1890 to about 6 per cent in 1894.

The decline of imports from Germany was due to the poor beet-sugar crops there in 1891 and 1892. The imports of sugar from Austria-Hungary were small prior to the act of 1890, and the remission of duty failed to stimulate the trade, except very slightly at the beginning of the reciprocity period. The reimposition of duties on sugar in 1894 caused Austrian sugar practically to disappear from the imports of 1895. The imports from Austria of reciprocity articles other than sugar were insignificant in amount.

THE EFFECT OF THE IMPOSITION OF PENALTY DUTIES.

The effectiveness of penalty duties as a check upon imports is evident in the experiences of the penalized countries: Colombia, Venezuela, and Haiti. The imports from these countries consisted more largely of coffee, hides, sugar, and molasses, than did the imports from the reciprocity countries. Immediately after the imposition of the penalty duties on the enumerated articles, their importation from the penalized countries fell to a small fraction of the former amounts. The penalty duties were levied from March 15, 1892, to August 27, 1894, so that the figures for the fiscal years 1893 and 1894 should best show their effect. In 1891, the first complete fiscal year immediately preceding the imposition of the penalty duties, the penalized countries furnished 7.32 per cent in value of the imports of the specified articles into the United States; in 1893 they furnished 2.29 per cent; and in 1894, 1.73 per cent. The fall in values was from $17,000,000 in 1891 to $4,000,000 in 1894. The removal of penalizing duties by the new tariff act of 1894 was followed by a marked increase in imports of the specified articles from these countries in the years 1895 to 1897, years during which similar imports from other countries, and especially from the reciprocity countries, were undergoing great reductions.

The influence of the penalty duties upon imports is directly traceable only in the experiences of the penalized countries. A more detailed analysis of the imports from these countries is, therefore, presented in Tables VII and VIII.

TABLE VII.—*Imports from penalized countries into the United States, 1888–1897.*
ALL PENALIZED COUNTRIES.

Year.	Total.		Reciprocity articles.			All other articles.	
	Value.	Per cent increase[1] over 3-year average, 1888–1890.	Value.	Per cent increase[1] over 3-year average, 1888–1890.	Per cent of total imports from penalized countries.	Value.	Per cent increase[1] over 3-year average, 1888–1890.
1888	$17,363,328		$14,719,751		84.77	$2,643,577	
1889	18,413,531		15,968,450		86.72	2,445,081	
1890	16,963,239	*3.51*	14,254,737		84.03	2,708,502	
1891	20,087,349	14.26	17,018,936	*4.85*	84.72	3,068,413	4.21
1892	17,644,953	37	14,632,235	13.60	82.92	3,012,718	18.06
1893	7,934,057	*54.87*	5,186,339	*2.33*	65.37	2,747,718	15.92
1894	6,539,414	*62.80*	4,085,050	*65.38*	62.47	2,454,364	5.72
1895	16,534,172	*5.95*	13,741,275	*72.73*	83.11	2,792,897	*5.56*
1896	16,317,621	7.18	13,911,508	*8.28*	85.25	2,406,113	7.46
1897	15,734,725	10.50	13,519,347	*7.14*	85.92	2,215,378	*7.42*

[1] Decreases in italics.

TABLE VII.—*Imports from penalized countries into the United States, 1888–1897*—Con.

VENEZUELA.

Year.	Total.		Reciprocity articles.			All other articles.	
	Value.	Per cent increase[1] over 3-year average, 1888–1890.	Value.	Per cent increase[1] over 3-year average, 1888–1890.	Per cent of total imports from Venezuela.	Value.	Per cent increase[1] over 3-year average, 1888–1890.
1888	$10,051,250	....	$9,771,020	....	97.21	$280,230	....
1889	10,392,569	....	10,000,473	....	96.23	392,096	....
1890	10,966,765	4.74	10,474,559	3.89	95.51	492,206	26.80
1891	12,078,541	15.36	11,713,366	16.18	96.98	365,175	5.93
1892	10,325,338	1.38	9,825,923	2.54	95.16	499,415	28.66
1893	3,625,118	65.38	3,110,884	69.14	85.81	514,234	32.47
1894	3,464,481	66.91	3,182,065	68.44	91.85	282,416	27.25
1895	10,073,951	3.78	9,736,944	3.42	96.65	337,007	13.18
1896	9,649,911	7.83	9,235,665	8.39	95.71	414,246	6.72
1897	9,543,572	8.85	9,109,193	9.65	95.45	434,379	11.90

COLOMBIA.

Year.	Total.		Reciprocity articles.			All other articles.	
	Value.	Per cent increase[1] over 3-year average, 1888–1890.	Value.	Per cent increase[1] over 3-year average, 1888–1890.	Per cent of total imports from Colombia.	Value.	Per cent increase[1] over 3-year average, 1888–1890.
1888	$4,393,258	....	$3,166,574	....	72.08	$1,226,684	....
1889	4,263,519	....	3,126,138	....	73.32	1,137,381	....
1890	3,575,253	18.31	2,479,540	15.20	69.35	1,095,713	4.99
1891	4,765,354	16.87	3,259,603	11.47	68.40	1,505,751	30.57
1892	4,116,886	.97	2,586,042	11.56	62.82	1,530,844	32.74
1893	3,572,918	12.37	2,057,482	29.64	57.59	1,515,436	31.40
1894	2,234,887	45.19	882,584	69.82	39.49	1,352,303	17.26
1895	3,713,682	8.92	2,182,484	25.36	58.77	1,531,198	32.77
1896	4,970,002	21.90	3,765,114	28.76	75.76	1,204,978	4.48
1897	4,730,933	16.03	3,429,669	17.29	72.49	1,301,264	12.83

HAITI.

Year.	Total.		Reciprocity articles.			All other articles.	
	Value.	Per cent increase[1] over 3-year average, 1888–1890.	Value.	Per cent increase[1] over 3-year average, 1888–1890.	Per cent of total imports from Haiti.	Value.	Per cent increase[1] over 3-year average, 1888–1890.
1888	$2,918,820	....	$1,782,157	....	61.06	$1,136,663	....
1889	3,757,443	....	2,841,839	....	75.63	915,604	....
1890	2,421,221	20.16	1,300,638	34.14	53.72	1,120,583	5.95
1891	3,243,454	6.96	2,045,967	3.60	63.08	1,197,487	10.93
1892	3,202,729	5.61	2,220,270	12.42	69.32	982,459	7.10
1893	736,021	75.73	17,973	99.09	2.44	718,048	32.11
1894	840,046	72.30	20,401	98.98	2.41	819,645	22.48
1895	2,746,539	9.43	1,821,847	7.75	66.33	924,692	12.57
1896	1,697,618	44.02	910,729	53.88	53.65	786,889	25.60
1897	1,460,220	51.85	980,485	50.35	67.15	479,735	54.64

[1] Decreases in italics.

TABLE VIII.—*Imports of coffee and hides from penalized countries into the United States, 1888–1897.*

ALL PENALIZED COUNTRIES.

Year.	Coffee.			Hides.		
	Value.	Per cent increase[1] over 3-year average 1888–1890.	Per cent of total imports of coffee into the United States.	Value.	Per cent increase[1] over 3-year average 1888–1890.	Per cent of total imports of hides into the United States.
1888	$12,324,990	....	20.37	$2,255,917	....	9.42
1889	14,105,748	....	18.88	1,830,963	....	7.29
1890	12,781,895	*2.21*	16.33	1,472,837	*20.53*	6.73
1891	15,295,628	17.02	15.91	1,690,264	8.79	6.05
1892	13,281,045	1.61	10.37	1,350,655	*27.12*	5.03
1893	3,865,524	*70.43*	4.80	1,320,815	*28.73*	4.66
1894	3,141,739	*75.97*	3.48	943,311	*49.10*	5.61
1895	12,376,733	*5.31*	12.88	1,361,195	*26.55*	5.20
1896	12,041,189	7.88	14.20	1,870,317	.92	6.13
1897	12,082,003	7.57	14.82	1,436,629	*22.48*	5.16

VENEZUELA.

Year.	Coffee.			Hides.		
	Value.	Per cent increase[1] over 3-year average 1888–1890.	Per cent of total imports of coffee into the United States.	Value.	Per cent increase[1] over 3-year average 1888–1890.	Per cent of total imports of hides into the United States.
1888	$8,863,599	....	14.65	$907,235	....	3.79
1889	9,138,591	....	12.23	861,882	....	3.43
1890	9,662,207	4.78	12.35	812,347	*5.59*	3.71
1891	10,814,874	17.28	11.25	898,492	4.42	3.22
1892	9,095,042	*1.37*	7.10	730,881	*15.08*	2.72
1893	2,472,343	*73.19*	3.07	638,541	*25.79*	2.25
1894	2,689,479	*70.83*	2.98	492,586	*42.75*	2.93
1895	8,872,179	*3.79*	9.23	864,765	*.50*	3.30
1896	8,128,254	*11.86*	9.59	1,107,411	28.70	3.63
1897	8,300,672	*9.99*	10.18	808,509	*6.04*	2.90

COLOMBIA.

Year.	Coffee.			Hides.		
	Value.	Per cent increase[1] over 3-year average 1888–1890.	Per cent of total imports of coffee into the United States.	Value.	Per cent increase[1] over 3-year average 1888–1890.	Per cent of total imports of hides into the United States.
1888	$1,749,862	....	2.89	$1,293,158	....	5.40
1889	2,170,963	....	2.91	927,866	....	3.69
1890	1,849,441	*3.85*	2.36	630,099	*33.70*	2.88
1891	2,491,811	29.55	2.59	767,743	*19.22*	2.75
1892	1,988,679	3.39	1.55	597,363	*37.14*	2.22
1893	1,392,252	*27.62*	1.73	665,230	*30.00*	2.35
1894	443,765	*76.93*	.49	438,819	*53.83*	2.61
1895	1,698,250	11.71	1.77	480,887	*49.40*	1.84
1896	3,029,947	57.53	3.57	735,165	*22.64*	2.41
1897	2,834,631	47.37	3.47	595,038	*37.39*	2.13

[1] Decreases in italics.

TABLE VIII.—*Imports of coffee and hides from penalized countries into the United States, 1888–1897.*

HAITI.

Year.	Coffee.			Hides.		
	Value.	Per cent increase over 3-[1] year average 1888-1890.	Per cent of total imports of coffee into the United States.	Value.	Per cent increase over 3-[1] year average 1888-1890.	Per cent of total imports of hides into the United States.
1888	$1,711,529		2.83	$55,524		0.23
1889	2,706,194		3.74	41,215		.16
1890	1,270,247	*34.05*	1.62	30,391	*28.28*	.14
1891	1,988,943	3.27	2.07	24,029	*43.80*	.08
1892	2,197,294	14.09	1.72	22,411	*47.12*	.08
1893	929	*99.99*		17,044	*59.78*	.06
1894	8,495	*99.56*	.01	11,906	*71.90*	.07
1895	1,806,304	*6.21*	1.88	15,543	*63.32*	.06
1896	882,988	*54.15*	1.04	27,741	*34.54*	.09
1897	946,700	*50.85*	1.16	33,082	*21.93*	.12

[1] Decreases in italics.

The imports from these countries consisted in great part of reciprocity articles, coffee and hides constituting almost the whole. Imports of coffee and hides, as well as of the other specified articles from each of these countries, underwent very great reductions during the operation of the penalty duties. From Colombia and Venezuela imports of other than the specified articles showed moderate increases. In Haiti political disturbances came at the same time as the penalty duties, and the imports from this country dwindled to a petty fraction of their former amount; but even here the reduction in the volume of imports was much greater for the penalized articles than for other articles. In all three countries the recovery of exports to the United States following the removal of the penalty duties in August, 1894, was immediate and sharp. The effect of the penalty duties is shown even more clearly in the figures given in Table VIII for individual commodities, especially coffee, of which the imports from the penalized countries fell from $12,700,000 in 1890 to $3,000,000 in 1894, and from 16.33 per cent of the total imports of coffee in 1890 to 3.48 per cent in 1894.

EFFECT UPON EXPORTS.

An analysis of the exports is presented in the following pages. Additional difficulties confront the attempt to analyze the exports in view of differences in the schedules of articles, the rates of concession, and the dates of enactment and termination of the various reciprocity agreements, no two of which were exactly alike. With the exception of Germany, however, all the reciprocity countries granted concessions covering the bulk of their imports from the United States, and, with the exception of Brazil, all the concessions became effective in the fiscal year 1892, and if withdrawn at all, were withdrawn in the fiscal year 1895. For summary analysis, the period 1892 to 1895 may, therefore, be taken as a rough approximation to the reciprocity period.

EXPORTS BY GROUPS OF COUNTRIES.

In Table IX the exports to the reciprocity countries are compared with the exports to all countries and with those to non-reciprocity countries.

TABLE IX.—*Domestic exports from the United States, by groups of countries, 1888–1897.*

Year.	Total exports.		American reciprocity countries.			American nonreciprocity, nonpenalized countries (excluding Canada and Newfoundland).		
	Value.	Per cent increase in value over 3-year average, 1888–1890.	Value.	Per cent increase in value over 3-year average, 1888–1890.	Per cent of total exports.	'Value.	Per cent increase in value over 3-year average, 1888–1890.[1]	Per cent of total exports.
1888	$683,862,104		$31,669,688		4.63	$25,721,018		3.76
1889	730,282,609		36,921,301		5.06	31,030,207		4.25
1890	845,293,828	12.24	41,837,234	13.66	4.95	35,049,135	14.54	4.15
1891	872,270,283	15.82	45,666,569	24.06	5.23	29,188,355	*4.61*	3.35
1892	1,015,732,011	34.87	50,285,700	36.61	4.95	29,150,191	*4.74*	2.87
1893	831,030,785	10.34	53,507,309	45.36	6.44	35,346,043	15.51	4.25
1894	869,204,937	15.41	52,874,013	43.64	6.08	27,430,669	*10.36*	3.16
1895	793,392,599	5.34	45,574,863	23.81	5.75	29,747,946	*2.78*	3.75
1896	863,200,487	14.61	41,242,347	12.04	4.78	36,593,224	19.59	4.24
1897	1,032,007,603	37.03	38,654,362	5.01	3.75	40,313,753	31.74	3.91

Year.	Penalized countries.			Germany.		
	Value.	Per cent increase in value over 3-year average, 1888–1890.[1]	Per cent of total exports.	Value.	Per cent increase in value over 3-year average, 1888–1890.	Per cent of total exports.
1888	$12,254,248		1.79	$55,624,264		8.13
1889	11,408,127		1.56	66,568,695		9.11
1890	11,608,095	*1.27*	1.37	84,315,215	22.49	9.98
1891	13,414,214	14.10	1.54	91,684,981	33.20	10.51
1892	12,020,804	2.25	1.19	104,180,732	51.35	10.26
1893	12,360,305	5.13	1.49	81,992,572	19.11	9.87
1894	12,134,468	3.21	1.40	90,065,108	30.84	10.36
1895	10,965,078	*6.73*	1.38	90,615,551	31.64	11.42
1896	11,195,043	*4.78*	1.30	96,364,368	39.99	11.16
1897	10,642,016	*9.48*	1.03	123,784,453	79.83	11.99

Year.	Austria-Hungary.			All other countries.		
	Value.	Per cent increase in value over 3-year average, 1888–1890.[1]	Per cent of total exports.	Value.	Per cent increase in value over 3-year average, 1888–1890.	Per cent of total exports.
1888	$331,662		0.05	$558,264,224		81.64
1889	720,825		.10	583,633,454		79.92
1890	945,703	41.98	.11	671,538,446	11.09	79.44
1891	1,215,540	82.50	.14	691,100,624	14.33	79.23
1892	1,485,233	122.99	.15	818,609,351	35.42	80.58
1893	542,073	*18.62*	.06	647,282,483	7.08	77.89
1894	526,721	*20.92*	.06	686,173,958	13.51	78.94
1895	2,059,742	209.24	.26	614,429,419	1.65	77.44
1896	2,370,901	255.96	.27	675,434,604	11.74	78.25
1897	3,759,700	464.47	.36	814,853,319	34.80	78.96

[1] Decreases in italics.

The reciprocity period was one of general industrial depression, and in Latin America of revolutionary disturbances as well. The total exports from the United States, therefore, showed no tendency to increase and, with the exception of 1892, were lower in all the years of the reciprocity period than in 1891. Exports in 1892, it is true, were much greater than those of any previous year. The explanation lies entirely in the bumper crops in the United States in 1891 and the partial crop failures in Europe which increased the prices of and the demand for American foodstuffs; for the year 1892 showed a large decrease in exports other than foodstuffs. During the reciprocity period the exports to the American non-reciprocity countries decreased in about the same proportion as the total exports. The figures of exports to the American reciprocity countries stand out in sharp contrast, showing considerable gains throughout the reciprocity period. The exports to Germany and to Austria-Hungary both decreased during the reciprocity period except in the abnormal year 1892. Upon the termination of reciprocity, the exports to American reciprocity countries again present a contrast, for they decreased sharply, although the years after 1895 marked expanding trade with all other groups of countries. On the other hand, the exports to Germany and Austria-Hungary show no effect of the termination of reciprocity, for while they decreased under reciprocity, they increased considerably upon its termination. But neither Germany nor Austria-Hungary withdrew the reductions in duties which they had granted in 1892, and American products continued after 1894 to receive the same tariff treatment from these countries that they had received during the period in which the agreements were effective.

In order to indicate to what extent increases in exports may be attributed to the reciprocity concessions, there is presented in Table X a comparison of the total exports with the exports of the more important articles figuring in the reciprocity agreements.

TABLE X.—*Domestic exports from the United States, by classes of articles, 1888–1897.*

Year.	Total exports.		Breadstuffs.			Selected provisions.[1]		
	Value.	Per cent increase over 3-year average, 1888–1890.	Value.	Per cent increase over 3-year average, 1888–1890.[2]	Per cent of total exports.	Value.	Per cent increase over 3-year average, 1888–1890.	Per cent of total exports.
1888	$683,862,104	....	$127,191,687	....	18.60	$70,463,601	....	10.32
1889	730,282,609	....	123,876,661	....	16.96	79,004,798	....	10.82
1890	845,293,828	12.24	154,925,927	14.48	18.33	103,531,338	22.72	12.25
1891	872,270,283	15.82	128,121,656	*5.33*	14.69	105,661,125	25.24	12.11
1892	1,015,732,011	34.87	299,363,117	121.21	29.47	102,711,812	21.74	10.11
1893	831,030,785	10.34	200,312,654	48.02	24.10	99,373,104	17.79	11.96
1894	869,204,937	15.41	166,777,229	23.24	19.19	106,480,313	26.21	12.25
1895	793,392,599	5.34	114,604,780	*15.32*	14.44	102,008,520	20.91	12.86
1896	863,200,487	14.61	141,356,993	4.45	16.38	97,511,000	15.63	11.30
1897	1,032,007,603	37.03	197,857,219	46.20	19.17	96,622,506	14.63	·9.37

[1] Beef, canned, salted or pickled, and other cured, tallow, bacon, hams, pickled pork, lard, mutton, poultry and game, and all other meat products except fresh beef, fresh pork, and oleomargarine.
[2] Decreases in italics

TABLE X.—*Domestic exports from the United States, by classes of articles, 1888–1897*—
Continued.

Year.	Iron and steel and manufactures thereof.			Wood and manufacturers thereof.			All others.		
	Value.	Per cent increase over 3-year average, 1888–1890.	Per cent of total exports.	Value.	Per cent increase over 3-year average, 1888–1890.[1]	Per cent of total exports.	Value.	Per cent increase over 3-year average, 1888–1890.[1]	Per cent of total exports.
1888	$20,948,321	....	3.06	$23,063,108	....	3.37	$442,195,387	....	64.65
1889	25,584,289	....	3.50	26,910,672	....	3.69	474,906,189	....	65.03
1890	30,530,345	18.85	3.61	28,274,529	8.40	3.34	528,031,689	9.62	62.47
1891	33,482,846	30.35	3.84	26,270,040	.72	3.01	578,734,616	20.15	66.35
1892	33,694,115	31.17	3.32	25,790,571	*1.12*	2.55	554,172,396	15.05	54.55
1893	35,774,097	39.27	4.30	26,666,439	2.24	3.21	468,904,491	*2.65*	56.43
1894	35,412,213	37.86	4.07	27,712,169	6.25	3.19	532,823,013	10.62	61.30
1895	39,049,769	52.02	4.92	27,115,907	3.96	3.42	510,613,623	6.01	64.36
1896	48,388,066	88.37	5.60	31,947,108	22.48	3.70	543,997,320	12.94	63.02
1897	63,461,240	147.05	6.15	39,624,800	51.92	3.84	634,401,838	31.70	61.47

[1] Decreases in italics.

The exports of specified articles show in some cases increases in years when total exports decreased, in other cases smaller decreases than those shown by the total exports. The gains were most marked in breadstuffs and in manufactures of iron and steel.

EXPORTS BY COMMODITIES.

Breadstuffs.—In Table XI are presented data relating to the exports of breadstuffs. As a rule the exports of such commodities as breadstuffs are for short periods more dependent upon crop conditions than upon rates of duty.

TABLE XI.—*Domestic exports of breadstuffs from the United States, 1888–1897.*

Year.	Total exports of breadstuffs.			To American reciprocity countries.		
	Value.	Per cent increase over 3-year average, 1888–1890.[1]	Per cent of total exports of all articles.	Value.	Per cent increase over 3-year average, 1888–1890.[1]	Per cent of total exports of breadstuffs.
1888	$127,191,687	....	18.60	$9,040,554	....	7.11
1889	123,876,661	....	16.96	10,541,712	....	8.51
1890	154,925,927	14.48	18.33	11,688,654	12.13	7.55
1891	128,121,656	*5.33*	14.69	11,943,952	14.59	9.33
1892	299,363,117	121.21	29.47	14,082,896	35.11	4.70
1893	200,312,654	48.02	24.10	12,876,526	23.53	6.43
1894	166,777,229	23.24	19.19	12,574,335	20.63	7.54
1895	114,604,786	*15.32*	14.44	9,232,877	*11.43*	8.05
1896	141,356,993	4.45	16.38	9,503,121	*8.83*	6.72
1897	197,857,219	46.20	19.17	9,953,632	*4.51*	5.03

[1] Decreases in italics.

TABLE XI.—*Domestic exports of breadstuffs from the United States, 1888–1897*—Contd.

Year.	To European reciprocity countries.			To all other countries.		
	Value.	Per cent increase over 3-year average, 1888–1890.[1]	Per cent of total exports of breadstuffs.	Value.	Per cent increase over 3-year average, 1888–1890.[1]	Per cent of total exports of breadstuffs.
1888	$1,423,366	....	1.12	$116,727,767	....	91.77
1889	2,415,740	....	1.95	110,919,209	....	89.54
1890	5,241,126	73.20	3.38	127,996,147	13.22	89.07
1891	2,528,038	*16.46*	1.97	113,649,666	*6.75*	88.70
1892	19,573,509	546.82	6.54	265,706,712	118.01	88.76
1893	6,806,976	124.91	3.40	180,629,157	48.20	90.17
1894	8,189,984	170.62	4.91	146,012,910	19.80	87.55
1895	4,107,259	35.72	3.58	101,264,644	*16.92*	88.37
1896	7,333,794	142.33	5.19	124,519,386	2.16	88.09
1897	18,042,026	496.23	9.12	169,861,561	39.37	85.85

[1] Decreases in italics.

The increases in the exports of breadstuffs in 1892 and 1893 were undoubtedly due to the coincidence of exceptionally good crops here with abnormally poor crops in Europe. Of the increase of $171,000,000 in the export of breadstuffs in 1892 as compared with 1891, only $2,000,000 is accounted for by increase in exports to American reciprocity countries, and $17,000,000 by increased exports to Germany. The exports to Austria were negligible throughout the reciprocity period. Exports of breadstuffs during the reciprocity period showed relatively smaller increases in the amounts sent to the American reciprocity countries than to other countries. Reciprocity apparently failed, therefore, to increase to any important extent the export of breadstuffs to American reciprocity countries. On the other hand, the large increases in total exports to these countries can not, for this reason, be attributed to exceptional crop conditions.

Manufactures of iron and steel.—The effect of the reciprocity concessions upon exports is most strikingly shown in the figures for manufactures of iron and steel given in Table XII.

TABLE XII.—*Domestic exports of manufactures of iron and steel from the United States, 1888–1897.*[1]

Year.	Total exports of manufactures of iron and steel.			To American reciprocity countries.			To all other countries.		
	Value.	Per cent increase over 3-year average, 1888–1890.	Per cent of total exports of all articles.	Value.	Per cent increase over 3-year average, 1888–1890.	Per cent of total exports of manufactures of iron and steel.	Value.	Per cent increase over 3-year average, 1888–1890.	Per cent of total exports of manufactures of iron and steel.
1888	$20,948,321	....	3.06	$3,058,525	....	14.60	$17,889,796	....	85.40
1889	25,584,289	....	3.50	4,123,246	....	16.12	21,461.043	....	83.88
1890	30,530,345	18.85	3.61	5,479,750	29.83	17.95	25,050,595	16.69	82.05
1891	33,482,846	30.35	3.84	7,813,849	85.14	23.34	25,668,997	19.57	76.66
1892	33,694,115	31.17	3.32	8,574,388	103.18	25.40	25,119,727	17.01	74.60
1893	35,774,097	39.27	4.30	10,672,505	152.89	29.83	25,101,592	16.93	70.17
1894	35,412,213	37.86	4.07	8,048,028	90.71	22.73	27,364,183	27.47	77.27
1895	39,049,769	52.02	4.92	8,151,562	93.15	20.87	30,898,207	43.93	79.13
1896	48,388,066	88.37	5.60	5,624,963	33.27	11.62	42,763,103	99.20	88.38
1897	63,461,240	147.05	6.15	4,577,290	8.46	7.22	58,883,950	174.79	92.78

[1] Includes also agricultural implements and scientific instruments. Excludes pig iron.

Total exports of these articles increased somewhat in 1891, but the greater part of this increase went to reciprocity countries. No concessions other than those made by Brazil came into effect until after the beginning of the fiscal year 1892; but the trade with Brazil, that country having made its concessions effective on April 1, 1891, accounted for more than half of the increase in the United States exports of these articles to reciprocity countries in 1891. The available data, however, do not indicate whether or not the increase in 1891 in the exports to Brazil resulted from reciprocity. After 1891 the total exports of iron and steel manufactures remained practically constant, whereas from 1891 on the exports to reciprocity countries were considerably greater than they had been in 1890. Upon the termination of the concessions, the exports to reciprocity countries dropped from the high level of more than $8,000,000 in each of the years 1894 and 1895 to $5,600,000 in 1896 and $4,500,000 in 1897. On the other hand, the exports of the same articles to non-reciprocity countries increased during the same years from $30,000,000 in 1895 to $42,000,000 in 1896 and to $58,000,000 in 1897. Again it is impossible to determine with certainty to what extent the changes in exports noted above resulted from the termination of reciprocity.

EXPORTS TO AMERICAN RECIPROCITY COUNTRIES.

In Table XIII are presented the figures of total exports to each of the American reciprocity countries.

The introduction of reciprocity was not followed in every case by an increase in exports. Only in the cases of Cuba, Porto Rico, and Brazil were such increases as occurred considerable. The exports to the British West Indies remained practically constant. In the case of three of the Central American Republics the introduction of reciprocity was marked by decreases in exports. But during this period there was taking place a general decline in imports into the West Indies, due, in part at least, to the commercial depression which resulted, in the sugar growing islands, from the glutting of the British market with the bounty-fed European beet sugar. The Central American reciprocity countries, Nicaragua, Honduras, and Guatemala, whose imports from the United States fell during the reciprocity period, were at this time feeling most keenly the effects of the prevalent industrial depression. Furthermore, these countries were so little developed economically and so lacking in the necessary commercial machinery, and the exports to them prior to reciprocity were so slight, that it would be unwarrantable to expect to find that there had been an appreciable response to tariff concessions which remained in force for so short a period. The panic of 1893 was felt most keenly in Brazil, Honduras, and Nicaragua, and it is to these countries that the exports showed the most marked reductions in amount in the fiscal years 1893 and 1894.

A more detailed analysis of United States exports to several of the more important reciprocity countries follows.

TABLE XIII.—*Domestic exports from the United States to American reciprocity countries, 1888-1897.*

Country.	Concessional period.	1888	1889	1890	1891	1892	1893	1894	1895	1896	1897
Brazil	Apr. 1, 1891–Jan. 1, 1895.	$7,063,892	$9,276,511	$11,902,496	$14,049,273	$14,240,009	$12,355,584	$15,827,914	$15,135,125	$14,222,934	$12,406,785
Per cent increase over 3-year average, 1888–1890.				26.43	49.23	51.26	31.02	46.88	60.77	51.08	31.79
Cuba	Sept. 1, 1891–Aug. 27, 1894.	$9,721,124	$11,297,198	$12,669,509	$11,929,605	$17,622,411	$23,604,064	$19,855,237	$12,533,260	$7,212,348	$7,599,757
Per cent increase over 3-year average 1888–1890.				12.82	6.23	56.92	110.18	75.80	11.60	*34.89*	*32.33*
Porto Rico	Sept. 1, 1891–Aug. 27, 1894.	$1,920,358	$2,175,458	$2,247,700	$2,112,334	$2,808,631	$2,502,788	$2,705,646	$1,820,203	$2,080,400	$1,964,850
Per cent increase over 3-year average 1888–1890.				6.30	*0.16*	32.83	18.36	27.96	*13.92*	*1.61*	*7.08*
Dominican Republic	Sept. 1, 1891–Sept. 24, 1894.	$792,560	$1,150,651	$926,651	$986,826	$984,188	$1,108,733	$1,715,782	$1,318,919	$1,019,242	$1,045,037
Per cent increase over 3-year average, 1888–1890.				*3.13*	3.15	2.88	15.99	79.36	37.87	6.55	9.24
British West Indies	Feb. 1, 1892–Aug. 27, 1894.	$7,450,018	$8,197,693	$8,074,433	$9,546,058	$8,886,137	$8,855,943	$9,287,496	$8,465,349	$9,460,989	$8,638,187
Per cent increase over 3-year average, 1888–1890.				2.11	20.72	12.38	9.24	19.65	7.06	17.45	12.00
Salvador	Feb. 1, 1892–	$645,302	$690,884	$886,231	$1,134,995	$1,274,021	$1,118,054	$1,059,292	$1,236,595	$1,582,217	$1,596,881
Per cent increase over 3-year average, 1888–1890.				19.65	53.21	71.98	50.92	42.99	66.93	113.58	115.56
Nicaragua	Mar. 12, 1892–Jan. 9, 1895.	$861,156	$900,813	$1,270,072	$1,592,013	$1,187,189	$812,654	$314,012	$967,329	$1,089,320	$1,058,664
Per cent increase over 3-year average, 1888–1890.				25.67	57.52	17.46	*19.59*	*19.46*	*4.29*	7.78	2.77
British Guiana	Apr. 1, 1892–Aug. 27, 1894.	$1,651,711	$1,643,249	$2,011,122	$1,761,350	$1,885,542	$1,953,012	$2,330,938	$1,684,830	$1,719,705	$1,532,115
Per cent increase over 3-year average, 1888–1890.				13.71	*0.42*	6.61	10.42	33.48	*4.74*	*2.77*	13.58
Honduras	May 25, 1892–	$672,796	$618,973	$522,631	$583,114	$478,947	$442,907	$537,463	$615,009	$556,893	$669,682
Per cent increase over 3-year average, 1888–1890.				*13.59*	3.69	*20.81*	*26.77*	11.15	1.69	7.92	10.73
Guatemala	May 30, 1892–Sept. 24, 1891.	$887,771	$969,871	$1,326,388	$1,971,001	$1,809,577	$1,713,142	$1,610,509	$2,596,032	$3,092,323	$2,992,118
Per cent increase over 3-year average, 1888–1890.				24.97	35.71	70.50	61.41	51.74	144.60	191.36	181.92
Total		$31,669,688	$36,921,301	$41,837,234	$45,666,569	$51,176,652	$54,450,911	$53,774,289	$46,372,651	$42,136,371	$39,484,056
Per cent increase over 3-year average, 1888–1890.				12.66	24.06	39.03	47.93	46.09	25.98	14.47	7.27

¹ Decreases in italics.   ² Includes Bermuda.

Exports to Cuba.—Cuba granted a long list of concessions, covering almost the entire range of the imports, both of natural products and of manufactures, which she took from the United States. The rates of concession varied from a reduction of 25 per cent to a complete remission of duty, and, owing to the generally high level of the Cuban duties, the concessions amounted to substantial reductions from the rates previously in force on American products. They were far from sufficient, however, to equalize the rates on imports from Spain and from the United States, and on many important articles the preference to the mother country remained substantial enough to be practically prohibitive of American imports. The rates granted to the United States were not extended to any other country, although one country, at least, Great Britain, made demands for such extension by virtue of her most-favored-nation treaty with Spain.

TABLE XIV.—*Domestic exports from the United States to Cuba, 1888–1897.*

(Concessional period, Sept. 1, 1891, to Aug. 27, 1894.)

Year.	All articles exported.		Concessional articles.					
			All concessional articles.			Iron and steel and manufactures thereof.		
	Value.	Per cent increase over 3-year average, 1888–1890.[1]	Value.	Per cent increase over 3-year average, 1888–1890.[1]	Per cent of all articles exported.	Value.	Per cent increase over 3-year average, 1888–1890.[1]	Per cent of all articles exported.
1888	$9,724,124	....	$8,911,752	....	91.65	$1,048,869	....	10.79
1889	11,297,198	....	10,349,604	....	91.61	1,760,845	....	15.59
1890	12,669,509	12.82	11,394,896	11.50	89.94	2,360,808	36.98	18.63
1891	11,929,605	6.23	10,419,929	1.97	87.34	2,446,185	41.93	20.51
1892	17,622,411	56.92	15,726,768	53.90	69.24	3,652,045	111.90	20.72
1893	23,604,094	110.18	20,915,743	104.69	88.61	5,275,190	206.07	22.35
1894	19,855,237	76.80	17,736,444	73.58	89.33	3,811,604	121.15	19.20
1895	12,533,260	11.60	11,124,644	8.87	88.76	2,228,028	29.27	17.78
1896	7,512,348	*55.11*	6,367,236	*57.69*	84.76	604,659	*64.92*	8.05
1897	7,629,757	*52.07*	6,260,937	*58.74*	82.06	310,417	*81.99*	4.09

Year.	Concessional articles.								
	Breadstuffs.			Provisions.			Wood and manufactures thereof.		
	Value.	Per cent increase over 3-year average, 1888–1890.[1]	Per cent of all articles exported.	Value.	Per cent increase over 3-year average, 1888–1890.[1]	Per cent of all articles exported.	Value.	Per cent increase over 3-year average, 1888–1890.[1]	Per cent of all articles exported.
1888	$1,387,752	....	14.27	$2,615,475	....	26.90	$1,320,536	....	13.58
1889	1,336,047	....	11.83	3,209,787	....	28.41	1,110,946	....	9.83
1890	1,520,617	7.48	12.00	2,853,968	*1.35*	22.53	1,208,476	*0.40*	9.54
1891	874,979	*58.16*	7.33	2,735,566	*5.44*	22.93	1,190,556	*1.88*	9.98
1892	2,305,031	62.92	13.08	4,128,817	42.71	23.43	1,528,953	26.01	8.68
1893	3,512,207	148.25	14.88	5,565,584	92.38	23.58	1,881,095	55.04	7.97
1894	3,164,541	123.67	15.94	5,008,532	73.12	25.22	1,571,297	29.50	7.91
1895	1,569,004	10.90	12.52	3,110,485	7.51	24.81	770,064	*56.55*	6.14
1896	774,792	*45.24*	10.31	2,340,939	*19.08*	31.16	490,396	*59.58*	6.53
1897	888,123	*57.23*	11.69	2,263,141	*21.77*	29.66	412,651	*65.99*	5.43

[1] Decreases in italics.

Table XIV.—*Domestic exports from the United States to Cuba, 1888–1897*—Cont'd.

| Year. | Concessional articles. | | | | All other articles. | |
| | Other concessional articles. | | | | | |
	Value.	Per cent increase over 3-year average, 1888–1890.[1]	Per cent of all articles exported.	Value.	Per cent increase over 3-year average, 1888–1890.	Per cent of all articles exported.
1888	$2,539,120	....	26.11	$812,372	....	8.35
1889	2,931,979	....	25.95	947,594	....	8.39
1890	3,451,027	16.04	27.24	1,274,613	26.09	10.06
1891	3,172,639	6.67	26.59	1,509,676	49.25	12.60
1892	4,111,925	38.26	23.33	1,895,643	87.80	10.76
1893	4,681,668	57.41	19.83	2,688,350	165.77	11.39
1894	4,180,460	40.56	21.06	2,118,793	109.46	10.67
1895	3,447,057	15.90	27.51	1,408,616	39.26	11.24
1896	2,156,450	*27.49*	28.71	1,145,112	13.21	15.24
1897	2,386,605	*19.75*	31.28	1,368,820	35.32	17.94

[1] Decreases in italics.

The American exports to Cuba, data for which are presented in Table XIV, fell somewhat from 1890 to 1891 (prior to reciprocity), but rose from about $12,000,000 in 1891 to over $23,000,000 in 1893 and over $19,000,000 in 1894. They fell again to $12,000,000 in 1895, during ten months of which year the concessions were no longer in effect. Prior to reciprocity the exports of concessional articles had generally formed over 90 per cent of the total exports of the United States to Cuba, and had been gradually declining, until in 1891 they were only 87 per cent. During the reciprocity period they rose again to about 89 per cent, but upon the termination of reciprocity they dropped to 85 per cent in 1896 and to 82 per cent in 1897. From 1895 to 1897 all classes of exports to Cuba showed great declines, due no doubt to the revolutionary disturbances, but the fall in exports of concessional articles was much greater than that in other articles, showing the effect of the termination of the reciprocity concessions. The increase in United States exports to Cuba during the reciprocity period was not more marked in breadstuffs than in other concessional commodities.

In order to determine whether or not the increased exports of the United States to Cuba are to be explained as simply part of a general increase in Cuban imports, there are presented in Tables XV to XVII statistics of exports to Cuba from European countries.

TABLE XV.—*Total domestic exports from the United States to Cuba and Porto Rico compared with exports from Spain, the United Kingdom, France, and Germany, 1889–1897.*[1]

Year.	Total exports to Cuba and Porto Rico from specified countries.	United States.		Spain.	
		Value.	Per cent of total exports from specified countries.	Value.	Per cent of total exports from specified countries.
1889	$49,865,794	$13,472,656	27.02	$19,127,072	38.36
1890	55,004,841	14,917,209	27.12	21,238,609	38.61
1891	55,311,717	14,041,939	25.39	25,473,293	46.05
1892	69,020,306	20,431,042	29.60	31,975,822	46.33
1893	69,856,462	26,106,882	37.37	29,342,396	42.00
1894	63,115,556	22,560,883	35.74	28,127,971	44.57
1895	59,634,303	14,353,463	24.07	34,871,045	58.48
1896	50,494,719	9,392,748	18.60	33,219,601	65.79
1897		9,564,607			

Year.	United Kingdom.		France.		Germany.	
	Value.	Per cent of total exports from specified countries.	Value.	Per cent of total exports from specified countries.	Value.	Per cent of total exports from specified countries.
1889	$13,466,360	27.00	$2,140,370	4.29	$1,659,336	3.32
1890	14,158,123	25.74	2,644,100	4.81	2,046,800	3.72
1891	12,108,140	21.89	1,989,016	3.60	1,699,320	3.07
1892	13,307,444	19.29	1,408,900	2.04	1,897,098	2.74
1893	11,001,079	15.75	1,290,047	1.85	2,116,058	3.03
1894	9,280,853	14.70	1,013,845	1.61	2,132,004	3.38
1895	8,001,567	13.42	752,700	1.26	1,655,528	2.77
1896	5,851,708	11.59	431,778	.86	1,598,884	3.13
1897	5,088,271		237,825		1,377,306	

[1] From data in U. S. Monthly Summary of imports and exports, February, 1899. Figures for United States are for fiscal years; all others are for calendar years.

TABLE XVI.—*Domestic exports of manufactures of iron and steel from the United States to Cuba and Porto Rico, compared with similar exports from the United Kingdom, Germany, and France, 1890–1897.*[1]

Year.	Total manufactures of iron and steel exported to Cuba and Porto Rico from specified countries.	United States.		United Kingdom.		Germany.		France.	
		Value.[2]	Per cent of total from specified countries.	Value.	Per cent of total from specified countries.	Value.	Per cent of total from specified countries.	Value.	Per cent of total from specified countries.
1890	$5,138,039	$2,936,651	57.16	$1,924,409	37.45	$342,958	6.67	$87,766	1.71
1891	5,292,812	3,303,639	62.42	1,862,882	35.20	360,570	6.81	72,003	1.29
1892	6,844,879	4,595,732	67.14	1,850,808	27.04	338,912	4.95	63,318	.93
1893	8,566,396	6,983,127	81.52	1,335,095	15.58	247,044	2.88	65,780	.77
1894	6,327,020	4,966,833	78.50	1,100,165	17.39	196,112	3.10	66,990	1.06
1895	4,168,249	2,884,107	69.19	1,074,314	25.77	176,596	4.24	24,217	.58
1896	2,057,761	946,782	46.01	704,888	34.25	405,552	19.71	17,324	.84
1897	1,614,906	614,522	38.05	922,450	57.12	76,160	4.72	13,487	.84

[1] From official reports of the several countries.
[2] Including agricultural implements.

TABLE XVII.—*Domestic exports of cotton goods from the United States to Cuba and Porto Rico, compared with similar exports from Spain, the United Kingdom, Germany, and France, 1890–1897.*[1]

Year.	Total cotton goods exported to Cuba and Poto Rico from specified countries.	United States.		Spain, value.	United Kingdom, value.	Germany, value.	France, value.
		Value.	Per cent of total from specified countries.				
1890	$7,423,630	$170,462	2.29	$3,703,904	$3,255,212	$143,276	$150,776
1891	6,480,948	124,328	1.92	3,883,345	2,303,159	125,188	44,928
1892	8,473,017	148,160	1.75	5,845,154	2,306,166	111,622	64,284
1893	9,279,398	163,922	1.77	6,793,353	2,055,872	103,530	161,293
1894	8,417,313	141,467	1.68	6,217,698	1,894,825	71,162	92,081
1895	7,359,152	82,721	1.12	5,891,039	1,261,299	52,598	71,495
1896	7,293,186	90,377	1.24	6,014,083	1,135,651	34,034	17,425
1897	1,204,242	79,454	6.60	....	725,306	20,706	7,898

[1] From official reports of the several countries.

These figures indicate that the concessions granted to the United States diverted a portion of Cuba's trade from the European countries to the United States, for the increases in the American exports to Cuba during the reciprocity period contrast with decreases in the exports of France, Germany, and the United Kingdom, and with relatively smaller increases in the exports of Spain. While the decreases in total exports to Cuba in 1896 and 1897—or after the termination of reciprocity—were relatively less for the United States than for the other countries, with the exception of Spain, the exports of the selected concessional articles show the effects of the termination of the concessions, for they underwent much greater reductions in these years than did the similar exports from European countries, again with the exception of Spain. As has been pointed out, the concessions to the United States were not sufficient to equal the preference in the Cuban tariff to the products of Spain.

Exports to Brazil.—Brazil granted to the United States the free admission of a long list of important commodities, including, among others, breadstuffs, meat products, fish, coal, agricultural implements, machinery, and tools, and she ceded in addition a 25 per cent reduction in the rates of duty on certain articles, including, among others, provisions, leather, lumber, furniture, wagons and carriages, and manufactures of rubber. The rates of the Brazilian tariff were high, and the preference to American products was therefore substantial. The reduced rates do not seem to have been extended to any other country.

TABLE XVIII.—*Domestic exports from the United States to Brazil, 1888-1897.*

(Concessions in effect from Apr. 1, 1891, to Jan. 1, 1895.)

Year.	All articles.		Concessional articles.					
			All concessional articles.			Breadstuffs.		
	Value.	Per cent increase over 3-year average, 1888-1890.	Value.	Per cent increase over 3-year average, 1888-1890.	Per cent of all articles.	Value.	Per cent increase over 3-year average, 1888-1890.[1]	Per cent of all articles.
1888	$7,063,892	....	$5,194,509	....	73.54	$2,779,492	....	39.35
1889	9,276,511	....	7,449,270	....	80.30	4,064,809	....	43.82
1890	11,902,496	26.43	9,907,094	31.80	83.24	4,940,765	25.77	41.51
1891	14,049,273	49.23	11,527,959	53.36	82.05	4,348,948	10.71	30.95
1892	14,240,009	51.26	11,558,916	53.78	81.17	5,158,138	31.31	36.22
1893	12,339,584	31.07	9,639,959	28.24	78.12	3,709,103	5.58	30.06
1894	13,827,914	46.88	11,277,191	50.02	81.55	3,540,585	9.87	25.60
1895	15,135,125	60.77	12,446,590	65.58	82.24	2,691,617	31.48	17.79
1896	14,222,934	51.08	11,177,065	48.69	78.58	3,450,446	12.17	24.26
1897	12,406,785	31.79	9,486,191	26.20	76.46	3,561,500	9.34	28.71

Year.	Concessional articles.								
	Iron and steel.[2]			Cotton manufactures.			Wood manufactures.		
	Value.	Per cent increase over 3-year average, 1888-1890.	Per cent of all articles.	Value.	Per cent increase over 3-year average, 1888-1890.[1]	Per cent of all articles.	Value.	Per cent increase over 3-year average, 1888-1890.	Per cent of all articles.
1888	$728,499	....	10.31	$665,986	....	9.43	$384,495	....	5.44
1889	1,003,056	....	10.81	631,094	....	6.80	443,506	....	4.78
1890	1,073,722	14.83	9.02	813,700	15.65	6.84	494,750	12.21	4.15
1891	2,583,169	176.25	18.39	581,974	17.29	4.14	873,631	98.14	6.22
1892	2,373,174	153.79	16.67	749,370	6.51	5.26	747,607	69.56	5.25
1893	2,050,888	119.32	16.62	1,402,569	99.34	11.36	806,033	82.81	6.53
1894	1,438,031	53.79	10.40	1,538,689	118.69	11.13	537,953	22.01	3.89
1895	3,123,374	234.02	20.64	1,702,518	141.97	11.25	671,992	52.41	4.44
1896	2,407,123	157.42	16.92	992,972	41.13	6.98	946,475	114.66	6.65
1897	1,804,550	92.98	14.54	674,994	4.06	5.44	815,211	84.89	6.57

Year.	Concessional articles.						All other articles.		
	Provisions.			Other concessional articles.					
	Value.	Per cent increase over 3-year average, 1880-1890.[1]	Per cent of all articles.	Value.	Per cent increase over 3-year average, 1888-1890.	Per cent of all articles.	Value.	Per cent increase over 3-year average, 1880-1890.	Per cent of all articles.
1888	$419,278	....	5.94	$216,759	....	3.07	$1,869,383	....	26.46
1889	593,268	....	6.40	713,537	....	7.69	1,827,241	....	19.70
1890	1,969,626	98.14	16.55	614,531	19.34	5.19	1,995,402	5.17	16.76
1891	2,116,013	112.87	15.06	1,024,224	98.90	7.29	2,521,314	32.89	17.95
1892	1,135,344	14.21	7.98	1,395,283	170.96	8.39	2,681,093	41.29	18.83
1893	857,117	13.78	6.95	814,249	58.12	6.60	2,699,625	42.29	21.88
1894	2,420,919	143.54	17.51	1,801,014	249.75	13.02	2,550,723	34.44	18.45
1895	3,289,684	230.94	21.73	967,405	87.87	6.39	2,688,535	41.71	17.76
1896	2,493,958	150.89	17.54	886,091	72.08	6.23	3,045,869	60.54	21.42
1897	1,765,037	77.56	14.23	864,899	67.96	6.97	2,920,594	53.93	23.54

[1] Decreases in italics.

[2] Iron and steel including agricultural implements and scientific instruments and excluding, band, hoop, and scroll iron, bar iron, ingots, and typewriters.

In Brazil the concessions were in effect for three months of the fiscal year 1891, in which year there appears a considerable increase in exports over the figures of 1890. The increase in 1891 was not as great for the concessional articles as for the non-concessional articles, because of decreases in exports of breadstuffs and manufactures of cotton. The other classes of concessional articles all showed very large increases in that year. The available data, however, do not indicate to what extent, if any, the increase in exports in 1891 resulted from the operation of reciprocity during the fiscal quarter of that year. There was a decline in the exports of breadstuffs to Brazil during the reciprocity period, in spite of the complete remission of duty on breadstuffs. The explanation is found in the development of Argentinian competition with American flour and wheat.

In Table XIX are presented the figures of exports of wheat and wheat flour to Brazil from the Argentine in the years 1890 to 1895. It will be seen that the increase in the imports from the Argentine more than made up for the decrease in the imports from the United States.[1]

TABLE XIX.—*Domestic exports of wheat and wheat flour from the United States to Brazil, compared with similar exports from the Argentine, 1889–1895.*

Year.	Wheat.		Wheat flour.	
	Argentine to Brazil.[1]	United States to Brazil.	Argentine to Brazil.[1]	United States to Brazil.
	Bushels.	*Bushels.*	*Barrels.[2]*	*Barrels.[2]*
1889	154,625	415,507	7,628	678,972
1890	3,365,829	1,768,234	67,669	687,342
1891	3,809,572	580,127	23,829	722,369
1892	4,160,311	164,622	116,552	918,547
1893	8,552,893	63,928	297,553	837,039
1894	17,457,235	63	366,481	920,869
1895	2,134,898	63	535,763	775,425

[1] From U. S. Monthly Summary, 1898, p. 1405, and official Argentine statistics.
[2] Computed on the basis of 196 pounds to the barrel.

All the concessional articles other than breadstuffs show increases both absolutely and as compared to the total exports and to the exports of non-concessional articles to Brazil. The increases were especially prominent in the manufactures of iron and steel and in cotton manufactures. The termination of reciprocity was marked by a decrease in the exports of the concessional articles for the years 1896 and 1897, in which years, on the other hand, the exports of non-concessional articles were still increasing.

In Tables XX to XXII is presented a comparison of American exports of selected concessional articles with exports of similar articles to Brazil by the United Kingdom, France, and Germany.

[1] See p. 293 seq., infra, for a discussion of the Brazilian trade in wheat and wheat flour.

TABLE XX.—*Total domestic exports from the United States to Brazil compared with exports from the United Kingdom, Germany, and France to Brazil, 1890–1897.*[1]

Year.	United States.			United Kingdom.		
	Total.	Per cent increase over 1890.	Per cent of total exports from the 4 specified countries.	Total.	Per cent increase over 1890.[2]	Per cent of total exports from the 4 specified countries.
1890	$11,902,496	....	15.60	$36,297,413	....	47.57
1891	14,049,273	18.04	16.06	40,343,475	11.15	46.12
1892	14,240,009	19.64	18.14	38,495,601	6.06	49.04
1893	12,339,584	3.67	15.52	37,829,412	4.24	47.58
1894	13,827,914	16.18	17.40	36,625,211	.91	46.08
1895	15,135,125	27.16	18.17	35,640,767	1.81	42.79
1896	14,222,934	19.50	19.15	32,430,375	10.65	43.68
1897	12,406,785	4.24	19.84	26,431,100	27.18	42.26

Year.	Germany.			France.		
	Total.	Per cent increase. over 1890.[2]	Per cent of total exports from the 4 specified countries.	Total.	Per cent increase over 1890.[2]	Per cent of total exports from the 4 specified countries.
1890	$12,470,962	....	16.34	$15,635,066	....	20.49
1891	13,209,000	5.92	15.11	19,866,431	27.06	22.71
1892	12,352,200	.95	15.73	13,417,378	14.18	17.09
1893	14,807,408	18.74	18.62	14,541,417	6.99	18.28
1894	13,566,000	8.78	17.07	15,462,553	1.10	19.45
1895	17,897,600	43.51	21.49	14,622,057	6.48	17.55
1896	14,360,206	15.15	19.34	13,236,321	15.34	17.83
1897	11,951,884	4.16	19.11	11,753,881	24.82	18.79

TABLE XXI.—*Domestic exports of manufactures of iron and steel, excluding fire-arms, from the United States to Brazil compared with similar exports from the United Kingdom, Germany, and France to Brazil, 1890–1897.*[1]

Year.	United States.			United Kingdom.		
	Total.	Per cent increase over 1890.	Per cent of total exports from the 4 specified countries.	Total.	Per cent increase over 1890.[2]	Per cent of total exports from the 4 specified countries.
1890	$958,015	....	7.48	$9,259,519	....	72.28
1891	2,270,014	136.95	11.99	11,918,083	28.71	62.93
1892	2,149,982	123.48	15.83	8,422,417	9.04	62.27
1893	1,832,797	91.31	14.40	8,021,121	13.37	63.01
1894	1,291,384	34.80	11.08	7,451,268	19.55	63.95
1895	2,892,051	201.88	20.23	7,611,688	17.80	53.26
1896	2,048,660	113.84	14.67	8,043,891	13.13	57.59
1897	1,323,171	38.12	14.11	5,395,124	41.73	57.52

Year.	Germany.			France.		
	Total.	Per cent increase. over 1890.	Per cent of total exports from the 4 specified countries.	Total.	Per cent increase over 1890.[2]	Per cent of total exports from the 4 specified countries.
1890	$1,775,004	....	13.86	$817,244	....	6.38
1891	3,181,346	79.23	16.80	1,569,513	92.05	8.29
1892	2,187,696	23.25	16.17	775,189	5.15	5.73
1893	2,241,484	26.28	17.61	635,261	22.27	4.99
1894	2,315,026	30.42	19.87	593,965	27.32	5.10
1895	3,137,316	76.75	21.95	651,784	20.25	4.56
1896	3,142,314	77.03	22.50	731,914	10.44	5.24
1897	2,008,720	13.17	21.42	652,683	20.14	6.96

[1] From official reports of the several countries. Figures for the United States are for fiscal years; all others are for calendar years.
[2] Decreases in italics.

TABLE XXII.—*Exports of cotton goods from the United States to Brazil compared with similar exports from the United Kingdom, Germany, and France to Brazil, 1890–1897.*[1]

Year.	United States.			United Kingdom.		
	Total.	Per cent increase over 1890.[2]	Per cent of total exports from the 4 specified countries.	Total.	Per cent increase over 1890.[2]	Per cent of total exports from the 4 specified countries.
1890	$813,700	....	4.39	$14,197,843	....	76.67
1891	581,974	*28.48*	3.65	12,253,317	*13.70*	76.82
1892	749,370	7.91	3.64	16,336,101	15.06	79.34
1893	1,402,569	72.37	5.99	17,285,759	21.75	73.94
1894	1,538,689	89.10	7.50	15,083,887	6.24	73.50
1895	1,702,518	109.23	8.98	12,904,337	*9.11*	67.99
1896	992,972	22.03	6.53	11,006,076	*22.48*	72.31
1897	674,994	*17.05*	5.88	8,619,715	*39.29*	75.14

Year.	Germany			France.		
	Total.	Per cent increase over 1890.[2]	Per cent of total exports from the 4 specified countries.	Total.	Per cent increase over 1890.[2]	Per cent of total exports from the 4 specified countries.
1890	$2,661,554	....	14.38	$834,440	....	4.56
1891	2,002,056	*24.79*	12.55	1,112,332	33.30	6.98
1892	2,601,816	*2.25*	12.63	904,266	8.37	4.39
1893	3,376,268	26.85	14.44	1,314,018	57.47	5.61
1894	2,742,474	3.03	13.36	1,157,688	38.74	5.64
1895	3,103,044	16.59	16.37	1,248,801	49.66	6.58
1896	2,159,374	*18.89*	14.19	1,061,102	27.16	6.97
1897	1,486,786	*44.15*	12.96	600,679	17.23	6.02

[1] From official reports of the several countries. Figures for the United States are for fiscal years; all others are for calendar years.
[2] Decreases in italics.

The increases, during the reciprocity period, of United States exports to Brazil contrast with decreases in exports to Brazil from the United Kingdom and France and smaller increases from Germany. In the years 1895 to 1897, after the termination of reciprocity, total United States exports to Brazil decreased, but the decrease in total United States exports was not as great as the decreases in the exports to Brazil of each of the specified countries. On the other hand, the United States exports to Brazil of manufactures of cotton and of iron and steel—articles in respect to which the United States had enjoyed a tariff preference under the reciprocity agreement—decreased to a much greater degree in the years immediately following the termination of reciprocity than did the similar exports to Brazil of the specified European countries.

Exports to British West Indies.—The agreements which were concluded with Great Britain on behalf of the British West Indies and British Guiana, provided, in each case, for the free admission into these colonies from the United States of a numerous list of natural and manufactured products and provided also for the admission of other important products at reductions of 25 or 50 per cent from the general rates of duty. The colonial tariffs were moderate in their rates, however, and all concessions granted to the

United States were enjoyed also by the mother country and by all nations entitled to favored-nation treatment. The concessions therefore were of limited significance.

TABLE XXIII.—*Imports into Barbados, Jamaica, Trinidad, and British Guiana, 1890–1897.*[1]

BARBADOS.

Year.	Total value.	From the United States.		From the United Kingdom.	
		Value.	Per cent of total.	Value.	Per cent of total.
1890	$5,801,494	$2,072,610	35.73	$2,472,272	42.68
1891	5,188,618	1,836,822	35.40	2,102,611	40.52
1892	5,256,440	1,836,852	34.94	2,280,885	43.39
1893	6,670,531	2,437,873	36.55	2,833,803	42.48
1894	6,217,568	2,281,819	36.70	2,466,615	39.67
1895	4,650,636	1,635,672	35.17	1,902,369	40.91
1896	5,097,591	1,735,433	34.04	2,272,774	44.58
1897	4,902,277	1,564,473	31.91	2,306,663	47.05

JAMAICA.

1890	$10,638,234	3,588,546	33.73	$5,987,933	56.29
1891	8,553,065	3,179,242	37.17	4,190,997	49.00
1892	9,435,598	3,287,863	34.85	4,865,968	51.57
1893	10,486,884	3,496,712	33.34	5,786,136	55.17
1894	10,651,881	3,904,237	36.65	5,376,540	50.48
1895	11,124,278	4,630,039	41.62	5,376,020	48.32
1896	9,021,997	3,552,130	39.37	4,506,746	49.95
1897	8,070,842	3,498,160	43.34	3,775,681	46.78

TRINIDAD.

1890	$10,929,620	$2,082,816	19.05	$3,996,281	36.56
1891	10,190,433	2,051,843	20.13	3,779,418	37.08
1892	10,154,387	2,220,932	21.87	3,691,359	36.35
1893	11,036,501	2,266,480	20.53	4,249,613	38.50
1894	10,463,011	2,169,441	20.73	4,058,999	38.79
1895	11,065,559	2,155,298	19.47	4,804,368	43.42
1896	11,972,732	2,228,213	18.61	4,755,826	39.72
1897	10,503,583	2,190,227	20.85	4,169,185	39.69

BRITISH GUIANA.

1890	$9,171,393	$1,843,738	20.10	$5,487,285	59.83
1891	8,299,762	1,822,184	21.95	4,507,149	54.30
1892	8,652,350	2,125,740	24.56	4,612,387	53.31
1893	9,334,651	2,339,278	25.06	5,087,749	54.50
1894	8,110,125	2,117,920	26.11	4,288,411	52.88
1895	7,015,668	1,854,804	26.44	3,838,511	54.71
1896	6,520,711	1,456,790	22.34	3,808,767	58.41
1897	6,285,263	1,660,852	26.63	3,600,667	57.74

FOUR SPECIFIED COLONIES.

1890	$36,540,741	$9,587,710	26.23	$17,943,771	49.10
1891	32,223,878	8,890,091	27.58	14,580,175	45.24
1892	33,498,775	9,471,388	28.26	15,450,601	46.12
1893	37,528,663	10,540,343	28.09	17,957,301	47.85
1894	35,442,585	10,473,417	29.55	16,190,565	45.68
1895	33,856,141	10,275,813	30.35	15,921,268	45.68
1896	32,613,031	8,972,566	27.51	15,344,113	47.05
1897	29,711,965	8,913,712	30.00	13,852,196	46.62

[1] From data in U. S. Monthly Summary, Feb., 1899. Converted at the rate of one pound sterling equaling $4.86.

Table XXIII presents in greater detail the data concerning the United States exports to the more important British colonies on whose behalf reciprocity agreements were concluded with Great Britain. This table indicates that no marked result followed upon the establishment of reciprocal relations. The reduced rates were enjoyed by practically all the commercial nations trading with the British West Indies, and in the islands the imports from the United States barely maintained their position both as to amount and in relation to total imports into these colonies. In the case of British Guiana, however, reciprocity was followed by a substantial increase in imports from the United States, and the termination of reciprocity was followed by a substantial decline in such imports. The proportion of American imports to total imports was greater in 1897. however, than in any single reciprocity year.

Exports to Germany.—Germany granted concessions on products of the farm and forest only. Crop conditions played a large part, therefore, in determining the volume of the exports of reciprocity articles to Germany. The agreement was effected just in time to permit considerable shipments of the record crop of 1891 to enter under the lower duties and thus to contribute toward relieving the shortage of foodstuffs in Germany which resulted from the partial crop failures in Europe in 1891. The agreement also involved the repeal of certain features in the German sanitary regulations by which American hogs and pork products had been practically excluded from the German market. Even if the figures of the year 1892, therefore, are set aside as accounted for by abnormal circumstances, there was, nevertheless, a substantial increase in the exports of concessional articles to Germany during the reciprocity period as a whole, as against -it is important to note—a decrease in the total exports to that country. The exports to Germany showed great increases after 1895. This was a period of trade expansion in Germany, but it is also to be remembered that when the agreement was abrogated by the United States, Germany did not cancel her concessions.

TABLE XXIV. —*Domestic exports from the United States to Germany.*

(Concessions in effect from Feb. 1, 1892.)

Year.	Total exports.		Concessional articles.			Breadstuffs.		
	Total value.	Per cent increase over 3-year average, 1888–1890.	Value.	Per cent increase over 3-year average, 1888–1890.[1]	Per cent of total value of all articles.	Value.	Per cent increase over 3-year average, 1888–1890.[1]	Per cent of total value of all articles.
1888	$55,621,264	....	$1,783,224	....	3.21	$1,424,666	....	2.56
1889	66,568,695	....	2,9 6,823	....	4.47	2,419,250	....	3.63
1890	84,315,215	22.49	6,232.790	70.09	7.39	5,242,495	73.09	6.22
1891	91,684,971	33.20	3,150.611	*13.77*	3.45	2,530.513	*16.45*	2.76
1892	104,180,732	51.35	20,229 683	4 2.08	19.42	19,642,640	546.28	18.79
1893	81,992,572	19.11	7, 93.937	9.06	8.89	6,807,252	124.75	8.30
1894	90,065,108	30.84	8,951,026	144.8	9.94	8,221,594	171.45	9.13
1895	90,615,551	31.64	4,8 5,426	33.5	5.8	4,108.164	35.64	4.53
1896	96,364,368	39.99	8,370,996	12.45	8.69	7, 40,646	130.58	7.62
1897	123,784,453	79.83	19,4 4,851	431.48	15.73	17,8 3,976	433.83	14.43

[1] Decreases in italics.

TABLE XXIV.—*Domestic exports from the United States to Germany*—Continued.

Year.	Other concessional articles.			All other articles.		
	Value.	Per cent increase over 3-year average, 1888–1890.[1]	Per cent of total value. of all articles.	Value.	Per cent increase over 3-year average, 1888–1890.	Per cent of total value of all articles.
1888	$358.558	....	0.65	$53,528,040	....	96.79
1889	557,573	....	.84	63,591,872	....	95.53
1890	990,295	55.84	1.17	78,082,425	19.81	92.61
1891	629,098	*1.00*	.69	88,525,360	35.84	96.55
1892	587,043	7.62	.56	83,951,049	28.82	80.58
1893	486,685	*23.41*	.59	74,698,635	14.63	91.10
1894	729,432	14.79	.79	81,114,082	24.48	90.06
1895	767.262	20 74	.85	85,740,125	31.56	94.62
1896	1,030 350	62 14	1.07	87,993,362	35 02	91 31
1897	1,610,875	153 49	1.28	104,309,602	60 06	84 27

[1] Decreases in italics.

Exports to Austria-Hungary.—The concessions made by Austria-Hungary covered the entire range of that country's imports. Unfortunately the United States statistics of exports to most countries which receive their imports to any considerable extent via the ports of a third country are unsatisfactory, and this applies especially to the figures of United States trade with Austria. The data available provide little information concerning the tendency of United States trade with Austria during the reciprocity period. By the agreement of 1892, Austria-Hungary extended to all the products of the United States the rates of the minimum (conventional) schedule of her new tariff. This minimum schedule was at the same time applied to the products of most of the commercial nations, so that the agreement made no tariff concessions particularly in favor of the United States. The United States figures of exports to Austria-Hungary for this period show some increase immediately following the conclusion of the agreement. There was a sharp drop in the years 1893 and 1894, coincident with the industrial depression, followed by a great increase in each of the next three years. Austria-Hungary did not, upon the abrogation of the agreement, withdraw her minimum rates from American products. The increase in the exports which took place during these years would scarcely have been possible had the very high maximum rates of the Austrian tariff been imposed on American products.

CONCLUSIONS AS TO EFFECT OF AGREEMENTS ON AMERICAN TRADE.

The foregoing analysis of imports and exports indicates that penalty duties were effective as a measure of retaliation and as a means of securing special tariff favors. The particular commodities upon which such duties could be imposed under the act of 1890, although few in number, constituted the bulk of the imports into the United States from a large number of American countries. In order to assure the continued free admission of their coffee, hides, sugar, and molasses into the United States, most of these countries complied with the request of the American Government that they make "reciprocal and equivalent" concessions of duty upon American products. The lists of articles upon which reductions or remissions of duty were so granted were long and varied, including almost every important article among United States exports to Latin America, and the reductions of duty were substantial in amount.

The imposition of penalty duties upon the coffee, hides, sugar, and molasses of Colombia, Venezuela, and Haiti, upon the failure of those countries to establish reduced rates of duty on American products, reduced almost to zero the export trade of these countries to the United States. The importance to an exporting country of the admission of its chief products into important markets free of duty or at reduced rates of duty, even though the favorable treatment is general and creates no preference in favor of that country, is shown by the experience of the sugar-producing countries after the remission of the duty on sugar by the United States. While imports into the United States were in general declining, the imports of sugar increased rapidly during the period of free admission. Such effectiveness as the penalty provision exhibited was due almost wholly to the inclusion of sugar in the list of articles upon which penalty duties might be imposed, together with the extraordinary conditions prevailing in the sugar industry during this period. At a time when there was a glut in the world sugar market and it was extraordinarily difficult for the sugar-producing countries to dispose of their stocks of sugar even at the low prices then current, a country would be willing to make, in return for the free admission of its sugar into the United States, concessions of duty on American products such as in normal times it might refuse even to consider.

The nature of the reciprocity provisions of 1890 was not such as would be expected extensively to affect import trade as a whole. The "reciprocity" provision was in reality simply a penalizing measure; it amounted, as has been pointed out, to a threat of especially unfavorable treatment by the United States for the products of any country which refused upon request to grant especially favorable treatment to the products of the United States. The main effect of those provisions was a marked decrease of imports from the penalized countries. In the total of United States imports of the specified articles, the proportion which came from the penalized countries, either before or during the period of the imposition of penalty duties, was small. Consequently the bulk of the imports of the articles enumerated in section 3 of the act entered free of duty. Had the situation been different, had most of these imports been subjected to penalty duties, the benefit of the remission of duties would have accrued chiefly to the favored foreign producers. But under the conditions which actually prevailed, the free admission of the enumerated articles inured to the benefit of the American consumer through the resultant fall in prices on the American market.

Provisions such as those of section 3 of the act of 1890 ought chiefly to affect exports. But the countries with which agreements were made took only a small fraction of the total exports of the United States, and during the reciprocity period these countries were laboring under the combined handicaps of severe industrial depression and widespread revolutionary disturbances. Nevertheless, on the whole, the exports to these countries, especially of articles on which concessions had been granted, showed substantial increases in the face of a general decrease in the total of exports to all countries.

While for several individual countries such increases were not apparent, these were countries in which the effects of the disturbed conditions of the time were most severe. If proper consideration be given to the limited extent of the field in which reciprocity operated and to the abnormal conditions prevalent during the period, the foregoing evidence indicates that the agreements resulting from section 3 of the act of 1890 exerted a favorable influence upon the export trade of the United States.

5. TREATIES AND AGREEMENTS UNDER THE TARIFF ACT OF 1897.

TREATIES AND AGREEMENTS UNDER THE TARIFF ACT OF 1897.

THE LEGISLATIVE RECORD.

In the Congressional elections of 1894 the Republican Party gained a majority in Congress. Reciprocity sentiment gained greatly in strength thereafter. The export trade of the United States was expanding, but found a serious obstacle in the discriminatory treatment to which it was subjected in European tariffs. Reciprocity appeared to offer a means of securing an equalization of the tariff treatment of American products and the products of other countries. In 1896 the House Ways and Means Committee conducted hearings upon the question of reciprocity and sent out circulars to the business interests of the country. The statements and evidence in the hearings, at which many of the important American industries were represented, strongly favored reciprocity. The results of the circular inquiry apparently showed the business men of the country to be overwhelmingly in favor of incorporating reciprocity provisions as a permanent feature of American tariff legislation.[1] Of fifty-two replies received by the committee, in answer to its questionnaire, from commercial and industrial associations, including boards of trade, chambers of commerce, etc., fifty-one supported a policy of reciprocity; and out of more than two hundred and fifty replies from manufacturers and merchants in all kinds of business scattered throughout the country, only fifteen opposed it. Following these evidences of business opinion, the Republican Party in the campaign of 1896 inserted a reciprocity plank in its platform. In 1896, William McKinley was elected President, and a Congress was elected which was largely Republican in both Houses. In his inauguration address, delivered on March 4, 1897, President McKinley said:

In the revision of the tariff especial attention should be given to the reenactment and extension of the reciprocity principle of the law of 1890. * * * The brief trial given this legislation amply justifies a further experiment and additional discretionary power in the making of commercial treaties, the end in view always to be the opening up of new markets for the products of our country, by granting concessions to the products of other lands that we need and can not produce ourselves, and which do not involve any loss of labor to our own people, but tend to increase their employment.

In a message dated March 6, 1897, President McKinley called upon Congress to meet on March 15 in extraordinary session, to consider the condition of the revenues of the Government. The only purpose of this special session stated in the message was the passage of a tariff law which should provide ample revenue, since the expenditures of the Government during the three preceding years had exceeded the receipts.

Introduction of the Dingley tariff bill.—On March 18, only three days after Congress met, Mr. Dingley, of Maine chairman of the

---

[1] 54th Cong., 1st sess., H. R. No. 2263, 295–545.

House Committee on Ways and Means, introduced "A bill to provide revenue for the Government and to encourage the industries of the United States."

Provisions for reciprocity in the original bill.—Section 3 of this bill made provision for reciprocity by two methods. The earlier portion of this section provided for the extension of authority to the President to proclaim certain specified reductions in duties on a specified list of articles, when coming from countries which made such concessions on the products of the United States as the President might adjudge reciprocal and equivalent. The articles upon which reduced duties could be levied under these conditions were the following: Argols, chicle, brandies, champagne and all other sparkling wines, still wines, laces of silk, mineral waters, drawings and statuary, sugar and molasses. The later portion of section 3, as originally proposed, provided further for the imposition, by proclamation of the President, of penalty duties of 3 cents per pound on coffee, 10 cents per pound on tea, and 1½ cents per pound on hides, when coming from countries which imposed upon the products of the United States duties which the President deemed, in view of the free admission of these products into the United States, unequal and unreasonable.

The provision for penalty duties in the second part of section 3 was similar to that of section 3 of the act of 1890, except that sugar and molasses, being no longer on the free list, were in the new proposal to be omitted from the list of articles upon which such duties could be levied. But the first portion of section 3 of the Dingley bill provided a very different form of reciprocity from that which had been authorized by section 3 of the McKinley Act. The act of 1890 had provided that duties should be levied on five specified articles in the free list, in cases where such articles were imported from countries that did not extend fair and reasonable tariff treatment to the products of the United States. By the first section of the Dingley bill the President was authorized to reduce the duties on certain specified commodities when these commodities were imported from countries which had granted to the United States reciprocal and equivalent concessions.

House debate on the reciprocity section.—The bill was debated in the House from March 22 to 31, but in the discussion very little attention was given to the reciprocity section. The only extended reference to this section was made by Mr. Hopkins, of Illinois, a member of the Ways and Means Committee, who spoke in part as follows:

In the present bill the principle of reciprocity has been enlarged and adapted to our commercial relations with France, Germany, Belgium, and other European countries, as well as Mexico and the Central and South American States. * * *

Let me illustrate: We furnish for Germany to-day her largest market for beet sugar. * * * In framing this bill, * * * we have imposed a certain rate of duty on sugar. * * * Now, we have provided in this reciprocity branch of the bill that only 92 per cent of this duty shall be collected from countries importing sugar here that enter into reciprocal agreements with the United States, and we believe that will be a sufficient inducement to the German Government to reopen her markets for all of the products of our farms and factories.

We, however, are not limited in the bill to sugar alone. There are other articles of German production, like champagne, and all sparkling wines, still wines, mineral water, etc., that are produced and shipped in large quantities from that country to this. They will all have a lower rate of duty under the conditions I have indicated than would otherwise be required. It is hoped * * * that the inducements we have placed in this bill will be sufficiently strong to cause the German Government to enter into the most friendly commercial agreements with the United States and permit again our cattle, sheep, and hogs to be sold freely in her markets. * * * * * * We stand for protection first and foremost, and we desire to couple with that the principle of opening foreign markets for our goods. * * * * * * I believe that the principle of reciprocity is in perfect harmony with the doctrine of protection. Reciprocity is scientific protection, and is adapted to our improved commercial conditions and civilization. It is a principle that to-day is recognized in the laws of France, Germany, Russia, and other European countries. It has given them the control of the markets of the world on many of the articles specified in these commercial or reciprocal agreements.

Mr. Kerr, of Pennsylvania, in reply to Mr. Hopkins, claimed that the inducements offered to other countries by the reciprocity section of the bill were trifling and were wholly insufficient to secure valuable concessions in return. He urged in its place a return to the McKinley plan of penalty duties on the products of countries whose tariff rates on American products were unreasonable and excessive. Other members, joining in the opposition to section 3, characterized it as inuring only to the benefit of the farm-implement and meat-packing trusts, and as involving no significant reductions in what they termed the excessively high rates of the general tariff.

The bill had strong support in the House, however, and with section 3 in the form in which it had been introduced, it was passed by the House of Representatives on March 31, less than two weeks after its introduction.

The bill in the Senate.—In the Senate, progress was slower. On April 1 the bill was referred to the Committee on Finance, which, on May 4, reported it back to the Senate, with sundry amendments. The committee disapproved of the form of reciprocity provided for in section 3 as the bill had passed the House, and declared its intention to introduce new reciprocity provisions of much broader scope than those provided in the House bill.

Senator Allison's amendment.—The discussion in the Senate was more thorough than that in the House. On June 30 and again with some modifications on July 21, Senator Allison, of Iowa, introduced as a substitute for section 3 a provision for reciprocity which was totally different in character. This substitute provided that the President should be authorized "by and with the advice and consent of the Senate" to enter, within two years from the date of the passage of the act, into the negotiation of commercial treaties with other countries. In return for the admission of American products by other countries at reduced rates of duty, the President would be authorized to grant reductions not exceeding 20 per cent of the duties on the products of the treaty countries prescribed in the regular schedule, and to grant the free admission from the reciprocity countries of natural products which were not natural products of the United States and which were on the dutiable list. The treaties would become effective after they had "been duly ratified and public proclamation made accordingly." The treaty period was not to exceed five years.

Senator Allison's proposed amendment gave rise to a long debate over its constitutional features. Much discussion centered about the right of the President "by and with the advice and consent of the Senate" to conclude treaties which, while they affected the revenues, were to come into effect upon ratification by the Senate and without action on the part of the House of Representatives. It was argued that this would involve a transfer to the President and the Senate of the power to levy revenue taxes which was conferred by the Constitution upon Congress as a whole. In reply to this, it was contended by supporters of the amendment that the right of the President and the Senate together to repeal revenue legislation by treaty with other countries had been frequently confirmed by the Supreme Court of the United States, and that the House of Representatives could, in case a treaty involved revenue legislation, exercise its constitutional prerogative to enact revenue legislation in either of two ways—by refusing to pass the legislation necessary to put such treaty into effect, or by initiating legislation to repeal such treaty.

The Senate finally accepted Senator Allison's amendment, which took the form of a new section to be inserted in lieu of section 3 as it had passed the House. The bill thus amended was passed by the Senate on July 7 and was sent to the conference committee.

Bill reported by conference committee.—The conference committee presented its report to the House on July 19. The committee had restored to the bill, as section 3, the reciprocity provision which had passed in the House, but this provision now embodied some important changes. From the list of articles upon which the duties could be reduced for reciprocity purposes the following were eliminated: Chicle, silk laces, natural or artificial mineral waters, and sugar and molasses. Upon some of the remaining articles the minimum duties were reduced. Coffee and tea were retained on the list of free articles on which penalty duties might be imposed; hides and skins were struck off; tonka and vanilla beans were added.

The conference report also retained, as section 4, the amendment providing for reciprocity on a more extensive scale, which had been introduced by Senator Allison in the Senate.

The conference committee had amended section 4, however, so as to require the approval of Congress in addition to the ratification of the Senate, before treaties negotiated in conformity with its provision could become binding.

In presenting the conference report to the House, Mr. Dingley gave the following account of the insertion of this amendment therein:

In substance, the agreement of the conferees combines the reciprocity clause of the House and that incorporated in the bill by the Senate, with certain amendments, which substantially united the two plans, so that both may be made available if desired. One of the amendments which has been adopted is vital in its effect. The Senate provided that the President might enter into commercial treaties with foreign countries, and when ratified by the Senate they should become binding on the country. The House conferees insisted upon an amendment that they should not become binding until ratified by Congress. In other words, the House conferees maintained that the House should approve as well as the Senate before any such commercial treaties should take effect, and the Senate conferees conceded the point.

Passing of the act.—The House of Representatives accepted the conference report, without much debate, on July 19, the same day it was submitted. When the conference report reached the Senate, Senator White, of California, after reading section 4, objected that it provided for a roundabout way of modifying the tariff, whereas the modification might be effected much more directly and easily by direct legislation of Congress. He referred to the amendment of section 4 of the conference bill, whereby the approval of Congress was necessary to the ratification of a treaty, as a "remarkable provision." After the President of the United States had gone through the effort of negotiating reciprocity treaties and after the Senate and the President together had made a treaty with some foreign power, he thought it should not be necessary to bring the treaty before Congress for their approval. But the conference bill had strong support in the Senate, and the reciprocity provisions were of minor importance as compared with the tariff provisions of the bill as a whole. On July 24, 1897, the bill was passed as the conference committee had reported it. It was signed by the President and became effective on the same day.

Reciprocity sections of the act.—The provisions for reciprocity constituted sections 3 and 4 of the act. They read as follows:

SEC. 3. That for the purpose of equalizing the trade of the United States with foreign countries, and their colonies, producing and exporting to this country the following articles: Argols, or crude tartar, or wine lees, crude; brandies, or other spirits manufactured or distilled from grain or other materials; champagne and all other sparkling wines; still wines, and vermuth; paintings and statuary; or any of them, the President, and he is hereby, authorized, as soon as may be after the passage of this act, and from time to time thereafter, to enter into negotiations with the Governments of those countries exporting to the United States the above-mentioned articles, or any of them, with a view to the arrangement of commercial agreements in which reciprocal and equivalent concessions may be secured in favor of the products and manufactures of the United States; and whenever the Government of any country, or colony, producing and exporting to the United States the above-mentioned articles, or any of them, shall enter into a commercial agreement with the United States, or make concessions in favor of the products, or manufactures thereof, which, in the judgment of the President, shall be reciprocal and equivalent, he shall be, and is hereby, authorized and empowered to suspend, during the time of collection of the duties mentioned in this act, on such article or articles so exported to the United States from such country or colony, and thereupon and thereafter the duties levied, collected, and paid upon such article or articles shall be as follows, namely:

Argols, or crude tartar, or wine lees, crude, five per centum ad valorem.

Brandies, or other spirits manufactured or distilled from grain or other materials, one dollar and seventy-five cents per proof gallon.

Champagne and all other sparkling wines, in bottles containing not more than one quart and more than one pint, six dollars per dozen; containing not more than one pint each and more than one-half pint, three dollars per dozen; containing one-half pint each or less, one dollar and fifty cents per dozen; in bottles or other vessels containing more than one quart each, in addition to six dollars per dozen bottles on the quantities in excess of one quart, at the rate of one dollar and ninety cents per gallon.

Still wines, and vermuth, in casks, thirty-five cents per gallon; in bottles or jugs, per case of one dozen bottles or jugs containing each not more than one quart and more than one pint, or twenty-four bottles or jugs containing each not more than one pint, one dollar and twenty-five cents per case, and any excess beyond these quantities found in such bottles or jugs shall be subject to a duty of four cents per pint or fractional part thereof, but no separate or additional duty shall be assessed upon the bottles or jugs.

Paintings in oil or water colors, pastels, pen and ink drawings, and statuary, fifteen per centum ad valorem.

The President shall have power, and it shall be his duty, whenever he shall be satisfied that any such agreement in this section mentioned is not being fully executed by the Government with which it shall have been made, to revoke such suspension and notify such Government thereof.

And it is further provided that with a view to secure reciprocal trade with countries producing the following articles, whenever and so often as the President shall be satisfied that the Government of any country, or colony of such Government, producing and exporting directly or indirectly to the United States, coffee, tea, and tonquin, tonqua, or tonka beans, and vanilla beans, or any such articles, imposes duties or other exactions upon the agricultural, manufactured, or other products of the United States, which, in view of the introduction of such coffee, tea, and tonquin, tonqua, or tonka beans, and vanilla beans, into the United States, as in this Act hereinbefore provided for, he may deem to be reciprocally unequal and unreasonable, he shall have the power and it shall be his duty to suspend, by proclamation to that effect, the provisions of this Act relating to the free introduction of such coffee, tea, and tonquin, tonqua, or tonka beans, and vanilla beans, of the products of such country or colony, for such time as he shall deem just; and in such case and during such suspension duties shall be levied, collected, and paid upon coffee, tea, and tonquin, tonqua, or tonka beans, and vanilla beans, the products or exports, direct or indirect, from such designated country, as follows:

On coffee, three cents per pound.

On tea, ten cents per pound.

On tonquin, tonqua, or tonka beans, fifty cents per pound; vanilla beans, two dollars per pound; vanilla beans, commercially known as cuts, one dollar per pound.

SEC. 4. That whenever the President of the United States, by and with the advice and consent of the Senate, with a view to secure reciprocal trade with foreign countries, shall, within the period of two years from and after the passage of this Act, enter into commercial treaty or treaties with any other country or countries concerning the admission into any such country or countries of the goods, wares, and merchandise of the United States and their use and disposition therein, deemed to be for the interests of the United States, and in such treaty or treaties, in consideration of the advantages accruing to the United States therefrom shall provide for the reduction during a specified period, not exceeding five years, of the duties imposed by this Act, to the extent of not more than twenty per centum thereof, upon such goods, wares, or merchandise as may be designated therein of the country or countries with which such treaty or treaties shall be made as in this section provided for; or shall provide for the transfer during such period from the dutiable list of this Act to the free list thereof of such goods, wares, and merchandise, being the natural products of such foreign country or countries and not of the United States; or shall provide for the retention upon the free list of this Act during a specified period, not exceeding five years, of such goods, wares, and merchandise not included in said free list as may be designated therein; and when any such treaty shall have been duly ratified by the Senate and approved by Congress, and public proclamation made accordingly, then and thereafter the duties which shall be collected by the United States upon any of the designated goods, wares, and merchandise from the foreign country with which such treaty has been made shall, during the period provided for, be the duties specified and provided for in such treaty and none other.

COMPARISON OF GENERAL RATES AND REDUCED RATES UNDER SECTION 3 OF THE ACT OF 1897.

In the following table is presented a comparison of the rates specified in the first part of section 3 on the articles enumerated therein, with the rates levied on these articles under the general tariff:

Article.	Rate under general tariff.	Rate under section 3.
Argols	1–1½ cents per pound	5 per cent ad valorem (equivalent to about $\frac{1}{10}$–$\frac{3}{4}$ cent per pound).
Brandies	$2.25 per proof gallon	$1.75 per proof gallon.
Champagne and all other sparkling wines.	$8 per dozen quart bottles	$6 per dozen quart bottles.
Still wines and vermuth	40–50 cents per gallon in casks; $1.60 per dozen quart bottles.	35 cents per gallon in casks; $1.25 per dozen quart bottles.
Paintings, drawings, and statuary.	20 per cent ad valorem	15 per cent ad valorem.

Reciprocity and the rates of the Dingley tariff.—On several occasions in later years the statement was made that the Dingley tariff had been prepared with higher rates than were really intended to be levied, with a view to their being reduced by reciprocity treaties with other countries. Mr. Kasson made such a statement in 1900 when he appeared before the Foreign Relations Committee of the Senate to urge the ratification of the treaties which he had negotiated under section 4 of the act.[1]

[1] 56th Cong., 1st sess., Sen. Doc. No. 225, p. 69.

Mr. John Ball Osborne, who was joint secretary of the reciprocity committee appointed by President McKinley to carry out the negotiations, has made the same claim, and in more specific terms:

When the rates of duty enumerated in the first section (of the Dingley tariff) were being formulated, it was clearly understood by the framers of the law and by the interested manufacturers that each and every rate was subject to reduction to the extent of one-fifth under the operation of the reciprocity section. The rates were consequently made one-fifth higher than would otherwise have been justified. If the present rates on highly protected articles are reduced by 20 per cent, and the results compared with the corresponding rates of the McKinley tariff of 1890, it will be found that in every instance an ample measure of protection is left to the article, often higher than the duty under the high tariff of 1890.[1]

Later, in the Senate discussion of the tariff bill of 1909, this question was again raised. Senator Bacon said that a general increase in the rates of the Dingley bill had been made with a view to their subsequent reduction by means of reciprocity treaties. Senator Aldrich and others denied this. They admitted that the duties on certain articles, and especially sugar, were higher in the bill than they would have been made had it not been the intention of the framers of the bill that the rates should be lowered by the establishment of reciprocity arrangements with other countries. But they denied that there was any deliberate intention to increase rates of duty upon all articles in order that they might be reduced in turn by the mechanism of reciprocity; the rates were, they claimed, not generally above the level deemed necessary for protection to domestic industry.[2]

NEGOTIATION OF TREATIES.

European resentment against American tariff policy.—The tariff policy of the United States was at this time deeply resented by many nations. The South American countries and Germany and Austria-Hungary had been seriously offended in 1894 by the abrupt termination by the United States of the reciprocity agreements which had been negotiated under authority of the act of 1890. The further raising of the American tariff level by the act of 1897 added to the resentment felt in Europe against the tariff methods of this country. It was generally held by the European States that their admission of American agricultural products at moderate rates was sufficient to warrant admission of their manufactured products into the United States at moderate rates of duty. The rapid development since 1895 of the American exports of manufactured products to Europe was alarming the European manufacturing interests, and newspapers and periodicals both in Europe and in the United States devoted much space to the discussion of what was termed "the American invasion." The fear of the United States as a growing competitor, and the feeling of hostility to its policy of high protective duties received their clearest and most formal expression when in 1897 the premier of Austria-Hungary, Count Goluchowski, proposed to the other European nations a scheme for an official combination of the commercial nations of Europe against the trade interests of the United States. This radical proposal received some serious attention, but among other considerations, the hope of favorable developments from the reciprocity provisions of the

[1] "Expansion through Reciprocity," in The Making of America, edited by Robert M. LaFollette, Vol. II, p. 382.
[2] 61st Cong., 1st sess., Cong. Rec., Vol. 44, pt. 4, pp. 4082–4085.

new Dingley tariff prevented the concerted adoption of any hostile course of action. Nevertheless the treatment accorded to American products by the tariffs of European countries was highly unsatisfactory to American exporters and was threatening to become more so.

Tariff discrimination against American products.—France had adopted, in 1892, a new tariff system, wherein there were established by law two schedules—a maximum and a minimum.[1] The rates of the maximum schedule were applied to the imports from all countries which had not the guarantee, in existing treaties, of most-favored-nation treatment. Most of the important commercial nations either already had favored-nation treaties with France, or hastened to negotiate for such agreements as would secure to their products the minimum rates of the French tariff. The result was that of all the important western countries, only Portugal and the United States were subjected to the rates of the French maximum tariff. In the case of the United States the application of the maximum rates was not complete. By temporary legislation, subject to termination at any moment, France had extended the lowest rates of her tariff to a few of the products of the United States.[1] The American exporters of the other products which were affected by the application of the maximum rates were making strong and repeated representations to the American Government, urging the initiation of measures whereby the removal of the discrimination against American products could be secured even at the cost of the concession to France of reductions from the rates of the American tariff.

Germany, Austria, Italy, Belgium, and Switzerland had in 1891-92 adopted another form of bargaining tariff, whereby concessions from their general tariffs were made only by treaty in return for reciprocal concessions. Under the operation of the most-favored-nation clause, which was a feature of all these treaties, any concession granted to one country at once became available to practically all of Europe. This meant that unless the United States took prompt action in the form of some modification of its tariff policy and tariff law, American products would soon be discriminated against by the tariffs of most European nations.

Germany had not withdrawn the concessions granted to the United States by the reciprocity agreement of 1892, but she was dissatisfied with the manner of the abrupt termination of the agreement by the United States and with the whole general status of her commercial relations with the United States.[2] It was well known that she was contemplating a tariff revision which would make it possible to deal more harshly with American products unless there should be extended to her own products treatment more favorable than that provided under the Wilson tariff of 1894. Furthermore, many of the countries of Europe, under the leadership of Germany, were at this time discriminating against the cattle and the meat products of the United States. Regulations were applied to cattle and meat imports from the United States which, under the guise of sanitary precautions, established effective protection for the domestic meat industries of these countries as against their strongest competitor.

---

[1] See page 155, infra.   [2] See Part II, p. 426, infra.

After the passage of the Dingley Act, the hostile movement against the products of the United States became widespread. Spain in 1898 augmented her maximum tariff and applied its rates to the products of the United States; Switzerland in 1900 pursued a like course, withholding from American products for the first time the benefits of her conventional tariff; and Russia in 1901, in retaliation against the high tariff of the United States and especially the countervailing duty upon Russian sugar, subjected American manufactures to the surtaxes of her general tariff, which were almost prohibitive, the increase in rates amounting to from 50 to 100 per cent.

Reciprocity commission.—American exporting interests were becoming apprehensive over the European situation, and strong pressure was brought to bear upon the administration to persuade it to initiate negotiations whereby there could be secured elimination of existing discriminations and the assurance that no further ones would be incorporated in pending tariff legislation. President McKinley had at once seen the desirability of pressing reciprocity negotiations. Acting upon the general authority vested in the President and not upon any authority particularly given by Congress, he appointed, on October 15, 1897, John A. Kasson, of Iowa, as special commissioner for the negotiation of reciprocity treaties. Mr. Kasson was provided with offices and a suitable personnel to be known as the "reciprocity commission."

The tariff act of 1897 made possible, as has been shown, three kinds of tariff bargaining. First, the President was empowered by section 3 to negotiate and to proclaim without reference to Congress treaties based upon concessions of duty on argols, brandies, sparkling and still wines, paintings, and statuary. These became familiarly known as the "argol agreements," taking their name from the first item in the specified list of articles upon which concessions could be granted by the United States. Second, the President was empowered to impose specified penalty duties on tea, coffee, and tonka and vanilla beans when imported from countries whose treatment of American products he deemed reciprocally unequal and unreasonable. Third, under section 4 of the act, the President was authorized to enter into negotiations on the basis of more general concessions.

"ARGOL AGREEMENTS," FIRST SERIES.

In conformity with the first of these bargaining provisions of section 3, two series of agreements were concluded with European countries. The first series, consisting of treaties with France, Portugal, Germany, and Italy, was negotiated by Mr. Kasson during the McKinley administration. An arrangement of somewhat exceptional character, account of which is given elsewhere in this report,[1] procured for Switzerland also, though only for a short time, the concessions granted by the argol agreements to other countries.

Argol agreement with France, 1898.—Negotiations for the conclusion of an agreement on the basis of the concessions provided in the first portion of section 3 were first initiated with France. Some account has already been given of the unsatisfactory state of the commercial relations of the United States with that country.[2] In

---

See Part II, p. 428, infra.   [2] See p. 204, infra.

addition to the discriminatory measures already in force against American products, the French Chamber had under consideration in 1898 a proposal to double the rate on cottonseed oil, and this seemed likely to be adopted. Cottonseed oil was at that time almost exclusively an American product and was exported in large quantities to Europe. It competes with other vegetable oils, originating in other countries, and higher duties on cottonseed oil divert consumption to the latter products. It was extremely important for the prosperity of the cottonseed oil industry of the United States that it should not be specially discriminated against in the chief European markets, and Mr. Kasson exerted every effort to obtain a suspension of the threatened increase in the French duties. He also sought a repeal of the measures already in force in France which discriminated against American products. It soon became evident that the only means available for securing any relaxation of these measures was the entrance into reciprocity negotiations promising to extend to France important reductions in the rates of the Dingley tariff. As the first result of the negotiations, an "argol agreement" between the two countries was concluded on May 28, 1898.

In the agreement of 1898 the United States granted to France the concessions authorized by the first portion of section 3, with the exception of the reductions on champagne and other sparkling wines, and secured in return a guarantee of the continuance of the concessions granted by France in 1893,[1] and in addition the newly established minimum rates on sausages and lard. Mr. Kasson refused to grant the authorized reductions on champagne and other sparkling wines, upon the ground that these were articles of luxury the consumption of which in the United States was not affected by the higher duties sufficiently to justify the considerable loss of revenue which would result from their reduction. Mr. Kasson inserted in the agreement the further reservation that the concession on still wines and vermuth could be withdrawn at the discretion of the President whenever France imposed on American products additional duties which he should deem unreasonable. As a result of the negotiations, the proposal to increase the duties on cottonseed oil had been dropped in the French Chamber, but there was no guarantee in the agreement that this suspension was to be permanent. Another proposal in the French Chamber, to withdraw from American petroleum the minimum rate, which had been granted freely to the United States at the time when it was given by convention to Russia (in 1893), was also dropped as a result of the negotiations; but here again no guarantee or assurance was offered against the imposition at any moment of the maximum rate. The minimum rates conceded to the United States by the agreement involved, for the articles specified, reductions in duty amounting, as compared with the rates of the maximum schedule, to from 15 to 20 per cent. The list of articles included a number of the important products of the United States—among others, canned meats, some wood products, and fruits. There seems no reason to doubt that it was not the concessions which Mr. Kasson was authorized to make in conformity with the provisions of section 3 that induced France to grant these important concessions in return. The negotiations were

---

[1] See p. 155, infra.

preliminary in character, and the deciding consideration for the French negotiators was the hope that the argol agreement would prove the first step to the conclusion of a reciprocity treaty upon the broader basis of the general reduction of duties authorized by section 4 of the act of 1897.[1]

Argol agreement with Portugal, 1899.—Portugal, by a reciprocal arrangement with Russia, had given to the mineral oils of that country preferential rates which threatened the extinction of the American export trade in petroleum with Portugal. Mr. Kasson succeeded in concluding with Portugal an agreement similar to that with France. It was signed on May 22, 1899, at Washington, but it was not until June 12, 1900, that it was ratified by the Cortes of Portugal and put into effect by proclamation. Portugal was granted the same concessions as those granted to France, with the exception of the reduction of duty on vermuth. In addition, Portugal secured the reduced rates on sparkling wines, a merely nominal concession since these wines are not produced in that country. In return for the concessions by the United States, Portugal granted the most-favored-nation rates (the rates to Spain and Brazil excepted) on oils, flour (other than wheat flour), corn, wheat, lard, various agricultural and other machinery and tools, and tar and mineral pitch. Portugal reserved the right to abrogate the agreement if the United States at any time imposed duties on cork or coffee. The mention of coffee was made in consideration of the interests of the Azores and the Madeira Islands, which exported coffee.

Argol agreement with Italy, 1900.—Mr. Kasson was successful in negotiating a reciprocity agreement with Italy, which was signed on February 8, 1900, and put into effect on July 18, 1900. This agreement was to continue until the end of the year 1903, and thereafter unless denounced by either party subject to one year's notice. In return for concessions identical with those granted to France, the treaty secured to the United States the free admission into Italy of her turpentine, natural fertilizer, and skins; a material reduction of the duty on cottonseed oil; and the admission at the minimum rates of her fish, agricultural and electrical machinery, and scientific instruments. But the Italian Government had already accorded the minimum rates of duty to all the imports of the United States, in conformity with its interpretation of the terms of the most-favored-nation provisions in the treaty of 1871 with this country. The agreement occasioned no change in these rates except in the cases of turpentine (which formerly had been dutiable), and of cottonseed oil and fish (the treaty rates on which were lower than the corresponding rates of the existing Italian conventional tariff). With these exceptions, the concessions to the United States consisted, therefore, not so much in an actual lowering of the rates, as in the guarantee that during the period of the agreement the rates on the articles specified in the agreement would not be raised.

Argol agreement with Germany, 1900.—Under the same authority of section 3, certain of the commercial difficulties between the United States and Germany were adjusted by an agreement similar to those which have been described above. This agreement, signed on July 10, 1900, was put into effect by proclamation on July 13. It was

---

[1] 56th Cong., 1st sess. Sen. Doc. No. 225.

made terminable on three months' notice by either party. Germany had recently concluded a series of treaties with other countries, which covered a large proportion of the articles which she imported or might import from the United States. In return for concessions identical with those granted to France and Italy, Germany bound herself to refrain during the treaty period from imposing upon the specified commodities when coming from the United States higher duties than weie stipulated in these treaties. Germany further conceded the repeal of the regulations requiring that the dried or evaporated fruits imported from the United States be inspected on account of the San José scale. The pledge was promptly made good, to the great satisfaction of American fruit exporters whose trade had been hampered by this requirement.

Extension of argol concessions to Switzerland, 1898.—The extension to Switzerland of the reductions of duty authorized by section 3 may be regarded as an indirect result of the reciprocity provisions of the Dingley Act. Upon the proclamation of the reciprocity agreement with France in 1898, Switzerland, on June 29, 1898, presented a claim that under the terms of her commercial treaty with the United States of November 25, 1850, wherein there was pledged unconditional most-favored-nation treatment, she was entitled to any concessions granted to France. The Secretary of State felt bound to acknowledge this claim, and ruled that the imports of Swiss products should be admitted at the same duty as the imports from France. This ruling took effect as of June 1, 1898, and provided for the reliquidation of all customs entries of such products which had been liquidated, after that date, at the higher rates. On March 23, 1899, the United States gave a year's notice of its intention to denounce those clauses of the treaty of 1850 which obligated her to extend unconditional most-favored-nation treatment to Switzerland, and on March 23, 1900, the full duties were again collected on Swiss products, and Switzerland thereupon applied to American products the rates of her maximum tariff.[1]

Nature of the concessions received by the United States.—The concessions obtained in these agreements in return for the few and scanty reductions of duty provided for in section 3 were much more generous and important than had been anticipated by the American public, and the final enactment of the treaties may be said, judging from the slight extent to which they gave occasion for comment or discussion, to have been received with general satisfaction. These agreements differed in one important respect from those negotiated under the act of 1890. In the agreements under the act of 1890 the United States received special concessions from the treaty countries, in return for her promise to abstain from the imposition of discriminatory duties on the products of these countries. In the agreements under the act of 1897 the United States obligated herself to grant special concessions in order to secure from other countries the suspension or repeal of discriminatory duties on her exports. Thus the situation was reversed, apparently to the disadvantage of the United States.

Different results of negotiations under the acts of 1890 and 1897.— The difference in the character of the concessions given by the United

---

[1] See Part II, p. 428, infra.

States in the agreements concluded under tariff acts of 1890 and 1897, respectively, was due to the difference in the form of the bargaining provisions in the two acts. No provision was made in the act of 1890 for special concessions by the United States and consequently no special concessions were granted in the agreements which were negotiated under the act. In section 3 of the act of 1897, on the other hand, the only effective bargaining provisions provided for special concessions, and such concessions were granted by the United States in every agreement which resulted from the act of 1897.

The difference in the character of the concessions received by the United States in the agreements concluded under the two acts resulted from the difference in situation, in relation to tariff bargaining, between the countries with which agreements were negotiated under the act of 1890 and the countries with which agreements were negotiated under the act of 1897. The reciprocity agreements concluded under the act of 1890 were made—with the exception of those with Germany and Austria-Hungary—with countries with single-schedule tariff systems. As a result, the reductions in rates which were made by the other parties—except Germany and Austria-Hungary—to the United States were established by special agreements outside the operation of their general tariff systems; they thus constituted concessions made especially in favor of products of the United States. In the case of the agreements with Germany and Austria-Hungary the United States gained no special concessions, because these countries employed bargaining tariff systems which provided for the application of the unconditional interpretation of the most-favored-nation clause, thus generalizing their tariff concessions. The agreements concluded under the act of 1897 were made with countries each of which had in its tariff system a provision for the generalization of concessions, and the consequence was that as soon as each of the countries had entered into commercial agreements with a number of other countries the concessions which it granted, if not already enjoyed by most-favored nations, were extended, by generalization, to such countries.

"ARGOL AGREEMENTS," SECOND SERIES.

After 1906, and during President Roosevelt's administration, the United States negotiated a second series of agreements upon the basis of section 3 of the act of 1897. In this series, there were granted to the treaty countries concessions of duty upon the articles specified in that section, similar in character to those granted by the earlier series of argol agreements; some of the older agreements requiring renewal were extended; and champagne and other sparkling wines were added to the list of articles upon which concessions were granted by the United States.

Arrangement with Switzerland, 1906.—The first arrangement of the new series was that made with Switzerland. This country, as has been indicated above, had in 1900 applied the rates of her maximum tariff to American products, because of the denunciation by the United States of the most-favored-nation clauses of the treaty of 1850. In 1905 Switzerland adopted a new tariff with maximum and minimum schedules, to take effect on January 1, 1906; and by a decree promulgated in 1905, to take effect immediately upon the coming into force of the new tariff, she extended the entire schedule of minimum rates to American products. President Roosevelt considered the extension of the Swiss minimum rates to American products a sufficient return for the concessions which had been extended under section 3 of the act of 1897 to France, Germany, and other countries; and by a proclamation of January 1, 1906, to take effect on the same day, he extended these reductions of duty to Swiss products. The reestablishment of reciprocal commercial relations between the two countries was thus effected through concurrent and independent action by the two Governments and without the negotiation of a formal agreement.

Supplementary agreement with Germany, 1907.—The commercial treaties of Germany with other European countries were to expire on March 1, 1906, upon which date the German tariff law of 1902 was to come into effect. But, on the basis of the new tariff, and explaining the motive for new tariff legislation long prior to the date on which the law could take effect, the German Government had negotiated with the most important countries of Europe a series of new commercial treaties to become effective on March 1, 1906. These treaties created a new conventional tariff with substantial reductions varying from 20 per cent to 33⅓ per cent from the rates of the statutory tariff. The United States had secured, by the agreement of 1900, some of the concessions which had been granted by Germany to a number of European countries by the treaties which were to expire in 1906, but these concessions would expire with the termination of European treaties. The treaty of 1828 with Prussia, which otherwise might have been expected to assure the United States most-favored-nation treatment, was the subject of controversy between the two countries with regard to both its status and its interpretation. No reliance, therefore, could be placed upon it as a means of securing the United States against tariff discrimination by Germany. Unless a new agreement should be concluded, there was every reason to suppose that Germany would apply the rates of her new maximum tariff to the products of the United States, to the serious injury of the growing American export trade with Germany. The United States succeeded in concluding, in February, 1906, a special arrangement which guaranteed for her until June 30, 1907, the concessions granted by Germany to Belgium, Italy, Austria-Hungary, etc., in the new treaties of 1904 and 1905. In return, the United States was to continue in force the reductions of duties granted to Germany by the agreement of 1900. In the meantime, President Roosevelt sent a commission of experts to investigate and report as to the facts bearing upon the commercial relations between the two countries. Upon the basis of the report of this commission, a further temporary agreement was concluded in April and May, 1907, whereby the United States extended to Germany the reduced duties on sparkling wines provided for by section 3 of the act of 1897 and obtained in return a guarantee of the extension to American products of almost all of the conventional rates of the new German tariff. Germany had found objectionable some phases of the American customs administration, especially the methods used to secure a check on the customs valuations of importers and the severe penalties imposed for slight and unintentional undervaluation. In the agreement of 1907 there was inserted an undertaking by the United States to remedy by specified modifications certain of the objectionable features of its customs administration. The agreement was to remain in force until June 30, 1908, and thereafter subject to six months' notice for termination by either party.

Commercial agreement with Spain, 1906.—In 1898 Spain had increased the rates of her maximum tariff and had immediately applied them to American products. Upon the proposal of Mr. William Collier, the American minister at Madrid, Spain agreed on August 1, 1906, to extend most-favored-nation treatment (Portugal excepted) to the United States in return for similar treatment (Cuba excepted) from the United States. This involved the concession to Spain of the reduced duties already granted under section 3 of the act of 1897 to other countries, in return for the application of the Spanish minimum tariff to American products.[1]

Commercial arrangement with Bulgaria, 1906.—Bulgaria in 1906 had concluded commercial treaties with Germany, Great Britain, Russia, France, and Italy, whereby considerable reductions from her autonomous tariff were granted to these countries. Following the conclusion of these treaties, Bulgaria decided to accord most-favored-nation treatment to the products of countries with which agreements had been made in the past and which continued to extend most-favored-nation treatment to Bulgarian products. The United States had never concluded a commercial agreement with Bulgaria, but no discrimination against American products had ever been made by that country. As some differences of opinion existed in official circles in Bulgaria as to the treatment to which American products were entitled under the new tariff legislation, the American diplomatic agent, Mr. Jackson, was authorized, on June 5, 1906, to propose that reciprocal most-favored-nation treatment should continue to be applied by each country to the products of the other.[2] The Bulgarian Government accepted the proposal, and the arrangement, securing for American products the conventional rates of the Bulgarian tariff, went into effect immediately in Bulgaria. In the United States, however, the President's proclamation confirming this informal arrangement was not made until September 15, 1906, to take effect on September 30, 1906.

Amendatory agreements with France, 1902 and 1908.—On August 20, 1902, an amendatory and additional agreement was signed with France which applied the provisions of the original agreement of May 28, 1898, to Algeria and to Porto Rico, and provided that until February 23, 1903, Porto Rican coffee should be admitted into France at the minimum tariff rate. France entered into this agreement in the anticipation of the ratification of the convention of 1899 (under section 4 of the act of 1897), which would continue the arrangement more permanently. France continued to admit Porto Rican coffee at the minimum rate for some time after February 23, 1903, at first in the hope that the convention of 1899 might yet be ratified and later "in a friendly spirit for nothing." [3]

The situation in regard to the treatment of American petroleum was similar to that in regard to coffee. According to the often repeated French claim, the minimum rates had in 1893 been applied to American petroleum without the formality of an agreement, in the expec-

[1] U. S. Foreign Relations, 1906, vol. 2, pp. 1341-1342.
[2] Ibid., 1906, Pt. I, p. 141.
[3] Ibid., 1908, P. 320.

tation that compensatory concessions would be granted by the United States. The Wilson tariff of 1894, which made considerable reductions in the rates of duty on silks, woolen and cotton manufactures, gloves, wines, jewelry, porcelain, and furniture, was more favorable to the products of France than the preceding tariff had been. France therefore continued to apply to American petroleum the rates of her minimum tariff. Then came the passage of the act of 1897, with its greatly increased duties on the important products of France, and especially on silks. But in the hope of securing reductions from the rates of the Dingley tariff by means of a reciprocity treaty under section 4, France still hesitated to apply the maximum rates on American petroleum.

Negotiations for a treaty in conformity with the provisions of section 4 were actually entered upon and an agreement between the negotiators was reached, but the American Senate took no action leading to ratification, the treaty not being reported from the Senate Committee on Foreign Affairs.[1] On March 26, 1907, after, it had become certain that the treaty would not be ratified, France gave notice that after August 1, 1907, Porto Rican coffee would be subjected to the rate of the maximum tariff, and at about the same time she also intimated that she intended to withdraw the minimum rates from American petroleum. The importance of the proposed increase of duty on Porto Rican coffee lay in the fact that for certain qualities of that product France was the only market, while the French maximum rate of 26 cents per pound—equivalent to an ad valorem rate of almost 300 per cent—would be absolutely prohibitive. The threatened action with regard to petroleum was also of serious moment. The exports of American petroleum to France had shown considerable growth during this period. This was due in part to natural development, in part to the decrease in Russian shipments because of the Russo-Japanese war and the internal disturbances in Russia following its termination; also in part to the exclusion by France of petroleum from the Dutch East Indies, through the application thereto of her maximum rate. The withdrawal of the minimum rates from the American product would destroy the advantage enjoyed by the latter over that of the Dutch East Indies, and the American representatives argued strongly against any action which would have such effect.

The American representatives further contended that since the United States extended most-favored-nation treatment to the products of France she should be given the same treatment in return. They cited Italy, Austria-Hungary, Roumania, Servia, and Bulgaria as instances of countries with bargaining tariffs that "grant and have always granted to American products the unqualified benefits of their respective conventional tariffs."[2] On July 1, 1907, the United States extended to Germany the reductions of duty on sparkling wines authorized by section 3 of the act of 1897. France thereupon requested the same reductions for her champagne and other sparkling wines, in exchange for the continued admission of Porto Rican coffee at the minimum rate of duty. After somewhat protracted negotiations, an agreement was finally reached on January 28, 1908, whereby, in return for the reduction of duties on French champagne and other sparkling wines, France was to admit at the minimum rates coffee, chocolate, vanilla, and the other food

---

[1] See p, 221, seq., infra.   [2] U. S. Foreign Relations, 1908, p. 323.

products classified in the French tariff as "colonial products" (excepting sugar and tobacco) when coming from the United States (including Porto Rico), and to guarantee the continued admission of American petroleum at the minimum rate. The agreement was proclaimed and came into effect on February 1, 1908.

Agreements with Portugal, Great Britain, Spain, Italy, and the Netherlands.—On November 19, 1902, an amendatory agreement was concluded with Portugal, taking effect by proclamation of the President on January 24, 1907, whereby the terms of the agreement of May 22, 1899, were applied to Porto Rico. An agreement was concluded with Great Britain on November 19, 1907, and proclaimed by the President in the United States on December 5, 1907, whereby in return for the free admission of samples of dutiable goods brought into Great Britain by American commercial travelers, the reductions of duties on paintings, drawings, statuary, etc., provided for by section 3 of the act of 1897, were applied to these articles when imported from that country. A supplementary arrangement was concluded with Spain on February 20, 1909, whereby Spanish sparkling wines were to enter at the reduced rates which had already been extended to France, Germany, and other countries, "in order to remove any possible ground for exercise by the Spanish Government of the right under Article III of the agreement of August 1, 1906, to rescind any of its concessions made therein to the United States." [1] A supplementary agreement was signed with Italy on March 2, 1909, coming into effect by proclamation of the President on April 24, 1909, whereby the reductions on sparkling wines previously extended to some other countries were likewise granted to Italy, in return for the guarantee that the Italian duty on mowers and tedders should not exceed the rate of 4 lire per 100 kilograms—this being the existing rate of the Italian conventional tariff. On May 16, 1907, a commercial agreement, to take effect on August 12, 1908, was concluded with the Netherlands; in accordance with its terms the reductions of duty authorized by section 3 of the act of 1897 upon brandies and other distilled spirits were granted to the Netherlands, in return for the reduction of the rates of duty on certain American meat products.

Conclusions as to the effect of the concessional provision.—Limited in scope as were the reductions in duty authorized by section 3 of the act of 1897, they had undoubtedly proved their bargaining value. They had secured in favor of American products the rates of the minimum tariffs of Germany, Spain, Portugal, and Bulgaria; special remissions or reductions of duty from Italy, Great Britain, and the Netherlands; and a considerable modification of the French tariff discrimination against American products. To France the American reductions were possibly of considerable importance; their value to the other countries was negligible. They were small in amount, and they applied to but a few articles, not very important in the trade of these countries with the United States. The European countries were not, as a rule, seeking special favors, but used their bargaining tariffs as a means of protecting their exports against unfair discrimination. As soon as the American negotiators succeeded in convincing the European Governments that the reductions which they offered were not exceeded in the commercial agreements of the United States with other countries, they were able, except in their negotiations

---

[1] U. S. Foreign Relations, 1909, p. 545.

with France, to secure most-favored-nation treatment for American products. It was acknowledged in the course of the negotiations with several of the countries with which agreements were concluded that the American concessions were nominal in character. All that was sought from the United States by most of the treaty countries was most-favored-nation treatment. Whether this meant in immediate application considerable reductions of duty or merely nominal concessions appeared to be a minor consideration.

The provisions of section 3 operated somewhat unequally in one respect, so far as countries with single tariff systems were concerned. There seemed to be no way, for instance, by which Great Britain could get the minimum rates under section 3, except by making concessions of duty from her limited tariff schedule, which schedule already treated American products with impartiality—in fact, allowing most of them, as those of all countries. to enter duty free. There was a contrast between the treatment by the United States of France and Switzerland, on the one hand, and of Great Britain on the other. France levied high duties against American products, higher in most cases than those imposed upon similar products when coming from other countries. Nevertheless, by granting on a few articles the rates of her minimum tariff she secured all the American concessions. Switzerland, by the simple process of imposing her maximum tariff upon American imports and then withdrawing it again, secured the American concessions, on the ground of having given reciprocal and equivalent concessions in return. But Great Britain, as a consequence of having never discriminated against American products—at least in recent years—had no tariff discriminations to remove, and was unable to secure these concessions.

It is true that upon certain products of the United States Great Britain did levy duties which might have been reduced as a reciprocal concession to the United States. Such, in fact, was the character of the reductions made by the Netherlands. But there is a clear distinction between the removal of a discriminatory duty and the reduction of a duty which is applied to the products of all countries alike. A country with a policy of maintaining a single schedule of duties can make reductions of the latter sort only, the result of such reductions being, of course, either the establishing of special treatment, or the lowering of the general tariff. This is one of the disadvantages in tariff bargaining sustained by a country whose tariff contains only a single schedule and no bargaining provision. Nevertheless, except for the occasional discrimination against them by the United States, both Great Britain and the Netherlands received most-favored-nation treatment from all the important commercial countries. With due consideration of the general European practice in regard to tariff treatment of the products of countries employing single schedule tariffs of low duties, section 3 might consistently have contained a provision whereby most-favored-nation treatment could be extended, without bargaining, to such countries.

THE PENALTY DUTIES PROVIDED FOR BY SECTION 3.

The second portion of section 3 of the act of 1897 authorized the President to impose penalty duties upon the imports of coffee, tea, tonka, and vanilla beans, when coming from countries whose treatment of American products was "unequal and unreasonable." In its wording, and in the character of the power which it conferred upon the President, this portion of section 3 was identical with section 3 of the act of 1890. It differed, however, in one important respect. The main force of the bargaining features of the act of 1890 had lain in the authorization of a discriminatory duty upon the imports of sugar from countries treating the products of the United States unfavorably. No other article was as well suited to the purpose in 1890, and probably the same was true in 1897. But under the act of 1890 sugar and molasses had entered free of duty, while under the act of 1897 they were subjected to rates of duty much too high to make practicable a proposal for further increases, even though these increases were to be contingent only. The substitution of tonka and vanilla beans—articles of very slight commercial importance—for hides, sugar, and molasses lessened the effectiveness of the section very considerably. It was not to be expected, therefore, that any great results would be obtained from the operation of the clause. With one exception the section played no part in the negotiation of reciprocity agreements. In the argol agreement with Portugal a provision for the free admission of coffee into the United States had been inserted in order to safeguard the interests of the Portuguese coffee-growing islands, the Azores and the Madeiras.[1] But, although it did not lead to the negotiation of any formal agreement, a much more important result of the provision was the understanding reached with Brazil, whereby that country was induced to make considerable tariff reductions on a number of important products and manufactures of the United States. An account of the Brazilian preferential arrangement and its working will appear in another portion of this report.[2] The penalty provision did not figure in any other negotiations.

Agreements under section 3.—The following table presents a list of the reciprocal agreements concluded under section 3 of the tariff act of 1897. The agreements are listed in the order in which they became effective.

Reciprocity agreements which were concluded under section 3 of the tariff act of 1897.

Country.	Original agreement.		Amendatory agreement.		Date terminated.
	Date effective.	Articles included.	Date effective.	Additional articles included.	
France.........	June 1, 1898	All specified in section 3, except sparkling wines.	Aug. 22, 1902 Feb. 1, 1908	None...... Sparkling wines.	Oct. 31, 1909
Portugal,......	June 12, 1900	All specified in section 3, except vermuth.	Jan. 24, 1907	None...........	Aug. 7, 1910
Germany.......	July 13, 1900	All specified in section 3, except sparkling wines.	July 1, 1907	Sparkling wines.	Feb. 7, 1910
Italy..........	July 18, 1900	....do................	Apr. 24, 1909	.....do.........	Aug. 7, 1910
Switzerland....	Jan. 1, 1906	By concurrent legislation or executive action (no diplomatic action). All specified in section 3, except sparkling wines.			Oct. 31, 1909
Spain..........	Sept. 1, 1906	All specified in section 3, except sparkling wines.	Feb 20, 1909	Sparkling wines.	Aug. 7, 1910
Bulgaria.......	Sept. 30, 1906	....do................			Oct. 31, 1909
United Kingdom.	(June 5, 1906) Dec. 5, 1907	Statuary, paintings, etc., only.			Feb. 7, 1910
Netherlands....	Aug. 12, 1908	Brandies and other spirits only.			Aug. 7, 1910

[1] See p. 207, infr. [2] See p. 285 seq., infra.

COMMERCIAL TREATIES NEGOTIATED (BUT NOT RATIFIED) UNDER SECTION 4 OF THE TARIFF ACT OF 1897.

Section 4, which authorized the President to reduce by 20 per cent or less the duties on any articles imported into the United States, and further, to transfer to the free list natural products of other countries which were not natural products of the United States, in return for equivalent concessions by other countries, provided a basis for the establishment of much broader and more extensive reciprocal arrangements. In conformity with the provisions of section 4, Mr. Kasson negotiated the following conventions: with France; with the United Kingdom—for Barbados, British Guiana, Turks and Caicos Islands, Jamaica, Trinidad, and Bermuda; with Nicaragua; with Ecuador; with the Dominican Republic; with Denmark—for the island of St. Croix; and with the Argentine. The treaty term was five years in all of these conventions save two, in which cases it was four years. These treaties attracted much more attention and were subjected to much more discussion than were the argol agreements. Their provisions were more comprehensive and more important. An account of the negotiations and of the attempt of the administration to secure the ratification of the treaties follows.

Negotiations with France.—The treaty with France was the first to be negotiated. By the imposition of most of the rates of her maximum tariff upon imports from the United States, France had established a measure of discrimination against American products to which she subjected no other important country. If the reciprocity provisions of the act of 1897 were to prove their effectiveness, it was important that Mr. Kasson should secure at least a modification, if not the complete removal, of this discrimination. The negotiations between France and the United States were initiated in the autumn of 1897 by a proposal of the French Ambassador at Washington, M. Patenôtre, that the United States grant the full reduction of 20 per cent, authorized by section 4, to the entire list of French merchandise imported into the United States, in return for a concession by France of the whole minimum tariff. Mr. Kasson carefully considered this offer, but he found it unacceptable, and the failure to arrive at a mutually satisfactory basis for an agreement brought the negotiations to a halt. The French Government therefore submitted to the Chamber of Deputies several measures which, if adopted, would have proven very disadvantageous to American trade. But the conclusion of the argol agreement in 1898 secured the suspension of these measures and led to a resumption of negotiations upon the basis of the provisions of section 4 of the act of 1897. The French Government again demanded the full 20 per cent reduction allowed by section 4, but this was refused. Mr. Kasson further refused to make any concessions whatsoever on woolen goods, in view of the fact that there was a high duty on wool under the tariff act of 1897; and he excluded from consideration many other articles upon which he was unwilling to reduce the existing duties. He confined his concessions, according to his own statement, to articles peculiarly French, and limited the reductions in a majority of cases to 5 and 10 per cent of the existing rates. He intimated to the French representatives that if France continued to shut out the products of American industries by discriminatory duties, the United States might not take part in the Paris Exposition of 1900 and to the effect of this representation he later attributed in part his success in securing an agreement.[1]

Signing of Kasson treaty with France, 1899.—After these protracted and intermittent negotiations, the convention was finally signed on July 24, 1899. France undertook to apply to the products of the United States the minimum rates upon all but 19 of the 654 items enumerated in her minimum schedule. Of the articles from which the minimum rates were still withheld, two only, boots and shoes and machine tools, were of much commercial importance to the United States. On the articles specified in the treaty, the average reduction of duty from the rates of the maximum tariff was 26.1 per cent, excluding reductions of duties on mineral and vegetable oils, and 48 per cent, including these reductions. Upon many items the reduction was 50 and even 60 per cent. The average reduction for 96 products of the soil was over 32 per cent.

The comparison of the amounts of concession to be granted by each side had an important influence both in France and in the United States upon the determination of official and of popular opinion toward the convention, especially since the negotiators on both sides emphasized such comparisons as the most vital factor in the whole discussion. Elaborate calculations of these concessions were made on both sides, and the French, by including petroleum in their list of concessions, claimed that they had granted more than they received. Mr. Kasson, in his statement before the Senate Committee on Foreign Relations, explained that he had refused to acknowledge as a concession the minimum rates on petroleum which the American product had already been enjoying for some years. But the French, by simply withdrawing the minimum rates on one or two articles, in order to be able to concede them by the treaty, could increase the apparent amount of their concessions.

The failure of the American representative to secure the entire minimum schedule from France later gave rise to some complaints from the producers of the commodities excluded and particularly from the boot and shoe interests of Massachusetts. Mr. Kasson explained his failure as follows:

They do not take into account that it required the consent of France. If the United States could have included them, it would have been done. A persistent effort was made to do it, but they said, "we must exclude some articles, as you have done, or we can not get the treaty approved. The United States are keeping out a great number of articles and we must keep out some." I endeavored to the best of my ability to get them in, but they absolutely refused to allow them, as obstinately as we, on our part refused concessions on woolen goods and some other articles they wanted.[2]

By the convention the United States was to admit a list of specified products of France or Algeria at reductions in duty varying from 5 to 20 per cent from the existing rates, the list comprising 126 of the 463 dutiable items enumerated in the United States tariff. France had already granted to all most-favored nations, and therefore to practically all Europe, the concessions

---

[1] 56th Cong., 1st sess., Sen. Doc. No. 225, p. 66.   [2] Ibid., p. 77.

extended to the United States by the treaty. The concessions offered by the United States to France had not as yet been extended or promised to any other country.

Treaties with Great Britain for the West Indies.—Of the other treaties negotiated under section 4, none approached in importance the proposed treaty with France. Nevertheless, the terms of these other treaties are of interest as they reveal both the plans of the administration in reference to the reciprocity provisions of the act of 1897 and the effectiveness of such provisions in securing more favorable treatment from other countries for the products of American industry. All of these proposed treaties were with American countries, namely: The Argentine, Ecuador, Nicaragua, the Dominican Republic, Denmark—for the island of St. Croix, Great Britain—for Barbados, British Guiana, Turks and Caicos Islands, Jamaica, and Bermuda.[1]

The first advance toward the establishment of reciprocity on the basis of section 4 of the act of 1897 had been made by Great Britain on behalf of the British West Indies. The negotiations did not prove difficult. As finally concluded and presented to the Senate Committee on Foreign Relations, the agreements made provision for reductions of duty to each colony by the United States on a very short list of articles, in return for reductions in the tariffs of each of the colonies on important and longer lists including both agricultural and manufactured products. The considerations were different for the different colonies. The treaty for Jamaica provided for reductions by the United States of: (a) 20 per cent of the duties on rum, citrus fruits, pineapples, and fresh vegetables, including potatoes and onions; and (b) of 12½ per cent on cane sugar and molasses. The treaty with Great Britain for British Guiana stipulated a reduction of 12½ per cent on cane sugars, fresh vegetables, and kaolin; for Barbados a reduction of 12½ per cent of the duties on cane sugar and molasses, fresh fruits, fresh vegetables, and asphalt; for Turks and Caicos Islands a reduction of 12½ per cent on salt and sponges, unmanufactured, and the free admission of sisal grass, not dressed or manufactured; for Bermuda 20 per cent on potatoes, onions, tomatoes, and other fresh vegetables, bulbs, and natural flowers. In return each of these colonies was to admit at a considerable reduction or with total remission of duty many of the most important agricultural and manufactured products of the United States.

Of the reductions in the duties of the tariff act of 1897 which the United States undertook to grant in these treaties, the only ones which affected important American industries were the reduction of 12½ per cent on sugar, which was conceded to all of these colonies except Bermuda, and that of 20 per cent on oranges extended to Jamaica. Of the total imports of sugar into the United States in 1898, amounting to 1,200,000 tons, only 103,000 tons came from the British West Indies. In the opinion of Mr. Kasson, a reduction of 12½ per cent from the high duties on sugar of the act of 1897 left a sufficient amount of protection to safeguard the interests of the domestic sugar industry. The duty on oranges under the Dingley

---

[1] A treaty was negotiated with Great Britain for Trinidad, but the period stipulated in the treaty for exchange of ratifications expired without the treaty having been submitted to the Senate, and extension of the period was refused by the colony.

tariff, even with the reduction stipulated by the Jamaica treaty, would still be twice as high as it had been under the act of 1890. Almost the entire Jamaican output already found its market in the United States, and according to Mr. Kasson the inferior quality of Jamaica oranges and the time of year at which they ripen would prevent their competing seriously with the California product. Nevertheless, both these items of tariff reduction aroused considerable opposition from the interests concerned and contributed to the hostile attitude of the Senate Committee on Foreign Relations toward the treaties.

Treaties with Denmark, for St. Croix, with the Dominican Republic, with Nicaragua, and with Ecuador.—By the treaty with Denmark for the island of St. Croix the United States was to reduce its duties on rum and sugar by $12\frac{1}{2}$ per cent, in return for which St. Croix was to admit a long list of American agricultural products and a few important manufactured articles free of duty or at considerably reduced rates. The treaties with the Dominican Republic, Nicaragua, and Ecuador were similar in character, involving concessions by the United States on short lists of articles in which these countries were interested, among which were sugar and hides, in return for important reductions of duties on American products.

Treaty with the Argentine.—The negotiations with the Argentine were carried on for the United States by the American minister, Mr. Buchanan, at Buenos Aires. Mr. Buchanan found it impossible to persuade the Argentine Government to enter into treaty relations except upon the basis of the reduction of the American duty on wool; and in the treaty which was finally signed the American concessions were practically confined to a reduction of 20 per cent on wool. In return there were obtained reductions of duty on a number of American products and a modification of the Argentine *aforo*. This latter was a system of arbitrary and variable customs valuations, whereby the specific duties could be and frequently were increased without legislative action. The repeated changes in actual rates which were thus effected were a cause of constant uncertainty and often of loss to importing interests.

Summary of concessions to be granted.—The American negotiators, seeing opportunities for a great development of the trade in coal with South America, made it a point to obtain in all these treaties provisions for the favorable treatment of American coal. Six of the treaties provided that coal should be duty free; the others provided for the reduction or limitation of the rates at which it was dutiable. The concessions which the American countries agreed to grant to the United States in these treaties were too many and too varied to be accounted for here in detail. For the more important commodities upon which the treaties specified reductions by the United States, a comparison between the rates of duty specified in the treaties and the rates of the tariff acts of 1890 and 1897 is presented in the following table.

Rates of duty upon selected commodities under Kasson treaties compared with rates under tariff acts of 1890 and 1897.

Commodity.	Treaty country.	Rates under tariff act of 1990.	Rates under tariff act of 1897.	Rates under treaties.	Imports from treaty country, 1898.
Asphalt	Barbados	Free	50¢ per ton	43⅓¢ per ton	$240,286
Fresh fruit	Barbados	Not on a comparable basis.	Citrus 1¢ per lb	⅞¢ per lb	[1] 506,642
	Jamaica		Pineapples $7 per thousand.	$5.60 per thousand	[1] 246,415
Fresh vegetables.	Barbados	Various	Various	12½% reduction	...
	Jamaica			20% reduction	[1] 1,215
	Bermuda			do	381,319
	British Guiana.			12½% reduction	...
Hides	Argentine	Free	15% ad valorem	12% ad volorem	2,928,597
	San Domingo.			do	53,327
	Ecuador			Free	95,433
	Nicaragua			do	62,833
Honey	San Domingo.	20¢ per gal	20¢ per gal	16¢ per gal	3,240
Rum	Jamaica	$2.50 per gal	$2.25 per gal	$1.70 per gal	[1] 42,834
	St. Croix			$1.97 per gal	811
Sponges	Turks and Caicos Islands.	20% ad valorem	20% ad valorem	17½% ad valorem	[1] 244,973
Sugar	Barbados, Jamaica	Free	1–2¢ per lb	⅞–1¾¢ per lb	[1] 4,551,282
	British Guiana.			do	3,045,666
	San Domingo.			⅞–1⅜¢ per lb	2,030,239
	St. Croix			⅘–1⅜¢ per lb	312,443
	Argentine			do	260,957
	Nicaragua			do	8,195
Molasses	Barbados, Jamaica	Free	3–6¢ per gal	2⅝–5¼¢ per gal	[1] 86,782
	San Domingo.			do	24
	St. Croix			do	939
Tobacco (leaf)	San Domingo.	35¢ per lb	35¢ per lb	28¢ per lb	21,295
Wool	Argentine	Class I, 11¢ per lb	Class I, 11¢ per lb	Class I, 8⅘¢ per lb	557,530
		Class II, 12¢ per lb	Class II, 12¢ per lb	Class II, 9⅗¢ per lb	18,813
		Class III, 32–50% ad valorem.	Class III, 4–7¢ per lb.	Class III, 3⅕¢–5⅗¢ per lb.	58,382

[1] From British West Indies.

Even after the reductions specified by the treaties the rates upon many of the articles remained higher, as will be seen from the figures of the above table, than they had been under the tariff act of 1890.

Unsuccessful negotiations with Russia.—The United States Government entered into negotiations with Russia whereby concessions of considerable value to the American exporters were to be granted by Russia in return for some minor reductions of duty on the part of the United States. By 1900 these negotiations were on the point of reaching a satisfactory conclusion. In 1901 the countervailing duty on bounty sugar which was authorized by the tariff act of 1897 was imposed by the Secretary of the Treasury on Russian sugar, on the ground that the omission of the Russian Government to collect, on a certain proportion of the output of each sugar factory when exported, the taxes which it would have levied thereon if sold for consumption in Russia, operated as an indirect bounty to the export of sugar.[1]

[1] The Russian sugar tax system was very complicated, and there was considerable difference of opinion in the United States as to whether or not it operated to subsidize export of sugar from Russia. The Treasury decision to the effect that there existed in effect in Russia a bounty on sugar export—the Appraiser General dissenting—is to be found in Treasury Decisions, vol. 4, pp. 405–419, Apr. 19, 1901. See also the decision of the Supreme Court in the case of Downs *vs.* United States.

The Russian Government denied that its tax legislation operated in any manner so as to result in a bounty to sugar export, and interpreted the imposition of the countervailing duty of the United States Government as a retaliatory measure which had only been withheld up to that time because of the expectation of a successful conclusion of the reciprocity negotiations then under way. Under the Russian customs regulations, "goods which form the basis of manufacture and trade in those countries which do not give Russia the most favored privileges of import and transit" were subject to customs surtaxes of 30 per cent above the minimum rates on certain schedules and 20 per cent on others. Under the authority of this regulation, the Russian Government increased by 30 per cent the duties on American manufactures. These increases came into effect on March 1, 1901.[1]

In 1903, a revision of the Russian tariff introduced additional increases of from 25 to 100 per cent in the duties on many articles. As most countries had commercial treaties with Russia which made impossible the alteration of the existing rates until those treaties should expire, the whole weight of these increases fell upon those countries which did not enjoy most-favored-nation treatment. They fell with especial severity upon the products of the United States because of the nature of the articles upon which these additional duties were to be levied. But in 1905 Count Witte, following the successful negotiation, with American assistance, of a Russo-Japanese peace, notified the American Government that all discrimination against American products would be removed and that most-favored-nation treatment would in the future be extended to the products of the United States.[2]

TREATIES SUBMITTED TO SENATE FOR RATIFICATION.

The President transmitted the French treaty to the Senate on December 6, 1899, and the other treaties soon after. The treaties were referred to the Senate Committee on Foreign Relations, which took up their study in January, 1900, and it was in this committee that the discussion of the treaties centered. Mr. Kasson appeared before the committee on January 10 in support of the French treaty, and made a long statement favoring its ratification.[3] In this statement Mr. Kasson declared the French treaty to be the most important and the most valuable to the United States. As he saw little likelihood of negotiating with European countries any others that would be more advantageous, he was awaiting the results of the submission of the French treaty to the Senate before carrying his European negotiations further. He had put his best efforts into the French treaty, and he could see no propriety in continuing the negotiations and adding to the embarrassment to which the Government would be subjected.

In a memorandum relating to the French treaty, Mr. Kasson presented to the committee an analysis of the French imports, purporting to show that the United States sold France 36 per cent of her duty-free imports, 35 per cent of the dutiable imports upon which there was

---

[1] U. S. Consular Report, July, 1901, p. 412.
[2] See Part II, p. 433, infra.
[3] Mr. Kasson's statement appears in 56th Cong., 1st sess., Sen. Doc. No. 225, pp. 63–81.

no tariff discrimination when coming from this country, and only 1.4 per cent of the imports upon which the maximum rates were levied when coming from the United States.[1] From these figures he drew the "inevitable" conclusion that, if the minimum rates were secured for the articles of American export which at the time were subjected to the maximum rates, the United States would furnish France with a large percentage also of this, the largest class of her imports.

There was no lack of popular interest in and discussion of the merits of the treaties, especially of the treaty with France. Those who were directly interested in the results of the negotiations conducted active campaigns in the press, at public meetings, and before the Senate Committeee on Foreign Relations. Mr. Kasson presented a collection of letters from American producers and exporters who had found their trade with France restricted by the tariff discriminations to which it was subjected. These interests anticipated a considerable development of the French trade, provided as favorable treatment could be secured for their products as that which was extended to their European competitors. Most prominent among the industrial interests who favored the ratification of the treaties were the manufacturers of agricultural implements. Pleas for the ratification of the treaty were also made by representatives of the manufacturers of various other iron and steel products and by smelting and refining companies.

The ability of the French Government, when not bound by treaties, to raise duties at will, and to transfer rates from the minimum to the maximum tariff, and its readiness to do this by way of retaliation—of which the United States already had had experience—made the ratification of the treaty important, in Mr. Kasson's view, in that, for the treaty period, it would relieve American export interests from the uncertainty caused by the constant apprehension of unfavorable tariff changes.

Debate on ratification.—The discussion of the treaty developed into a contest between two groups of interests. On the one side were representatives of the American industries which were on an export basis, together with other persons who were less directly concerned but who favored any measure which would bring about a reduction in the rates of the tariff of 1897. On the other side were both domestic producers who feared the giving of any encouragement to foreign competition, and those who objected to a reduction of duties, not because of any personal interest they might have in its immediate effect, but because reductions in duties by treaty—"reciprocity"—seemed to them a dangerous precedent and an infringement of the principle of protection.

The chief opposition to the ratification of the French treaty came from the manufacturers of certain articles which either were already in competition with French articles of similar character or seemed to the American producers thereof to be likely to offer competition if the duties were lowered in the slightest extent. Mr. Kasson maintained, however, that in most of these cases the imports from France formed but a small part either of the total imports or of the domestic production. He claimed that, even with the reductions of duty specified in the treaty, the remaining rates would still be higher in

---

[1] 56th Cong., 1st sess., Sen. Doc. No. 225, p. 110.

most cases than the rates of the tariffs of 1890 and 1894. In any case, he maintained that the total injury which could possibly accrue to American industries through the intensified competition of imports from France with their products would be more than offset by the gains to American industry resulting from the increased exports to France.

Reductions of American duties in the treaty with France.—The following table presents data relating to the industries which would have been most affected had the French treaty been ratified.

Rates of duty on French products specified in Kasson treaty with France as compared with rates of the tariff acts of 1890 and 1897.[1]

Article.	Rates under the tariff act of 1890.	Rates under the tariff act of 1897.	Rates under treaty.	Imports from France, 1898.
Brushes	40 per cent	40 per cent	36 per cent	$476,433
Electric and gas fixtures.	45 per cent	45 per cent	40.5 per cent	480,000
Jewelry	50 per cent	60 per cent	57 per cent	908,807
Knit goods (cotton)	35 per cent ad valorem to $2 per dozen stockings plus 40 per cent ad valorem.	50–71 per cent	40–57 per cent	241,278
Optical instruments and spectacles.	60 per cent	45 per cent	40.5 per cent	245,167
		80 per cent	72 per cent	188,969
Paper	25–35 per cent	20–50 per cent	18–45 per cent	256,424
Perfumes	$2 per gallon and 50 per cent ad valorem.	50–68 per cent	45–61 per cent	367,841
Tiles and fire bricks, etc.	25–40 per cent	40–73 per cent	35–65 per cent	(2)

[1] 56th Cong., 1st sess., Sen. Doc. 225, pp. 146–160.   [2] Less than $30,000 from all countries.

In the table are included only those articles on the ground of whose inclusion in the treaty the American producers protested against ratification. The table exhibits for comparison the rates as reduced by the treaty and the rates of the tariffs of 1890 and 1897. It also shows the value of the imports from France in the year 1898. In some cases the comparison of rates is difficult because in the one case specific or partly specific duties were imposed, while in the other the duties were *ad valorem*. In no case, with the exception of tiles and fire bricks, were the imports from France insignificant.

Ratification of treaties urged by Mr. Kasson.—While the treaties were still before the Senate Committee on Foreign Relations, awaiting ratification, Mr. Kasson was invited to deliver before the Illinois Manufacturers' Association an address on the question of reciprocity. In the course of this address he answered the claim made in various quarters that the treaty with France involved a repudiation by the Republican administration of the protective principle upon which the party had gone before the people in the election of 1896. He contended that the treaties were unquestionably consistent with the principles of protection, but he distinguished between two types of protectionism, the reasonable and the unreasonable, the former of which recognized the plain fact that protection for the export trade had become equally important with protection of the home market. He admitted that the United States was not yet sufficiently sure of its foreign markets to abandon a policy of reasonable protection of the home market; but, on the other hand, he contended that the home market was so safeguarded for American producers as to justify moderate concessions of rates to aid the export trade.[1]   Following this speech, the Illinois Manufacturers' Association adopted a resolution strongly urging upon the Senate the early ratification of the pending treaties.

Failue to secure approval of the Senate.—The administration failed in its attempt to secure, during this session, the ratification of the French treaty. Senator Aldrich, the chairman of the Committee on Foreign Affairs, succeeded, with others, in preventing any action by the committee. President McKinley gave the reciprocity treaties his continued support. In his annual message to Congress in 1900 he urged upon the Senate the speedy ratification of the treaties which had been submitted and referred to the reciprocity policy in the following words:

The policy of reciprocity so manifestly rests upon the principles of international equity, and has been so repeatedly approved by the people of the United States that there ought to be no hesitation in either branch of Congress in giving to it full effect.[2]

But the interests unfavorable to reciprocity maintained active opposition, and no progress towards ratification was made during the short session of 1900–1901. In the meantime the period originally stipulated in the treaties for the exchange of ratifications had expired in the case of all of these treaties; but supplementary conventions extending the period during which such ratifications could be obtained were signed for all except that affecting Trinidad. In the case of Trinidad, the extension was refused by the colony upon advice of the British authorities.

Reference to an address by Senator F. E. Warren may help to explain the disinclination of the Senate Committee on Foreign Relations to report favorably on the treaties. In the course of this address, Senator Warren made the following statement regarding the history of the treaties in the committee:

When the (Argentine) treaty was transmitted to the Senate it was referred to the Committee on Foreign Relations, and I violate no propriety when I state that that committee gave the Argentine, as well as other reciprocity treaties submitted to it, a thorough, complete and full hearing, with the result that the treaties submitted were found to be not in accord with the principle of the reciprocity provision of the Dingley Act. According to the theory of the great apostle of reciprocity, James G. Blaine, and according to the contention of William McKinley and a majority of the American people we should exchange only commodities which one country or the other does not produce; but in the Argentine treaty this important principle was apparently lost sight of by its framers.[3]

Resignation of Mr. Kasson.—Disheartened by his failure to secure action from Congress on the treaties which he had so successfully negotiated, Mr Kasson, on March 9, 1901, tendered his resignation as special commissioner of the President, the resignation to become effective on April 19, 1901. The reciprocity commission continued in existence for some time as a special bureau of the State Department, intrusted with the duties of attention to the negotiation of reciprocity agreements; but as no such agreements were concluded or attempted during the next few years its activity was confined to matters of routine.

The Republican Party and reciprocity.—President McKinley continued to give the Kasson treaties his faithful support. But in spite

---

[1] Delivered at Chicago, Oct. 4, 1901, and later printed in book form under the title, "Reciprocity."
[2] U. S. Foreign Relations, 1900, p. xxvii.
[3] Reported in The Protectionist, Sept., 1901, vol. 13, No. 5, p. 288.

of his personal popularity, and in spite of the growing demand for broader foreign markets, upon which he based his support of reciprocity, the President could not carry his party with him. The Republican Party favored reciprocity only as it had been outlined in their platform of 1900, reciprocity "so directed as to open our markets on favorable terms for what we do not ourselves produce in return for free foreign markets."

Reciprocity convention called by manufacturers.—By the summer of 1901 no further progress toward the ratification of the treaties had been made. The continued desire for the broadening of foreign markets for American manufactures and the anxiety caused by the discriminatory legislation of the European Governments were again arousing the American exporting interests to a sense of the necessity for a careful consideration of reciprocity. On September 4 the National Association of Manufacturers issued a call for a reciprocity convention "for the purpose of clear comprehension and expression of public sentiment."

President McKinley's last speech.—On the next day President McKinley delivered the famous Buffalo speech, his last address, in which he presented his views of the relation of reciprocity to protection and committed himself more strongly than ever to reciprocity. He spoke in part as follows:

By sensible trade arrangements, which will not interrupt our home production, we shall extend the outlets for our increasing surplus. A system which provides a mutual exchange of commodities is manifestly essential to the continued and healthful growth of our export trade. We must not repose in fancied security that we can forever sell everything and buy little or nothing. If such a thing were possible, it would not be best for us or for those with whom we deal. We should take from our customers such of their products as we can use without harm to our industries and labor. Reciprocity is the mutual outgrowth of our wonderful industrial development under the domestic policy now firmly established. * * *

The period of exclusiveness is past. The expansion of our trade and commerce is the pressing problem. Commercial wars are unprofitable. A policy of good will and friendly trade relations will prevent reprisal. Reciprocity treaties are in harmony with the spirit of the times; measures of retaliation are not.

If perchance some of our tariffs are no longer needed for revenue or to encourage and protect our industries at home, why should they not be employed to extend and promote our markets abroad? [1]

The President's speech gave a great impetus to the agitation for reciprocity, which immediately became widespread. But the ranks of the party in power were divided on the question, and it soon became evident that the decision of the manufacturers' reciprocity convention would have considerable influence in determining what action should be taken in respect to the treaties awaiting ratification.[2]

The manufacturers' reciprocity convention.—The manufacturers' "reciprocity convention" met in Washington on November 19. As soon as it had assembled, all doubt disappeared as to what its verdict would be. The final resolution of the convention recommended to Congress the maintenance of the principle of protection for the home market and the extension by reciprocity of opportunities for increased

[1] 58th Cong., 2d sess., Sen. Doc. No. 268, pp. 8 and 9. Delivered at the Pan-American Exposition at Buffalo, Sept. 5, 1901.

[2] The New York Tribune on Nov. 13, 1901, expressed itself in regard to the Kasson treaties and the manufacturers' convention as follows: "It is confidently predicted that the convention will define the attitude and expectations of the business interests of the Nation on the reciprocity question so clearly * * * that there will no longer be cause for anybody to misunderstand the program, policies, and purpose by which a new Congress overwhelmingly Republican in both branches will be guided."

foreign trade by special reductions of the tariff in special cases, but only where it could be done without injury to any of the domestic interests of manufacturing, commerce, or farming.[1] The resolution rendered it certain that the Republican Party would not push the ratification of the Kasson treaties and would take no further steps for the extension of the reciprocity policy.

There are several factors to account for the defeat of the reciprocity movement so soon after it had been proclaimed with apparent enthusiasm and unity of sentiment. Undoubtedly a potent reason was the inevitable difference between reciprocity in theory and reciprocity in practice. Reciprocity as a theory stimulated many hopes of trade expansion and injured no one. But reciprocity incorporated in agreements stipulating specific reductions of duty threatened the profits of some and gave only a vague promise of gains to others. Moreover, the American export trade was expanding without the aid of any thoroughgoing establishment of reciprocity, and this fostered the general and growing disposition to let well enough alone.

President Roosevelt and reciprocity.—President Roosevelt in his first annual message to Congress adhered to the position taken by his predecessor, but in less emphatic terms. He emphasized the consistency of reciprocity with protection. In this message he said:

Reciprocity must be treated as the handmaiden of protection. Our first duty is to see that the protection granted by the tariff in every case where it is needed is maintained, and that reciprocity be sought for so far as it can safely be done without injury to our home industries. * * * The natural line of development for a policy of reciprocity will be in connection with those of our productions which no longer require all of the support once needed to establish them upon a sound basis, and with those others where either because of natural or of economic causes we are beyond the reach of successful competition.

I ask the attention of the Senate to the reciprocity treaties laid before it by my predecessor.[2]

But in this session also, no action was taken by the Senate toward the ratification of the treaties. In his message of the following year President Roosevelt, after discussing the necessity of tariff adjustments, referred to reciprocity as follows:

One way in which the readjustment sought can be reached is by reciprocity treaties. It is greatly to be desired that such treaties may be adopted. They can be used to widen our markets and to give a greater field for the activities of our producers on the one hand, and on the other hand to secure in practical shape the lowering of duties when they are no longer needed for protection among our own people, or when the minimum of damage done may be disregarded for the sake of the maximum of good accomplished. If it prove impossible to ratify the pending treaties, and if there seem to be no warrant for the endeavor to execute others, or to amend the pending treaties so that they can be ratified, then the same end—to secure reciprocity—should be met by direct legislation.[3]

Lapsing of treaties.—The extended periods for the ratification of the treaties were allowed to expire, and no further attempt was made to continue the negotiations with the countries concerned. After four years' delay without its being submitted to the Senate, the French treaty negotiated in 1899 was considered by the administration to have been finally abandoned, and the French embassy was

---

[1] The New York Tribune interpreted the resolution as a "complete repudiation of the work done by the reciprocity commissioner, John A. Kasson, and an even plainer note warning the Senate no longer to consider the Kasson treaties now pending." (Nov. 21, 1901.)
[2] U. S. Foreign Relations, 1901, p. xxiii.
[3] U. S. Foreign Relations, 1903, p. xvi.

so informed in June, 1903.[1] In his annual message to Congress for 1903, President Roosevelt made no reference to reciprocity. The treaties remained pigeonholed in the Senate Committee on Foreign Affairs and no further action was ever taken regarding them.

ARGOL AGREEMENTS TERMINATED BY THE TARIFF ACT OF 1909.

The Payne-Aldrich tariff bill.—The Payne-Aldrich tariff bill, as submitted to the House in 1909, contained a provision instructing the President to give notice within ten days after the passage of the act to all foreign countries with which, in conformity with section 3 of the act of 1897, reciprocity agreements had been concluded, of the intention of the United States to terminate such agreements. The length of the period of notice was to be governed in each case by the stipulations regarding termination contained in the agreement. This provision remained unchanged and was not made the occasion for debate until the bill reached the conference committee.

The conference committee added the further provision that in the cases where commercial agreements contained no stipulations in regard to their termination, they were to terminate on October 31, 1909. As the agreement with France contained no provision regarding its own termination, the reductions of duty authorized by section 3 of the act of 1897 would be withdrawn sooner in the case of France than in the case of those countries whose agreements stipulated one year's notice, and it was pointed out in the Senate that this would operate as a discrimination against France.

Provision in the act of 1909 for termination of agreements.—The provision in the tariff act of 1909 for the termination of existing commercial agreements which had been concluded under the act of 1897 was as follows:

SEC. 4. That the President shall have power, and it shall be his duty to give notice, within ten days after the passage of this act, to all foreign countries with which commercial agreements in conformity with the authority granted by section three of the act entitled "An act to provide revenue for the Government and to encourage the industries of the United States," approved July twenty-four, eighteen hundred and ninety-seven, have been or shall have been entered into, of the intention of the United States to terminate such agreement at a time specified in such notice, which time shall in no case, except as hereinafter provided, be longer than the period of time specified in such agreements respectively for notice for their termination; and upon the expiration of the periods when such notice of termination shall become effective the suspension of duties provided for in such agreements shall be revoked, and thereafter importations from said countries shall be subject to no other conditions or rates of duty than those prescribed by this act and such other acts of Congress as may be continued in force: *Provided,* That until the expiration of the period when the notice of intention to terminate hereinbefore provided for shall have become effective, or until such date prior thereto as the high contracting parties may by mutual consent select, the terms of said commercial agreements shall remain in force: *And provided further,* That in the case of those commercial agreements or agreements made in accordance with the provisions of section three of the tariff act of the United States approved July twenty-four, eighteen hundred and ninety-seven, which contain no stipulations in regard to their termination by diplomatic action, the President is authorized to give to the Governments concerned a notice of termination of six months, which notice shall date from April thirtieth, nineteen hundred and nine.

---

[1] U. S. Foreign Relations, 1903, p. 318.

Termination of agreements.—The provisions in the tariff act of 1909 which carefully stipulated the method of termination of the commercial agreements concluded under section 3 of the act of 1897 were intended to remove all danger of controversies and protests, such as those which resulted from the abrupt termination by the tariff act of 1894 of the agreements concluded under the act of 1890. Preliminary notice of the intended termination of the agreements had been given on April 30, 1909, or prior to the passage of the tariff act of 1909, to all countries with which commercial agreements under section 3 of the act of 1897 had been concluded. Final notice was given to these countries on August 6 and 7. Of these agreements, two stipulated six months' prior notice for termination; four stipulated one year's notice; and two—those with France and Bulgaria—contained no provisions for termination. The arrangement whereby Switzerland had been granted the concessions authorized by section 3 of the act of 1897 had no tbeen established through diplomatic action and therefore required no notice of termination; but the State Department followed the same procedure regarding this arrangement as that which had been adopted for the agreements which contained no provisions for. their termination.

Controversy with France regarding termination of agreement of 1908.—The only difficulty which arose from this method of terminating the agreements was experienced with France. The French Government claimed that the agreement of 1908 had been made in permanent form, that its termination required a diplomatic understanding, and that the allowing of a shorter period of notice to France than to the other reciprocity countries was unfriendly. It intimated that the French laws which had been suspended by the agreement with the United States would be reenacted immediately upon its termination, but suggested the probability of the continued application to the products of the United States of the minimum rates enumerated in the agreement, provided this agreement were not terminated in advance of the other agreements. The American Government took the position, however, that the act of 1909 prescribed a definite procedure which left no opportunity for discretion and gave no authority whereby the admission of the French products enumerated in the agreement could be continued at the reduced rates beyond the date set by the law. Upon the termination of the agreement, on November 1, 1909, France applied all the rates of her maximum tariff to American products.[1]

EFFECT OF AGREEMENTS CONCLUDED UNDER SECTION 3.

The influence on American trade of the reciprocity agreements which were concluded under section 3 of the act of 1897 is to be studied, as has been that of the agreements concluded under the act of 1890, with a view to both the results upon imports and the results upon exports. In this case, as in that of the agreements under the act of 1890, the nature of the concessions made by and to the United States was such that reciprocity exerted a much greater influence upon exports than upon imports.

---

[1] U. S. Foreign Relations, 1909, pp. 248–250.

EFFECT UPON IMPORTS.

In the case of imports, reciprocity, by causing a reduction of the duties on a large portion of the imports of the articles which are the subjects of the various agreements, may lower the price to the consumer and may thereby lead to an increase of the gross amount of imports. Even if the imports which come in at the reduced duties are not in sufficient quantity to effect a reduction of price to the consumer, they may nevertheless represent a considerable diversion of trade from non-reciprocity to reciprocity countries, and may therefore be of distinct advantage to the latter.

The articles upon which reductions of duties were made in the agreements concluded under section 3 of the act of 1897 were few, but in amount of imports they were not unimportant. The agreements came into effect soon after the revision of the tariff in 1897, and they terminated soon after another revision in 1909. It is necessary, therefore, that caution be exercised lest there be attributed to the influence of the agreements that which was more probably the result of the legislative changes in the tariff.

Table I shows the rates of duty on reciprocity articles in the tariff schedules of 1894, 1897, and 1909 as compared with the rates specified in the agreements.

TABLE I.—*Rates of duty on articles specified in section 3 of the tariff act of 1897, as compared with general rates under the tariff acts of 1894, 1897, and 1909.*

Article.	Tariff act of 1894.	Tariff act of 1897.		Tariff act of 1909.
		General rates.	Rates under section 3.	
Argols...................	Free................	1 to 1½ cents per lb. (=16%. ad valorem circa).	5% ad valorem (= $\frac{7}{10}$-$\frac{2}{3}$ cent per lb. circa).	5% ad valorem (= $\frac{2}{3}$ cent per lb. circa).
Brandies and other distilled spirits.	$1.80 per proof gallon.	$2.25 per proof gallon.	$1.75 per proof gallon.	$2.60 per proof gallon.
Champagne and all other sparkling wines.	$8 per dozen quart bottles.	$8 per dozen quart bottles.	$6 per dozen quart bottles.	$9.60 per dozen quart bottles.
Still wines..............	$1.60 per dozen quart bottles.	$1.60 per dozen quart bottles.	$1.25 per dozen quart bottles.	$1.85 per dozen quart bottles.
Works of art (not for exhibition purposes nor the work of American artists).	Free...............	20% ad valorem...	15% ad valorem...	Free, if 20 years old or over.

From the data presented in this table it will be seen that in the case of argols and art works even the treaty rates under the act of 1897 were higher than the rates effective previous to the passage of the act; in the case of brandies the treaty rate was practically the same as the general rate under the act of 1894; in the case of still wines the treaty rate was lower than the old rate by only 35 cents per dozen quart bottles. There remain only sparkling wines and brandy as the commodities upon which, by means of reciprocity agreements, a considerable reduction of duty could be effected. Except in the case of these two last-named commodities there should, therefore, be no reason to expect to find, as a consequence of reciprocity, a considerable increase in the imports of the specified commodities.

The reciprocity agreements created a preference in favor of the treaty countries even in the case of the articles which were taxed at a higher rate than that to which they had been subject under the tariff act of 1894. The preference in favor of treaty countries amounted to about 70 per cent of the general rates in the case of argols, about 22 per cent for brandies, 25 per cent for champagne, 20 per cent for still wines, and 25 per cent for works of art. Percentage reductions of duties become more important as the basic rates of duty increase, and, conversely, they diminish in importance as the basic rates of duty decrease. Thus a preference of 20 per cent is of much more significance when the rate of duty is 50 per cent than when the rate of duty is only 10 per cent. In the case of still wines the rate of duty was so low that even the complete remission of duty to the reciprocity countries would not have been of very great importance. The general rate of duty on still wines amounted to $1.60 per dozen quart bottles, while the rate of duty under section 3 was about $1.25 per dozen quart bottles. A preference of only 3 cents on each quart bottle of wine could not be expected to exert great influence on the course of trade. The general duties on sparkling wines, argols, brandies, and works of arts were on a much higher level, however, and the relative percentages of preference established upon these articles by the reciprocity agreement were also higher. Diversion of trade to the countries with which agreements were concluded would be expected, therefore, to have been more marked in the case of these last-named articles than in that of still wines.

Imports by commodities.—In the course of the following analysis of imports by commodities the reciprocity countries are grouped for each commodity in such a manner as to bring together countries for which the treaty periods correspond most closely and which exported in large amounts the articles under examination at the moment.

ARGOLS.

Table II.—*Imports of argols into the United States, 1896–1902; 1907–1912.*

(Treaty periods: France, June 1, 1898, to Oct. 31, 1909; Portugal, June 12, 1900, to Aug. 7, 1910; Italy, July 18, 1900, to Aug. 7, 1910.)

Year.	From all countries (value).	From France, Italy, and Portugal.	
		Value.	Per cent of imports from all countries
1896	$2,724,709	$2,493,863	91.53
1897	1,967,042	1,848,799	93.99
1898	1,591,027	1,435,197	90.21
1899	1,914,450	1,788,623	93.43
1900	2,388,693	2,263,353	94.75
1901	2,476,482	2,431,363	98.18
1902	2,263,588	2,200,853	97.23
1907	2,562,384	2,543,384	99.26
1908	2,305,185	2,270,603	98.50
1909	2,641,867	2,535,135	95.96
1910	2,220,657	2,101,781	94.65
1911	2,938,337	2,790,280	94.96
1912	2,225,180	2,095,024	94.15

With the price of argols about 8 cents per pound and the general rate 1 cent to 1½ cents per pound—according to the percentage content of bi-tartrate of potash—the preference to the reciprocity countries amounted to from seven-tenths of a cent to 1⅕ cents per pound. The imposition of a duty on argols by the tariff act of 1897 was followed by a fall in the imports in 1897 and 1898, but in the following years, during which reciprocity agreements were concluded with the important argol-producing countries, France, Portugal, and Italy, the absolute amounts of imports of argols from all countries and from these three countries, as well as the percentage of the total imports which came from these three countries, showed considerable increases. Thus the share of the trade in argols going to these countries increased from 90 per cent in 1898 to 93 per cent in 1899—in which fiscal year the French treaty first became effective—and to 98 per cent in 1901—in which year the treaties with Portugal and Italy became effective. The new tariff act of 1909 maintained the rate of 5 per cent ad valorem on argols as the general rate and consequently imports increased still further. The generalization of the reciprocity rate immediately destroyed the preference in favor of the reciprocity countries, with the result that there was a decrease in the share of the total imports which came from these countries.

SPARKLING WINES.

TABLE.III.—*Imports of champagne and other sparkling wines into the United States, 1905–1912.*

(Treaty periods: Germany, July 1, 1907, to Feb. 7, 1910; France, Oct. 1, 1908, to Oct. 31, 1909; Spain, Feb. 20, 1909, to Aug. 7, 1910; Italy, Apr. 24, 1909, to Aug. 7, 1910.)

Year.	From all countries.	From France, Germany, Italy, and Spain.	
	Value.	Value.	Per cent of imports from all countries.
1905	$5,723,764	$5,353,969	93.54
1906	6,127,062	5,716,508	93.30
1907	6,229,281	5,688,142	91.33
1908	5,221,070	4,955,623	94.92
1909	6,863,785	6,791,311	98.94
1910	6,302,377	6,163,172	97.79
1911	3,566,824	3,154,282	88.43
1912	4,688,090	4,217,246	89.96

No reductions of duty on sparkling wines were granted in any of the agreements concluded prior to 1907 except in the case of the agreement with Portugal of June, 1900. As Portugal produces only a negligible amount of sparkling wines, the reduction of duty extended to Portugal was purely nominal. In 1907 the reduced rates on sparkling wines were granted to Germany, and in 1908 to France. The share of the imports of sparkling wines which came from the four reciprocity countries exporting this product—France, Germany, Italy, and Spain—increased from 91 per cent of the whole in 1907 to 95 per cent in 1908. In 1909 the reduced rates were extended also to Spain and Italy, and in that year the share of the imports coming from the

four countries increased to 99 per cent. As the treaty periods with
France and Germany extended into the fiscal year 1910, and those
with Spain and Italy into 1911, the drop in imports from these countries, both in amount and in the share of the total, did not come into
evidence until the fiscal year 1911. But the influence of reciprocity
can be clearly deduced from the fact that whereas in 1910 the imports
from France, Germany, Italy, and Spain were 98 per cent of the total,
they declined in 1911, when no preference was granted, to 88 per
cent, and in 1912 to 90 per cent.

WINES AND LIQUORS OTHER THAN SPARKLING WINES.

TABLE IV.--*Imports of wines and liquors other than sparkling wines into the United States
1896–1902; 1907–1912.*

Year.	From all countries.		From France, Germany, Italy, and Portugal.	
	Value.		Value.	Per cent of imports from all countries.
1896	$5,616,320		$3,587,110	63.88
1897	6,501,017		3,981,496	61.24
1898	4,104,750		2,539,598	61.87
1899	5,231,546		3,086,905	59.01
1900	6,284,844		3,570,628	56.82
1901	6,997,297		3,903,560	55.79
1902	7,685,837		4,345,479	56.54
1907	12,305,119		6,678,543	54.27
1908	11,925,624		6,399,326	53.66
1909	12,940,877		7,021,421	54.26
1910	13,693,641		8,009,974	58.49
1911	11,041,718		5,340,131	48.36
1912	11,366,589		5,553,056	48.85

The total imports of wines and liquors other than sparkling wines
increased after the conclusion of the more important reciprocity
agreements. At no period, however, during the duration of the
reciprocity agreements was the share of the imports of these articles
which came from the important treaty countries equal to what it had
been prior to the conclusion of the agreements. This would suggest
that the agreements were without effect. That reciprocity was nevertheless not totally without influence is to be seen in the figures for
the later years, which show a drop of over 10 per cent in the share of
the trade accruing to these countries upon the termination of the
arrangements,—from 58 per cent in 1910 to 48 per cent in 1911 and to
49 per cent in 1912. The share of the treaty countries was greater
in 1910 than it had been for some time previous, but this was due
to the fact that the reciprocity countries were able during the fiscal
year 1910 to pass their goods into the United States at the reduced
rates of duty specified in section 3 of the act of 1897, whereas
other countries were obliged to pay the much higher rates of duty of
the tariff act of 1909.

TABLE V.—*Imports of wines and liquors other than sparkling wines into the United States, 1896–1902; 1907–1912.*

(Treaty periods: France, June 1, 1898, to Oct. 31, 1909; Germany, July 13, 1900, to Feb. 7, 1910; Italy, July 13, 1900, to Aug. 7, 1910; Portugal, June 12, 1900, to Aug. 7, 1910.)

Year.	Distilled spirits, except brandy.			Still wines.			Brandy.		
	From all countries.	From France, Germany, Italy, and Portugal.		From all countries.	From France, Germany, Italy, and Portugal.		From all countries.	From France, Germany, Italy, and Portugal.	
	Value.	Value.	Per cent of imports from all countries.	Value.	Value.	Per cent of imports from all countries.	Value.	Value.	Per cent of imports from all countries.
1896	$1,446,873	$274,699	18.99	$3,478,686	$2,685,642	77.20	$690,761	$626,769	90.74
1897	2,074,835	404,276	19.48	3,514,461	2,742,304	78.03	911,721	834,816	91.56
1898	1,004,135	192,025	19.12	2,704,857	1,994,140	73.72	395,758	353,433	89.31
1899	1,683,256	299,556	17.80	2,921,415	2,202,779	75.40	626,875	584,570	93.25
1900	2,282,717	419,502	18.38	3,305,587	2,518,847	76.20	696,540	632,279	90.77
1901	2,524,237	466,782	18.49	3,629,742	2,649,756	73.00	843,318	786,959	93.32
1902	2,784,048	627,644	22.54	3,990,370	2,867,320	71.86	911,419	850,515	93.32
1907	5,037,146	1,042,096	20.69	5,580,500	4,066,856	72.88	1,687,473	1,569,591	93.01
1908	4,876,325	1,039,452	21.32	5,525,457	3,957,852	71.63	1,523,842	1,402,122	92.01
1909	5,566,879	1,182,184	21.24	5,412,828	3,982,361	73.57	1,961,170	1,856,876	94.68
1910	5,098,704	1,442,904	28.35	6,704,916	4,779,484	71.28	1,899,021	1,787,586	94.13
1911	5,058,547	881,613	17.43	4,964,789	3,570,915	71.92	1,018,382	887,603	87.16
1912	5,147,197	862,354	16.75	4,903,361	3,515,070	71.69	1,316,031	1,175,632	89.33

Table V gives in greater detail the figures of imports of wines and liquors other than sparkling wines. In the case of distilled spirits there was in 1902 an increase in the share of the trade going to the reciprocity countries, and this was maintained during the remaining years of the reciprocity period. In the year 1910 the imports from the reciprocity countries reached their highest point. This was due to the fact that the reciprocity countries had more to gain from rushing in their imports at the reduced rates of duty, and, furthermore, had a longer period of warning of the impending increase. In 1911 and 1912, following the termination of reciprocity, there was a sharp drop in the share of the imports coming from these countries.

In the case of still wines, there was not apparent in the share of the trade going to the reciprocity countries any appreciable tendency toward increase, and there followed upon the termination of reciprocity no marked change. But, as has been pointed out, the preference on still wines amounted only to 3 cents a quart.

In the case of brandy the preference amounted to 50 cents a gallon, and, in the short period during which the rates of the new tariff of 1909 were in effect for imports from the non-reciprocity countries but not yet applied to the reciprocity countries, the differential between the rate specified in section 3 of the act of 1897 and that specified in the tariff act of 1909 amounted to 85 cents a gallon. The share coming from the selected reciprocity countries increased after the conclusion of the first agreements and fell sharply when the agreements became ineffective.

ART WORKS.

TABLE VI.—*Imports of art works into the United States, 1896–1902; 1907–1912.*

(Treaty periods: France, June 1, 1898, to Oct. 31, 1909; Germany, July 13, 1900, to Feb. 7, 1910; Italy, July 18, 1900, to Aug. 7, 1910.)

| Year. | All art works. | | | Works of art not for exhibition purposes nor the work of American artists. | | |
| | From all countries. | From France, Germany, and Italy. | | From all countries. | From France, Germany, and Italy. | |
		Value.	Per cent of imports from all countries.		Value.	Per cent of imports from all countries.
1896	$4,972,361	$3,095,620	62.26			
1897	4,424,533	2,978,282	67.31	$375	$340	
1898	2,263,427	1,376,800	60.83	1,562,219	912,824	58.43
1899	2,739,576	1,914,804	69.89	2,040,121	1,473,024	72.20
1900	2,881,816	1,924,419	66.78	2,264,218	1,633,285	72.13
1901	3,723,883	2,530,657	67.96	2,823,444	1,909,071	67.61
1902	5,067,938	3,333,678	65.78	3,179,913	2,056,589	64.67
1907	7,516,527	5,375,195	71.51	5,160,569	3,763,448	72.93
1908	5,067,245	3,578,326	70.62	3,911,125	2,944,794	75.29
1909	4,991,724	2,727,565	54.64	3,239,168	1,516,936	46.83
1910	23,282,006	11,576,023	49.72	20,335,324	10,592,720	52.09
1911	23,137,667	13,959,305	60.33	21,855,282	13,030,397	59.54
1912	36,952,738	19,579,729	52.99	35,292,041	18,582,549	52.65

The figures presented in Table VI indicate that the imports of works of art not imported for exhibition purposes and not the work of American artists were, prior to 1897, practically nil; that although subject to a higher duty under the act of 1897 they were nevertheless imported in large amounts after 1897; and that after the total remission of duty by the act of 1909 they increased over tenfold. In 1899 the imports showed a considerable increase. During the fiscal year 1899 France was the only country enjoying the reduced rates of duty authorized in section 3 of the act of 1897, but the increase from France alone (see Table VIII) for that year was $625,000—an increase greater than the increase in that year in total imports from all countries. The fall in 1909 in the imports of art works from the selected reciprocity countries was probably due in part to the anticipation of the remission of duty by the impending tariff, in part to the increased imports from the United Kingdom which first entered at the reduced rates in the fiscal year 1908. The remission of duties by the act of 1909 was apparently followed by a great increase of imports. But in the comparison of imports in years during which there occurred important tariff changes, the recorded figures for articles such as works of art may be misleading, as their valuation for the customs or for other purposes is always more or less arbitrary.

Imports by Countries.—The following analysis of the imports of reciprocity articles by separate countries makes possible a more detailed study of the influence of reciprocity upon the amount and the source of the imports.

TABLE VII.—*Imports into the United States of the articles specified in section 3 of the act of 1897 (champagne and other sparkling wines omitted), 1896–1902; 1907–1912.*

(Treaty periods: France, June 1, 1898, to Oct. 31, 1909; Germany, July 13, 1900, to Feb. 7, 1910; Italy, July 18, 1900, to Aug. 7, 1910; Portugal, June 12, 1900, to Aug. 7, 1910.)

Year.	From all countries.	From four specified countries.		From France.	
	Value.	Value.	Per cent of imports from all countries.	Value.	Per cent of imports from all countries.
1896	$8,341,029	$6,081,406	72.91	$2,658,398	31.87
1897	8,468,434	5,830,635	68.85	2,613,966	30.87
1898	7,257,996	4,878,179	67.21	2,260,149	31.14
1899	9,186,117	6,348,567	69.11	3,819,989	41.58
1900	10,937,755	7,467,216	68.26	4,540,607	41.51
1901	12,297,223	8,244,318	67.04	4,950,306	40.25
1902	13,129,338	8,604,899	65.53	5,044,833	38.42
1907	20,028,072	12,985,402	64.83	7,444,137	37.16
1908	18,141,934	11,615,224	64.03	6,500,363	35.83
1909	18,821,912	11,073,894	58.84	5,510,675	29.28
1910	36,249,652	20,707,853	57.12	13,419,397	37.02
1911	35,835,337	21,164,227	59.05	14,348,225	40.03
1912	48,883,810	26,233,574	53.67	20,312,955	41.55

Year.	From Germany.		From Italy.		From Portugal.	
	Value.	Per cent of imports from all countries.	Value.	Per cent of imports from all countries.	Value.	Per cent of imports from all countries.
1896	$1,390,147	16.67	$1,800,426	21.58	$232,435	2.79
1897	1,450,251	17.12	1,556,150	18.38	210,268	2.48
1898	1,016,927	14.01	1,418,812	19.55	182,201	2.51
1899	1,219,497	13.28	1,172,940	12.77	136,141	1.48
1900	1,323,791	12.10	1,394,963	12.75	207,855	1.90
1901	1,419,581	11.54	1,561,473	12.69	312,958	2.56
1902	1,604,093	12.22	1,629,823	12.41	326,150	2.48
1907	1,854,476	9.26	3,318,499	16.57	368,290	1.84
1908	1,641,002	9.05	3,060,296	16.87	413,563	2.28
1909	1,746,367	9.28	3,413,861	18.14	402,991	2.14
1910	2,711,000	7.48	4,069,486	11.22	507,970	1.40
1911	2,391,472	6.67	3,976,096	11.10	448,434	1.25
1912	2,466,773	5.05	3,093,144	6.33	360,702	0.74

The establishment of reciprocity with the four countries accounted for in Table VII brought no increase in the combined share of these countries in the total imports of the reciprocity articles into the United States, although it was followed by a considerable increase in the amounts imported from these countries. The influence of reciprocity is to be seen, however, in the decline of imports from the reciprocity countries upon the ending of the various agreements. The imports from each of the countries specified in Table VII, except France, formed a smaller share of the total imports of the reciprocity articles into the United States after the termination of reciprocity. As a later table (Table VIII) will indicate, the great increase in the imports of the specified articles from France in 1910 and 1911 consisted almost wholly of art works, which were free under the new tariff.

In order to escape the higher duties of the new tariff the non-reciprocity countries shipped wines and liquors into the United States from March to August, 1909, in large quantities. The reciprocity countries on the other hand could continue to ship their wines and liquors into the United States at the reduced rates until later dates, ranging from October 31, 1909, for France, to August 7, 1910, for Spain, Portugal, and Italy. In 1909 the imports from the non-reciprocity countries were consequently greater than they would have been in the normal course of trade, and in 1910 and 1911 the imports from the reciprocity countries underwent a similar exceptional increase.

FRANCE.

TABLE VIII.—*Imports from France into the United States of articles specified in section 3 of the act of 1897 during 1896–1912.*

Year.	Wines and liquors other than sparkling wines.			Champagne and other sparkling wines.			Argols or wine lees.		
	Value.	Per cent of total imports from France.	Per cent of total imports of wines, etc., into the United States.	Value.	Per cent of total imports from France.	Per cent of total imports of champagne, etc., into the United States.	Value.	Per cent of total imports from France.	Per cent of total imports of argols or wine lees into the United States.
1896	$1,770,431	2.67	31.52	$3,313,752	5.00	91.34	$887,967	1.34	32.59
1897	2,048,039	3.03	31.50	3,132,959	4.64	93.58	565,927	.84	28.77
1898	1,239,106	2.35	30.19	3,066,999	5.82	93.96	396,830	.75	24.94
1899	1,615,950	2.60	30.89	3,423,716	5.51	93.31	952,742	1.53	49.78
1900	1,875,619	2.57	29.84	3,853,547	5.28	93.62	1,219,699	1.67	51.05
1901	2,029,072	2.69	29.00	4,251,218	5.63	92.64	1,252,428	1.66	50.58
1902	2,327,872	2.81	30.29	4,529,837	5.46	91.86	1,023,782	1.24	45.22
1903	2,294,910	2.55	27.40	5,428,431	6.03	92.60	1,173,987	1.30	42.94
1904	2,342,005	2.88	26.49	4,607,479	5.65	92.71	1,064,162	1.31	41.73
1905	2,431,810	2.71	26.44	5,248,050	5.84	91.69	1,047,757	1.17	45.71
1906	2,693,115	2.48	26.45	•5,613,311	5.18	91.62	1,087,173	1.00	46.11
1907	3,260,752	2.55	26.49	5,562,695	4.35	89.32	1,020,365	.80	39.83
1908	2,998,323	2.94	25.13	4,839,764	4.75	92.70	1,020,883	1.00	44.29
1909	3,598,550	3.32	27.81	6,670,810	6.15	97.19	989,384	.91	37.45
1910	3,529,449	2.67	25.78	5,986,864	4.52	95.00	854,436	.65	38.47
1911	2,210,522	1.92	20.02	3,036,860	2.63	85.14	1,158,910	1.00	39.45
1912	2,806,436	2.25	24.68	4,085,398	3.28	87.15	811,991	.65	36.49

Year.	Art works.			Total specified in section 3.			Total imports.	
	Value.	Per cent of total imports from France.	Per cent of total imports of art works into the United States.	Value.	Per cent of total imports from France.	Per cent of imports of specified articles into the United States from all countries.	Value.	Per cent of imports into the United States.
1896				$5,972,150	9.01	49.90	$66,266,967	8.50
1897				5,746,925	8.51	48.64	67,530,231	8.83
1898	$624,213	1.18	39.96	5,327,148	10.10	50.64	52,730,848	8.56
1899	1,251,297	2.01	61.34	7,243,705	11.65	56.37	62,146,056	8.91
1900	1,445,289	1.98	63.84	8,394,154	11.50	55.78	73,012,085	8.59
1901	1,668,806	2.21	59.11	9,201,524	12.19	54.48	75,458,739	9.17
1902	1,693,179	2.04	53.24	9,574,670	11.55	53.02	82,880,036	9.18
1903	2,539,429	2.82	63.26	11,436,757	12.70	54.50	90,050,172	8.78
1904	1,464,334	1.80	54.60	9,477,980	11.64	49.78	81,410,347	8.21
1905	1,494,119	1.66	37.39	10,221,736	11.38	48.19	89,830,445	8.04
1906	2,371,188	2.19	57.25	11,764,787	10.85	51.58	108,415,350	8.84
1907	3,163,020	2.47	61.29	13,006,832	10.17	49.53	127,803,407	8.91
1908	2,481,157	2.43	63.44	11,340,127	11.12	48.54	101,999,541	8.54
1909	922,741	.85	28.49	12,181,485	11.23	47.42	108,387,337	8.26
1910	9,035,512	6.82	44.44	19,406,261	14.66	45.61	132,363,346	8.50
1911	10,978,793	9.51	50.25	17,385,085	15.06	44.12	115,414,784	7.56
1912	16,694,528	13.42	47.31	24,398,353	19.50	45.54	124,548,458	7.53

The imports from France show to a slight extent the influence of the reduced rates established by the reciprocity agreements. The reductions had no visible effect on the imports of wines and liquors. There were great increases, however, in the imports of champagne in the two years 1909 and 1910. during which champagne entered at the reduced rates specified in section 3. But a considerable part of the increase in imports of champagne in these two years was undoubtedly due to the desire of French exporters and American importers to escape the increased duties provided for by the new tariff. The effect of reciprocity is most clearly to be seen in the figures of imports of argols and of art works. The share of the total American imports of argols which came from France increased from 25 per cent of the whole in 1898 to 50 per cent in 1899; of art works from 40 per cent in 1898 to 61 per cent in 1899.

After the termination of the agreement in 1910 both the amount of imports of reciprocity articles and the share of the total coming from France declined. The ending of the agreement was also followed by an increase in the imports of works of art from France, both in absolute amount and relatively to the total imports of these articles into the United States. After August 5, 1909, works of art over twenty years old entered the United States free of duty, and the recorded import figures showed a tremendous increase in 1910 and 1911 over the figures for the previous years.

PORTUGAL.

Table IX.—*Imports from Portugal into the United States, 1896–1912.*

(Treaty period: June 12, 1900–Aug. 7, 1910.)

| Year. | Articles specified in section 3 of the act of 1897. | | | | | | Articles specified in section 3 of the act of 1897. | | | All articles. | |
| | Wines and liquors. | | | Argols or wine lees. | | | Total specified in section 3.[1] | | | | |
	Value.	Per cent of total imports from Portugal.	Per cent of total imports of wines, etc., into the United States.	Value.	Per cent of total imports from Portugal.	Per cent of total imports of argols into the United States.	Value.	Per cent of total imports from Portugal.	Per cent of imports of specified articles into the United States from all countries.	Value.	Per cent of imports into the United States from all countries.
1896	$115,017	5.10	1.25	$117,418	5.20	4.31	$232,435	10.30	1.94	$2,255,731	0.29
1897	116,507	5.21	1.18	93,761	4.20	4.77	210,268	9.41	1.78	2,234,291	.29
1898	104,413	4.01	1.42	77,878	2.99	4.89	182,291	7.00	1.73	2,605,370	.42
1899	104,647	3.52	1.18	31,479	1.06	1.64	136,141	4.58	1 06	2,975,504	.43
1900	109,095	2.91	1.05	98,760	2.64	4.13	207,855	5.55	1.38	3,743,216	.44
1901	153,098	4.54	1.32	159,860	4.74	6.46	312,958	9.29	1.85	3,370,430	.41
1902	146,537	4.61	1.16	178,609	5.62	7.89	326,150	10.26	1.81	3,179,449	.35
1903	156,156	4.48	1.10	189,007	5 45	6.95	346,230	9.94	1.65	3,483,562	.34
1904	161,408	3.08	1.17	149,730	2.85	5.87	311,143	5.93	1.03	5,243,587	.53
1905	155,859	2.42	1.04	121,321	1.88	5 29	277,180	4.30	1.31	6,439,207	.58
1906	166,333	3.24	1.02	136,245	2.65	5.78	302,588	5.89	1.32	5,139,708	.42
1907	178,530	2.75	.96	189,741	2.93	7.41	368,290	5.68	1.40	6,479,500	.45
1908	188,618	3.80	1.10	224,935	4.53	9.76	413,563	8.33	1 77	4,967,922	.42
1909	209,346	3.36	1.06	193,645	3.10	7.33	402,991	6.46	1.57	6,240,562	.48
1910	310,572	4.77	1.55	195,394	3.00	8.80	507,970	7.80	1.19	6,507,733	.42
1911	150,730	2.15	1.03	296,262	4.22	10.08	448,434	6.40	1.14	7,015,358	.46
1912	138,852	2.24	.87	219,045	3.50	0.84	360,702	5.82	1.67	6,200,190	.38

[1] Including art works

Imports of wines and liquors from Portugal declined in 1899, in relation to total import of these articles from all countries, due possibly to the diversion of American purchases to France following the conclusion of the United States-France reciprocity agreement in 1898. This decline was not checked until 1901, the first year in which reciprocity with Portugal was effective. In 1907 the imports of wines and liquors from Portugal were again at a low level, to be explained possibly by a diversion of trade to Spain owing to the establishment of reciprocity relations between that country and the United States. The imports for 1910 were especially high, due no doubt to the fact that the Portuguese agreement did not end until August 7, 1910, which enabled the Portuguese exporters to ship their wines into the United States at the old duties for a whole year after the passage of the tariff act of August 5, 1909. In 1911 and 1912 the share of imports of these articles coming from Portugal decreased considerably. The American imports of argols from Portugal declined from 1898 to 1900, during which years French argols were entering at the reduced rates. After the conclusion of the Portuguese agreement in 1901, Portugal recovered and retained her former share of the trade. The imports of works of art from Portugal were small and infrequent.

GERMANY.

TABLE X.—*Imports from Germany into the United States, 1896–1912.*

(Treaty period: July 13, 1900, to Feb. 7, 1910; champagne, July 1, 1907, to Feb. 7, 1910.)

Year.	Articles specified in section 3 of the act of 1897.					
	Wines and liquors other than sparkling wines.			Sparkling wines.		
	Value.	Per cent of total imports from Germany.	Per cent of total imports of wines, etc., into the United States.	Value.	Per cent of total imports from Germany.	Per cent of total imports of champagne, etc., into the United States.
1896	$1,390,147	1.48	24.75	$37,979	0.04	1.05
1897	1,450,251	1.30	22.31	30,084	.03	.90
1898	901,945	1.29	21.97	48,048	.07	1.47
1899	1,101,214	1.31	21.05	36,852	.04	1.00
1900	1,214,232	1.25	19.32	53,619	.05	1.30
1901	1,298,539	1.29	18.56	82,040	.08	1.79
1902	1,404,919	1.38	18.28	64,049	.06	1.30
1903	1,586,855	1.33	18.95	74,394	.06	1.27
1904	1,502,439	1.38	17.00	109,403	.10	2.20
1905	1,554,961	1.32	16.91	99,329	.08	1.74
1906	1,541,964	1.14	15.15	93,973	.07	1.53
1907	1,623,776	1.00	13.19	111,348	.07	1.79
1908	1,511,145	1.06	12.67	104,759	.07	2.01
1909	1,453,097	1.01	11.23	109,803	.08	1.60
1910	1,773,291	1.05	12.95	160,994	.09	2.55
1911	1,216,150	.75	11.02	99,227	.06	2.78
1912	1,240,352	.72	10.91	116,680	.07	2.49

Year.	Articles specified in section 3 of the act of 1897.						All articles.	
	Art works.			Total specified in section 3.[1]				
	Value.	Per cent of total imports from Germany.	Per cent of total imports of art works into the United States.	Value.	Per cent of total imports from Germany.	Per cent of total imports of specified articles into the United States from all countries.	Value.	Per cent of imports into the United States from all countries.
1896				$1,428,126	1.52	11.93	$94,240,833	12.09
1897				1,480,335	1.33	12.52	111,210,614	14.54
1898	$114,982	0.17	7.36	1,064,975	1.53	10.12	69,697,378	11.31
1899	118,283	.14	5.80	1,256,349	1.49	9.78	84,225,777	12.08
1900	109,559	.11	4.84	1,377,410	1.41	9.15	97,374,700	11.46
1901	120,718	.12	4.28	1,501,621	1.49	8.89	100,445,902	12.20
1902	198,461	.19	6.24	1,668,142	1.63	9.24	101,997,523	11.29
1903	188,229	.15	4.69	1,849,478	1.54	8.81	119,772,511	11.67
1904	245,658	.22	9.16	1,857,528	1.70	9.76	109,188,554	11.01
1905	171,436	.14	4.29	1,825,777	1.54	8.61	118,268,356	10.59
1906	225,191	.17	5.44	1,861,285	1.38	8.16	135,142,996	11.01
1907	230,692	.15	4.47	1,965,824	1.22	7.49	161,543,556	11.27
1908	129,466	.09	3.31	1,745,761	1.22	7.47	142,935,547	11.97
1909	292,868	.20	9.04	1,856,170	1.29	7.23	143,525,828	10.94
1910	936,335	.56	4.60	2,871,994	1.70	6.75	168,805,137	10.84
1911	1,173,360	.72	5.37	2,490,699	1.53	6.32	163,242,560	10.69
1912	1,226,281	.72	3.47	2,583,453	1.51	4.82	171,380,380	10.37

[1] Including argols.

Germany's share of American trade in wines and liquors other than sparkling wines had been steadily declining before 1900, and reciprocity did not stop the decline or apparently cause any check to it. In the case of sparkling wines, Germany was the first country to receive the reduced rates of duty—from July 1, 1907—and her exports to the United States showed thereafter some increase. They were small in volume, however, and the increase was not maintained after the reductions were extended to other countries. Imports of the other articles enumerated in section 3 of the act of 1897 were unimportant in amount.

ITALY.

TABLE XI.—*Imports from Italy into the United States, 1896–1912.*

(Treaty period: July 18, 1900, to Aug. 7, 1910; sparkling wines, Apr. 24, 1909, to Aug. 7, 1910.)

Year.	Articles specified in section 3 of the act of 1897.					
	Wines and liquors other than sparkling wines.			Argols or wine lees.		
	Value.	Per cent of total imports from Italy.	Per cent of total imports of wines etc., into the United States.	Value.	Per cent of total imports from Italy.	Per cent of total imports of argols or wine lees into the United States.
1896	$311,948	1.41	5.55	$1,488,478	6.72	54.62
1897	366,699	1.92	5.64	1,189,111	6.24	60.45
1898	291,134	1.45	7.17	951,019	4.72	59.77
1899	265,094	1.07	5.07	804,402	3.24	42.03
1900	371,032	1.33	5.91	941,894	3.38	39.55
1901	422,851	1.72	6.04	1,019,075	4.14	41.16
1902	466,412	1.53	6.07	998,462	3.27	44.10
1903	702,023	1.94	8.38	1,356,461	3.74	49.61
1904	819,092	2.47	9.26	1,324,795	4.00	51.95
1905	971,435	2.51	10.56	1,054,982	2.73	46.03
1906	1,168,802	2.88	11.48	1,076,221	2.65	45.64
1907	1,615,485	3.20	13.12	1,333,278	2.64	52.04
1908	1,701,340	3.79	14.26	1,024,785	2.29	44.46
1909	1,760,428	3.57	13.60	1,352,106	2.74	51.18
1910	2,396,662	4.81	17.51	1,051,951	2.11	47.36
1911	1,762,744	3.72	15.97	1,335,108	2.82	45.44
1912	1,367,416	2.85	12.03	1,063,988	2.21	47.82

Year.	Articles specified in section 3 of the act of 1897.						All articles.	
	Art works.			Total specified in section 3.				
	Value.	Per cent of total imports from Italy.	Per cent of total imports of art works into the United States.	Value.	Per cent of total imports from Italy.	Per cent of total imports of specified articles into the United States from all countries.	Value.	Per cent of imports into the United States from all countries.
1896				$1,802,510	8.14	15.06	$22,142,487	2.84
1897	$340		90.67	1,557,700	8.17	13.18	19,067,352	2.49
1898	173,629	0.86	11.12	1,421,472	6.99	13.51	20,332,637	3.30
1899	103,444	.42	5.07	1,174,168	4.73	9.14	24,832,746	3.56
1900	78,437	.28	3.46	1,397,018	5.00	9.28	27,924,176	3.29
1901	119,547	.48	4.23	1,564,318	6.35	9.26	24,618,384	2.99
1902	164,949	.53	5.19	1,634,773	5.35	9.05	30,554,931	3.33
1903	227,319	.63	5.66	2,289,823	6.32	10.91	36,246,412	3.53
1904	232,647	.70	8.67	2,381,390	7.18	12.51	33,158,042	3.34
1905	310,777	.80	7.78	2,343,587	6.06	11.05	38,628,579	3.46
1906	434,842	1.07	10.50	2,689,058	6.62	11.79	40,597,556	3.31
1907	369,736	.73	7.16	3,332,322	6.60	12.69	50,455,157	3.52
1908	334,171	.75	8.54	3,071,296	6.85	13.15	44,844,174	3.76
1909	301,327	.62	9.30	3,424,097	6.95	13.33	49,287,894	3.76
1910	620,873	1.24	3.05	4,081,997	8.18	9.59	49,868,367	3.20
1911	878,244	1.86	4.02	3,991,707	8.43	10.13	47,334,809	3.10
1912	661,740	1.38	1.87	3,102,176	6.46	5.79	48,028,529	2.91

The imports of the reciprocity articles from Italy all showed increases in 1901, the first year of the reciprocity period, and these increases were maintained in the following years. In 1901 the total imports from Italy showed, on the contrary, a decrease. After the termination of reciprocity, the share of Italy in the American import trade in wines and liquors fell considerably.

SWITZERLAND.

TABLE XII.—*Imports from Switzerland into the United States, 1896 to 1912.*

(Concessional periods: June 1, 1898, to Mar. 23, 1900; Jan. 1, 1906, to Oct. 31, 1909.)

	Articles specified in section 3 of the act of 1897, excluding sparkling wines.			All articles.	
	Value.	Per cent of total imports from Switzerland.	Per cent of total imports of specified articles into the United States from all countries.	Value.	Per cent of total imports into the United States from all countries.
1896	$34,262	0.24	0.28	$14,080,033	1.80
1897	44,675	.32	.37	13,849,782	1.81
1898	17,363	.15	.16	11,380,835	1.84
1899	32,068	.21	.25	14,826,480	2.12
1900	32,376	.18	.21	17,393,268	2.04
1901	16,425	.10	.09	15,799,400	1.91
1902	14,516	.09	.08	17,784,855	1.96
1903	25,471	.12	.12	21,183,328	2.06
1904	19,069	.10	.10	19,534,439	1.97
1905	22,730	.11	.11	20,415,268	1.83
1906	18,946	.08	.08	23,421,242	1.91
1907	21,071	.08	.08	26,830,474	1.87
1908	21,255	.09	.09	24,698,036	2.07
1909	32,636	.14	.13	23,831,492	1.82
1910	30,766	.12	.07	25,209,159	1.62
1911	41,994	.16	.11	25,652,299	1.68
1912	38,814	16	.07	23,958,697	1.45

The reductions of duty authorized by section 3 of the act of 1897 were granted to Switzerland from June 1, 1898, to March 23, 1900, and again from January 1, 1906, to October 31, 1909. The imports from Switzerland of the articles specified in section 3 were very small throughout the entire period under investigation. In 1899 and 1900, during which years the reduced duties were in effect, the imports of these articles were over twice as great, however, as in 1898, the first fiscal year in which the general rates of the Dingley tariff were in effect. The increases consisted largely in greater imports of distilled spirits. In 1906 and 1907, when the reduced rates were again in effect for Swiss products, the imports of the reciprocity articles from Switzerland showed no increase as compared with the imports of the preceding years.

SPAIN.

TABLE XIII.—*Imports from Spain into the United States, 1903–1912.*

(Treaty period: Sept. 1, 1906, to Aug. 7, 1910; sparkling wines, Feb. 20, 1909, to Aug. 7, 1910.)

| | Articles specified in section 3 of the act of 1897. | | | | | | | | All articles. | |
| | Wines and liquors other than sparkling wines. | | | Art works. | | | Total specified in section 3.[1] | | | |
Year.	Value.	Per cent of total imports from Spain.	Per cent of total imports of wines, etc., into the United States.	Value.	Per cent of total imports from Spain.	Per cent of total imports of art works into the United States.	Value.	Per cent of total imports from Spain.	Per cent of total imports of specified articles into the United States from all countries.	Value.	Per cent of imports into the United States from all countries.
1903....	$686,124	8.09	8.19	$5,412	0.07	0.13	$692,771	8.17	3.30	$8,478,587	0.83
1904....	759,354	9.10	8.59	16,276	.19	.61	775,730	9.29	4.07	8,346,173	.84
1905....	732,052	8.33	7.96	2,729	.03	.07	734,978	8.36	3.47	8,786,507	.79
1906....	855,847	8.00	8.41	9,244	.08	.22	865,122	8.08	3.79	10,689,653	.87
1907....	977,739	7.28	7.94	4,894	.04	.09	982,909	7.32	3.74	13,426,665	.94
1908....	987,124	6.98	8.27	4,119	.03	.11	991,359	7.01	4.24	14,152,712	1.19
1909....	1,010,919	7.24	7.88	442,842	3.15	13.67	1,463,223	10.39	5.70	14,077,064	1.07
1910....	1,483,532	8.04	10.84	89,022	.48	.44	1,582,368	8.58	3.72	18,453,278	1.18
1911....	879,995	4.45	7.97	527,755	2.67	2.42	1,410,352	7.13	3.58	19,784,998	1.30
1912....	764,478	3.48	6.72	31,846	.15	.09	808,605	3.69	1.51	21,931,434	1.33

[1] Including sparkling wines and argols.

The imports of wines and liquors from Spain showed a marked increase following the establishment of reciprocity in the year 1907, but they had been rising rapidly prior to this, and it is impossible to determine to what extent the later advance should be attributed to the influence of the reductions of duty. In 1909 and 1910 there occurred great increases, but these were undoubtedly due mostly to the desire of the American importers and the Spanish exporters to get their wares into the United States in time to escape the high duties of the new tariff. Spain produces sparkling wines only to a very trifling extent, and the preference on still wines was too small to be of much effect. The imports from Spain of other reciprocity articles were unimportant and apparently were unaffected by reciprocity.

THE NETHERLANDS.

TABLE XIV.—*Imports from the Netherlands into the United States, 1905 to 1912.*

(Treaty period: Aug. 12, 1908, to Aug. 7, 1910.)

| | Distilled spirits. | | | All articles. | |
Year.	Value.	Per cent of total imports from Netherlands.	Per cent of total imports of distilled spirits into the United States.	Value.	Per cent of imports into the United States from all countries.
1905.........	$124,812	0.57	2.67	$21,718,748	1.94
1906.........	109,625	.41	2.06	27,007,107	2.20
1907.........	128,659	.40	1.91	32,455,612	2.26
1908.........	112,230	.55	1.75	20,305,864	1.70
1909.........	195,653	.75	2.60	26,086,336	1.99
1910.........	363,900	1.15	5.21	31,713,766	2.04
1911.........	246,729	.75	4.06	32,926,492	2.16
1912.........	69,623	.20	1.08	35,568,436	2.15

In the agreement with the Netherlands, the United States conceded only the reduced rates on distilled spirits. The imports of this commodity from the Netherland showed a sharp increase in 1909 and 1910—the only reciprocity years—but this increase was probably due, as in the case of the other countries, more to the endeavor to escape the higher duties of the new tariff than to the effect of the reductions in rates from the old duties secured by the reciprocity agreement.

UNITED KINGDOM.

TABLE XV.—*Imports of art works from the United Kingdom into the United States, 1905–1912.*)

(Treaty period: Dec. 5, 1907, to Feb. 7, 1910.)

Year.	Art works.[1]			All articles.	
	Value.	Per cent of total imports from United Kingdom.	Per cent of total imports of art works into the United States.	Value.	Per cent of imports into the United States from all countries.
1905	$1,019,147	0.58	25.50	$175,811,918	15.73
1906	740,016	.35	17.87	210,029,437	17.12
1907	995,080	.40	19.28	246,112,047	17.16
1908	777,048	.41	19.87	190,355,475	15.94
1909	1,160,472	.56	35.83	208,612,758	15.90
1910	8,721,881	3.22	42.90	271,029,772	17.41
1911	7,029,691	2.69	32.17	261,289,106	17.11
1912	15,082,167	5.53	42.74	272,940,700	16.51

[1] Works of art, etc., for exhibition purposes, etc., and art works, the production of American artists, not included.

The reciprocity agreement with the United Kingdom obtained for that country the reductions on works of art only. The imports of these articles showed some increase during the reciprocity period, but a much greater increase followed the remission of duties by the new tariff of 1909.

EFFECT UPON EXPORTS.

Trade by countries.—In return for the concessions made in accordance with section 3 of the act of 1897, the various reciprocity countries granted tariff favors ranging from guarantees of the maintenance of rates already effective on American products, or minor reductions of duty on a few unimportant articles, to the extension for the first time of a complete schedule of minimum rates to American products. In not a single case, however, did any of the reductions of duty which the agreements assured to the United States constitute exclusive concessions. In most cases the reductions had been granted to a number of other countries before being extended to the United States, and in the few instances in which the reductions were made for the first time, they were immediately extended, by virtue of most-favored-nation agreements, to practically all of the European countries.

FRANCE.

The French tariff treatment of American products offered a conspicuous case of unfavorable discrimination. The especially disadvantageous position of the American exporters in the French market, and the protracted character of the negotiations which Mr. Kasson initiated on behalf of the American Government in the endeavor to secure a more general application of the minimum rates of the French tariff to American products, rendered the effect of the agreement which was finally reached an object of greater interest than that of any other of the argol agreements.

A limited list of American products had been admitted into France since 1893 at the minimum rates of the French tariff. The French Government extended the rates of the minimum tariff by law of January 27, 1893, to a short list of meat and wood products and of fruits, and by decree of July 7, 1893, mineral oils were added to this list. By the agreement of May 28, 1898, the French Government guaranteed the admission at the minimum rates of the products previously mentioned, with the exception of mineral oils, and with the addition of sausages and lard. On August 22, 1902, the minimum rate on coffee (established by law of Feb. 24, 1900) was extended by agreement to coffee from the United States and Porto Rico.[1]

These concessions to the United States, although not numerous, covered items figuring to an important extent in the export trade of the United States, and represented, it has been estimated, from one-third to one-half of all the dutiable imports into France from the United States.[2] The agreements in which the concessions were incorporated were abrogated by the United States, the termination to take effect on October 31, 1909. During the next five months all imports from the United States were subject to the rates of the French general tariff. As a result of the negotiations conducted in accordance with the provisions of the act of 1909, an account of which is given elsewhere,[3] France agreed to extend to the United States all the minimum rates which she had previously granted and in addition a considerable number of others.

TABLE XVI.—*Exports of domestic merchandise from the United States to France, 1896–1912.*

Year.	To Europe.	To France.	
		Value.	Per cent of exports to Europe.
1896	$663,244,677	$45,352,724	6.83
1897	804,207,623	56,287,631	7.00
1898	962,202,778	93,790,717	9.74
1899	925,165,326	59,069,112	6.38
1900	1,026,703,241	81,993,909	7.96
1901	1,121,909,593	76,431,378	6.81
1902	994,321,959	69,244,213	6.96
1903	1,014,949,869	75,092,466	7.39
1904	1,046,075,474	83,207,554	7.95
1905	1,008,467,292	74,413,272	7.37
1906	1,189,254,885	96,453,755	8.11
1907	1,286,657,982	111,338,555	8.65
1908	1,270,016,773	113,802,055	8.96
1909	1,135,586,011	107,464,412	9.46
1910	1,118,402,094	114,665,589	10.25
1911	1,289,354,924	132,869,150	10.30
1912	1,325,896,164	131,132,613	9.89

[1] See p. 211, infra. [2] U. S. Tariff Series No. 25, Customs Tariff of France, p. 9. [3] See p. 272, infra.

From 1896 to 1912 the exports of American merchandise to France underwent a rapid and fairly steady increase. The fluctuations which did occur were largely to be accounted for by fluctuations in the movement of breadstuffs due to the varying crop conditions in the United States and France. As has been indicated, most of the minimum rates of the French tariff which were guaranteed to the United States by the commercial agreement of 1898 were already being enjoyed by American exporters prior to the conclusion of the agreement. No sudden rise in the volume of total exports to France was therefore to be expected. The figures in Table XVI, on the other hand, indicate a marked fall in exports in 1899 as compared with 1898, the fiscal year 1899 being the first full year in which the agreement was in effect.

TABLE XVII.—*Exports of breadstuffs from the United States to France, 1896–1912.*

Year.	Value.	Year.	Value.	Year.	Value.
1896	$2,081,480	1902	$3,397,960	1908	$2,654,356
1897	3,390,563	1903	3,471,215	1909	4,029,641
1898	40,510,974	1904	909,057	1910	1,182,845
1899	3,934,387	1905	1,495,112	1911	4,521,681
1900	4,380,016	1906	6,788,928	1912	426,943
1901	4,498,449	1907	4,635,983		

If the figures in Table XVI be compared with the figures for exports of breadstuffs to France, given in Table XVII, it will be seen at once that the explanation of the decline in total exports to France from 1898 to 1899 lies in the fact that the United States export to France of the item breadstuffs was in 1898 unusually large.

TABLE XVIII.—*Imports (special trade) into France, by countries, 1897–1912.*[1]

Year.	From all countries.	From United Kingdom.		From United States.		From Germany.		From Belgium.	
		Value.	Per cent of imports from all countries.	Value.	Per cent of imports from all countries.	Value.	Per cent of imports from all countries.	Value.	Per cent of imports from all countries.
1897	$763,508,000	$93,682,000	12.27	$84,438,000	11.06	$59,676,000	7.82	$55,623,000	7.29
1898	863,193,000	97,446,000	11.29	120,316,000	13.94	64,462,000	7.47	60,718,000	7.03
1899	872,032,000	114,044,000	13.08	82,469,000	9.46	69,480,000	7.97	64,153,000	7.36
1900	906,675,000	130,198,000	14.36	98,334,000	10.85	82,411,000	9.09	81,446,000	8.98
1901	843,256,000	116,167,000	13.78	88,220,000	10.46	77,567,000	9.20	69,036,000	8.19
1902	848,046,000	109,401,000	12.90	81,993,000	9.67	80,713,000	9.52	63,706,000	7.51
1903	926,632,000	107,289,000	11.58	104,162,000	11.24	85,731,000	9.25	62,725,000	6.77
1904	868,943,000	101,036,000	11.63	93,180,000	10.72	82,758,000	9.52	59,135,000	6.81
1905	922,329,000	114,353,000	12.40	98,874,000	10.72	92,100,000	9.99	60,390,000	6.55
1906	1,086,050,000	144,847,000	13.34	113,465,000	10.45	112,596,000	10.37	72,761,000	6.70
1907	1,201,039,000	170,458,000	14.19	129,485,000	10.78	123,173,000	10.26	82,334,000	6.86
1908	1,088,616,000	153,030,000	14.06	126,820,000	11.65	117,248,000	10.77	79,034,000	7.26
1909	1,205,497,000	171,095,000	14.19	140,446,000	11.65	127,592,000	10.58	84,746,000	7.03
1910	1,384,447,000	179,548,000	12.97	118,521,000	8.56	166,077,000	12.00	90,671,000	6.55
1911	1,556,699,000	191,746,000	12.32	159,572,000	10.25	189,082,000	12.15	104,722,000	6.73
1912	1,588,544,000	202,341,000	12.74	171,828,000	10.82	192,846,000	12.14	104,374,000	6.57

[1] From France: Tableau Général du Commerce et de la Navigation.

French statistics of imports into France also show the effect of the unusually large United States exports of breadstuffs in 1898. Only in the figures for the year 1910 does the effect of reciprocity appear conspicuously in this series of returns. During three months of this year the maximum rates were in effect upon all articles of American origin, including those which in the recently terminated agreement had entered at the minimum rates. In this year there occurred a large decrease in the percentage of the total imports into France which came from the United States. Not all of this decline, however, is to be attributed to the effect of the application of the maximum duties during a few months of the year. The fluctuations in the total imports from the United States are again largely capable of explanation as the result of fluctuations in the exports of foodstuffs from the United States. Nevertheless, an examination of the figures of imports for the individual commodities which entered at the minimum rates prior to the termination of the reciprocity agreement makes it clear that the imposition of the maximum rates during two months of the calender year 1909 and three months of the calender year 1910 resulted in large decreases in the volume of imports into France from the United States of the articles affected.

The French official statistics of imports for separate commodities are based upon official valuations and give simply the quantities of imports and the officially estimated values per unit. The following analysis of French imports of articles affected by the argol agreements is based consequently upon the figures of quantities instead of the figures of values.

APPLES AND PEARS.

TABLE XIX.—*Imports into France of apples and pears, dried or preserved, 1906–1912.*[1]

[Expressed in thousands of killos.]

Year.	For table use.			For cider and perry.		
	Total from all sources (including French colonies).	From the United States.		Total from all sources (including French colonies).	From the United States.	
		Quantity.	Per cent of total.		Quantity.	Per cent of total.
1906	797	702	95.61	2,611	2,175	83.30
1907	838	826	98.57	2,285	1,804	81.58
1908	407	382	93.86	3,275	2,684	81.95
1909	246	174	70.74	2,214	1,497	67.62
1910	372	208	55.91	4,383	2,961	67.56
1911	436	392	89.91	4,136	2,826	68.33
1912	427	392	91.80	3,444	2,837	82.38

[1] From France: Tableau Général du Commerce et de la Navigation.

The imports into France of apples and pears were almost wholly from the United States except in the years 1909 and 1910 when such imports from the United States were subjected to the French maximum rates. Even after the reestablishment of the minimum rates on April 1, 1910, the United States did not regain her former share of the trade.

CANNED MEATS.

TABLE XX.—*Imports of canned meats into France, 1907–1912.*[1]

Year.	Total from all sources (including French colonies).	From the United States.		From French colonies.	
		Quantity.	Per cent of total.	Quantity.	Per cent of total.
	Kilos.	*Kilos.*		*Kilos.*	
1907	220,496	124,293	56.37	44,209	20.05
1908	473,495	146,124	30.86	224,053	47.32
1909	538,300	144,500	26.84	247,600	46.00
1910	1,194,500	50,300	4.21	968,500	81.08
1911	1,691,400	82,900	4.90	1,357,300	80.25
1912	2,284,200	81,700	3.57	1,906,900	83.48

[1] From France: Tableau Général du Commerce et de la Navigation.

The imports of canned meats from the United States fell sharply in 1910, both in amount and relatively to the total imports from all sources, and did not, in the two following years, regain their former proportions. This was due to a combination of causes. In the French tariff act of 1892 the general duty on canned meats was equivalent to $1.75 per hundred pounds, and the minimum rate to $1.31. Canned meats entered free of duty from Algeria, so that the extension of the minimum rate on canned meats to the United States still left a tariff preference amounting to $1.31 per hundred pounds in favor of the Algerian product. From November 1, 1909, to April 1, 1910, the maximum duty of $1.75 per hundred pounds was imposed upon the American product, thus increasing the preference in favor of the Algerian product. By the French tariff revision of 1910, effective on April 1 of that year, the general rate was raised to $2.01 and the former general rate was made the minimum rate. Thus after November 1, 1909, the preference in favor of the Algerian product was $1.75 per hundred pounds. To this factor can be attributed in part at least the great increase in imports from the French colonies—chiefly Algeria—and the fall in the imports from the United States. Crop conditions in the United States were, however, a contributing factor. The years 1908 and 1909 were marked in the United States by small corn crops of poor feed value, and as a result the exports of meats and meat products, as well as of breadstuffs, fell in 1910 to a fraction of their former amount.

LARD.

TABLE XXI.—*Imports into France of lard, 1897–1901; 1907–1912.*[1]

[Expressed in thousands of kilos.]

Year.	Total from all sources.	From the United States.	
		Quantity.	Per cent of total.
1897	21,484	19,993	93.08
1898	16,470	14,842	90.12
1899	15,417	14,632	94.90
1900	12,708	12,128	95.43
1901	7,240	6,727	92.92
1907	7,184	6,307	87.80
1908	6,977	6,386	91.54
1909	1,566	1,246	79.57
1910	791	163	20.71
1911	11,974	9,617	80.35
1912	11,016	9,461	85.86

[1] From France: Tableau Général du Commerce et de la Navigation.

The situation in regard to the trade in lard was very similar to that in canned meats. Before 1898 there had been in the French tariff only one rate on lard, namely, $1.27 per hundred pounds. In 1898 a new minimum rate was established of $2.19 per hundred pounds and the maximum rate was raised to $3.15 per hundred pounds. By the agreement of 1898 the minimum rate was granted to the United States. In 1910 the minimum rate was raised to $2.63, the maximum rate remaining unchanged. From the figures in Table XXI it will be seen that, in spite of the extension of the minimum rate in 1898 to the United States, the imports of American lard into France decreased, this being due, in part, if not wholly, to the great increase in the rate in the minimum schedule. The imposition of the maximum rate from November 1, 1909, to April 1, 1910, the increase in the minimum rate after April 1, 1910, and the poor crops in the United States in 1908 and 1909 all co-operated to reduce the imports of American lard into France in 1909 and 1910 to a very small amount. The years 1911 and 1912 showed a partial recovery.

MINERAL OILS.

TABLE XXII.— *Imports into France of crude mineral oils, 1906–1912.*[1]

[Quantity expressed in hectoliters.]

Year.	Total from all sources.	From United States.		From Russia.		From Roumania.	
		Quantity.	Per cent of total.	Quantity.	Per cent of total.	Quantity.	Per cent of total.
1906	2,214,830	1,657,770	74.84	63,995	2.889	493,065	22.26
1907	2,524,168	1,756,173	69.57	135,699	5.37	632,296	25.05
1908	2,454,516	1,516,222	61.76	304,331	12.39	631,930	25.74
1909	2,217,413	1,020,521	46.03	699,908	31.57	496,982	22.41
1910	1,988,301	340,583	17.13	954,375	48.00	693,343	34.87
1911	2,408,726	934,206	38.78	966,484	40.12	508,023	21.09
1912	2,154,243	1,104,023	51.25	473,510	21.98	576,706	26.77

[1] From France: Tableau Général du Commerce et de la Navigation.

TABLE XXIII.—*Imports into France of refined mineral oils, 1906–1912.*[1]

[Quantities expressed in thousands of hectoliters.]

Year.	Total from all sources.	From United States.		From Russia		From Roumania.		From Austria-Hungary.	
		Quantity.	Per cent of total.	Quantity.	Per cent of total.	Quantity.	Per cent of total.	Quantity.	Per cent of total.
1906	2,167	1,307	60.28	90	4.15	623	28.74	(²)	....
1907	2,820	1,543	54.73	315	11.17	675	24.94	(²)	....
1908	2,355	1,932	82.00	20	0.86	70	2.97	(²)	....
1909	5,391	3,570	66.22	377	7.00	857	15.91	518	9.61
1910	3,151	937	29.76	405	12.88	1,158	36.75	557	17.68
1911	4,212	2,157	51.21	500	11.87	952	22.62	456	10.83
1912	4,811	2,569	53.40	436	9.07	961	19.97	584	12.15

[1] From France: Tableau Général du Commerce et de la Navigation.   ² Not separately stated.

Minimum rates on mineral oils were first established by France in 1893 in preparation for the negotiation of a commercial agreement with Russia. The Russian product was the chief competitor of American petroleum in the French market. The minimum rates were extended by France to the United States in 1903, although not by agreement. The effect of the imposition in 1909 of the maximum rates is shown in the figures for 1909 and 1910 by the great decline in the imports from the United States and the increase in the imports from Russia. In the French tariff revision of 1910 the rates on very heavy mineral oils (paraffin, etc.) were increased. In spite of the re-extension of the minimum rates to the United States from April 1, 1910, American petroleum had not by 1912 succeeded in regaining its former share of the French trade.

COFFEE. .

TABLE XXIV.—*Imports of coffee into France, 1897–1912.*[1]

Year.	From all countries.	From Brazil.		From Porto Rico.	
	Quantity.	Quantity.	Per cent of imports from all countries.	Quantity.	Per cent of imports from all countries.
	Kilos.	*Kilos.*		*Kilos.*	
1897	77,474,095	30,367,754	39.20	2,665,674	3.44
1898	79,404,795	29,364,432	36.98	3,395,719	4.28
1899	81,418,492	29,294,993	35.98	4,705,680	5.78
1900	81,998,764	33,703,476	41.10	2,373,973	2.89
1901	84,265,279	37,787,498	44.84	1,135,070	1.35
1902	85,839,747	42,171,779	49.12	3,024,402	3.52
1903	111,635,767	56,365,104	50.50	4,309,064	3.86
1904	76,290,170	37,555,181	49.22	2,629,396	3.45
1905	90,985,491	44,926,577	49.37	2,191,364	2.41
1906	97,843,065	49,888,327	50.98	1,893,027	1.93
1907	101,570,992	53,510,601	52.66	2,148,716	2.11
1908	102,761,921	56,387,458	54.87	2,083,200	2.03
1909	107,942,000	63,917,200	59.23	1,591,300	1.47
1910	111,827,600	66,295,800	59.29	1,103,400	0.99
1911	111,056,600	57,185,500	51.47	1,169,600	1.05
1912	111,238,600	55,925,000	50.29	1,036,100	0.93

[1] From France: Tableau Général du Commerce et de la Navigation.

New rates on the tropical products—coffee, cocoa, chocolate, spices, etc.—were established by the French law of February 24, 1900. On coffee, the new rates were equivalent to 27 cents a pound as the maximum and 12 cents a pound as the minimum. By the agreement of 1902 with the United States, the minimum rates were extended to Porto Rican coffee from August 22 of that year. Brazil, the chief source of the French supply, had received the minimum rates on July 17, 1900, very shortly after those rates were established. The adverse effect of these tariff changes on the Porto Rican exports of coffee to France is shown by the figures of Table XXIV. Prior to 1900 the Porto Rican coffee had been gaining in the French market, and the Brazilian article was scarcely holding its own. But the establishment in 1900 of a preference in favor of Brazilian coffee, by the creation of maximum and minimum rates and the extension of the minimum to Brazil, reversed the tendency and brought about a considerable increase in the imports to France of Brazilian coffee and a decrease in the imports of Porto Rican coffee. The extension of the minimum rates to Porto Rican coffee in 1902 enabled Porto Rico to regain a considerable part of the trade which she had previously enjoyed. But the ensuing years showed as a whole a tendency for the Brazilian trade to increase at the expense of the Porto Rican. The imposition of the maximum rates on Porto Rican coffee during the five-month interval from November 1, 1909, to April 1, 1910, effected a very marked reduction in the imports from Porto Rico.

Estimate of the effect of the agreements with France.—The exports to France from the United States of those articles which were affected by the argol agreements with that country thus show in almost every case a favorable influence. The articles upon which reductions of duty were made in the agreements were not a sufficiently great proportion of the total American export trade to France to affect appreciably the American share in the total imports into France from all sources. Even the considerable increase in 1910 in the number of articles of American production which were admitted into France at the minimum rates did not result in an increase in the proportion of the French imports which derived their origin from the United States.

PORTUGAL.

The following tables show the effect of the reciprocity agreements upon the trade between the United States and Portugal.

TABLE XXV.—*Domestic Exports to Portugal from the United States, 1895–1912.*

Year.	Total exports.	Specified articles.						Total.	
		Corn.	Wheat.	Lard.	Agricultural implements.	Tools.	Mineral oils.	Value.	Per cent of total exports.
1895.........	$2,960,526	....	$1,739,384	$377	$6,553	$6,231	$323,618	$2,076,163	70.13
1896.........	3,156,991	$13,050	2,127,700	490	1,606	2,745	341,845	2,487,436	78.79
1897.........	2,510,453	47,867	1,319,905	132	1,573	4,583	358,314	2,395,101	95.06
1898.........	3,532,057	65,312	1,953,924	304	4,125	6,726	364,710	2,395,101	67.81
1899.........	4,130,730	774,450	1,750,956	231	3,487	2,954	232,757	2,764,835	66.93
1900.........	5,886,542	605,186	3,505,425	3,104	4,142	28,341	210,459	4,356,657	74.01
1901.........	5,289,460	51,145	3,061,077	2,458	5,277	17,260	339,547	3,476,764	65.73
1902.........	3,044,206	....	1,468,798	2,436	5,490	33,836	356,779	1,867,339	61.34
1903.........	3,651,804	34,990	1,845,462	....	7,362	12,885	304,863	2,205,562	60.41
1904.........	1,934,975	....	339,495	224	13,895	7,489	150,709	511,812	26.45
1905.........	2,089,448	235,786	....	181	18,156	8,162	300,143	562,428	26.92
1906.........	1,461,843	75,286	342,844	605	8,026	8,751	313,873	749,385	51.26
1907.........	2,787,179	13,004	511,530	718	9,065	3,927	358,057	896,301	32.16
1908.........	3,078,498	....	323,018	540	11,989	12,709	561,845	910,101	29.56
1909.........	3,890,555	....	1,248,408	862	23,479	3,706	447,540	1,723,995	44.21
1910.........	3,223,724	....	8,649	....	19,037	4,152	446,618	478,456	14.84
1911.........	2,663,401	600	98,000	22	7,833	6,851	354,835	468,141	17.58
1912.........	2,755,001	....	211,690	760	7,058	21,031	524,223	767,762	27.87

TABLE XXVI.—*Imports into Portugal of mineral oils, 1898–1912.*[1]

Year.	From all sources.	From United States.		From Russia.	
		Value.	Per cent of imports from all sources.	Value.	Per cent of imports from all sources.
1898...	$681,507	$626,788	91.97	....	....
1899...	781,801	381,287	48.77	$382,394	45.29
1900...	775,303	347,270	44.79	371,393	47.90
1901...	841,045	518,038	61.57	270,119	32.83
1902...	728,998	528,096	72.43	165,372	22.68
1903...	782,969	355,229	45.35	387,778	49.52
1904...	632,789	338,490	53.48	248,075	39.20
1905...	657,964	455,935	69.29	124,183	18.87
1906...	714,942	586,711	82.07	44,312	6.20
1907...	737,294	610,336	82.78	46,029	6.24
1908...	704,858	628,119	89.10	18,333	2.59
1909...	725,771	540,391	75.55	110,606	15.24
1910...	737,153	555,402	75.31	131,074	17.70
1911...	789,400	502,317	63.61	121,954	15.45
1912...	919,055	778,591	84.72	42,236	4.60

[1] From Portugal: Comercio e Navegação,

TABLE XXVII.—*Imports of corn into Portugal, 1898-1912.*[1]

Year.	From all sources.	From United States.		Year.	From all sources.	From United States.	
		Value.	Per cent of imports from all sources.			Value.	Per cent of imports from all sources.
1898	$987,327	$416,600	42.19	1906	$288,072	$10,818	3.76
1899	2,346,086	1,389,133	59.21	1907	447,873	48,343	10.79
1900	1,882,591	980,396	52.08	1908	1,899,585	11,414	.60
1901	335,996	105,722	31.47	1909	1,984,579	343,252	17.30
1902	574,596	53,933	9.39	1910	394,105	11	.00
1903	297,580	30,407	10.22	1911	332,018	30,920	9.31
1904	401,899	76,153	18.95	1912	789,896	21,251	2.69
1905	1,962,349	508,661	25.92				

[1] From Portugal: Comercio e Navegação.

TABLE XXVIII.—*Imports of wheat into Portugal, 1898-1912.*[1]

Year.	From all sources.	From United States.		Year.	From all sources.	From United States.	
		Value.	Per cent of imports from all sources.			Value.	Per cent of imports from all sources.
1898	$3,950,804	$3,850,835	97.47	1906	$4,591,045	$366,576	7.98
1899	4,554,355	4,104,161	90.11	1907	1,115,105	789,849	70.83
1900	5,370,478	4,564,130	84.99	1908	6,224,693	1,654,819	26.58
1901	3,396,230	3,081,035	90.72	1909	5,581,606	645,319	11.56
1902	450,689	413,668	91.79	1910	4,355,862	466,022	10.70
1903	3,285,117	3,198,633	97.37	1911	629,011	144,828	23.02
1904	4,012,189	569,580	14.19	1912	3,319,239	874,449	26.34
1905	5,515,111	235,010	4.26				

[1] From Portugal: Comercio e Navegação.

Portugal granted to the United States under the agreement of 1900 reduced rates of duties upon a short list of commodities, of which only the articles accounted for in Table XXV were important in the exports from the United States to Portugal. The American statistics of exports do not reveal any effect of reciprocity except in the case of mineral oils. In 1898 Portugal had granted a special reduction of duty on Russian petroleum, which resulted in increased imports from Russia and decreased imports from the United States during the years 1899 and 1900. The American agreement with Portugal in 1900 established an equalization of the rates on Russian and American mineral oils, and in the following years the imports from the United States regained their former volume.

The Portuguese statistics of imports of mineral oils (Table XXVI) show more clearly the influence which reciprocity had upon the trade in this article. In the two years, 1899 and 1900, during which the tariff differential in favor of Russia was effective, the American share of the Portuguese imports of mineral oils was 49 and 45 per cent, respectively. In 1901 it increased to 62 per cent and in 1902 to 72 per cent, and although it fluctuated somewhat in the following years, on the whole it remained at the level attained immediately after the conclusion of the agreement.

TABLE XXIX.—*Total Imports into Portugal, 1898 to 1912.*[1]

[Values expressed in thousands.]

Year.	From all sources.	From the United States.		From the United Kingdom.		From France.		From Germany.	
		Value.	Per cent of imports from all sources.	Value.	Per cent of imports from all sources.	Value.	Per cent of imports from all sources.	Value.	Per cent of imports from all sources.
1898.......	$52,494	$7,606	14.49	$16,823	32.05	$5,066	9.65	$7,157	13.63
1899.......	54,691	8,705	15.92	18,185	33.25	4,699	8.59	7,844	14.34
1900.......	64,502	9,679	15.00	20,643	32.00	5,409	8.39	9,307	14.43
1901.......	62,449	8,154	13.06	19,058	30.52	6,135	9.82	9,687	15.51
1902.......	60,044	4,308	7.18	18,729	31.19	6,132	10.21	9,958	16.59
1903.......	63,510	6,664	10.40	18,819	29.63	6,055	9.53	10,675	16.81
1904.......	67,006	4,780	7.13	19,601	29.25	6,480	9.67	11,291	16.85
1905.......	65,532	3,745	5.71	18,443	28.14	6,572	10.03	10,376	15.83
1906.......	65,223	5,056	7.75	18,825	28.86	6,945	10.65	11,108	17.03
1907.......	66,369	6,549	9.87	20,052	30.21	7,236	10.90	11,852	17.86
1908.......	72,628	7,817	10.76	19,260	26.52	6,682	9.20	11,151	15.35
1909.......	69,939	7,471	10.68	18,847	26.95	6,226	8.90	10,785	15.42
1910.......	75,068	8,022	10.69	21,534	28.69	6,749	8.99	11,432	15.23
1911.......	73,577	6,302	8.56	20,950	28.47	5,657	7.69	13,097	17.80
1912.......	80,584	8,617	10.69	22,705	28.18	7,498	9.30	13,428	16.66

[1] From Portugal: Comercio e Navegação.

The American share of the total Portuguese import trade declined in 1901—the first complete year of reciprocity—and it continued to decline in the following years. This decline in the share of the United States in the import trade of Portugal is accounted for almost wholly by a decrease in the imports into Portugal of corn and wheat. Both of these products were included in the list of articles upon which Portugal, by virtue of the agreement of 1900, established reduced rates of duty; but the trade in breadstuffs is governed rather by relative crop conditions than by tariff legislation. Except in the case of mineral oils there is not apparent any influence of the agreement of 1900 on the course of this trade.

GERMANY.

The effect of the reciprocity agreements upon the trade between the United States and Germany is shown by Tables XXX to XXXIV.

TABLE XXX.—*Domestic exports from the United States to Germany, 1896–1915.*

Year.	Value.	Per cent of total exports to Europe.	Year.	Value.	Per cent of total exports to Europe.
1896.................	$96,364,368	14.52	1906.................	$232,403,778	19.54
1897.................	123,784,453	15.39	1907.................	254,329,306	19.76
1898.................	153,171,100	15.91	1908.................	274,178,712	21.58
1899.................	153,265,513	16.56	1909.................	232,797,756	20.50
1900.................	184,648,094	17.94	1910.................	246,786,846	22.06
1901.................	188,350,919	16.78	1911.................	283,022,029	21.95
1902.................	170,222,737	17.11	1912.................	303,495,338	22.88
1903.................	190,896,447	18.80	1913.................	328,029,906	22.44
1904.................	212,367,144	20.30	1914.................	341,875,820	23.23
1905.................	191,271,367	18.96	1915.................	28,656,206	1.47

The United States enjoyed, prior to 1900, on many of its important export products the minimum rates of the German tariff. The concession by Germany of the minimum rates in the agreement of 1900 guaranteed the continuance of the treatment formerly in force and extended its scope somewhat. The steady growth of American exports to Germany which had occurred in the nineties continued during the years of the reciprocity period. After 1906 some of the conventional rates were withheld from the United States, but these were not sufficiently important to cause any check to the increase in American exports as a whole. As a result of the negotiations carried on in accordance with the provisions of the act of 1909, American products were in 1910 given by Germany the benefit of the full minimum schedule.

TABLE XXXI.—*Imports into Germany, 1898–1912.*[1]

[Values expressed in thousands.]

Year.	From all sources.	From the United States.		From Russia.	
		Value.	Per cent of imports from all sources.	Value.	Per cent of imports from all sources.
1898	$1,209,194	$208,520	17.25	$172,626	14.28
1899	1,304,977	212,731	16.30	147,733	11.32
1900	1,372,216	238,858	17.41	159,622	11.63
1901	1,290,254	234,629	18.19	159,142	12.34
1902	1,340,178	212,534	15.86	180,622	13.48
1903	1,428,640	222,414	15.56	195,717	13.70
1904	1,512,328	224,435	14.84	191,557	12.67
1905	1,696,661	236,082	13.91	231,463	13.64
1906	1,909,210	294,252	15.41	254,271	13.32
1907	2,082,192	314,120	15.09	263,756	12.67
1908	1,824,640	305,368	16.73	225,050	12.34
1909	2,027,790	300,490	14.81	324,613	16.01
1910	2,126,322	282,652	13.29	330,013	15.52
1911	2,309,947	319,634	13.84	388,951	16.85
1912	2,544,636	377,468	14.83	363,664	14.29

Year.	From Austria-Hungary.		From the United Kingdom.		From France.	
	Value.	Per cent of imports from all sources.	Value.	Per cent of imports from all sources.	Value.	Per cent of imports from all sources.
1898	$149,273	12.35	$134,786	11.15	$62,234	5.15
1899	170,290	13.05	160,166	12.27	70,969	5.44
1900	167,652	12.22	171,167	12.48	72,011	5.25
1901	162,701	12.61	131,539	10.20	64,794	5.02
1902	165,526	12.35	132,640	9.90	72,263	5.39
1903	172,339	12.06	141,379	9.89	78,614	5.50
1904	167,312	11.07	146,348	9.68	86,963	5.75
1905	178,980	10.55	170,971	10.07	95,708	5.64
1906	192,727	10.10	196,196	10.28	103,134	5.40
1907	193,553	9.30	232,592	11.17	108,083	5.19
1908	178,907	9.80	165,971	9.09	99,996	5.48
1909	179,607	8.85	172,129	8.48	115,551	5.69
1910	180,686	8.50	182,444	8.58	121,099	5.70
1911	180,686	7.82	192,497	8.33	124,810	5.40
1912	197,540	7.76	200,634	7.88	131,376	5.16

[1] From Auswartiger Handel.

Although American exports to Germany increased both in amount and relatively to the increase in exports to all Europe, the official German statistics show that the proportionate share of the United States in the total import trade of Germany was steadily decreasing throughout the reciprocity period.

The articles upon which the maximum rates were imposed during the period in which the agreement of 1907 was in effect were considerable in number, but the German tariff is so detailed in its classification that it is difficult to compare items of import with those listed in the American export statistics. Tables XXXII to XXXIV present the figures of exports to Germany for a few of the selected articles which were subjected from 1907 to 1909 to the maximum duties.

TABLE XXXII.—*Domestic exports of silk and silk waste from the United States to Germany, 1904-1912.*

Year.	To Europe.	To Germany.		Year.	To Europe.	To Germany.	
		Value.	Per cent of exports to Europe.			Value.	Per cent of exports to Europe.
1904	$52,896	$24,540	46.39	1909	$105,534	$13,201	12.50
1905	35,736	6,660	18.63	1910	132,207	20,026	15.14
1906	37,742	7,341	19.45	1911	272,495	42,410	15.56
1907	57,498	7,154	12.44	1912	288,592	46,927	16.26
1908	72,744	9,538	13.11				

TABLE XXXIII.—*Domestic exports of wood alcohol from the United States to Germany, 1904-1912.*

Year.	To Europe.	To Germany.		Year.	To Europe.	To Germany.	
		Value.	Per cent of exports to Europe.			Value.	Per cent of exports to Europe.
1904	$561,596	$186,783	33.25	1909	$376,112	$161,534	42.94
1905	584,811	209,010	35.73	1910	549,993	258,588	47.01
1906	457,204	164,754	36.03	1911	851,720	410,316	48.17
1907	860,662	367,704	42.72	1912	634,476	337,450	53.18
1908	811,961	241,660	29.76				

TABLE XXXIV.—*Domestic exports of tanning materials from the United States to Germany, 1904-1912.*

Year.	To Europe.	To Germany.		Year.	To Europe.	To Germany.	
		Value.	Per cent of exports to Europe.			Value.	Per cent of exports to Europe.
1904	$181,476	$54,125	29.82	1909	$90,563	$22,015	24.30
1905	234,042	71,602	30.59	1910	96,716	18,184	18.80
1906	217,351	49,799	22.91	1911	123,131	10,350	8.40
1907	155,911	54,141	34.72	1912	141,652	11,741	8.28
1908	131,641	34,523	26.22				

Silk and silk waste, and wood alcohol show increases after the reestablishment of the minimum rates in 1910, and tanning materials show a decline following the withdrawal of the minimum rates in 1907. To what extent these changes are to be attributed to the influence of the tariff, the available data do not sufficiently indicate.

ITALY.

Tables XXXV to XXXIX present figures for the trade between the United States and Italy during the reciprocity period.

TABLE XXXV.—*Exports of domestic merchandise from the United States to Italy, 1897–1912.*

Year.	To Europe.	To Italy.		Year.	To Europe.	To Italy.	
		Value.	Per cent of exports to Europe.			Value.	Per cent of exports to Europe.
1897	$804,207,623	$21,377,761	2.65	1905	$1,008,467,292	$38,429,738	3.81
1898	962,202,778	23,067,997	2.39	1906	1,189,254,885	47,362,491	3.98
1899	925,165,326	24,892,037	2.69	1907	1,286,657,892	61,137,155	4.75
1900	1,028,793,341	33,059,005	3.21	1908	1,270,016,773	53,599,773	4.22
1901	1,121,909,593	34,277,491	3.05	1909	1,135,586,011	58,078,454	5.11
1902	994,321,959	30,888,503	3.10	1910	1,118,402,094	53,048,326	4.74
1903	1,014,949,869	34,692,263	3.41	1911	1,289,354,924	59,993,525	4.65
1904	1,046,075,474	35,434,448	3.38	1912	1,325,896,164	64,892,006	4.89

TABLE XXXVI.—*Imports into Italy, excluding gold and bullion, 1897–1912, from all sources.[1]*

Year.	From all countries.	From the United States.		From Germany.	
		Value.	Per cent of exports from all countries.	Value.	Per cent of exports from all countries.
1897	$229,979,000	$24,103,000	10.48	$29,023,000	12.62
1898	272,774,000	32,072,000	11.76	30,347,000	11.12
1899	290,766,000	32,511,000	11.18	37,454,000	12.88
1900	328,146,000	43,679,000	13.31	39,261,000	11.97
1901	331,668,000	45,229,000	13.64	39,685,000	11.96
1902	342,823,000	40,740,000	11.88	42,791,000	12.48
1903	350,819,000	40,931,000	11.67	44,559,000	12.70
1904	362,366,000	46,073,000	12.72	48,569,000	13.40
1905	389,046,000	45,912,000	11.54	55,409,000	14.24
1906	485,270,000	59,997,000	12.37	76,026,000	15.67
1907	555,969,000	75,839,000	13.64	101,643,000	18.28
1908	562,262,000	78,164,000	13.90	100,548,000	17.88
1909	600,560,000	75,307,000	12.54	97,169,000	16.18
1910	626,473,000	70,053,000	11.18	101,254,000	16.16
1911	654,135,000	80,149,000	12.25	105,181,000	16.08
1912	714,461,000	99,462,000	13.92	120,873,000	16.91

Year.	From the United Kingdom.		From France.		From Austria-Hungary.	
	Value.	Per cent of exports from all countries.	Value.	Per cent of exports from all countries.	Value.	Per cent of exports from all countries.
1897	$43,110,000	18.74	$31,041,000	13.50	$25,887,000	11.26
1898	48,909,000	17.96	22,459,000	8.23	25,082,000	9.19
1899	57,811,000	19.88	29,393,000	10.11	31,031,000	10.67
1900	69,242,000	21.10	32,300,000	9.84	36,939,000	11.26
1901	53,917,000	16.25	34,591,000	10.43	34,433,000	10.38
1902	55,420,000	16.17	35,498,000	10.35	33,987,000	9.91
1903	54,533,000	15.57	37,302,000	10.65	33,650,000	9.51
1904	61,623,000	17.02	36,256,000	10.65	36,170,000	9.98
1905	67,132,000	17.27	39,658,000	10.19	37,607,000	9.67
1906	86,906,000	17.92	43,990,000	9.07	43,673,000	9.00
1907	100,956,000	18.16	49,345,000	8.88	43,141,000	7.76
1908	96,674,000	17.19	53,319,000	9.48	58,032,000	10.32
1909	94,694,000	15.77	63,517,000	10.58	59,695,000	9.94
1910	91,920,000	14.67	64,454,000	10.29	55,921,000	8.92
1911	98,397,000	15.04	63,146,000	9.65	55,760,000	8.52
1912	111,386,000	15.59	55,891,000	7.82	56,834,000	7.95

[1] From Movimento Commerciale del Regno d'Italia.

The total American export trade with Italy showed a steady increase; this began prior to the agreement of 1900 and continued after its termination. Italy had extended most-favored-nation treatment to American products prior to the conclusion of the agreement of 1900, and she continued such treatment after the termination of the agreement. The only change caused in the commercial relations of the two countries by the reciprocity arrangement was that duties were reduced by the United States on those of Italy's products which were among the articles enumerated in section 3 of the act of 1897, while the Italian Government established several new conventional rates which were lower than the old general rates. The effect of reciprocity is therefore to be sought mainly in the trend of exports to Italy of those articles upon which new minimum rates were made effective by the agreement. These articles were preserved fish, cottonseed oil, and turpentine.

PRESERVED FISH.

TABLE XXXVII.—*Imports of preserved fish into Italy, 1897–1902, 1907–1912.*[1]

Year.	From all sources.	From the United States.		Year.	From all sources.	From the United States.	
		Value.	Per cent of imports from all sources.			Value.	Per cent of imports from all sources.
1897.........	$5,184,597	$16,899	0.33	1907.........	$10,750,453	$1,228,637	11.43
1898.........	5,100,388	84,163	1.65	1908.........	13,622,374	1,921,060	14.10
1899.........	4,932,299	124,483	2.52	1909.........	14,384,344	1,892,820	13.15
1900.........	5,179,560	108,891	2.10	1910.........	10,223,082	346,328	3.39
1901.........	5,901,135	193,716	3.28	1911.........	9,677,721	228,391	2.36
1902.........	6,738,861	374,280	5.55	1912.........	10,552,566	159,321	1.51

[1] From Movimento Commerciale del Regno d'Italia.

The general rate of duty on preserved fish was 30 lire per quintal (equivalent to about 2.6 cents per pound), while the rate established by the agreement was from 15 to 25 lire per quintal (or from 1.3 to 2.2 cents per pound). The Italian importation of preserved fish from the United States increased in amount to a very marked extent after the conclusion of the agreement in 1900, and fell in 1910 and subsequent years when the conventional rate established by the agreement was no longer effective. Imports of fish from the United States amounting in value in 1900 to only $108,000, increased to $374,000 in 1902 and to $1,893,000 in 1909, but fell to $346,000 in 1910 and to $159,000 in 1912.

COTTONSEED OIL.

TABLE XXXVIII.—*Imports of cottonseed oil into Italy, 1897–1902; 1907–1912.*[1]

| Year. | From all sources. | From the United States. | | Year. | From all sources. | From the United States. | |
		Value.	Per cent of imports from all sources.			Value.	Per cent of imports from all sources.
1897.........	$236,475	$181,771	76.86	1907.........	$395,519	$364,482	92.15
1898.........	843,691	728,316	86.33	1908.........	1,564,994	1,494,848	95.52
1899.........	661,901	602,195	90.96	1909.........	4,846,823	4,670,300	96.35
1900.........	1,185,097	1,101,538	92.96	1910.........	690,959	661,450	95.72
1901.........	1,090,964	1,038,345	95.17	1911.........	2,055,705	2,018,429	98.18
1902.........	366,837	343,411	93.62	1912.........	3,006,807	2,965,040	98.61

[1] From Movimento Commerciale del Regno d'Italia.

The general rate of duty on cottonseed oil was 24 lire per quintal (equivalent to 2.1 cents per pound), whereas the conventional rate established by the agreement was 21.50 lire per quintal (equivalent to about 1.9 cents per pound). The imports of cottonseed oil, most of which came from the United States, fluctuated considerably in amount from year to year. The reduction in duty was small and apparently had no influence on imports. The reduction was not sufficient to put cottonseed oil on a parity with other vegetable oils in so far as tariff treatment was concerned.

TURPENTINE.

TABLE XXXIX.—*Imports of turpentine into Italy, 1897–1902, 1907–1912.*[1]

| Year. | From all sources. | From the United States. | | From France. | |
		Value.	Per cent of imports from all sources.	Value.	Per cent of imports from all sources.
1897.........	$242,180	$176,711	72.97	$1,405	0.58
1898.........	351,096	290,482	82.74	1,973	.56
1899.........	234,451	115,946	49.45	29,822	12.71
1900.........	457,245	337,062	73.72	7,280	1.59
1901.........	315,406	261,677	82.96	5,075	1.60
1902.........	317,694	211,689	66.63	33,326	10.48
1907.........	580,698	211,084	36.35	287,724	49.54
1908.........	642,999	229,207	35.65	357,475	55.59
1909.........	519,788	160,634	30.90	310,611	59.75
1910.........	647,114	169,462	26.19	374,289	57.83
1911.........	731,323	207,560	28.38	202,920	27.75
1912.........	688,807	194,021	28.17	419,844	60.95

[1] From Movimento Commerciale del Regno d'Italia.

The imports of turpentine likewise showed considerable fluctuations from year to year. The general rate of duty on turpentine was 8 lire per quintal; under the agreement it entered free. The remission of this duty, which had been equivalent to but seven-tenths of 1 cent per pound, was not sufficient to cause any significant change in the amount of turpentine imported. The imports of turpentine into Italy during the first year of reciprocity actually showed an increase over the figure of the preceding year, but the imports in the latter year had been abnormally low. With the ending of the agreement and the reestablishment of the old general rate, a smaller proportion of the Italian imports of turpentine came from the United States.

SWITZERLAND.

Imports into Switzerland from the United States, as compared with those from other countries, are shown in the following table:

TABLE XL.—*Imports into Switzerland, 1898–1912.*[1]

(Values expressed in thousands.)

Year.	From all sources.	From the United States.		From Germany.	
		Value.	Per cent of imports from all sources.	Value.	Per cent of imports from all sources.
1898	$205,604	$14,102	6.86	$60,720	29.53
1899	223,869	11,935	5.33	66,138	29.54
1900	214,444	11,015	5.14	67,619	31.54
1901	202,650	11,833	5.84	61,179	30.20
1902	217,803	11,890	5.46	62,616	28.75
1903	230,860	11,067	4.79	68,670	29.74
1904	239,334	10,388	4.34	72,657	30.36
1905	266,311	10,986	4.13	85,074	31.95
1906	283,528	11,287	3.98	92,543	32.64
1907	325,673	13,538	4.16	106,406	32.67
1908	287,020	11,707	4.08	98,951	34.48
1909	309,213	12,266	3.97	103,025	33.32
1910	336,789	13,283	3.94	109,184	32.42
1911	347,855	14,491	4.17	112,209	32.26
1912	381,966	16,166	4.23	124,962	32.70

Year.	From France.		From Italy.		From Austria-Hungary.		From the United Kingdom.	
	Value.	Per cent of imports from all sources.	Value.	Per cent of imports from all sources.	Value.	Per cent of imports from all sources.	Value.	Per cent of imports from all sources.
1898	$39,359	19.14	$30,072	14.63	$12,780	6.22	$9,835	4.78
1899	41,289	18.44	36,929	16.49	14,769	6.60	10,891	4.86
1900	40,019	18.67	31,268	14.58	13,344	6.22	12,025	5.61
1901	39,669	19.58	30,464	15.04	12,335	6.09	9,076	4.48
1902	41,892	19.23	34,313	15.75	13,009	6.25	10,432	4.79
1903	42,750	18.51	34,921	15.12	14,993	6.49	11,022	4.77
1904	46,113	19.27	32,691	13.66	15,851	6.62	11,101	4.64
1905	52,940	19.88	34,142	12.82	17,664	6.63	13,279	4.99
1906	54,295	19.15	38,732	13.66	17,704	6.24	16,156	5.70
1907	57,469	17.65	44,446	13.65	19,878	6.10	22,759	6.99
1908	54,730	19.07	33,167	11.56	19,075	6.65	16,793	5.85
1909	59,083	19.11	35,738	11.56	19,700	6.37	17,499	5.66
1910	66,892	19.86	39,105	11.64	21,374	6.35	21,747	6.46
1911	65,549	18.85	34,861	10.02	21,968	6.32	19,272	5.54
1912	72,632	19.01	37,176	9.73	23,617	6.18	22,536	5.90

[1] From Statistik des Warenverkehrs der Schweiz mit dem Auslande.

The Swiss imports from the United States appear to have been smaller in the years during which the rates of the conventional tariff were applied to the products of the United States than in the years during which American products were subjected to the maximum rates. No effect whatsoever of the reciprocal arrangements with the United States can be deduced from the available Swiss data. The American statistics of exports to Switzerland do not indicate the actual movement of trade, as the bulk of the exports which actually go to Switzerland are credited to Holland, France, Germany, the United Kingdom, and the other countries of first destination.

SPAIN.

The effect of the reciprocity agreements upon the trade between the United States and Spain may be gauged by the statistics given in Tables XLI and XLII.

TABLE XLI.—*Exports of domestic merchandise from the United States to Spain, 1903-1912.*

Year.	To Europe.	To Spain.		Year.	To Europe.	To Spain.	
		Value.	Per cent of exports to Europe.			Value.	Per cent of exports to Europe.
1903	$1,014,949,869	$17,674,109	1.74	1908	$1,270,016,773	$21,882,992	1.72
1904	1,046,075,474	15,725,308	1.50	1909	1,135,586,011	19,653,427	1.73
1905	1,008,467,292	17,020,286	1.68	1910	·1,118,402,094	18,899,125	1.68
1906	1,189,254,885	19,091,070	1.60	1911	1,289,354,924	24,760,914	1.92
1907	1,286,657,982	21,284,312	1.65	1912	1,325,896,164	25,030,211	1.88

TABLE XLII.—*Imports into Spain, 1898-1912.*[1]

[Values expressed in thousands.]

Year.	From all sources.	From the United States.		From the United Kingdom.		From France.		From Germany.	
		Value.	Per cent of imports from all sources.	Value.	Per cent of imports from all sources.	Value.	Per cent of imports from all sources.	Value.	Per cent of imports from all sources.
1898	$73,918	$11,388	15.41	$15,275	20.66	$10,646	14.40	$5,461	7.39
1899	147,691	18,532	12.55	36,474	24.69	22,181	15.02	9,996	6.77
1900	139,885	15,764	11.27	36,665	26.21	20,260	14.48	11,591	8.29
1901	125,754	16,721	13.29	27,772	22.08	18,646	14.82	11,207	8.91
1902	124,253	16,508	13.28	26,596	21.40	19,859	15.98	12,564	10.11
1903	131,374	16,936	12.89	26,246	19.97	20,793	15.83	13,526	10.29
1904	·134,218	15,008	11.18	25,325	18.87	19,125	14.25	13,655	10.17
1905	154,136	17,523	11.37	24,590	15.96	21,565	13.99	12,428	8.06
1906	172,491	24,072	13.95	29,739	17.24	24,586	14.25	15,808	9.16
1907	163,972	23,513	14.34	31,118	18.97	22,551	13.75	16,969	10.35
1908	167,858	23,686	14.11	33,549	19.98	24,412	14.54	17,941	10.69
1909	167,471	21,292	12.71	35,991	21.49	23,209	13.86	19,965	11.92
1910	180,007	19,840	11.02	36,613	20.34	23,994	13.33	20,692	11.50
1911	178,082	23,202	13.03	30,074	16.89	23,471	13.18	22,781	12.79
1912	190,454	28,097	14.75	36,202	·19.00	24,220	12.72	24,820	13.03

[1] From Estadistica general del comercio exterior de Espana.

The agreement of 1906 with Spain secured for the United States most-favored-nation treatment (Portugal excepted) on the part of Spain. The American exports to Spain increased immediately following the conclusion of reciprocity, and the American share of the Spanish import trade also showed an increase. The exports to Spain increased from $19,000,000 in the fiscal year 1906 to $21,000,000 in the fiscal year 1907, which was the first year of the treaty period. The Spanish figures of imports show that in the calendar year 1906, during the latter part of which the agreement was effective, the imports from the United States were $24,000,000, or 14 per cent of the total imports into Spain, whereas in 1905 the imports from the United States were only $17,500,000, or 11 per cent of the total imports into Spain. During the five years preceding reciprocity the Spanish imports from the United States averaged $16,410,000; during the five years from 1906 to 1910 they averaged $22,480,000. This was the one case in which the reciprocity agreement secured for the United States a new and full extension of complete most-favored-nation treatment, and the increase in the American exports to Spain which resulted was therefore especially significant.

BULGARIA.

Reciprocity introduced no new factors into the commercial relations of the United States with Bulgaria, as the United States had always enjoyed most-favored-nation treatment from Bulgaria. The American exports to Bulgaria were small in amount and formed only a very small percentage of the total Bulgarian imports, but they showed a steady growth throughout the period.

TABLE XLIII.—*Imports into Bulgaria, 1902–1911.*[1]

(Treaty period: Sept. 30, 1906, to Oct. 31, 1909.)

[Values expressed in thousands.]

Year.	From all countries.	From the United States.		From Austria-Hungary.		From Great Britain.		From Germany.		From France.	
		Value.	Per cent of imports from all countries.	Value.	Per cent of imports from all countries.	Value.	Per cent of imports from all countries.	Value.	Per cent of imports from all countries.	Value.	Per cent of imports from all countries.
1902	$13,751	$59	0.45	$3,501	25.46	$2,937	21.36	$1,651	12.00	$764	5.56
1903	15,788	73	.46	4,406	27.90	2,864	18.14	2,107	13.34	650	4.12
1904	25,030	111	.44	7,367	29.43	3,638	14.53	3,856	15.41	2,064	8.25
1905	23,594	274	1.16	6,376	27.03	3,895	16.51	4,059	17.21	1,413	5.99
1906	20,935	90	.43	5,366	25.64	3,783	18.07	3,092	14.77	1,037	4.95
1907	24,060	175	.73	6,695	27.83	4,135	17.19	3,794	15.77	1,272	5.29
1908	25,119	111	.44	6,859	27.30	4,478	17.83	4,023	16.01	1,355	5.39
1909	30,963	114	.37	7,501	24.23	5,213	16.84	5,638	18.21	2,155	6.96
1910	34,230	165	.48	9,181	26.82	4,378	12.79	6,585	19.24	2,962	8.65
1911	38,474	327	.85	9,306	24.19	5,797	15.07	7,689	19.99	4,811	12.51

[1] From Statistique du Commerce du Royaume de Bulgarie avec les pays étrangers.

THE UNITED KINGDOM.

The agreement with the United Kingdom involved no tariff changes affecting American exports to the United Kingdom, with the exception that travelers' samples, which formerly were subject to duty upon entrance into the United Kingdom, were made free of duty.

THE NETHERLANDS.

The imports into the Netherlands from the United States of the few articles upon which special rates were established by the agreement—mutton, pork, and bacon—decreased in the years 1908 to 1910, during which the agreement was effective, both in amount and in relation to the total imports of these articles into the Netherlands. The decrease is to be explained by the general decline which took place in these years in the American exports of foodstuffs, owing to poor crop conditions in the United States. The concessions which the Netherlands had granted on these products were unimportant, and they were ·generalized to all countries entitled to most-favored-nation treatment. In so far as the American export trade was concerned, the agreement with the Netherlands was, therefore, of little significance.

TABLE XLIV.—*Imports of mutton, pork, and bacon into the Netherlands, 1906–1913.*[1]

(Treaty period: Aug. 12, 1908, to Aug. 7, 1910.)

Year.	From all countries.	From the United States.		Year.	From all countries.	From the United States.	
		Value.	Per cent of imports from all countries.			Value.	Per cent of imports from all countries.
1906	$1,649,747	$1,356,607	82.2	1910	$228,430	$170,330	74.6
1907	866,137	716,965	82.8	1911	561,844	455,793	81.1
1908	737,952	640,372	86.5	1912	960,512	841,843	87.9
1909	296,377	244,463	82.5	1913	392,848	344,054	87.6

[1] From Statistiek van den In-, Uit- en Doorvoer, the Netherlands.

RESUMÉ OF TRADE WITH FRANCE, ITALY, PORTUGAL, AND GERMANY.

TABLE XLV.—*Domestic exports from the United States, 1897–1912.*

(Treaty periods: France, June 1, 1898, to Oct. 31, 1909; Portugal, June 12, 1900, to Aug. 7, 1910; Germany, July 13, 1900, to Feb. 7, 1910; Italy, July 18, 1900, to Aug. 7, 1910.)

Year.	To Europe.	To France, Italy, Portugal, and Germany.		Year.	To Europe.	To France, Italy, Portugal, and Germany.	
		Value.	Per cent of exports to Europe.			Value.	Per cent of exports to Europe.
1897	$804,207,623	$203,969,298	25.36	1905	$1,008,467,292	$306,203,825	30.36
1898	962,202,778	273,561,871	28.43	1906	1,189,254,885	377,681,867	31.75
1899	925,165,326	241,357,392	26.08	1907	1,286,657,982	429,592,195	33.38
1900	1,028,793,341	305,587,550	29.70	1908	1,270,016,773	444,659,038	35.01
1901	1,121,909,593	304,349,248	27.12	1909	1,135,586,011	402,240,177	35.42
1902	994,321,959	273,399,659	27.49	1910	1,118,402,094	417,724,485	37.35
1903	1,014,949,869	304,332,980	29.98	1911	1,289,354,924	478,548,105	37.11
1904	1,046,075,474	332,944,121	31.82	1912	1,325,896,164	502,274,958	37.88

TABLE XLVI.—*Total imports into France, Italy, Portugal, and Germany, 1898–1912.*

[Expressed in thousands.]

Year.	From all countries.	From United States.		Year.	From all countries.	From United States.	
		Value.	Per cent of imports from all countries.			Value.	Per cent of imports from all countries.
1898	$2,397,655	$368,514	15.36	1906	$3,545,762	$472,770	13.33
1899	2,522,466	336,416	13.33	1907	3,905,569	525,993	13.45
1900	2,671,539	390,547	14.61	1908	3,548,146	518,169	14.60
1901	2,527,627	376,232	14.88	1909	3,903,786	523,724	13.41
1902	2,591,091	339,575	13.15	1910	4,212,310	479,248	11.33
1903	2,769,601	374,171	13.51	1911	4,594,358	565,677	12.31
1904	2,810,646	368,468	13.11	1912	4,874,205	654,230	13.42
1905	3,073,567	384,613	12.51				

Table XLV shows that the amount of the combined exports to the four reciprocity countries with which the agreements were of longest duration, and also the percentage which these exports formed of the total exports to all Europe, underwent steady growth during the entire period under investigation. Neither the introduction of reciprocity nor its termination was accompanied by any marked change in the amount of trade with these countries. Table XLVI presents combined figures of imports into the same four countries and likewise indicates that reciprocity brought about no very important expansion or diversion of trade. The share of the United States in the import trade of these four countries showed no tendency to increase during the reciprocity period. In 1910 and 1911, when reciprocity had terminated, the percentage of imports from the United States to total imports declined. Few of the reductions which had been granted to the United States in the various agreements were withdrawn by the reciprocity countries upon their termination. Of the countries included in this table the most important—France and Germany—granted to the United States after 1909 a larger percentage of the rates of their minimum schedules than they had granted under reciprocity.

ESTIMATE OF THE EFFECT OF THE AGREEMENTS.

The foregoing analysis of trade with the countries with which reciprocity agreements were concluded under section 3 of the act of 1897 presents various instances of increases in imports from and exports to these countries, some of which resulted apparently from the reductions of duties effected by the agreements. In most cases, however, the collected statistics indicate that the tariff arrangements established by the agreements in question had little effect upon the general course of trade. The reductions of duty were often small in amount and, in the cases both of those granted by and of those received by the United States, were not exclusive but were extended to most of the important competing countries. The concessions made to the United States in the various agreements were, with a few exceptions, continued after the termination of the agreements. This being the case, the treatment of a given United States product upon importation into most of the "reciprocity" countries was not different after the reciprocity period from that extended to it during the period. Hence it is difficult to determine what increases in United States exports were properly attributable to reciprocity and what are sufficiently to be accounted for by the general expansion of American trade. The one general conclusion which seems deducible from the data presented in the preceding pages is that concession-making agreements in which the number of articles upon which reductions are made is not great, in which reductions are small in amount, and in connection with which the favors are extended to other competing countries, exert but little influence upon the course of trade.

THE TARIFF ACT OF 1909.

THE TARIFF ACT OF 1909.

HISTORY OF THE BILL.

Reciprocity sentiment after 1897.—At the close of the last and during the opening years of the present century a number of factors combined to weaken the public support of reciprocity. Foremost among these factors were the continued discrimination against American products in European tariffs, the refusal of the Senate to ratify the Kasson treaties, the scant consideration given by the American public to the "argol agreements," and the fears of domestic producers that reciprocity would involve a reduction of the protection which their industries received. When the time for tariff revision again drew near there was little enthusiasm for the reciprocity policy.

As far as their official programs were concerned, in the interval between 1897 and 1908, the two great parties reversed their positions. The Democratic platform in 1904 definitely indorsed reciprocity for the first time since 1892, whereas the Republican platform of 1904 contained no mention of it for the first time in a number of years. In 1908 the platforms of both parties were silent upon reciprocity, while the Republicans proposed in its stead "the establishment of maximum and minimum rates to be administered by the President under limitations fixed by the law, the maximum to be available to meet the discrimination by foreign countries against American goods entering our markets, and the minimum representing the normal measure of protection at home." The Republicans succeeded in winning the election of 1908, with large majorities in both houses.

Introduction of the tariff bill of 1909.—The new Congress proceeded in 1909 without delay to consider the revision of the tariff. On March 17, 1909, Mr. Payne, of New York, chairman of the House Committee on Ways and Means, presented a bill in the House to "provide revenue, equalize duties, and encourage the industries of the United States, and for other purposes." This was at once referred to the Committee on Ways and Means and was reported back the following day without amendment.

Maximum and minimum schedules.—Section 1 of the bill contained a general schedule of duties, and section 2 a free list. Section 3 enumerated a long list of articles, specifying rates thereon, to form the maximum schedule. These rates exceeded those of the general tariff by 20 per cent on some articles, 25 per cent on others, and 40 per cent on still others. Section 3 further enumerated a number of articles (which in the general tariff were on the free list) upon which the maximum duties were to be 20 per cent ad valorem.

Section 4 provided that imports into the United States from any country which did not discriminate against American products should pay the rates of duty prescribed in section 1, and in case the articles were mentioned in section 2 they should be admitted free of duty. This section further provided that in case after 60 days from the passage of the act any country failed to admit any article imported from the United States on terms as favorable as those accorded to any similar article imported from any other country, there should be levied upon the imports from such country the rates of duty prescribed in section 3.

The bargaining features of the Payne bill were thus given the form of penalizing provisions. They differed, however, in some important respects from the penalizing provisions of the acts of 1890 and 1897. In the Payne bill the number of articles upon which penalizing duties could be imposed was much greater, and the penalizing provisions were therefore of correspondingly greater severity. The decision as to whether the tariff treatment accorded to American products by another country called for the application of the penalty duties was placed in the hands of the Treasury Department and ultimately in the hands of the courts, instead of being left to the President. The purpose of the provisions was not the securing of special tariff favors from other countries, but, on the contrary, the removal of discriminations against American products.

House debate on maximum and minimum clauses.—Mr. Payne, in opening the discussion on the maximum and minimum clauses of the bill, expressed confidence that all the important nations would take advantage of the minimum rates by so arranging their own rates as to entitle them to the minimum tariff. The bargaining features, he said, were not intended to secure preferential treatment for American products from other countries. "We gave them rates," he said, "by which they may pay our tariff and come in, sometimes in equal competition and sometimes in not quite equal competition, with our manufacturers, and all we ask of them is that they shall do the same thing to us, and leave it to the skill and enterprise of our manufacturers to go into their markets and pay tariff rates on even terms with every other foreign country and seek an open competition for their trade."[1]

Opposition to the bill.—From the Democratic side of the House the opposition to the Payne bill was very forceful, but it was directed more against the high level of the duties stipulated therein than against the special bargaining features. The objection was brought against section 2 that, by establishing maximum rates averaging 20 per cent above the rates of the Dingley tariff and by transferring 68 items from the Dingley free list to the list of articles dutiable in the maximum schedule of the Payne bill at 20 per cent ad valorem, the level of duties would be made unduly high. The Democrats gave the bargaining features of the bill no support. They claimed that the special reciprocity arrangement between the United States and Cuba was itself an example of discrimination such as the sections under debate were intended to penalize when that discrimination was directed against the United States; that sections 3 and 4 embodied a threat to which no country would yield after it had established, as the result of study and long negotiations, a complex system of commercial relationship; that the short period of delay stipulated in section 4—sixty days from the passage of the bill—before the maximum scale should become effective was unjust for countries which had with other countries special commercial treaties which could not be

---

[1] 61st Cong., 1st sess., Cong. Rec., Vol. 1, p. 143.

easily abrogated or modified within that time. Many Democratic speakers urged a revision of the bargaining features of the bill so as to provide for "true reciprocity"—that is, actual concessions from the general tariff schedule in return for special favors received from other countries. They interpreted the maximum and minimum features, not as a provision making possible the grant of concessions in return for equivalent concessions, but as a threat of penalties to be applied alike to foreign producers and home consumers whenever a foreign country withheld from the United States concessions which had been granted to another country. They believed that the framers of the bill should have taken into consideration the special circumstances of geographical proximity, political or racial affiliations, historical usage, or commercial intercourse, which might dictate the commercial relations between foreign countries. They criticized as a defect the fact that the bill attempted to secure the desired results by creating a mechanism which would automatically supplant the method of negotiation.

On April 9 Mr. Champ Clark, Democratic leader in the House, made a motion to re-submit the bill to the Committee on Ways and Means with instructions to amend by making the rates of duty then stipulated in the bill the maximum rates, with provision for a lower schedule of minimum rates which could be allowed to countries in return for equivalent concessions. This motion was defeated, and on the same day the House passed the bill with the maximum-minimum clause as originally introduced by Mr. Payne.

The bill in the Senate.—The bill reached the Senate on April 10, 1909, and was at once referred to the Committee on Finance, of which Mr. Aldrich, of Rhode Island, was chairman. On April 19 it was sent back from the committee with sections 1 and 2 merged into one section and with sections 3, 4, 6, and 7 struck out.

Senator Aldrich's amendment.—On April 30 Senator Aldrich submitted as a substitute for sections 3 and 4 of the House bill a new amendment, to be known as sec. 2, likewise proposing to establish both maximum and minimum schedules. The free list and the rates in section 1 of the dutiable list were together to constitute the minimum schedule; the rates of the dutiable list plus 25 per cent *ad valorem*, and, in addition, special rates of 5 cents per pound on coffee and 10 cents per pound on tea—which in the minimum schedule were on the free list—were to constitute the maximum schedule. The rates of the maximum schedule were to be imposed on and after March 1, 1910, on all imports into the United States, but in case the President was satisfied that any country did not "unduly discriminate," directly or indirectly, against products of the United States, he might by proclamation cause the imports from such country to be admitted at the rates of the minimum schedule.

Comparison of the Aldrich amendment with the bargaining provision of the Payne bill.—Senator Aldrich's substitute for sections 3 and 4 of the House bill, although similar in purpose, was radically different from these sections both in form and in substance. In the Aldrich amendment the articles of the free list in the minimum schedule were not included—except coffee and tea—in the list of articles upon which the duties were to be imposed under the maximum schedule, but were to enter free of duty from all countries under all circumstances. The provision in the Aldrich amendment for a maximum schedule was simpler than the corresponding provision in the House bill in that the rates of the maximum schedule exceeded the rates of the minimum schedule by the uniform amount of 25 per cent *ad valorem*. It authorized the President to extend the minimum rates only to countries which did not discriminate directly or indirectly against the products of the United States, and it further differed from the House bill in that it completely reversed the procedure for applying the maximum rates. In the House bill the minimum rates were intended to be the general tariff and to be applied to the imports from countries, except such as the Treasury officials found to be unduly discriminating against products of the United States; but the Aldrich amendment proposed that the maximum rates should be the general schedule and that they should be applied to the imports from all countries, except such as the President found not to be discriminating against the products of the United States.

Debate in the Senate on the Aldrich amendment.—The debate on the bargaining features of the bill was not begun in the Senate until July 3, 1909. On that day Mr. Aldrich explained that the provisions for a maximum schedule as they had appeared in the House bill, and as he had amended them, were intended to empower the administration to inform a foreign government that it must either permit the import of American products without unjust discrimination or suffer the higher rates of duty to be imposed upon its exports to the United States. A number of amendments were submitted which were intended to make the bargaining features of the bill correspond more closely to the similar provisions of the Dingley Act, but these amendments were all rejected.

Successful amendments.—Upon a motion of Senator Aldrich, the Senate reinserted in the bill sections 5 and 6 as they had appeared in the House bill, providing for the exemption of the reciprocity treaty of 1903 with Cuba from the operation of the act and making provision for notice of termination of the other existing commercial agreements. The proposal contained in the Aldrich amendment for penalty duties on coffee and tea was struck out by agreement. Senator Heyburn submitted two amendments affecting the application of the maximum rates, the first of which stipulated that 30 days' notice be given before the maximum rates were reimposed upon the products of a country to which the minimum rates had previously been granted; the second, that the minimum rates be not imposed upon any country until after the 31st day of March, 1910. These amendments were accepted by agreement.

Unsuccessful amendments.—There were submitted a number of amendments which proposed radical changes in the Aldrich amendment, but these were all rejected. Senator Gore introduced an amendment to the effect that section 4 of the tariff act of 1897 [1] be substituted for section 2 of the proposed bill. Senator Bacon criticized the Aldrich amendment on the ground that it proposed to enact as a general tariff a schedule of rates which was intended to meet exceptional cases of discrimination only. He thought it preferable to provide a general tariff to meet the normal situation and to add thereto a provision for special duties to meet the exceptional cases of discrimination as they arose. He suggested, therefore, that the minimum rates be made the general schedule, and that provision be

---

[1] See p. 202, infra.

made for the application of the maximum rates only by special proclamation to meet cases of unfair discrimination against American products. Senator Cummins proposed an amendment to the effect that the authority to levy the maximum rates be assigned to the President and not to the Treasury, and further, in order to give the bargaining provisions greater elasticity, that the President be authorized to levy at his discretion all or part of the rates of the maximum schedule. Senator Daniel criticized the Aldrich amendment on the ground that its terms were vague and left too much to the personal discretion of the Executive, with the possibility as a consequence that personal pique, prejudice, and partiality might be the ruling factor in deciding the attitude of the United States Government in its commercial relations with other countries.

Senator La Follette submitted an amendment proposing an additional section in which the President should be authorized, in return for special reductions from the existing tariffs of foreign countries on the products of the United States, to grant additional reductions of duty, but in no case to bring the rates to more than 20 per cent less than those provided for in the tariff act of 1897. He explained that the object of the amendment was to authorize the President to initiate negotiations with foreign countries which had no minimum rates in their existing tariffs or whose minimum rates were not sufficiently low. It would revive section 4 of the act of 1897 in respect to all those articles upon which rates had not been reduced by 20 per cent in the bill then under consideration, and it would give the President the means to obtain for American products special tariff reductions which could not otherwise be secured.

These four amendments were rejected, in most cases with little or no debate. They served, however, to indicate the considerations upon which rested such dissatisfaction with the Aldrich plan of bargaining tariff as existed in the Senate.

Conference committee and enactment.—On July 5 Senator Aldrich's amendment was accepted by the Senate. Three days later the bill passed the Senate and was sent to a conference committee of both Houses. The committee adopted the Senate provision for a maximum-and-minimum tariff in preference to the plan of the House. The conference report was accepted by the House without debate on the bargaining features and by the Senate after little discussion. The act was approved by the President and became law on August 5, 1909.

Sections 2, 3, and 4 of the tariff act of 1909.—In the act of 1909, section 2 contained the provisions for maximum and minimum schedules, section 3 provided for exemption of the reciprocity treaty with Cuba from the operation of the act, and section 4 stipulated the time and method of termination of the existing commercial agreements.[1] Sections 2 and 3 read as follows:

SEC. 2. That from and after the thirty-first day of March, nineteen hundred and ten, except as otherwise specially provided for in this section, there shall be levied, collected, and paid on all articles when imported from any foreign country into the United States, or into any of its possessions (except the Philippine Islands and the islands of Guam and Tutuila), the rates of duty prescribed by the schedules and paragraphs of the dutiable list of section one of this Act, and in addition thereto twenty-five per centum ad valorem; which rates shall constitute the maximum tariff of the United States: *Provided*, That whenever, after the thirty-first day of March, nineteen hundred and ten, and so long thereafter as the President shall be satisfied, in view of

---

[1] For the legislative record and the text of sec. 4, see p. 227, seq., infra.

the character of the concessions granted by the minimum tariff of the United States, that the government of any foreign country imposes no terms or restrictions, either in the way of tariff rates or provisions, trade, or other regulations, charges, exactions, or in any other manner, directly or indirectly, upon the importation into or the sale in such foreign country of any agricultural, manufactured, or other product of the United States, which unduly discriminate against the United States or the products thereof, and that such foreign country pays no export bounty or imposes no export duty or prohibition upon the exportation of any article to the United States which unduly discriminates against the United States or the products thereof, and that such foreign country accords to the agricultural, manufactured, or other products of the United States, treatment which is reciprocal and equivalent, thereupon and thereafter, upon proclamation to this effect by the President of the United States, all articles when imported into the United States, or any of its possessions (except the Philippine Islands and the islands of Guam and Tutuila), from such foreign country shall, except as otherwise herein provided, be admitted under the terms of the minimum tariff of the United States as prescribed by section one of this Act. The proclamation issued by the President under the authority hereby conferred and the application of the minimum tariff thereupon may, in accordance with the facts as found by the President, extend to the whole of any foreign country, or may be confined to or exclude from its effect any dependency, colony, or other political subdivision having authority to adopt and enforce tariff legislation, or to impose restrictions or regulations, or to grant concessions upon the exportation or importation of articles which are, or may be, imported into the United States. Whenever the President shall be satisfied that the condition which led to the issuance of the proclamation hereinbefore authorized no longer exist, he shall issue a proclamation to this effect, and ninety days thereafter the provisions of the maximum tariff shall be applied to the importation of articles from such country. Whenever the provisions of the maximum tariff of the United States shall be applicable to articles imported from any foreign country they shall be applicable to the products of such country, whether imported directly from the country of production or otherwise. To secure information to assist the President in the discharge of the duties imposed upon him by this section, and the officers of the Government in the administration of the customs laws, the President is hereby authorized to employ such persons as may be required.

SEC. 3. That nothing in this Act contained shall be so construed as to abrogate or in any manner impair or affect the provisions of the treaty of commercial reciprocity concluded between the United States and the Republic of Cuba on the eleventh day of December, nineteen hundred and two, or the provisions of the act of Congress heretofore passed for the execution of the same.

Abandonment of reciprocity.—The act of 1909 marked an important reversal of practice by the United States in regard to tariff bargaining: the policy of giving concessions for concessions was abandoned for that of penalizing countries which made discriminations unfavorable to the United States.

OPERATION OF THE MAXIMUM AND MINIMUM CLAUSE IN THE TARIFF ACT OF 1909.

President Taft's message, December, 1909.—Fear had been expressed, both in Congress and in the press, that the provision in section 2 which authorized the President to apply the maximum duties to all countries which discriminated unduly against the United States would lead to tariff wars and, in application, to an increase of the import duties above the high level already fixed in the minimum schedule. In his message to Congress of December 7, 1909, President Taft made it clear that he would use caution in applying these rates and expressed the hope and belief that the United States would not be led into tariff wars as a result of the authority conferred upon him. He pointed out that the term, "unduly discriminatory," used in section 2 allowed him wide discretion; before applying the maximum duties upon the imports from a country it was necessary that he should find not only that that country discriminated against the trade of the United States, but that the discriminations were "undue," that is, without good and fair reason. He expressed the belief that this authorization had been conferred in the hope that there would never be occasion to apply the maximum duties and in the expectation that the power to apply them would enable the President and the State Department through friendly negotiations to secure the elimination of whatever was unduly discriminatory against the United States from the laws and practices of foreign countries.

Investigation by State Department.—In order properly to carry out the intent of the maximum and minimum features of the act of 1909, it was necessary to ascertain authoritatively in what manner the tariff laws, as well as other legislative or administrative acts of foreign governments, were affecting the commerce of the United States. The State Department accordingly issued general instructions to the diplomatic and consular officials of the United States directing them to report fully upon this matter. In response to these instructions the State Department received detailed and comprehensive reports, the contents of which suggested a basis for negotiations for the removal of unfair discrimination against American trade.[1] These reports disclosed a number of instances of differential treatment against products of the United States. They also brought out the fact that in many cases the tariff rates imposed on certain products distinctively American were so much in excess of the rates on competing products of other countries as to constitute definite obstacles to American commerce.

Negotiations to secure removal of discriminations.—Negotiations were at once entered upon in order that these discriminations might be eliminated and the necessity of applying the maximum rates to the products of any country be avoided.

The Tariff Board, which had been appointed in September, 1909, under authority of section 2 of the act of 1909,[2] co-operated with the Department of State both in investigating the question of discrimination on the part of foreign countries and in the negotiations which followed, aiming at the removal of such discriminations where they existed.

Negotiations with Germany.—By the argol agreement of 1907 Germany had granted to the United States her conventional rates of duty upon all but a few articles. It was estimated that, under this agreement, no more than 4 per cent of the imports into Germany from the United States were subject to the maximum rates of duty. The negotiations in conformity with the act of 1909 resulted in Germany's granting to the United States her full conventional rates in return for the minimum tariff of the United States. The German law of February 5, 1910, which put these rates into operation, contained the following proviso:

Should the United States of America by means of laws, treaties with other countries, or in any other way modify to the detriment of Germany the present conditions concerning the exchange of merchandise between the German Empire and the United States, the Bundsrath will, at its discretion, withdraw, in whole or in part, the favors granted to the products of the United States.

Subsequently the United States, by the act of July 26, 1911, granted admission to Canadian wood pulp and paper at lower rates

---

[1] A summary of the material in these reports is contained in a report of the Secretary of State and the Secretary of the Treasury relative to tariff negotiations carried on in accordance with the provisions of the act of Aug. 5, 1909, printed as H. Doc. No. 956, 61st Cong., 2d sess.

[2] See p. 272.

of duty than were imposed upon similar products from Germany.[1] This caused much criticism in Germany and led to retaliatory action by the German Government. The conventional rates of duty in force in Germany by virtue of existing treaties were not withdrawn from the United States, but the new rates established by the German treaties with Japan and Sweden, which came into force toward the end of 1911, were not granted to the United States. Upon certain products—for example, boots and shoes of india rubber—the rates established by the new Swedish treaty were the same as the rates in the old treaty with that country. But, acting upon the theory that the concessions of conventional rates to the United States expired with the termination of the conventions originally establishing such rates, and that the United States was not entitled to conventional rates established in new treaties, Germany, in December, 1911, subjected American boots and shoes of india rubber to the rates of its maximum tariff. Thus, without any alteration in the rates either of the general or of the conventional tariff, and without any change in its avowed policy in regard to commercial relations with the United States, the German Government nevertheless in effect imposed upon a number of American products rates higher than those which had been previously in force, and higher, also, than those which were imposed upon similar products coming from other countries.

Most-favored-nation agreement with Portugal.—The negotiations with Portugal led to the conclusion on June 28, 1910, of a most-favored-nation commercial arrangement by exchange of notes at Washington. Upon agreement of the United States to extend the minimum tariff to Portugal, that country agreed to extend most-favored-nation treatment (Spain and Brazil excepted) to the United States.

Negotiations with France.—Under the commercial agreements of 1898 and 1908 France had granted to the United States the benefit of her minimum rates on 25 items in the French tariff. On the many and important products of the United States not included in these 25 items, France imposed the discriminatory rates of her maximum tariff. Upon the termination of the agreement of 1908, on November 1, 1909, the French Government applied its complete maximum tariff to all imports from the United States.

As a result of the negotiations initiated by the State Department, and conducted with the assistance of the Tariff Board, with the intent to secure more favorable treatment from France in return for the extension to her of the minimum schedule of the new 1909 tariff, France agreed to grant her minimum tariff rates to the United States on about 80 items. The list of articles to which the minimum rates of the French tariff were to be applied included a number of the manufactured articles which figured most prominently in the export trade of the United States, such as agricultural and other implements, tools, and machinery. Furthermore, the French rates on all edible oils were equalized, thus removing the discrimination against American cottonseed oil.

Agreement with Austria-Hungary.—The Government of Austria-Hungary, in exchange for the minimum tariff of the United States, continued to grant its complete conventional tariff rates to the products of the United States and further agreed to reduce the duties on cottonseed oil.

---

[1] Two years later this rate was extended by decision of the courts to Germany and other countries. See Part III, p. 487, footnote, infra.

Arrangement with Brazil.—Through the representations of the State Department, Brazil agreed to add to the previous list of American products in favor of which preferential reduction had been granted the following additional articles: Cement, corsets, dried fruits, and school furniture and desks.[1]

Arrangement with Canada.—Under the terms of the Franco-Canadian treaty of February 1, 1910, there were conceded to France a number of the rates of the Canadian intermediate tariff and in addition a number of special rates. By the operation of the favored-nation clause in British treaties, the treaty rates were extended automatically to many other countries, some of whose products competed with the products of the United States in the Canadian market. A partial adjustment between the United States and Canada was reached by the extension on the part of Canada of the intermediate rates of the Canadian tariff to various exports of the United States.

Elimination of discrimination against American cottonseed oil.—The negotiations entered upon by the State Department served the useful purpose of securing in some cases a removal and in others a mitigation of the discrimination against American cottonseed oil as compared with vegetable oils produced by other countries. The tariff treatment of cottonseed oil in Europe affords an interesting illustration of the manner in which a country may indirectly discriminate against the products of another country without imposing higher rates upon the products of that country than are imposed upon the identical products coming from other countries. Cottonseed oil, the product of a growing industry in the United States, competes with other edible vegetable oils, and is predominantly an American product. It was an almost universal feature of European tariffs that the rates on the competing vegetable oils were lower than the rates on cottonseed oil. This discrimination had developed from a number of causes. The duties on other vegetable oils in some cases had been reduced in commercial treaties with other countries of which these oils were a special product, without a corresponding reduction in the duty on cottonseed oil. In other cases, the foreign producers of vegetable oils, who could not hold their domestic market unless protected, feared most of all the competition of the American substitute, and persuaded their Government to discriminate against it. In still other cases, the extraction of the oil from American or Egyptian cottonseed had become in some European countries a domestic industry, and higher duties were put upon the oil than upon the seeds in order to protect the manufacturers who crushed the oil from imported seed. An additional reason for the high tariff rates on cottonseed oil is to be found in its adaptability for mixing with olive oil. It became customary as early as the eighties of the last century for the peasants in the olive oil producing countries to mix the olive oil with the cheaper cottonseed oil in the proportions of two parts of the former to one part of the latter. The resemblance of the mixture to pure olive oil was so great that even the experts could not always distinguish between them. This seemed a menace to the whole olive oil industry and led to the imposition by the countries of southwestern Europe of what were intended to be prohibitory tariff rates on cottonseed oil.

---

[1] See p. 287, infra.

The part which the French duties on cottonseed oil had played in the commercial negotiations of the United States with France since 1890, and the concession made by Italy in the commercial agreement of 1900, whereby the Italian duty on cottonseed oil was reduced, have already been mentioned. The negotiations in 1909 resulted in the securing of legislation or of promises of legislation intended to equalize the tariff treatment of cottonseed and other vegetable oils from France, Austria-Hungary, Greece, Servia, Roumania, and Bulgaria. But some of these promises, conspicuously those of Austria, were never redeemed.

Proclamations applying the minimum rates.—The President issued, prior to April 1, 1910, 134 proclamations applying the minimum rates to the products of as many countries or colonies. This series of proclamations embraced the entire commercial world, and in no instance were the maximum rates of the tariff of 1909 applied.

Effectiveness of the maximum and minimum clauses.—In his message to Congress on December 6, 1910, President Taft declared that section 2 of the tariff law of 1909 had operated satisfactorily, and had thus far proved a guarantee of continued commercial peace. The provision for a schedule of maximum rates did not, however, secure total elimination of discrimination against American products. Germany found means of evading her most-favored-nation agreement of 1910 with the United States and imposed upon some American products the rates of her maximum tariff. France still discriminated against the products of the United States by applying to American imports the maximum rates on 520 of the 600 articles in her tariff. The negotiations for the removal of excessive duties on cottonseed oil were only partially successful. In some of the cases where legislation to equalize the duties on cottonseed oil and other vegetable oils had been promised, the promise was not lived up to. In the case of Italy, the reciprocity agreement of 1900 had established certain new conventional rates which ceased to apply when the agreement terminated. Important among the articles upon which Italy lowered her rates as a result of that agreement had been cottonseed oil, and in 1910 Italy reimposed her old rate upon that article. The President acknowledged in his message of 1910 that there remained instances in which foreign governments dealt arbitrarily and inequitably with American commercial interests within their jurisdiction. It appeared that the maximum and minimum provisions of the act of 1909 were not sufficient or, what is more probable, were not elastic enough, to secure total elimination of discrimination against American products in European markets. The administration finally decided to bring its observations to the attention of Congress and to suggest amendments to the tariff act.

Secretary of State Knox on section 2 of the act of 1909.—On December 13, 1911, Secretary of State Knox, in a lengthy letter to Mr. Underwood, then chairman of the House Committee on Ways and Means, presented some additional information concerning the negotiations which had been carried on under section 2 of the tariff act of 1909.[1] Mr. Knox pointed out some of the defects of the section which had become apparent in the course of negotiations, and he gave some account of the tariff and administrative discriminations, the removal of which had not been secured. His general conclusion was that the section had operated advantageously. "The remarkable

---

[1] This letter appears in full in the New York Herald of Dec. 15, 1911, pp. 3 and 4.

growth of this country's export trade in the past two years is of itself evidence of the enlarged markets obtained under equalized opportunity made possible by section 2 of the tariff law."

But there remained features in foreign practices which were adverse to the development of the United States export trade and which were of serious import to the American enterprises directly concerned. To solve the problem of their removal Mr. Knox believed that it would be necessary to amend section 2 so as to provide for the imposition of penalty duties which could be varied to suit the offenses whose removal was sought.

The department feels that * * * provision should be made for varying rates of tariff to be added to the minimum rates * * * applicable by proclamation when, through the investigations made at the instance of the President, he shall become satisfied that another nation's laws or practices as relating either to tariffs or commercial methods having governmental sanction are inimical to the equal opportunity in trade and commerce to which American enterprise is fairly entitled.

Only by a practicable means of offsetting adverse action of other countries could injustice to American foreign commerce be overcome. "The State Department," Mr. Knox continued, "is convinced that equal opportunity for enjoying the minimum tariff of the United States and the abundance of commercial opportunity thus vouchsafed should not be conceded to such nations as deny to American citizens rights and privileges granted to others. It is realized that the gravity of the offense should be met by a suitable remedy—one that may be graduated to meet the degree of embarrassment sought to be corrected." The removal of unfair measures might demand in one instance the imposition of a few additional duties upon a few commodities, in another instance it might be necessary that all of a nation's exports to the United States should be subjected to penalty rates, and in aggravated cases it might even become necessary totally to prohibit imports from the offending country. The State Department believed that if a proper provision were inserted in the tariff law, the instances of actual application of increased rates would prove to be exceedingly rare.

State Department's proposed amendment to section 2 of the act of 1909.—Mr. Knox inclosed with his letter a draft amendment to section 2 of the act of 1909 embodying the suggestions which he had made. The suggested amendment—which was never submitted to the House—was as follows:

A BILL To amend section 2 of an act entitled "An act to provide revenue, equalize duties, and encourage the industries of the United States, and for other purposes," approved August 5, 1909.

Be it enacted by the Senate and House of Representatives of the United States in Congress assembled, That section two of an act entitled "An act to provide revenue, equalize duties, and encourage the industries of the United States, and for other purposes," be, and is hereby, amended so as to read as follows:

"SEC. 2. That from and after the passage of this act, and so long thereafter as the President of the United States shall be satisfied that the government of any foreign country imposes any terms or restrictions, either in the way of tariff rates or provisions, trade or other regulations, charges, exactions, or in any other manner, directly or indirectly, upon the importation into or the sale in such foreign country of any agricultural, manufactured, or other product of the United States, which unduly discriminate against the United States or the products thereof, and that such foreign country pays no export bounty or imposes no export duty or prohibition upon the exportation of any article to the United States which unduly discriminates against the United States or the products thereof, and that such foreign country accords to the agricultural, manufactured, or other products of the United States treatment which is reciprocal and equivalent, all articles when imported into the United States, or any of its possessions (except the Philippine Islands and the islands of Guam and Tutuila), from such foreign country shall be admitted under the terms of the minimum tariff of the United States as prescribed by section one of the tariff act of August fifth, nineteen hundred and nine. Any proclamation issued by the President under the authority herein conferred and the application of the minimum or other tariff rates may, in accordance with the facts as found by the President, extend to the whole of any foreign country, or may be confined to or exclude from its effect any dependency, colony, or other particular subdivision having authority to adopt and enforce tariff legislation, or to impose restrictions or regulations, or to grant concessions upon the exportation or importation of articles which are, or may be, imported into the United States: *Provided,* That whenever the President of the United States shall be satisfied that the conditions with respect to any country, which led to the application of the minimum tariff hereinafter authorized, no longer exist, or that the government of any foreign state, by repressive, discriminatory, or confiscatory measures, either of legislation or of administration, jeopardizes, impairs, or destroys the capital of citizens of the United States legitimately invested in such foreign state; or whenever the President shall be satisfied that new discriminations are made or that relative treatment not equivalently favorable is given by or under the authority of any foreign state adversely affecting the importation into or sale in such foreign state of any product of the United States; or that the government of such foreign state, whether by law or by administrative measures, imposes exactions, regulations or limitations restrictive of or harmful or amounting to relative treatment not equivalently favorable to the commerce of the United States with such foreign state with respect to the imports into or exports from such state; or if a foreign state, with respect to its exports to other foreign or neutral markets, seeks, by law or by administrative measures, to provide for the payment of bounties, rebates of duties or allowance upon exports in such a manner as to affect adversely the commerce of the United States established with foreign or neutral markets, he shall direct that such increased ad valorem rates of duty as he shall determine are equivalent to the injury inflicted upon American capital or commerce shall be imposed upon imports of all or such duty-free products of such foreign state as he may deem proper, provided that in no case shall the additional duty so imposed be less than five per centum nor more than twenty-five per centum ad valorem; or he may direct that the like ad valorem rates of duty shall be imposed upon importations of all such duty-free products of such foreign state as he may deem proper, or upon both dutiable and duty-free importations, or, in what the President shall be satisfied are extreme cases of new discrimination and unjust treatment of the commercial or foreign interests of citizens of the United States on the part of such foreign state, he may direct that such products of such foreign state as he may deem proper shall be excluded from importation to the United States; that whenever the President shall be satisfied that any of the above-described conditions exists he shall issue a proclamation to this effect, and ninety days thereafter all the dutiable imports into the United States from the offending foreign state, or such of the dutiable products as are named in the proclamation, being the product of such foreign state, shall be subject to the increased rates of duty specified in the proclamation; or in the case of duty-free imports from such foreign state, all such imports or such of them as are named in the proclamation, being the product of the offending foreign state, shall become dutiable at the rates of duty specified in the proclamation; or, in the case of the prohibition of importation, such articles of merchandise as the President shall have selected and named in his proclamation, being the product of the said offending foreign state, shall not be entitled to entry at any of the ports of the United States, and the importation thereof shall be prohibited. All articles of merchandise imported contrary to this act shall be forfeited to the United States, and shall be liable to be seized, prosecuted, and condemned, in like manner and under the same regulations, restrictions, and provisions as have been heretofore established for the recovery, collection, distribution, and remission of forfeitures to the United States by the several revenue laws. Whenever the provisions of this act shall be applicable to importations into the United States of the products of any foreign state, they shall be applicable thereto whether such products are imported directly from the country of production or otherwise. The President may at any time by proclamation, which shall be effective upon a date to be specified therein, revoke, modify, terminate, or renew any such direction hereinbefore authorized as, in his opinion, the public interest may require. To secure information to assist the President in the discharge of the duties imposed upon him by this section and the officers of the Government in the administration of the customs laws, the President is hereby authorized to employ such persons as may be required."

Nothing in this act contained shall be so construed as to abrogate or in any manner, impair or affect the provisions of any act of Congress to promote the reciprocal trade relations of the United States with another country.

7. THE TARIFF ACT OF 1913.

THE TARIFF ACT OF 1913.

New tariff bill introduced, 1913.—In March, 1913, the Democratic party came into control of both the executive and the legislative branches of the Government. The new administration prepared at once to revise the tariff. In the report which the House Committee on Ways and Means presented with the tariff bill, there appeared the following comment upon the maximum and minimum provisions of the act of 1909:

> The minimum and maximum tariff provisions adopted in the Payne bill have not been productive of any effective expansion of our foreign trade and commerce. The conventional tariff being the minimum rate and the President being authorized to enforce the maximum rate against foreign nations resulted in an attempt to expand our commerce by force. We went to the nations of the world with the demand that they stand and deliver or we would punish them. Many years ago this system of expanding trade and commerce was abandoned by the enlightened nations. We are of the opinion that the only true course that can be pursued to expand our foreign trade along rational lines is through mutual concessions that may prove beneficial to both of the contracting parties, free from coercion.

As it was drafted by the House Committee on Ways and Means the bill contained no provision for maximum and minimum schedules, but it included a reciprocity section as follows:

> That for the purpose of readjusting the present duties on importations into the United States and at the same time to encourage the export trade of this country, the President of the United States is authorized and empowered to negotiate trade agreements with foreign nations, wherein mutual concessions are made looking toward freer trade relations and further reciprocal expansion of trade and commerce: *Provided, however,* That said trade agreements before becoming operative shall be submitted to the Congress of the United States for ratification or rejection.[1]

The bill in the House.—When the bill was presented to the House for debate, Mr. Towner offered as an amendment an additional paragraph providing for maximum and minimum tariff schedules; also for notice of termination of all agreements which had been negotiated under the act of 1897. Both these proposed provisions were identical in wording with the similar provisions in section 2 of the act of 1909.[2] Mr. Towner, in support of his amendment, spoke in part as follows:

> In this reprocity provision of the original bill the President is authorized to negotiate trade agreements with foreign nations provided such agreements shall be submitted to Congress for ratification. But such power already exists without this provision. Under it President Roosevelt negotiated our present Cuban treaty. Under it President Taft negotiated the ill-fated Canadian reciprocity agreement.
>
> In order to be effective under a system where individual tariff agreements must be made with each Government, power should be lodged in some executive department to negotiate such treaties and make such changes. This we are unwilling to do. The Congress will not relinquish its power to control this great source of revenue, and would have no constitutional power to do so if it desired. With our present system we are almost necessarily precluded from individual trade agreements or reciprocity treaties with every nation from which we receive imports. To place ourselves at their mercy unless such agreements are made is certainly not wise.
>
> It would appear almost self-evident that the system best adapted to our condition is the maximum and minimum system. It is the simplest, subject to the least fric-

---

[1] Par. A, Sec. V, in the original blil and Par. II, Sec. IV, in the act as passed.
[2] The second provision was altogether redundant, for all the agreements which had been concluded under the act of 1897 had already been terminated by the act of 1909.

tion, not open to misconception, not subject to "most-favored-nation" objections, is more stable and uniform in operation, is most easily administered and most generally understood. Besides it has been tried and has been found not only successful, but notably and exceptionally so. * * *

The committee [on Ways and Means] declares that the only way to expand our foreign trade "along rational lines is through mutual concessions."[1] That is just what the maximum and minimum provision enables us to do. But our only chance for "mutual concessions" under the proposed law will be to still further reduce rates which the sponsors of the bill declare are already as low as they dare make them. If, after the passage of this bill, France shall again seek to impose her maximum rates against our commerce, what can we do? Protest? We did that before and without avail. Grant her still further reductions from the rates fixed in the present bill? Then every nation with a "most-favored-nation" clause in its treaty, and nearly every one contains such clause, will demand like reductions. In this condition we shall be at the mercy of our eager and strenuous rivals, begging favors where experience has taught us no favors will be granted. In what a humiliating condition this will place us! At the last we shall be compelled to adopt this provision, for it will be our only measure of protection. How much better to do it now.

There was no discussion of Mr. Towner's proposed amendment, and, on a division, it was rejected by 62 yeas to 107 noes.

In the course of the debate in the House on the administrative features of the bill, Mr. Payne expressed regret at the omission of maximum and minimum provisions. He regarded the clause which empowered the President to negotiate treaties as of no significance since it added nothing to the constitutional authority which already lay with the President to negotiate treaties subject to ratification by the Senate. Mr. Underwood, in reply, claimed that the maximum and minimum provisions of the act of 1909 had been ineffective, inasmuch as they provided for penalties, not concessions, as the means of securing more favorable tariff treatment from foreign countries. Foreign countries had generally refused to submit to threats, and the particular failure with reference to paper and wood pulp had forced President Taft to the procedure of negotiating a commercial agreement with Canada. This action, he went on to say, was a repudiation of the maximum and minimum tariff provisions of the act of 1909. He admitted that the rates in the bill then before the House could have been made a maximum schedule, and that concessions could have been allowed therefrom in favor of developing foreign commerce, but the Committee on Ways and Means had decided that it would be more effective to leave the hands of the President free and to authorize him to go to foreign countries by warrant of law and negotiate trade agreements. This authorization, he claimed, was not merely nominal. Tariff agreements negotiated by the President solely by virtue of his constitutional authority must be referred to the House and they become there subject to amendment; they must take the course of independent legislation. In distinction, trade agreements negotiated in conformity with the reciprocal trade provisions in the bill under discussion would be subject, when referred to the House, only to ratification or rejection.

There was no further debate in the House on the bargaining features of the bill, and the bill passed the House with the reciprocity section unchanged.[2]

---

[1] See p. 279, infra.

[2] On May 7, 1913, in the course of the House debate on the administrative features of the bill, an amendment to the reciprocity clause had been proposed providing further, "that the act entitled 'An act to promote reciprocal trade relations with the Dominion of Canada and for other purposes,' approved July 26, 1911, be and is hereby repealed." This was ruled out of order. It was, however, again proposed later in the day and came to a vote. In the first division it was defeated by 107 yeas to 213 noes, and upon a demand for tellers it was again defeated, this time by 121 yeas to 222 noes.

The bill in the Senate.—In the Senate the bill was first referred to the Committee on Finance. The committee proposed that there be added to the reciprocity section a provision authorizing the President to substitute for the rates of the general tariff higher penalty duties on a number of specified products when imported from countries whose treatment of American products was not "reciprocal and equivalent."[1]

In presenting their report the committee called special attention to this provision. They characterized the bargaining features of the act of 1909 as embarrassing, clumsy, and inadequate, and as having given rise to a situation less satisfactory than that which had previously existed. They claimed, for the substitute provision which they recommended, that it would place in the hands of the President powers extensive enough to be effective, yet circumscribed enough to permit of their being put into application without disturbing the general fiscal system of the country. They believed that wise use of the retaliatory power would bring about equitable arrangements with those countries which were not extending fair treatment to the United States, and that the weapon thus provided would prove effective without its ever becoming necessary actually to apply it.

This proposal of the Committee on Finance differed from the provisions of similar type in the tariff acts of 1890 and 1897 (sec. 3 in each of these acts), not only in the greater comprehensiveness of the list of articles upon which penalty duties could be imposed, but also in that the President was left free to proclaim such duties upon all or on a part only of the articles enumerated. Some criticism of the proposed amendment was offered on the ground that it was too limited in scope. It was suggested that there were countries none of whose important export products were included in the list of enumerated articles, and that such countries, in case they should discriminate against American products, could not within the provisions of the amendment be adequately penalized. The amendment was agreed to, however, without a division.

The passing of the bill.—In the conference committee, the Senate amendment was given up. This left in the bill as its sole general bargaining feature the provision—unchanged from the form in which it had been introduced originally—which authorized the President to negotiate commercial treaties subject to the approval of Congress.

---

[1] This added provision read as follows: "*And provided further,* That whenever the President shall ascertain as a fact that any country, dependency, colony, province, or other political subdivision of government imposes any restrictions, either in the way of tariff rates or provisions, trade or other regulations, charges or exactions, or in any other manner, directly or indirectly, upon the importations into or sale in such foreign country of any agricultural, manufactured, or other product of the United States which unduly or unfairly discriminate against the United States or the products thereof; or whenever he shall ascertain as a fact that any such country, dependency, colony, province, or other political subdivision of government imposes any restriction or prohibition upon the exportation of any article to the United States which unduly or unfairly discriminates against the United States; or whenever he shall ascertain as a fact that any such country, dependency, colony, province, or other political subdivision of government does not accord to the products of the United States reciprocal and equivalent treatment, he shall have the power and it shall be his duty to suspend by proclamation the operation of the provisions of this act relative to the rates of duty to be assessed upon the importation of the following specified articles, or such of them as he may deem just, and to substitute therefor the rates of duty hereinafter prescribed upon such articles when imported directly or indirectly from such country, dependency, colony, province, or other political subdivision of government. * * *."

The specified articles and the penalty duties to be imposed thereon were as follows: On fish, 1 cent per pound; on coffee, 3 cents per pound; on tea, 10 cents per pound; on the following articles one and one-fourth times the rate specified in sec. 1 of the bill: on earthen, stone, and china ware; expressed oils; lemons; cheese; wines of all kinds; malt liquors; knitted goods; silk dresses and silk goods; leather gloves; laces and embroideries, and articles made wholly or in part of the same; toys; jewelry and precious, semiprecious, and imitation precious stones; on the following, in addition to the duties as provided in sec. 1 of this act, the duties specified below: on sugars, testing by the polariscope not above 75°, fifteen-hundredths cent per pound, and for every additional degree by the polariscope test, one one-hundredth cent per pound; on molasses, 2 cents per gallon; on wool, 15 per cent ad valorem.

Without any further debate on this provision, the bill was passed by both Houses, and on October 3, 1913, it was approved by the President and became law.

Provision for the reciprocal free admission of certain foodstuffs.— In the act of 1913 potatoes, wheat, and wheat products were on the free list, but with the provision that, when imported from countries which themselves imposed import duties upon them, these products should be taxed at certain specified rates. The provision for the conditional free admission of wheat and wheat products is similar to the corresponding provision in regard to potatoes, and is as follows:

[To be admitted free of duty:] Wheat, wheat flour, semolina, and other wheat products, not specially provided for in this section: *Provided*, That wheat shall be subject to a duty of 10 cents per bushel, that wheat flour shall be subject to a duty of 45 cents per barrel of one hundred and ninety-six pounds, and semolina and other products of wheat, not specially provided for in this section, ten per centum ad valorem. when imported directly or indirectly from a country, dependency, or other subdivision of government which imposes a duty on wheat or wheat flour or semolina imported from the United States.

Free admission of wheat and potatoes under the above provision.— On April 16, 1917, Canada removed, by order in council, her duties on wheat, wheat flour, and semolina, thus taking advantage of the clause in the United States tariff providing for the reciprocal free admission of these products.

The Argentine Republic has also removed the duties on wheat, and in Australia wheat enters free of duty. In conformity with the provision in the United States act of 1913, wheat from these three important producing countries is entitled to free admission into the United States.

In 1918 Canada's yield of potatoes was the highest on record. In the fall of the year it was officially estimated that there were available for export in Canada, chiefly in Ontario, Quebec, and Manitoba, about 30,000,000 bushels. By an order in council of November 7, 1918, the Canadian government placed potatoes on the free list, thus taking advantage of the reciprocal provision, in regard to the free admission of potatoes into the United States, in the tariff act of 1913.

8. PREFERENTIAL TREATMENT OF CERTAIN AMERICAN PRODUCTS BY BRAZIL.

PREFERENTIAL TREATMENT OF CERTAIN AMERICAN PRODUCTS BY BRAZIL.

Brazilian tariff treatment of American products.—There has been no commercial treaty of any kind between Brazil and the United States since the termination, by the tariff act of 1894, of the reciprocity agreement of July 31, 1891. Since 1904, however, with the single exception of the period from January 1, 1905 to July 1, 1906, Brazil has granted to the United States a tariff preference upon a number of important articles.

Almost all of the Brazilian exports to the United States have consisted of articles which enter the latter country free of duty, as the accompanying table indicates.

Free and dutiable imports into the United States from Brazil.

Year.	Tariff act in effect.	Free of duty.		Dutiable.		Total.
		Amount.	Per cent of total.	Amount.	Per cent of total.	
1900	Act of 1897	$55,204,311	95.1	$2,869,146	4.9	$58,073,457
1911	Act of 1909	100,457,075	99.6	410,109	.4	100,867,184
1915	Act of 1913	96,910,776	97.7	2,267,952	2.3	99,178,728

Of the Brazilian output of coffee, over 50 per cent is sold to the United States, and this country is also the chief market for Brazilian rubber. These two commodities constitute the bulk of the Brazilian exports, and coffee has been admitted into the United States free of duty since 1872, rubber since 1870. American exports to Brazil, on the other hand, have always been subjected to extremely heavy import duties. In view of this situation, the American representatives in Brazil had been insisting for some time prior to 1904 upon more favorable tariff treatment of American products.

American representations to Brazil for reductions of duty.—Section 3 of the act of 1897, in addition to the provision for reduction of duties on argols, brandies, etc., which formed the basis for the negotiation of the so-called "Argol Agreements" with various European countries, also empowered the President to impose a duty of 3 cents a pound upon coffee coming from a country imposing duties upon American products which "in view of the admission of such coffee * * * into the United States" free of duty "he may deem to be reciprocally unequal and unreasonable." This gave the American representative a bargaining instrument, whereby he could enter into negotiations with Brazil based upon the guarantee of a continued suspension of the authorized penalty duty on coffee.

A long, energetic, and persistent campaign, extending over five years, was made by the State Department, through the American

Legation in Brazil, before the Brazilian Government finally consented to grant some reductions of the tariff rates in favor of American products.

Establishment of the preference in 1904.—As a result of protracted negotiations, the Brazilian Government in 1903 introduced a bill in the Brazilian Congress, providing for considerable reductions of duty upon a number of imports from the United States, the most important of which was wheat flour.

The bill met with strong opposition. English interests which had invested large amounts of capital in the development of flour milling in Brazil united with the importers of flour from other countries to bring strong political pressure to bear upon the Brazilian Congress in opposition to the measure. The Brazilian Senate formally refused to confirm the arrangement. As a result, the administration failed to secure the passage of this bill. Nevertheless, the Brazilian President, taking advantage of an old law which empowered him to give, without resort to Congress, a 20 per cent preference on any articles coming from countries admitting Brazilian coffee free of duty, established a measure of preferential treatment for American products. His plan was put into operation by a decree issued on April 16, 1904, reducing by 20 per cent the duties on the following articles when coming from the United States: Wheat flour, manufactures of india rubber, watches and clocks, inks and colors (except writing inks), varnishes, and condensed milk. This action of the administration was actively opposed by the Brazilian Congress, by the press, and by the public generally. The chief importance of the arrangement lay in the reduction of duty on American flour. The flour-milling and wheat-importing interests of Brazil were powerful and influential, and did their utmost to bring the measure into popular disrepute. Their efforts succeeded, and there was soon no question but that at the next session of Congress steps would be taken to prevent the renewal of the arrangement.

Preference on American products withdrawn, 1905.—The Brazilian Congress met in December, 1904. It immediately took up the question of the preference extended to the United States. Not only did both houses vote against renewing the preferential arrangement for the following year, but they revoked the authority of the President to make concessions of any kind to any countries without reference to Congress. As a consequence, no preference of any kind was given by Brazil to American products during the year 1905.

Preference reestablished, 1906.—In 1905 the prices of wheat and flour were so much higher in the United States than in the Argentine that any amount of tariff concession to American flour at that time, even to the extent of a total remission of duty, would not have attracted increased imports from the United States. As a consequence the opposition of the Brazilian milling interests to such an arrangement was less energetic than before, and the President of Brazil succeeded, in December of that year, in obtaining a grant of authority from Congress to renew the preferential concessions which had been granted to the United States in 1904, and to add to the previous list of concessional products five more articles, as follows: Typewriters, refrigerators, pianos, scales, and windmills. The decree making the reductions effective was not issued, however, until the 1st of July following. Since 1906 this preferential arrangement, although it has often been the subject of vigorous debate in the Brazilian Congress and in the press, has regularly been authorized by the Brazilian Congress by incorporation in the annual budget. In 1907 linotypes and cash registers were added to the preferred list under the classification of "typewriters," and paints were included under "varnishes." In 1908 and 1909 the arrangement was re-enacted without modification.

Negotiations in 1909.—Upon the passage in the United States of the tariff act of 1909 the State Department immediately opened negotiations with Brazil, as with other countries, in order to secure such tariff treatment of American products as would justify the President in extending to imports from Brazil the rates of the minimum tariff. The existing Brazilian preference was not considered sufficiently comprehensive, and in response to urgent requests by the American representatives the Brazilian Government, on January 1, 1910, added to the list of commodities upon which it granted reductions of duty several additional articles of American manufacture, as follows: Cement, dried fruits, desks, corsets, and school furniture. Subsequently the Brazilian Congress passed an act granting authority to the Executive to extend the preferential list at his option.

Preferential arrangement since 1911.—On January 1, 1911, the preference in favor of American flour was increased to 30 per cent. Since that date there has been no change either in the list of preferred articles or in the extent of the preference. In 1916, however, the wording of the decree was altered so as to specify, for the first time, that the articles upon which reductions of duty were granted must be the products of the United States. Formerly it had been possible for goods which reached Brazil via the United States, even though not grown or manufactured in the latter country, to enjoy the advantages of the tariff reductions.

For the year 1917 the concessions were authorized by section I of Article II of Law No. 3213 of December 30, 1916, which reads as follows:

There is hereby continued in force the authority given to the Government to adopt a differential tariff in favor of one or more articles of foreign production, the reduction [on other articles] being limited to 20 per cent, and on wheat flour to 30 per cent, made in exchange for concessions to articles of Brazilian production, especially rubber and tobacco.[1]

It will be seen that the power of the Brazilian President to reduce the duties is not limited to any specified articles, and that the only products expressly named, for which favorable tariff treatment is sought by Brazil, are rubber and tobacco. In the Brazilian budget for 1904, when the present preferential arrangement was first applied in favor of American products, coffee alone had been so mentioned. Sugar and alcohol were added in the budget for 1911; herva matte (yerba mate), in 1912; and cocoa, tobacco, and cotton in the budget for 1913.

In the year 1917 the articles of American production to be entitled to the preference were specified in the presidential decree No. 12334 of January 1, 1917, which reads as follows:

The President of the Republic of the United States of Brazil, * * * decrees:

ARTICLE 1. During the current year, to count from the first day of the present month, the articles mentioned hereinbelow, when produced in the United States of America,

---

[1] Brazil Diario Oficial, Dec. 31, 1916, p. 14781

shall enjoy the following reductions in import duties: 30 per cent on wheat flour and 20 per cent on condensed milk, manufactures of rubber under Schedule 1033 of the tariff, clocks and watches, paints and inks under Schedule 173 of the tariff (except writing inks), varnishes, typewriters, refrigerators, pianos, scales, windmills, Portland cement, corsets, dried fruits, school furniture, and desks.

For the year 1918 the preference has been renewed without change by presidential decree No. 12812 of January 9.

EFFECT OF THE PREFERENCE ON AMERICAN EXPORTS TO BRAZIL.

Total imports into Brazil.—The data, both from Brazilian and American official compilations, available for a statistical study of the influence of the Brazilian preferential on American trade, are fairly complete; the classifications of commodities in the commercial statistics of the two countries correspond sufficiently to permit of approximate comparisons; and tariff changes and other incidental factors which tend to complicate such an inquiry have been few and their effect is calculable. In the ensuing analysis separate studies will appear of the trade in each commodity upon which a preferential reduction was established, and the articles will also be considered in appropriate groupings.[1]

TABLE I.—*Total Imports into Brazil, by countries, 1902–1916.*[2]

[Preferential effective from Apr. 16, 1904, to Dec. 31, 1904, and since July 1, 1906.]

Year.	Value of total imports from all countries.	From the United States.		From Great Britain.		From Germany.	
		Value.	Per cent of total.	Value.	Per cent of total.	Value.	Per cent of total.
1902	$113,491,392	$13,894,208	12.24	$31,947,114	28.15	$12,981,585	11.44
1903	117,778,973	13,298,550	11.29	33,372,349	28.33	14,512,154	12.32
1904	126,096,621	14,050,119	11.14	34,996,562	27.75	15,984,387	12.68
1905	147,600,240	15,276,827	10.35	39,219,687	26.57	19,642,471	13.31
1906	161,968,695	18,557,971	11.46	45,379,405	28.02	23,796,969	14.69
1907	197,157,468	25,161,983	12.76	59,140,335	30.00	30,252,754	15.34
1908	172,734,213	20,920,200	12.11	49,762,241	28.81	25,656,907	14.85
1909	180,708,583	22,375,651	12.38	48,479,869	26.83	28,145,513	15.58
1910	231,577,204	29,740,518	12.84	65,923,059	28.47	36,819,921	15.90
1911	257,481,615	34,342,673	13.34	74,787,809	29.05	43,234,140	16.79
1912	308,624,285	48,168,710	15.61	77,711,370	25.18	53,083,534	17.20
1913	326,831,508	51,353,003	15.71	79,979,626	24.47	57,114,178	17.48
1914	169,117,807	30,686,725	18.15	40,500,819	23.95	26,258,241	15.53
1915	145,749,024	46,968,238	32.23	31,886,695	21.88	2,202,507	1.51
1916	194,582,153	76,238,664	39.18	39,667,499	20.39	86,186	.04

[1] The American data are from United States Commerce and Navigation Reports. The Brazilian data are obtained from official publications of the Brazilian Government, directly for the years up to and including 1914, and indirectly for the years 1915 and 1916, from the compilation made therefrom in the United States Supplement to Commerce Reports 40b, of Dec. 28, 1917. The conversions from the Brazilian currency have been made with proper allowances for the rate of depreciation of the paper milreis from its nominal value, the rate of depreciation being calculated by a comparison of the totals in the Brazilian commerce statistics as expressed in paper milreis and in English pounds sterling. In 1902 the paper milreis was equivalent to 24.09 cents in gold, in 1903 to 24.21 cents, in 1904 to 24.60 cents, in 1907 to 30.57 cents, in 1908 to 30.45 cents, in 1909 to 30.48 cents, and in 1914 to 30.1 cents. The figures for 1915 and 1916 have been obtained, already converted, from the Commerce Report mentioned above. In the years not specifically mentioned, the paper milreis was worth its nominal value, 32.44 cents.

[2] From Estatistica Commercial, Commercio Exterior do Brasil.

TABLE I.—*Total imports into Brazil, by countries, 1902–1916*—Continued.

Year.	From the Argentine.		From France.		From Portugal.	
	Value.	Per cent of total.	Value.	Per cent of total.	Value.	Per cent of total.
1902	$10,176,167	8.97	$9,965,621	8.78	$7,859,721	6.93
1903	10,540,065	8.95	10,369,473	8.80	8,487,381	7.21
1904	12,965,901	10.28	11,270,010	8.94	9,252,044	7.34
1905	17,375,727	11.77	13,247,711	8.98	10,833,653	7.34
1906	17,065,348	10.54	14,923,457	9.21	10,583,798	6.53
1907	17,660,140	8.96	17,028,140	8.64	11,456,550	5.81
1908	17,502,482	10.13	15,569,685	9.01	8,937,670	5.17
1909	18,141,008	10.04	18,702,437	10.35	10,044,044	5.56
1910	19,791,814	8.55	21,800,421	9.45	12,881,491	5.56
1911	19,618,677	7.62	22,772,919	8.84	13,849,477	5.39
1912	23,145,738	7.50	27,785,355	9.00	14,607,181	4.73
1913	24,323,704	7.44	31,979,184	9.78	14,345,255	4.39
1914	16,203,359	9.58	12,932,907	7.65	8,770,935	5.19
1915	23,143,815	15.88	7,205,798	4.94	7,219,814	4.05
1916	27,364,520	14.06	10,117,764	5.20	9,049,044	4.65

TABLE II.—*Domestic exports from the United States, 1900–1917.*

Year.	Total value of exports to all countries.	To Brazil.		To South America, except Brazil.	
		Value.	Per cent of exports to all countries.	Value.	Per cent of exports to all countries.
1900	$1,394,483,082	$11,578,119	0.83	$27,367,644	1.96
1901	1,407,761,001	11,663,574	.78	32,736,621	2.20
1902	1,381,719,401	10,391,130	.75	27,662,487	2.00
1903	1,420,141,679	10,736,748	.75	30,401,124	2.14
1904	1,460,827,271	11,046,856	.75	39,708,171	2.71
1905	1,518,561,666	10,985,096	.72	45,909,035	3.02
1906	1,743,864,500	14,530,471	.83	60,629,310	3.47
1907	1,880,851,078	18,697,547	.99	63,459,627	3.37
1908	1,860,773,346	19,490,077	1.04	64,093,797	3.44
1909	1,663,011,104	17,527,692	1.05	59,033,997	3.54
1910	1,744,984,720	22,897,890	1.31	70,348,930	4.03
1911	2,049,320,199	27,240,146	1.32	81,654,748	3.98
1912	2,204,322,409	34,678,081	1.57	107,632,370	4.88
1913	2,465,884,149	42,638,467	1.72	103,509,526	4.19
1914	2,364,579,148	29,963,914	1.26	94,575,995	3.99
1915	2,768,589,340	25,629,555	.92	73,694,402	2.66
1916	4,333,482,885	40,572,197	.93	139,603,177	3.22
1917	6,290,108,394	56,727,234	.90	202,753,137	3.23

From 1902 to 1916 the imports into Brazil from the United States showed a steady and considerable increase both in amount and in relation to the total imports into Brazil. No very conspicuous effect of the preferential arrangement appears in the figures of the imports into Brazil. The preference was withdrawn during 1905 and the first half of 1906; in the year 1905 the figures of total imports show a slight increase in amount over the preceding year, but a decrease in percentage of total imports into Brazil from all countries. The corresponding figures, from the American official statistics, of exports from the United States to Brazil likewise reveal no apparent effect of the preferential arrangement. In the year ending June 30, 1906—during the whole of which year the preferential reductions were withheld—the American exports showed an increase as compared with the previous year from about $10,985,000 to about

$14,530,000; that is, of approximately $3,545,000. The articles upon which a preferential reduction was granted in 1904 formed but a small percentage of the aggregate imports of Brazil from the United States. The failure of the preference to have any marked effect on the gross exports from the United States to Brazil is of significance, therefore, only in so far as it reveals the slight importance of the arrangement. To judge of the effectiveness of the arrangement within the limits to which it was confined, it is necessary to study the figures for the individual articles affected.

Imports into Brazil of Preferred Articles.

The imports into Brazil of the articles upon which the preference was granted on April 16, 1904, are compared, in Table III, with the total imports into Brazil. The imports of the preferred articles from the United States decreased without interruption from 1902 until 1906. After 1907, when the preferential rates were again effective, there came a gradual recovery, and in 1910 imports of these articles from the United States were at a point higher than they had previously reached during the period studied. The importance of the trade in these articles relatively to the total imports from the United States was not so great during the period of the arrangement as it had been prior to 1904. Until the course of trade was changed by the abnormal conditions which began with the war, in 1914, the percentage of these articles coming from the United States was also less during the preferential period than it had been prior to 1904.

TABLE III.—*Imports into Brazil of the articles upon which a preference was granted on Apr. 16, 1904, compared with total imports into Brazil, 1902–1916.*

[Preferential effective Apr. 16, 1904, to Dec. 31, 1904, and since July 1, 1906.]

ALL ARTICLES.

Year.	Grand total from all countries.	From the United States.	
		Value.	Per cent of grand total.
1902	$113,491,392	$13,894,208	12.24
1903	117,778.973	13,298,550	11.29
1904	126,096,621	14,050,119	11.14
1905	147,600,240	15,276,827	10.35
1906	161,968,695	18,557,971	11.46
1907	197,157,468	25,161,983	12.76
1908	172,734,213	20,920,200	12.11
1909	180,708,583	22,375,651	12.38
1910	231,577,204	29,740,518	12.84
1911	257,481,615	34,342,673	13.34
1912	308,624,285	48,168,710	15.61
1913	326,831,508	51,353,003	15.71
1914	169,117,807	30,686,725	18.15
1915	145,749,024	46,968,238	32.23
1916	194,582,153	76,238,664	39.18

TABLE III.—*Imports into Brazil of the articles upon which a preference was granted on April 16, 1904, compared with total imports into Brazil, 1902–1916*—Continued.

ARTICLES UPON WHICH PREFERENCE WAS GRANTED ON APR. 16, 1904.

Year.	Total specified articles from all countries.		From the United States.		
	Value.	Per cent of total imports from all countries.	Value.	Per cent of total imports of all articles from the United States.	Per cent of total imports from all countries.
1902	$7,083,340	6.24	$2,816,020	20.27	39.75
1903	7,525,614	6.39	2,411,797	18.13	32.05
1904	9,227,137	7.32	2,431,578	17.30	26.35
1905	10,003,607	6.78	1,783,989	11.68	17.83
1906	10,532,354	6.50	1,778,607	9.58	16.89
1907	11,852,913	6.01	2,259,441	8.98	19.06
1908	11,045,971	6.39	2,249,161	10.75	20.36
1909	11,730,668	6.49	2,486,128	11.11	21.19
1910	13,303,295	5.74	3,576,782	12.03	26.89
1911	13,252,621	5.15	3,845,379	11.20	29.02
1912	15,669,972	5.08	4,529,305	9.40	28.90
1913	15,230,145	4.66	4,497,783	8.76	29.53
1914	11,083,045	6.55	4,883,789	15.91	44.06
1915	11,897,592	8.16	6,777,066	14.43	56.96
1916	12,137,818	6.24	5,310,523	6.97	43.75

ARTICLES UPON WHICH PREFERENCE WAS GRANTED ON APR. 16, 1904, EXCLUDING WHEAT FLOUR.

Year.	Value.	Per cent	Value.	Per cent	Per cent
1902	$1,286,243	1.13	$123,091	0.89	9.57
1903	1,475,840	1.25	128,135	.96	8.68
1904	1,575,152	1.25	219,153	1.56	13.91
1905	1,872,668	1.27	232,651	1.52	12.42
1906	1,855,255	1.14	204,953	1.10	11.05
1907	2,163,383	1.10	284,817	1.13	13.17
1908	2,019,312	1.17	310,438	1.48	15.37
1909	2,414,975	1.34	278,892	1.25	11.55
1910	3,372,903	1.46	450,517	1.51	13.36
1911	3,531,542	1.37	510,392	1.49	14.45
1912	3,907,282	1.27	512,352	1.06	13.11
1913	4,842,105	1.48	542,759	1.06	11.21
1914	2,816,076	1.66	300,215	.98	10.66
1915	2,257,619	1.55	721,236	1.54	31.95
1916	3,340,133	1.72	1,454,979	1.91	43.56

The imports of wheat flour were so much greater in amount than were those of the other articles upon which a preference was granted that they dominate the figures. The third part of Table III affords data for a comparison with wheat flour excluded. The figures indicate that the preference was immediately effective for the specified articles, excepting wheat flour. The imports from the United States of these specified articles, wheat flour excepted, increased from 9 per cent of the imports of similar articles from all countries, in 1903, to 14 per cent in 1904. They did not maintain this relative rate of increase, however, and, as will appear later, the increase in the year 1904 was due mainly to unusually great imports of condensed milk. The imports from the United States of the preferred articles other than flour increased considerably in amount during the period under investigation, but there was as marked an increase in the total of the imports of similar articles from all countries.

EXPORTS OF PREFERENTIAL ARTICLES FROM THE UNITED STATES.

In Table IV is presented a comparison of the United States exports to Brazil, to South American countries with the exception of Brazil, and to all countries, of the articles upon which a preferential reduction was granted by Brazil in 1904.

TABLE IV.—*Domestic exports from the United States of the articles upon which a preference was granted on Apr. 16, 1904, 1902–1916.*

ALL PREFERENTIAL ARTICLES.

Year.	To all countries.	To Brazil.		To South America, except Brazil.	
		Value.	Per cent of total to all countries.	Value.	Per cent of total to all countries.
1902	$74,071,243	$2,255,418	3.04	$2,212,566	2.99
1903	82,494,974	2,229,257	2.70	2,158,197	2.62
1904	78,462,726	1,861,335	2.37	2,620,825	3.33
1905	50,973,225	1,431,308	2.81	2,963,810	5.81
1906	70,892,807	1,337,417	1.89	3,590,860	5.05
1907	75,507,267	1,546,757	2.05	2,583,627	3.42
1908	77,861,197	1,836,749	2.36	2,477,692	3.18
1909	63,171,941	1,869,476	2.96	2,385,316	3.78
1910	61,977,111	2,349,024	3.79	3,030,802	4.89
1911	66,179,551	3,189,541	4.82	3,477,962	5.26
1912	69,203,470	3,677,972	5.31	3,315,484	4.85
1913	72,777,661	3,593,060	4.94	3,622,875	4.98
1914	71,656,117	3,991,878	5.51	3,513,261	4.87
1915	116,409,449	4,298,690	3.69	4,377,609	3.78
1916	144,673,491	5,236,709	3.60	7,319,543	5.05

ALL PREFERENTIAL ARTICLES EXCEPT WHEAT FLOUR.

Year.	To all countries.	To Brazil.		To South America, except Brazil.	
1902	$8,409,269	$68,066	0.81	$224,219	2.67
1903	8,738,570	80,915	.93	245,015	2.80
1904	9,567,890	75,629	.79	313,465	3.28
1905	10,797,089	205,743	1.90	354,300	3.28
1906	11,785,938	125,536	1.06	438,626	3.64
1907	13,331,870	163,776	1.23	508,423	3.81
1908	13,690,689	195,975	1.43	491,154	3.59
1909	12,014,575	197,973	1.65	465,999	3.89
1910	14,355,644	244,515	1.70	560,588	3.90
1911	16,792,605	348,753	2.08	673,393	4.01
1912	18,203,673	399,991	2.20	707,360	3.89
1913	19,606,124	487,821	2.49	917,706	4.68
1914	17,201,942	239,773	1.39	819,791	4.76
1915	21,540,106	326,000	1.50	825,814	3.83
1916	57,325,686	1,020,384	1.78	2,430,423	4.23

In the fiscal year 1905, during six months of which year the specified articles were admitted into Brazil at the reduced rates, the exports of these articles to Brazil showed a decrease in amount, in comparison with a considerable increase in similar exports to the remainder of South America, but a great decrease in total exports of these articles. The effects of the Brazilian reductions of duty were visible, however, in 1907, the first year after the renewal of the preference, when there was, as compared with the year 1906, an increase both in the amount of the exports of these articles to Brazil and in their relative proportion to the total exports of these articles and to the exports to the rest of South America, and this increase was thereafter constant.

The general tendency toward increase on the part of the exports of the preferred articles to Brazil appears more clearly when the figures of these exports are made up with the exclusion of wheat flour. The exports to Brazil of the preferred articles other than wheat flour increased from $75,000 in 1904 to $205,000 in 1905, during six months of which year the preference was in effect. This, as has been explained elsewhere, was due largely to an exceptional Brazilian import of condensed milk. In the following year, during which the preference was not in effect, there was a decrease, but, from 1907 on, the exports of the specified articles increased rapidly, both in absolute amount and relatively to the export of these articles to all countries and to the remainder of South America.

THE EFFECT OF THE PREFERENCE ON THE WHEAT FLOUR TRADE.

On account both of the volume of the trade involved and of the amount of interest stimulated thereby, the reduction of the Brazilian duty on American wheat flour from 25 reis to 20 reis per kilogram was the most important feature of the preferential arrangement. The history of the American flour and grain exports to Brazil affords an illustration of a decline in trade between two countries resulting from the development of a competing industry in the importing country and the rise of a new source of supply in a third country more advantageously situated than the exporting country with which it begins to compete.

TABLE V.—*Imports into Brazil of wheat flour, 1902–1916.*[1]

Year.	Value of total imports of wheat flour.	From the United States.		From Argentina.		From Uruguay.		From Austria-Hungary.	
		Value.	Per cent of total.	Value.	Per cent of total.	Value.	Per cent of total.	Value.	Per cent of total.
1902	$5,797,097	$2,692,929	46.45	$1,868,688	32.24	$412,060	7.11	$518,623	8.94
1903	6,049,774	2,283,662	37.75	3,144,595	51.98	72,986	1.21	493,190	8.15
1904	7,651,985	2,212,425	28.91	4,546,311	59.41	207,034	2.71	651,240	8.51
1905	8,130,939	1,551,038	19.08	5,802,829	71.37	280,307	3.45	490,250	6.02
1906	8,677,099	1,573,654	18.14	6,632,073	76.43	39,814	.46	430,102	4.95
1907	9,689,350	1,074,694	20.38	6,789,350	70.07	328,614	3.39	590,847	6.00
1908	9,026,659	1,938,723	21.48	6,144,002	68.07	390,649	4.33	550,432	6.09
1909	9,315,693	2,207,236	23.69	6,268,483	67.29	555,567	5.96	244,006	2.62
1910	9,930,392	3,126,265	31.48	6,163,884	62.07	374,802	3.77	212,323	2.13
1911	9,721,079	3,334,987	34.31	5,694,019	58.57	495,176	5.09	110,179	1.13
1912	11,762,690	4,016,953	34.16	6,288,019	53.48	1,257,139	10.69	134,174	1.14
1913	10,388,040	3,955,024	38.07	5,821,418	56.05	339,793	3.28	98,396	.94
1914	8,266,969	4,583,574	55.44	3,165,152	38.28	97,277	1.18	15,450	.19
1915	9,639,973	6,055,830	62.82	3,198,846	33.18	243,757	2.53	....	....
1916	8,797,685	3,855,544	43.82	4,035,450	45.87	799,570	9.09	....	....

[1] From Estatistica Commercial, Commercio Exterior do Brasil.

TABLE VI.—*Exports of wheat flour from the United States, 1900–1917.*

Year.	Total value of wheat flour exported.	To Brazil.		To South America, except Brazil.	
		Value.	Per cent of total.	Value.	Per cent of total.
1900	$67,760,886	$2,549,065	3.76	$1,789,527	2.64
1901	69,459,296	2,687,786	3.86	2,178,283	3.13
1902	65,661,974	2,187,352	3.33	1,988,347	3.02
1903	73,756,404	2,148,342	2.91	1,913,182	2.59
1904	68,894,836	1,785,406	2.59	2,307,360	3.33
1905	40,176,136	1,225,565	3.05	2,609,510	6.49
1906	59,106,869	1,211,881	2.05	3,152,234	5.33
1907	62,175,397	1,382,981	2.22	2,075,204	3.33
1908	64,170,508	1,640,774	2.55	1,986,538	3.09
1909	51,157,366	1,671,503	3.26	1,919,317	3.75
1910	47,621,467	2,104,509	4.41	2,470,214	5.18
1911	49,386,946	2,840,788	5.75	2,804,569	5.67
1912	50,999,797	3,277,981	6.42	2,608,124	5.11
1913	53,171,537	3,105,239	5.84	2,705,169	5.08
1914	54,454,175	3,752,105	6.89	2,693,470	4.94
1915	94,869,343	3,972,690	4.18	3,551,795	3.74
1916	87,337,805	4,216,205	4.82	4,889,120	5.59
1917	93,198,474	2,743,818	2.94	4,294,653	4.60

Prior to 1890 the United States had been by far the leading source of the wheat and wheat flour imports into Brazil. But the development of the fertile wheat lands of the Argentine in close proximity to the Brazilian markets, together with the lower scale of prices for wheat which generally prevails in the Argentine because of the greater distance of that country from the important European markets, enabled the Argentine soon to equal, and in more recent years to surpass, the exports of wheat to Brazil from the United States. By 1890 the Argentine had become the chief source of the imports of wheat into Brazil, and during the following decade Argentine wheat completely displaced American wheat in the Brazilian market.

Wheat growing in the Argentine was followed by the development of flour milling. Argentine flour soon became a serious competitor of American flour in the Brazilian market; by 1903 the Brazilian imports of flour from the Argentine had surpassed in amount the imports from the United States. But even more serious became the competition from Brazilian mills using Argentine and Uruguayan wheat. To a smaller extent there was also competition from the flour of Austria-Hungary.

Competition from Argentine flour.—In 1904 Brazil granted a preference of 20 per cent to American flour. There was, in addition, a customs regulation which allowed 20 per cent tare for the weight of the barrels when flour entered Brazil in such containers. Barrels are too expensive in the Argentine to be used as containers, but a considerable proportion of the flour imported from the United States to Brazil comes packed in barrels. The net weight of a barrel of flour is approximately 196 pounds, and the weight of the container is ordinarily about 16 pounds. The 20 per cent allowance for tare therefore resulted in a substantial tariff differential in favor of American flour in barrel packages in addition to the formal preference of 20 per cent. In 1911 the tariff preference was increased to 30 per cent.

TABLE VII.—*Brazilian tariff differential in favor of American flour.*

	Rate on Argentine flour.	American flour.			
		Under 20 per cent preferential.		Under 30 per cent preferential.	
		Rate.	Differential.	Rate.	Differential.
Nominal duties—reis per kg....................................	25. 0	20. 0	5. 0	17. 5	7. 5
1. Duties paid 35 per cent in gold, 65 per cent in paper (paper milreis=32.11 cents; gold milreis=54.60 cents):					
(a) Not including surtax—reis per kg. (no allowance for tare)...	31. 0	24. 8	6. 2	21. 7	0. 3
(b) Including surtax ¹—reis per kg. (no allowance for tare)...	39. 4	33. 2	6. 2	30. 1	9. 3
(c) Including surtax ¹—cents per 196 pounds net (no allowance for tare)................................	113. 6	95. 7	17. 9	86. 8	26. 8
(d) Including surtax ¹—cents per barrel of 196 pounds net, 212 pounds gross (20 per cent allowance for tare)²..		82. 8	30. 8	75. 1	38. 5
2. Duties since Jan. 1, 1916, paid 40 per cent in gold, 60 per cent in paper:					
(a) Not including surtax—reis per kg. (no allowance for tare)...	31. 8	....	....	22. 3	9. 5
(b) Including surtax ¹—reis per kg. (no allowance for tare)...	40. 2	....	....	30. 7	9. 5
(c) Including surtax ¹—cents per 196 pounds net (no allowance for tare)................................	115. 8	....	....	88. 4	27. 4
(d) Including surtax ¹—cents per barrel of 196 pounds net, 212 pounds gross (20 per cent allowance for tare)²		....	....	76. 5	39. 3

¹ The surtax is 2 per cent ad valorem, payable in gold milreis, and is based on the official value of flour, which is equal to 10 times the nominal duty.
² Argentine flour, which is always packed in sacks, is not subject to the allowance for tare.

As will be seen from the figures in Table VII, the tariff differential in favor of American flour, when allowance is made for the payment of 35 per cent of the duties in gold, amounted to 17.9 cents per 196 pounds (30.8 cents for flour packed in barrels) under the 20 per cent preference, and to 26.8 cents per 196 pounds (38.5 cents for flour packed in barrels) under the 30 per cent preference. In 1906 it was estimated that the advantage in freight rates on flour to Rio de Janeiro amounted in favor of the Argentine, as compared with the United States, to about 75 cents per (barrel of) 196 pounds, net.¹ The tariff preference in favor of American flour, even if allowance is made for the excess tare for the barrels, was therefore insufficient to offset the advantage in freight rates enjoyed by the Argentine shippers to the southern ports of Brazil.

In the southern ports the demand is only for flour packed in sacks. In the trade with these ports no advantage accrues to the American exporters from the excess tare allowed for the weight of barrels. In the northern ports, however, barrels are used extensively as containers for commodities of domestic commerce, and as a consequence they have a substantial commercial value. A considerable proportion of the imports of flour into the northern ports is packed in barrels, and in the trade with these ports the American exporters of flour benefit from the tare allowance for the barrels.

Beginning with 1916 the Brazilian Government has required payment of duties to be made to the extent of 40 per cent in gold milreis. This change resulted in a slight increase in the tariff differential in favor of American flour. If allowance is made for the deprecia-

¹ U. S. Consular Reports, Oct. 8, 1906, No. 2386.

tion of the paper milreis, the preference in 1916 on a bag of American flour was 31 cents and on a barrel was 45 cents. On the other hand, because of the general advance in transportation costs since the outbreak of the war, the freight differential in favor of the Argentine has undoubtedly increased in even greater ratio, so that the relative position of American flour in the Brazilian market is now, as compared with the flour of the Argentine, worse than it was prior to 1916.

TABLE VIII.—*Exports of wheat flour from the Argentine, showing percentage sent to Brazil, 1906–1910.*

Year.	Total.	To Brazil.	Per cent of total.
	Metric tons.	*Metric tons.*	
1906	129,000	114,784	88.9
1907	127,500	118,332	92.8
1908	113,500	99,232	87.4
1909	116,487	102,358	87.8
1910	115,408	99,949	86.6

TABLE IX.—*Wheat prices and ocean freights.*[1]

	February—			
	1916	1915	1914	1913
Cash prices, per bushel, on or about Feb. 15: No. 2 hard winter wheat, at—				
Liverpool, England	$1.87	$1.90	$1.07	$1.07
New York, United States	1.38	1.70	1.03	1.04
Difference	.49	.20	.04	.03
"Rosafe" wheat, at—				
Liverpool, England	[2]2.40	1.94	1.06	1.11
Buenos Aires, Argentina	[2]1.04	1.36	.99	.88
Difference	1.36	.58	.07	.23

[1] From U. S. Department of Agriculture, Monthly Crop Report, March, 1916, p. 26.   [2] Jan., 1916.

It is claimed for American flour that it is of better quality, makes finer bread, and, in equal competition with Argentine flour, could command a slightly higher price in the Brazilian market. But, as is indicated by the figures in Table VIII, Brazil is the sole important export market for Argentine flour. The price of wheat and consequently of flour is generally much lower in the Argentine market than in New York because of the greater transportation cost to the important European markets. (See Table IX.) To keep their mills in operation and to retain their sole important export market, the millers of the Argentine would undoubtedly meet any reduction of the American price to the Brazilian consumer by a corresponding reduction in the price of their own product.

The decline in the Brazilian imports of flour from the United States, both absolutely and in relation to the imports from the Argentine, continued, therefore, for some time after the establishment of the preference of 20 per cent in 1904. But the increase of the preference in 1911 to 30 per cent, by further reducing the disadvantage under which American flour was laboring in its competition with Argentine flour, regained for American flour, at the expense of the Argentine product, a larger share of the Brazilian import trade. The American share in the Brazilian imports increased from 31 per cent in 1910 to 34 per cent in 1911 and to 38 per cent in 1913, whereas the share of the Argentine decreased from 62 per cent in 1910 to 59 per cent in 1911 and to 56 per cent in 1913. (See Table V.)

Competition from Austria-Hungary.—The Brazilian imports of flour from Austria-Hungary showed a decline throughout this period, falling from about 9 per cent of the total in 1902 to about 1 per cent in 1913. (See Table V.) Although the preference to American flour probably contributed to this decline, the most important factors undoubtedly were the competition of the Argentine flour and the development of a more extensive market in Austria and in other European countries for the Austrian product.

Competition from Brazilian flour.—

TABLE X.—*Brazilian tariff differential between flour and wheat—in favor of wheat*

I. DUTIES PAID 35 PER CENT IN GOLD, 65 PER CENT IN PAPER.

	Rates of duty.—Flour in sacks (no tare allowance).—Surtax of 2 per cent ad valorem included.[1]			Rates of duty.—Flour in barrels of 196 pounds net, 212 pounds gross (allowance for tare of 20 per cent of duty).—Surtax of 2 per cent ad valorem included.[1]		
	Under general tariff.	Under 20 per cent preferential on American flour.	Under 30 per cent preferential on American flour.	Under general tariff.	Under 20 per cent preferential on American flour.	Under 30 per cent preferential on American flour.
Flour—reis per kg.	39.4	33.2	30.1	34.1	28.7	26.0
Wheat—reis per kg.	15.7	15.7	15.7	15.7	15.7	15.7
Differential in favor of wheat:						
(a) In reis per kg.	23.7	17.5	14.4	18.4	13.0	10.3
(b) In cents per (bushel of) 60 pounds.	20.9	15.4	12.7	16.2	11.5	9.1
(c) In cents per (barrel of) 196 pounds.	68.3	50.4	41.5	53.0	37.4	29.7

II. DUTIES SINCE JAN. 1, 1916, PAID, 40 PER CENT IN GOLD, 60 PER CENT IN PAPER.

	Rates of duty.—Flour in sacks (no tare allowance).—Surtax of 2 per cent ad valorem included.[1]			Rates of duty.—Flour in barrels of 196 pounds net, 212 pounds gross (allowance for tare of 20 per cent of duty).—Surtax of 2 per cent ad valorem included.[1]		
	Under general tariff.	Under 20 per cent preferential on American flour.	Under 30 per cent preferential on American flour.	Under general tariff.	Under 20 per cent preferential on American flour.	Under 30 per cent preferential on American flour.
Flour—reis per kg.	40.2	....	30.7	34.8	....	26.5
Wheat—reis per kg.	16.1	....	16.1	16.1	....	16.1
Differential in favor of wheat:						
(a) In reis per kg.	24.1	....	14.6	18.7	....	10.4
(b) In cents per (bushel of) 60 pounds.	21.2	....	12.8	16.4	....	9.1
(c) In cents per (barrel of) 196 pounds.	69.4	....	42.0	53.8	....	30.0

[1] The surtax is payable in gold reis, and is based on the official values of flour and wheat, equal in both cases to 10 times the general rate of duty. The nominal duty on wheat is 10 reis per kilogram.

The most serious competitor of American flour, however, was the flour milled in Brazil from Argentine and Uruguayan wheat. As is indicated by the data in Table X, the Brazilian import duties on flour and on wheat result in a tariff differential in favor of wheat which amounted, under the general tariff and when payment of duties was required to be 35 per cent in gold reis, to approximately 68 cents per 196 pounds. The 30 per cent preference on flour effected a considerable reduction in the amount of this differential, but it still left the duty on a barrel of flour 41.5 cents higher than on an equivalent weight of wheat.[1]

Flour is imported from the United States in barrels in the northern ports only. The northern ports import practically no wheat. The tare allowance for flour in barrels is not of any aid, therefore, in reducing the differential between the duties on flour and on wheat.

The change in the method of paying duties instituted in 1916, whereby 40 per cent of the duties instead of 35 per cent is required to be paid in gold, increased the differential in favor of wheat, i. e., between the duties on flour and those on wheat, to 69.4 cents per 196 pounds, under the general tariff, and to 42 cents under the 30 per cent preferential. If allowance is made for the depreciation of the paper milreis, the differential, in 1916, was 80 cents per 196 pounds, under the general tariff, and 49 cents under the 30 per cent differentials.

The cost of transportation of flour from the ports of the United States to those of southern Brazil is much greater than the cost of transportation of wheat from the River Plate to southern Brazil. Moreover, the price of wheat is generally lower in the Argentine than in the United States. There thus results an additional factor favoring the Brazilian milling of Argentine wheat, as compared with the importation of flour from the United States. The Brazilian mills are financially strong and in operation very successful. Dividends of over 20 per cent are common, and the mills have accumulated in addition great reserves from undistributed profits. There is undoubtedly, under the protection afforded by the tariff differential between flour and wheat, a large margin of profit in flour milling in Brazil. The amount of the protection to Brazilian flour (Table X) is approximately 44 cents per barrel, which is not far from the total cost of milling in the United States. The cost of the raw material is less in Brazil than in the United States. If it should be necessary in order to meet keener American competition, the Brazilian millers could afford, it may be presumed, to make considerable reductions in the price of their product.

Table XI demonstrates the success of the Brazilian tariff differential in favor of wheat in encouraging the domestic milling of flour.

---

[1] In calculating the differential on wheat and on flour it is customary to add to the stated duty on wheat an amount sufficient to offset the difference in weight between a given quantity of wheat and the flour which is obtained therefrom. Thus, on the assumption that from 100 pounds of wheat there are obtained 70 pounds of flour, a duty of 10 reis per kilogram on wheat is generally calculated as equivalent to 14.3 reis per kilogram on flour. If bran entered free of duty in Brazil this would be a proper basis for calculation. But, in point of fact, the duty on bran is 20 reis per kilogram—or twice as high as the duty on wheat—and this is not a merely nominal duty, since very considerable quantities of bran are imported into Brazil each year. To make the calculation accurate it might even be necessary, therefore, to deduct from the duty on wheat the saving of duty on its bran content which is effected when wheat enters in the grain. The milling of wheat involves the waste, however, of about 4 per cent in bulk exclusive of the flour and bran obtained, and the addition of 4 per cent to the estimate of the real duty on the flour content of wheat approximately offsets the saving in duty on its bran content. In the calculations upon which the figures in Table X are based, the duty of 10 reis per kilogram on wheat is accepted as representing a duty of approximately 10 reis per kilogram on the flour to be obtained from it.

TABLE XI.—*Imports of flour into Brazil compared with flour milled in Brazil from imported wheat, 1902–1914.*[1]

Year.	Total consumption of wheat flour.	Flour milled in Brazil.[2]		Flour imported into Brazil.		Imports of wheat in the grain.
		Quantity.	Per cent of total consumption.	Quantity.	Per cent of total consumption.	
	Kilos.	*Kilos.*		*Kilos.*		*Kilos.*
1902	210,394,000	104,803,000	49.81	105,591,000	50.19	149,719,000
1903	235,254,000	118,120,000	50.21	117,134,000	49.79	168,745,000
1904	266,541,000	135,492,000	50.83	131,049,000	49.17	193,561,000
1905	290,461,000	149,997,000	51.64	140,464,000	48.36	214,282,000
1906	316,093,000	162,147,000	51.29	153,946,000	48.71	231,639,000
1907	343,050,000	172,797,000	50.37	170,253,000	49.63	246,853,000
1908	333,039,000	181,963,000	54.63	151,076,000	45.37	259,948,000
1909	317,817,000	171,512,000	53.97	146,304,000	46.03	259,304,000
1910	380,374,000	221,418,000	58.21	158,956,000	41.79	316,313,000
1911	391,962,000	233,292,000	59.49	158,761,000	40.51	333,146,000
1912	456,555,000	266,900,000	58.46	189,655,000	41.54	381,286,000
1913	477,058,000	306,898,000	64.33	170,160,000	35.67	438,426,000
1914	401,196,000	267,606,000	66.70	133,589,000	33.30	382,295,000

[1] From Estatistica Commercial, Commercio Exterior do Brasil.
[2] The figures of quantities of flour milled in Brazil are obtained from the total imports of wheat in the grain, which are reduced to their potential flour content on the assumption that the weight of wheat is to the weight of the flour obtainable therefrom as 100 is to 70. The domestic production of wheat in Brazil is not taken into consideration.

Whereas at all times since 1903 more wheat flour has been milled in Brazil than has been imported, the proportion of the domestic milled flour to total consumption of flour has increased from 49.8 per cent in 1902 to 58.2 per cent in 1910 and 64.3 per cent in 1913. The establishment of the 20 per cent preference in favor of American flour and its increase in 1911 to 30 per cent may, perhaps, have checked the tendency toward dominance of the Brazilian market by the domestic mills. But the counteracting forces were powerful enough to render the preference to American flour largely ineffective.

The figures in Table XI take no account of the flour milled in Brazil from domestic wheat. The Brazilian production of wheat is small, but it has been increasing very rapidly in recent years. No crop figures for wheat are published for Brazil as a whole. Such statistics as exist for the individual States indicate that Brazil produced about 52,000,000 kilos (1,900,000 bushels) in 1911, and that production had about doubled by 1917. All of the wheat grown in Brazil is milled and consumed there, and it therefore replaces corresponding amounts of foreign wheat or wheat flour which otherwise would be imported. If allowance is made for the flour milled from domestic wheat on the basis of the crop figures for 1911 given above, the proportion of flour milled in Brazil to total flour consumed in Brazil was, in 1911, 62 per cent instead of 59 per cent. The greatly increased attention which is now being paid to wheat growing in southern Brazil promises to result in checking still further the imports of flour from other countries, including the United States.

The development of milling in Brazil might, at first glance, be expected to cause a shifting of imports from the United States from flour to wheat. But the American exports of wheat to Brazil had declined even more rapidly than the exports of flour, and from 1894 until 1914 were practically negligible. The geographical location of the flour mills and of the large consuming markets in Brazil wholly explain this situation. Distances in Brazil are very great, and the populous provinces south of Maceio (for example the district surrounding and including Rio de Janeiro) are too near the Argentine and too far from the wheat-growing and flour-milling districts of the United States to permit of American competition becoming effective. Moreover, as has been indicated above, an increasing proportion of the wheat needed for milling in southern Brazil is being produced there. Milling in Brazil is wholly confined to the southern provinces. The ports of Brazil from Maceio north import almost no wheat, but purchase about 40 per cent of the total amount of wheat flour imported into Brazil. The farther north a Brazilian port is situated, the greater is the approach toward equalization between the transportation costs from the River Plate on the one hand and from New York on the other. Consequently a large proportion—probably the bulk—of the imports of wheat flour into the northern ports of Brazil come from the United States. But these northern ports, as has been indicated, import practically no wheat. It is, therefore, a direct consequence of the localization of milling in southern Brazil that the wheat imports come wholly from the River Plate region. If flour milling were to be developed in the northern ports of Brazil, there would result an increase in the exports of wheat from the United States to Brazil, but at the cost of the exports of flour.

Conclusions as to effect of preference on flour exports.—The circumstances are unfavorable for the American exports both of wheat and of flour. The preference of 20 per cent in favor of American flour improved the situation somewhat for the northern ports of Brazil, and the increase of the preference to 30 per cent probably enabled American flour to compete with the Argentine product in ports farther south. But Argentine flour possesses in southern Brazil an advantage of proximity which is too great to be overcome by tariff favors. Even if Brazil were to grant a total remission of duty on American flour and to maintain at the same time the present duties on Argentine flour, the difference in transportation costs to the important Brazilian markets would still tend to prevent a considerable diversion of trade from the Argentine to the United States. The failure of the preference to effect any appreciable change in the proportions in which the Brazilian imports of flour are divided between the Argentine and the United States has been due, therefore, to natural economic factors operating in a direction counter to the influence of the preference. The real issue, however, which the American flour export trade to Brazil has to face is not so much the competition of Argentine flour as the development of Brazilian milling under the stimulus of the tariff differential and other advantages favoring the Brazilian millers.

EFFECT OF THE PREFERENCE ON ARTICLES OTHER THAN WHEAT FLOUR.

Preference granted on articles other than wheat flour on April 16, 1904.—The other articles upon which the Brazilian Government established in 1904 a preference in favor of the United States were comparatively unimportant items in the export trade of the United States with Brazil. But the imports into Brazil of some of these commodities were considerable. The Brazilian consumer had long been accustomed to European patterns, styles, and brands, but it was thought that the preference, by reducing the cost of the American substitutes, would divert a portion of the trade to American exporters.

The extent to which the American export trade with Brazil was able to gain from the special reductions in duty will appear from the following analysis of the statistics covering the articles affected The articles, in addition to wheat flour, upon which a preferential reduction of 20 per cent was granted in 1894 were as follows: Inks, colors and varnishes; watches and clocks; condensed milk; and manufactures of india rubber.

MANUFACTURES OF INDIA RUBBER.

TABLE XII.—*Imports into Brazil of manufactures of india rubber, 1902-1916.*[1]

[Preferential effective from Apr. 20, 1904, to Dec. 31, 1904, and since July 1, 1906.]

Year.	From all countries.	From the United States.		From Germany.		From Great Britain.		From France.	
		Value.	Per cent of total.	Value.	Per cent of total.	Value.	Per cent of total.	Value.	Per cent of total.
1902	$499,307	$27,374	5.48	$163,896	32.82	$186,348	37.32	$72,133	14.45
1903	571,945	36,503	6.35	211,416	36.77	185,765	32.31	70,057	12.18
1904	561,067	38,533	6.87	196,225	34.97	175,648	31.31	67,798	12.08
1905	715,426	41,472	5.80	213,399	29.83	259,791	36.31	88,200	12.33
1906	587,468	40,194	6.84	188,623	32.11	220,855	37.59	77,908	13.26
1907	512,277	57,995	11.32	155,571	30.37	178,566	34.85	74,008	14.45
1908	432,760	46,877	10.83	132,808	30.69	141,259	32.64	69,787	15.13
1909	535,567	78,137	14.59	172,750	32.25	146,729	27.21	75,706	14.14
1910	755,319	155,670	20.61	210,543	27.87	204,471	27.07	85,020	11.26
1911	926,692	170,477	18.39	263,392	28.31	259,040	27.95	109,207	11.03
1912	964,646	183,280	19.00	289,647	30.03	279,242	28.95	111,634	11.57
1913	1,776,603	181,915	10.24	543,186	30.57	353,439	19.89	471,933	26.56
1914	886,239	66,741	7.53	203,355	22.95	211,937	23.91	249,650	28.17
1915	948,625	363,584	38.33	3,436	.36	216,308	22.80	112,958	11.91
1916	1,583,787	871,958	55.06	322	.02	241,242	15.23	170,231	10.75

[1] Estatistica Commercial, Commercio Exterior do Brasil.

TABLE XIII.—*Domestic exports from the United States of manufactures of india rubber, 1902-1917.*

Year.	To all countries.	To Brazil.		To South America, except Brazil.	
		Value.	Per cent of total.	Value.	Per cent of total.
1902	$3,462,402	$15,961	0.45	$58,338	1.68
1903	4,176,351	22,057	.52	82,117	1.96
1904	4,436,124	27,894	.62	93,743	2.11
1905	4,780,817	46,795	.97	138,241	2.89
1906	5,692,385	29,849	.52	157,590	2.76
1907	6,214,910	15,221	.90	195,820	3.15
1908	6,705,105	59,867	.89	211,436	3.15
1909	6,615,074	84,462	1.27	205,512	3.10
1910	9,060,895	105,145	1.16	305,370	3.37
1911	10,947,248	150,465	1.37	412,450	3.76
1912	11,167,229	209,239	1.87	391,335	3.51
1913	12,511,548	251,260	2.00	514,449	4.11
1914	11,808,462	119,272	1.09	516,199	4.37
1915	13,819,641	182,556	1.32	554,820	4.01
1916	34,282,112	690,156	2.01	1,730,575	5.06
1917	30,875,460	1,154,381	3.74	3,309,302	10.72

Brazilian imports of manufactures of india rubber from the United States increased under the preference, but it was several years before the increase became considerable. In 1902 and 1903—prior to the establishment of the preference—the import from the United States amounted to 6 per cent of the total imports, in 1910 to 20 per cent, and stood in 1912 at 19 per cent. Under the stimulus of the abnormal war conditions it increased to 38 per cent in 1915 and to 55 per cent in 1916. The expansion of this trade in manufactures of india rubber has undoubtedly been fostered by the especially favorable terms upon which the American products are admitted to Brazil. The Brazilian duties on india-rubber products are very high, ranging from $0.40 to $5 per pound; the preference, therefore, is of substantial amount. (On products made of para rubber, however, there are very great reductions of duty from the general rates.) From Table XIII it will be seen that the exports of the manufactures of india rubber from the United States to Brazil increased in greater proportion than the exports of similar articles to all countries and to the remainder of South America.

CLOCKS AND WATCHES.

TABLE XIV.—*Imports into Brazil of clocks and watches, 1902–1916.*[1]

[Preferential effective from Apr. 20, 1904, to Dec. 31, 1904, and since July 1, 1906.]

Year.	From all countries.	From the United States.		From Switzerland.		From Germany.	
		Value.	Per cent of total.	Value.	Per cent of total.	Value.	Per cent of total.
1902	$229,838	$55,478	24.14	$129,575	56.38	$27,588	12.00
1903	226,142	52,998	23.44	127,431	56.35	30,421	13.45
1904	251,767	82,193	32.65	115,175	45.75	38,609	15.34
1905	311,031	81,489	26.20	140,889	45.30	69,380	22.31
1906	341,720	83,886	24.55	139,535	40.83	92,670	27.12
1907	463,653	111,490	24.05	200,860	43.32	116,804	25.19
1908	366,304	128,926	35.20	135.366	36.95	79.625	21.74
1909	357,825	83,511	23.34	182,832	51.10	60.638	16.95
1910	483,321	156,063	32.29	213,847	44.25	81,200	16.80
1911	543,147	159,857	29.43	247,524	45.57	100,142	18.44
1912	475,762	111,782	23.50	216,431	45.49	107,911	22.68
1913	484,001	124,086	25.64	224,486	46.38	102,566	21.19
1914	210,407	51,086	24.28	109,235	51.92	30,708	14.59
1915	105,855	57,164	54.00	33,426	31.58	3,234	3.05
1916	165,197	108,878	65.91	42,115	25.49		

[1] Estatistica Commercial, Commercio Exterior do Brasil.

TABLE XV.—*Domestic exports from the United States of clocks and watches, 1902–1917.*

[Preferential effective Apr. 16, 1904, to Jan. 1, 1905, and since July 1, 1906; on alarm clocks, only since Jan. 1, 1909.]

CLOCKS AND WATCHES.

Year.	To all countries.	To Brazil.		To South America, except Brazil.	
		Value.	Per cent of total.	Value.	Per cent of total.
1902	$2,144,490	$46,077	2.15	$124,139	5.79
1903	2,133,529	47,080	2.21	113,413	5.32
1904	2,281,195	39,205	1.72	151,228	6.63
1905	2,316,414	64,010	2.76	153,397	6.62
1906	2,598,441	71,968	2.77	187,269	7.21
1907	3,169,272	96,582	3.05	163,170	5.15
1908	2,848,725	113,714	3.99	181,575	6.37
1909	2,487,332	90,819	3.65	150,945	6.07
1910	2,588,931	105,937	4.09	132,916	5.13
1911	3,126,771	153,165	4.90	137,875	4.41
1912	3,542,145	124,611	3.52	191,610	5.41
1913	3,608,257	120,025	3.33	239,205	6.63
1914	3,013,149	66,015	2.19	150,846	5.01
1915	2,574,809	41,710	1.66	59,552	2.31
1916	4,118,264	60,529	1.47	110,235	2.68
1917	4,276,399	146,721	3.43	357,932	8.37

CLOCKS.

Year.	To all countries.	To Brazil.		To South America, except Brazil.	
		Value.	Per cent of total.	Value.	Per cent of total.
1902	$1,146,381	$17,669	1.54	$50,006	4.36
1903	1,091,724	33,828	3.10	50,421	4.62
1904	1,186,279	30,824	2.60	76,001	6.42
1905	1,192,246	46,684	3.92	63,129	5.30
1906	1,304,451	50,612	3.88	97,554	7.48
1907	1,445,290	60,049	4.16	94,966	6.57
1908	1,461,989	68,564	4.69	118,227	8.09
1909	1,235,795	65,526	5.30	113,079	9.15
1910	1,360,218	85,825	6.31	98,884	7.27
1911	1,565,901	119,219	7.61	100,219	6.40
1912	1,661,468	107,056	6.45	135,368	8.15
1913	1,823,008	111,449	6.11	168,677	9.25
1914	1,552,725	59,865	3.85	80,686	5.20
1915	1,660,033	38,004	2.29	43,847	2.64
1916	2,593,826	58,265	2.25	88,896	3.43
1917	2,532,266	141,854	5.60	272,841	10.78

WATCHES.

Year.	To all countries.	To Brazil.		To South America, except Brazil.	
		Value.	Per cent of total.	Value.	Per cent of total.
1902	$998,109	$28,408	2.85	$74,133	7.43
1903	1,041,805	13,252	1.27	62,992	6.05
1904	1,004,016	8,381	.77	75,137	6.86
1905	1,124,168	17,326	1.54	90,268	8.03
1906	1,293,990	21,356	1.65	89,715	6.93
1907	1,723,982	36,533	2.12	68,204	3.96
1908	1,386,736	45,150	3.26	63,348	4.57
1909	1,251,537	25,293	2.02	37,866	3.02
1910	1,228,713	20,112	1.64	34,032	2.77
1911	1,560,870	33,946	2.17	37,556	2.41
1912	1,880,677	17,555	.93	56,242	2.99
1913	1,783,249	8,576	.48	70,528	3.96
1914	1,460,424	6,150	.42	70,160	4.81
1915	914,776	3,706	.41	15,705	1.72
1916	1,524,438	2,264	.15	21,339	1.40
1917	1,744,133	4,867	.28	85,091	4.88

The chief imports entering Brazil from the United States under the classification "clocks and watches" are cheap watches—commonly known as "dollar watches"—and alarm clocks. Alarm clocks were not admitted at the reduced rates until 1909. On both of those articles the general duty is 2 milreis each—equal to about 75 cents—and the duty under the preference is reduced to 1 milreis, 600 reis—equal to about 60 cents. The first year of the preference, 1904, marks a relatively great increase in the imports of clocks and watches from the United States. Since 1904 the imports have fluctuated, and the American share in the trade, although it has on the whole increased, has not developed conspicuously.

The exports from the United States to Brazil of clocks and watches formed a larger proportion of the total exports of these articles from the United States in the fiscal year 1905, and even more so in the years 1907 and after, than they had formed in the years previous to the establishment of the preference. The exports of clocks to Brazil increased greatly after 1909—it will be remembered that alarm clocks were not subject to the preference until 1909. The exports of these articles to Brazil increased more rapidly than the exports of the sam articles to all countries, and more rapidly also than the same exports to all the rest of South America.

INKS, PAINTS, AND DYESTUFFS.

TABLE XVI.—*Imports into Brazil of inks, prepared paints, and varnish, 1902–1916.*[1]

[Preferential effective: Inks and colors and varnish from Apr. 20, 1904, to Dec. 31, 1904, and since July 1, 1906; prepared paints since Jan. 1, 1907.]

Year.	From all countries.	From the United States.		From the United Kingdom.		From Germany.	
		Value.	Per cent of total.	Value.	Per cent of total.	Value.	Per cent of total.
1902	$284,229	$39,815	14.00	$154,300	54.29	$46,579	16.39
1903	319,334	37,893	11.86	194,457	60.89	51,933	16.26
1904	371,810	52,809	14.20	224,293	60.32	49,673	13.36
1905	371,987	49,458	13.29	221,044	59.42	55,970	15.05
1906	357,962	68,255	19.07	185,263	51.75	52,961	14.79
1907	470,370	92,872	19.74	244,335	51.94	65,835	14.00
1908	468,524	94,862	20.24	235,797	50.33	66,688	14.23
1909	564,014	94,156	16.69	331,774	58.82	88,172	15.63
1910	902,974	118,095	13.07	474,912	52.59	173,270	19.19
1911	837,558	163,306	19.49	422,207	50.41	168,463	20.11
1912	1,066,999	198,703	18.62	512,677	48.05	204,702	19.18
1913	1,155,313	231,759	20.06	524,148	45.37	229,816	19.89
1914	511,733	105,913	20.69	220,410	43.07	81,446	15.91
1915	461,636	176,604	38.25	207,267	44.90	8,713	1.89
1916	803,677	346,755	43.14	380,470	47.34		

[1] From Estatistica Commercial, Commercio Exterior do Brasil.

TABLE XVII.—*Domestic exports from the United States of varnishes, 1902–1917.*

Year.	To all countries.	To Brazil.		To South America, except Brazil.	
		Value.	Per cent of total.	Value.	Per cent of total.
1902	$607,685	$3,796	0.62	$17,636	2.90
1903	667,475	4,998	.75	21,604	3.24
1904	726,585	4,024	.55	26,617	3.66
1905	791,578	2,880	.36	26,860	3.39
1906	839,070	9,777	1.16	44,764	5.33
1907	961,291	5,489	.57	75,853	7.89
1908	940,699	11,936	1.27	40,140	4.27
1909	821,027	11,939	1.45	56,059	6.83
1910	976,238	18,274	1.87	68,150	6.98
1911	1,050,290	21,494	2.05	63,822	6.08
1912	1,118,004	40,166	3.59	103,974	9.30
1913	1,267,860	81,809	6.45	90,056	7.10
1914	1,038,864	30,057	2.89	50,661	4.88
1915	682,352	26,646	3.90	52,904	7.76
1916	838,339	64,652	7.71	63,982	7.63
1917	1,104,698	82,738	7.49	126,177	11.42

TABLE XVIII.—*Domestic exports from the United States of printing inks, 1902-1917.*

Year.	To all countries.	To Brazil.	To South America, except Brazil.	Year.	To all countries.	To Brazil.	To South America, except Brazil.
1902	$189,903	$2,055	$8,020	1910	$325,744	$7,018	$26,328
1903	220,544	6,019	10,856	1911	406,672	10,062	38,735
1904	238,314	3,263	14,094	1912	409,722	13,335	37,281
1905	276,330	2,434	23,472	1913	439,955	21,134	36,046
1906	275,105	1,450	32,916	1914	443,377	10,699	39,467
1907	308,678	3,514	44,749	1915	384,847	14,453	40,501
1908	303,024	8,128	36,052	1916	682,165	37,822	145,055
1909	305,154	6,458	30,950	1917	715,411	55,308	242,014

TABLE XIX.—*Domestic exports from the United States of dyes and dyestuffs, 1902-1917.*

Year.	To all countries.	To Brazil.	To South America, except Brazil.	Year.	To all countries.	To Brazil.	To South America, except Brazil.
1902	$531,225	$120	$4,695	1910	$380,203	$146	$5,978
1903	619,645	364	3,665	1911	325,519	13	3,879
1904	517,878	383	5,081	1912	314,694	480	1,907
1905	475,334	132	2,665	1913	347,656	301	2,238
1906	491,247		2,707	1914	356,919	65	3,779
1907	486,608	186	4,394	1915	1,177,925	3,976	36,899
1908	437,950	112	2,006	1916	5,102,002	71,246	193,554
1909	380,884		3,875	1917	11,709,287	1,203,140	583,838

TABLE XX.—*Domestic exports from the United States of paints[1], 1905 1917.*

Year.	To all countries.	To Brazil.		To South America, except Brazil.	
		Value	Per cent of total.	Value.	Per cent of total.
1905	$2,520,791	$35,848	1.42	$125,522	4.98
1906	2,658,192	48,717	1.83	151,167	5.69
1907	2,934,909	59,932	2.04	163,540	5.57
1908	2,951,376	75,565	2.56	160,225	5.44
1909	3,027,411	68,869	2.27	186,973	6.18
1910	3,770,105	75,332	2.00	240,813	6.39
1911	4,245,295	125,285	2.95	290,639	6.84
1912	4,871,930	109,231	2.24	391,676	8.04
1913	5,249,489	158,205	3.01	385,236	7.34
1914	5,002,088	95,962	1.92	343,319	6.86
1915	4,924,401	89,849	1.82	398,582	8.09
1916	8,617,401	239,519	2.78	963,736	11.18
1917	10,840,783	317,716	2.93	1,227,631	11.32

[1] Dry colors included; varnish and zinc oxide excluded.

The Brazilian duties on inks, paints, colors, and varnish are very high, so that the 20 per cent preference constitutes a considerable reduction from the general rates, but prepared paints were not admitted at the preferential rates until January 1, 1907. A considerable increase in the Brazilian imports of all these articles from the United States occurred in 1904, the first year of the preferential arrangement, but it was followed by only a slight drop in 1905, during which year the preference was withheld. In 1906 there was again a considerable increase in the imports of these articles from the United States, but the total imports into Brazil were increasing more rapidly than the imports from the United States.

The American figures of exports of varnishes and printing inks showed a considerable growth in the trade with Brazil under the preferential arrangement. Exports to Brazil of dyes and dyestuffs were almost negligible, however, until the outbreak of the war, when they underwent great expansion. Thus, in 1913 they amounted to only $301, in 1916 they reached $71,000, and in 1917 they had attained the surprising amount of $1,203,000. But the increase in United States exports of dyestuffs since 1914 is in no way related to the preference, and is due to the effect of the war in cutting off European supplies. The exports of varnishes to Brazil increased more rapidly than the exports of varnishes to all countries, and also than the same exports to South America, excluding Brazil. Exports of paints—which did not enter Brazil at the reduced'rates until January 1, 1907—showed a slight increase in that year and the increase continued during the following years of the period until the outbreak of the war. This increase was relatively greater than the increase of the exports to all countries, but it developed at about the same rate as the increase of the exports to the remaining countries of South America.

CONDENSED MILK.

TABLE XXI.—*Imports into Brazil of condensed milk, 1902–1916.*[1]

[Preferential effective from Apr. 20, 1904, to Dec. 31, 1904, and since July 1, 1906.]

Year.	From all countries.	From the United States.		From Switzerland.	
		Value.	Per cent of total.	Value.	Per cent of total.
1902	$272,869	$424	0.16	$246,575	90.35
1903	355,419	741	.21	328,403	92.40
1904	390,508	45,618	11.68	313,969	80.40
1905	474,224	60,232	12.70	369,830	77.98
1906	568,105	12,618	2.22	482,588	84.94
1907	717,083	22,460	3.13	633,176	88.30
1908	751,724	39,773	5.29	666,488	88.66
1909	957,569	23,088	2.41	845,209	88.27
1910	1,231,289	20,689	1.68	1,107,429	89.94
1911	1,224,145	16,752	1.37	1,139,908	93.12
1912	1,399,875	18,587	1.33	1,289,211	92.10
1913	1,426,188	4,999	.35	1,271,579	89.16
1914	1,207,697	76,475	6.33	1,024,263	84.81
1915	741,503	123,884	16.71	591,653	79.79
1916	787,472	127,388	16.18	633,547	80.45

[1] From Estatistica Commercial. Commercio Exterior do Brasil.

TABLE XXII.—*Domestic exports from the United States of condensed milk, 1902–1917.*

Year.	To all countries.	To Brazil.		To South America, except Brazil.	
		Value.	Per cent of total.	Value.	Per cent of total.
1902	$1,473,564	$157	0.01	$11,391	0.77
1903	921,026	397	.04	13,360	1.45
1904	1,367,794	860	.06	12,592	.92
1905	2,156,616	89,492	4.14	9,665	.44
1906	1,889,690	12,492	.66	13,380	.70
1907	2,191,111	1,993	.09	24,437	1.12
1908	2,455,186	2,218	.09	19,945	.81
1909	1,375,104	4,295	.31	18,658	1.35
1910	1,023,633	7,995	.78	21,846	2.13
1911	936,105	13,554	1.44	16,672	1.78
1912	1,651,879	12,160	.73	27,871	1.74
1913	1,432,848	3,292	.92	35,712	2.49
1914	1,341,140	3,665	.27	58,904	4.39
1915	3,066,642	56,659	1.84	81,138	2.64
1916	12,712,952	95,979	.75	187,012	1.47
1917	25,136,641	146,798	.58	394,830	1.57

The Brazilian rate on condensed milk is 500 reis per kilogram—equivalent to 7.2 cents a pound. The preferential rate is equivalent to about 5.8 cents a pound, the preference thus being slightly less than 1.4 cents a pound. A very great increase in the Brazilian imports from the United States occurred in 1904, but the imports of 1905, during which year the preference was not in effect, were even greater. The bulk of the imports came and continue to come from Switzerland, and the Swiss brands which are most popular in Brazil are said to be controlled by an American company. The unusually large imports in 1904 and 1905 were due, according to a consular statement, to a surplus production in the United States in these years.

After July 1, 1906, when the preference was again established, there were substantial imports from the United States, although these were far from equal in amount to the imports of 1904 and 1905. Brazilian import statistics classify as "American" all products shipped from an American port. The American figures of exports to Brazil show that there were abnormal shipments in the fiscal year 1905, but account for a much smaller volume of trade during the following years than is indicated in the Brazilian figures. The discrepancy is to be explained largely by the fact that one of the popular brands of milk imported into Brazil from the United States, and listed under imports from the United States, is manufactured at Goderich, Ontario, and is, therefore, not included in the American "domestic export" figures.

ADDITIONAL ARTICLES PLACED ON PREFERENTIAL LIST, 1906.

The Brazilian Government in 1906 added to the list of articles upon which the preferential reduction of 20 per cent was granted the following articles: Scales and balances, typewriters, pianos, refrigerators, and windmills. These articles, though important among the products of the United States, play a very small part in the trade of the United States with Brazil. In several cases the imports of these articles into Brazil from Europe were very considerable, and the preference was expected to divert a portion of this trade to American exporters. In other cases, in which the Brazilian consumption of these articles was very limited, it was hoped that the preference would enable the American producers to place their products in the Brazilian market under circumstances so advantageous that an important market would thus be developed. The course of the United States-Brazilian trade in these articles is shown in the following tables:

SCALES AND BALANCES.

TABLE XXIII.—*Imports into Brazil of scales and balances, 1902-1916.*

[Preferential effective since July 1, 1906.]

Year.	From all countries.	From the United States.		From the United Kingdom.		From Germany.	
		Value.	Per cent of total.	Value.	Per cent of total.	Value.	Per cent of total.
1902	$44,053	$14,903	33.83	$9,244	20.98	$12,773	28.99
1903	46,857	18,280	39.01	7,900	16.86	10,498	22.40
1904	68,669	22,765	33.15	17,136	24.95	15,930	23.20
1905	70,762	28,593	40.41	16,407	23.19	16,589	23.44
1906	83,181	28,861	34.70	25,341	30.46	20,607	24.77
1907	99,858	34,712	34.76	19,369	19.39	31,279	31.32
1908	85,637	37,506	43.80	17,909	20.91	22,666	26.47
1909	76,188	27,267	35.79	19,320	25.36	23,711	31.12
1910	131,411	56,742	43.18	37,320	28.40	30,340	23.09
1911	120,569	49,791	41.30	30,407	25.22	31,550	26.17
1912	135,509	67,503	49.81	24,073	17.76	32,018	23.63
1913	147,065	57,765	39.28	27,822	18.92	46,790	31.82
1914	57,846	24,340	42.08	15,404	26.63	13,331	23.05
1915	32,078	21,381	66.65	8,626	26.89	840	2.62
1916	63,792	42,832	67.14	17,709	27.76	....	....

TABLE XXIV.— *Domestic exports from the United States of scales and balances, 1904-1917.*

Year.	To all countries.	To Brazil.		To South America, except Brazil.	
		Value.	Per cent of total.	Value.	Per cent of total.
1904	$652,303	$22,189	3.40	$108,411	16.62
1905	674,771	22,836	3.38	133,174	19.73
1906	845,870	28,650	3.38	154,869	18.31
1907	976,383	21,873	2.24	217,777	22.34
1908	984,695	42,469	4.31	189,294	19.22
1909	751,230	17,322	2.30	160,312	21.33
1910	834,890	33,701	4.03	196,389	22.80
1911	1,061,389	53,387	5.02	225,499	21.24
1912	1,074,630	46,907	4.36	250,112	23.27
1913	1,184,685	58,317	4.92	239,315	20.20
1914	1,128,764	32,994	2.92	209,433	18.55
1915	661,073	18,787	2.84	84,011	12.70
1916	1,083,380	23,626	2.18	144,219	13.31
1917	1,456,090	34,624	2.37	197,286	13.55

The Brazilian duties on scales and balances vary considerably according to the weight and size of the article, but in general they are very high. Brazilian imports from the United States increased in 1907, the first complete calendar year in which the reduced duties were effective, but it was several years before the full effect of the preference became apparent, either absolutely or in relation to total imports, in increased imports of these articles from the United States.

The American figures of exports of scales and balances to Brazil indicate a decrease in the fiscal year 1907, the first fiscal year in which the preference was effective, and abnormally low shipments in 1909. In all other years of the period during which the special reductions of duty were in effect, however, the American exports to Brazil were greater in amount and in proportion to total exports of these articles from the United States than they had been prior to the establishment of the preference. The exports to Brazil during the preferential period increased at a more rapid rate than did those to the remainder of South America.

TYPEWRITING MACHINES.

TABLE XXV.—*Imports of typewriting machines into Brazil, 1904–1916.*[1]

[Preferential effective since July 1, 1906.]

Year.	From all countries.	From the United States.		Years.	From all countries.	From the United States.	
		Value.	Per cent of total.			Value.	Per cent of total.
1904	$34,147	$27,195	79.63	1911	$376,558	$320,199	85.03
1905	60,904	50,313	82.60	1912	424,541	356,302	83.92
1906	72,984	61,659	84.48	1913	362,354	287,711	79.42
1907	122,646	107,469	87.62	1914	122,327	101,471	82.98
1908	130,399	117,358	89.98	1915	90,983	87,976	96.68
1909	196,067	171,354	87.39	1916	207,512	204,102	98.36
1910	272,990	237,255	86.91				

[1] Estatistica Commercial, Commercio Exterior do Brasil.

TABLE XXVI.—*Domestic exports of typewriters from the United States, 1904–1917.*

Year.	To all countries.	To Brazil.		To South America except Brazil.	
		Value.	Per cent of total.	Value.	Per cent of total.
1904	$4,537,125	$17,771	0.39	$151,152	3.33
1905	4,745,285	35,227	.74	235,135	4.95
1906	5,126,374	60,445	1.17	243,986	4.75
1907	6,274,400	69,167	1.10	326,843	5.20
1908	6,495,756	116,539	1.79	341,102	5.25
1909	6,800,069	112,484	1.63	377,568	5.47
1910	8,239,510	181,205	2.10	526,032	6.38
1911	9,778,498	289,419	2.95	727,280	7.40
1912	11,423,691	312,638	2.73	716,780	6.27
1913	11,532,364	351,640	3.04	745,483	6.46
1914	10,575,573	125,598	1.18	631,917	5.97
1915	5,315,134	62,334	1.17	232,010	4.36
1916	9,104,189	119,817	1.31	416,230	4.57
1917	11,162,423	232,309	2.08	682,342	6.11

The preference established in 1906 on American typewriters amounted to about $4 reduction in duty on each typewriter, but apparently did not change the price to the consumer. The extra profit to the merchants may have increased their willingness to stock American machines and to push their sales. The Brazilian returns for imports include typewriters, adding machines, and linotypes in one class as "typewriting machines." The imports of "typewriting machines" from the United States prior to the establishment of the preference already formed the bulk of the imports of these articles into Brazil. The establishment of the preference on typewriters was followed by an appreciable increase in imports of "typewriting machines" in 1906, during six months of which year the reductions were effective, and by much greater increases in the following years, until the depression of 1914. On January 1, 1907, the reductions were extended for the first time to linotypes and adding machines, and the considerable increase in the imports of typewriting machines into Brazil from the United States in that year may have resulted from this extension of the preferred class.

The American figures of exports to Brazil of typewriters showed a marked increase in amount from 1908 on. This increase was relatively greater than the increase in the total exports of typewriters from the United States to all countries and in exports of typewriters to other portions of South America.

PIANOS.

TABLE XXVII.—*Imports of pianos and piano players into Brazil, 1904-1916.*[1]

[Preferential effective since July 1, 1906.]

Year.	From all countries.	From the United States.		From Germany.		From France.	
		From all countries.	Per cent of total.	Value.	Per cent of total.	Value.	Per cent of total.
1904	$155,367	$9,817	6.32	$105,053	67.61	$27,182	17.50
1905	263,785	9,813	3.72	168,393	63.84	64,581	24.48
1906	258,707	13,242	5.12	175,601	67.88	58,101	22.46
1907	292,541	13,120	4.48	192,301	65.74	62,208	21.27
1908	351,149	25,624	7.30	227,415	64.76	78,542	22.37
1909	361,238	32,628	9.03	256,717	71.06	51,149	14.16
1910	513,446	56,748	11.05	352,610	68.67	72,178	14.06
1911	777,313	109,315	14.06	549,712	70.72	81,438	10.48
1912	868,690	127,208	14.64	608,592	70.06	79,992	9.21
1913	700,056	118,202	16.88	459,198	65.59	76,139	10.88
1914	238,137	49,521	20.80	139,994	58.78	34,849	14.63
1915	69,133	32,960	47.68	15,687	22.69	10,951	15.84
1916	137,476	81,191	59.06	522	.38	24,408	17.75

[1] Estatistica Commercial, Commercio Exterior do Brasil.

TABLE XXVIII.—*Domestic exports of pianos from the United States, 1904-1917.*

Year.	To all countries.	To Brazil.		To South America except Brazil.	
		Value.	Per cent of total.	Value.	Per cent of total.
1904	$1,294,405	$8,699	0.67	$26,525	2.04
1905	1,356,542	6,105	.45	46,688	3.44
1906	1,417,898	11,782	.83	66,093	4.66
1907	1,483,103	10,164	.68	83,539	5.63
1908	1,903,084	29,057	1.52	84,148	4.42
1909	1,267,849	30,598	2.41	75,178	5.92
1910	1,902,732	46,826	2.46	162,393	8.53
1911	2,102,616	57,194	2.72	173,814	8.26
1912	2,185,880	107,322	4.90	247,958	11.34
1913	2,239,685	99,715	4.45	272,484	12.16
1914	1,929,870	52,136	2.70	214,298	11.09
1915	1,245,524	22,956	1.84	146,427	11.75
1916	2,160,212	41,937	1.94	356,643	16.50
1917	2,776,825	89,598	3.22	524,954	18.90

The Brazilian duties on pianos are very high; on those types which are commonly produced in the United States the rates of the general tariff range from about $108 to $180 each, while the preferential reductions range from about $22 to $36 each.   During the first two years of the preference the imports of pianos into Brazil from the United States showed no increase.   But the American pianos differed in style and shape from the European pianos to which the Brazilian consumers had been accustomed, and at the time when the preference was established no commercial house in Brazil handled American pianos.   In 1908 there appeared some signs of an expansion of the imports from the United States under the stimulus of the preference, and in the following years the purchases from the United States increased very markedly both in absolute amount and in relation to the imports from other countries.

The American figures likewise showed no increase in exports of pianos to Brazil until the fiscal year 1908, but from 1908 until the depression of 1914 the exports of pianos to Brazil were much greater, both absolutely and in relation to total exports, than they had been in the period prior to the preference.   The American exports of pianos to Brazil also increased more rapidly than did similar exports to South America, excluding Brazil, during the years immediately following the establishment of the preference.

WINDMILLS.

TABLE XXIX.—*Domestic exports of windmills and parts from the United States, 1907-1917.*

[Preferential effective since July 1, 1906.]

Year.	To all countries.	To Brazil.		To South America except Brazil.	
		Value.	Per cent of total.	Value.	Per cent of total.
1907	$999,069	$20,026	2.00	$481,443	48.10
1908	1,354,900	25,756	1.90	833,710	61.53
1909	1,196,508	16,433	1.37	764,183	63.86
1910	1,484,813	22,569	1.52	1,028,619	69.28
1911	1,929,991	37,611	1.94	1,230,882	63.77
1912	1,876,164	35,966	1.91	1,144,671	61.01
1913	1,318,771	22,847	1.73	617,436	46.81
1914	1,618,349	24,278	1.50	735,768	45.46
1915	709,607	13,006	1.83	286,056	40.30
1916	1,087,964	10,035	.92	625,714	57.51
1917	895,277	12,376	1.38	415,190	46.37

The Brazilian duty on windmills is 8 per cent *ad valorem*, which makes the preferential reduction amount to less than 2 per cent *ad valorem*.   The imports of windmills are not separately entered in the Brazilian figures and have been given separately in the American figures only since 1907. There is thus no means of comparing the imports prior to the establishment of the preference with those under the preference.   During the years from 1907 on, when American figures are available, not much expansion was shown in the exports to Brazil, whereas the exports to the remainder of South America were increasing during most of the period.

Trade in refrigerators.—In the statistics of neither country do there appear separate figures for imports or exports of refrigerators. There is as yet a very limited use of ice in Brazil, and the market for this article is at present unimportant.

ADDITIONAL ARTICLES PLACED ON PREFERENTIAL LIST, 1910.

In the Brazilian budget law for 1910 there were included in the list of commodities of American manufacture upon which preferential reductions of duty were granted several additional articles, as follows: Cement, dried fruits, desks, corsets, and school furniture. For these articles no separate Brazilian figures appear for desks, corsets, or school furniture, and the imports of fruits have been separately entered only since 1911. The exports of all of these articles to Brazil prior to 1910 were undoubtedly small in amount. Of the Brazilian importation of fruits, only a small percentage comes from the United States, even under the preferential arrangement. The most important of the articles which were added to the list in 1910, in so far as the trade between the two countries is concerned, was cement.

CEMENT.

TABLE XXX.—*Imports of cement into Brazil, 1908–1916.*[1]

[Preferential effective since Jan. 1, 1910.]

Year.	From all countries.	From the United States.		From Germany.		From Belgium.		From the United Kingdom.	
		Value.	Per cent of total.	Value.	Per cent of total.	Value.	Per cent of total.	Value.	Per cent of total.
1908	$2,683,076	$2,115	0.08	$1,258,553	46.90	$505,567	18.84	$677,409	25.24
1909	2,535,551	4,856	.19	1,317,282	51.95	406,975	15.99	657,152	25.92
1910	3,316,976	7,116	.21	1,355,932	40.88	577,568	17.41	1,167,529	35.20
1911	3,637,241	33,872	.93	1,651,767	45.41	622,661	17.12	1,104,628	30.37
1912	5,276,974	276,624	5.24	2,531,426	47.98	962,499	18.24	1,140,862	21.62
1913	7,137,861	766,915	10.75	2,986,278	41.84	908,772	12.77	1,923,224	27.02
1914	2,554,991	364,907	14.28	1,092,754	42.77	218,385	8.55	583,952	22.85
1915	2,611,315	1,180,501	45.21	84,667	3.24	6,012	.23	678,024	25.96
1916	4,327,307	1,036,658	23.96					1,629,127	37.65

[1] Estatistica Commercial, Commercio Exterior do Brasil.

The imports of cement into Brazil have been considerable. Prior to 1910 practically none of these imports came from the United States, but by 1913 over 10 per cent of the total import of cement into Brazil came from the United States. With imports from Europe largely cut off since the war, the imports of American cement into Brazil have increased greatly.

CONCLUSION AS TO EFFECT OF BRAZILIAN PREFERENTIAL ON AMERICAN EXPORTS.

The foregoing analysis indicates that the preferential arrangement, in so far as its object was to secure an increase in the American share of the imports into Brazil, has been attended by a moderate measure of success. It has not succeeded in increasing the proportion of the Brazilian consumption of wheat flour which is provided by American mills, nor has it effected a substantial increase in the share of the Brazilian imports of wheat flour coming from the United States, but it has undoubtedly tended to check the decline which the economic situation was bringing about. The other preferred articles were less important, and even in the aggregate constituted only a small fraction of the total American exports to Brazil. The preference on these articles, however, had much more effect. In almost every instance the establishment of the preference was followed shortly by an appreciable increase in the American exports to Brazil, both absolutely and in relation to the total amount of Brazilian imports from all sources. The statistics indicate that the trade with Brazil in several articles, notably pianos and cement, practically owed its establishment to the influence of the preference. To some extent the growth of the trade with Brazil in the preferred articles was undoubtedly due to the effect of the special tariff treatment of American products in directing the attention of American exporters more closely to the Brazilian market. Another contributing factor was the general growth of American exports to Brazil, which showed itself in the increased Brazilian import from the United States of articles upon which no reductions of duty at all were granted. But even when allowance is made for these contributing factors, the increases in the exports of the preferred articles to Brazil, which followed upon the establishment of the reductions, and which contrast both with the smaller increases in the exports of similar articles to the rest of South America and with the relatively smaller increases in imports into Brazil of these articles from other countries, indicate that the prefer-. ential arrangement was moderately effective in securing an expansion of American trade with that country in the articles affected by the arrangement. The tariff preference to American wheat flour, to which most importance was attached in both Brazil and the United States, failed, however, to show any important positive results.

9. THE CUBAN RECIPROCITY TREATY OF 1902.

THE CUBAN RECIPROCITY TREATY OF 1902.

NEGOTIATION OF THE COMMERCIAL CONVENTION WITH CUBA.

The Cuban revolution and reconstruction.—Cuba, the most important of the islands of the Caribbean, became independent of Spain and passed temporarily under the control of the United States in 1898. In accordance with the treaty of peace concluded between the United States and Spain on December 10, 1898, American officials assumed the difficult task of administering the affairs of the island. Two years of revolution had reduced Cuba to a deplorable state, and its economic, political, and social conditions demanded immediate attention.

In the work of reconstruction, the new administration set about establishing schools, improving sanitation, constructing highways, placing the currency upon a sound basis, and endeavoring to increase as extensively and rapidly as possible the general welfare of the Cuban people. These efforts could not be immediately of very great effect; the agriculture of Cuba, which was the mainstay of its community life, revived but slowly, and privation among the masses of the people threatened to become general and acute.

In the hope of hastening the work of alleviation by the improvement of Cuban commerce, a commission of Cuban planters and merchants went to Washington in January, 1901.[1] But the representations of the commissioners did not receive adequate consideration, because the attention of Congress was occupied by the adjustment of the more strictly political relations between the two countries. During the summer of 1901 the demand on the part of the Cubans for a commercial treaty with the United States became steadily more insistent and this was especially true in the case of the influential sugar and tobacco interests. The demand also received support from the Provisional Military Government which still controlled the Island; this body even financed a campaign in the United States to inform the country "of the desires of the people of Cuba as to * * * trade relations."[2] In December, 1901, another group of prominent Cubans petitioned the United States Senate for the enactment of a law which would effect a reduction of 50 per cent from the Cuban tariff rates in return for a reduction of similar amount in the American tariff on Cuban raw sugar (up to a certain grade) and molasses. From the very beginning this movement met with a cordial response from President Roosevelt and the administration generally. In his annual report for 1901, Mr. Root, Secretary of War, expressed emphatic approval of the policy of extending tariff concessions to Cuba. He declared that

aside from the moral obligation to which we committed ourselves when we drove Spain out of Cuba, and aside from the ordinary considerations of commercial advantage involved in a reciprocity treaty, there are the weightiest reasons of American

---

[1] 57th Cong., 1st sess., II. Doc. No. 535, p. 408. [2] 57th Cong., 1st sess., H. Doc. No. 679.

public policy pointing in the same direction; for the peace of Cuba is necessary to the peace of the United States; the independence of Cuba is necessary to the safety of the United States. The same considerations which led to the war with Spain now require that a commercial agreement be made under which Cuba can live. The condition of the sugar and tobacco industries in Cuba is already such that the earliest possible action by Congress upon this subject is desirable. [1]

Congress opposed to tariff reductions in favor of Cuba.—At the opening of the Fifty-seventh Congress, President Roosevelt called attention in even more emphatic terms to the obligations resting upon the American Government.

In the case of Cuba * * * there are weighty reasons of morality and of national nterest why the policy should be held to have a peculiar application, and I must earnestly ask for your attention to the wisdom, indeed to the vital need, of providing for a substantial reduction in the tariff duties on Cuban imports into the United States. Cuba has in her Constitution affirmed that she should stand, in international matters, in closer and more friendly relations with us than with any other power; and we are bound by every consideration of honor and expediency to pass commercial measures in the interest of her material well-being.[2]

But Congress received the suggestion coldly and no action was taken during the December session. A majority of the members who supported a protectionist policy looked upon reductions of duty in favor of Cuba as a possible starting point for revisions in other directions. Furthermore, the domestic beet-sugar and cane-sugar producers exerted what influence they could to prevent the granting of concessions upon Cuban products.

Introduction of a reciprocity bill.—When Congress again convened on January 6, 1902, public opinion had begun to develop in favor of some readjustment of the commercial relations between the two countries. The Ways and Means Committee sat for nine days hearing arguments presented on both sides of the matter.[3] At these hearings the Cuban case was not effectively organized or presented, whereas the opposition was ably supported by representatives of American beet and cane-sugar interests, and tobacco interests. Hawaiian and Porto Rican representatives also contributed their opposition. The Cuban side was presented in a communication from Military Governor Wood to Chairman Payne of the Ways and Means Committee, in which it was pointed out that the planters had exhausted their resources and that a crisis was imminent. In the judgment of General Wood, one of the foremost obstacles to the recovery of Cuban agriculture was the uphill competition with the bounty-fed sugar of Europe and the highly protected product of the United States. "Relief," he declared, "must be granted and granted quickly, or a condition will arise which will render the establishment and maintenance of a stable government highly improbable."[4]

The committee finally reported in favor of a reciprocity arrangement, and Chairman Payne introduced such a measure in the House of Representatives on March 19, 1902. After considerable discussion the proposal was reported back on March 31 with a favorable recommendation. The measure as it was then drafted contemplated a reciprocal reduction of duties of 20 per cent upon the condition that Cuba should first adopt immigration laws "as fully restrictive of im-

[1] 57th Cong., 1st sess., H. Rept. No. 1276, p. 1.
[2] 57th Cong., 1st sess., Sen. Doc. No. 405, p. 1.
[3] Reciprocity with Cuba, Hearings before Committee on Ways and Means. 57th Cong., 1st sess., H. Doc. No. 535.
[4] 57th Cong., 1st sess., H. Doc. No. 535, p. 648-9. Also 57th Cong., 1st sess., Cong. Rec. 35, 1902, p. 4629.

migration as the laws of the United States." The arrangement would be effective only until December 1, 1903.[1]

The reciprocity bill in the House.—Discussion of the measure in the House of Representatives was opened by Mr. Payne on April 8. After outlining the situation produced in the world's sugar market by the giving of bounties to producers of beet sugar and describing the distress in Cuba resulting therefrom, Mr. Payne emphasized the moral obligation of the United States toward the Island, declaring that the United States would be recreant to its duty if it failed to create conditions which, by assuring Cuba a favorable market, would render her prosperous. In the debate which ensued, the arguments in support of the proposed agreement went at great length into the consideration of ethical and of political principles, while the discussion of the economic possibilities was, in the main, limited to showing that no injury would be done to domestic producers. The greatest emphasis upon the purely commercial advantages which were to be expected from the arrangement was in a speech by Mr. McCall, of Massachusetts, who nevertheless thought the attention devoted to this feature was disproportionate to its importance. The opposition argued, in part, that the distress in Cuba had been greatly exaggerated, and that there was no moral obligation to do more than had already been done.[2] If relief was needed it might be given, they held, by an appropriation from the Treasury or by means of a rebate system whereby the full duties on imports from Cuba would be collected and a lump sum refunded to the Cuban Government, thus causing no interference with American industry. Representatives of those regions of the United States which are particularly interested in the production of sugar and tobacco declared that these industries would be ruined by the competition of Cuban products, while at the same time the Government would suffer a serious diminution in its revenues. It was asserted that the treaty would not help the Cuban planters, nor would it reduce the price of sugar to American consumers; that the price of sugar was fixed in Hamburg, and the chief beneficiary of the proposed arrangement would be the American sugar-refining interests.

Failure of the bill in the Senate.—After a long discussion the bill finally passed the House of Representatives on April 18, 1902, by a decisive vote. It failed, however, to come to a vote in the Senate. The committee reports showed the same division of opinion which had appeared in the House of Representatives. Some members opposed any action whatever; others favored the appropriation of a lump sum to relieve the distress; and still others were convinced that the proposed measure would benefit only the Sugar Trust.[3] But legislative matters concerning the Philippines and the Panama Canal crowded out other business, and on July 1, 1902, Congress adjourned without having acted upon the Cuban bill. Meanwhile, on May 20, 1902, the government of the Island had been turned over to the Cuban people.

The failure of the bill to reach a vote in the Senate occurred in spite of appeals from the Presidents both of Cuba and of the United

---

[1] 57th Cong., 1st sess., II. Rept. No. 1276, part 4, p. 2. (Report of Committee on Ways and Means.)
[2] 57th Cong., 1st sess., 1902, Cong. Rec. 35, pp. 4019, 4333.
[3] 57th Cong., 1st sess., Sen. Docs. Nos. 388, 474, pp. 1–3. The evidence presented on the actual conditions in Cuba and the claims of the beet-sugar industry as to the effect of the treaty upon its future are detailed in 57th Cong., 1st sess., Sen. Doc. No. 439.

States. On June 12, when the chances were already slight that the bill would be acted upon, President Palma cabled to President Roosevelt an earnest petition for legislative relief before it was "too late and the country was financially ruined."[1] President Roosevelt immediately sent a special message to Congress in which he again drew attention to the exceptional circumstances of the case: "We expect Cuba to treat us on an exceptional footing politically and we should put her in the same position economically. * * * I ask that the Cubans be given all possible chances to use to the best advantage the freedom of which Americans have such a right to be proud and for which so many American lives have been sacrificed." But the President's appeal was of no avail, and the attempt to secure an adjustment of the commercial relations with Cuba by legislative action failed.

Negotiation of a treaty.—The President next sought to attain the same end by the negotiation of a treaty. The result of the President's new efforts was the signing, on December 11, 1902, of a commercial convention "to strengthen the bonds of friendship between the two countries, and to facilitate their commercial intercourse by improving the conditions of trade between them." It was agreed to preserve unchanged the free lists then in force in the two countries. All Cuban goods not on the free list were to be allowed to enter the United States at a reduction of 20 per cent from the tariff rates which were at any time imposed on foreign merchandise. Dutiable American goods imported into Cuba were to be divided into four classes, entering at rates which were 20, 25, 30, and 40 per cent, respectively, below the regular Cuban duties.

Ratification of the treaty by the Senate.—An extraordinary session of the Senate was called to meet March 5, 1903, for the purpose of considering, among other matters, the Cuban and Isthmian treaties. On the last day of the session, March 19, the ratification of the Cuban treaty was advised by the Senate. Shortly thereafter the Cuban Government signified its approval of the treaty.

Discussion of the treaty in Congress.—The final article contained a provision that the convention was not to take effect until it should have received the approval of Congress. Anxious to have final action taken upon the measure, the President convened the first session of the Fifty-eighth Congress on November 9, 1903. On the second day of the session he submitted the commercial treaty with Cuba to Congress for its approval. The President declared in his message that the legislation was "demanded not only by our interest but by our honor"; he pointed out further that the conditions under which the withdrawal of American authorities from Cuba had been arranged had brought Cuba into close political relations with the United States, and that it necessarily followed that Cuba must also to a certain degree become included within the lines of American economic policy.

The discussion in the House gave rise to the same arguments that had been used in the previous Congress. The opposition again turned chiefly upon the damage which the measure would bring to American interests; the supporters urged the moral duty of the United States toward Cuba, the political importance to the United States of a government able to maintain order in the island, and, in less positive terms, the commercial advantages which would follow.

---

[1] 57th Cong., 1st sess., Sen. Doc. No. 405, pp. 1-3.

Approval and proclamation of the treaty.—When the measure came up for a decision in the House on November 19 it was passed by a vote of 335 yeas to 21 nays. In the Senate the discussion began on December 7. The arguments offered resembled those in the previous debates. The bill was passed on December 16 by a vote of 75 to 18. On December 17, 1903, the treaty was formally proclaimed.

This treaty is the only agreement of its kind found in the engagements of either of the two countries. It provided for mutual reductions of customs charges from whatever rates might be in force in the two countries, but did not fix a definite schedule of duties. As indicated above, no change was to be made in the free lists as they stood in 1902. The Cuban free list contains few major articles of commerce, the important items being coal, agricultural tools, fresh fish, unfinished pine wood, cattle for breeding purposes, and direct importations by publishers of unglazed print paper. In return for a uniform reduction by the United States of 20 per cent in the rates on all dutiable imports from Cuba, the Cuban Government agreed to make reductions on various groups of American products. The important items composing these groups are as follows:

Reduction in duty of 20 per cent:
    Machinery and apparatus (in which copper is not the chief article of value).
    Copper and copper products (other than apparatus and machines).
    Nickel, zinc, and tin, and products of.
    Vegetable and animal oils.
    Artificial or chemical fertilizers.
    Wood and manufactures of wood.
    Meats and meat products.
    Candles.
    Tin and manufactures of.
    Horses, mules, asses.
    Swine, sheep, and goats.
    Hides, skins, and leather.
    Glue, lard, and bristles.
    Rubber manufactures, etc.
Reduction of 25 per cent:
    Earthen and stone ware.
    Salted, pickled, and preserved fish.
    Glassware.
    Iron and steel products (except machinery and cutlery).
    Spirits, etc.
Reduction of 30 per cent:
    Breadstuffs.
    Chemicals and medicines.
    Cotton and cotton goods.
    Window glass.
    Boots and shoes.
    Cutlery.
    Butter.
    Turpentine, paints, and colors.
    Bottled malt liquors.
    Canned vegetables, etc.
    Paints, etc.
Reduction of 40 per cent:
    Cattle (except for breeding).
    Watches.
    Chinaware and porcelain.
    Canned fruits and nuts.
    Cheese.
    Silk and silk manufactures.
    Wool and woolens.
    Toilet and fancy soaps.
    Rice, etc.

Cuba granted to the United States no reduction from her duties on tobacco and tobacco manufactures. In Article VIII of the treaty it was stipulated that the reductions should not be extended to any other countries. In the same article it was provided that during the continuance of the treaty no Cuban sugar should be admitted to the United States at a rate of duty lower by more than 20 per cent than the duty imposed by the tariff act of 1897, and no sugar from countries other than Cuba should be admitted by treaty or convention into the United States at a lower rate of duty than that provided by the act of 1897. The proviso in Article VIII containing these stipulations in respect to the duties on sugar was abrogated and repealed by Section IV–B of the United States tariff act of 1913. With this exception, the agreement has been in force continuously since 1903.

SECOND TREATY WITH CUBA.

In addition to this treaty, which was concerned with commercial adjustments, another treaty with Cuba had been negotiated while the commercial treaty was in process of ratification. This second treaty, signed May 22, 1903, stated the conditions under which American military authority might be withdrawn from or be reinstated in the island; its provisions embodied the principles of the Platt amendment to the Army appropriation bill of March 2, 1901.[1] The original discussions of the amendment had contemplated a commercial as well as a political arrangement with Cuba; but the treaty of 1903 was solely political in its character. Nevertheless it had an influence upon Cuban industry and commerce no less important than that exercised by the commercial convention of the previous year. After making provision for the assurance of Cuban independence, it proceeds:

The Government of Cuba consents that the United States may exercise the right to intervene for the preservation of Cuban independence, the maintenance of a government adequate for the protection of life, property, and individual liberty * * *

Ratifications were exchanged July 1, 1903, and the treaty was proclaimed on July 2, 1904. It is important to recognize that without this guarantee of public order assuring labor and capital the enjoyment of the fruits of industry, the great commercial development which has subsequently occurred in the Island would have been impossible. This assurance of protection has resulted in the investment of large amounts of foreign capital in Cuba, has made possible the development of the natural resources of the Island, and has aided in the creation of a large and profitable foreign trade and a body of taxable wealth which, through the public income thereby provided, enables the authorities more easily to fulfill their obligation to maintain an efficient government. The United States has greatly profited by the opportunity for profitable investment of capital in Cuba. To be sure, the establishment of order opened up a field for investment to all foreign capital; but the proximity of Cuba to the American market, the American preference for many Cuban products, the ease with which developments could be supervised because of the frequent sailings and the short transit period, have all contributed to give American investments a position of growing importance.

---

[1] U. S. Statutes, Vol. 31, pp. 897–898.

TREATY BETWEEN CUBA AND ITALY.

The only other commercial treaty entered into by Cuba has been that concluded on December 29, 1903, with Italy.[1] This treaty guaranteed reciprocal "most-favored-nation" treatment, but Article XXVIII contains the following special stipulation: "It is understood that the provisions laid down in the foregoing articles do not cover the cases in which Cuba may grant special reductions on its customs duties to the produce of other American States. Consequently, such concessions can not be claimed by Italy on the grounds of its being the most favored nation, except when they be granted to another State which is not American." This clause is similar to those found in several Latin-American treaties by which there is reserved the right to make special agreements with neighboring States, or with any States of Latin America. Under the interpretation of the "most-favored-nation" clause adopted by the United States, an express statement of the right to make special agreements of this sort would be unnecessary.[2] Its presence in this treaty permits of no question being raised concerning Cuba's freedom to enter into such agreements.

THE PRESENT TARIFF SYSTEM OF CUBA.

The existing tariff system of Cuba is founded upon a law of 1897 enacted by the Spanish authorities. This law originally granted the minimum duties only to the imports from Spain. On August 8, 1898, the President of the United States made a radical change in the system by a proclamation extending the minimum rates to imports from all countries into such Cuban ports as were then in possession of the United States. Later proclamations of December 17, 1898, and of March 31, 1900, further modified the measure.[3] After the negotiation of the reciprocity treaty with the United States, Cuba adopted, on January 16, 1904, a surtax law, supplemented by decree on February 1 of the same year. The surtax increased most of the rates of the tariff by 25 or 30 per cent, and operated to enhance the preferential advantages enjoyed by the United States. A tariff system thus built up of Spanish, American, and Cuban contributions is naturally complicated. Upon dutiable imports from the United States there are imposed at the present time the rates of the tariff of 1900 as modified by subsequent decrees, plus the surtax rates, and minus the reductions provided for by the reciprocity treaty. Compared with many Caribbean tariffs the Cuban system contains, in addition to specific rates, a large number of *ad valorem* duties; there were very few of these in the old Spanish tariffs, and their appearance in the present system is due to American influence. There are only a few instances of compound specific and *ad valorem* charges.

THE INFLUENCE OF RECIPROCITY UPON CUBAN TRADE WITH THE UNITED STATES.

Skepticism as to the probable effect of the treaty.—At the time when the reciprocity agreement of 1902 was being negotiated, many persons in close touch with Cuban commercial affairs believed that

---

[1] Convenios y Tratados Celebrados por la Republica de Cuba desde, 1903 a 1908, Habana, 1908, p. 135.
[2] See Part II, p. 392, infra.
[3] There have been many subsequent modifications of individual rates by decree: See Tariff Series No. 27, U. S. Department of Commerce and Labor.

the treaty would not materially affect either the distribution of the staple Cuban exports or the sources of the Cuban imports. The major portion of the Cuban export trade already found its market in the United States; and it did not appear likely that great benefits would be derived from increasing the share of the Cuban imports contributed by the United States. Even the supporters of the treaty, it will be recalled, placed but little emphasis upon its possible commercial results. In 1902 Gen. Bliss, the collector of customs at Habana, expressed the opinion in a report that the preference would not be capable of producing any great increase in the trade between the two countries. When the treaty was under discussion in the Cuban Senate, Señores Gamba and Rodrigues, of the Merchants' Union, expressed the opinion that following the ratification of the measure there would not be much falling off of Cuban trade with Europe. To what extent these views proved to be correct will be shown by a statistical examination 'of the trade during the past quarter century, and particularly since 1900.

Method of procedure in studying effects of reciprocity.—Any study of trade relations in which it is desired to trace the influence of a single factor, such as a reduction of tariff duties, must be made with great caution, because of the numerous other elements which inevitably enter into the problem. . In the particular case of Cuban trade it is difficult to find for the purpose of comparison a period, before reciprocity existed, in which Cuban production and trade were subject to the same general conditions as those which prevailed in the period after the conclusion of the treaty. During the period from the close of 1891 to the middle of 1894, an earlier reciprocity arrangement, similar (especially as regards the Cuban imports) to the one under discussion, had been in effect between Cuba and the United States.[1] The years from 1895 to 1899 had been marked by the Revolution and the serious disruption of Cuban economic life. And for several years after 1898 Cuban trade, especially the import trade, was in some degree affected by the occupation of the Island by American military forces, which fact would naturally have the effect of drawing an increased proportion of Cuban imports from the United States. The pre-reciprocity period with which even an approximate comparison can be made is limited to the years 1900 to 1903.

In the presentation of the statistical data for the Cuban-American trade, the exhibit of figures for the trade as a whole will be supplemented by a more detailed analysis of the important commodities composing it and also of groups of commodities. This is desirable because the aggregate values of a trade may reflect the influence of a small number of large values representing commodities which may in a given case be quite independent of tariff conditions. The Cuban study is favored in one respect in that, after·1902 Cuba entered into no other reciprocity agreements, while at the same time the relations between the United States and Cuba's competitors have undergone no important modification through the conclusion of commercial treaties.

The trade in general.—A survey of the total trade between Cuba and the United States from 1888 to 1916 is presented in Chart I.

---

[1] See p. 182 seq, infra.

CHART I.—*Trade of United States with Cuba, 1888 to 1916.*

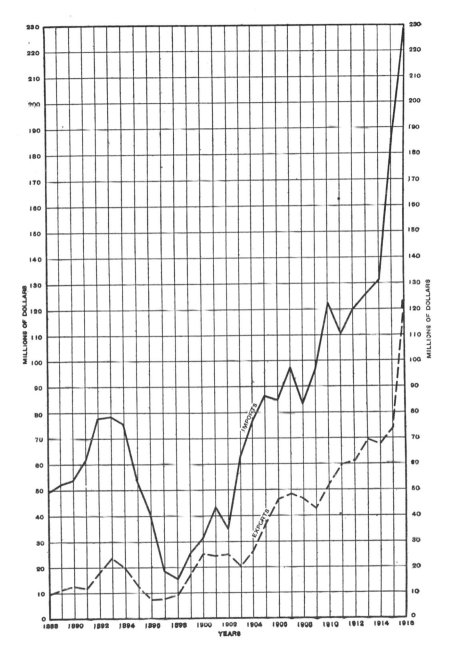

The fact is at once apparent that the United States purchases more from Cuba than Cuba purchases from the United States. The curves, in Chart I, for both the American exports to and imports from Cuba reflect the influence of the earlier reciprocity agreements (in effect from September 1, 1891, to August 27, 1894), and of the second revolution which began early in 1895 and continued for nearly four years. The period from 1904 to 1907 (the fiscal year 1904 being taken as the first year in which the new reciprocity agreement was operative) · shows a decided increase over the preceding period. This is due not alone to reciprocity, but also to the fact that the years immediately preceding the treaty were a period of gradual and halting recovery in Cuban industry. After 1908 there is evident a continued tendency toward increased values in both phases of the trade, with a slight advantage in favor of the American imports.

From Table I it appears that after the conclusion of reciprocity the average share of the United States in both the import and export commerce of Cuba increased.

TABLE I.—AVERAGE ANNUAL IMPORTS OF ALL MERCHANDISE INTO CUBA, BY COUNTRIES, FOR FOUR-YEAR PERIODS, 1900–1914.[1]

[Values expressed in thousands.]

Country from which imported.	1900–1903.		1904–1907		1908–1911		1912–1914 [2]	
	Average value.	Per cent of total.	Average value.	Per cent of total.	Average Value.	Per cent of total.	Average value.	Per cent of total.
United States........	$27,471	42.1	$40,842	46.0	$49,023	50.6	$68,044	53.3
Germany.............	3,303	5.1	5,694	6.4	7,043	7.3	8,442	6.6
Spain...............	9,822	15.1	9,403	10.6	8,343	8.6	9,677	7.6
France..............	3,138	4.8	4,952	5.6	5,429	5.6	6,687	5.2
United Kingdom.....	10,013	15.3	13,405	15.1	15,122	15.6	15,171	11.9
All other............	11,459	17.6	14,470	16.3	11,814	12.3	19,673	15.4
Total imports..	65,206	100.0	88,766	100.0	96,774	100.0	127,694	100.0

AVERAGE ANNUAL EXPORTS OF ALL MERCHANDISE FROM CUBA TO VARIOUS COUNTRIES, 1900–1914.

Country from which imported.	1900–1903.		1904–1907		1908–1911		1912–1914 [2]	
United States........	$44,678	75.3	$87,235	85.5	$104,181	85.8	$130,647	81.3
Germany.............	4,181	7.0	4,092	4.0	4,064	3.3	4,874	3.0
Spain...............	946	1.6	716	.8	769	.6	717	.4
France..............	1,251	2.1	1,173	1.1	1,465	1.2	2,329	1.4
United Kingdom.....	5,664	9.5	5,598	5.5	6,551	5.4	14,991	9.3
All other............	2,601	4.5	3,248	3.1	4,385	3.7	7,150	4.6
Total exports...	59,321	100.0	102,062	100.0	121,416	100.0	160,708	100.0

[1] Cuba: Comercio Exterior.   [2] Three-year period.

In the period 1900–1903 Cuba sent 75.3 per cent of all her exports to the United States; in 1904–1907, 85.5 per cent; in 1908–1911, 85.8 per cent. In 1912–1914 the percentage fell to 81.3 per cent. The average proportion of the Cuban exports sent to the principal European countries declined practically without exception in the two periods following reciprocity. As for the Cuban imports, the average share contributed by the United States has shown constant gains, rising in the same period from 42.1 to 46 per cent, then to 50.6 per cent, and finally to 53.3 per cent of the average imports. The figures for 1915 and 1916, while interesting as showing how the trade has been affected by the great war, are of no positive value in the study of reciprocity and may therefore be omitted from the discussion. The data for individual years are presented in Tables II and III.

TABLE II.—TOTAL IMPORTS OF MERCHANDISE INTO CUBA FROM PRINCIPAL COUNTRIES, 1900–1916.[1]

[Expressed in thousands.]

Year.	From all countries.	From United States.	From Germany.	From Spain.	From France.	From United Kingdom
1900	$71,681	$30,087	$2,630	$11,008	$3,600	$11,955
1901	65,107	28,136	3,403	9,536	2,923	9,281
1902	65,204	28,020	3,456	9,483	3,054	9,585
1903	58,831	23,640	3,724	9,262	2,974	9,232
1904	70,155	28,659	4,642	8,940	3,844	12,494
1905	83,843	37,686	5,107	9,737	4,619	12,500
1906	104,395	48,830	6,593	10,647	5,564	14,987
1907	96,668	48,192	6,433	8,286	5,781	13,639
1908	96,993	46,450	7,762	8,816	5,854	14,550
1909	83,856	42,612	6,350	7,239	4,793	20,639
1910	98,239	49,955	6,850	8,825	5,530	12,539
1911	108,006	57,075	7,208	8,489	5,538	12,758
1912	118,970	62,441	7,533	9,464	6,543	14,833
1913	132,289	70,705	9,515	9,412	6,580	16,097
1914	131,821	70,985	8,275	10,155	6,937	14,581
1915	122,810	74,052	2,218	10,224	3,840	14,098
1916	171,809	120,378	64	12,100	5,358	15,684

[1] Cuba: Comercio Exterior.

PERCENTAGES OF TOTAL CUBAN IMPORTS FROM PRINCIPAL COUNTRIES, 1900–1916.

Year.	United States.	Germany.	Spain	France.	United Kingdom
1900	41.96	3.66	15.35	5.02	16.67
1901	43.21	5.22	14.64	4.48	14.25
1902	42.97	5.30	14.54	4.68	14.70
1903	40.18	6.33	15.74	5.05	15.69
1904	40.84	6.61	12.74	5.49	17.80
1905	44.95	6.09	11.61	5.50	14.90
1906	46.77	6.30	10.18	5.32	14.34
1907	49.85	6.66	8.57	5.98	14.11
1908	47.89	8.00	9.09	6.04	15.00
1909	50.81	7.57	8.63	5.72	24.61
1910	50.85	6.97	8.98	5.63	12.76
1911	52.84	6.67	7.86	5.13	11.81
1912	52.47	6.33	7.95	5.50	12.47
1913	53.44	7.10	7.11	4.97	12.17
1914	53.86	6.28	7.71	5.26	11.06
1915	60.30	1.81	8.33	3.13	11.48
1916	70.07	.04	7.04	3.12	9.13

TABLE III.—TOTAL EXPORTS OF MERCHANDISE FROM CUBA TO PRINCIPAL COUNTRIES, 1900–1916.

[Expressed in thousands.]

Year.	To all countries.	To United States.	To United Kingdom.	To Germany.	To Spain.	To France.
1900	$45,229	$34,622	$4,345	$2,298	$818	$1,156
1901	63,133	45,508	5,881	6,722	579	1,402
1902	51,074	35,828	5,994	3,939	1,238	1,324
1903	77,849	62,758	6,434	3,766	1,150	1,120
1904	93,122	77,100	5,884	5,144	1,001	1,188
1905	99,161	84,717	6,189	3,782	682	922
1906	105,199	88,981	5,869	4,309	768	1,580
1907	110,764	98,141	4,446	3,130	413	1,002
1908	97,447	81,715	5,145	3,741	795	1,768
1909	115,637	99,973	4,959	4,484	1,017	1,296
1910	144,036	122,198	11,014	4,336	537	1,389
1911	128,542	112,834	5,086	3,691	725	1,405
1912	140,787	122,909	11,066	3,689	480	2,509
1913	165,207	132,581	15,663	6,497	690	1,825
1914	170,129	136,388	18,242	4,436	980	2,651
1915	214,913	182,962	24,218	644	1,475	854
1916	301,954	229,859	52,138	....	2,418	8,306

PERCENTAGES OF TOTAL CUBAN EXPORTS SENT TO PRINCIPAL COUNTRIES, 1900-1916.

Year.	To United States.	To United Kingdom.	To Germany.	To Spain.	To France.
1900	76.54	9.60	5.08	1.80	2.55
1901	72.07	9.31	10.64	.91	2.20
1902	70.13	11.73	7.71	2.42	2.59
1903	80.61	8.26	4.83	1.47	1.43
1904	82.80	6.32	5.52	1.09	1.28
1905	85.43	6.24	3.81	.69	.93
1906	84.58	5.58	4.10	.73	1.50
1907	88.57	4.01	2.83	.37	.90
1908	83.85	5.28	3.84	.82	1.82
1909	86.48	4.29	3.88	.88	1.12
1910	84.83	7.65	3.01	.37	.96
1911	87.77	3.96	2.87	.56	1.09
1912	83.77	7.54	2.51	.33	1.71
1913	80.25	9.48	3.93	.42	1.10
1914	80.16	10.72	2.61	.58	1.56
1915	85.13	11.27	.30	.69	.40
1916	76.12	17.27	....	.80	2.75

INDIVIDUAL ARTICLES IMPORTED FROM CUBA.

The chief export products of Cuba are raw cane sugar, tobacco and its manufactures, fruits, cabinet woods, molasses, and iron ore. All of these articles, except leaf and manufactured tobacco and molasses, have long been shipped almost exclusively to the United States; hence, reciprocity could be of but limited influence in changing the distribution of Cuban exports. Moreover, little is to be gained, except in the case of sugar, from a calculation of the proportion of the total United States imports coming from Cuba, since the commodities are mainly specialties, the values of which are relatively small and easily affected by extraneous circumstances. And of the fruits exported by Cuba the most important—bananas—were not properly a reciprocity article, inasmuch as bananas from all countries have been admitted into the United States free of duty. The same would apply to pineapples prior to 1909, when a very low duty was placed upon them. Thus the usual methods of studying the effects of reciprocity can properly be applied to only a small number of the important American imports from Cuba, and to these attention will be mainly directed.

THE SUGAR TRADE.

The reduction of 20 per cent in the duties on Cuba sugar was the most important of the American concessions in the treaty. Most of the sugar imported from Cuba grades approximately 95° polariscope test. Sugar of this grade paid a duty of 1.65 cents per pound under the tariff acts of 1897 and 1909 and the reduction on Cuban 95° sugar amounted to 0.33 cent. All raw sugar, however, is bought and sold on a 96° polariscope basis, and the most useful price quotations are also on that basis. For the purposes of this investigation, it will therefore be convenient to make all calculations refer to 96° sugar. Under the tariff acts of 1897 and 1909, 96° sugar paid a duty of 1.685 cents, and the reduction on Cuban 96° sugar therefore amounted to 0.337 cent. Since March 1, 1914, the general duty on 96° sugar has been 1.256 cents, and the reduction on Cuban sugar 0.2512 cent. As this reduced duty was in effect for only a few months prior to the outbreak of the war, there will be little occasion to refer to it in this report.

TABLE IV.—*Exports of raw sugar from Cuba, 1900–1917.*[1]

Year.	Total.	To the United States.	
		Quantity.	Per cent of total.
	Pounds.	*Pounds.*	
1900	696,283,249	696,159,715	99.98
1901	1,121,027,008	1,120,915,937	99.99
1902	1,020,594,994	1,020,544,317	99.99
1903	2,348,250,038	2,308,883,557	98.32
1904	2,811,179,575	2,799,720,733	99.59
1905	1,968,761,285	1,968,700,177	99.99
1906	2,787,035,583	2,777,094,209	99.64
1907	3,111,350,864	3,097,887,850	99.57
1908	2,168,259,307	2,168,252,685	99.99
1909	2,861,120,758	2,860,969,029	99.00
1910	3,655,469,213	3,445,731,365	94.26
1911	3,311,638,408	3,307,515,646	99.88
1912	3,546,603,593	3,285,417,936	92.64
1913	4,886,430,625	4,407,168,288	90.19
1914	5,672,756,583	4,920,658,845	86.74
1915	5,299,183,789	4,693,975,251	88.58
1916	6,746,622,964	5,146,896,503	76.29
1917	6,122,086,016	4,696,703,147	76.72

[1] Cuba: Comercio Exterior.

Prior to reciprocity, in years when conditions were not unusual, all of the surplus sugar of Cuba was exported to the United States. The reciprocity arrangement did not result in any diversion to the United States of sugar which but for reciprocity would have gone elsewhere. It created no new source of supply for the American market, for even without specially favorable treatment the United States was the most advantageous market for Cuban sugar. On the other hand, there have been in every year since 1910, with but one exception, fairly substantial exports of sugar from Cuba to countries other than the United States.

TABLE V-A.—IMPORTS OF SUGAR INTO THE UNITED STATES, 1900–1916.

[In thousands of pounds.]

Fiscal year.	Total imports of sugar.	From Cuba.[1]		From noncontiguous territories of the United States.[2]		From all other countries, paying full duty.	
		Amount.	Per cent of total.	Amount.	Per cent of total.	Amount.	Per cent of total.
1900	4,018,087	705,456	17.55	626,762	15.60	2,685,869	66.85
1901	4,803,088	1,099,404	22.86	832,773	17.34	2,870,911	59.80
1902	3,936,286	984,217	25.00	915,794	23.27	2,036,275	51.73
1903	5,217,077	2,396,498	45.93	1,019,742	19.55	1,800,837	34.52
1904	4,696,348	2,819,558	60.04	1,057,294	22.51	819,496	17.45
1905	4,784,974	2,057,684	42.99	1,182,038	24.70	1,545,252	32.31
1906	5,136,479	2,781,901	54.26	1,226,521	23.93	1,128,057	21.81
1907	5,621,005	3,236,466	57.58	1,254,330	22.31	1,130,209	20.11
1908	4,918,773	2,309,189	46.94	1,585,184	32.23	1,024,400	20.83
1909	5,700,675	2,862,260	50.21	1,594,965	27.98	1,243,450	21.81
1910	5,774,098	3,509,658	60.78	1,855,504	32.13	408,936	7.09
1911	5,594,985	3,347,606	59.83	1,887,402	33.74	359,977	6.43
1912	6,044,323	3,186,634	52.72	2,375,325	39.30	482,364	7.98
1913	6,590,787	4,311,782	65.42	2,053,944	31.17	225,061	3.41
1914	6,822,781	4,926,606	72.21	1,872,752	27.45	23,423	.34
1915	7,290,730	4,784,888	65.63	2,196,629	30.13	309,213	4.24
1916	7,619,878	5,150,852	67.59	2,204,114	28.93	264,912	3.48

[1] 20 per cent preference since Dec. 17, 1903.
[2] Duty free from Hawaii and Porto Rico; 25 per cent reduction from the Philippines until 1909, free, since 1909.

[In thousands of pounds.]

Fiscal year.	Total.	Cane sugar from the Dutch East Indies.	Cane sugar from the West Indies other than Cuba and Porto Rico.	Beet sugar mainly from Europe.	Sugar above No. 16 Dutch standard from various sources.	All other.
1900	2,685,869	1,162,203	347,730	701,539	11,459	462,938
1901	2,870,911	777,987	360,051	908,683	109,737	714,453
1902	2,036,275	636,710	322,653	255,030	91,093	730,789
1903	1,800,837	891,758	347,046	87,130	53,342	421,561
1904	819,496	440,370	186,524	2,414	16,305	173,883
1905	1,545,252	899,395	202,639	233,945	22,802	186,471
1906	1,119,057	781,892	151,477	48,549	9,177	127,962
1907	1,130,209	448,680	113,084	397,745	7,585	163,115
1908	1,024,400	589,680	142,143	221,037	6,938	64,602
1909	1,243,450	916,858	95,747	98,626	5,874	126,345
1910	408,936	314,851	20,078	1	6,107	67,889
1911	359,977	228,079	28,021	24,669	4,203	75,005
1912	482,364	340,396	41,289	6,504	5,984	88,191
1913	225,061	12,760	3,930	182,648	3,344	22,379
1914	23,423	....	4,519	3,368	(1)	15,736
1915	309,213	22	97,988	878	(1)	210,325
1916	264,912	32	111,076	2	(1)	153,802

[1] Not separately enumerated since 1914.

The imports of sugar from Cuba have always been an important portion of the total imports into the United States. Imports from Cuba have increased greatly under reciprocity. Since 1906 they have formed more than half the total imports of sugar into the continental United States in every year but one. The imports from the non-contiguous territories, under the stimulus of the favored treatment which they enjoy, have likewise shown great increases. As a consequence, the amount of the full-duty-paying imports has been undergoing rapid diminution. In the three years immediately preceding reciprocity, they averaged, excluding the Cuban imports, 48 per cent of the total imports; in the three years following reciprocity they averaged only 24 per cent. In 1910 they fell to only 7 per cent of the total imports, and since that year they have never risen above 8 per cent. By 1913 they had fallen to a little over 3 per cent, and in 1914 they had practically disappeared.[1]

Not only have the full-duty-paying imports been under reciprocity a small and rapidly diminishing fraction of the total sugar imports, but in each year, and especially since 1909, the bulk of the favored sugars has come in during a period of the year when there are no substantial imports of full-duty sugar. Java has been the most important source of imports of full-duty sugars, and the imports of Javan sugar have been confined mainly to the months from August to December. The full-duty-paying beet sugar from Europe has also been imported mainly in the latter half of each year. During the first half of each year practically all of the sugar imports have been from Cuba. In the early years of reciprocity, it is true, there continued to be substantial imports from other West Indian islands, and these sugars are available for import at about the same time of the year as Cuban sugars. But it is significant that the imports of the former exhibited a pronounced decrease in 1904, the first year of Cuban reciprocity. From 1909 to the outbreak of the war in 1914

[1] The figures of imports are for fiscal years.

very little full-duty-paying West Indian sugar was imported. During the first six months of the year Cuban sugar dominates the American market. It is in this period of the year that the bulk of the domestic sugar is offered for sale. If the preference to Cuban sugar inures to the benefit mainly of the Cuban producer, the amount of protection to the domestic producers, including the producers in the noncontiguous territories, is not reduced by Cuban reciprocity. On the other hand, if the reduction of duty on Cuban sugar results in a reduction of price to the American purchaser of raw sugar, the protection to the American producer is reduced by a corresponding amount.

Sugar prices in New York compared with sugar prices at Hamburg in different months of the year.—A comparison of the prices—and especially of the relative fluctuations in the prices—of sugar in an important foreign market on the one hand and in New York on the other, if carried back to a period antecedent to Cuban reciprocity, should aid in determining the extent, if any, to which reciprocity resulted in a change in the relation of the American to the world price of sugar. For the purpose of such a comparison the best available price data are the quotations of Willett & Gray for 96° centrifugal cane sugar in New York and the reports by the same firm of the London quotations for 88 per cent analysis beet sugar f. o. b. Hamburg. The last-named sugar is inferior to 96° centrifugal cane sugar in refining value. The two sugars are consequently not altogether comparable. But the variations from year to year in the allowances which would have to be made for the 88 per cent analysis beet sugar to bring it to parity with 96° centrifugal cane sugar would be so small as to render calculation thereof unnecessary at this point in the investigation.[1]

In Chart II the average excess, in different months of the year, of the New York price for 96° centrifugal sugar over the Hamburg price for 88 per cent analysis beet sugar—no allowance being made for the difference in grades—is charted for three separate periods. In the period 1901 to 1903, which was prior to reciprocity, there was no marked difference at different seasons of the year between the relations of the New York price to the Hamburg—or world—price. The excess of the New York over the Hamburg price was in this period greatest during months in which Cuban sugar came upon the market. In the second period, from 1904 to 1909, Cuban sugar was admitted at a reduced rate, but the full-duty-paying imports were still a substantial fraction of the total imports. During this period the average excess of the New York over the Hamburg price was less throughout the year than in the first period. Furthermore, there was, in this period, a pronounced difference between the average amount of the excess of the New York price over the Hamburg price in the months from July to November—when most of the full-duty-paying imports entered—and the average amount of the excess in the remainder of the year —when Cuban sugar dominated the market. Relative to the Hamburg price the New York price was much lower during the months when there were substantial imports of Cuban sugar than in the remainder of the year. In the third period, 1910 to 1913, the imports of full-duty sugar were small, and in each year they had a significant influence on price only for a few weeks during the late summer when sugar from other sources was scarce. In this period

---

[1] See page 332, infra.

the price levels showed tendencies similar to those of the second
period, but more pronounced.   The excess of the New York over the
Hamburg price was much lower throughout most of the year than
it had been in the previous periods; there was a greater variation in
the amount of the excess of the New York over the Hamburg price
between the months of heavy Cuban imports and the months when
the full-duty-paying imports came in; and the average period of
relatively high excess of the New York over the Hamburg price—
the period when full-duty-paying imports were an important factor

CHART II.—*Monthly average excess of New York price of 96° centrifugal sugar over
the Hamburg price of 88 per cent analysis beet sugar. Averaged for the periods 1901
to 1903; 1904 to 1909; 1910 to 1913.*

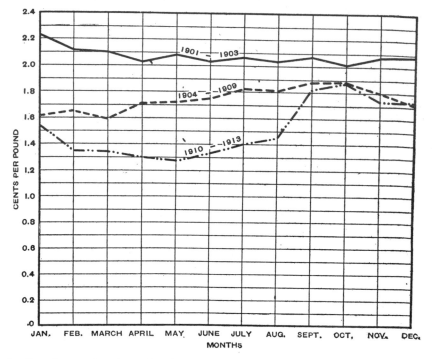

in the determination of price—was much shorter in this than in the
two preceding periods.

The data exhibited in this chart indicate that during the months
when Cuban sugar dominated the market, a substantial portion
of the reduction of duty established by reciprocity inured to the
benefit of the American consumer.   They also indicate both that the
share of the reduction which went to the American consumer was
greater, and that the period of the year during which the American
price was on the basis of the Cuban duty was longer, in the years
after 1909, when there were only small full-duty-paying imports,
than in the years 1904 to 1909, when the full-duty-paying imports
constituted a larger share of the total imports.

NEW YORK PRICES AND "HAMBURG PARITY."

Chart III[1] presents confirmatory evidence. In this chart there is shown by weeks, for the period from 1900 to the outbreak of the war in 1914, the relation of the New York price of 96° centrifugal sugar to "Hamburg parity"—or the equivalent, in cents per pound for 96° centrifugal, after allowances have been made for the difference in grades, of the price at which 88 per cent analysis Hamburg beet sugar can be laid down in New York with the duty paid.[2]

As long as there were substantial imports of European beet sugar, the New York price of sugar was based on the Hamburg price (itself determined at London, the ruling market) and normally was approximately equal to Hamburg parity in New York. The freight from Hamburg to New York is generally about the same as the freight from Hamburg to London. If the customs duties of both countries be disregarded, the London price would under these conditions be equal to the New York price. But the freight from Cuba to New York is substantially less than the freight from Cuba to London. As a consequence, when the New York price was equal to Hamburg parity, the New York bid for Cuban sugar f. o. b. Havana would be higher than the London bid.[3]

Prior to 1903 it had been necessary every year, at least for many years, to import European beet sugar in order to meet the American demand. In 1903, on the other hand, the domestic production of cane and beet sugar, the imports from the favored possessions of the United States, and the Cuban exportable surplus were all unusually large and, together with the imports from Java and the British West Indies, were much more than sufficient to satisfy the American demand at a price equivalent to Hamburg parity. As a consequence, the American price fell below Hamburg parity. As has been indicated, a fall below Hamburg parity would result in the diversion of Cuban exports to London only if great enough completely to offset the advantages in regard to freight rates which the New York market offered, compared with the London market, for Cuban sugar. In the spring of 1903 this was the case—for the first time in twenty years—and as a consequence there were Cuban sales to London and there were practically no imports of beet sugar into the United States.[4] (See Tables IV and V).

---

[1] Facing p. 335, infra.

[2] The following illustration of the method by which Hamburg parity is calculated is taken from Willett & Gray, Oct. 3, 1912, p. 395:

Parity of 88 per cent analysis beet and 96° polarization cane sugar, duty paid, without bounty or countervailing duty; exchange at $4.88 per pound sterling. When beet is quoted by London at 9s. per hundredweight (112 pounds) f. o. b. Hamburg, add 7½d. for freight and lighterage to refinery— Cents.

say 9s. 7½d. net per hundredweight c. and f. to New York	2.098
Insurance, bank commission, lost weight, together with 1½ per cent	.031
Duty (88 per cent analysis outturn, 94° polarization)	1.615
Difference in value to refiners between beet and cane	.19

Beet, 88 per cent f. o. b. Hamburg, parity of centrifugals, 96° at New York, per pound 3.934

[3] When the New York price was equal to Hamburg parity, the amount of the excess of the New York over the London bid for Cuban sugar would be equal to freight Havana to London minus freight Havana to New York. It would be profitable to export Cuban sugar to England only when the New York price fell below Hamburg parity by the amount of freight Havana to London minus freight Havana to New York. As a result of the differences in freight costs, there would be no exports to London from Cuba when there were imports into New York from Hamburg, and there would be no imports into New York from Hamburg when there were exports from Cuba to London. It is assumed here that freight Hamburg to New York is equal to freight Hamburg to London.

[4] This indicates that in 1903 the New York price, minus freight from Havana to New York, was as low as, or lower than, the Hamburg price, plus freight Hamburg to London minus freight Havana to London, i. e., the New York bid for Cuban sugar f. o. b. Havana was as low as, or lower than, the London bid, allowance being made, of course, for differences in grade between Hamburg beet and Cuban cane sugars.

A fall in the price of sugar below Hamburg parity is not conclusive evidence, therefore, that the price of sugar to the American consumer is lower than it would have been in the absence of Cuban reciprocity. It may merely indicate conditions in the American market of supply in relation to demand which result in there accruing to the American consumer instead of to the Cuban producer the principal gain from the lower cost of transportation from Havana to New York as compared with the cost from Havana to London. In 1903, there were, as has been shown, some exports of sugar from Cuba to London. The average amount (0.36 cent) by which the New York price was below Hamburg parity from February to May, 1903, may be taken as approximately the maximum possible amount of excess of Hamburg parity over the New York price under equal tariff treatment of the European and Cuban sugar, and with shipping costs on the various trade routes remaining as they were in 1903. If the New York price had fallen below this point, Cuban sugar would have been diverted to London until the New York price rose again.

Under reciprocity, the New York price may fall to a point more than 0.36 cent below Hamburg parity, to the amount by which the duty on Cuban sugar is less than the duty on German sugar, i. e., 0.337 cent until March 1, 1914, 0.2512 cent since March 1, 1914. This makes the lowest possible New York price under Cuban reciprocity equal to 0.697 cent below Hamburg parity under the tariff acts of 1897 and 1909 and to 0.61 cent per pound since March 1, 1914, under the tariff act of 1913. Not until this point is reached will Cuban sugar be diverted to London. This statement, however, requires some qualification. It is based on the assumption, as stated above, that freight rates and other expenses incidental to transportation have remained constant since 1903. In fact, these charges had increased even prior to the war, and in the years preceding the outbreak of the war the freight advantage in favor of Cuban sugar was somewhat over 0.36 cent per pound. The New York price under normal conditions could therefore fall below Hamburg parity prior to March 1, 1914, by somewhat over 0.697 cent and since March 1, 1914, by somewhat over 0.61 cent. During short periods of time, moreover, and especially if shipping conditions from Cuba to Europe should be unfavorable, the Cuban exporters would accept bids below what would be for them a profitable basis during longer periods. With the Cuban sales organization and shipping schedules adapted to the prospective marketing of the Cuban sugar crop in the United States, the sudden transfer to another market would always involve inconvenience and costs, and these considerations would lead to the acceptance by Cuban exporters of what might otherwise be considered unacceptable bids for their sugar. On the other hand, the New York bids are often out of harmony with the Cuban offers and at such times the New York market quotations may be merely nominal, no business being done at the quoted prices. Nevertheless, the length of the period in 1910 during which the New York quotations were exceeded by Hamburg parity by approximately 0.90 cent indicates that with shipping costs as they were prior to the war the New York price of sugar could fall below Hamburg parity by at least 0.90 cent per pound, without diverting Cuban shipments to London.

When the New York price under Cuban reciprocity is lower than Hamburg parity by more than 0.36 cent, it is safe to conclude that the American consumer is getting a portion of the remitted duty on

The average proportion increased in the second period (1904–1907), but this was due to an unusually high value in a single year. Molasses is a commercial product to a less degree than sugar; and the market for it in Cuba is not as completely organized as in some of the other producing localities. Moreover, the improvement of refining technique in Cuba, whereby more of the sugar content is removed from the molasses, has lowered the quality of Cuban molasses and the demand for it in the United States has declined correspondingly.

TOBACCO AND TOBACCO PRODUCTS.

The tobacco trade occupies the second place in value among the commodities which Cuba furnishes to the United States. The effect of reciprocity upon a commodity such as leaf tobacco cannot be satisfactorily determined because the tobaccos from different regions are regarded as being more or less distinct varieties. The share contributed by Cuba to the total imports of tobacco into the United States would, therefore, be of no significance. The values of the leaf imported from Cuba have increased steadily and with no indication of any stimulus due to reciprocity (Table VII–A). The distribution of the Cuban exports of leaf tobacco, on the other hand, gives a somewhat more trustworthy view of the situation; but the figures in Table VII–B show only moderate gains in the percentage of the Cuban exports of leaf sent to the United States after the conclusion of reciprocity.

TABLE VII–A.—IMPORTS OF LEAF TOBACCO INTO THE UNITED STATES, 1900–1916.[1]

[In thousands of dollars.]

Year.	From all countries.	From Cuba.	From Netherlands.	From Turkey.	From Germany.
1900	$13,297	$7,615	$4,569	$275	$138
1901	16,290	9,834	5,609	293	166
1902	15,211	8,578	4,835	1,176	289
1903	17,234	9,967	4,355	1,766	547
1904	16,939	9,793	5,251	735	438
1905	18,038	10,825	5,024	1,044	579
1906	22,447	13,510	6,235	1,258	994
1907	26,055	13,590	8,270	2,428	1,272
1908	22,870	13,114	6,157	2,105	1,170
1909	25,400	15,797	5,073	2,049	1,134
1910	27,751	14,128	6,222	4,309	2,067
1911	27,857	14,203	6,180	6,392	497
1912	31,918	14,705	7,835	8,596	234
1913	35,933	16,295	8,038	10,086	753
1914	35,032	16,385	7,461	9,837	212
1915	27,160	11,259	9,027	5,398	73
1916	24,629	12,109	7,080	38	....

[1] U. S. Commerce and Navigation.

TABLE VII-B.—CUBAN EXPORTS OF UNMANUFACTURED TOBACCO, 1900–1916.[1]

[In thousands of dollars.]

Year	To all countries.	To United States.	Per cent to United States.	Average per cent to United States.
1900	$9,720	$8,395	86.3	
1901	16,055	10,690	66.5	
1902	11,556	9,261	80.1	
1903	12,655	10,744	85.0	
				78.2
1904	12,088	9,137	75.6	
1905	12,651	11,113	87.8	
1906	15,753	13,778	87.5	
1907	15,496	14,585	94.1	
				86.8
1908	16,006	14,083	88.0	
1909	20,073	16,486	82.1	
1910	17,789	14,626	82.2	
1911	16,889	14,319	84.8	
				84.1
1912	17,396	14,954	86.0	
1913	21,650	16,251	75.1	
1914	19,007	16,011	84.2	
				81.3
1915	14,637	11,469	78.3	
1916	16,264	12,567	77.3	

[1] Cuba: Comercio Exterior.

In the field of tobacco manufactures—cigars, cigarettes, and cheroots—Cuba had almost a monopoly of the American import market even before the reciprocity period (Table VIII–A). For more than a decade since 1903 imports of Cuban tobacco goods have remained practically unchanged. The free admission into the United States of Philippine tobacco products after 1909 added considerably to the total imports, but did not do so at the expense of the imports from Cuba. The proportion of the Cuban exports of all varieties of tobacco manufactures shipped to the United States (Table VIII–B) has shown some tendency to increase, but not sufficiently to permit the conclusion that the treaty was the leading cause. In general, the tobacco trade can not be said to afford positive evidence of the working of reciprocity.

TABLE VIII-A.—IMPORTS OF CIGARS, CIGARETTES, AND CHEROOTS INTO THE UNITED STATES, 1900–1916.[1]

[In thousands of dollars.]

Year.	From all countries.	From Cuba.	From United Kingdom.	From Egypt.	From Philippine Islands.[2]
1900	$2,299	$2,185	$74	$4	$1
1901	2,401	2,292	59	7	14
1902	2,411	2,317	56	4	6
1903	3,271	3,175	49	9	8
1904	3,054	2,970	40	12	6
1905	4,028	3,931	55	10	2
1906	4,031	3,964	25	11	4
1907	3,995	3,889	28	47	3
1908	4,245	4,163	19	40	1
1909	3,519	3,460	20	18	2
1910	5,581	3,829	24	25	1,665
1911	5,212	4,218	24	23	921
1912	5,291	3,882	17	22	1,339
1913	7,753	4,000	25	25	2,327
1914	5,193	3,684	25	26	1,385
1915	4,368	2,978	20	29	1,318
1916	4,815	3,349	19	27	1,383

[1] U. S. Commerce and Navigation   [2] Free after Aug. 6, 1909.

TABLE VIII–B.—CUBAN EXPORTS OF ALL MANUFACTURED TOBACCO, 1900–1916.[1]

[In thousands of dollars.]

Year.	To all countries.	To United States.	Per cent to United States.	Average per cent to United States.
1900	$11,992	$4,539	37.5	
1901	12,853	2,586	20.1	
1902	13,091	2,544	19.4	
1903	12,821	3,234	25.2	
				25.4
1904	12,718	3,055	24.0	
1905	14,141	3,899	27.6	
1906	15,851	4,583	28.9	
1907	13,426	4,932	36.7	
				29.3
1908	15,273	4,522	29.6	
1909	12,939	3,767	29.1	
1910	12,370	4,021	32.5	
1911	13,099	4,311	32.9	
				31.0
1912	13,061	3,863	29.6	
1913	13,914	3,994	28.7	
1914	13,773	3,924	28.5	
				28.9
1915	8,312	3,071	36.9	
1916	9,495	3,411	35.9	

[1] Cuba: Comercio Exterior.

IRON ORE: MAHOGANY.

Although sugar and tobacco constitute over 90 per cent of the American imports from Cuba, one or two of the leading miscellaneous articles may be briefly considered. Of the total imports of iron ore into the United States, Cuba provides over 50 per cent (Table IX). All of the Cuban product goes to the United States. One steel plant near Baltimore relies wholly upon Cuban ore, and other plants near Philadelphia use it to a considerable extent. The proportionate supply from Cuba increased at a rapid rate until 1910; the United States tariff act of 1909 reduced the duty on iron ore to a very nominal rate so that other ore producing countries thereafter found it possible to increase their exports to the United States. It must be noted, however, that iron ores imported from other sources than Cuba are for the most part of a different variety, especially in regard to phosphorus content. Furthermore, the value of the imports of Cuban ore began to increase in a marked degree several years before reciprocity became effective. In any case the Cuban iron ore trade is not quantitatively important and represents another case of a specialized commodity, the commerce in which is relatively independent of tariff duties.

No definite effect of reciprocity is apparent in the case of mahogany, the leading cabinet wood which Cuba supplies to the United States. The imports of mahogany into the United States from Cuba have decreased both in absolute amounts and in relation to total imports (Table X).

TABLE IX.—IMPORTS OF IRON ORE INTO THE UNITED STATES, 1900–1916.[1]

[Values expressed in thousands.]

Year.	Total value of iron ore imported from all countries.	From Canada.	From Spain.	From New-foundland and Labrador.	From Sweden.	From Cuba.		
						Value.	Per cent of total.	Average per cent of total.
1900	$1,497	$5	$650	$122	....	$479	32.03	....
1901	1,135	76	351	116	....	573	50.40	....
1902	2,362	685	406	72	....	1,109	46.90	....
1903	2,351	320	238	92	....	1,622	68.90	....
								51.5
1904	1,593	283	141	64	....	1,087	68.20	....
1905	1,670	245	252	5	....	1,153	69.00	....
1906	2,728	220	437	35	....	1,952	71.50	....
1907	3,360	52	626	117	$12	2,137	63.60	....
								67.7
1908	2,949	55	355	81	15	2,275	77.10	....
1909	2,714	12	567	102	32	1,915	70.50	....
1910	6,763	97	1,009	385	983	3,997	59.10	....
1911	6,691	264	602	288	1,636	3,665	54.70	....
								62.0
1912	6,119	89	355	309	1,754	3,533	57.70	....
1913	7,035	282	439	238	1,461	4,408	62.60	....
1914	6,984	360	273	261	1,946	3,717	53.20	....
								57.9
1915	3,833	121	273	26	1,060	2,178	56.80	....
1916	4,618	471	311	....	1,163	2,422	52.40	....

TABLE X.—IMPORTS OF MAHOGANY INTO THE UNITED STATES, 1900–1916.[1]

[Values expressed in thousands.]

Year.	Total value of mahogany imported from all countries.	From United Kingdom.	From Mexico.	From Nicaragua.	From Cuba.			Value of exports of mahogany from Cuba.	
					Value.	Per cent of total.	Average per cent of total.	Total.	Average.
1900	$1,572	$557	$424	$252	$212	13.5	....	$446	....
1901	1,752	418	549	386	302	17.2	....	457	....
1902	2,361	830	445	657	308	13.0	....	457	....
1903	2,783	1,120	410	418	490	17.6	....	634	....
							15.5		$512
1904	2,690	814	591	281	303	11.2	....	762	....
1905	1,977	748	326	223	88	4.4	....	404	....
1906	2,470	1,189	434	158	120	4.8	....	466	....
1907	3,263	1,425	686	104	187	5.7	....	570	....
							6.7		550
1908	2,566	766	603	264	150	5.8	....	669	....
1909	2,479	920	554	174	112	4.5	....	398	....
1910	3,224	1,469	720	52	108	3.3	....	510	....
1911	3,171	1,161	706	24	187	5.9	....	810	....
							4.9		597
1912	3,038	1,072	617	47	201	6.6	....	802	....
1913	4,839	2,062	664	21	338	7.0	....	1,121	....
1914	4,925	1,539	785	290	193	3.9	....	860	....
							5.7		927
1915	2,640	527	488	307	98	3.7	....	213	....
1916	2,781	770	623	218	147	5.2	....	286	....

[1] U. S. Commerce and Navigation.

That this was not due to a general decline in the mahogany industry of Cuba is demonstrated by the fact that the exports of this article from Cuba to all countries have increased.

EFFECT OF CUBAN RECIPROCITY AS REFLECTED BY IMPORTS OF INDIVIDUAL ARTICLES.

The increases in the imports from Cuba since 1903 are due very largely to one important factor—the increased imports of Cuban sugar, the annual values of which are of sufficient magnitude to dominate figures of the entire trade. In the case of sugar, the benefit of the remission of duties by the reciprocity treaty has been shared with the American consumer by the Cuban exporter. In 1913, and in 1914 up to the outbreak of the war, the American consumer appeared to be gaining the whole of the reduction in the sugar duties. In the case of tobacco the Cuban products meet in the American market with practically no competition from other foreign sources, and the reduction of duty on the Cuban product was therefore only to a limited extent a special favor to a Cuban product in competition with the products of other countries. The other imports upon which the United States conceded reduced duties were of considerably less importance, and formed only a small share of the total imports of similar articles into the United States. The remissions of duty on the small Cuban shares in these imports could not, therefore, appreciably affect their prices in the United States, and the benefit of these remissions accrued solely to the Cuban exporters.

EXPORTS FROM THE UNITED STATES TO CUBA.

Figures have already been given which show that the total American exports to Cuba increased upon the establishment of reciprocity, and, further, that the relative position of the United States in the Cuban import trade unquestionably improved. It may next be considered whether these results would not have been brought about in any case, irrespective of tariff conditions, owing to the abnormal conditions prevailing in Cuba during the pre-reciprocity period and because of the proximity of Cuba to the United States, the investment in the islands of large sums of American capital, and the quasi-political guardianship exercised by the United States since the expulsion of Spain.

A comparison may first of all be made of the course of the exports to Cuba with the exports to certain other similarly located countries which did not grant tariff favors to the United States. Chart IV[1] presents the domestic exports from the United States to Cuba and to eight other countries of the Caribbean group which in a general way resemble Cuba in point of location, climatic conditions, and state of economic development (p. 342).

The exports to Cuba immediately after the conclusion of the treaty expanded, whereas those to the other countries did not. But the depression after 1907 exerted a more marked effect on the Cuban than on the other Caribbean trade. Since 1909 the growth represented by the two curves has been approximately equal, and it must be noted that during recent years serious political disturbances have occurred in several of the Caribbean countries, whereas Cuba has enjoyed a considerable measure of orderly progress.

Groups of exported articles.—It will be recalled that under the provisions of the treaty of 1902 four classes of commodities were admitted into Cuba at reductions of duty—20, 25, 30, and 40 per

---

[1] See p. 342, infra.

cent respectively. This classification offers an opportunity to compare the values of one group with those of another and thereby to determine whether the progress made by the several groups varied directly with the degree of preference extended to the articles which they embraced.

The fact that the Cuban customs classifications do not entirely correspond with those specified in the reciprocity treaty, and the fact that many important classes were not established by the cus-

CHART IV.—*Domestic exports from the United States to Cuba, and to eight Caribbean countries, namely: Colombia, Costa Rica, Guatemala, Honduras, Nicaragua, Salvador, Dominican Republic, and Venezuela.*

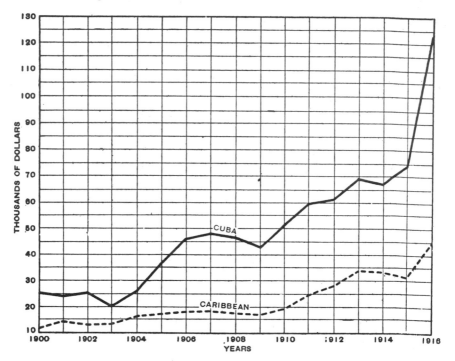

toms until 1903, render it impossible to obtain complete Cuban data for the tariff groups. The plan adopted, therefore, has been, first, to arrange the exports of the United States to Cuba according to the four complete tariff groups for the ten years 1902–1911, and secondly, to obtain from the Cuban sources statistics for selected articles representing the treaty groups, this being for the purpose of observing the proportion of these contributed from time to time by the United States. The former method has yielded the figures brought together in Table XI.

TABLE XI.—*Average annual exports of domestic merchandise from United States to Cuba.*[1]

[Arranged by tariff groups.]

	1	2	3	Average percentage increase.	
	Average, 1902–3.	Average, 1904–1907.	Average, 1908–1911.	2 over 1.	3 over 2.
Articles on free list and with 20 per cent reduction	$14,262,683	$23,812,284	$30,624,338.	66.4	21.1
Articles with 25 per cent reduction	2,068,306	3,980,951	5,944,167	92.4	39.4
Articles with 30 per cent reduction	4,860,006	9,297,747	13,187,868	91.3	41.3
Articles with 40 per cent reduction (not including cattle and rice)[2]	80,319	209,607	375,920	160.9	76.9

[1] Figures compiled from U. S. Commerce and Navigation.
[2] The inclusion of cattle would distort the figures for the group by reason of a sudden falling off after 1907 due probably to sanitary restrictions. Rice exports are intermittent. In view of the small absolute amount of the exports in this group, little importance can be attached to the figures of percentage increase for this group.

It will be observed that the increase in the American exports varied directly with the amount of tariff preference. This points to the conclusion that the reciprocity treatment had some tangible and definite influence. The results derived by the second method referred to are given in Table XII.

TABLE XII.—*Imports into Cuba of groups of representative commodities, showing average values in thousands of dollars coming from the United States and from all countries, 1904–1907: 1908–1911.*[1]

Selected articles and amount of reduction from Cuban tariff.	Average, 1904–1907.		Average, 1908–1911.		Percentage of total coming from the United States.	
	From the United States.	From all countries.	From the United States.	From all countries.	1904–1907	1908–1911
Reduction of 20 per cent: Copper products, sugar machinery, barrels and hogsheads, tin and manufactures of, leather and hides, stearin candles	$2,219	$3,825	$2,587	$4,318	58.01	59.91
Reduction of 25 per cent: Steel bars and rods, herring, glassware, earthenware, and stoneware	224	872	329	958	25.68	34.4
Reduction of 30 per cent: Chemicals, paints, plain cottons, cotton prints, boots and shoes, butter, bottled beer	3,754	11,169	5,789	13,171	33.61	43.9
Reduction of 40 per cent: Watches, preserved fruits, silk clothing, wool clothing, cheese	147	947	226	858	15.5	26.3

[1] Cuba: Comercio Exterior.

From each of the four groups a number of typical commodities were selected, the principal basis of selection being that these should represent articles in the export of which to Cuba the United States has encountered competition from one or more countries. This prevents the data from being affected by the values of a few important commodities which Cuba obtains almost exclusively from the United States. Reciprocity could have little effect, if any, in increasing the proportionate amounts brought into Cuba of such articles as wheat flour, lard, steel rails, and certain other railway equipment, barbed wire, sewing and typewriting machines, and mineral oil—in all of which lines the United States dominated the Cuban market before the reciprocity period.   Table XII indicates that the shares which the United States contributed to the average values of the representative groups increased between the periods 1904–1907 and 1908–1911 in proportion to the tariff favors enjoyed by the groups—a result which supplements the conclusions drawn from the previous table.   Since we are dealing here with selected commodities, the precise percentages are of less significance than the fact that they form a series ascending from the group of lowest to the group of highest tariff reductions.

In the Appendix will be found tables containing the complete statistics for the individual selected articles which are grouped in Table XII.   These tables give the imports into Cuba of each article from the countries principally contributing that article; the total imports; the proportions of the total imports contributed by the United States; and the total exports of each article from the United States.

GENERAL CONCLUSIONS.

From the foregoing analysis certain general conclusions may be drawn.   The imports into the United States from Cuba appear to reflect the influence of reciprocity to a much less significant degree than do the exports of the United States to Cuba.   The principal gains made by the imports have been due to the fact that several important staple articles of Cuban production have found a steady and growing market in the United States, a market which would probably have developed in some measure without the extension of tariff advantages.   The export trade to Cuba developed during the four years following the establishment of reciprocity more rapidly than did the export trade to other Caribbean countries; the exports from the United States to some extent displaced the products of other countries in the Cuban market, and the expansion of the export trade in the important commodities appeared to be approximately in proportion to the amount of tariff reduction which Cuba granted.   It must not be overlooked, however, that these results were due not only to the treaty of 1902, but also in considerable part to the favorable influence upon Cuba of the reconstruction program and the assurance of law and order guaranteed by the treaty of 1903.   Allowance must be made also for the tendency for a development in the trade to occur, in view of the political relations existing between Cuba and the United States, the investments of American capital in Cuba, the development in the United States of a great export commerce in manufactures, and the settlement of American citizens upon the Island, all of which were promoted by the assurances contained in the second treaty.   It appears that upon the whole the export trade of the United States to Cuba has been positively and favorably affected by the treaty of 1902, but to an extent which has been moderate and which is not susceptible of precise measurement.

APPENDIX.

[Values expressed in thousands of dollars.]

Copper and its products (20 per cent), including brass and bronze, 1900–1916.

Year.	Cuban imports from—						Per cent from United States.	Average per cent from United States.	Total exports from United States.
	All countries.	United States.	Germany.	Spain.	France.	United Kingdom.[1]			
1900......	$499	$334	$29	$4	$34	$94	67.0	....	$57,853
1901......	214	149	13	1	9	41	69.6	....	43,267
1902......	253	142	16	3	27	64	56.0	....	41,218
1903......	303	164	34	5	37	62	54.1	....	39,667
								62.2	
1904......	441	191	100	5	43	92	43.2	....	57,142
1905......	470	234	114	4	41	70	49.8	....	86,225
1906......	767	505	99	.7	51	100	65.8	....	81,283
1907......	819	590	82	3	36	103	72.0	....	94,762
								60.9	
1908......	665	356	152	3	35	115	53.5	....	104,065
1909......	583	365	119	2	23	67	62.6	....	85,290
1910......	736	524	72	4	30	97	71.2	....	88,004
1911......	802	540	82	2	39	132	67.3	....	103,813
								64.1	
1912......	887	624	103	1	46	100	70.3	....	113,959
1913......	1,102	829	104	1	31	124	75.2	....	140,165
1914......	1,109	837	116	2	30	99	75.4	....	146,223
								73.9	
1915......	734	611	28	.5	12	53	83.1	....	99,558
1916......	952	858	1	20	18	40	90.0	....	173,946

[1] England only in 1900, 1901, 1902, and 1904.

Sugar machinery (20 per cent).

Year.	Cuban imports from—[1]					Per cent from United States.	Average per cent from United States.	Total exports from United States.
	All countries.	United States.	United Kingdom.[2]	Germany.	Belgium.			
1900..............	$252	$224	$4	$18	....	88.7	....	....
1901..............	467	440	16	8	....	94.3	....	....
1902..............	1,521	1,236	182	47	$16	81.3	....	....
1903..............	603	449	95	31	26	74.5	....	....
							82.7	
1904..............	616	388	113	32	78	62.9	....	....
1905..............	1,465	1,072	133	125	122	73.1	....	....
1906..............	3,758	2,105	577	417	564	56.0	....	....
1907..............	1,623	1,075	224	175	125	66.2	....	....
							62.3	
1908..............	1,392	753	525	92	21	54.0	....	....
1909..............	1,272	910	216	54	62	71.5	....	....
1910..............	2,041	1,285	487	85	109	62.9	....	....
1911..............	4,257	2,313	983	267	579	54.8	....	$2,59
							58.7	
1912..............	3,801	2,047	685	313	326	52.5	....	1,783
1913..............	5,575	2,977	731	746	1,102	53.3	....	2,889
1914..............	4,279	2,402	520	275	852	56.1	....	2,548
							54.0	
1915..............	2,339	1,788	182	13	78	76.4	....	2,092
1916..............	8,873	8,357	390	1	....	94.1	....	5,987

[1] Includes accessories as well as sugar machinery.   [2] England only in 1900–1902.

[Values expressed in thousands of dollars.]

Barrels and hogsheads (20 per cent).

Year.	Cuban imports from—				Per cent from United States.	Average per cent from United States.	Total exports from United States.
	All countries.	United States.	United Kingdom.[1]	Spain.			
1901	$478	$218	$32	$214	45.6		$117
1902	461	213	28	204	46.2		127
1903	472	177	37	239	37.5	43.0	175
1904	498	206	38	226	41.4		215
1905	544	240	28	233	44.1		188
1906	573	256	33	239	44.7		243
1907	605	294	30	230	48.6	44.9	345
1908	564	258	27	226	45.9		267
1909	536	252	18	215	47.0		282
1910	560	279	26	208	49.9		565
1911	570	290	45	195	50.9	48.5	
1912	579	325	24	196	56.2		321
1913	597	357	25	179	59.8		383
1914	605	382	22	162	63.1	59.7	914
1915	579	381	23	154	65.8		1,114
1916	819	593	23	161	72.4		583

[1] England only in 1901–02.

Tin and manufactures of (20 per cent).

Year.	Cuban imports from—					Per cent from United States.	Average per cent from United States.	Total exports from United States.
	All countries.	United States.	United Kingdom.[1]	Spain.	Germany.			
1900	$137	$75	$41	$9	$5	55.1		$387
1901	135	73	37	8	8	69.4		566
1902	116	54	41	9	8	46.6		525
1903	52	13	12	3	13	26.5	49.1	663
1904	70	19	15	3	24	27.9		262
1905	93	16	22	4	39	18.0		752
1906	119	24	40	4	37	20.1		1,069
1907	123	27	38	2	39	22.5	21.6	1,181
1908	122	24	36	3	47	20.0		1,043
1909	77	19	22	4	21	25.5		877
1910	126	32	36	3	38	25.8		944
1911	147	38	43	4	48	26.2	24.3	1,047
1912	152	59	37	5	33	39.4		1,311
1913	187	70	45	4	43	37.6		1,474
1914	182	51	58	7	39	28.0	34.7	1,553
1915	104	55	21	7	11	53.1		1,873
1916	152	106	39	2		69.9		2,962

[1] England only in 1900–1902.

[Values expressed in thousands of dollars.]

Hides, skins, and leather [1] *(20 per cent).*

Year.	All countries.	United States.	Ger-many.	Spain.	France.	United King-dom.[2]	Per cent from United States.	Average per cent from United States.	Total exports from United States.
1900	$180	$67	$2	$79	$24	$7	37.3	....	$22,602
1901	196	88	2	69	29	4	44.8	....	22,386
1902	165	73	1	68	20	1	44.7	....	23,257
1903	232	115	(3)	91	23	1	49.4	44.4	24,739
1904	362	213	1	120	24	2	58.6	....	28,098
1905	469	288	1	116	27	5	61.4	....	29,110
1906	491	323	1	136	27	2	65.8	....	30,540
1907	515	379	1	105	24	4	77.0	66.5	33,818
1908	379	285	2	71	15	6	75.2	....	28,506
1909	442	358	1	67	11	3	81.1	....	31,684
1910	532	423	3	78	12	5	79.5	....	38,938
1911	577	485	5	64	13	5	84.0	80.4	42,002
1912	620	513	6	70	18	4	82.8	....	44,057
1913	704	585	17	78	16	6	83.1	....	45,834
1914	817	629	6	142	16	5	77.0	80.7	39,476
1915	757	658	3	71	8	4	86.9	....	69,915
1916	1,114	988	(3)	92	7	5	88.7	....	83,949

[1] Cuba: Comercio Exterior. [2] England only in 1900–1902. [3] Less than $1,000.

Stearin candles [1] *(20 per cent).*

Year.	All countries.	United States.	Germany.	Belgium.	Spain.	Per cent from United States.	Average per cent from United States.	Total exports from United States
1901	$323	$5	$6	$3	$296	1.5	....	$237
1902	249	15	2	4	194	6.0	....	287
1903	305	36	19	28	213	11.6	6.3	515
1904	179	66	2	28	80	36.8	....	510
1905	246	105	(²)	24	112	42.7	....	701
1906	186	97	1	7	78	52.2	....	609
1907	267	159	2	16	86	59.3	48.6	473
1908	261	191	8	13	44	72.9	....	366
1909	216	104	1	9	65	61.7	....	353
1910	205	105	2	1	85	51.1	....	295
1911	204	122	1	....	69	60.2	62.3	291
1912	199	114	2	(²)	67	57.3	....	255
1913	156	71	(²)	(²)	71	45.5	....	246
1914	174	72	1	....	86	41.3	48.6	283
1915	205	85	1	1	105	41.3	....	417
1916	168	84	....	....	75	49.8	....	576

[1] Cuba: Comercio Exterior. [²] Less than $1,000.

[Values expressed in thousands of dollars.]

Glass containers (25 per cent).

Year.	Imports into Cuba from—						Per cent from United States.	Average per cent from United States.	Total exports from United States.[2]
	All countries.	United States.	Germany.	Spain.	France.	United Kingdom.[1]			
1901.......	$162	$73	$13	$36	$12	$24	45.4	....	....
1902.......	150	36	14	40	16	37	23.9	....	....
1903.......	162	24	16	50	21	41	14.7	....	....
								28.1	
1904.......	135	27	16	45	18	22	20.3	....	....
1905.......	208	55	22	68	26	32	26.5	....	....
1906.......	327	65	82	93	34	37	19.9	....	....
1907.......	256	73	24	79	37	32	28.6	....	....
								23.9	
1908.......	234	53	24	84	35	34	22.4	....	....
1909.......	204	39	20	79	36	22	20.0	....	....
1910.......	189	32	12	77	37	21	16.9	....	....
1911.......	209	32	14	82	47	17	15.2	....	....
								18.7	
1912.......	240	37	15	92	51	25	15.4	....	....
1913.......	285	58	21	105	41	40	20.3	....	....
1914.......	321	47	35	99	55	42	14.7	....	....
								16.6	
1915.......	214	47	6	91	31	26	21.7	....	....
1916.......	296	67	....	136	37	35	22.7	....	....

[1] England only in 1901 and 1902.   [2] Not separately reported.

Earthenware and stoneware (25 per cent).

Year.	Imports into Cuba from—						Per cent from United States.	Average per cent from United States.	Total exports from United States.
	All countries.	United States.	Germany.	France.	United Kingdom.[1]	Belgium.			
1900.......	$138	$28	$32	$35	$25	....	20.0	....	$519
1901.......	169	16	51	12	65	$6	9.7	....	460
1902.......	194	18	55	14	89	2	9.4	....	550
1903.......	121	5	54	11	45	5	3.7	....	519
								10.7	
1904.......	175	3	100	7	55	9	1.8	....	614
1905.......	193	4	109	9	60	8	2.0	....	796
1906.......	245	8	104	12	101	18	3.1	....	957
1907.......	187	18	65	10	64	27	9.5	....	987
								4.1	
1908.......	231	7	59	11	85	67	3.1	....	1,058
1909.......	118	9	25	5	32	45	7.9	....	730
1910.......	146	7	32	10	47	50	4.7	....	802
1911.......	231	16	64	15	86	45	7.0	5.5	1,134
1912.......	276	31	49	23	96	76	11.1	....	1,493
1913.......	283	38	48	28	106	61	1?.3	....	456
1914.......	294	60	49	23	103	57	20.3	....	413
								15.1	
1915.......	239	47	38	4	106	11	19.9	....	294
1916.......	372	93	3	1	190	....	24.9	....	427

[1] England only in 1900–2.

[Values expressed in thousands of dollars.]

Bars and rods of steel (25 per cent).

Year.	Imports into Cuba from—						Per cent from United States.	Average per cent from United States.	Total exports from United States.
	All countries.	United States.	Germany.	Belgium.	France.	United Kingdom.[1]			
1901	$109	$77				$32	70.4		$2,988
1902	68	12	$12	$4	$14	27	17.5		1,222
1903	167	26	35	33	12	61	15.3		1,861
								33.3	
1904	268	36	43	32	22	123	13.4		1,518
1905	308	73	35	37	19	116	23.7		2,064
1906	533	241	42	76	16	148	45.3		1,467
1907	532	225	42	83	18	159	42.3		3,091
								34.9	
1908	504	243	15	91	22	131	48.2		3,323
1909	380	198	5	102	11	65	52.1		2,649
1910	493	268	16	114	3	88	54.4		4,258
1911	779	368	10	222	4	173	42.2		5,016
								49.9	
1912	1,015	762	6	128	6	112	75.0		6,812
1913	935	729	12	110	4	78	78.0		10,565
1914	1,130	757	8	190	2	172	67.0		7,392
								73.0	
1915	689	653		3	2	31	94.7		10,830
1916	1,007	995				9			37,693

[1] England only in 1901 and 1902.

Herring (25 per cent).

Year.	Imports into Cuba from			Per cent from United States.	Average per cent from United States.	Total exports from United States.
	All countries.	United States.	Spain.			
1901	$16	$11	$4	70.1		$84
1902	7	5		75.2		57
1903	44	18	25	41.8		34
					52.1	
1904	30	13	14	43.7		44
1905	32	19	8	58.9		54
1906	29	16	10	56.4		56
1907	29	19	6	67.0		38
					56.7	
1908	27	18	6	65.1		32
1909	34	14	17	42.4		33
1910	23	7	10	31.9		28
1911	31	7	16	21.4		51
					39.9	
1912	48	13	20	27.4		160
1913	51	15	13	28.3		209
1914	64	25	15	39.2		242
					32.3	
1915	87	54	7	62.0		114
1916	162	60	14	36.9		154

[Values expressed in thousands of dollars.]

Chemicals (30 per cent).

Year.	Cuban imports from—						Per cent from United States.	Average per cent from United States.	Total exports from United States.
	All countries.	United States.	Germany.	Spain.	France.	United Kingdom.[1]			
1900	$980	$415	$58	$110	$245	$93	42.3	....	$13,203
1901	960	418	61	65	241	104	43.4	....	14,384
1902	1,013	438	69	59	260	95	43.3	....	13,288
1903	1,001	437	59	76	272	122	43.6	43.3	13,697
1904	1,062	455	76	66	290	125	42.9	....	14,480
1905	1,232	626	54	46	359	113	50.8	....	15,859
1906	1,496	752	64	44	462	135	50.3	....	18,798
1907	1,571	865	74	33	398	147	55.0	50.3	20,373
1908	1,711	886	100	37	446	180	51.8	....	20,873
1909	1,753	957	76	26	493	158	54.6	....	19,131
1910	2,393	1,420	91	52	576	174	59.3	....	21,415
1911	3,062	1,983	123	50	584	232	64.7	58.9	23,007
1912	3,999	2,593	121	60	775	334	64.9	....	25,117
1913	4,246	2,546	108	61	921	469	60.0	....	26,574
1914	4,159	2,199	229	82	850	573	52.9	59.2	27,079
1915	5,119	3,310	155	58	668	648	64.7	....	46,380
1916	6,834	5,121	13	89	936	581	74.9	....	124,362

[1] England only in 1900–2.

Paints (30 per cent).

Year.	Cuban imports from—					Per cent from United States.	Average per cent from United States.	Total exports from United States.[2]
	All countries.	United States.	Germany.	France.	United Kingdom.[1]			
1900	$264	$94	$23	$11	$111	35.7	....	$1,902
1901	225	101	15	5	88	44.8	....	2,036
1902	215	86	12	14	75	39.9	....	2,096
1903	216	84	6	15	100	38.9	39.7	2,350
1904	233	82	7	16	117	35.3	....	2,756
1905	246	113	9	13	99	46.0	....	3,126
1906	353	172	13	13	140	48.7	....	4,612
1907	391	187	20	16	155	47.9	45.2	4,893
1908	343	167	16	18	126	48.8	....	4,942
1909	359	180	18	17	132	50.4	....	4,780
1910	450	254	12	15	147	56.6	....	5,702
1911	525	314	19	11	155	59.7	54.4	6,294
1912	538	299	11	9	196	55.6	....	7,072
1913	645	386	10	10	213	59.9	....	7,681
1914	622	378	10	9	177	60.8	58.8	7,256
1915	547	383	3	2	141	70.1	....	7,415
1916	836	708	....	3	110	84.6	....	11,416

[1] England only in 1900–2.   [2] The classification as reported is not comparable.

[Values expressed in thousands of dollars.]

Cotton goods, plain (30 per cent).

Year.	Cuban imports from—						Per cent from United States.	Average per cent from United States.	Total exports from United States.
	All countries.	United States.	Ger-many.	Spain.	France.	United King-dom.			
1903......	$2,868	$226	$35	$669	$124	$1,760	7.9	....	$16,909
1904......	3,968	272	70	827	182	2,527	6.9	....	9,256
1905......	4,903	650	113	816	247	2,923	13.3	....	33,995
1906......	4,432	764	86	1,117	188	2,099	17.2	....	36,252
1907......	3,780	570	56	735	146	2,040	15.1	....	13,737
								12.45	
1908......	5,308	550	153	1,105	299	2,063	10.4	....	8,459
1909......	4,305	954	53	780	219	2,095	22.2	....	14,527
1910......	4,691	621	58	1,039	241	2,355	13.2	....	11,450
1911......	4,017	846	36	681	208	1,830	21.1	....	13,812
								16.2	
1912...,....	5,957	1,539	40	939	445	2,712	25.8	....	19,804
1913......	6,309	1,307	49	830	532	2,912	20.7	....	18,090
1914......	4,146	929	18	803	155	1,679	22.4	....	17,230
								23.0	
1915......	4,233	1,847	8	580	57	1,378	43.6	....	16,146
1916......	6,086	2,788	....	1,007	84	1,679	45.8	....	23,479

Cotton goods, colored (30 per cent).

Year.	Cuban imports from—				Per cent from United States.	Average per cent from United States.	Total exports from United States.
	All countries.	United States.	Spain.	United King-dom.			
1903....................	$764	$101	$128	$455	13.3	....	$8,440
1904....................	1,125	155	125	722	13.8	....	5,439
1905....................	1,504	299	242	745	19.9	....	7,325
1906....................	1,621	350	230	867	21.6	....	6,929
1907....................	1,391	325	111	781	23.4	....	7,502
						19.3	
1908....................	1,674	341	135	939	20.4	....	5,809
1909....................	1,326	355	70	703	26.8	....	7,165
1910....................	1,797	389	119	972	21.7	....	8,521
1911....................	1,785	495	130	909	27.7	....	10,575
						24.0	
1912....................	2,100	524	209	1,078	25.0	....	11,584
1913....................	2,359	533	324	1,129	22.6	....	12,578
1914....................	2,210	518	247	1,097	23.4	....	11,613
						23.3	
1915....................	2,053	820	200	807	40.0	....	12,536
1916....................	2,509	1,289	168	866	51.4	....	22,902

[Values expressed in thousands of dollars.]

Boots and shoes (30 per cent).

Year.	All countries.	United States.	Spain.	Per cent from United States.	Average per cent from United States.	Total exports from United States.
1900	$2,291	$473	$1,768	20.7		$4,276
1901	1,638	405	1,226	24.8		5,526
1902	1,790	573	1,213	32.0		6,182
1903	1,762	614	1,145	34.8		6,665
					27.6	
1904	2,554	1,050	1,501	41.1		7,239
1905	2,857	1,418	1,436	49.6		8,057
19 6	3,281	2,191	1,088	66.8		9,142
1907	3,574	2,786	779	77.9		10,666
					60.7	
1908	3,435	2,742	690	79.8		11,469
19 9	3,146	2,630	509	83.6		10,305
1910	3,615	3,012	589	83.3		12,408
1911	4,003	3,339	649	83.4		13,746
					82.6	
1912	3,767	3,017	738	80.1		16,009
1913	4,980	4,064	907	81.7		18,196
1914	4,249	3,398	835	80.0		17,867
					80.6	
1915	4,676	4,021	643	86.0		24,696
1916	5,976	5,269	701	88.6		47,224

Butter (30 per cent).

Year.	Cuban imports from—				Per cent from United States.	Average per cent from United States.	Total exports from United States.
	All countries.	United States.	Denmark.	Spain.			
1900 [1]	$227	$114	$26	$65	50.2		$3,143
1901	108	29	25	44	27.1		4,014
1902	128	33	41	32	26.4		2,885
1903	122	20	49	37	16.5		1,604
						23.2	
1904	158	25	67	42	15.9		1,768
1905	205	36	95	35	18.0		1,648
1906	275	48	131	54	17.6		4,922
1907	302	70	149	47	23.3		2,429
						19.1	
1908	350	56	203	45	16.2		1,407
1909	274	60	123	54	21.9		1,268
1910	352	72	202	42	20.7		785
1911	424	68	271	34	16.2		1,059
						18.3	
1912	306	55	188	38	18.1		1,468
1913	328	55	216	31	16.9		872
1914	357	60	191	64	16.9		877
						17.0	
1915	408	60	241	57	14.8		2,392
1916	388	59	243	67	15.3		3,590

[1] Including oleomargarine.

[Values expressed in thousands of dollars.]

Bottled beer (30 per cent).

Year.	Cuban imports from—				Per cent from United States.	Average per cent from United States.	Total exports from United States.
	All countries.	United States.	Germany.	United Kingdom.¹			
1901	$554	$286	$52	$209	51.6	....	$1,643
1902	438	176	34	227	40.2	....	1,199
1903	403	121	29	251	30.2	....	1,082
						41.7	
1904	322	85	32	203	26.6	....	769
1905	345	163	29	320	31.7	....	932
1906	695	231	43	417	33.4	....	1,059
1907	619	264	38	315	42.6	....	1,128
						34.4	
1908	516	166	27	318	32.3	....	964
1909	403	137	26	239	34.0	....	964
1910	319	67	13	236	21.2	....	877
1911	333	81	15	229	24.3	....	990
						28.6	
1912	351	89	26	232	25.6	....	1,101
1913	449	146	27	272	32.5	....	1,301
1914	397	122	17	252	31.0	....	1,405
						29.8	
1915	293	116	8	165	39.7	....	1,010
1916	410	192	....	217	46.8	....	969

¹ England only in 1901 and 1902.

Silk clothing (40 per cent).

Year.	Cuban imports from—			Per cent from United States.	Average per cent from United States.	Total exports from United States.¹
	All countries.	United States.	France.			
1903	$77	$21	$43	28.14	....	....
1904	56	2	29	3.79	....	....
1905	60	....	42	.86	....	....
1906	160	40	62	25.29	....	....
1907	117	23	60	20.18	....	....
					17.3	
1908	184	24	109	13.21	....	....
1909	80	36	35	45.71	....	....
1910	34	22	3	64.74	....	....
1911	150	67	33	44.67	....	....
					33.0	
1912	216	110	67	51.10	....	....
1913	223	124	36	55.66	....	....
1914	204	58	30	28.01	....	....
					45.3	
1915	153	72	25	47.00	....	....
1916	306	177	31	58.10	....	....

¹ Not separately reported.

[Values expressed in thousands of dollars.]

Wool clothing (40 per cent).

Year.	Cuban imports from—					Per cent from United States.	Average per cent from United States.	Total exports from United States.
	All countries.	United States.	Ger-many.	France.	United King-dom.[1]			
1900								$570
1901	$48	$13	$13	$7	$2	27.46		805
1902	82	13	9	39	6	16.05		852
1903	96	13	5	65	5	14.35		1,290
							17.6	
1904	43	4	1	31	4	9.37		1,457
1905	72	2	8	55	3	3.81		1,624
1906	135	22	1	89	11	16.82		1,618
1907	48	21	2	10	3	45.57		1,688
							17.3	
1908	97	38	3	48	1	39.57		1,717
1909	91	71		12	3	78.66		1,420
1910	91	69	1	5	2	76.88		1,555
1911	98	55	17	19	1	56.00		1,450
							62.2	
1912	163	68	18	63	3	41.90		1,743
1913	180	98	19	51	1	54.77		2,460
1914	176	93	16	51	2	53.20		2,148
							50.9	
1915	84	59	1	4	1	70.08		9,108
1916	132	121		6	3	91.45		19,368

[1] England only in 1901 and 1902.

Cheese (40 per cent).

Year.	Cuban imports from—			Per cent from United States.	Average per cent from United States.	Total exports from United States.
	All coun-tries.	United States.	Holland.			
1900	$577	$92	$391	16.03		4,943
1901	460	59	298	12.87		3,950
1902	373	53	249	14.43		2,745
1903	393	35	321	9.00		2,250
					13.1	
1904	364	37	286	10.35		2,452
1905	481	23	404	4.82		1,084
1906	591	41	413	7.03		1,940
1907	488	55	352	11.30		2,012
					8.1	
1908	535	41	420	7.80		1,092
1909	357	41	279	11.49		857
1910	417	58	309	13.97		441
1911	408	46	298	11.33		1,288
					10.9	
1912	380	45	284	11.96		898
1913	414	59	309	14.34		441
1914	472	74	338	15.67		414
					14.0	
1915	417	108	280	26.07		8,463
1916	524	298	198	56.82		7,430

[Values expressed in thousands of dollars.]

Preserved fruits (40 per cent).

Year.	Cuban imports from—			Per cent from United States.	Average per cent from United States.	Total exports from United States.
	All countries.	United States.	Spain.			
1900	$76	$24	$44	31.5		3,190
1901	61	18	38	29.4		3,077
1902	63	15	44	24.5		1,289
1903	49	17	24	34.8		1,806
					29.0	
1904	62	21	33	34.0		2,752
1905	90	39	42	43.9		2,612
1900	162	64	83	39.7		2,437
1907	170	76	77	44.8		1,685
					41.3	
1908	151	69	61	46.1		1,687
1909	155	96	45	61.9		2,977
1910	134	59	59	43.9		2,832
1911	152	88	46	58.1		2,892
					52.7	
1912	194	126	46	64.9		4,149
1913	226	140	67	61.7		5,781
1914	201	130	57	64.8		5,088
					63.8	
1915	190	144	37	75.8		6,333
1916	374	323	37	86.4		8,028

Watches (40 per cent).

Year	Cuban imports from—					Per cent from United States.	Average per cent from United States.	Total exports from United States.
	All countries.	United States.	Germany.	France.	Switzerland.			
1900	$51	$6	$17	$10	$15	12.78		787
1901	86	18	19	15	30	21.05		1,044
1902	75	14	31	14	14	18.65		998
1903	75	13	26	24	9	18.07		1,041
							17.8	
1904	134	29	36	51	16	22.13		1,094
1905	171	41	56	55	16	24.13		1,124
1906	250	33	90	88	35	13.37		1,293
1907	124	5	44	57	16	4.67		1,723
							16.0	
1908	99	2	48	30	13	2.79		1,386
1909	55	3	12	33	6	6.06		1,251
1910	73	3	9	51	9	4.58		1,228
1911	64	5	17	30	10	8.12		1,560
							5.5	
1912	149	4		35	8	2.83		1,880
1913	45	11	4	21	7	24.48		1,783
1914	42	5	7	21	8	13.89		1,460
							8.9	
1915	30	6	1	5	10	22.40		914
1916	49	12	1	12	22	25.70		1,524

10. COMMERCIAL RELATIONS OF THE UNITED STATES WITH NEWFOUNDLAND.

357

COMMERCIAL RELATIONS OF THE UNITED STATES WITH NEWFOUNDLAND.

The fisheries question and commercial relations with Newfoundland.—The commercial relations of the United States and Newfoundland have always been very closely connected with the fisheries question, and any tariff arrangements which have been negotiated between the two countries have always been either a product of the fisheries question or in some other way associated therewith. It has been the constant desire of Newfoundland to secure as the price of fishing privileges in her waters the free admission of the products of her fisheries into the United States.

Negotiations, 1783–1854.—It is not necessary here to enter upon a history or discussion of the complicated fisheries question. The treaty of Versailles, 1783, had made provision for American rights in the Newfoundland fisheries, but the War of 1812, according to the British claims, terminated those provisions of the treaty which dealt with the fisheries. In 1816 a new treaty, containing new tariff provisions, was concluded, which governed the rights and privileges of American fishermen in the North Atlantic fisheries until the conclusion of the reciprocity treaty in 1854 between the United States and Great Britain on behalf of the British North American Colonies, including Newfoundland. The treaty of 1854 provided among other things for the mutual free exchange of natural products, including the products of the fisheries.[1]

The treaty of Washington, 1871.—The reciprocity treaty of 1854 was terminated by the United States on March 17, 1866, and its termination again revived the fisheries question. A new settlement of this question was consummated by the treaty of Washington, of 1871, in which, among other things, provision was made, in Articles XVI and XXXII, for the reciprocal free admission of the products of the fisheries of the United States on the one hand and those of the British North American Colonies on the other. In 1883 the United States gave due notice of termination of the fisheries articles in the treaty of Washington, and those provisions ceased to operate in 1885.

The Bayard-Chamberlain treaty, 1888, unratified.—On February 15, 1888, there was negotiated a new arrangement, the Bayard-Chamberlain treaty. In this treaty the United States Government undertook to recommend to Congress the enactment of legislation to remove the duties on the fisheries products of Canada and Newfoundland. After a long and forceful debate in open session of the Senate, the treaty failed of ratification. A two-year *modus vivendi* had been arranged, however, and this continued to regulate the fisheries.

The Bond-Blaine convention, 1890, unratified.—In 1890, when the *modus vivendi* was about to expire, the State Department negotiated a new arrangement with Newfoundland, the Bond-Blaine convention. To expedite the acceptance of the new arrangement, the *modus vivendi* was continued meanwhile. By the terms of the Bond-Blaine

---

[1] For a discussion of this treaty, see p. 63 seq, infra.

convention, various fisheries products from Newfoundland were to be
admitted free into the United States in return for the free admission
into Newfoundland of printing presses, gas engines, raw cotton,
crushing mills, and certain other articles from the United States;
rates were established which were not to be exceeded, for imports
into Newfoundland of American flour, pork, bacon and hams, beef,
Indian meal, salt, kerosene, and certain other articles, and Newfoundland was to concede to American fishermen the right to touch and trade
on Newfoundland shores.

Canada, which was not included in the compact, protested against
the convention on the ground that, as all British subjects had common
property rights in the fisheries, no one group could barter the fisheries
away for concessions to be enjoyed by itself alone, and further, that
if this convention were ratified it would operate to discriminate
against Canadian fishermen, in that, while they paid the regular high
duties of the American tariff, the Newfoundland fishermen would pay
lower duties.   The agreement could not become effective without
ratification on the one side by the American Senate and on the other
by the British Government.   Yielding to the insistent representations
of the Canadian Government, the British Government let it be understood that it would not ratify the convention.   Meanwhile, the *modus
vivendi* regulating the use of the fisheries by Americans was extended
from time to time.

The Bond-Hay convention, 1902, unratified.—In 1902 Canada withdrew her objections to a reciprocal arrangement between the United
States and Newfoundland, and there was negotiated the Bond-Hay
convention, similar in its terms to the Bond-Blaine convention of
1890.   After being held by the Senate Committee on Foreign Relations for two sessions, the convention was there so amended in February, 1905, as to become unacceptable to Newfoundland.   In 1910 the
fisheries question was finally settled by arbitration proceedings between the United States and Great Britain, the fisheries privileges
being governed in the interval by the yearly extension of the *modus
vivendi.*

11. THE ATTEMPT TO ESTABLISH A RECIPROCITY ARRANGEMENT WITH CANADA, 1910-11.

THE ATTEMPT TO ESTABLISH A RECIPROCITY ARRANGEMENT WITH CANADA, 1910–11.

CANADA'S TWENTIETH CENTURY POLICY.

The "national policy" in the hands of the Liberal Party.—The first decade of the twentieth century was the most prosperous period that the Dominion of Canada had yet experienced. Economic well-being encouraged and was reflected in a general feeling of optimism and self-confidence, stirrings of national pride, and emphasis of Imperial loyalty. The time was ripe for the realization of the ideal of constructive nationalism; opportunity stimulated the making of plans for developing a rich and productive nation. The prosecution of these plans required a program of activity on the part of the Government. Thus it happened that the Liberal Party, when it came into power under Sir Wilfred Laurier, in 1896, took over the "national policy" of the Conservatives—which it had formerly denounced—and further developed it in various directions.

The primary aim to which the new administration committed itself was the fostering and promoting of domestic industry and commerce. For the benefit of domestic industries it framed a protective tariff little less exclusive than that of the previous administration. A free list was constructed with a view to providing raw materials for manufacturing; but where the producers of raw or partly manufactured materials were thought to require protection, duties were put upon their products also. In the case of a few manufactured articles the producers were indemnified for such duties on their materials, not by additional compensatory duties on their own products, as in the United States, but by direct bounties and by drawbacks upon re-exportation. Such bounties were conspicuous in the iron and steel industries. Under this fostering care some branches of industry grew beyond existing needs, as was also the case with the railroads; and a market for their output, as well as for the constantly increasing agricultural surplus, had to be sought in other countries.

Canadian preference upon British imports.—Barred from the United States by the rates of the tariff of 1897, Canadian producers turned their attention to developing better markets in the mother country and in the other British colonies. As an aid in this direction the Canadian Government provided in its tariff act of 1897 for a system of preferential duties upon British imports.

The preferential arrangement, as revised in 1898, applied to imports from the United Kingdom and such British colonies and possessions as gave equally favorable treatment to their imports from Canada. The preference was originally a uniform fraction of the general duties; later it was reduced on a few commodities—especially woolens—owing to complaints of domestic manufacturers; and in 1907 the preferential duties were made a separate schedule, independent of the general rates,

Tariff war with Germany.—In the early years of the twentieth century, Canada's trade with Germany suffered the injurious effects of a tariff war, for which the preferential system was indirectly responsible. Germany, objecting to the preferential treatment of British goods, withdrew from Canada the benefit of her conventional tariff rates and subjected Canadian goods to the higher rates of her general tariff. Several years of negotiation and correspondence brought no concession from Germany. Accordingly the Dominion, by the act of October 24, 1903, adopted what amounted to a maximum tariff, intended for retaliatory purposes. Germany was not named in the act, but German goods were subjected to the surtax, while the measure was never used—nor intended to be used—against any other country.

The tariff law of 1907.—Both the preferential tariff and the surtax of 1903 were adopted with the intention that they should be applied only to particular countries. After an extensive investigation by a special tariff commission a general revision was made in a new tariff act passed in 1907. The rates upon some manufactures were slightly raised—none more than 5 per cent ad valorem—and some rates were slightly reduced. The British preferential rates were somewhat lowered, and were made an independent schedule. But the most important feature was the adoption of an intermediate schedule—for bargaining purposes—with rates higher than those of the British preferential, but lower, upon the most important articles, than the rates of the general tariff. In addition to, and distinct from the schedules above mentioned, the surtax provision was maintained as a possible retaliatory device. The so-called "general" rates formed the maximum rates of the tariff proper. [On the whole, it may be said that if the average reduction by the preferential schedule be taken as one-third of the general rates, that effected by the intermediate schedule averaged less than one-sixth.] The intermediate schedule was intended to be used in negotiating for concessions by treaty with foreign countries.

Convention with France and its effect.—Immediately after the passage of the act, its efficacy was tested by the opening of negotiations with France. In September, 1907, a commercial convention was signed, which, after considerable revision, went into effect in February, 1910.[1] Under this convention Canada acquired from France the concession of the rates of the French minimum tariff upon several hundred items, giving in return the rates of her intermediate tariff and, upon a few items, still lower rates. It was mutually stipulated that if the duties upon the enumerated articles were further lowered by either of the parties in favor of any other country, the other should be given the benefit of the additional reduction.

The observable direct results of this treaty were insignificant indeed. France raised the rates in her tariff schedules so that even the minimum duties were high enough to check Canadian exports; and the changes in the Canadian schedule were too small to offer any particular attraction to French trade.

The British preference and the French treaty may have benefited Canada indirectly by attracting to her the attention of foreign governments, producers, and commercial interests, but the direct and immediate effect of these measures upon the actual trade fell far short of expectations.

---

[1] Denounced by France December, 1918.

CANADA'S COMMERCE WITH THE UNITED STATES IN THE TWENTIETH CENTURY.

The American tariff act of 1897.—In the United States, there was enacted in 1897 the Dingley Tariff Act. This act affected commercial relations with Canada in several ways. It contained a provision for increasing the import duties upon lumber by an amount equal to the export duty which Canada had imposed upon logs. The threat was sufficient to cause Canada to remove her export duty. But the United States gained practically no advantage thereby, for in 1900 the Province of Ontario, and later British Columbia, Quebec, and New Brunswick enacted requirements that timber cut on the Crown lands should be manufactured in Canada. These laws proved more effective than the Dominion's export duty and actually encouraged a very considerable transfer of American capital and enterprise to the forests of these Provinces. No other provision of the Dingley Act was aimed specifically at Canada, but the rates named in the act were so high as to be, under normal conditions, almost prohibitive for some Canadian products, such as barley. The influence of the act was shown not in an actual decrease of American imports from Canada, but in the failure of those imports to increase in proportion to the growing ability of Canada to compete in the American market.

Protectionist measures in Canada.—Meanwhile, the policy of the Canadian Government had become, as already explained, as strongly protectionist as was that of the United States. It is true that the Canadian duties were usually not so high as the American, but, according to the evidence of the debate in the House of Commons, they were arranged so as to discriminate as far as possible against American imports; and the tariff was supplemented by other measures, some intended to discourage imports from the United States and some certain to have that effect, whether so intended or not. Prominent among the latter were an extremely stringent patent law; the imposition of a tax of 15 cents a pound upon the admission of foreign circulars, advertising matter, etc.; and the addition to the tariff act (in 1904) of an "anti-dumping" clause.

Mention has already been made of the encouragement given by the Canadian Government to the construction of railway lines east and west rather than north and south. Such routes as were thereby afforded were, however, considerably more expensive and involved greater delay than transportation to and from the American centers. Therefore neither politics nor sentiment was able to prevent the gradual multiplication of branch lines across the border. In 1910 not only had the direct trade with the United States increased enormously, but of Canada's exports to other countries no less than 27 per cent was still shipped through the ports of the United States.[1] But Canada's railways had opened for her producers a substitute for the American market which was especially useful when that market was oversupplied, unduly manipulated, or closed by the tariff.

Obstacles to and character of the trade between the two countries.—A more fundamental economic obstacle to the growth of commerce was the fact that among Canadian products there were but a limited number which the American consumer desired. This had a counter-

---

[1] Kyte, Geo. W., House of Commons Debates, Feb. 21, 1911, p. 1045.

part in the fact that there were some Canadian needs which American producers could not supply. The following table gives the chief Canadian exports to the United States, grouped in the order of their importance, in 1910:

Principal Canadian exports of home produce to the United States.[1]

Forest produce:
 Principal items: Unmanufactured wood, planks and boards, shingles
  and laths. $31, 835, 326
Mineral produce: [2]
 Principal items: Copper ore and copper, coal, nickel ore and matte,
  and asbestos. 15, 552, 732
Manufactures:
 Principal items: Wood pulp, household effects, and paper. 15, 350, 280
Animals and their produce:
 Principal items: Hides and skins, furs, and live stock 10, 629, 614
Agricultural produce:
 Principal items: Grains, seeds, and bran. 8, 204, 250
Fisheries produce:
 Principal items: Fresh fish and lobsters 4, 627. 051

The unequal industrial development of the two countries placed a limit to the kinds and quantities of goods which Canada could sell to the United States. Of nearly all the manufactured articles which figured in the trade, with the exceptions· of paper and flour, Canada bought more from the United States than she sold there.

On the other hand, an examination of the figures of Canadian imports from the United States makes it abundantly evident that the growth of Canadian industry and the establishing and maintenance of protective duties aimed principally at the wares of the United States had remarkably little effect in reducing imports from that country, although it is possible that the duties may have retarded the rate of increase of these imports. How great the development of Canadian industry has been, it is difficult to say with accuracy; a recent writer places the annual output of her factories in 1890 at $368,000,000, from which it increased by 1900 to $481,000,000, and by 1910 to $1,165,000,000.[3] But it is noteworthy that the greater part of this expansion was in directions in which, owing to natural causes, the competition of American products had never been particularly serious. Most of it was found in flour and sawmilling, meat packing, canning, paper making, and certain branches of the iron and steel industry. It was only in the last of these that some actual displacement of American goods was evident, and this was of no serious consequence.

Factors tending to offset artificial restrictions.—That the trade between the United States and Canada underwent an unprecedented development in spite of these deterring factors is a notable illustration of the weakness of artificial barriers against the potent economic forces controlling commerce between neighboring countries. The more important of these forces in this instance may be briefly indicated. Of primary importance: Commerce between the United States and Canada was in many essential respects more in the nature of domestic than of foreign trade. Propinquity, similarity of speech, of commercial law, of business methods, and of monetary units

---

[1] From Canada Year Book, 1911, pp. 68–83.
[2] Does not include gold-bearing quartz, dust, nuggets, etc., and silver ore, concentrates, etc., amounting to $17,935,732.
[3] Skelton, O. D., in Canada and its Provinces, Vol. 9, p. 252.

facilitated the transaction of business. Trade descriptions, price quotations, credit systems, commercial ratings, were developed in like manner and put to like uses in both countries. Similarity of environment, racial relationship, and frequency of intercourse resulted in an identity of fashions, habits, and wants. There was an active movement of tourists and settlers in both directions. All these things contributed to make the trade between Canadians and Americans the same as the trade of each with their fellow countrymen, and thereby tended to foster it.

Side by side with the interests and habits thus shared in common, there were differences in the physical resources and technical development of the two countries that made exchange of many articles profitable and, indeed, necessary. This was eminently true of such things as Indian corn, tobacco, certain fruits from the south, and furs from the north. While Canada's resources in many varieties of timber were enormous, she produced little hardwood, and this is indispensable for certain purposes. The United States, while some of its timber resources were approaching exhaustion, was yet able to supply the very varieties which Canada needed. Again, the growing iron and steel industry of Canada required increasing supplies of coke, which had to be imported because the Nova Scotian coal contained too much sulphur for economical coking. Canada lacked Bessemer ore, and imported quantities of it from Minnesota, sending her own ore to the furnaces of Ohio and Pennsylvania. In like manner Canadian hard wheat, spruce, asbestos, nickel, and gypsum furnished or supplemented the raw materials needed in the United States.

There were other more special reasons for commercial growth. Investments of American capital in Canadian industries often took the form of the establishment or purchase (in whole or in part) of enterprises to be controlled and officered by American business men. Sir George E. Foster has stated that in 1910 American capital in new plants, branch factories, and factory equipment amounted to $226,000,000.[1] Such enterprises created more trade than they displaced. Their initial installations of machinery and equipment were almost invariably bought from the United States, and parts for repair and renewal were constantly ordered from the same source. Partly finished products were frequently shipped for completion across the border.

There was an extensive similarity of industrial requirements and needs in the two countries. Many patterns and devices created in the United States to meet special American needs were produced nowhere else. Thus, the only serious competition in the market for agricultural tools and machinery was such as grew up on Canadian soil. The sawmilling machinery adapted to the methods of Canadian sawyers was procurable only in the United States, with the exception of a few German imitations. Many branches of Canadian industry had their inception in the United States, and the builders, managers, superintendents, and skilled laborers, even when native Canadians, had frequently been trained across the border. When to these reasons are added the unapproached excellence of some American

---

[1] House of Commons Debates, Feb. 14, 1911, p. 3606. In May, 1911, F. W. Field, the Toronto correspondent of the British Board of Trade, estimated that Americans had invested in Canada almost $420,000,000. Quoted from P. T. McGrath, American Review of Reviews, XLIX, p. 598.

products, such as machine tools, and the originality and special suitability of many others, such as ranges, heating plants and fixtures, and plumbers' supplies, the preference of Canadian consumers as indicated in the import statistics is readily understood.

Many American industries were able to retain and extend their market in Canada in spite of Canadian competition, because of their greater capital, their more highly developed organization, and their incomparably greater market at home—the last named being probably the most important of these factors. The increased market enabled them to effect economies and to specialize.

The advantage of financial strength and larger scale operations was as apparent in the selling as in the technical departments of business. The organization for advertising, soliciting, packing, and delivery that was effective in the United States could be extended to Canada at little additional cost. American traveling salesmen and agents were familiar figures in every Canadian province; the effective methods of selling were those for which they had been trained at home; they understood the Canadian situation better than did their British and German competitors; they could fill orders promptly; and they could make deliveries in quantities and forms to suit their customers. The efforts and activities of American consuls and commercial agents were also a distinctly advantageous contribution.

Under these circumstances the greater part of Canada's import trade was supplied by the United States. What Canadians purchased from other countries was, in the main, precisely what the people of the United States also had to import. The most notable exception was afforded by woolen manufactures. Though this industry had attained a great expansion in the United States, it had not been lifted to the plane upon which it stood in Europe, and its whole output, except for an insignificant amount of ready-made clothing which went to Canada, was sold, under the protection of very heavy duties, in the United States. In other directions, however, the Canadian imports from the United States grew in proportion as American industry expanded so as to embrace what had previously been the specialties of other countries.

In sum, the growth of Canada's prosperity and population was reflected in her trade with the United States. While Canada's legislative restrictions may have modified the character of the trade, they seem, however formidable in appearance, to have had little effect upon its volume. The development of her domestic industries displaced some American products, but it created a new demand for others. Upon the whole, history probably affords no better example of the degree to which the growing prosperity of one country accrues to the benefit of its neighbors.

THE RECIPROCITY MOVEMENT IN 1911.

The tariff act of 1909 in the United States.—In the United States it was left to the friends and framers of the tariff law of 1897, after they had admitted that readjustments were necessary to meet new conditions, to revise the tariff law. The Republican Party carried the country, for the fourth time in succession, in 1908. One of the first concerns of Congress during the next year was the revision of the tariff.

In the framing and exactment of the tariff act of 1909 Congress made an approach, as has been explained elsewhere, to the two-schedule tariff system. The rates of the maximum schedule were to be applied to all countries not found to be extending satisfactory treatment to the products of the United States, and those rates amounted to a penalty duty of 25 per cent ad valorem—in addition to the regular duties—on all goods on the dutiable list.

Efforts to prevent tariff war with Canada.—Canada found herself, along with other countries, threatened with the maximum duties; their application would without doubt very nearly have put an end to her export trade with the United States and would probably have brought on a disastrous tariff war. Hoping to avert this needless blow to the business interests of both countries, President Taft sent to Ottawa early in 1910 Prof. Henry C. Emery, chairman of the United States Tariff Board, and Mr. Charles M. Pepper, commercial adviser—representing the State Department—to discuss the situation with the Canadian authorities. These representatives were received by Sir Wilfrid Laurier, premier, and Mr. Fielding, Minister of Finance, and informal conferences ensued. The American representatives did not raise the question of the British preference; rates applicable only within the Empire were regarded as a "domestic" arrangement with which foreign countries were not concerned. They did take up, as a matter of friendly discussion, the provincial restrictions upon timber export, especially in their application to pulp wood; but that was represented to them as a matter with which the Dominion Government had no power to deal. This left as the only cause of American complaint the French treaty which was about to go into effect. Upon the ground that the United States gave Canada her lowest rates, it was urged that Canada in turn should reciprocate with the treatment accorded to the most favored nation. To this the Canadian representatives replied that the favors extended to France had been granted in return for equivalent concessions made by that country, and that the United States might have them, if they so desired, upon the granting of equivalent reductions in the general rates of the new tariff act. The discussion from this point turned upon the difference between the "American" and the "English" interpretation of the most-favored-nation clause, and, no agreement having been reached as to the rights of the United States in the case in question, the conference ended.[1]

President Taft then arranged that he himself should meet Mr. Fielding at Albany, and the conference occurred on March 19. Assuring Mr. Fielding of his desire to cultivate friendly commercial relations with Canada, the President explained that the terms of the tariff act left him no discretion; he could extend the benefit of the minimum rates only if Canada made concessions; he suggested that the reductions in the French treaty be extended to the United States. Mr. Fielding replied that Canada would be willing to discuss the proposal only if the United States were prepared to make direct concessions from the rates of her tariff. In the course of the conference the President emphasized his desire that the two Governments should cooperate to bring about better trade relations; and he added that for the present the difficulty with regard to applying the maximum tariff to Canada would be relieved if she would grant moderate concessions.

On most-favored-nation practices, see Part II, p. 394 seq., infra.

A few days later negotiations of a more formal character were opened at Washington. The conferences were most friendly; but Mr Fielding and his colleague, Mr. Graham, were firm in the contention that responsibility for the threatened tariff war rested solely with the United States, and that, therefore, the concessions made by Canada to avoid the conflict should not be numerous, should involve nothing disadvantageous to any Canadian industry, and should not be made specifically to the United States, but should apply equally to all countries. It was at length agreed that the United States Government was to be satisfied with the extension by Canada of the intermediate instead of the general rates in application to thirteen articles imported from the United States. Among these articles were soap, tableware, cottonseed oil, leather, perfumery, watch movements, and photographs. These reductions would have very little fiscal effect; in the previous fiscal year the articles of the group in question had been imported into Canada from the United States to the value of $4,814,293, and the proposed reduction in the duties would—it was estimated—involve a loss of revenue to Canada, assuming imports to remain the same, of only $192,814.[1]

Slight though the concessions were, the plan was attacked by the Conservatives in the Canadian Parliament upon the grounds that the Government had yielded to the bullying threat of a club; that it had bound itself not to alter without the consent of the United States the duties upon thirteen tariff items; and that any concession at all was an admission in principle that the French treaty was discriminatory against the United States—an admission which would expose Canada to the likelihood of demands for further concessions in case she ever made further commercial treaties with any other country.[2] Sir Wilfrid Laurier defended the Government's action as necessary if a tariff war was to be avoided, and maintained that Canada had not agreed and never would agree to the American contention that, whenever two nations made a commercial treaty by which they exchanged favors, the United States had the right to ask from both the most-favored-nation treatment. He said the concessions were of no importance; that in return for them Canada secured peace and good relations with her neighbor; and he added, significantly, "The first thing we shall do is to endeavor to negotiate with our neighbors and if possible to get a treaty of commerce with them."[3]

This statement of the prime minister was made in accordance with an understanding reached in the course of the friendly conferences just concluded. On March 26 Secretary Knox, in a letter congratulating Mr. Fielding on the adjustment of the immediate difficulty, had written: "Let me take this opportunity to express by his direction the desire of the President that your Government will find it convenient to take up with this Government, at such time and in such manner as may be mutually satisfactory, the consideration of a readjustment of our trade relations upon the broader and more liberal lines which should obtain between countries so closely related geographically and racially, as indicated by the President in his

[1] Statement of Hon. William Paterson. Minister of Customs, House of Commons debates, May 3, 1910, p. 8755.

[2] Speeches of Mr. Currie, Mr. Maclean, and Mr. R. L. Borden, House of Commons debates, Mar. 30 and May 3, 1910.

[3] Speech of Sir Wilfrid Laurier, Ibid., Mar. 30, 1910, p. 5993.

recent public utterances." [1]   To this Mr. Fielding responded that the Canadian people would receive with pleasure the formal confirmation of the President's public utterances thus conveyed; and that his Government would avail itself of the invitation.

It was in this manner that the new movement for reciprocity had its origin; but when once under way it was given momentum in the United States by the operation of another provision of the tariff act of 1909, namely, that imposing retaliatory duties upon Canadian wood, pulp, and paper.   The use of news-print paper in the United States had been growing very rapidly, but the imports of paper and pulp from Canada, which had a practically unlimited potential capacity for producing both, had amounted to but an insignificant percentage of the consumption.[2]   It was generally believed by American consumers (principally the press) that their interests had been sacrificed in the tariff for the benefit of a manufacturing combination.   By the tariff act of 1909, a sliding scale of duties upon paper had been arranged to reduce the rates generally applicable.   But the reductions did not affect Canada, since it was expressly provided that the rates of the previous tariff should continue to apply against any country or dependency which levied an export duty upon wood, pulp, or paper; and in addition that a countervailing duty be collected equivalent to the export duty of the producing country.   This provision had been framed for the particular purpose of retaliating against the export duties of the Canadian provincial governments.   Furthermore, no reduction was made in the rates upon chemical wood pulp; and the duty was removed from mechanically ground pulp only when imported from a country which imposed no export restrictions of the kind mentioned.   The average cost of producing news-print paper was less in Canada than in the United States by $5.35 a ton, owing chiefly to the lower cost of pulp wood.[3]   This difference was greatly magnified in popular estimation, and it was widely believed that the retention of the duties was solely responsible for the rise in prices by which the "paper trust" had benefited, and that their removal would effect a saving to the newspapers of at least six or eight million dollars a year.   There was, therefore, a widespread and cordial expression of approval in the reception by the press of President Taft's proposal for reciprocity.

Negotiations of a reciprocity agreement.—A reciprocity arrangement was finally negotiated at Washington in January, 1911.   The Canadian agents were Mr. Fielding, Minister of Finance. and Mr. Paterson, Minister of Customs, with the cooperation of Ambassador Bryce. For the United States, the matter was in charge of Mr. Knox, Secretary of State, and Mr. Hoyt, Counselor of the State Department, with certain expert assistants.   As far as possible, diplomatic forms and ceremonies were dispensed with; there was very little official correspondence, and the negotiations were almost entirely verbal and informal.   After the arrangement had been concluded, Mr. Fielding and Mr. Paterson addressed a formal letter to Secretary Knox setting forth their understanding of what had been agreed upon.

---

[1] House of Commons debates, Mar. 30, 1910, p. 5972.
[2] By 1910 the annual consumption had attained a value of $54,000,000; but the imports from Canada had amounted to but $3,021,347 worth of wood pulp and $2,019,089 worth of paper, crude paper stock, and all manufactures of paper.
[3] Report of U. S. Tariff Board, May 15, 1911, Pt. V.

This letter and Secretary Knox's reply are the only important official documents relating to the conference. -

Two points had been settled quickly to the satisfaction of both sides. One was that the arrangement should take the form of concurrent legislation instead of a treaty, for the reason that the Canadians wished to be free at any time to annul it if it should prove after trial to be unfavorable to their interests.[1] The other was that Canada would not exchange the right to the inshore fisheries for the free admission of fish to the United States. The Canadian representatives consented, however, to annul the license charges which had been required of American fishermen under the *modus vivendi* of 1887, and to retain only the nominal fee of a dollar a year upon each vessel as an evidence of unimpaired national control.

Regarding the pulp and paper duties, the conferees were unable to reach a satisfactory agreement. The Dominion Government had not the power to remove the export restrictions imposed by the individual Provinces. The best that could be done was to agree that the United States should admit free of duty all Canadian wood pulp and paper made of wood pulp when valued at not more than 4 cents a pound, upon the condition precedent that no export duty, fee, or charge of any kind should have been imposed upon the paper or the pulp or wood of which it was made. This provision became section 2 of the act which later passed Congress, and as the operation of that section was not made dependent upon the fate of the reciprocity measure, it went into effect in spite of the subsequent defeat of that arrangement.[2]

Proposed changes in the tariff rates.—The proposed changes in the general tariff rates were listed in four schedules. Schedule A embraced the articles that were to be duty free in both countries. It included practically all agricultural products except wool; fish and fish oil of all kinds (except sardines and fish preserved in oil); hewn timber, sawed lumber, posts, ties, poles, staves, and palings; unmanufactured asbestos, gypsum, talc, mica, feldspar, and fluorspar. Very few manufactured products were included in this schedule, the most important of those that were included being galvanized or tinned iron and steel sheets, galvanized wire and wire rods of certain gauges, all barbed fencing wire, cream separators, carbon electrodes, typesetting and typecasting machines, coke, and cottonseed oil.

Schedule B included articles to be admitted into each country from the other at identical rates of duty, which were generally lower than those at the moment then prevailing in either country. Many of the items were secondary products and manufactures of which the chief component materials were made free in Schedule A. Under this head came such articles as flour, barley-malt, canned vegetables, fresh and canned meats, lard, bacon, prepared cereals, biscuits, and fruit juices. Schedule B also included agricultural implements and machinery, monumental and building stone (except marble and onyx), cutlery and plated ware, clocks and watches, motor vehicles, bathroom fixtures, and some other manufactures of minor importance.

Schedule C included six articles that were to be admitted at special rates by the United States: Aluminum, laths, shingles, planed or finished lumber, iron ore, and coal slack.

---

[1] Mr. Fielding, House of Commons Debates, Jan. 26, 1911, p. 2502.   [2] See Part II, p. 411, infra.

Schedule D contained seven articles upon which Canada was to make reductions: Cement, fruit trees, condensed milk, unsweetened biscuits, canned fruits, peanuts, and bituminous coal.

Estimate of provisions and potential effects.—The arrangement affected nearly one-half of all the imports into the United States from Canada, but only one-fifth of the imports into Canada from the United States. The articles placed upon the free list included more than 40 per cent of the United States imports from Canada and less than 10 per cent of the Canadian imports from the United States. Of the articles placed on the free lists, there had been on the dutiable list in the United States over 76 per cent, in Canada less than 17 per cent. The previous United States duties were to remain on less than 5 per cent of the imports from Canada; and the Canadian duties were to remain on more than 35 per cent of the imports from the United States. The Canadian imports from the United States were, however, of much greater total value than the United States imports from Canada; and the absolute values of the imports to be affected in each direction were almost the same.

The following tables show how the arrangement would have operated if applied to the trade as it stood in 1909–10:

Canadian imports (affected by the agreement) from the United States, fiscal year ended March 31, 1910.

	Value.	Per cent of total imports.	Per cent of dutiable imports.	Duties previously levied.	Amount of duties to be remitted.
Articles to be made free	$21,957,605	9.19	16.51	$1,476,129	$1,476,129
Articles to be reduced in duty	25,870,354	10.82	19.45	6,300,107	1,084,450
Total affected	47,827,959	20.01	35.96		
Remaining dutiable at the previous rate	85,198,178	35.65	64.04		
Total previously dutiable	133,026,137	55.64	100.00		
Total previously free	106,044,412	44.36			
Grand total	239,070,549			7,776,236	2,560,579

American imports (affected by the agreement) from Canada, fiscal year ended June 30, 1910.

	Value.	Per cent of total imports.	Per cent of dutiable imports.	Duties previously levied.	Amount of duties to be remitted.
Articles to be made free	$39,811,560	40.67	76.40	$4,256,988	$4,256,988
Articles to be reduced in duty	7,521,598	7.68	14.44	1,412,838	612,945
Total affected	47,333,158	48.35	90.84		
Remaining dutiable at the previous rates	4,770,780	4.87	9.16		
Total previously dutiable	52,103,938	53.22	100.00		
Total previously free	43,024,372	46.78			
Grand total	95,128,310	100.00		5,649,826	4,849,933

Except for the articles included in Schedule A, reductions in the other schedules were very moderate, averaging approximately 8 per cent ad valorem on the part of the United States and a little more than 4 per cent on the part of Canada—reductions which in each case left protection practically unimpaired.   To the American representatives the scope of the arrangement was a disappointment.   They had hoped to secure much more extensive concessions, but the Canadian representatives were unwilling to take away the tariff protection from manufactured articles.

Upon the whole the Canadian duties fixed in the agreement corresponded closely with the rates of the Canadian intermediate tariff of 1907.   The explanation of this is simple.   The prime object of the conferees was to arrange for the admission to the United States of Canadian agricultural produce, fish, and raw materials.   Having settled upon this, the conferees took the Canadian intermediate tariff and selected from it certain items which the United States exported in considerable quantities and upon which the American members asked for the lowest rates possible.   But upon nearly all of these the Canadians would consider no reductions below the terms of the intermediate tariff.   The only important exceptions were cottonseed oil, galvanized or tinned sheets, and typesetting and typecasting machines, all of which were added to the free list.   Considering the nature of the articles and the very small difference between the proposed rates and the old, it is difficult to see how the export of American manufactures could have been materially affected.

Many of the items in Schedule A were already duty free in Canada. In addition to the few manufactures already mentioned, the only other articles made free of which Canada had imported considerable quantities during the previous fiscal year were horses and sheep, vegetables, fruits and berries, barley, seeds, and oysters; of all these (excepting barley and oysters) she had sold to the United States more than she had bought from them.   The truck farmers of Ontario and the fruit growers of British Columbia were practically the only Canadian agricultural interests opposed to the arrangement.

Schedule A was more important to the United States, where it was expected and primarily intended to encourage imports.   Aside from pulp wood, pulp, and paper, concerning which no satisfactory settlement was reached, the articles in the free list which were most prominent in the minds of the conferees, and about which the discussion chiefly turned in both countries, were meat, animals, wheat, fish, and lumber.   Most agricultural products sold at a rather lower price in Canada than across the border, but, except in the case of wheat, the Canadian export surplus was so small in comparison with the annual product of the United States, that it could not materially have affected American markets except to some slight extent in the towns near the border.

Although much the same considerations also apply to the trade in meat animals, the extension of the free list to cover this trade encountered special opposition on both sides.   In the United States the sheep raisers feared that it would cut into the advantage to which they were accustomed under the tariff; in Canada the meat packers objected because they feared a possible rise in the prices of their supplies.   On the whole, the most that could reasonably have been expected of the arrangement in this connection was that the widening of the sources of supply would contribute somewhat toward stabilizing prices by preventing abrupt fluctuations arising from local causes.

The case of wheat was different.   Both countries produced a large wheat surplus and they were competitors in the European market:

yet there was room for a considerable trade in this commodity between the two. This was due in part to the location of their respective wheat fields and to differences in quality of the grain. An even more important practical reason was that in Canada the increase in the production of grain had outstripped the development of milling, while in the United States the milling industry had been developed to such an extent that the grain crops were frequently insufficient to keep the mills running at full capacity. Therefore Canada exported much wheat and comparatively little flour, while the United States exported chiefly flour. The Canadian price of wheat was fixed in Liverpool, but this was not always true of the American price even of export wheat. Furthermore, much of the product of both countries did not grade for export. "Macaroni" wheat and certain other grades were consumed mainly in the domestic market, and the price was determined by the demand in that market. In view of these facts and of the transportation situation the repeal of duties would doubtless materially have stimulated American purchases of wheat from Canada.

In regard to the trade in fish, it would seem that Canada could readily have met the demand in the American market and still have had a surplus. But much of the Canadian output would not have been salable in America and, even with duties removed in the United States, must have continued to go to Europe and the West Indies. Some benefit would have accrued to the Nova Scotia fishermen and to consumers in Boston and other North Atlantic cities, but the total effect would have been local and in no case considerable.

The most important results of the agreement would have arisen from the free admission of rough lumber and the reduction of duties upon dressed lumber, laths, and shingles. Only upon these articles could the agreement possibly have lowered American prices by anything like the amount of the export duties which Schedule A would have removed, and even in this case the effect of the remission of duties would have been limited to New England and the regions adjacent to the lower Great Lakes. The continuous exploitation of the forests and the concentration of ownership of most of the timber were reflected in rising prices which were felt by practically all classes. The proposal of free lumber was therefore widely popular. The repeal of the lumber duties at an early date was expected even by the lumber interests. Their opposition to the reciprocity arrangement was due, therefore, rather to their wish to use the repeal as a means to force the abolishing of the provincial restrictions upon timber export than to any expectation that resistance would be permanently successful.

Such, then, were the character and the possibilities of the agreement. It should be noted that its provisions were addressed exclusively to import duties. By this arrangement Canada was to obtain practically everything that she had formerly sought by way of reciprocity, while her concessions were to be little more than those which she had already extended to most countries, but not to the United States, through the operation of her conventional tariff.

On January 26, 1911, legislation to carry the arrangement into effect was introduced concurrently in the House of Representatives in the United States and in the House of Commons in Canada.

Passage of the reciprocity bill in Congress.—In the United States protests against the proposed tariff revision came from every interest upon whose products the duties had been lowered. The farmers in the border States—particularly the wheat-growing States of the Northwest—the fishermen of New England, the sheep and cattle men of the Mountain States, and the lumbermen of the Pacific coast and the South, formed the chief groups who believed their future prosperity jeopardized. But the most effective opposition came from the advocates of protectionist principles. Argumentative illustrations and statistics were brought up to date, but neither in Congress nor in the press was there advanced against the measure a single argument that had not appeared among those which had sufficed for the rejection of reciprocity in the later decades of the nineteenth century. It was soon manifest that although the measure had been initiated by a Republican President, it would be opposed by the majority of his party in Congress. The fate of the bill rested upon the action of the Democrats, and what this action would be was not long left in doubt. With the combined support of Democrats, Progressives, and some Republicans, the bill passed the House on February 14, 1911, by a vote of 221 to 93.

In the Senate, the Committee on Finance reported the bill on February 24, in the form in which it had passed the House, and without recommendation. The majority of the committee were known to be opposed to it. Of the short session, only seven legislative days remained. Sentiment in the Senate was more evenly divided than it had been in the House, and it was doubtful what the result of a vote would be. Control of the Senate's procedure was, however, still in the hands of opponents of the measure, and the bill was not allowed to come to a vote before the Sixty-first Congress expired.

Disappointed at the failure of the Senate to take action, President Taft summoned Congress to meet on April 4, for the particular purpose of enacting the reciprocity legislation. The composition of the new, Sixty-second, Congress removed all doubt as to what would be the result. On April 21, the measure passed the House for the second time, by a vote of 268 to 89. The action of the Senate was more deliberate, but, in spite of strenuous opposition, the combination support gave the measure a majority. The bill passed on July 22, by a vote of 53 to 27, and it was approved by the President on July 26, 1911.

The bill in the Canadian Parliament.—When the Canadian representatives reached home, it was with a feeling of keen satisfaction that in return for the conventional tariff they had opened the way for the free admission of nearly all important Canadian products, except manufactures, into a market of more than 90,000,000 consumers. When charged, during the ensuing debate in Parliament, with having neglected to provide detailed information and estimates showing the probable operation of the measure, Mr. Fielding justified the omission upon the ground that:

What we have done is no departure from the policy of Canada for forty years. * * * There is an important difference in the position of the United States Government then and now. They were proposing a radical departure from the policy of the country, and they may have needed information of that sort to support their case, but we certainly did not.[1]

---

[1] House of Commons Debates, Apr. 6, 1911, p. 6782.

But the Canadian Government seems somewhat to have overlooked the inevitable effect of economic conditions in Canada upon public opinion. During the preceding twenty years, the growth of cities, the building of east and west railways, the establishing of interprovincial traffic, the diversification of industries, and the development of overseas markets, had been attained in spite of the refusal of reciprocity. Business had adjusted itself to prevailing conditions; there was greater and more general prosperity than Canada had ever known before. Conservative leaders contended that a sudden change of policy was uncalled for and ill advised at a time when Canada's production was greater than ever before, when markets and transportation facilities were adequate and the prices received by Canadian producers the highest they had ever been. They even asserted that any benefits which might be expected to flow from the conclusion of the arrangement would probably soon come to Canada without concessions, through changes to be made in the American tariff by the Democratic Party.

The Government felt itself in a position to contend that the agreement involved no change of policy, inasmuch as neither party had formally repudiated its once eager advocacy of reciprocity, each having merely refrained from action until the attitude of the United States should indicate that negotiations would be fruitful. Furthermore, the Canadian intermediate tariff had been adopted in 1907 for the special purpose of opening foreign markets, and the use to which it was put in this case could be pointed to as a culminating success. But the opposition claimed that when the conventional tariff was enacted, no Canadian had anticipated its application to the United States; that, on the contrary, its chief purpose had been to procure substitute markets and to give an advantage to imports from other countries in retaliation for American illiberality; and that to use it now to promote trade with a country that had always been commercially hostile would constitute a violation of the Parliament's mandate from the people. Upon this latter ground it was urged that to proceed with the measure without first appealing to the country would even be unconstitutional.[1]

It soon became apparent, both in Parliament and in the press, that resentment at the rejection by the United States of former proposals would play an important part in determining the issue. It was widely believed in Canada that in earlier times the United States had made use of its commercial policy with intent to force Canada into a surrender of her economic and even her political independence. This feeling was sedulously cultivated by a certain section of the press, and Americans who read the Canadian papers were surprised and chagrined at the animosity and bitterness displayed. Resentment at past behavior was readily transmuted into distrust of present intentions. It was darkly hinted that the United States would gain advantages not yet discernible in the terms of the treaty. All sorts of ulterior motives were suggested for the change in American policy.

Nor was the apprehension lacking that closer trade relations with the United States would injure commerce within the British Empire. According to a resolution of the Montreal Board of Trade, "it [reciprocity] might easily prove to be the entering of a wedge that would

---

[1] Mr. Armstrong, Sir Clifford Sifton, Mr. Harris, Mr. MacLean and others, House of Commons Debates, Feb. 22, 24, 28, Mar. 8, etc., 1911, pp. 4144–4480.

eventually result in the separation of our interests from those of the motherland."[1]   The United States already had more of Canada's commerce than all the rest of the world; if that share were increased, what would remain for the mother country and the other British colonies?   Canada had initiated the policy of imperial preference; she took a parental pride in it, and many of her statesmen still cherished the hope that England would yet adopt the system.   To such a hope the agreement seemed to threaten a deathblow, for if England should ever establish a preference, American products would be poured into Great Britain through Canada to take advantage of it.   Against this, the Liberal supporters pointed out that the policy of British preference was in no way impaired but might be carried to any length the Government desired.   They further indicated that the measure under discussion affected altogether little more than $6,000,000 worth of British imports, and that even upon this amount the preference was but slightly lessened.   They urged that the idea of "tariff reform"— that is, of abandoning the free-trade system—and "imperial preference" had been irretrievably repudiated in England in the elections of 1906.   But Canadians are extremely sensitive to anything which may reflect upon their loyalty and attachment to the Empire, and the argument that more commerce with the United States would mean less with the mother country carried great weight.

The opponents of reciprocity did not confine themselves to appeals to sentiment.   Perhaps the most telling point they made against the proposed arrangement was the insecurity as to the length of its duration.   Based as it was to be upon concurrent legislation in the two countries, it would be subject to abrogation at the pleasure or caprice of either.   The United States would be free, with or without cause or pretext, to put an end to the arrangement at any time.   Through its adoption, the trade of Canada would be diverted from its present channels; European markets for Canadian produce would be neglected for that of the United States, and other countries would occupy those markets; the entire structure of Canada's business would be readjusted to reciprocity; if, then, after this process was completed, the arrangement should be terminated, Canada's commerce would be suddenly paralyzed.   This possible objection to the agreement had not escaped its authors upon either side, but they had believed it impossible to persuade their respective legislatures to ratify a treaty for a definite period and they were convinced that a few years of operation would show the arrangement to be so beneficial to both countries that its continuance would be desired by both. The opposition pointed, however, to the precipitate abrogation of the former reciprocity treaty and expressed strong distrust of the American plan for the future.   Should Canada accept the proposed arrangement, she would be bound hand and foot, since, having sacrificed her other markets, she would be utterly dependent upon the good will of the United States.[2]   She would be unable to make any change in her tariff without the consent of Washington—her commercial agreements would be subject to approval or veto by the United States Senate; even the British preference might, upon the demand of Congress, have to be sacrificed; the enforcement of quarantine regu-

---

[1] Quoted by Mr. Blain, House of Commons Debates, Feb. 27, 1911, p. 4385.
[2] See statement of eighteen Toronto Liberals, Industrial Canada, II, p. 834, House of Commons Debates, Mr. Borden, Feb. 9, 1911, p. 3300.

lations would be declared an infringement of the agreement; and one concession after another might be wrung from Canada until commercial union under the tariff laws of the United States would be the final result.   It was claimed that approval of the arrangement had been put through at Washington only by an unstable coalition of heterogeneous elements and that a change in party alignment would bring about its repeal.

Even more effective with the electorate, though less well founded, was the argument that reciprocity would be a fatal blow to Canada's industries and would undo all that had been achieved by the "national policy"; Canada would be reduced to the condition of a producer of raw materials, while all the skilled and highly paid labor would be performed in the United States   "My count against this measure, stronger and deeper than any," said Mr. Foster, "is that it threatens the best and highest production in this country, that it threatens thereby the stream of interprovincial trade, which is absolutely the life and essence of this country as a whole; it also vitally affects and changes the channels of trade and the great transport routes.   *   *   * It vitally affects the labor interests by shifting one-half of our production to the United States, and that half employs the most labor at the highest wages." [1]   Canadian wheat would be ground at Minneapolis; the Canadian meat packers would be put out of business by the American trust;[2] the duty reduction of 8 cents a ton on coal would crowd the Nova Scotia companies from the markets of Quebec and Ontario;[3] the British Columbia lumber mills would lose their markets;[4] the Trent River Paper Co. could not compete with American mills, on account of the cost of coal and other supplies;[5] according to a memorial of the American Newspaper Publishers Association, Canada would produce only pulp and the United States would turn this into paper;[6] and the arrangement would cause the wasteful exploitation, for American profit, of Canadian resources. Great insistence was also placed upon the probable effect of the agreement in stemming the inflow of British capital.[7]

In meeting these arguments the Liberals were upon strong ground, for they had carefully refrained from so far lowering the rates upon manufactures as to affect Canadian prices.   With regard to the diversion of traffic, Sir Wilfrid Laurier pointed out that the growth of the Northwest insured the prosperity of the railways, that the Canadian lines provided a route from Winnipeg to Liverpool 600 miles shorter than that by way of New York, and that under the bonding privilege all the traffic that was likely to go through the United States already went that way.[8]   Business men in general were not frightened by the prospect of reciprocity.   Within three weeks after the introduction of the bill, Canadian Pacific stock rose five points; Grand Trunk also went up; and for all the 49 stocks listed on the Montreal Exchange there was an average increase in value of 2¼ per cent.[9]

---

[1] House of Commons Debates, Feb. 9, 1911, pp. 3409–3411.
[2] Toronto Monetary Times, XLVI, 1213.
[3] House of Commons Debates, Mr. Maddin, July 28, 1911.
[4] Toronto News, Feb. 14, 1911.
[5] Communication submitted by Mr. Porter, House of Commons Debates, Feb. 23, 1911, p. 4118.
[6] Mr. Borden, House of Commons Debates, Mar. 8, 1911, p. 4931.
[7] House of Commons Debates, Feb. 9, 1911, Mr. Foster et al., p. 3409.
[8] House of Commons Debates, Mar. 7, 1911, p. 4758.
    Mr. McPhail, in Montreal Witness, Feb. 21, 1911.

The fear of annexation.—It is not likely that the agreement would have been defeated in Canada upon economic grounds alone, for in reality it offered no threat to any existing Canadian industry, and it promised benefit to the farmers, fishermen, and lumbermen, whose political influence was very great. Mr. Fielding declared that there had been no serious effort to discuss it from an economic point of view and that its opponents, unable to deal with it upon its merits, "beat the big drum of imperialism." [1]

The manufacturers and protectionists of course, based their opposition on economic grounds. But, with full recognition of the strategic possibilities which the opportunity for attack offered, the whole force of the Conservative Party was directed against the reciprocity measure, while the Liberals were weakened by defections within their own ranks. Sir Wilfrid Laurier's naval policy, for instance, had alienated a portion of the Quebec electorate, a constituency which usually gave him its almost undivided support. So far as reciprocity was the real question with the voters, there is little doubt that the decisive factor was the fear that commercial intimacy would lead to annexation. The friends of the agreement protested in vain that Canadians did not export their loyalty in sacks of wheat or packages of gypsum, and that the prediction of political union was an insult to their intelligence. Nevertheless the opposition maintained that "* * * the far-reaching effect of business affiliation, the close proximity and constant efflux and influx, the seductions of commercialism, the constant intercourse of business, social, and official life will inevitably weaken the ties of empire, and wean the thoughts of our newer generations, if not of ourselves, toward the predominant power and create new attachments. * * * The dominant sentiment in the United States that is pushing reciprocity through to a successful enactment is not economic, it is political. It is still the conquest of Canada." [2] Old and new assertions of American publicists and journalists favoring political union were republished broadcast throughout the Provinces. There have always been and there are to-day a great number of Canadians who honestly believe that the United States has been constantly on the watch for an opportunity to annex the Dominion. This is, of course, not at all in accordance with the facts. The real opinion of an overwhelming majority of Americans upon this matter was that expressed by Secretary Knox in a public address in Chicago: "The United States," he said, "recognizes with satisfaction that the Dominion of Canada is a permanent North American political unit and that her autonomy is secure." [3] But for one Canadian who read this speech, there were ten who read the statement of the New York Journal: "We look forward to the day when this whole North American Continent will be one great nation, as it should be." [4] Such remarks stung the national pride of Canadians to the quick and were interpreted as the indiscreet voicing by individuals of a sentiment cherished by all Americans.

---

[1] House of Commons Debates, Feb. 9, 1911, p. 3359.
[2] Mr. Foster, House of Commons Debates, Feb. 14, 1911, p. 3635.
[3] 61st. Cong., 3d sess., H. Doc. No. 1418, p. 6.
[4] See this and other extracts from the Hearst newspapers, reproduced in the British Trade Journal, XLIX, p. 351.

Defeat of the bill.—In the House of Commons the debate over the reciprocity measure continued for several months. The Liberal majority was strong; indeed, only three members "bolted" the party on the reciprocity issue. But the opposition was alert, resourceful, and determined to make the most of their opportunity. Obstructive tactics finally compelled the prime minister to appeal to the country; on July 29 Parliament was dissolved. In the elections which followed the Conservatives carried the day by a popular vote of 669,000 as against 625,000 for the Liberals. In the new House of Commons the Conservatives had 133 seats, the Liberals, 88. The victory was really won in the single Province of Ontario, where the Conservatives elected 73 members and the Liberals only 13. In the Maritime Provinces, in Quebec, and in the Prairie Provinces, the Liberals had a popular majority of nearly 30,000, but this was more than counterbalanced by a minority in Ontario of 63,000.[1] It is the unanimous judgment of observers who watched without prejudice the progress of events in Canada that the fear of annexation was more potent than all other causes combined in defeating the Liberals, on the basis of reciprocity. The result of the elections of course put an end to further consideration of the reciprocity measure.

Canada vetoes the arrangement.—The events of 1911 constituted an interesting reversal. Whereas in previous years reciprocity had had the active support of the Canadian people, it was now rejected by popular majority at the polls. In an earlier period it had been made by Canadian statesmen the subject of repeated overtures and proposals, which had fallen upon deaf ears in the United States. In 1911 both the administration and the legislature in the United States gave the project their approval, only to see it rejected in Canada by the electorate.

The reciprocity legislation still stands in the United States.—Upon the statute books of the United States the act providing for reciprocity with Canada still stands as a law; the passage of a like act by the Canadian Parliament would still put the arrangement, as it was negotiated, into effect.

---

[1] Skelton, O. D. The Day of Sir Wilfrid Laurier, p. 269.

PART II. THE MOST-FAVORED-NATION CLAUSE.

PART II. THE MOST-FAVORED-NATION CLAUSE.

THE MOST-FAVORED-NATION CLAUSE.

1. CHARACTER, PURPOSE, AND FORMS OF THE MOST-FAVORED-NATION CLAUSE.

The most-favored-nation clause and the practice of reciprocity.—No single feature of modern commercial treaties has occasioned more or greater difficulties of interpretation than the conspicuous pledge known as "the most-favored-nation clause." This clause has been frequently referred to in the preceding sections of this report. It is, as has been indicated, a provision intended to assure to each (or one) of the parties to a treaty that it has been put by the other in a position as advantageous as that accorded to any other nation, and that it shall not subsequently be put in a less advantageous position in the event that greater favors or privileges be granted to a third or other States.

Occurring almost universally, under widely differing conditions, in both the unconditional and the conditional forms, each of which appears in a variety of types (see *supra* and *infra*) and in a veritable network of treaties, this clause has contributed at once to the solution of some and to the creation without solution of other serious problems in commercial relations. Obviously a variety of such problems will arise where and when some States do and some others do not make reciprocity treaties. In the construction of the most-favored-nation clause, two schools of interpretation have developed. The adherents of one view, that which has become known as the "American" interpretation, have insisted on maintaining the distinction between favors given gratuitously and concessions granted expressly in return for present and recognized compensation; the adherents of the other view have sought to negative or to eliminate this distinction, insisting that most-favored-nation treatment calls for the extension, to States entitled thereto, of all concessions made to any other States.

Appearance in treaties.—The most-favored-nation provision should not be thought of as necessarily a separate and isolated treaty article. In a given treaty it may appear as a separate article, or it may appear as a clause in one or in several articles. In most treaties it appears in at least two connections. Frequently, in treaties of modern date generally, there comes first a clause or clauses providing for most-favored-nation treatment in respect to specified matters, after which a separate article covering comprehensively and collectively the particular provisions which have preceded.[1] This covering article, thought of as particularly the most-favored-nation clause, often provides sweepingly for general most-favored-nation treatment. Ordinarily a reference to "the most-favored-nation clause" in a given treaty is a reference particularly to the covering article.

---

[1] The order of appearance is often reversed.

In phraseology the provision may be either positive or negative; in some treaties it is worded affirmatively; in some, negatively; in many, both. Favored-nation treatment may be pledged without specific employment of the term "most-favored-nation."

Limitations as to intent.—The effect which the favored-nation provision is intended to have either in generalizing or in restricting State action applies, of course, only to international relationships. It has never been intended that it should operate so as to interfere with internal policies of States. The provision is not usually considered as comprehending, and it is frequently specified that it does not comprehend special relations between a colony and a mother country. The same is true of special arrangements growing out of special relations between nations, due to proximity or unusual circumstances. In some cases application or non-application to certain nations is specified. In some cases the articles, activities, or transactions to which the clause shall or shall not apply are specified.

The unconditional and the conditional forms.—Both as regards interpretation, as already suggested, and as regards phraseology, there have developed in modern times two distinct and conflicting usages. Up to the time of the American Revolution, the favored-nation provision had appeared in but one form, that of a pledge wherein no conditions were laid down as to the circumstances under which the concessions granted should extend as between the contracting parties. In the first American treaty, that made with France in 1778, there was attached to the usual pledge the qualifying conditional provision—" * * * freely, if the concession (to the third State) was freely made, or on allowing the same compensation, if the concession was conditional." From that time forward the most-favored-nation pledge has been made sometimes with and sometimes without the qualifying stipulation. Where no such stipulation is attached, it is customary to speak of the clause as being "unconditional"; when the stipulation appears that there shall be compensation the clause is spoken of as "conditional." It has been the practice of the United States, almost without exception, to employ the conditional form. It is the practice of European States to-day, but it has not always been, to employ, almost without exception, the unconditional form.

Relation between form and interpretation.—In reference to any given treaty, the interpretation to be applied in practice to a particular obligation, must necessarily depend to a considerable extent upon the form which the pledge has been given in the particular clauses wherein it is established. It thus becomes necessary in a study of most-favored-nation obligations to distinguish the various forms which the favored-nation clause has assumed. For this purpose, it is possible to make a classification of forms according to the character and extent of the grant which the phraseology employed implies. Such a classification will appear in Appendix A of this section. For present purposes it will suffice to indicate briefly certain characteristics of, differences between, and pertinent facts with regard to the unconditional and the conditional forms of the clause.

The unconditional form.—Among unconditional forms there are distinguishable at least four, and possibly five types. The first distinction to be made is that between the "unlimited" and the "limited" pledges; next that between the unilateral and the reciprocal.

In the unlimited but unilateral type, one State undertakes to give to the other (without reciprocity) any (or all) favors and privileges which it has granted or may grant to any other (the "most-favored") nation. Provisions of this type are found chiefly in treaties between States of which one is relatively strong and advanced and the other relatively weak and backward. In the reciprocal and unlimited type, the contracting parties agree mutually that each shall grant to the other any (or all) favors or privileges (in all matters referred to or not excluded) which it has granted or may grant to any other (the "most-favored") nation. This type appears particularly in the contemporary treaties of European States between themselves; it is characteristically that of the "unconditional" most-favored-nation clause. It is gradually being superseded by a type which may be looked upon either as distinct or as a mere variation, a type which employs the same phraseology, but with the addition of the provision that the favors, etc., referred to shall be granted "immediately and without condition." This has been more and more used in recent years; in the treaties of some countries it has become the standard type and is employed almost exclusively. The "immediate and unconditional" provision appears in three only of the treaties to which the United States has been a party. Of these account will be given in due course.

To the favored-nation pledge, whether in the unconditional or in the conditional form, there is frequently added a limitation, in the form of a provision to the effect that it is not to apply to or be invoked in connection with special arrangements such as those between a mother country and its colonies, those between limitrophe countries, or those established, for reason specified, with countries named. Instances of special arrangements which are thus excepted from the operation of the favored-nation clause and which are not regarded as constituting discriminations against third countries appear in the relations of Spain and Portugal, Russia and Persia, Russia and China, China and British India, China and French India, Thibet and British India, China and Korea, Mozambique and the Transvaal, Abyssinia and France, Morocco and France, Brazil and Ecuador, Chile and Latin-American countries, the countries of Central America, the United States and Cuba.[1]

The following examples may be taken as illustrative of the unconditional types[2] described above:

A. Unilateral and unlimited, unconditional.—United States-Siam treaty, May 29, 1856, Article IX:

> The American Government and its citizens will be allowed free and equal participation in any privileges that may have been, or may hereafter be granted by the Siamese Government to the Government, citizens, or subjects of any other nation.

B. Reciprocal and unlimited, unconditional.—France-Great Britain convention of November 16, 1860 (complementary to the Cobden treaty), Article V:

> Each of the high contracting powers engages to extend to the other any favor, any privilege or diminution of tariff which either of them may grant to a third power in regard to the importation of goods, whether mentioned or not mentioned in the treaty of 23d of January, 1860.

---

[1] See Memorandum presented to the House of Representatives by Mr. McCall on Jan. 18, 1912, 62d Cong., 2d sess., Cong. Rec., Vol. 48, part 2, p. 1096.
[2] For more detailed classification and examples, see Appendix A, p. 445, infra.

C. Reciprocal and unlimited, immediate and unconditional.—
Great Britain-Japan treaty, April 3, 1911, Article XXIV:

> The high contracting parties agree that, in all that concerns commerce,
> navigation, and industry, any favor, privilege, or immunity which either high
> contracting party has actually granted, or may hereafter grant, to the ships,
> subjects, or citizens of any other State, shall be extended immediately and
> unconditionally to the ships or subjects of the other high contracting party,
> it being their intention that the commerce, navigation, and industry of each
> country shall be placed in all respects on the footing of the most-favored
> nation.

D. Reciprocal but limited, unconditional.—Cuba-Italy treaty,
December 29, 1903, Article XXVIII (most-favored-nation clause,
plus):

> It is understood that the provisions laid down in the foregoing Articles do
> not cover the cases in which Cuba may grant special reductions on its customs
> duties to the produce of other American States. Consequently, such conces-
> sions can not be claimed by Italy on the grounds of its being the most-favored
> nation, except when they be granted to another State which is not American.

The conditional form.—There are at least three distinguishable
types of the conditional form. First, there are rare instances of
unilateral most-favored-nation pledges in the conditional form.
Second, the most-favored-nation pledge may be reciprocal, expressly
conditional, and general (unlimited). This is the type in which the
conditional form most frequently appears: The contracting parties
agree mutually that each shall grant to the other any (or all) favors
and privileges (or all specified or not specifically excepted) which it
has granted or may grant to any other (the " most-favored " nation),
freely, if the concession (to the third State) is freely made, or on
allowing the same compensation (or an equivalent), if the concession
has been conditional. Third, a reciprocal pledge in the conditional
form may be limited, as may the unconditional, by special specified
exceptions.

The following examples may be taken as illustrative of the conditional types described above:

A. Unilateral, unlimited conditional.—United States-Korea
treaty, May 22, 1882, Article XIV:

> The high contracting powers hereby agree that, should at any time the King
> of Chosen grant to any nation, or to the merchants or citizens of any nation,
> any right, privilege or favor, connected either with navigation, commerce,
> political or other intercourse, which is not conferred by this treaty, such right,
> privilege and favor shall freely inure to the benefit of the United States, its
> public officers, merchants and citizens, provided always, that whenever such
> right, privilege or favor is accompanied by any condition, or equivalent conces-
> sion granted by the other nation interested, the United States, its officers and
> people shall only be entitled to the benefit of such right, privilege or favor
> upon complying with the conditions or concessions connected therewith.

B. Reciprocal and unlimited, but conditional.—United States-
France treaty, February 6, 1778, Article II:

> The most Christian King and the United States engage mutually not to
> grant any particular favor to other nations, in respect to commerce and navi-
> gation, which shall not immediately become common to the other party, who
> shall enjoy the same favor, freely, if the concession was freely made, or on
> allowing the same compensation, if the concession was conditional.

C. Reciprocal and limited, conditional.—United States-Brazil
treaty, December 12, 1828, Article II:

> The United States of America and His Majesty the Emperor of Brazil,
> desiring to live in peace and harmony with all the other nations of the earth,
> by means of a policy frank and equally friendly with all, engage mutually not
> to grant any particular favor to other nations, in respect of commerce and
> navigation, which shall not immediately become common to the other party,
> who shall enjoy the same freely, if the concession was freely made, or on
> allowing the same compensation if the concession was conditional. It is under-
> stood, however, that the relations and conventions which now exist, or may
> hereafter exist, between Brazil and Portugal, shall form an exception to this
> article.

The clause appears in the conditional form in almost all of the major commercial treaties of the United States; in many of the treaties of Central and South American States; in those made between American States and Japan; in many between American and European States; in several made between European States in the period preceding 1860; and in some made between European States since 1860—the favors, privileges, and concessions contemplated being especially those relating to commerce and navigation.

The essential distinction between the conditional and the unconditional forms.—The conditional form, unlike the unconditional, recognizes and records a distinction between " concessions freely made " and " concessions made in return for equivalent." It contains the express stipulation that favored-nation treatment is to be accorded on a basis, constantly, of reciprocal concessions.

2. THE CLAUSE IN USE—THEORY AND PRACTICE.

Theory.—A study of the use and construction of the most-favored-nation clause discloses promptly the necessity for distinguishing between theory and practice. There actually exist to-day (1) a so-called " European " theory; (2) a " European " practice; and (3) an "American" theory and practice. According to the " European " theory, most-favored-nation treatment should be unconditional. This theory does not admit the principle that each State must give compensation in order that it shall be entitled under the provisions of the clause to the benefit of concessions made to other States; or, from another point of view, it assumes that compensation has been given once and for all in the conclusion of the original treaty in which the favored-nation treatment is pledged. In practice, however, the States which hold to the European theory recognize, when they have employed phraseology which puts a clause within the description of the conditional form, and when they are dealing with States which cling to the "American" theory, that continued most-favored-nation treatment is to be based on some form of (present and future) exchanging of definite and recognizable concessions.

In the American theory and practice, as represented most conspicuously in the position which has been taken and maintained by all departments of the Government of the United States, most-favored-nation treatment, no matter by what form of the clause prescribed, presupposes reciprocation in the form of giving a quid pro quo. In application, any favors or concessions which one of the parties to a treaty may extend to a third nation can be claimed by the other contracting party, " freely " only if they are " freely granted" to the third nation, and can be claimed on a basis of compensation only if there is offered by the claimant a satisfactory equivalent.

In brief, the European theory does not approve conditional most-favored-nation treatment; but European practice recognizes and admits it in reference to certain treaties and countries. American theory does not approve unconditional most-favored-nation treatment; and American practice has refused to recognize it as logical or practical, though it has accorded it in certain exceptional instances.[1] In the European view the function of the clause is

[1] See p. 402, infra.

automatically to distribute or generalize advantages. In the American view its proper function is to safeguard against the denial of opportunities; that is, to prevent discrimination.

Practice.—In making commercial or other treaties, every nation has desired to secure the maximum of advantage obtainable for itself, and to grant the minimum of such concessions as may be costly or disadvantageous to itself. That any and finally all nations have accepted and employed the most-favored-nation clause has been due to the fact that the clause has proved the most convenient instrument yet devised for insuring each of the parties to a treaty, they being satisfied with the terms agreed upon at the moment of its signing, against the possibility of being placed subsequently in a position of disadvantage in comparison with a third or other nations through the exclusive extension by the other party of additional, greater, or more valuable favors or concessions to such nation or nations.

Different periods disclose different attitudes both on the part of individual nations and among groups of nations. Thus, as has already been stated, during the eighteenth century the most-favored-nation clause appeared in the unconditional form, but commercial treaty practice exhibited a decided disinclination to give except on condition of receiving. In 1778, with the making of the first American treaty, the most-favored-nation clause was for the first time given the conditional phraseology.

During the first quarter of the nineteenth century there was a decided tendency toward the general adoption of more liberal attitudes in commercial policy. At the same time, the American specification for " compensation " was written into a considerable number of the increasing circle of treaties wherein commercial privileges were extended and concessions made, the principle followed being that of giving for equivalents. In 1824 the United States made a treaty with Colombia which was the beginning of the adoption of the conditional clause in South American practice. This was followed in 1825 by a similar treaty with the Central American Confederation, and thenceforth for twenty-five years South and Central American treaties regularly embodied the conditional form of the clause. Between 1826 and 1830 this form was followed in a number of treaties concluded between American and European States. After 1830, as American commerce grew and the influence of American practices began to be felt, there appeared a series of treaties between European States in which the favored-nation provision was phrased in the conditional form. In the period from 1830 to 1859, the guiding principle in commercial treaty making was that of individual bargaining. England and some of the northern European States were disposed to be conservative, but even they employed the conditional form of the clause in some of their treaties. Of the treaties which were made in that period, not a few are still in force.

Between 1850 and 1865 European tariff and commercial treaty policies underwent a radical transformation. The outstanding event was the conclusion of the Cobden treaty between England and France on January 23, 1860. In this treaty (in Article XIX) each of the contracting parties agreed to give the other every favor, etc., in relation to the articles " mentioned in the present treaty," which it might grant to any third power. This pledge was supplemented by the

" covering " most-favored-nation clause which appeared in Article V of the complementary convention of November 16, 1860:

Each of the high contracting powers engages to extend to the other any favor, any privilege or diminution of tariff which either of them may grant to a third power in regard to the importation of goods whether mentioned or not mentioned in the treaty of 23d of January, 1860.

Other European nations promptly followed the example of England and France and began removing various artificial obstacles to commercial intercourse. The most-favored-nation clause appeared the most efficient single instrument for hastening the process. It would operate, in the unconditional form and with the unconditional interpretation, automatically to generalize each concession made by one to any other nation, thus lowering tariff walls gradually, uniformly, and without shock. As the leading States of Europe applied themselves to the remaking of their commercial agreements, a characteristic feature of the new treaties was the employment of the most-favored-nation clause in the unconditional form. In the free-trade movement of the sixties, these States practically abandoned the use of the conditional form of the clause. When the leading States of of the Continent subsequently returned, after 1875, to the principles and practices of protection, they did not resume the use of the conditional form. This can be explained in part by the development of " maximum-and-minimum " and " general-and-conventional " tariff systems, with the correlated use of the tariff treaty.[1] But, explanations apart, since 1860 European States have employed, with but few exceptions, the unconditional form of the most-favored-nation clause and have insisted among themselves upon the unconditional construction: they hold that all favors or concession which either party to a most-favored-nation agreement extends to a third State are due at once and without special compensation to the other party.

American States.—While European States have shifted, as has been shown, first from the use of the unconditional to that of the conditional, and then back to the use of the unconditional, the United States has employed throughout the conditional form and the conditional construction of the clause. The practices of South and Central American States have varied. Especially in late years there has appeared a tendency in treaties between these and European States to use the unconditional form; but it may be said that the principle of requiring compensation has on the whole prevailed in the treaties of American States *inter se* and in a majority of the treaties which these countries have made with European, Asiatic, and African States.

Japan.—The practice of Japan, since that country assumed a position of equality in treaty-making, has varied. The treaties which Japan has made with European States contain the unconditional form of the clause; those which she has made with American States contain, practically without exception, the conditional form.

Other States.—Other Asiatic countries, and Turkey among European States, have had acquaintance chiefly with the unilateral and unconditional form, wherein the pledge for favored-nation treatment is made, not reciprocally, but in favor of the Occidental States.

---

[1] See Part III, p. 457, seq., infra.

Points of special importance.—Two facts stand out with special prominence:

First, with all the changing of commercial policy, tariff systems, and treaty forms, and in spite of controversy, the most-favored-nation clause in one form or another has come to be regarded almost as a constant feature in commercial treaties;

Second, favored-nation usage has varied with some nations, and has remained practically constant with some others.

3. THE UNITED STATES—PRACTICE IN TREATY MAKING.

American theory of commercial agreements—" Reciprocity."—The parties to any sort of a commercial agreement may be considered as endeavoring each to secure for himself something which he conceives to be to his own advantage. It does not follow that either need entertain the idea of securing an advantage over the other party or an advantage over and against third parties. An agreement with regard to a right, a privilege, or a favor, or any specified treatment need not imply that the position sought or obtained is one of superiority or to be enjoyed exclusively; the essential is that the party to whom it is extended shall conceive himself benefited by its acquisition and possession.

A commercial transaction involves an exchange; a commercial agreement implies the giving of something for something. One of the greatest of the advantages which one nation may gain at the hands of another without injury to the moral or the fundamental legal rights, either of the other or of third nations, is the assurance that its subjects and its commerce will be treated as well by and within the jurisdiction of the other as are those of any third nation. Put negatively, this advantage may be gained in the form of an assurance against artificial exclusion or discrimination.

The United States has from the outset based its commercial treaty relations on the principle of give and take. It has sometimes refused to give, and it may in some instances have appeared to be taking more than it has given; but reciprocity has been its guiding principle in commercial policy. American statesmen have contended for an "equality of opportunity" in negotiation, but this has not connoted in their conception identity of treatment. They have sought to secure the removal of restrictions and discriminations which interfere with commerce, but not to secure the same terms for all States and at all times and in relation to all trade. In the use of the most-favored-nation clause, the United States adopted at the outset the principle, and it has since contended consistently, that the right under the most-favored-nation provision, to participate in the privileges (advantageous treatment) extended to third States, is not absolute but is conditional upon the offering of an acceptable and approved equivalent.

EARLY TREATIES.

With France, 1778.—The first treaty which the American Confederation made, that concluded with France on February 6, 1778, contained the first example of the "American" form of the most-favored-nation clause.

In the preamble of this treaty the contracting parties declared that they were taking—

for the basis of their agreement the most perfect equality and reciprocity * * *; leaving, also, each party at liberty to' make, respecting commerce and navigation, those interior regulations which it shall find most convenient to itself; * * * founding the advantage of commerce solely upon reciprocal utility and the just rules of free intercourse; reserving * * * to each party the liberty of admitting at its pleasure other nations to a participation of the same advantages.

The favored-nation clause, Article II, read:

The Most Christian King and the United States engage mutually not to grant any particular favor to other nations, in respect of commerce and navigation, which shall not immediately become common to the other party, who shall enjoy the same favor, freely, if the concession was freely made, or on allowing the same compensation, if the concession was conditional.

The statesmen who negotiated and signed this agreement obviously intended to make possible, but not automatically to effect, the acquisition by each of the contracting parties of favors which the other might give to a third power. As here worded, the favored-nation pledge amounts, not to a guarantee of a free gift of advantages, but to a promise by each party that the co-contractant shall not be denied the opportunity to purchase upon reasonable terms such advantages as may be extended to other nations. The clause thus becomes, not an instrument for acquisition, but a preventive of discrimination.

With the Netherlands, 1782.—The next American treaty, that with the Netherlands, October 8, 1872, contained in its preamble the same declaration regarding intent, and the same reservations. It then provided, in Articles II and III, that the subjects of the contracting parties "shall pay in the ports," etc., each of the other,

no other or greater duties or imposts of whatever nature * * * than those which the nations the most favored are or shall be obliged to pay; and they shall enjoy all the rights, liberties, privileges, immunities and exemptions in trade, navigation and commerce which the said nations do or shall enjoy.

It is to be noticed, first, as stated above, that the preambles to these two treaties were the same; second, that in the Netherlands treaty the most-favored-nation clause just quoted did not contain specific provision for compensation. This treaty, moreover, did not contain a separate "covering" most-favored-nation clause. The third treaty, made with Sweden in 1783, contained a covering conditional clause, calling for compensation. The fourth treaty, made with Prussia in 1785, contained in Article IV provision for mutual access to markets for the goods of each, whether in its own or other vessels, on the most-favored-nation basis, with the reservation that either party might establish "retaliating regulations" against nations which in certain particulars might discriminate against it. There appeared no covering most-favored-nation clause. When this treaty was renewed in 1799, the above-mentioned provision was retained; and when the next treaty with Prussia was concluded, in 1828, the regular American form of the covering most-favored-nation clause was inserted.[1]

With Great Britain, 1794.—In the treaty made with Great Britain on November 19, 1794, the preamble declared it the desire of the contracting parties to "regulate the commerce and navigation between (themselves) * * * in such a manner as to render the same reciprocally beneficial and satisfactory;" but there appeared no most-favored-nation clause.

With France, 1800.—In the treaty with France of September 30, 1800, Article VI provided that—

Commerce between the parties shall be free. The vessels of the two nations * * * shall be treated in their respective ports as those of the nation most favored; and, in general, the two parties shall enjoy the ports of each other, in regard to commerce and navigation, the privileges of the most favoured nation.

Further, in Article XI, the citizens of each shall pay "no other or greater duties," etc., than are required of the most favored nation.

With France, 1803.—In the treaty concluded with France on April 30, 1803, for the Louisiana purchase, it was provided in Article VIII that—

In future and forever after the expiration of the twelve years (provided for elsewhere), the ships of France shall be treated upon the footing of the most favoured nations in the ports above mentioned * * *

With Algiers, 1815.—In a treaty made with Algiers on September 5, 1795, there appeared no most-favored-nation clause; but in the treaty made with Algiers on June 30, 1815, Article I contained a most-favored-nation pledge, with the conditional provision—

* * * When the grant is conditional it shall be at the option of the contracting parties to accept, alter, or reject such conditions, in such manner as shall be most conducive to their respective interests.

With Great Britain, 1815.—In a treaty signed within the same week with Great Britain, on July 3, 1815, the preamble declared it the intention of the contracting parties to regulate commerce, etc., " in such manner as to render the same reciprocally beneficial and satisfactory "; and Article II provided for most-favored-nation treatment, in the form, "no higher or other duties," etc., shall be charged; but there appeared no covering clause specifying compensation.

With Sweden-Norway, 1816.—The treaty concluded with Sweden-Norway on September 4, 1816, contained, in Article II, the same type of provision, "no higher or other duties," etc.; but in Article XII it provided that Article II and others of the treaty of 1783 be renewed, and the Article II thus retained had provided for compensation in connection with most-favored-nation privileges. This provision was reaffirmed in a new treaty concluded with Sweden-Norway on July 4, 1827.

---

[1] United States-Prussia Treaty, May 1, 1828, Art. IX. See p. 422, seq., infra.

TREATIES WITH SOUTH AND CENTRAL AMERICAN COUNTRIES.

In 1824 the United States made the first of an extensive series of treaties with American States. This and all the treaties which belong to this group contained the most-favored-nation clause in the conditional form.

Typical "American" wording of the clause.—The first of the series, the treaty of October 3, 1824, with Colombia, contained the clause (Article II) in the following wording:

[The contracting parties] desiring to live in peace and harmony with all the other nations of the earth, by means of a policy frank and equally friendly with all, engage mutually not to grant any particular favor to other nations, in respect to commerce and navigation, which shall not immediately become common to the other party, who shall enjoy the same freely if the concession was freely made, or on allowing the same compensation if the concession was conditional.

This may be considered a typical "American" wording. There followed, in Article III, the provision that citizens of the contracting parties shall pay no higher or other duties, etc., than are or shall be paid by those of any other nation. This provision appears in later treaties regularly.

In the course of the next fifty years, treaties containing provisions similar to the above, though with occasional variations in the wording and occasional stipulations for exceptions to the application, were made between the United States and South and Central American countries, as follows:[1] With the Central American Republic, December 5, 1825; Brazil, December 12, 1828; Mexico, April 5, 1831; Chile, May 16, 1832; Venezuela, January 20, 1836; Peru-Bolivia, November 30, 1836; Ecuador, June 13, 1839; Colombia, December 12, 1846; Guatemala, March 3, 1849; Salvador, January 2, 1850; Peru, July 26, 1851; the Argentine, July 10, 1853, and July 27, 1853; Bolivia, May 13, 1858; Paraguay, February 4, 1859; Venezuela, August 27, 1860; Haiti, November 3, 1864; Dominican Republic, February 8, 1867 (this contained no covering clause); Nicaragua, June 21, 1867; Peru, September 6, 1870; Salvador, December 6, 1870. The last of this series, the treaty of 1870 with Salvador, contained in its covering most-favored-nation clause wording identical with that employed in the first, that of 1824 with Colombia, quoted above.

OTHER TREATIES WITH EUROPEAN STATES.

Turning again to relations with European States, reference to the texts shows that here, also, after 1824, it was the regular practice of the American Government to employ the most-favored-nation clause, and that in a few cases, but only a few, it subscribed to a deviation from the conditional form which it had previously adopted.

Treaties made with Denmark on April 26, 1826, and with the Hanseatic Republics on December 20, 1827, contained the same wording of the clause as that found in the treaty of 1824 with Colombia.

A convention signed with Great Britain on August 6, 1827, continued in force the treaty of 1815. This would seem to indicate that the United States was satisfied with the most-favored-nation

---

[1] For examples of variations in wording see Appendix B to this section, p. 451, infra.

plédge made in the earlier treaty, although that treaty did not contain specifically the provision for compensation.

The treaty made with Prussia on May 1, 1828, which renewed portions of the treaties of 1785 and 1799, spoke in the preamble of " perfect reciprocity," and provided in Article IX:

If either party shall hereafter grant to any other nation any particular favor in navigation or commerce, it shall immediately become common to the other party, freely, where it is freely granted to such other nations, or on yielding the same compensation, when the grant is conditional.

Treaties made with Austria-Hungary on August 27, 1829, and with Russia on December 18, 1832, contained wording identical with this.

More than forty years later, in the treaty made with Italy on February 26, 1871, the phraseology of the favored-nation provision remained similar to, and the import was identical with, that of the treaties made with European States' and with American States during the twenties.

[The two contracting countries] mutually engage not to grant any particular favor to other nations, in respect to commerce and navigation, which shall not immediately become common to the other party, who shall enjoy the same freely if *   *   *   or on allowing the same compensation if *   *   *   conditional.[1]

TREATIES WITH FAR-EASTERN STATES.

With Japan.—In the first treaty between the United States and Japan, 1854, which was, incidentally, the first treaty concluded between Japan and any occidental country, it was provided that privileges and advantages given by Japan to third nations should be given to the United States " without any consultation or delay." (Treaty of Mar. 31, 1854, Article IX.) The favored-nation provisions in all the early treaties between Japan and occidental countries were unilateral (see provisions from United States-Japan treaties of 1858 and 1878, in Appendix B); but in the making of treaties during and since the year 1894 Japan has treated with all occidental nations upon a basis òf equality. The United States-Japan treaty of 1894 contained in Article I the provision that citizens or subjects of the contracting parties should enjoy each in the territories of the other the same privileges, etc., and should be subject to " no higher imposts or charges in these respects than the citizens or subjects of the most favored nation." This was followed, in Article XIV, by a covering clause providing that—

in all that concerns commerce and navigation, any privilege, *   *   * shall be extended *   *   *   gratuitously, if *   *   *   and on the same or equivalent conditions if the concession shall have been conditional.

And to this was added—

it being their intention that the trade and navigation of each country shall be placed, in all respects, by the other upon the footing of the most favored nation.[2]

When the United States and Japan made their next commercial treaty in 1911, this broad statement with regard to intention was not retained. The treaty of February 21, 1911, contains various express limitations, and in the covering most-favored-nation clause there is

---

[1] United States-Italy treaty, Feb. 26, 1871, Article XXIV.
[2] This final clause was adopted bodily from the form used extensively by European States *inter se*, a phraseology which appeared in all of the treaties made between Japan and European States in the series which began in 1894.

a deviation at the beginning and an omission at the end from the phraseology used in the treaty of 1894:

Except as otherwise expressly provided in this treaty, * * * any privilege, * * * shall be extended * * * gratuitously, if * * * and on the same or equivalent concessions, if the conditions shall have been equivalent.

With China.—Nearly all of the favored-nation pledges which appear in treaties to which China has been a party have been unilateral.

The United States-China treaty of July 3, 1844, contains in Article II the provision:

* * * And if additional advantages or privileges, of whatever description, be conceded hereafter by China to any other nation, the United States, and the citizens thereof, shall be entitled thereon to a complete, equal, and impartial participation in the same.

The treaty of June 18, 1858, contains in Article XXX the provision:

The contracting parties hereby agree that should at any time the Ta Tsing Empire grant to any nation * * * any right, privilege or favor, connected either with navigation, commerce, political or other intercourse which is not conferred by this treaty, such right, privilege and favor shall at once freely inure to the benefit of the United States * * *.[1]

In the United States-China treaty of October 8, 1903, in Article V, the pledge is made mutually and reciprocally:

It is expressly agreed * * * that citizens of the United States shall at no time pay other or higher duties than those paid by the citizens or subjects of the most-favored nation.

Conversely, Chinese subjects shall not pay higher duties on their imports into the United States than those paid by the citizens or subjects of the most-favored nation.[2]

It will be noticed that this provision is not conditional; at the same time the fact should not be overlooked that this is not a " covering " clause. In the light of the interpretation by the United States Government of other treaties, this article would not constitute a pledge of unconditional most-favored-nation treatment.[3]

CASES OF DEVIATION OR APPARENT DEVIATION FROM THE REGULAR UNITED STATES PRACTICE.

There are a few instances in which the negotiators of American treaties have obtained or have acceded to pledges which have constituted in form, and in one or two cases in the intention of the signers, exceptions to the regular American practice. As regards principle, however, the deviation from the general rule has been in most cases apparent rather than real.

Unilateral treaties (exceptional).—The United States has made treaties in which some if not all of the provisions have been unilateral and unconditional, with: China, Egypt, Japan, Morocco, Muskat, Samoa, Siam, Tunis, Turkey, and the Congo. In these the United States has not guaranteed in all respects the same treatment

---

[1] See, however, the United States-China treaty of July 28, 1868, Arts. VI and VII, and that of Nov. 17, 1880, Art. III.
[2] Compare and contrast with provisions in the Great Britain-China treaty of Sept. 5, 1902, Art. XV, and the Japan-China treaty of Oct. 8, 1903, Art. IX.
[3] See p. 405, infra.

that is to be extended to it; the parties in negotiating have not been on a basis of complete international equality. In such agreements, stipulations which are unilateral may and should be regarded as intended to secure unconditional most-favored-nation treatment for the United States. (See, however, the opinion of ·Mr. Olney, Secretary of State, quoted infra.) But, in view of the exceptional circumstances under which a unilateral treaty is made, this can not legitimately be considered as an evidence of inconsistency in American practice.

In by no means all of the treaties made between the United States and less advanced States have the most-favored-nation pledges been unilateral. In many of them the arrangements have been identical with those which prevail between States fully equal.

Treaties in which the compensation clause does not appear (equivocal).—It will have been observed that in several of the treaties cited above, the " compensation " clause does not appear. Such omission has occurred in treaties with: Holland, 1782; Great Britain, 1794 and 1815; France, 1800; the Ottoman Empire, 1830; Greece, 1837; Hanover, 1840 (but the Hanover treaty of 1846, superseding that of 1840, contained the clause); Persia, 1856; China, 1903; and Abyssinia (Ethiopia), 1903; and three others. (See next paragraph.) Several of this group are no longer in force. Some of this group contained provision for most-favored-nation treatment stated in the negative form only; none of those above listed contained the words, " immediate or unconditional." They form exceptions, on the basis of what they omit, to the usual phraseology employed in United States treaties, but the omission by no means indicates, in the absence of other evidence, that they were meant to guarantee unconditional most-favored-nation treatment.

Real exceptions (specifying unconditional most-favored-nation treatment).—The United States has been a party to three treaties which must be admitted to have contained, as regards form, pledges for absolute and unconditional most-favored-nation treatment: the treaty with Switzerland, November 25, 1850; the treaty with the Orange Free State, December 22, 1871; and the treaty with Serbia, October 14, 1881. In each of these the contracting parties guaranteed to each other the immediate enjoyment of commercial favors and advantages which either might grant to third nations; in none of them did there appear the " compensation " clause.

Only one of these has ever been made the basis of a demand by the other party that the United States accord it unconditional most-favored-nation treatment. This was the Swiss treaty, and very shortly after the claim was presented the favored-nation provision in that treaty was abrogated at the instance of the United States.[1]

The treaty with the Orange Free State is no longer in force.

The treaty with Serbia may be said to stand alone in the exhibition today of a pledge calling for " unconditional " most-favored-nation treatment on the part of the United States. In this treaty, signed on October 14, 1881, it is provided:

I. There shall be reciprocally full and entire liberty of commerce and navigation between the citizens and subjects of the two high contracting powers.

   *   *   *   *   *   *   *

---

[1] See p. 428, infra.

* * * and all the rights, privileges, exemptions and immunities of any kind enjoyed with respect to commerce and industry by the citizens or subjects of the high contracting parties, or which are or may be hereafter conceded to the subjects of any third power, shall be extended to the citizens or subjects of the other.

VI. As to the amount, the guarantee and the collection of duties on imports and exports, as well as regards transit, re-exportation, warehousing, local dues and custom-house formalities. each of the two high contracting parties binds itself to give to the other the advantage of every favor, privilege or diminution in the tariffs on the import or export of the articles mentioned or not in the present convention, that it shall have granted to a third power. Also every favor or immunity which shall be later granted to a third power shall be immediately extended and without condition, and by this very fact to the other contracting party.

SPECIAL AFFIRMATION.

The following example is peculiarly interesting because of the special affirmation which the favored-nation clause contains with regard to the principle of favored-nation treatment.

Treaty with Tonga (the Friendly Islands), October 2, 1886, Article II:

* * * and no rights, privileges or immunities shall be granted (to third States) which shall not be also equally and unconditionally granted by the same to the other High Contracting Party * * *; it being understood that the parties hereto affirm the principle of the law of nations that no privilege granted for equivalent or on account of propinquity or other special conditions comes under the stipulations herein contained as to favored nations.

CONCLUSIONS WITH REGARD TO PRACTICE IN TREATY MAKING.

A survey of the treaty list of the United States and a comparison with the lists of other States discloses several interesting facts:

The United States has employed the clause by no means as regularly in its later agreements as it did before 1890. It has employed it in a smaller proportion of its agreements than have some other States. Among United States treaties which contain the clause and which are in force, a relatively large proportion were made at dates preceding 1860. The clause is by no means as essential an instrument in the operation of the American tariff and commercial treaty systems as it is in the corresponding systems of several European States.

In late years the United States has made various commercial agreements in the form of reciprocity treaties in which most-favored-nation clauses have not been included; also, other types of commercial treaties and conventions, wherein, because of previous difficulties over the interpretation of the most-favored-nation clause, it has apparently seemed advisable to both parties not to include the most-favored-nation pledge specifically.

But the prevailing form of the pledge, where the most-favored-nation clause appears in treaties of the United States which are in force, continues to be that based on the principle of continuous reciprocity, specifying that compensation must be offered for favors (advantageous treatment) claimed, unless these have been given " freely " to third nations.

The following list constitutes an index to most-favored-nation clauses recently in force in commercial treaties of the United States.

MOST-FAVORED-NATION CLAUSES IN TREATIES OF THE UNITED STATES.

Table indicating provisions in conventions of the United States in force in 1914 respecting most-favored-nation treatment of imports and exports.[1]

(1) WITH THE COMPENSATION CLAUSE.

Countries.	Concluded.	Articles.
Argentine Republic	27 July, 1853	III and IV.
Austria-Hungary	27 Aug. 1829	V and IX.
Belgium	8 Mar. 1875	XII.
Bolivia	13 May, 1858	II and VI.
Colombia (New Grenada)	12 Dec. 1846	II and V.
Costa Rica	10 July, 1851	III and IV.
Denmark	26 Apr. 1826	I and IV.
Hanseatic Republics	20 Dec. 1827	II and IX.
Honduras	4 July, 1864	III and IV.
Italy	26 Feb. 1871	VI and XXIV.
Japan	21 Feb. 1911	XIV.
Liberia	21 Oct. 1862	VI.
Mecklenburg-Schwerin	9 Dec. 1847	VI and VII.
Oldenburg (accession to treaty of commerce and navigation with Hanover of 10 June, 1846).	10 Mar. 1847	VI and VII.
Paraguay	4 Feb. 1859	III and IV.
Prussia	1 May, 1828	V and IX.
Sweden and Norway	4 July, 1827	IX and XVII, and II of treaty with Sweden 1783 revived.
Tripoli	4 June, 1805	I.

(2) WITHOUT THE COMPENSATION CLAUSE.

China	8 Oct. 1903	V.
Congo (Belgium)	24 Jan. 1891	I, XI, XII.
Ethiopia (Abysinia)	27 Dec. 1903	III.
Great Britain	3 July, 1815	II.
Greece	10–22 Dec. 1837	VIII.
Ottoman Empire	7 May, 1830	I.
Persia	13 Dec. 1856	IV.
Portugal	28 June, 1910	Exchange of Notes.
Serbia	14 Oct. 1881	VI, VII, IX, XIII.
Tonga	2 Oct. 1886	II, IV.
Zanzibar	21 Sept. 1833	IV.
Zanzibar (Great Britain)	31 May 1902	II, III.

(3) UNILATERAL CLAUSE.

Egypt	16 Nov. 1884	Sole article: also Article I of commercial treaty of 3 Mar., 1884, between Greece and Egypt.
Morocco	16 Sept. 1836	XIV.
Siam	29 May, 1856	IX (general language).

[1] Sixty-second Cong., 1st sess., Sen. Doc. vol 28, Misc. II, Doc. No. 29, 1911, pp. 4–5.

4. THE UNITED STATES: PRACTICE IN TREATY CONSTRUCTION—THE "AMERICAN" INTERPRETATION.

American officials, both in the executive and in the judicial departments, have maintained with but rare deviation that, in the application of the most-favored-nation clause as it stands in American treaties, even though the clause itself may not contain an express stipulation calling for compensation, either party may always require an equivalent before granting concessions which the other claims on the strength of the clause, except in those cases where concessions have been made " freely " to third parties.

Conspicuous among Secretaries of State who have maintained and expounded this view appear the names of John Jay, Thomas Jefferson, John Quincy Adams, Albert Gallatin, Henry Clay, Edward Livingston, Martin Van Buren, Caleb Cushing, Edward Everett, Frederick T. Frelinghuysen, John Sherman, Richard Olney, and John Hay. The following instances are illustrative of American diplomatic opinions and decisions.

A. CONSTRUCTION BY UNITED STATES OFFICIALS—OPINIONS AND DECISIONS IN DIPLOMATIC CASES.

John Jay—Claims of the Netherlands Government, 1787—Formulation of the American interpretation.—The "American interpretation" was formulated as early as 1787 by John Jay, then Secretary for the Department of Foreign Affairs. The treaty between the United States and the Netherlands of 1782 had provided in Articles II and III that the subjects of the contracting States should pay in the ports each of the other "no other nor greater duties or imposts of whatever nature * * * than those which the nations the most favored are or shall be obliged to pay;" and that they should "enjoy all the rights (etc.) in trade, navigation, and commerce which the said nations do or shall enjoy." This contained no conditional qualification. In 1787 the minister for the Netherlands protested against an act of the Legislature of Virginia which exempted French brandies imported in French and American vessels from certain duties to which like commodities imported in Netherlands vessels remained liable. Mr. Jay, in a report to Congress concerning the matter, in October, 1787, said:

It is observable that this article takes no notice of cases where compensation is granted for privileges. Reason and equity, however, in the opinion of your Secretary, will supply this deficiency. * * * Where a privilege is gratuitously granted, the nation to whom it is granted becomes in respect to that privilege, a favored nation. * * * But where the privilege is not gratuitous, but rests on compact, in such case the favor, if any there be, does not consist in the privilege yielded but in the consent to make the contract by which it is yielded. * * * The favor therefore of being admitted to make a similar bargain is all that in such cases can reasonably be demanded under the article. Besides, it would certainly be inconsistent with the most obvious principles of justice and fair construction, that because France purchases at a great price, a privilege of the United States, that therefore the Dutch shall immediately insist not on having the like privileges at the like price, but without any price at all.[1]

It was at the same time Mr. Jay's opinion that, in the controversy in question, inasmuch as the reduction in duties had been made by the State of Virginia in favor of France gratuitously, the subjects of the Netherlands were entitled to the same reduction.

Reciprocity in regard to duties on ships, 1815—Claims of the French Government, 1817, and following—Opinions of J. Q. Adams, Monroe, Gallatin, and others.—In the treaty between the United States and France of April 30, 1803, Article VIII provided: "In future and forever after the expiration of the twelve years, the ships of France shall be treated upon the footing of the most-favored-nation in the ports above mentioned." In 1815, Congress passed an act offering reciprocity in the matter of duties upon ships. Great Britain took advantage of this and removed her discriminating duties against

---

[1] See Crandall, S. B., Am. Jour. Int. Law, 1913, p. 709.

American ships. Then, under the operation of the treaty between the United States and Great Britain of July 3, 1815, the ships of Great Britain were given a national treatment in the harbors of the United States. The French took no action similar to that of the British; but in a note of December 15, 1817, the French minister claimed, by virtue of the favored-nation provision in the treaty of 1803, an exemption for French ships similar to that granted British ships.

John Quincy Adams, Secretary of State, in reply of December 23, 1817, said:

> The eighth article of the treaty * * * stipulates that the ships of France shall be treated on the footing of the most-favored nations * * *; but it does not say, and can not be understood to mean, that France should enjoy as a free gift that which is conceded to other nations for a full equivalent.
>
> *　　　*　　　*　　　*　　　*　　　*　　　*
>
> It is true that the terms of the eighth article are positive and unconditional; but it will readily be perceived that the condition, though not expressed in the article is inherent in the advantage claimed under it. If British vessels enjoyed, in the ports of Louisiana, any gratuitous favors, undoubtedly French vessels would, by the terms of the article, be entitled to the same.[1]

The French Government, insisting on the unconditional interpretation of the most-favored-nation clause, contended that " a clause which is absolute and unconditional can not be subject to limitation or any modification whatever." The American Government emphasized the requirement of an equivalent. The French replied that an equivalent had been given at the time of the cession of Louisiana. The United States contended for a more specific equivalent, declaring that if there were given to France freely that for which England had paid, France would be enjoying a treatment more favored than that of the "most-favored nation."

In a note dated March 29, 1821, Mr. Adams said:

> It is no exception * * * that the vessels of England, Prussia, the Netherlands, and the Hanseatic cities pay * * * no other or higher duties than the vessels of the United States, This is not a favor, but a bargain. It was offered to all nations by the act of Congress of March 3, 1815. Its only condition was reciprocity. * * * Special, indeed, would be the favor which should yield to a claim of free gift to one, of that which had been sold at a fair price to another.[2]

Mr. Gallatin, minister to France, in a note to Viscount de Chateaubriand of February 27, 1823, took the same position. Mr. Gallatin stated expressly that in the American view the extension of favors to a third party is dependent upon the giving of an equivalent in compensation.

> * * * When not otherwise defined the right of most-favored-nation treatment is that, and can only be that, of being entitled to that treatment gratuitously, if such nation enjoys it gratuitously, and on paying the same equivalent if it has been granted in consideration of an equivalent.[3]

The American doctrine was clearly worded by President Monroe in his message to Congress on December 3, 1821. Referring to the claim of France, he said:

> If this should be so construed as that France shall enjoy the right, and without paying the equivalent, or the advantages of such conditions as might be allowed to other powers in return for important concessions made by them, then

---

[1] Am. St. Pap., U. S. For. Rel., V, pp. 152–153; see also citations in Moore's Dig., V, p. 258.
[2] Am. St. Pap., U. S. For. Rel., V, p. 163; see Moore's Dig., V, p. 258.
[3] Am. St. Pap., U. S. For. Rel., V, p. 673.

the whole character of the stipulations would be changed. She would not only be placed on the footing of the most favored nation, but on a footing held by no other nation.[1]

Mr. Clay and Mr. Van Buren, as Secretaries of State, continuing the discussion, maintained the views of their predecessors. Ultimately, after the interposition of various other issues and a settlement, France relinquished her claims with regard to Article VIII of the treaty of 1803.[2]

The United States grants an "equivalent" to Colombia, 1832.—The treaty of the United States with Colombia of October 3, 1824 [cited on page 399], had provided for favored-nation treatment on the basis of compensation if the concession was conditional. Later the United States claimed the right to certain advantages which Central America was enjoying under the latter's treaty with Colombia. When the Colombian Government pointed out that its treaty with Central America was made upon a reciprocity basis, the United States conceded that the claim which it had urged was unwarranted, and proceeded (in 1832) to arrange to grant to Colombia an equivalent for the advantages which it was demanding.[3]

Mr. Livingston, in reference to claims made by Austria, 1832.—The United States treaty with Austria of August 27, 1829, provided for conditional most-favored-nation treatment. [Cited on page 400.] Austria subsequently claimed that her wines should enter the United States at the same rate as that extended to French wines under the operation of the treaty with France of 1831. The French treaty in question provided, in Article VII, that the United States duties on the wines of France should not exceed a rate specified, while France in return abandoned her contentions for unconditional most-favored-nation treatment under the treaty of 1803 and agreed to a specified duty on United States long-staple cottons. Mr. Livingston, Secretary of State, pointed to the difference between favors freely granted and advantages extended reciprocally, and at the same time suggested that no nation intends to bind itself by a condition which will render it unable to make further treaties, declaring it to be a fair interpretation of the most-favored-nation clause, that if duties be lessened in favor of any other nation, the contracting parties should obtain a like reduction for the same equivalent.[4] Mr. Livingston advised President Jackson, on January 6, 1832:

A covenant to give privileges to the "most-favored nation" only refers to gratuitous privileges and does not cover privileges granted on the condition of a reciprocal advantage.[5]

Opinions and views of the Department of State in later years.—The opinion and position of the State Department in regard to the relation between most-favored-nation obligations and the special concessions between the United States and Hawaii in the reciprocity treaty of 1875, the views expressed by Secretary of State Frelinghuysen when several reciprocity treaties were being considered in 1884, the views expressed by Secretary of State Sherman in 1898, the opinion of the State Department in reply to claims presented by Switzerland

---

[1] See Moore's Dig., V, p. 258.
[2] Ibid., pp. 259–260. Art. VII of the treaty between the United States and France of July 4, 1831, provided for reciprocal special concessions.
[3] Ibid., p. 260.
[4] Ibid., p. 261.
[5] Ibid., p. 315.

in 1898, views expressed in discussions with Germany, and others, will be accounted for in a later section.

Conclusion with regard to diplomatic construction.—A full survey of diplomatic opinions and decisions warrants the conclusion and assertion that throughout and at the end of the period of a century and a quarter from the time of the making of the earliest United States treaties, the State Department held, with relatively few and unimportant exceptions, to the conception of favored-nation treatment which was entertained by the negotiators of the first treaties. By no other Government has there been maintained so consistent and so prolonged an allegiance to a conception and a precedent once established in the interpretation of the favored-nation clause.

B. CONSTRUCTION BY AMERICAN COURTS—OPINIONS AND DECISIONS IN JUDICIAL CASES.

Questions calling for the construction of most-favored-nation clauses and decisions as to obligations which they do or do not create have been brought in a number of instances before courts of the United States. The views of the judiciary as to the nature of the pledge in treaties to which the United States has been a party have been in conformity, generally speaking, with the views of the State Department; and the courts have held, in agreement with the Executive, that the making of special reciprocity agreements is not inconsistent with most-favored-nation treatment, the latter being conditional. The following brief accounts of certain of the most important and most interesting of the leading cases will show how the issue has been presented and what have been the conception and the rulings of the courts.

Bartram v. Robertson (1887)—Favored-nation pledges not intended to interfere with reciprocity arrangements or to generalize their benefits.—The United States-Denmark treaty of 1826, renewed by that of 1857, provided in Article IV that " No higher * * * duties shall be imposed on the importation into the United States of any article the produce or manufacture of * * * Denmark * * * than are * * * payable on the like articles being the produce or manufacture of any other foreign country; " and its Article I was a " covering " most-favored-nation clause, conditional in form, phrased as were the majority of the treaties of the period in which it had been concluded.

After the conclusion of the United States-Hawaiian treaty of reciprocity, a firm importing sugar and molasses from the Island of St. Croix (Danish) claimed that its imports should be admitted duty free as were like articles the products of Hawaii.

The claim was presented for adjudication in the case of Bartram v. Robertson, in the Circuit Court for the Southern District of New York.[1] On the construction of the favored-nation provision in the Danish treaty, the Court said:

" The meaning of the stipulation is that there shall be no unfriendly discrimination in the imposition of duties between the duties of Denmark and those of other countries. The stipulation is satisfied when there is no discrimination, according to the rule and policy observed with foreign nations in general. * * *

---

[1] 21 Blatch., 211 ; 15 Fed. Rep., 212 (1883).

" There is a broader view of the controversy, however, which can not be slighted. Stipulations like the one relied on are found in upwards of forty treaties made between the United States and foreign powers since 1815. * * * If the argument for the plaintiffs is sound, all these treaty stipulations are to be deemed embodied in the tariff act so as practically to exempt from duty the importations of all these foreign countries whenever the products of a single country may be exempted from duty.

" Can it be for a moment supposed that a stipulation in a treaty with a single power, exempting the products of that country from the payment of duty when imported here, made in the interest of our own commerce or manufactures, or designed upon special considerations of comity between the two nations, could be intended to affect such a far-reaching abrogation of our own revenue laws as would thus ensue? The proposition is too startling to be entertained."

Judgment was ordered for the defendant, and the plaintiffs appealed.

The Supreme Court of the United States, upholding the decision of the Circuit Court, declared that the most-favored-nation provisions in the United States-Denmark treaty of 1826 " do not cover concessions like those made to the Hawaiian Islands for a valuable consideration. * * * They imposed an obligation upon both countries to avoid hostile legislation in that respect " to imposition of duties, etc. " But they were not intended to interfere with special arrangements with other countries founded upon a concession of special privileges. * * *

" The treaty with the Hawaiian Islands * * * stipulates for the exemption from duty of certain goods * * * in consideration of and as an equivalent for certain reciprocal concessions on the part of the Hawaiian Islands to the United States. There is in such exemption no violation of the stipulations in the treaty with Denmark. * * * It does not appear that Denmark has ever objected. * * *

" Our conclusion is, that the treaty with Denmark does not bind the United States to extend to that country, without compensation, privileges which they have conceded to the Hawaiian Islands in exchange for valuable concessions. On the contrary, the treaty provides that like compensation shall be given for such special favors * * *."

(*Bartram* v. *Robertson* (1887), 122 U. S., 116.)

Whitney v. Robertson (1888)—The absence of an express provision for " compensation " does not imply that favors granted on a reciprocity basis are to be generalized.—A similar suit was brought by an importer of sugar and molasses from the island of San Domingo. The counsel for the plaintiff attempted to differentiate the case by pointing to omission from the most-favored-nation provision in the treaty between the United States and the Dominican Republic of the " compensation " clause, contending, essentially, for unconditional construction of a clause not expressly conditional in form. The Supreme Court said: " We do not think that the absence of this provision changes the obligations of the United States." Pointing to Article IX of the treaty with the Dominican Republic (1867), which provided, as did Article IV of the Danish treaty, that " no higher or other duties," etc., should be charged, the court declared: * * * " it is a pledge of the contracting parties that there shall be no discriminating legislation.   *   *   *   It had no greater extent. It was never designed to prevent special concessions upon sufficient considerations touching the importation of specific articles.   *   *   *   It would require the clearest language to justify a conclusion that our Government intended to preclude itself from such engagements with other countries which might in the future be of the highest importance to its interests." Furthermore, "if there be any conflict between the stipulations of the treaty and the requirements of the law, the latter (being of later date) must control." For an infraction of the provisions of the treaty, the remedy would have to be sought by the State claiming injury, by diplomatic procedure. (*Whitney* v. *Robertson* (1888), 124 U. S., 190.[1]

In 1897 the Dominican Republic gave notice of its denunciation of the treaty of 1867, this was accepted by the United States, and the treaty terminated on January 13, 1898.

Shaw v. United States (1911)—Application of favored-nation clause to reciprocity agreements—The reciprocity provisions in the tariff act of 1897 and in agreements made thereunder gave no special favor to any country.—In pursuance of the provisions of section 3 of the tariff act of 1897, the United States made reciprocity agreements with France, Portugal, Germany, Italy, and later with other nations, in which, among other things, special rates of duty lower than those in the tariff schedule were provided for brandies or other spirits, etc., imported from the various cocontracting parties, respectively, into the United States.[2] Subsequently a firm importing similar articles from England claimed the right to the same rates, contending the applicability of the most-favored-nation clause in the United States-Great Britain treaty of 1815. The case was carried from the United States Circuit Court for the Southern District of New York to the Court of Customs Appeals, where it was decided on April 10, 1911. The court, after quotation from and consideration of the tariff act of 1897, the terms of the various treaties involved and concerned, and the decisions of the Supreme Court in the cases of *Bartram* v. *Robertson* and *Whitney* v. *Robertson*, proceeded:

The question   *   *   *   is presented in this case   *   *   *   whether or not section 3 of the tariff act of 1897 was in conflict with the most-favored-nation clause of the treaty of 1815 with His Britannic Majesty. We think not.

Section 3 of the tariff act of 1897 was a general law; its attitude toward every nation was uniform. It offered no special favor to France, or Germany, or Italy, or any other country. Every foreign nation was treated alike by the terms of the law. It was equally within the opportunity of England to negotiate a reciprocity treaty as it was within the opportunity of France. The act itself in this particular was but a uniform authorization, means to effect the purpose, that was executed in the Danish treaty, the subject of consideration in the Bartram case. The two high contracting parties had by signed treaty in that case effected no more than what Congress had authorized with every nation by section 3 of the act of 1897.   *   * *

Moreover, we think that in logic or effect the negotiation of a treaty upon a consideration does no violence to that treaty provision with His Britannic Majesty. The reciprocity treaty with France is one founded upon mutual considerations. This country gave considerations for the considerations given in exchange therefor by France. If, therefore, this country should concede to Great Britain *without* consideration what it has conceded to France *for* consideration, it would not be conceding to England a favor it conceded to

---

[1] See also *Shaw* v. *U S.*, 20 Treas. Dec., and 1 Ct. of Customs Appls., 426 (1911); and Crandall, S. B., in Am. Jour. Int. Law, October, 1913, p. 710.
[2] See p. 408, infra.

the other country, but it would be conceding to England more than it conceded to the other country, because England in such case gives no consideration for the concession for which France gave a consideration.

* * * * * * * *

* * * We think the Bartram and Whitney cases, cited and quoted, *supra,* conclusive of this case. * * *[1]

American Express Co. et al. v. United States, and Bertuch & Co. et al. v. United States (1913)—Benefit of duty-free provision for wood pulp and paper from Canada extended to other countries, 1913.—In expectation of the conclusion of the reciprocity arrangement negotiated with Canada in January, 1911, Congress passed on July 2, 1911, an act in which section 2 provided that pulp wood and paper, the kinds therein described, when exported duty free from Canada, should be admitted duty free to the United States. The conclusion of the reciprocity arrangement was ultimately negatived by the failure of Canada to pass the necessary legislation.

Subsequently the commodities in question, exported free of duty from Canada, were admitted, upon importation to the United States, free of duty. Importers of similar products from Norway, Russia, Austria-Hungary, and Germany claimed, on the basis of most-favored-nation clauses in their treaties, the benefit of the same treatment. The United States General Appraisers held with regard to section 2 of the act of 1911 that, although the agreement had not been concluded, nevertheless the provision in section 2 was a valid law in force, and that under it the articles described, when exported duty free from Canada, were duty free upon importation into the United States. But, addressing themselves to the question, Can this specific provision which is made by Congress to apply to paper and wood pulp imported directly from Canada be interpreted to make free similar goods imported into this country from each of the forty-odd countries with whom we have favored-nation treaties? they held that the treaty-making power could not so invade the constitutional prerogative of the House of Representatives as thus to participate in the making of revenue laws, and that, therefore, the claims of plaintiff importers, based simply on the most-favored-nation clauses in the treaties could not be allowed.[2]

The case then went to the Court of Customs Appeals.

The court assumed that, for treaty purposes, Canada is a nation; that no distinction need be made among the States claiming favored-nation treatment because of differences in the language in the treaty clauses; that the position of each of the nations entitled to claim favored-nation treatment was equal to that of the one having the most advantageous treatment; and that section 2 of the act of 1911 was operative notwithstanding the fact that Canada had not taken the action necessary to establish reciprocity as to other importations provided for in the act.

The court held that it was within its province and was its duty to declare the force and effect of the treaties; that the treaty provisions in question were self-executing, and therefore to be applied; and that the privilege extended to Canada under section 2 of the act in question had been extended freely and without compensation. It declared that section 2 was " wholly independent of the reciproc-

---

[1] See *Shaw* v. *U. S.,* T. D. 31500. Treas. Dec., vol. 20, p. 718 (1911) ; 1 Ct. of Cust. Appls., 426.
[2] T. D. 32423–G. A. 7354, Treas. Dec., vol. 22, p. 647 (1912).

ity provision of the act. It is an act of Congress standing by itself."
The benefit which it extended to Canada was given freely and without compensation, whence, " It follows that non-prohibited exportation, from any nation entitled to the benefit of the favored-nation provision, of an untaxed material of the same kind and character answers all the requirements and should stand upon the same footing as accorded to goods so imported from Canada."

The decisions below were reversed and the articles in question were declared duty free.[1]

Justice De Vries presented a lengthy and forceful dissenting opinion, in the course of which he traversed the whole history of the construction of most-favored-nation obligations by the courts and by executive officials of the United States.

According to the decision in this case, together with that handed down by the same court (Justice De Vries dissenting) earlier on the same day in the case of *Cliff Paper Co.* v. *United States*,[2] section 2 of the act of 1911 is absolute, being wholly independent of the reciprocity provision of the act; the wood pulp and paper of the types specified, when imported from Canada, not having paid export duties, are admitted to the United States duty free; this favorable treatment has been extended to Canada freely and without compensation; hence, by virtue of the most-favored-nation clause, this clause being self-executing, the like products from other countries entitled to favored-nation treatment by the United States are duty free.

5. EUROPEAN PRACTICE, NOW UNCONDITIONAL, HAS VARIED.

While the practice of the United States as regards both the form and the construction of the clause has been on the whole uniform and consistent, that of the leading commercial countries of Europe has moved, as shown in a previous section, in one period from the unconditional toward the conditional and later back to the unconditional. In European policy, most-favored-nation treatment has now, as it had before 1825, a different meaning from that which attached to it between 1825 and 1860. At the same time the universalizing of concessions which the unconditional usage theoretically entails is to no small extent modified by the mechanism of the new tariff systems which have been developed in recent years. This will be shown in the section of this report which treats of tariff systems of Continental Europe.[3]

Inasmuch as Great Britain stands in a somewhat peculiar and a particularly conspicuous position in reference to tariff policies and commercial practices, and as British practice exhibits with greater regularity, greater consistency, and in greater simplicity than does that of any other State the possibilities of the unconditional most-favored-nation treatment, a brief examination of British practice will suffice as an illustration of the contemporary European conception of the purposes and intent of the favored-nation clause.

---

[1] 4 Ct. of Cust. Appls., 146 (1913).
[2] Ibid., 186 (1913).
[3] See Part III, p. 457 seq., infra.

British practice and experience.—Great Britain has employed, with probably fewer exceptions than any other State, the unconditional form of the clause, and has stood more prominently than have any others for the application of the " European " interpretation. Early British treaties stipulated simply for " reciprocal liberty of commerce." Where the most-favored-nation clause was used in British treaties in the eighteenth century, it appeared invariably in the unconditional form. This form prevails apparently in all British treaties at present in force. On January 1, 1907, the clause was to be found in no less than eighty-three British treaties, conventions, and agreements.[1]

In construction, British statesmen have insisted that the most-favored-nation treatment is, or should be, unconditional, their record upon this point being, since 1860, substantially as consistent as that of American statesmen in maintaining, so far as the United States has been concerned, that the treatment is and should be conditional.

After the conclusion of the Cobden treaty, the British, having committed themselves to the practice and the advocacy of free trade, found the most-favored-nation clause both a necessary and a particularly valuable instrument. British statesmen, no longer possessing an extensive tariff schedule as an instrument which they might use for bargaining and for championing commercial liberalism, were naturally desirous of securing for British commerce unconditional most-favored-nation treatment at the hands of all countries. In the attempt to secure unconditional favored-nation pledges, they were highly successful. In the process they generalized the concessions which they had made, giving, regardless of specific compensation, to the whole circle of commercial States the concessions which had been given to France on the basis of reciprocity.

Although the combination of free-trade policy and unconditional most-favored-nation practice has been largely to British advantage, it has also been not without its inconveniences. For instance, when Spain and Portugal demanded for concessions asked of them that special concessions be given in return, Great Britain was unable to offer such concessions, whereupon these countries adopted measures which involved discrimination against England. When the United States offered special reciprocity to States which would make reductions in duty in favor of its products, Great Britain had no reductions to offer—she could offer none without revising her whole fiscal plan—hence she did not secure the benefit of the concessions which the United States made to countries which entered with her into reciprocity agreements.

Again, with the rise of the sugar-bounties question, the British Government found its desire to establish countervailing duties inconsistent with its views with regard to the requirements of most-favored-nation treatment. Before long it modified these views to the extent of deciding that the use of such duties was not in conflict with the principles of most-favored-nation treatment.[2]

Still more embarrassing to the British Government has been the problem which has arisen with the development of preferential tariff views and practices within the Empire. This has led in recent years to agitation in the colonies, especially Canada, involving even the

---

[1] See Parl. Pap., Commercial No. 3 (1907) (Cd. 3395).
[2] See p. 433, infra.

suggestion from some quarters that the use of the conditional most-favored-nation clause be resorted to, and from others that the clause be dropped and be debarred altogether from British treaties. On April 23, 1897, Canada passed a tariff act which provided for preferential treatment, by means of a " reciprocal tariff," the purpose of which was to extend lower rates to imports from the British Empire than to those from foreign countries. The Belgian and the German Governments protested that this was inconsistent with the guarantee of most-favored-nation treatment made to them in their treaties with Great Britain. In the Colonial Conference of 1897, the premiers agreed that the demands of other nations for the benefit of the preferential treatment could not be allowed. In order that the provisions of the Canadian law might go into effect, the British Government gave notice in June, 1897, for termination of the Belgian and the German treaties. Other nations then accepted, for the time being at least, the contention that arrangements made between England and Canada were of a special nature such that the ordinary application of most-favored-nation pledges was not to be expected. It is to be noticed, however, in judging of the soundness of that contention, that British self-governing colonies possess tariff autonomy and there is no British imperial tariff system.

British construction—Attitude toward reciprocity and favored-nation rights and obligations.—The following illustrations serve to show that the British Government has at different times entertained differing views with regard to special engagements on a reciprocity basis. The quotation from Lord Granville stands, also, as an assertion of the most extreme claims of the " European " theory of most-favored-nation treatment.

(*A*) *The British view in 1854.*—During the negotiations of 1854 between the United States and Great Britain, which resulted in the Canadian reciprocity treaty of 1854, Mr. Crampton, British chargé d'affaires at Washington, under instructions from his Government, wrote to Mr. Clayton, Secretary of State:

It has been objected that if certain agricultural articles (more particularly wheat), the productions of Canada, were to be admitted free of duty into the United States, under a convention with the British Government for a reciprocal free trade between that Province and the United States in such productions, the like productions of other nations having " reciprocity treaties " of commerce with the United States must be admitted on the same terms.

To this it may be replied that no nation could claim for itself an advantage under a convention between Great Britain and the United States which Great Britain herself had not obtained under that convention. Had any other nation a colony similarly situated, she might then be borne out in claiming that such colony should be equally favored; otherwise not.

A precedent has already been established which involves this principle, and makes a distinction between an inland colony and an independent State. * * * In the year 1831 the United States passed "An act to regulate foreign trade on the northeast and northwest boundary,"[1] remitting all fees on British vessels entering their ports on that boundary; consequently, up to the present moment no fees are exacted there on either side, whereas they still exist in the Atlantic ports on all foreign vessels.[2]

Lord Clarendon, two years later, held apparently the same view with regard to the proposed United States-Hawaiian reciprocity treaty, and in 1878 Lord Derby conceded the principle, "under the

---

[1] Chap. 98, March, 1831.
[2] 31st Cong., 1st sess., H. Ex. Doc. 65.

peculiar circumstances of the case," in the contentions which grew out of the conclusion between the United States and Hawaii of the reciprocity treaty of 1875.[1]

(B) *The British view in 1885.*—The opinion which the British Government expressed twenty years later was quite different from the above. In 1884 Secretary of State Frelinghuysen submitted to the British ambassador at Washington a project for a reciprocity agreement between the United States and Great Britain in reference to the British West Indies.[2] Lord Granville, Secretary of State for Foreign Affairs, his Government having for some time expressed its dissent from the American construction of the United States-Hawaiian reciprocity treaty, made this the occasion to express his opinion of the American interpretation and his view of the proper construction in accordance with the British (European) practice. He wrote:

Article XIII expressly provides that the privileges conceded by this treaty are not to be granted by either party to other nations by reason of the most-favored-nation clause existing in any treaty with such nations, unless any such nation give what, in the opinion of the other party, is equivalent. But Her Majesty's Government are decidedly of the opinion that the exception to the most-favored-nation treatment thus contemplated would be an infraction of the most-favored-nation clause as hitherto interpreted in the law of nations * * *. The interpretation * * * involved in the United States proposals is, that concessions granted conditionally and for a consideration can not be claimed under it. From this interpretation Her Majesty's Government entirely and emphatically dissent. The most-favored-nation clause has now become the most valuable part of the system of commercial treaties, and exists between nearly all the nations of the earth. It leads more than any other stipulation to simplicity of tariffs and to ever-increasing freedom of trade * * *. Its effect has been, with few exceptions, that any given article is taxed in each country by practically one rate only * * *. But should the system contemplated by the United States be widely adopted, there will be a return to the old and exceedingly inconvenient system under which the same article in the same country would pay different duties according to its country of origin, nationality of the importing ship, and, perhaps at some future time, varying also with the nationality of the importer himself. It is, moreover, obvious that the interpretation now put forward [exactly that which had always been applied by the United States] would nullify the most-favored-nation clause; for any country, say, France, though bound by the most-favored-nation clause in her treaty with Belgium, might make treaties with any other country involving reductions of duty on both sides, and, by the mere insertion of a statement that these reductions were granted reciprocally and for a consideration, might yet refuse to grant them to Belgium unless the latter granted what France might consider an equivalent.

Such a system would press most hardly on those countries which had already reformed their tariffs, and had no equivalent concessions to offer, and, therefore, Great Britain, which has reformed her tariff, is mostly deeply interested in resisting it.[3]

In passing, it may be pointed out that Lord Granville's claim that the British interpretation represented that of the "law of nations" is as little to be accepted in the one direction as is a similar claim which was made by Secretary of State Bayard in 1886 on behalf of the American interpretation.[4]

Change in British sentiment.—In view of the changes since 1880 in commercial policy and in tariff and tariff-treaty making practices

---

[1] See pp. 418, 419, infra.
[2] See p. 141, infra.
[3] Earl Granville, Sec. of State for For. Affairs, to Mr. West, British Minister, Feb. 12, 1885. Parl. Pap., Commercial No. 4 (1885), 21–22 ; Moore's Dig., V, 271.
[4] See Appendix C, p. 453, infra.

among the continental European States, and as a consequence of the necessity of considering seriously the growing problems of imperial readjustment, British thought with regard to commercial policy has undergone during the past three decades a significant modification, of which by no means the least indication has been the changing attitude of the foreign office toward the possibility of employing more than one form and more than one construction of the most-favored-nation clause. The most recent development is the announcement that the British Government intends to terminate all its treaties which contain most-favored-nation pledges.[1]

The practice of continental European States.—Among the treaties in which since 1860 States of continental Europe have pledged themselves to unconditional most-favored-nation treatment the one which has been probably the most far-reaching in its effect was the Frankfort treaty, concluded between France and Germany on May 10, 1871, at the end of the Franco-Prussian War. Here, in Article XI, it was agreed that, in reference to importation, exportation, transit, customs administration, and the administration and treatment of subjects and officials, " * * * the French Government and the German Government will take for a basis of their commercial relations the régime of reciprocal treatment on the footing of the most favored nation. * * * However, there shall be excepted from the above rule the favors which either of the contracting parties has accorded or shall accord to other States than the following: England, Belgium, the Netherlands, Switzerland, Austria, Russia."

This most-favored-nation clause was unique in that it appeared in a political, rather than in a commercial, treaty and with the intention that it should endure permanently or until a new provision, mutually agreed upon, should supersede it. It is typical, however— in that it constituted a pledge for unconditional most-favored-nation treatment between the two leading commercial States of the Continent—of the practice which has prevailed during the past half century among the nations of continental Europe, whether free trade or protectionist in the matter of tariff policy, along with Great Britain. To the practices and experiences, the tariff machinery and commercial treaty methods of European States generally, attention will be devoted in Part III of this report.

6. THE MOST-FAVORED-NATION CLAUSE AND THE NEGOTIATION AND APPLICATION OF RECIPROCITY AGREEMENTS — EXPERIENCE OF THE UNITED STATES.

The American theory—Mr. Sherman's explanation of the relation between most-favored-nation pledges and reciprocity agreements, 1898.— The American conception of the proper functions of the most-favored-nation clause and reciprocity agreements, and of the rela-

---

[1] For evidence illustrative of contemporary British thought in reference to commercial policy, see final report of the Committee on Commercial and Industrial Policy after the War, Parl. Pap., Cd. 9035, 1918, especially pp. 48–53.

tion between the two has been set forth in many statements. Among official expositions, that given in 1898 by Mr. Sherman, Secretary of State, is, because of its comprehensiveness, its conciseness, and its date, especially noteworthy. The negotiations which Mr. Kasson had undertaken, as plenipotentiary for the making of reciprocity agreements under authority of section 3 of the tariff act of 1897, were under way. Mr. Buchanan, minister to the Argentine, had expressed the opinion in a communication to the State Department, dated June 15, 1897, that:

While any arrangement might be carried through here contemplating a general tariff reduction on *articles*, the most-favored-nation clause in the treaties between this country [the Argentine] and Europe would be a bar to a plan specifically specifying concessions to a *country*.

Mr. Sherman replied:

The plenipotentiary [Mr. Kasson] is of opinion, and this department gives its sanction to the proposition, that the foregoing construction of the most-favored-nation clause is erroneous; that it [the clause] does not control the right of the nations adopting it to make exclusive compensatory agreements in just reciprocity with other nations.

'The clauses referred to are expressed in various forms * * *; but the intent is the same in all the conventions between civilized countries, whether the clause stands alone, or is qualified by the other customary clause excepting particular favors. That intent is to secure for the contracting party equality with all competing nations in the conditions of access to the markets of the other * * *

It is clearly evident that the object sought in all the various forms of expression is equality of international treatment, protection against the willful preference of the commercial interests of one nation over another. But the allowance of the same privileges and the same sacrifice of revenue duties, to a nation which makes no compensation, that had been conceded to another nation for an adequate compensation * * * destroys that equality of market privileges which the * * * clause was intended to secure. And it concedes for nothing to one friendly nation what the other countries secure only for a price * * *

The neighborhood of nations, their border interests, their differences of climate, soil, and production, their respective capacity for manufacture, their widely different demands for consumption, the magnitude of the reciprocal markets, are so many conditions which require special treatment. No general tariff can satisfy such demands. * * *

What will be an equivalent compensation is to be honorably determined by the governments concerned. * * *

* * * The right of the other nations to enjoy the same special concessions depends on their ability to offer an equivalent compensation. When they do this the favored-nation clause is rightly invoked.

Such is the construction of the treaty clauses in question which the Government of the United States adopts in carrying out the late provisions of law for reciprocal commercial conventions with other States.[1]

It may be pointed out in passing that the United States has in practice not always lived up to the full implication, in all its details, of this theory. There will appear in the following pages instances illustrative of the problems and controversies which have arisen from the fact that the United States has given special concessions, on the basis of reciprocity, and has refused, following the conditional practice in most-favored-nation treatment, to generalize, and in some cases even to consider giving " for compensation," these concessions.

---

[1] See Mr. Sherman, Secretary of State, to Mr. Buchanan, minister to the Argentine, Jan. 11, 1898, Apr. 9, 1898, MS. Inst. Arg. Rep. XVII, pp. 306–337 ; Moore's Dig., v. p. 281,

THE HAWAIIAN RECIPROCITY TREATY.

Great Britain and Germany yield to the argument of "special circumstances."—The treaty between the United States and Hawaii of January 30, 1875, was a bargaining agreement wherein the contracting parties exchanged unusual favors on the basis of strict reciprocity. In Articles I and II, the two countries agreed that each, "in consideration of rights and privileges granted" in return, would admit certain specified articles from the other free of duty. In Article IV, the King of Hawaii undertook not to lease or dispose of any port, harbor, or other territory in his dominions or grant any special privileges or rights therein to any other State, and not to "make any treaty by which any other nation shall obtain the same privileges, relative to the admission of any articles free of duty," thereby secured to the United States. The English Government protested. Several other European governments also protested on the basis of their treaties with Hawaii, and Germany protested, although she had no such treaty.

Great Britain had a treaty with Hawaii (of July 10, 1851), wherein it was provided that neither country should charge higher duties upon articles from the other than upon the same articles from any third nation. It had been the usual conception of the American interpretation of favored-nation obligations that, as between two States subscribing to a favored-nation treaty, each might demand and secure favors given by the other to a third State, provided it was willing to grant concessions equivalent to those granted by the third State. But under the provisions of the new treaty between the United States and Hawaii the latter country was no longer free to extend to Great Britain even the opportunity to purchase concessions. Hence it appeared that, in order to fulfill her treaty obligations to the United States, it would be necessary for Hawaii to break her promise to Great Britain and to give the United States exclusive preferential treatment. From this fact, it was possible to argue that the action of the United States was not in agreement with the doctrine which it had maintained. The American Government pointed out that "special privileges had been given in return for special, valuable considerations," and took the position that this was, because of geographical and political circumstances, a special and extraordinary case. During the discussion it was shown that Lord Clarendon, British Secretary of State for Foreign Affairs, had in 1856 informed the Hawaiian Government with reference to the unratified reciprocity treaty, which had been signed at Washington in the preceding year, that, "as the advantages conceded to the United States by the Sandwich Islands are expressly stated to be given in consideration of and as an equivalent for certain reciprocal concessions on the part of the United States, Great Britain can not, as a matter of right, claim the same advantages for her trade under the strict letter of the (British-Hawaiian) treaty of 1851." Lord Clarendon had apparently yielded to the American interpretation. In the course of the discussions which followed the making of the treaty of 1875, the validity of the American contention was recognized by the British Government. In an instruction to the British representative at Honolulu on January 25, 1878, Lord Derby took the position that "only under the peculiar circumstances of the case " could the British Government agree to the differential treatment of British goods by Hawaii in favor of the United States.[1] The logic of the situation was likewise accepted by other Governments. When a commercial treaty was made between Germany and Hawaii in 1879, the provision was inserted that the special advantages which had been granted to the United States would not be invoked in favor of the relations sanctioned between the contracting parties.[2]

Later the Hawaiian Government made a treaty with Portugal containing a like declaration.

In 1884 Lord Granville, British Secretary of State for Foreign Affairs, asked that the advantages which the United States had conceded to Hawaii and was considering ceding to several American States with whom negotiations were in progress, especially those in regard to the importation of sugar, be extended to the West Indies. Lord Granville's request was based on the claim that Article II in the United States-Great Britain treaty of 1815—a most-favored-nation clause without the specific provision for compensation—was a pledge of unconditional most-favored-nation treatment.

Mr. Frelinghuysen, Secretary of State, replied:

It is clear that the second article of the treaty of 1815 has not authorized, and could not authorize, Great Britain to ask for the products or shipping of the United Kingdom favors identical with or equivalent to those which Spanish-American and West India colonial products and shipping may receive in the ports of the United States by reason of special reciprocity treaties. * * *

It may * * * be premature to assume that his lordship contemplates the negotiation of a reciprocity treaty which shall secure for the trade of the West Indian colonies with the United States special favors, although the negotiation of the Canadian reciprocity treaty of 1854 would show that this class of international engagements, applying only to particular colonies, is not in violation of the policy of Her Majesty's Government.[3]

In a very clearly worded decision of the United States Supreme Court in the case of *Bartram* v. *Robertson*,[4] the Hawaiian reciprocity arrangement was held exceptional. The court declared:

Those stipulations * * * [in the treaty with Denmark] do not cover concessions like those made to the Hawaiian Islands for a valuable consideration. They were pledges * * * that * * * there should be no discrimination * * * in favor of goods of like character imported from any other country * * * they were not intended to interfere with special arrangements with other countries founded upon a concession of special privileges.[4]

In this connection it is interesting to turn to the treaty made between the United States and Tonga (the Friendly Islands) on October 2, 1886. In Article II, after provision for most-favored-nation treatment, there appears the following, defining clause:

it being understood that the Parties hereto affirm the principle of the law of nations that no privilege granted for equivalent or on account of propinquity

[1] Moore's Dig., V, pp. 264-265.

[2] Hawaiian treaty with the German Empire, Sept. 19, 1879, separate article: " Certain relations of proximity and other considerations having rendered it important to the Hawaiian Government to enter into mutual agreements with the Government of the United States of America, by a convention concluded at Washington the 30th day of January, 1875, the two high contracting parties have agreed that the special advantages granted by said convention to the United States of America, in consideration of equivalent advantages, shall not in any case be invoked in favor of the relations sanctioned between the two high contracting parties by the present treaty." [See 56th Cong., 2d sess., Sen Doc., vol. 26, 231, p. 234 ; U. S. For Rel., 1878, p. 382 ; and Moore's Dig., V, p. 265.]

[3] Ms. notes to Great Britain, XIX, 514 ; Moore's Dig., V, p. 269.

[4] *Bartram* v. *Robertson*, 122 U. S., 116, 1887 ; p. 408 ; also see U. S. For. Rel., 1881, 622 ff, and Herod, Favored-Nation Treatment, 116 ff ; also see infra.

or other special conditions come under the stipulations herein contained as to favored nations.

(Compare and contrast with this United States-Tonga treaty, the treaty between Great Britain and Tonga of Nov. 29, 1879, Art. II.) This was undoubtedly inserted on account of the difficulties which had arisen from the Hawaiian treaty, and the interesting assertion which it contains in regard to the law of nations represents the view expressed elsewhere by Secretary Bayard.[1]

Explanation of the Hawaiian treaty—Mr. Gresham and Mr. Adee, to Russian representatives, 1895.—Later, in the course of a discussion with Russia, Mr. Gresham, Secretary of State, wrote to Prince Canta-cuzène, Russian minister at Washington, on February 16, 1895:

> It has been uniformly held by this Government that other countries with which we have treaties containing the most-favored-nation clause can derive no benefit from this reciprocal commercial arrangement with Hawaii.

Mr. Adee, Acting Secretary of State, explained to Mr. Somow, Russian chargé d'affaires, on July 30, 1895:

> The exceptional advantages granted to the Hawaiian Islands by the tariff laws of the United States, in conformity with the provisions of the reciprocity treaty * * * have been yielded to that Government in return for certain valuable and exclusive considerations and by reason of the peculiar geographical and commercial relations that exist between the two countries. The course of this Government has been consistent in holding that such privileges do not fall within the favored-nation clause of any treaty. * * *[2]

OFFICIAL VIEWS AND NEGOTIATIONS, 1883–84.

In the course of the correspondence which followed the negotiation in 1883 of reciprocity treaties with Mexico, with the Dominican Republic, with Spain (for Cuba and Porto Rico), and with Great Britain (for the British West Indies), and while the revision of Japan's commercial treaties was under discussion, Mr. Frelinghuysen, Secretary of State, expressed the opinion that there was no inconsistency between the American interpretation of the most-favored-nation clause and the making of special reciprocity treaties.[3] Nevertheless, President Cleveland saw fit, a few months later, to withdraw the pending Spanish and Dominican treaties from the Senate, one of his reasons for doing so being that embarrassing questions would arise through the existence of favored-nation pledges and treaties with other countries.

Controversies and discussions in connection with the reciprocity agreements negotiated after 1890.—The application of the unconditional interpretation would have rendered of little effect the provisions of the tariff acts of 1890 and 1897 which authorized the negotiation of reciprocity agreements. Under the unconditional interpretation, the concessions granted in the process of securing or acknowledging reciprocal favorable treatment would have become at once the due of all countries having the right to claim most-favored-nation treatment from the United States and (or) from the co-contracting parties. In order to render effective the policy of special reciprocity, it is essen-

---

[1] 1886. See Moore's Dig., V, p. 273; see Appendix C., p. 453, infra.
[2] U S. For Rel., 1895, II, pp. 1119, 1121. Moore's Dig., V, pp. 275–277.
[3] See Moore's Dig., V, pp. 267–268.

tial that the "American" interpretation of favored-nation obligations be applied.

Penalty duties in relation to most-favored-nation pledges.—The peculiar form of the "reciprocity" provisions of the act of 1890 presented difficulties which even the conditional interpretation could not and can not obviate. By section 3 of this act it was authorized that penalty duties be imposed upon certain specified products when coming from countries whose treatment of American products the President might deem to be "reciprocally unequal and unreasonable." The principle upon which the penalty duties were actually applied to the products of certain countries—by comparison of the relative height of the tariff rates of the United States and those of the countries to be penalized—is, however, altogether different from the principle of exchanging concessions upon which conditional most-favored-nation treatment rests. It may lead to consequences quite inconsistent with most-favored-nation treatment. Thus: A country which levied on products of the United States duties higher than those which it levied on the similar products of other countries, but at the same time lower than those to which its own products were subjected upon their importation into the United States, might, because of the latter fact, escape the application of the penalty duties. At the same time, another country, which was considered to be extending most-favored-nation treatment, in the usual sense, to the United States, might be levying on American products duties higher than the duties levied in the United States upon its products. Under these circumstances the President would be expected to impose penalty duties on the products of the latter country, unless it lowered its duties on American products; and this would be clearly inconsistent with most-favored-nation obligations. Unless it was undertaken to impose the penalty duties upon imports of the articles specified in section 3 from each and every country which failed to grant preferential treatment to products of the United States, the intention of the penalizing provision could not be carried out without involving the violation of a number of most-favored-nation pledges.

The imposition of penalty duties under the act of 1890.—Such situations did in fact arise in connection with the operation of the act of 1890. The United States made reciprocity agreements with four European and six South and Central American countries. At the same time certain imports from Mexico and the Argentine, which countries had not entered into reciprocity agreements with the United States, enjoyed the benefit of the free list. Colombia refused to negotiate for a special reciprocity agreement, on the ground that she was entitled by the treaty of 1846 to most favored-nation treatment. She claimed the right, in respect to commodities on the free list, to the same treatment that Mexico and the Argentine were enjoying. Her representatives expressed the view that the negotiation of a special agreement to obtain treatment to which they were already entitled by treaty would amount to the waiving of important rights. To the Colombian claim and contentions Mr. Gresham, Secretary of State, replied that the application of the law of 1890 did not violate any of the most-favored-nation obligations of the United States, since "it applied the same treatment to all countries whose tariffs the President found to be unreasonable and unequal." As has been pointed out, most-favored-nation relations do not rest upon such a basis as was implied in Mr. Gresham's statement. His answer can not be regarded as having been a sufficient reply to the claims which it was intended to refute; but the tone of the correspondence on the Colombian side was by no means conciliatory, and, in spite of the continued insistence of the Colombian representative that the discriminatory duties on the products of his country be removed, no action was taken.[1]

Haiti made a claim, when penalty duties were imposed upon her products, that this was in violation of her rights under the most-favored-nation provision in the treaty of 1864. This claim of Haiti, like that of Colombia, was rejected. In response to representations made by the American minister to Haiti in reference to the rights of Venezuela, the State Department pointed out that Venezuela had abrogated her commercial treaty with the United States and therefore had no basis upon which to advance a claim for favored-nation treatment.[2]

The protests of Colombia and Haiti against the imposition of the penalty duties appear to have been justified. The levying of such duties upon their products when they were not imposed upon similar products coming under similar circumstances from the Argentine, Mexico, and some other countries, would seem not in keeping with the ordinary American interpretation of favored-nation pledges, for, unless it could be shown, as it apparently was not, that the other countries cited were extending special treatment to the United States, Colombia and Haiti were entitled to the free enjoyment of such advantages as were enjoyed by those States.

Controversies with Germany, 1890–1894.—Of controversies arising from the fact that divergent interpretations of the most-favored-nation clause have prevailed contemporaneously in the United States and in Europe, respectively, the most important have been those between the United States and Germany.

The uncertain status and the different interpretations of the treaty of 1828 with Prussia were the source of constant misunderstanding and irritation between the United States and the German Government, from the early years of the German Empire. The articles of the Prussian treaty of 1828 whose construction was the chief subject of contention, read as follows:

ART. V. No higher or other duties shall be imposed on the importation into the United States of any article the produce or manufacture of Prussia, and no higher or other duties shall be imposed on the importation into the Kingdom of Prussia of any article the produce or manufacture of the United States, than are or shall be payable on the like article being the produce or manufacture of any other foreign country. Nor shall any prohibition be imposed on the importation or exportation of any article the produce or manufacture of the United States, or of Prussia, to or from the ports of the United States, or to or from the ports of Prussia, which shall not equally extend to all other nations.

ART. IX. If either party shall hereafter grant to any other nation any particular favor in navigation or commerce, it shall immediately become common to the other party, freely, where it is freely granted to such other nation, or on yielding the same compensation, when the grant is conditional.[3]

[1] U. S. Foreign Relations, 1894, p. 198.
[2] Ibid., p. 336.
[3] The treaty with the Hanseatic towns was similar to that of Prussia and need not be considered separately. Similar treaties were concluded between the United States and Hanover, in 1840 and 1846; Oldenburg, in 1847; and Mecklenburg-Schwerin, in 1847.

These two articles are practically identical with Articles V and IX of the United States-Austria-Hungary treaty of August 27, 1829, and the United States-Russia treaty of December 18, 1832. It will be observed that the limiting clause, "* * * where it is freely granted to such other nations, or on yielding the same compensation where the grant is conditional," which appears in the covering clause (Article IX), of the Prussian treaty, is not present in Article V. The German interpretation has stressed Article V, insisting that it is absolute and is neither modified nor limited by Article IX; whereas the United States has always contended that the two articles must be read together and that Article IX qualified Article V.

The first test' of the applicability and meaning of the treaty of 1828 came in 1883. The German Empire had adopted the European or unconditional interpretation of the most-favored-nation clause. It should be noticed, however, that the treaty whose interpretation became the subject of difference between the United States and the Government of the German Empire had been concluded thirty-two years before the conclusion of the Cobden treaty and forty-two years before the formation of the German Empire, and that the contracting parties had been Prussia and the United States. It can be shown that "reciprocity" was the guiding principle with both parties to the treaty at the time when it was made; in fact, the treaty so stated in its preamble.[1] In 1883 the German Government concluded commercial treaties with Italy and Spain, and immediately extended the concessions granted thereby to the other European nations with which it had most-favored-nation treaties. But in the official list of eighteen countries to which these concessions were granted, the United States was not included. If the German Government considered the treaty of 1828 in force and applicable to the relations of the Empire, consistency should have required, inasmuch as that Government was committed to the unconditional interpretation of the most-favored-nation pledges, that the United States be considered entitled to the benefit of these concessions. Two years later during the debate in the Reichstag on February 10, 1885, Bismarck made the following statement:

The previous speaker has assumed that the United States does not belong among the States treated on the most-favored-nation basis. As a matter of fact, it does belong in that group, not by reason of treaties of the Empire, but on the basis of treaties with Prussia and with several other German States which can not be considered distinct from the Empire. Practically we and the United States treat each other reciprocally as most-favored nations, which gives us reason, for example, to claim the same advantages in the United States for our sugar imports as those extended to Cuba and Porto Rico in the treaty between Spain on behalf of her colonies and the United States, if that treaty be put into effect.[2]

On February 20, 1885, the German Government expressly included the United States in a list of the twenty-four most-favored nations to which it extended the benefit of a reduction of duty on rye which it had just conceded to Spain. Thus, within two years, although no change had occurred in the treaty relations with the United States, the German Government reversed its position. It is not difficult to find an explanation for this alteration. In 1883 Germany had apparently had

---

[1] See Glier, Die Meistbegünstigungsklausel.
[2] Translation from Stenographic Report of the German Reichstag, 1884-85, Vol. II, p. 119a.

nothing to gain by extending to the United States the tariff concessions which were given to other European countries. But in 1885 the United States was in the midst of negotiations with Spain (for Cuba), whereby Cuban sugar would be admitted into the United States on preferential terms as compared with sugar coming from other countries. The interest of the German sugar producers in gaining access to the American market on terms at least as favorable as those secured by their chief competitors undoubtedly had some connection with the change of attitude described above. It would be of little avail for Germany to claim unconditional most-favored-nation treatment from the United States as a treaty right, if it could be shown either that she had denied the force and applicability of the treaty or that she was not herself acting in accordance with the unconditional interpretation in construing the treaty. Nothing was actually gained by Bismarck's maneuvering of the moment, for the treaty with Cuba was not ratified, and German sugar continued without question to enter the United States on as favorable terms as did any other sugar.

The next test came in 1891. From 1883 to 1891 Germany had prohibited the importation of American hogs, pork, and sausages, officially on sanitary grounds, but in reality as a measure of protection to her own agrarians. After repeated attempts to secure the repeal of this prohibition, and after a thorough demonstration of its unfairness to American producers, the United States finally enacted several measures which it was hoped would lead Germany to adopt a more liberal policy in regard to the importation of meat products from the United States. Of these measures, the most important appeared in the act of August 30, 1890, providing for the inspection of meat products destined for export, which contained in addition the following clauses:

SEC. 4. That whenever the President is satisfied that there is good reason to believe that any importation is being made, or is about to be made, into the United States, from any foreign country, of any article used for human food or drink that is adulterated to an extent dangerous to the health or welfare of the people of the United States, or any of them, he may issue his proclamation suspending the importation of such articles from such country for such period of time as he may think necessary to prevent such importation; and during such period it shall be unlawful to import into the United States from the countries designated in the proclamation of the President any of the articles the importation of which is so suspended.

SEC. 5. That whenever the President shall be satisfied that unjust discriminations are made by or under the authority of any foreign State against the importation to or sale in such foreign State of any product of the United States, he may direct that such products of such foreign States so discriminating against any product of the United States as he may deem proper shall be excluded from importation to the United States; and in such case he shall make proclamation of his direction in the premises, and therein name the time when such direction against importation shall take effect, and after such date the importation of the articles named in such proclamation shall be unlawful. The President may at any time revoke, modify, terminate, or renew any such direction as, in his opinion, the public interest may require.

Congress had thus provided another weapon which the President might use very effectively. Before 1890 the United States had possessed simply a single tariff with no bargaining or penalizing devices whereby favorable treatment could be encouraged and discriminations made unprofitable. By the legislation of 1890 and 1891, however, the Government was equipped with powerful bargaining instruments with which to invite or to compel fair treatment for the American export trade; and from this time on the United States was in a better position to bargain with Germany than had previously been the case.

During the years 1891, 1892, and 1893, Germany concluded with European countries a series of bargaining treaties which became known generally as the "Caprivi treaties."[1] If the United States-Prussia treaty of 1828 was still in force, the concessions granted by Germany in these new treaties to a number of the important countries of Europe should have been extended immediately to the United States. This was true no matter which interpretation of the most-favored-nation clause Germany chose to apply. Under the unconditional interpretation there could be no question: the United States would be entitled to any concessions granted to any other country under any circumstances whatsoever. Under the conditional interpretation, if Germany chose to apply that in dealing with the United States, the following considerations were applicable in support of the claim that the United States was entitled to the benefit of the concession. Germany had undertaken, by the Frankfort treaty, to extend to France immediately and unconditionally all concessions which she made to England, Belgium, Holland, Switzerland, Austria, and Russia. With or without compensation, it may be argued either way, Germany did so extend to France the concessions which she made to those countries. Further, Germany generalized her concessions in favor of European countries, among them Great Britain, even though on the part of Great Britain there was no giving of concessions in return by way of compensation. Hence, in Germany's most-favored-nation treatment either of France or of Great Britain, or of both, there was a " free " granting of favors without compensation. It would follow that even under the conditional interpretation of the most-favored-nation pledge the United States was entitled to the concessions—which Germany generalized in Europe—of the Caprivi treaties.

The Saratoga convention, 1891.—The United States did not, however, claim these concessions as her right, and Germany took no steps to extend them of her own accord. Instead, the Governments entered into negotiations which resulted in the conclusion of the Saratoga convention, of August 22, 1891, which was put into effect by President Harrison's proclamation of February 1, 1892.[2] By this special agreement the United States secured concessions identical with some of those which had been made to European States in the Caprivi treaties; also, the removal of the objectionable German sanitary regulations. But these concessions were granted as a bargain: the United States had undertaken by the act of March 3, 1891, to make a thorough inspection of meat destined for export, and it promised not to exercise against Germany the discretionary penalizing authority which had been placed in the hands of the President by section 3 of the tariff act of 1890 and by sections 4 and 5 of the act of March 3, 1891. Throughout the documents and correspondence connected with the negotia-

[1] See Part III, p. 470 seq., infra.
[2] The Saratoga convention consisted of an exchange of notes by representatives of the two countries. These were published in 52d Cong., 1st sess., Sen. Ex. Doc. No. 119, p. 110. See p. 154.

tion of the convention, the exchange of concessions was uniformly treated as a matter of agreement, in which a consideration was granted only in return for a consideration. In other words, the United States was obliged to pay for what, if the treaty of 1828 was still in force and applicable, it should have received gratuitously.

Significant in its bearing on the question of the status of the treaty of 1828 was the fact that, as a result of the Saratoga convention, Germany granted to the United States not all but only a part of the Caprivi concessions, those on agricultural products. While these were the most important of the concessions made in these treaties, the additional reduction of duties on a number of manufactured articles, which had been granted in 1891 to Austria-Hungary, Italy, Belgium, in 1892 to Switzerland, and in 1893 to Servia, Spain and Roumania, were withheld from the United States. Thus, even for compensation, the United States did not secure all that was due to her—if the treaty was still in effect—gratuitously.

Tariff act of 1894—Claims which followed.—The tariff act of 1894, by reimposing a duty on sugar and omitting the provisions for penalty duties, automatically ended, so far as the United States was concerned, the reciprocity agreements negotiated under the preceding tariff law. Among other things, the act of 1894 imposed an additional countervailing duty on bounty-fed sugar. This led to charges from the bounty-paying countries of unfair discrimination. The protests made by Germany are of interest, because they were made to rest at one moment on the Saratoga convention and at another upon the treaty of 1828.

Was the Saratoga convention a reciprocity agreement?—The communication of the American ambassador at Berlin, transmitting to the State Department the first German protest, gave evidence of the prevailing German conception that the Saratoga convention was a special bargain. A memorandum submitted by the German embassy at Washington stated:

The excitement which prevails in German agricultural and manufacturing circles on account of this inequitable treatment of a German production is the more vehement and less easily to be resisted inasmuch as it is generally believed that the United States, in the agreement of August 22, guaranteed exemption to Germany from the duty on sugar in return for the concession of the conventional duties on American agricultural products and the removal of the restrictions on the importation of swine.[1]

Shortly after, however, it was declared officially in Germany that the Saratoga convention was merely an explanatory or declaratory interchange of notes, confirming the treaty of 1828. In a speech before the Reichstag on December 14, 1894, the Secretary of State for Foreign Affairs, Baron Marschall von Bieberstein, made the following statement:

Representative Count Kanitz has expressed his regret that we have for three years allowed to inure to the advantage of the United States, without equivalence, the concessions which we had granted to the agricultural products of Austria-Hungary and other States by our commercial treaties. To defend the Imperial Government in this respect I possess only one argument, but that argument is conclusive. We have granted this concession to the United States without equivalent because we were under a treaty obligation to do so, because by force of Articles V and IX of the treaty concluded between Prussia

---

[1] U. S. Foreign Relations, 1894, p 234.

and the United States in the year 1828 we were bound to unconditional most-favored-nation treatment according to the interpretation which we have always given to this treaty.[1]

But later in the same speech the Secretary in a measure contradicted himself, as follows:

In respect to the concessions granted to Austria-Hungary, however, we do not extend the most-favored-nation treatment to the United States as the previous speaker thinks, presenting it unconditionally upon a tray. On the contrary, we had them give us certain guarantees, indeed by this very exchange of notes of August 22, 1891.[2]

The German protests did not avail to secure the removal of the countervailing duty on sugar. Owing to the crippling of the Cuban sugar industry by the Cuban revolution of 1896, the German exports of sugar to the United States increased in spite of the duty, and nothing more was heard in protest until the passage, in 1897, of the Dingley tariff act, which also provided for a countervailing duty on bounty sugar. Since the Saratoga convention was terminable by either party, the German Government applied itself even more energetically than before to the task of establishing the impression that its provisions were not a bargain, but merely a reaffirmation of the treaty of 1828. The fact that neither the treaty of 1828 nor most-favored-nation relations were anywhere mentioned in the convention, and the more important fact that the special terms of the convention were not consistent with the broader pledges of the treaty of 1828, were both ignored. The German Government formally protested against the provisions of the Dingley tariff on the grounds, first, that it violated the most-favored-nation clause of the treaty of 1828, and, second, that it was "incompatible with the provisions of the Saratoga convention."[3]

In a speech before the Reichstag on May 3, 1897, Baron Marschall made the following statement:

* * * The Imperial Government could have had no doubt, when it made the commercial treaty of 1891 with Austria-Hungary, that it was under obligation to allow to the United States unconditionally the reductions of duty granted to Austria-Hungary. It would have violated honesty and good faith, if, repeatedly claiming from the United States rights in our favor, we had denied our interpretation of these rights when our own obligation was in question. If then, in spite of this clear situation, negotiations with the United States took place, which led later to the exchange of notes at Saratoga, this was due entirely to the fact that the pending American legislation, comprehended under the name of the McKinley Act, permitted considerable doubt whether we could reckon upon full reciprocity in our interpretation. * * * In order to secure ourselves in this regard these negotiations took place whose results were ratified in the exchange of notes at Saratoga. It follows therefore that by this exchange of notes no new rights and no new duties were created; that the previous right to most-favored-nation treatment was not widened, but merely confirmed; in other words, that the exclusive purpose was to make clear what form the most-favored-nation treatment already existing by treaty should assume when applied to the later commercial legislation of the two States.[4]

Herein appears and stands a careful exposition of the revised German interpretation of the Saratoga convention. But the American Government refused to accept the German interpretation and continued to construe the Saratoga convention as a reciprocal agree-

---

[1] Translation from Stenographic Report of the German Reichstag, 1894–5, Vol. I, p. 122c.
[2] Ibid. p. 122d.
[3] U. S. For. Rel., 1897, p. 178.
[4] Stenographic Report of the German Reichstag, 1895–1897, Vol. VIII, p. 5757c,

ment, which, as such, had ceased to have effect from the moment of the termination of the law upon which, on the American side, it had been based.

Salt—Germany claims the benefit of the free list—American construction of a conditional provision for reciprocal removal or a retaliatory imposition of duty.—By the tariff act of 1894 salt was put on the free list. There was, however, a provision that—

> If salt is imported from any country * * * which imposes a duty upon salt exported from the United States, then there shall be levied * * * upon such salt the rate of duty existing prior to the passage of this act.[1]

Germany claimed, under the free-list provision of the act, and by virtue of the favored-nation provisions in the treaty of 1828, the right of free entry for her salt. At the same time American salt was subject to duty in Germany. Attorney General Olney, in declaring the German claim untenable, pointed to the American practice of accepting equivalents. Further, the tariff act, he said—

> enacts, in substance and effect, that any country admitting American salt free shall have its own salt admitted free here, while any country putting a duty upon American salt shall have its salt here dutiable. * * * In other words, the United States concedes "free salt" to any nation which concedes "free salt" to the United States. Germany, of course, is entitled to that concession upon returning the same equivalent. But otherwise she is not so entitled.
> * * * *[2]

THE EXTENSION OF SPECIAL CONCESSIONS, BY RECIPROCITY, UNDER THE ACT OF 1897.

The Swiss claim for unconditional most-favored-nation treatment, 1898—The United States concedes the claim, but cancels the favored-nation clauses in the treaty of 1850.—An example of the inconvenience of the unconditional most-favored-nation pledge in connection with the successful operation of reciprocity agreements is afforded in the history of the experience of the United States with Switzerland after the conclusion by the former of the reciprocity treaty with France, on May 28, 1898. As soon as the agreement in question went into force, the Swiss Government demanded for Swiss imports into the United States the benefit of the concessions which had just been extended to France. In presenting the demands of his Government, on June 29, 1898, the Swiss minister at Washington invoked the application of Articles VIII, IX, X, and XII, of the treaty of November 25, 1850, between the United States and Switzerland.

The articles read as follows:

> ART. VIII. In all that relates to the importation, exportation, and transit of their respective products, the United States of America and the Swiss Confederation shall treat each other, reciprocally, as the most-favored nation, union of nations, state, or society, as is explained in the following articles.
> ART. IX. Neither of the contracting parties shall impose any higher or other duties upon the importation, exportation, or transit of the natural or industrial products of the other, than are or shall be payable upon the like articles, being the produce of any other country, not embraced within its present limits.
> ART. X. In order the more effectually to attain the object contemplated in Article VIII, each of the contracting parties hereby engages not to grant any favor in commerce to any nation, union of nations, State, or society, which shall not immediately be enjoyed by the other party.

---

[1] Act of Aug. 27, 1894, Free List, 608.
[2] Olney, At. Gen., Nov. 13, 1894, 21 Op. 80, 82–83 ; Moore's Dig., V, p. 274.

ART. XII. The Swiss territory shall remain open to the admission of articles arriving from the United States of America; in like manner, no port of the said States shall be closed to articles arriving from Switzerland, provided they are conveyed in vessels of the United States, or in vessels of any country having free access to the ports of said States. Swiss merchandise arriving under the flag of the United States, or under that of one of the nations most favored by them, shall pay the same duties as the merchandise of such nation; under any other flag it shall be treated as the merchandise of the country to which the vessel belongs.

*   *   *   *   *   *   *

The United States consent to extend to Swiss products, arriving or shipped under their flag, the advantages which are or shall be enjoyed by the products of the most-favored nation arriving or shipped under the same flag.

It is hereby understood that no stipulation of the present article shall in any manner interfere with those of the four aforegoing articles, nor with the measures which have been or shall be adopted by either of the contracting countries in the interest of public morality, security, or order.

These articles called for immediate most-favored-nation treatment, and contained no conditional provisions calling for compensation. There was no conditional clause anywhere in the treaty. It was shown from the records of the original negotiations that the American minister at Berne, who had represented the United States, had proposed a limiting clause to which the Swiss Government had objected, and that finally Switzerland had been given " a full and unlimited guarantee of the usage of the most-favored nation."[1] Mr. Hay, Secretary of State, having thoroughly examined the evidence, felt bound to acknowledge the validity of the Swiss claim and declared that " justice and honor require that the common understanding of the high contracting parties at the time of the executing of the treaty should be carried into effect," although this formed an exception to the otherwise uniform policy of the United States. At the same time, Mr. Hay intimated that notice might be given of the termination of the articles in the treaty of 1850 upon which the Swiss claim was based. In the meantime the Treasury Department instructed the customs officials to apply to imports from Switzerland the rates which were imposed upon similar French goods under the terms of the recent reciprocity agreement.[2] Germany and other States soon claimed the same treatment. On March 23, 1899, the United States gave notice of denunciation of the most-favored nation articles in the treaty of 1850, and on March 23, 1900, these articles ceased to have effect. The regular duties were then again levied upon Swiss products. The Swiss Government in return applied its maximum tariff to imports from the United States.

In 1905 Switzerland adopted a new tariff law to take effect on January 1, 1906. When the new tariff came into effect, Switzerland, voluntarily and without there having been concluded between the two countries a new treaty, extended the application of her minimum schedule to the products of the United States. Simultaneously, by proclamation of January 1, 1906, President Roosevelt extended to Swiss products the reductions authorized by section 3 of the act of 1897, which had already been extended to a number of other countries. Thus, without the formality of a treaty, the commercial relations of the two countries were reestablished on a basis of most-

---

[1] Moore's Dig., V, pp. 283–285.
[2] Ibid., p. 285.

favored-nation treatment, with no surrender on the part of the United States of the principle of the conditional interpretation.

German claims on the basis of the reciprocity agreement with France and the extension of its benefits to Switzerland, 1898.—On the ground that the concessions granted to France had been extended gratuitously to Switzerland, the German Government claimed from the United States the extension of the same concessions in favor of German products, basing the claim on the most-favored-nation clauses of the United States-Prussia treaty of 1828. The State Department, without questioning the status of the treaty of 1828, adhered to the conditional interpretation of the most-favored-nation provisions. The gratuitous grant of concessions to Switzerland was to be considered an exception to the regular practice of the United States and would be no longer effective after the early termination of the treaty clauses upon which the obligation to Switzerland rested. That Germany might expect the benefit of the concessions because they had been granted to France was denied, on the ground that France had received these concessions only in return for reciprocal concessions.

The status of the treaty of 1828.—Meanwhile the applicability of the treaty of 1828 had been brought into question. As already mentioned, Bismarck had declared in 1885 that the United States was classed among the most-favored nations, not on the basis of a treaty with the German Empire but on the basis of treaties made with Prussia and other German States. The phrase which he used, " practically we treat each other as most-favored nations," implied that legally there was no obligation on either side. There has been, since, not a little consideration, some official, some academic, of the question whether Prussian rights and obligations under the treaty devolved, as a part of its legal inheritance, upon the German Empire. Thus, for instance, Mr. Olney, Secretary of State, requested in 1896 that he be " informed of the grounds, if any, for regarding the treaty stipulations with Prussia in 1828 as now operative with respect to the whole German Empire."[1] It is not within the province of this report to give an account of contributions to the discussion or to analyze the arguments, but the importance of the question warrants reference to the fact that Dr. Glier, a German authority, after a careful and exhaustive study of the evidences, expressed the opinion (1905) that the treaty never applied to the Empire, and, further, that the new relation which Prussia assumed at the time of the making of the Empire abrogated the treaty altogether.[2]

Negotiation of a new reciprocity agreement between Germany and the United States, 1900.—Upon the continued refusal of the United States to acknowledge itself obligated by the treaty of 1828 to grant unconditional most-favored-nation treatment, the German Government attempted to find a solution of the grievances of German exporters by negotiating an agreement with the United States, whereby the desired concessions might be obtained in return for reciprocal concessions.

Such a reciprocity agreement was concluded on July 10, 1900. Without determining the status or the interpretation of the treaty of '1828, it removed temporarily the main causes of irritation be-

---

[1] U. S. Foreign Relations, 1896, pp. 208–209.
[2] Glier, Die Meistbegünsklausel, pp. 303–307.

tween the United States and Germany; it provided for the extension to American products of all the tariff advantages which Germany had granted by the Caprivi treaties to various European countries, in return for which the United States gave Germany the benefit of the reductions of duty authorized by section 3 of the tariff act of 1897. This agreement was terminable by either party and made mention neither of the treaty of 1828 nor of most-favored-nation treatment. Since the agreement of 1900 was strictly in accordance with the requirements of conditional most-favored-nation practice, it implied either the acceptance by the German Government of the American interpretation of the treaty of 1828, or disregard of the existence of that treaty. In 1903, on January 15, Count Posadowsky declared, " the United States no longer enjoys most-favored-nation treatment in Germany." [1]

German claims in connection with the United States-Cuba reciprocity treaty of 1902.—By the treaty concluded with Cuba in December, 1902, all Cuban articles not admitted duty free into the United States were given 20 per cent reduction from the general duty, and articles from the United States were given reductions up to 40 per cent from the general Cuban duty. Article VIII provided that the reduction given by each to the other shall continue during the duration of the treaty " preferential in respect to all like imports from other countries," and that the United States shall admit " no sugar the product of any other foreign country * * * at a lower rate than that provided by the tariff act * * * [of 1897]."

The German Government subsequently pointed out that, even though the relations of Cuba and the United States are unusually close, nevertheless Cuba is a sovereign State and the United States bargains with her as such; and that so long as Germany and the United States have most-favored-nation relations, the United States should give Germany the opportunity to offer a concession through which to secure the advantage granted to Cuba. The validity of such a claim is contingent, first, of course, upon the existence of the most-favored-nation relations. The right, assuming such relation, to claim the opportunity to offer equivalent concession would depend upon the soundness or unsoundness of the general contention that the peculiar circumstances and relationships invoked warrant preferential and exclusive arrangements. The circumstances in this case are not unlike those which prevailed in Hawaiian-American relations in 1875, in regard to which Germany as well as Great Britain had admitted that " extraordinary circumstances" made preferential treatment warrantable. In the course of a memorandum presented to the House of Representatives in 1912 while reciprocity with Canada was under discussion, Mr. McCall, of Massachusetts, referred to the similarity of the " special circumstances" in the Hawaiian and the Cuban cases, as follows:

One of the grounds upon which the exclusive character of the mutual tariff concessions made by the United States and Cuba in the reciprocity treaty of December 11, 1902, is maintained is the relations of proximity between them. The special considerations underlying this treaty were partly geographical and partly political. The former may be described as " relations of proximity," and are similar to those which existed formerly between the United States and Hawaii and which appeared in a treaty between the Governments of the two

---

[1] See Glier, Die Meistbegünstigungsklausel, p. 267.

countries on January 30, 1875. * * * recognition of the "relations of proximity" involved in that treaty appears in a declaration annexed to a treaty between Germany and Hawaii concluded March 25–September 19, 1879.[1]

New reciprocity agreement with Germany, 1907.—The German tariff law of 1902 was to become effective on March 1, 1906. Toward the end of 1905 the German Government presented to the United States certain demands by meeting which the latter could secure the transitory extension to its commerce of the benefit of the reduced rates established in the tariff treaties which had been negotiated. A *modus vivendi* was forthwith concluded, to continue in force until June 30, 1907. When, subsequently, Germany made further tariff reductions in treaties with Sweden and Bulgaria, she did not extend the additional conventional rates to the United States. It was evident that on neither side was any unconditional most-favored-nation obligation considered to be in existence.

In 1906 tariff commissioners were sent by the American Government to Germany. After several months of study on the ground, these commissioners made a report, as the result of which there was concluded on May 2, 1907, a new agreement, which went into effect on July 1, 1907. By this agreement, Germany granted to American products most, but not all, of the rates of her new conventional schedule. In return the United States, in conformity with provisions in section 3 of the act of 1897, made concessions in the matter of customs and consular regulations along lines requested by Germany. Although the number of the articles upon which Germany did not grant the conventional rates was small and their importance negligible, nevertheless the fact of the exception amounted to a withholding of most-favored-nation treatment in the European sense. No mention was made, either in the negotiations or in the agreement itself, of the treaty of 1828 or of most-favored-nation treatment.

Provisions of the treaty of 1828 no longer effective.—The treaty of 1828 had never been formally abrogated; the question whether it extended to the whole Empire or only to Prussia had never been decided; the question whether it called for unconditional or for conditional most-favored-nation treatment was never settled officially. But neither in theory nor in practice were its terms applied to German-American commercial relations after, say, 1891. So far as its most-favored-nation clauses were concerned, the treaty was a dead letter. When the British Government published in 1908 a list of "commercial treaties in force," this treaty was not included.

After the beginning of the European war, both the United States and Germany appear to have considered the treaty in force and applicable to the relations of the United States and the whole German Empire. When the United States entered the war, those portions of the treaty which had to do with relations in time of peace became, without question, no longer effective.

---

[1] Text quoted in section on Hawaii, p. 419.

For further discussion of the Cuban-American reciprocity treaty, see p. 315 seq., infra. By section IV B, of the United States tariff act of October 3, 1913, the proviso in Article VIII of the treaty with Cuba was abrogated and repealed. The proviso had read as follows: "* * * *Provided.* That while the convention is in force, no sugar imported from the Republic of Cuba, and being the product of the soil or industry of the Republic of Cuba, shall be admitted into the United States at a reduction of duty greater than 20 per centum of the rates of duty thereon as provided by the tariff act of the United States approved July 24, 1897, and no sugar, the product of any other foreign country, shall be admitted by treaty or convention into the United States, while this convention is in force, at a lower rate of duty than that provided by the tariff act of the United States approved July 24, 1897."

COUNTERVAILING DUTIES.

Controversies with Russia—Countervailing duties not inconsistent with favored-nation pledges.—The question of the right, in connection with most-favored-nation treatment, to levy countervailing duties on bounty-fed products has occasioned difficulties in relation with a number of nations, and the right to levy such duties has been successfully vindicated, not alone by the United States, following conditional most-favored-nation practice, but by such States as Great Britain, following the unconditional practice.

Duties on sugar.—After the removal of the British duties on sugar, the British sugar-producing colonies and sugar refiners petitioned their Government for the imposition of a countervailing duty upon bounty-fed sugar coming from continental States. The law officers of the Crown then took the position, in 1880, that countervailing duties would be incompatible with the requirements of most-favored-nation treatment, and the Government felt that it could not undertake to impose such duties. But in 1889 the new Conservative ministry advocated legislation to prohibit importation of bounty-fed sugar. Ten years later, by the tariff amendment act of 1899, countervailing duties were established to be levied upon bounty-fed sugar imported into India. In correspondence with the Russian Government, the British Foreign Office declared that these duties were not in violation of most-favored-nation obligation. Lord Salisbury contended that the Russian system of refunding excise duties on sugar destined for export had the same effect as a "bounty of a more direct nature"; that it was the intention of the most-favored-nation clause that goods should enjoy equality of treatment, but not preferential advantages; and that the remedy for the adverse effects of a countervailing duty lay with the country whose legislation had created the artificial situation which necessitated the levying of such duty. This was adopted as the conclusive view of the British Government, and in 1902 Lord Lansdowne even offered to abrogate the treaty with Russia.

In the United States, later official conclusions, as had been the case in England, reversed earlier opinions. When in 1894 Congress laid countervailing duties upon bounty-fed sugar,[1] Mr. Gresham, Secretary of State, was of the opinion that this was in violation of the treaty obligations of the United States, and President Cleveland recommended, but did not secure, the repeal of the portion of the act which imposed this duty. Mr. Olney, Attorney General, took the position that the most-favored-nation clause could not be invoked to interfere with the internal regulations of a country, and pointed out that representatives of Great Britain and Germany had expressly declared at the conference of 1888 that the export sugar bounty of a country might be counteracted by an import sugar duty of another country without causing any discrimination which could be deemed a violation of the terms of the most-favored-nation clause.[2] In section 5 of the tariff act of 1897 Congress provided:

That whenever any country * * * shall pay * * *, directly or indirectly, any bounty * * * upon the exportation of any article * * *,

[1] Act of Aug. 27, 1894, schedule E, 182½.
[2] Olney, At. Gen., Nov. 13, 1894. 21 Op., 80, p. 82; Mr. Sherman, Secretary of State, to Mr. von Reichenau, German chargé d'affaires, Sept. 22, 1897. U. S. For. Rel., 1897, p. 178. Moore's Dig., V, pp. 305–306.

and such article * * *   is dutiable under the provisions of this act * * *, there shall be levied * * *   an additional duty equal to the net amount of such bounty * * *

The European protests of 1894 were repeated. Mr. Sherman, Secretary of State, abandoning the view of Mr. Gresham of three years before, denied the validity of the Russian, German, and Austro-Hungarian contentions, relying especially on the opinion expressed by Attorney General Olney in 1894.

The countervailing duty was also assessed on imports of Russian beet sugar. In 1901, in avowed retaliation, the Russian Government withdrew the benefit of its conventional tariff from important classes of American manufactures.

In 1902, by the Brussels sugar convention, the leading commercial States of Europe agreed to prohibit the importation into their territories of bounty-fed sugar. Russia, not a party to this convention, subsequently protested vigorously against the countervailing duties levied by Great Britain and the United States, but both powers insisted on the legality of the duties.

The position of the United States Government was defined in the decision rendered by the Supreme Court in the case of *Downs* v. *United States*, in 1903. A cargo of refined sugar had been imported from Russia, and the customs collectors at the port of Baltimore had imposed the countervailing duty. The importers had appealed, the decision of the collector had been affirmed by the General Appraisers, by the Circuit Court, and by the Circuit Court of Appeals. The Supreme Court went at length into the facts with regard to the method by which the production and exportation of sugar were officially encouraged in Russia. The Court affirmed the decision of the Circuit Court of Appeals. The substance of the decision may be summarized as follows: " When a tax is imposed on all sugar produced, but is remitted upon all sugar exported," and the exporter obtains from his government, " solely because of such exportation," a certificate which possesses an actual value and is salable in the open market, the remission of the tax is in effect a bounty upon the exportation. Sugar exported under such circumstances and imported into the United States is subject, under the provisions of the act of Congress of July 24, 1897 (30 Stat., 205), to an additional duty equal to the entire amount of such bounty. (*Downs* v. *U. S.* (1903), 187 U. S., 496.)

Duties on petroleum.—By the tariff act of 1897, petroleum was made free of duty. Section 2, paragraph 626, contained the provision that,

if there be imported into the United States crude petroleum, or the products of crude petroleum produced in any country which imposes a duty on petroleum or its products exported from the United States, there shall in such cases be levied a duty upon said crude petroleum or its products so imported equal to the duty imposed by such country.

In accordance with this provision a duty was levied upon imports of Russian petroleum; and, in order to guard against the free admission of petroleum products manufactured in England from the crude Russian product, the American collectors of customs were instructed, in 1901, to require the attachment of United States consular certificates of origin to invoices of naptha imported into the United States. The Russian Government, considering this unwarranted, withdrew the benefit of its conventional tariff rates from certain other classes of American products. Attempts of the American ambassador, in 1901, to secure the removal of these discriminatory duties failed. In 1905 the American ambassador reopened the discussion. In addition to the contention that the sugar and the petroleum duties constituted a deliberate discrimination against Russia, the Russian Ministry of Finance took the position, first, as to principle, that when countries are carrying on their trade subject to most-favored-nation treatment, a duty should not be changed without consultation between the two; and second, as to fact, that the United States was wrong in considering that sugar received a bounty in Russia. The American ambassador attempted to convince the Minister of Finance that the duties on sugar and petroleum were levied as a part of a general policy, not particularly against Russia; and he offered to negotiate a reciprocity treaty based upon section 3 of the act of 1897. The following note, handed to President Roosevelt by Count Witte on September 9, 1905, ended the misunderstanding to the satisfaction of the United States, and indicates that the Russian Government had altered its views:

Some years ago, in consequence of a misunderstanding in the interpretation of the most-favored-nation clause, there were established in Russia on several articles of American production customs duties on a higher scale than those levied on the same articles when imported from other countries.

His Majesty the Emperor of Russia has commanded me to inform the President of the United States that he has been pleased to order the discontinuance of the levying of such higher duties on American products in order that henceforth the American manufacturers should pay the same duties as importers from other countries.[1]

In 1907 Russia signed the sugar convention.

THE ARGOL AGREEMENTS AND MOST-FAVORED-NATION RELATIONS.

Several of the argol agreements negotiated in conformity with the provisions of section 3 of the act of 1897 [2] were either put into the form of most-favored-nation agreements or were made to reaffirm older most-favored-nation treaties.

Most-favored-nation treatment of American products by Italy—Reciprocity agreement, 1900.—A reciprocity agreement was negotiated with Italy on February 8, 1900, on the basis of section 3 of the act of 1897. In return for the identical concessions granted to France and Germany by the United States, the treaty secured the free admission into Italy of turpentine, which formerly had been dutiable even under the minimum tariff, the admission of cottonseed oil at a reduced rate of duty, and the admission of certain other American products at the minimum rates. But, as a matter of fact, the Italian Government had already accorded its minimum rates to all the imports of the United States upon the basis of the United States-Italy treaty of 1871 and in conformity with the European interpretation of the most-favored-nation clause. Upon the termination of the agreement by the United States in 1910, Italy continued to apply the rates of her minimum tariff to American products, but withdrew the special rates established by the agreement.

Most-favored-nation agreement with Spain, 1906.—On August 1, 1906, a commercial agreement was concluded with Spain which assumed a

---

[1] U. S. Foreign Relations, 1905, pp. 801–806.
[2] See Part I, p. 205 seq., infra.

broader character, in the matter of its phraseology, than that of a mere argol agreement in conformity with section 3 of the act of 1897. After making provision for what would amount to mutual unconditional most-favored-nation treatment, the agreement specified in Article III that—

Each of the high contracting parties * * * shall have the right to rescind forthwith any of its concessions herein made by it, if the other at any time shall withhold any of its concessions or shall withhold any of its tariff benefits now or hereafter granted to any third nation, exception being made of the special benefits now or hereafter given by Spain to Portugal and those now or hereafter given by the United States to Cuba.

In 1909 the Spanish Government requested that the reduction of duty on sparkling wines, which had been granted to France in 1908, be extended also to Spain in accordance with the agreement of 1906. A supplementary agreement was effected by an exchange of notes on February 20, 1909, whereby, without any additional concessions on her part, Spain was given the benefit of the reduction in question. Mr. Bacon, Secretary of State, wrote to the Spanish minister at Washington:

* * * In order to remove any possible ground for the exercise by your [the Spanish] Government of the right under Article III of the Commercial Agreement signed between the two countries on August 1, 1906, to rescind any of its concessions made therein to the United States, I have the honor to inform you that the President of the United States deems the concessions made by Spain in favor of the products and manufactures of the United States as reciprocal and equivalent to the grant by the Government of the United States of the reduced duties on all the articles of Spanish production and exportation enumerated in section 3 of the tariff act of the United States approved July 24, 1897.[1]

The agreement of 1906 had not required compensation. It called for most-favored-nation treatment without condition; but the statement that the concessions made by Spain were accepted as reciprocal and equivalent to the grant of the reduced duties on all the articles enumerated in section 3 of the act of 1897 was not merely formal or superfluous. It served two useful purposes. On the one hand, it brought the agreement of 1906 into harmony, at least in language, with the terms of section 3 of the tariff act under which it had been concluded. The tariff act of 1897 did not authorize the President to conclude unconditional most-favored-nation agreements without reference to the Senate. It authorized entering into agreements whereby duties on the articles enumerated in section 3 of the act of 1897 would be reduced only upon the concession of " reciprocal and equivalent " reductions by the other parties to the agreement. The acceptance of the original concessions made by Spain as " reciprocal and equivalent " to all the concessions authorized by section 3 was therefore necessary to fulfill the intent of the act of 1897. On the other hand, the statement served the further purpose of forestalling an attempt on the part of other nations to claim the reduction of duty on sparkling wines, without offering equivalent concessions in return, on the ground that this reduction had been extended gratuitously to Spain. No further concessions were made to other countries by the United States during the life of the Spanish agreement.[2]   Had such been

---

[1] Malloy, Treaties, Conventions, etc., Vol. II, p. 1721.
[2] The agreement with Spain was terminated on Aug. 7, 1910, on notice given by the United States.

made, it would have been necessary, in order to conform with the agreement of 1906, for the United States to concede them to Spain. This agreement with Spain was therefore, in a sense, a temporary departure from the American practice in regard to most-favored-nation treaties. Only the absence of reciprocity negotiations with other countries involving concessions not already made to Spain prevented the development of complications in the commercial relations of the United States with other countries entitled to most-favored-nation treatment. Even in case such treaties had been made, the provision in the Spanish agreement for the rescinding of concessions by either country immediately upon the failure of the other to live up to its terms offered a means of escape from controversies which otherwise might have taken a course similar to those which followed the gratuitous extension of tariff concessions to Switzerland in 1898.

Most-favored-nation arrangement with Bulgaria, 1906.—The United States had always enjoyed most-favored-nation treatment by Bulgaria, but such treatment was never, until June 5, 1906, guaranteed to her by any agreement or otherwise. The new Bulgarian tariff law of 1906 provided that the conventional rates of the Bulgarian tariff should be extended only to countries with which Bulgaria had commercial treaties. In order to secure the benefit of the conventional rates of the new Bulgarian tariff, the United States proposed that the reciprocal most-favored-nation principle should continue to govern the commercial relations of the two countries. The Bulgarian Government accepted the suggestion, and such an arrangement was put into effect by executive decrees in both countries. No formal agreement was signed, but in President Roosevelt's proclamation of September 15, 1906, applying to the products of Bulgaria the reductions authorized by section 3 of the act of 1897, it was explicitly stated that these reductions were granted in return for the extension of the Bulgarian minimum tariff to American products. Most-favored-nation relations were thus continued on a temporary basis and in a conditional form. The agreement was terminated by the United States tariff act of 1909 on October 31, 1909.

Agreement with Great Britain, 1907.—An agreement was concluded with Great Britain on November 19, 1907, whereby, in return for the free admission into that country of travelers' samples, otherwise dutiable, the concessions on works of art authorized by section 3 of the act of 1897 were extended to these articles when imported into the United States from Great Britain. Great Britain had been the most consistent supporter of the unconditional interpretation of the most-favored-nation clause in commercial treaties. The treaty of 1815 had established most-favored-nation relations between the United States and Great Britain, and this had always been given the conditional interpretation by the former country, and the unconditional by the latter. By the agreement of 1907, Great Britain accepted a partial grant of the " argol " concessions which had been given to other countries; but in order to preclude any future contention that she had thereby receded from her claim for the unconditional interpretation of the treaty of 1815, she introduced into the agreement the statement that it was entered into " without prejudice to the views held by each of them [the two Governments] as to the interpretation of the 'most-favored-nation' article" in the treaty of 1815.

Most-favored-nation treaties and reciprocity negotiations.—The presence of most-favored-nation clauses in various treaties thus introduced difficulties and complications in connection with the negotiation and administration of reciprocity agreements in accordance with the provisions of the tariff acts of 1890 and 1897. The combination gave rise to a number of protests, and led in the cases of Switzerland and Germany to retaliatory measures which, if the most-favored-nation clause had been absent, might not have been forthcoming. Little positive benefit was derived from the most-favored-nation clause during this period. Most European countries had established their tariff systems upon such a basis that every country of commercial importance which did not discriminate against them should receive full and unconditional most-favored-nation treatment. In the view of European countries, the primary purpose and function of most-favored-nation clauses has been automatically to insure uniformity and equality of treatment rather than to effect the securing of special treatment. Those countries of Europe which have single-tariff systems, especially when these are only moderately protective, have not been discriminated against, except at times by the United States; whereas there have been periods, as in the late nineties, when American products have received harsher treatment both directly and indirectly from the commercial nations of Europe than that to which the products of other countries have been subjected. A policy of reciprocity is likely to lead to discrimination by countries outside the reciprocity agreements, especially when this policy is accompanied by the conditional interpretation of existing most-favored-nation treaties. There have been occasions in the course of the reciprocity experiences of the United States—for instance, in the difficulty in 1900 over the treaty with Switzerland—when the conclusion of a reciprocity agreement with one country has led to the adoption of retaliatory measures against the United States by another country whose trade with the United States would be or was unfavorably affected by the agreement. There have been other occasions when, in order to avoid the likelihood that such retaliatory measures would be taken by the country affected, the United States has extended the concessions, granted in an agreement with one country, to other countries upon terms largely dictated by them, for instance, the agreement with Spain in 1909.

Most-favored-nation obligations and the projected reciprocity arrangement with Canada of 1912.—When the arrangement for reciprocity with Canada, agreed upon between the executive departments of the two Governments, but rejected by the Canadian electorate in 1912, was under discussion, it was made clear in both countries that the benefits reciprocally extended were not to be generalized. The considerations were very succinctly stated in a memorandum presented to the House of Representatives by Mr. McCall, of Massachusetts, on January 18, 1912, in the course of which appeared the following:

. Whatever tariff concessions in favor of imports into the United States from Canada the Congress shall adopt, in return for equivalent tariff concessions by Canada in favor of American products, will constitute, on the part of the United States, an exclusive and strictly preferential trade arrangement, which will involve no violation of the tariff treatment of the most favored nation offered to the world in the statutory minimum tariff of the United States. The benefits of this preferential-tariff treatment can not be justly claimed by any third country that is unable to offer to the United States substantial equivalency. It is impossible for any country of Europe, and perhaps any country which is not contiguous to the United States, to duplicate the conditions of economic relationship with the United States that are offered by Canada. This peculiar situation is based upon the following considerations: (the common boundary, homogeneity of populations, identity in material interests, facility of rapid communication by rail and waterway—which have contributed to bring about extensive and intimate commercial relations). * * * This peculiar relationship is not paralleled in our relations with any country of Europe. Consequently the Government of no European country can logically demand identity of commercial treatment.[1]

7. ESSENTIAL CHARACTER, ADVANTAGES, DISADVANTAGES, AND POSSIBLE DEVELOPMENTS.

Each of the several tariff systems has its peculiar characteristics and requirements. When a country equipped with a single schedule protective tariff attempts at once to pursue a policy of special bargaining and to extend most-favored-nation treatment it is bound to encounter much inconvenience, and it must constantly be combating the claims of other nations. Where special bargaining and most-favored-nation practice are associated, the latter must take the conditional form.

Efforts to insure and to secure equality of treatment by the method of making and taking special concessions, with conditional favored-nation treatment, have not been successful. A State which desires to make tariff bargains ought either to employ a tariff system in which there appears an alternative statutory schedule—which may be concessional, or may be defensive—or to generalize its concessions. A State may, on the other hand, if it is willing to do without the making of tariff bargains, retain a single-schedule tariff and refrain from making favored-nation pledges, in which case it will of course lose the guaranty from other States that it will not be discriminated against. Or, it may retain the single-schedule system and commit itself to the unconditional form of the most-favored-nation pledge, thus giving and accepting the general guaranty that it will not discriminate and shall not be discriminated against. This guaranty was the original intent of the most-favored-nation provision, and it is still the chief of its possible benefits—in no matter what form the clause has appeared.

Most of the disagreement over the interpretation of favored-nation provisions has been due to the fact that one or both of the parties to a given agreement have lost sight of or have failed to make adequate allowance for historical backgrounds, both political and economic. European States, in particular, having later adopted commercial policies and a form of the pledge different from those to which they were earlier committed, have since wished to make the interpretation of all favored-nation treaties, both new and old, conform to their later policies. Such terms as " favor," " privilege," " concession," and " reciprocity " assume different meanings in different periods, in different countries, and from the points of view of different tariff policies.

---

[1] 62d Cong., 2d sess., Cong. Rec., vol. 48, pt. 2, p. 1095.

So many have been the inconveniences of favored-nation practice and so extensive have become the difficulties and controversies arising therefrom, that it has been frequently and vigorously suggested that the pledge be done away with. As early as 1889 there were in France advocates of the omission of the most-favored-nation clause from all future treaties. Spain and Portugal at one time attempted to make treaties without the use of the clause. Swiss statesmen manifested dissatisfaction with the clause, but continued to use it. Some South American publicists and statesmen have argued against its use and have even urged the denunciation of existing treaties in order to eliminate it. Not a few Canadians have urged that the clause be dropped from the British treaties affecting Canada. The States of Salvador and Honduras have recently made a treaty (March 12, 1918) in which they pledge mutually very special treatment and undertake that each shall denounce any other of its treaties with third nations which may clash with the present agreement or under whose terms any third nations shall claim the benefits of this agreement. More recently (1918) France, Great Britain, and Italy have announced their intention to terminate all their commercial agreements containing the clause, this, however, with the explanation that they wish to have their hands free, and not with the intimation that they will in the future refrain from the use of the clause.

It is to be expected that at and after the conclusion of the present war the important commercial States will establish between or among themselves new treaty foundations for their commercial relations. Many of the commercial treaties of European States were due to terminate in 1915 or 1917. The beginning of the war terminated those between States which became enemies; the lapse of time has terminated many of the remainder. In the course of the war there have been formed or projected at least two European economic alliances. In 1916, at the Economic Conference in Paris, the representatives of the entente powers adopted principles implying the intention to abandon, for a term of years at least, the unconditional most-favored-nation practice. In their resolutions appeared the following:

Whereas the war has put an end to all treaties of commerce between the allies and the enemy powers, and it is of essential importance that during the period of economic reconstruction the liberty of none of the allies should be hampered by any claim put forward by enemy powers to most-favored-nation treatment, the allies agree that the benefit of this treatment will not be granted to those powers during a number of years to be fixed by mutual agreement among themselves During this number of years the allies undertake to assure each other, as far as possible, compensatory outlets for trade in case consequences detrimental to their commerce should result from the application of the undertaking referred to in the preceding clause.[1]

Reference to these resolutions calls for emphasis of the fact that two years have elapsed and there has been much thinking on these subjects since the date of that conference.

Could the most-favored-nation clause be done without, to advantage; or would it be possible, retaining it, to add to its usefulness and diminish its inconvenience? Any proposal entirely to eliminate the clause would call for very careful scrutiny of arguments presented for its condemnation. Among the actual or the alleged disadvantages

---

[1] Resolutions of the Economic Conference of the Allied Governments, 1916, Section B. Transitory Measures for the Period of the Commercial, Industrial, Agricultural, and Maritime Reconstruction of the Allied Countries, Article II.

which attend its use, it has been declared: that if strictly interpreted, it interferes with freedom of action; that if not strictly interpreted, it renders treaty relations uncertain, vague, and insecure; that it operates with no assurance of equal advantage to the two contracting parties, it makes it possible for some nations to gain free of cost favors as great as or greater than those for which others have paid highly; that the operation is affected by alterations in circumstances which can not be estimated adequately in advance; that the effect, beneficial or adverse, is dependent upon relations entered into with third states; that the consequence of its application is not infrequently loss of revenue; that it reduces the value of particular concessions for bargaining purposes; that the extending of the same concessions to one country which have been extended to another does not have identical effects upon the trade of the country which so extends the concessions. These criticisms are expressive, in every case, of the nationalistic viewpoint; they make no allowance for the probability that in such a relationship in the long run profit and loss will balance; they evidence no appreciation of the possibilities of generosity and liberal dealing in the promotion of cordial good will and larger commercial intercourse.

As an offset to such of these objections as will stand the test, the clause has in its favor the record of beneficial functions which it has unquestionably performed. It has been very useful as a stabilizer. Its effect has been to foster equality of treatment. It has discouraged individualistic and dualistic commercial practices, and it has promoted a general sense of security. As an essential part of the machinery of the widely employed general-and-conventional tariff system, and with the unconditional interpretation, it has in a measure counteracted the effects of the general tendency of European States since 1870 to increase their tariff rates; and it has been an obstacle to discriminatory practices. Through its operation the lowest rate conceded by each European country to any other has become, with a few exceptions, the rate extended by the former to all.

Any type of agreement imposes, of course, some restrictions upon the freedom of action of the contracting parties. Those commercial treaties which contain the most-favored-nation clause impose restrictions not only in respect to the relations of the parties with each other, but also in respect to their relations with third States. At the same time the degree of general security which the operation of the most-favored-nation clause has hitherto afforded, the assurance against discrimination, has been without question a feature of great practical value; it has much more than compensated for the limitations which the clause has imposed upon freedom of action. The fact that it has had its inconveniences is not a sufficient reason for abandoning the use of the clause.

If in the general revision of commercial treaties an attempt be made to do away with and to do without the favored-nation clause, the consideration of that proposal should be made contingent at the very outset on the offer therewith of some substitute which would give promise of performing the valuable functions which have been discharged by the clause and of affording relatively more of advantage and less of disadvantage than has attached to its use.

If, however, the favored-nation provision is to be retained, what can be done to eliminate and obviate the difficulties to which its use has in the past given rise? It has been suggested that the nations might agree by common stipulation upon the meanings to be attached to each of the various forms and types when and where they appear. While this would remove one of the chief opportunities for misunderstanding, it would not remove the fundamental source of contention, the fact that contracting parties are not of one mind as to the function which the favored-nation pledge ought to perform. Difficulty from the latter source can be obviated only by arriving at a general understanding which will involve definition, specification, and limitation.

This consideration has been made the point of departure for another suggestion, more sweeping and more difficult of execution, that, as between the two usages, the " European " unconditional and the " American " conditional, one or the other be adopted exclusively. Action in accordance with such a proposal would require a decision as to the relative merits of the two usages. There are several difficulties in the way of arriving at such a conclusion. A practice which is at a given moment advantageous to one State is not necessarily at the same moment advantageous to another or at a later moment advantageous to the first. For no two States are their relations to other States identical. As long as tariff walls exist, so long will there be differences in the actual effects of a given duty upon the trade of different States. So long also will a given concession, whether made to one State only or to all, affect differently the trade of the several States concerned. The imposition, for instance, by the State A of a given duty upon the commodity X, though that duty be levied equally upon the importations of X from all quarters, may affect the trade of but one State, B, since B may be the sole producer of X. A reduction or the removal of a duty upon, say, the commodity Y, though the concession be extended in favor of that commodity coming from no matter what States, may affect the trade of but one State, C, since C alone may be a producer of the commodity Y. Thus, unconditional most-favored-nation treatment, involving the generalizing of each specific favor, need by no means necessarily result in equality of treatment; and, conversely, conditional most-favored-nation treatment, with its special reciprocity agreements, need by no means necessarily result in discrimination.

The effect of either practice depends largely upon the circumstances of the nations among and between whom it is practiced, and upon the honesty, consistency, and rigidity or liberality with which the application is made to conform to the theory. The full application, in all that it implies, of the theory either of unconditional or of conditional favored-nation treatment, would tend to establish equality of treatment, estimated from the point of view of total net effect. But neither practice, if the requirements of the theory be followed only in part, if the clause be made simply to supplement a policy of commercial opportunism, will go far toward anything other than the elimination of some and the creation of other forms of discrimination.

Assuming as an original condition that no discriminations exist, unconditional most-favored-nation treatment will tend to preserve equality. But assuming, as has been the case, that there prevails at the outset a régime of discriminations, unconditional most-favored-nation treatment leaves the balance of advantage, as among States some of whose discriminatory practices are extensive and others of whose discriminatory practices are not extensive, with the former; while, on the other hand, conditional most-favored-nation treatment may enable the more liberal States to reduce the extent of the discriminatory practices of the less liberal, but will in the process probably lead to an increase in the extent of such practices on the part of the former.

For unconditional most-favored-nation practice to effect an actual and real equality of treatment, it is essential that a large number of concessions be made, the total involving a considerable number of particular concessions to each of a considerable number of (individual) nations, these particular concessions to individual nations all being generalized, with the result that there follows an actual general distribution of appreciable advantages. On the other hand, for conditional most-favored-nation practice to effect an actual and real equality of treatment, it is necessary that, when a special concession is made in favor of a given State, not only shall a special concession be required in return—thus increasing, internationally, the number of concessions granted—but the grantor State in each case must be willing to extend the same or equivalent concessions to any and all States which, desiring them, are willing—by concessions—to give an adequate return.

There have appeared recently evidences of an inclination on the part of statesmen of the European powers to give up the unconditional and adopt the conditional usage. There have also been some evidences that the United States would not be adverse to the acceptance of the unconditional usage. It would be unfortunate if, at a moment when the statesmen of all nations are striving to improve international relations, an alteration made in a practice as vital as that of most-favored-nation treatment should consist merely of a change of sides between the adherents of two conflicting usages. For the European nations to adopt preferential tariff arrangements and conditional most-favored-nation treatment would be essentially a step backward. For the United States to give up the policy of making special reciprocity arrangements and to adopt the unconditional most-favored-nation practice would be, assuming that European nations did not take the reversionary course to which some seem inclined, a distinct contribution to the cause of harmony and progress in international relations.

Whatever the relative advantages and whatever the difference in net results, "preference," "reciprocity," and conditional most-favored-nation treatment necessitate frequent and repeated special negotiations, constant bargaining, inevitable delays, actual inequality of treatment; they are essentially individualistic practices; while a uniform and sincere acceptance of the unconditional principle would result in the automatic and immediate generalization of all and whatever concessions any State agrees to make to any other.

The strongest arguments and the clearest cases for preferential and reciprocity practices rest on "special circumstances." There are situations which warrant special consideration and which may perhaps warrant special treatment. General principles may have to be modified to take account of geographical proximity or peculiar political connections. This has been recognized even by the States whose favored-nation practice is unconditional. Such exceptions are inconsistent with the pure theory, but not with the modifications which have been made in the practice, of unconditional most-favored-nation treatment. Where, however, there are no special circumstances or special relations, special treatment may be looked upon as a procedure whose effect, no matter what its intention, will be to create uncalled for and unwarranted distinctions, to perpetuate rather than to remove discriminations.

The American conception of commercial treaties as instruments for securing specific advantages by a process of reciprocal exchange has required, of course, as regards most-favored-nation treatment, that it be conditional. The situation of the United States in 1778 and for a long time thereafter was peculiar. The American Government embarked upon a commercial policy intended to offer and to secure equality of treatment. The United States has, however, actually established, repeatedly, commercial relationships with individual nations, of which the net effect has been inequality; her treatment of various nations, individually, has been "special." In some cases the circumstances appear to have warranted the special treatment, and the special treatment was consistent with principles recognized not only in conditional but in unconditional most-favored-nation practice. In others, the circumstances were not special, and, except as the position of the United States as a new country may be considered to have been peculiar, were not consistent with the logical requirements of a policy posited on the principle of "equality of opportunity." If now the policy of special and exclusive bargaining has been or is to be given up, the conditional most-favored-nation practice is no longer necessary.

The most-favored-nation clause will undoubtedly receive attention at the peace conference. There, or in some other international assembly authorized to deal with questions which have contributed to, arisen out of, or been suggested by the present war, it should be possible to frame a model pledge or pledges intended to secure equality of treatment. It may be found necessary to retain both the conditional and the unconditional practices; it may be found possible to adopt one or the other exclusively; but in any case, the phraseology of the most-favored-nation clause should be made unequivocal and unmistakable, the construction to be given should be predetermined, making it possible for all States, when treaties are being negotiated, to accept or to reject the clause with full understanding and agreement as to its import, intent and obligations.

Further, it should be possible to devise machinery for equitable construction and enforcement of this along with other pledges between nations. Provisions for arbitration have appeared in connection with not a few most-favored-nation clauses in modern treaties.[1] That is not enough. It has been suggested that engagements should be entered into, placing cases of disagreement as to the interpretation or the fulfillment of obligations within the jurisdiction of the Hague court. This also is not enough. Pledges of the type under consideration should have behind them in international relations the sanction of forms and methods of procedure as definite and as effective as those which stand in municipal affairs behind a legal contract.

---

[1] See, e. g., the treaty between Great Britain and Italy of June 15, 1883, protocol; treaty between Japan and Siam, Feb. 25, 1899; treaty between Austria-Hungary and Germany, Jan. 25, 1905, and other of the German treaties; treaty between Great Britain and Serbia, Mar. 31, 1908, XIV.

APPENDICES TO THE MOST-FAVORED-NATION CLAUSE.

APPENDIX A.

FORMS OF THE MOST-FAVORED-NATION CLAUSE.

From among many arrangements which have been attempted, the following classification, developed in the course of this inquiry, will serve at once to describe the distinguishable types, to locate each within one or the other of the two forms—the conditional and the unconditional—and to establish, by terminology and example, the essential difference between these forms:

CLASSIFICATION OF MOST-FAVORED-NATION CLAUSES ACCORDING TO CHAR-
ACTER AND EXTENT OF THE PLEDGE.

I. Unconditional forms.
    A. Unilateral.
        1. Unilateral and unlimited (general).
        2. Unilateral and limited.
    B. Reciprocal and unlimited (general), but not expressly immediate and unconditional.
    C. Reciprocal, unlimited, and expressly immediate and unconditional (general and absolute).
    D. Reciprocal and limited.
II. Conditional forms.
    A. Unilateral and unlimited (general), but expressly conditional.
    B. Reciprocal and unlimited (general), but expressly conditional.
    C. Reciprocal and limited, but expressly conditional.

The terminology employed in this classification is descriptive rather than designative; the recognition and the description of the types indicated is based upon an examination and comparison of actual treaty clauses—it is not intended or considered to be comprehensive of all possible forms.

Representative examples of actual clauses are exhibited in the amplification which follows herewith. For convenience, to avoid confusion, and because the "covering" clause is relatively far more important than the less comprehensive clauses which specify favored-nation treatment in respect to individual matters, this exhibit is made up of "covering" clauses. The dates given are, in most cases, those of signature. The italics are supplied for purpose of calling attention to particular features; they do not appear in the originals.

445

A. 1. *Unilateral and unlimited (general).*—In this form, one state undertakes to give to the other (without reciprocity) any (all) favors and privileges which it has granted or may grant to any other (the most-favored) nation. For instance:

United States-Siam Treaty, May 29, 1856, Article IX:

The American Government and its citizens will be allowed free and equal participation in any privileges that may have been, or may hereafter be granted by the Siamese Government to the Government, citizens, or subjects of any other nation.

United States-China Treaty, June 18, 1858, Article XXX:

The contracting parties hereby agree that should at any time the Ta Tsing Empire grant to any nation, or the merchants or citizens of any nation, any right, privilege or favor, *connected either with navigation, commerce, political or other intercourse,* which is not conferred by this treaty, such right, privilege and favor shall at once *freely inure* to the benefit of the United States, its public officers, merchants and citizens.

Great Britain-China Treaty, September 5, 1902, Article XV:

* * * *Any tariff concession* which China may hereafter accord to articles of the produce or manufacture of any other State shall *immediately be extended to similar articles* of the produce or manufacture of His Britannic Majesty's dominions by whomsoever imported.

A. 2. *Unilateral and limited.*—A unilateral pledge may be particularized by the presence of some inclusive or exclusive provision. Thus:

Great Britain-Japan Treaty, October 14, 1854, Article V:

In the ports of Japan either now open or which may hereafter be opened to the ships or subjects of any foreign nation, British ships and subjects shall be entitled to admission and to the enjoyment of an equality of advantages with those of the most-favored nation, *always excepting the advantages accruing to the Dutch and Chinese from the existing relations with Japan.*

Provisions of the above types are to be found chiefly in treaties, especially those of earlier days, but of which many are still in force, between Christian or highly civilized, or occidental, or powerful states, and those which are not Christian, or are semicivilized, or oriental, or comparatively weak.

In various recent treaties between Latin American and European States there appear in connection with reciprocity arrangements provisions which are, as respects the particular concession to which they apply, unilateral. Thus, in the treaty between France and Haiti of July 31, 1900, Article I:

The coffee and other colonial products enumerated in the schedule annexed, originating in Haiti, shall benefit on importation into France and Algeria by customs duties the most reduced applicable to similar products of any other foreign origin.

This may or may not be regarded, according to the point of view, as a unilateral favored-nation provision. It stands as a pledge on the part of France to extend constantly her minimum rates in favor of the Haitian products specified. In subsequent articles of the treaty, Haiti reciprocates, but not by the same method, in favor of French products specified. The favored-nation provision, as such, is therefore unilateral; and, applying to specified articles only, it is limited.

B. *Reciprocal and unlimited (general), but not expressly immediate and unconditional.*—In this the contracting parties agree mutually that each shall grant to the other any (all) favors or privileges (in all matters referred to) which it has granted or may grant to any other (the most-favored) nation; for instance, France-Great Britain convention of November 16, 1860 (complementary to the Cobden treaty), Article V:

Each of the High Contracting Powers engages to extend to the other any favor, any privilege or diminution of tariff which either of them may grant to a third power in regard to the importation of goods whether mentioned or not mentioned in the treaty of 23d of January, 1860.

Great Britain-Spain Treaty, October 5, 1750, Article VII:

His Catholic Majesty does hereby allow and consent that * * * all the rights, franchises, exemptions, and immunities that are or shall be granted or allowed to any other nation should be likewise granted and allowed to the said British subjects; and His Britannic Majesty that the same be granted and allowed to the subjects of Spain in His Britannic Majesty's Kingdoms.

Great Britain-Sweden-Norway Treaty, March 18, 1826, Article IX:

The High Contracting Parties engage that all articles the growth, produce, or manufacture of their respective dominions shall be subject to no higher duties, upon their admission from one country into the other, than are paid by the like article, the growth, product, or manufacture of any other foreign country, * * *; and, generally, that in all matters and regulations of trade and navigation each of the high contracting parties will treat the other upon the footing of the most favored nation.

Provisions of these types appear in many treaties, particularly those of European countries *inter se*. This type is characteristically that of " the unconditional " most-favored-nation clause. It is being superseded by the more specific type which follows.

C. *Reciprocal, unlimited, and expressly immediate and unconditional.*—In this, the contracting parties agree mutually that each shall grant to the other " immediately and without condition " all favors, etc., as in Form 4.

Great Britain-Paraguay Treaty, October 16, 1884, Article II:

The contracting parties agree that, in all matters relating to commerce and navigation, any privilege, favor, or immunity whatever, which either * * * has actually granted or may hereafter grant to the subjects or citizens of any other State shall be extended immediately and unconditionally to the subjects or citizens of the other contracting party; it being their intention that the trade and navigation of each country shall be placed, in all respects, by the other on the footing of the most-favored nation.

This has been a favorite form in British practice. With sometimes slight variations in wording it appears in the majority of British treaties in force. With the above there may be compared at random the provisions in the British treaties with Italy, June 15, 1883 (Art. XI); Honduras, January 21, 1887 (Art. I); Mexico, November 27, 1888 (Art. II); Japan, July 16, 1894 (Art. XV), and April 3, 1911 (Art. XXIV).

The " immediate and unconditional " form of the clause has been used in three treaties (only) of the United States. The following is the wording employed in one of the three:

United States-Servia treaty, October 14, 1881, Article VI:

* * * Also every favor or immunity which shall be later granted to a third power shall be immediately extended and without condition and by this very fact to the other contracting party.

Provisions of the above type appear in a large number of treaties, especially those made in recent years between or at the instance of European States. They appear in all the recent treaties between Japan and European countries and in the treaty of latest date between Japan and Siam. The treatment promised is the same as in type 4, but the words " immediately and unconditionally " strengthen the pledge by adding definiteness and assurance.

D. *Reciprocal and limited.*—In this, the contracting States agree mutually that each shall give to the other any (all) favors or privileges other than such as are specifically excepted (or of a type specified) which it has granted or may grant to any other (the most-favored) nation. The limitation is usually in respect to countries or regions rather than in respect to the type of treatment conceded. Exceptions in favor of trade with neighboring States, especially those that are limitrophe, are common. Thus:

Great Britain-Uruguay Convention of July 15, 1899, renewing the treaty of November 13, 1885:

* * * the stipulations contained in the treaty which is to be renewed do not include cases in which the Government of * * * Uruguay may accord special favors, exemptions, and privileges to the citizens or products of the United States, of Brazil, of the Argentine Republic, or of Paraguay in matters of commerce.

Such favors can not be claimed on behalf of Great Britain on the ground of the most-favored nation rights as long as they are not conceded to other States.

In the treaty between Austria-Hungary and Great Britain, December 5, 1876, provision was made for reciprocal most-favored-nation treatment, but it was specified that this shall not apply,

1. To those special and ancient privileges which are accorded to Turkish subjects for the Turkish trade in Austria-Hungary.

2. To those advantages which are or may be granted on the part of the Austro-Hungarian Monarchy to the neighboring countries solely for the purpose of facilitating the frontier traffic, or to those reductions of, or exemptions from, customs duties which are only valid in the said Monarchy for certain frontiers or for the inhabitants of certain districts.

3. To the obligations imposed upon either of the High Contracting Parties by a customs union already concluded, or which may hereafter be concluded.

In the treaty of Frankfort, May 10, 1871, Article XI, France and Germany agreed to reciprocal most-favored-nation treatment, but—

There shall be excepted from the above rule the favors which either of the contracting parties have accorded, or shall accord to other States than the following: England, Belgium, the Netherlands. Switzerland, Austria, Russia.

In the treaty of December 29, 1903, between Cuba and Italy, provision is made for reciprocal most-favored-nation treatment, but in Article XXVIII there is added the stipulation:

It is understood that the provisions laid down in the foregoing articles do not cover the cases in which Cuba may grant special reductions on its customs duties to the produce of other American States. Consequently, such concessions can not be claimed by Italy on the grounds of its being the most favored nation, except when they be granted to another State which is not American.

In the treaty between Great Britain and Japan of April 3, 1911, it is provided that the most-favored-nation provisions, etc., of the treaty shall not apply to " concessions granted by either high contracting party to contiguous States solely to facilitate frontier traffic within a limited zone " (Art. XXV), and they shall not apply to any of the British (colonial) dominions unless notice of adhesion shall have been given according to certain conditions specified. Provisions of the above types appear in many treaties, the limitations and particularizations being sometimes few and sometimes many; sometimes certain countries are excepted or specifically included; sometimes special relations arising out of propinquity are excluded; sometimes certain articles are specifically excluded or included.

II. CONDITIONAL FORMS.

Here, although the provision appears in a variety of wordings, and although the pledge may be general or limited, it is always conditional.

A. Unilateral and unlimited, but expressly conditional.—It happens in rare instances that one State undertakes to give the other (with no such pledge in return) any (all) favors and privileges which it has granted or may grant to any other (the most-favored) on condition that the State in whose favor this pledge is made shall meet the conditions or concessions, if any, which have attached to the granting of the same to the third nation. For instance:

United States-Korea treaty, May 22, 1882, Article XIV:

The High Contracting Powers hereby agree that, should at any time the King of Chosen grant to any nation or to the merchants or citizens of any nation, any right, privilege or favor, connected either with navigation, commerce, political or other intercourse, which is not conferred by this Treaty, such right, privilege and favor shall freely inure to the benefit of the United States, its public officers, merchants, and citizens, *provided* always, that whenever such right, privilege or favor is accompanied by any condition or equivalent concession granted by the other nation interested, the United States, its officers and people shall only be entitled to the benefit of such right, privilege or favor upon complying with the conditions or concessions connected therewith.

B. Reciprocal and unlimited, but expressly conditional.—In this type the contracting parties agree mutually that each shall grant to the other any (all) favors and privileges (or all specified or not specifically excepted) which it has granted or may grant to any other (the most-favored) nation, freely, if the concession (to the third State) is freely made, or upon allowing the same compensation (or an equivalent) if the concession has been conditional. For instance:

United States-France Treaty, February 6, 1778, Article II:

The most Christian King and the United States engage mutually not to grant any particular favor to other nations, in respect of commerce and navigation, which shall not immediately become common to the other party, who shall enjoy the same favor freely if the concession was freely made, or on allowing the same compensation if the concession was conditional.

United States-Colombia Treaty, October 3, 1824, Article II:

The United States of America and the Republic of Colombia, desiring to live in peace and harmony with all the other nations of the earth, by means of a policy frank and equally friendly with all, engage mutually not to grant any particular favor to other nations, in respect to commerce and navigation which shall not immediately become common to the other party, who shall enjoy the same freely if the concession was freely made, or on allowing the same compensation if the concession was conditional.

Great Britain-Netherlands Treaty, October 27, 1837, Article I:

* * * and Her Majesty the Queen of the United Kingdom of Great Britain and Ireland, and His Majesty the King of the Netherlands do hereby bind and engage themselves not to grant any favor, privilege, or immunity in matters of commerce and navigation to the subjects of any other State which shall not be also, and at the same time, extended to the subjects of the other high contracting party gratuitously, if the concession in favor of that other State shall have been gratuitous, and on giving as nearly as possible the same compensation or equivalent, in case the concession shall have been conditional.

The phrasing in the United States-Salvador treaty of December 6, 1870, Article II, is identical with that of the treaty with Colombia of 1824, quoted above. A variation in phrasing, but with the same meaning, is illustrated in the following:

United States-Japan Treaty, November 22, 1894, Article XIV:

The high contracting parties agree that in all that concerns commerce and navigation, any privilege, favor, or immunity which either * * * has actually granted or may hereafter grant to * * * any other State shall be extended to * * * the other high contracting party, gratuitously, if the concession in favor of that other State shall have been gratuitous, and on the same or equivalent conditions if the concession shall have been conditional; it being their intention * * *

C. Reciprocal and limited, but expressly conditional.—The pledge may be limited by localization or in some other way, thus:

United States-Brazil Treaty, December 12, 1828, Article II:

The United States of America and His Majesty the Emperor of Brazil, desiring to live in peace and harmony with all the other nations of the earth, by means of a policy frank and equally friendly with all, engage mutually not to grant any particular favor to other nations, in respect of commerce and navigation, which shall not immediately become common to the other party, who shall enjoy the same freely, if the concession was freely made, or on allowing the same compensation if the concession was conditional. It is understood, however, that the relations and conventions which now exist, or may hereafter exist, between Brazil and Portugal, shall form an exception to this article.

United States-Chile Treaty, May 16, 1832, Article II:

The United States of America and the Republic of Chili, desiring to live in peace and harmony with all the other nations of the earth, by means of a policy frank and equally friendly with all, engage mutually, not to grant any particular favor to other nations in respect of commerce and navigation, which shall not, immediately, become common to the other party, who shall enjoy the same freely, if the concession was freely made, or on allowing the same compensation if the concession was conditional. It is understood, however, that the relations and convention which now exists, or may hereafter exist, between the Republic of Chili and the Republic of Bolivia, the Federation of the Centre of America, the Republic of Colombia, the United States of Mexico, the Republic of Peru, or the United Provinces of the Rio de la Plata, shall form exceptions to this article.

In the treaty between the United States and Japan of February 21, 1911, Article XIV reads:

Except as otherwise expressly provided in this treaty, the high contracting parties agree that, in all that concerns commerce and navigation, any privilege, favor, or immunity which either contracting party has actually granted, or may hereafter grant, to the citizens or subjects of any other State shall be extended to the citizens or subjects of the other contracting party gratuitously, if the concession in favor of that other State shall have been gratuitous, and on the same or equivalent conditions if the concession shall have been conditional.

APPENDIX B.

EXHIBIT OF VARIOUS MOST-FAVORED-NATION PLEDGES OF THE UNITED STATES.

The following excerpts from a few of the treaties to which the United States has been a party are illustrative of variations in phraseology and of certain exceptions to the regular United States practice.

In the treaty of December 12, 1828, with Brazil, there appeared after the most-favored-nation pledge (Article II) the provision:

> It is understood, however, that the relations and conventions which now exist, or may hereafter exist, between Brazil and Portugal, shall form an exception to this (most-favored-nation) article.

A similar provision appeared in the treaty with Chile of 1832, excepting relations between Chile and various Central and South American States. (See preceding page.)

The treaty of July 27, 1853, with the Argentine contained in Article III the following positive and careful wording of the favored-nation clause:

> The two high contracting parties agree that any favor (etc.) whatever, in matters of commerce or navigation, which either of them has actually granted, or may hereafter grant, to the citizens (etc.) of any other government, nation, or state shall extend, in identity of cases and circumstances * * * gratuitously, if * * * gratuitous; or in return for an equivalent compensation if * * * conditional.

In the treaty of February 8, 1867, with the Dominican Republic there was no covering favored-nation clause.

The treaty with Nicaragua of June 21, 1867, contained in Article III the following variation in wording:

> It being the intention * * * to treat each other on the footing of the most favored nations, it is hereby agreed between them that any favor, privilege, or immunity whatever, in matters of commerce and navigation, which either contracting party has actually granted, or may grant hereafter, to the subjects or citizens of any other State, shall be extended to the subjects or citizens of the other contracting party; gratuitously, if * * *, or in return for a compensation, as nearly as possible of a proportionate value and effect, to be adjusted by mutual agreement, if the concession shall have been conditional.

The treaty with Salvador of December 6, 1870, contained, in its covering most-favored nation clause, wording identical with that which had appeared in the first of the treaties with American States, that of 1824 with Colombia (noted on p. 399.)

In the United States-China treaty of July 28, 1868, in Articles VI and VII, there appeared a mutual and reciprocal guarantee of most-favored-nation treatment in respect to travel, residence, and attendance at public institutions and the establishing and maintaining of schools.

In the United States-China treaty of November 17, 1880, in Article III, there appeared the mutual pledge that " no other kind or higher rate of tonnage duties or duties on imports " (or exports) shall be levied " than are imposed or levied on vessels " (or cargoes) " of other nations " (which make no discrimination) " or on those of subjects " (or citizens).

In the treaty concluded with the Two Sicilies on December 1, 1845, it was provided in Article I that there should be " reciprocal liberty of commerce," and—

the [High Contracting Parties] * * * engage that the subjects or citizens of any other State shall not enjoy any favor, privilege, or immunity whatever, in matters of commerce and navigation, which shall not also and at the same time be extended to the subjects or citizens of the other high contracting party, gratuitously, if the concession in favor of that other State shall have been gratuitous, and in return for a compensation, as nearly as possible of proportionate value and effect, to be adjusted by mutual agreement, if the concessions shall have been conditional.

In the treaty between the United States and Persia of December 13, 1856, Article IV read:

The merchandise imported or exported by the respective citizens or subjects of the two High Contracting Parties shall not pay in either country, on their arrival or departure, other duties than those which are charged in either of the countries on the merchandise or products imported or exported by the merchants and subjects of the most favored nation, and no exceptional tax, under any name or pretext whatever, shall be collected on them in either of the two countries.[1]

In the treaty between the United States and Japan of July 29, 1858, in the last paragraph of Article IV, appeared the provision:

No higher duties shall be paid by Americans on goods imported into Japan than are fixed by this treaty, nor shall any higher duties be paid by Americans than are levied on the same description of goods if imported in Japanese vessels, or the vessels of any other nation.

In the treaty between the United States and Japan of July 25, 1878, Article II, it was agreed that—

No other or higher duties shall be imposed on the importation into Japan of all articles of merchandise from the United States, than are or may be imposed upon the like articles of any other foreign country * * *

In the following three cases the United States has subscribed to an unconditional most-favored-nation pledge.

The treaty between the United States and Switzerland of November 25, 1850, in Article X, read:

* * * each of the contracting parties hereby engages not to grant any favor in commerce to any nation, union of nations, State, or society, which shall not immediately be enjoyed by the other party.

In the treaty between the United States and the Orange Free State of December 22, 1871, Article VI, read:

Neither of the contracting parties shall impose any higher or other duties [etc.] * * * than are or shall be payable on the like articles being the produce of any other country ;

and Article VII read:

Each of the contracting parties hereby engages not to grant any favor in commerce to any nation, which shall not immediately be enjoyed by the other party.

In the treaty between the United States and Serbia of October 14, 1881, in Article VI, after a specified favored-nation provision, there follows:

also every favor or immunity which shall be later granted to a third power shall be immediately extended and without condition, and by this very fact, to the other contracting party.

---

[1] See case of *Powers* v. *Comly* (1879), 101 U. S. 789, Appendix D, p. 454, infra.

APPENDIX C.

ADDITIONAL EXCERPTS, FROM STATEMENTS OF SECRETARIES OF STATE, ON THE INTENT, OPERATION, AND INTERPRETATION OF THE MOST-FAVORED-NATION CLAUSE.

I. Exceptions to the prevailing United States view.—In some cases, American officials, even while following the uniform interpretation, have expressed views which indicate that their conception of the clause differed somewhat from that generally entertained by their predecessors and successors. Secretary of State Fish seems even to have considered, in 1869, that there must be applied to United States treaties the current European interpretation, that is, that most-favored-nation treatment was "unconditional." He expressed the opinion that it would be necessary, in the event of providing by treaty for fixed rates of duty, to extend the same rates to third countries, and that for that reason among others it would be inadvisable to make a treaty proposed by the Argentine Government to establish such rates.[1]

President Cleveland declared, in his message to Congress on December 8, 1885, his belief in the inexpediency of concluding reciprocity treaties which were being considered between Spain and the United States in reference to Cuba and Porto Rico and between the Dominican Republic and the United States. One of his reasons was that embarrassing questions would arise under the most-favored-nation clause in treaties with other countries.[2] Mr. Gresham, Secretary of State, held, in 1895, a view different from that which subsequently prevailed concerning most-favored-nation obligations in connection with countervailing duties; and the position which he took regarding the mutually exclusive character of Articles VI and XI of the United States treaty with Russia of 1832 was not in accordance with the accepted American view.[3] Mr. Olney, Secretary of State, went so far, in 1896, as to declare that the unilateral favored-nation provision in the treaty of 1854 with Japan was by implication conditional.[4] Mr. Buchanan, Minister to the Argentine, was of the opinion, in 1897, that the most-favored-nation clause would be a bar to making a reciprocity treaty between the United States and the Argentine.[5]

II. Mr. Clay, on the "equivalent."—Mr. Clay, Secretary of State, wrote to Mr. Poinsett, American Minister to Mexico, in 1825, while a commercial treaty was under consideration between the United States and Mexico:

The rule of the most-favored nation can not be, and scarcely ever is, equivalent in its operation between the two contracting parties * * *. In order to ascertain the quantum of a favor * * * it is necessary that the claimant should be accurately informed of the actual state of the commercial relations between the nations on which the claim of the equal favor is preferred and all the rest of the commercial world.[6]

---

[1] Mr. Fish, Secretary of State, to Mr. Garcia, Argentine Minister, May 14, 1869, MS. notes to Argentine Legation VI, Moore's Dig., V, p. 262.
[2] U. S. Foreign Relations, 1885, XVI; Moore's Dig., V, pp. 271, 272.
[3] See Mr. Gresham, Secretary of State, to Prince Cantacuzene, Russian Minister, Feb. 16, 1895; Moore's Dig. V, pp. 274–276.
[4] Mr. Olney, Secretary of State, to Mr. Dun, Minister to Japan, Nov. 12, 1896 U. S. Foreign Relations, 1896, 429 ff.; Moore's Dig., V, p. 316.
[5] See Moore's Dig., V, p. 277. The State Department did not agree with Mr. Buchanan.
[6] Am. St. Pap., U. S. Foreign Relations, p. 579.

III. Mr. Bayard, on policy and law, 1886.—

In its commercial aspects the expediency of an unqualified favored-nation clause is questionable. The tendency is toward its formal qualification, by recognizing in terms (what most nations hold in fact and in practice, whether the condition is expressed in the clause or, not) that propinquity and neighborliness may create special and peculiar terms of intercourse not equally open to all the world; or by providing that the most-favored treatment, when based on special or reciprocal concessions, is only to be extended to other powers on like conditions.

You will doubtless have understood that where the words "qualified" and "unqualified" are   * * *   applied to the most-favored-nation treatment, they are used merely as a convenient distinction between the two forms (which) such a clause generally assumes in treaties, when containing the proviso that any favor granted by one of the contracting parties to a third party shall likewise accrue to the other contracting party, freely if freely given, or for an equivalent if conditional—the other not so amplified. This proviso, when it occurs, is merely explanatory, inserted out of abundant caution. Its absence does not impair the rule of international law that such concessions are only gratuitous, (and so transferable) to third parties when not based on reciprocity or mutually reserved interest as between the contracting parties. This ground has been long and consistently maintained by the United States.[1]

Needless to say, Mr. Bayard was going beyond the facts in claiming for the rule of American policy the character of a rule of international law.[2]

IV. Mr. Sherman, on most-favored-nation obligations and reciprocity, 1898.—In the course of a lengthy statement in connection with the negotiation of reciprocity treaties under the provision of the tariff act of 1897, Mr. Sherman, Secretary of State, declared, in 1898:

[The most-favored-nation clause] does not control the right of the nations adopting it to make exclusive compensatory agreements in just reciprocity with other nations.

V. Mr. Hay, in discussion with Switzerland, 1899.—In explaining the necessity for denouncing the most-favored-nation clause in the treaty with Switzerland of 1850, a clause in which the American negotiator had bound the United States to unconditional most-favored-nation treatment, Mr. Hay wrote, in 1898:

Should this Government continue to give to Swiss products gratuitously the advantages which other countries only acquire for an equivalent compensation, it would expose itself to the just reproaches of other governments for its exceptional favoritism. We desire that our friendly international policy should be maintained in its uniform application to all our commercial relations.[3]

APPENDIX D.

ADDITIONAL DECISIONS OF FEDERAL COURTS, INVOLVING INTERPRETATION AND APPLICATION OF THE MOST-FAVORED-NATION CLAUSE.

Taylor v. Morton (1846–1862)—Most-favored-nation provision in treaty with Russia executory, not self-executing.—Among leading cases where decisions have been rendered in American courts with regard to the application of most-favored-nation provisions, one of the earliest was that of *Taylor* v. *Morton.* Here a suit had been brought

---

[1] Mr. Bayard, Secretary of State, to Mr. Hubbard, Minister to Japan, July 7, 1886; MS. Inst. Japan, III, p. 425; Moore's Dig., V, p. 273. Cf. Whitney v. Robertson (1888), 124 U. S., p. 190.

[2] Compare with the opinion expressed by Lord Granville, in 1885, quoted in the text.

[3] See U. S. Foreign Relations, 1899, p. 748.

to recover an alleged excess of duties exacted by the collector of customs of the port of Boston on an importation of hemp from Russia (in 1846). The United States-Russia commercial treaty of 1832 contained, in Articles VI and IX, the most-favored-nation pledges usual to treaties of the United States, the latter of the two articles being conditional. The tariff act of 1842 contained a provision that hemp should pay a duty of $40 per ton, except that manila, sunn, and other hemps of India should pay $25 per ton. An importer of Russian hemp claimed, by virtue of the most-favored-nation provision in the treaty with Russia, the benefit of the lower rate.

The Circuit Court of the District of Massachusetts held that the terms of the treaty implied a contract and were in effect not self-executing, but executory; that, if there was any conflict between the provisions of the act of 1842 and those of the treaty of 1832, the provisions of the act, being later, abrogated those of the treaty; and, that the question of the rights of Russia or Russian subjects under the treaty was one to be disposed of by the political, not by the judicial departments of the United States Government. "The truth is that this clause (the most-favored-nation clause) in the treaty is merely a contract, addressing itself to the legislative power. The distinction between such treaties and those which operate as laws in courts of justice is settled in our jurisprudence." The conclusion was that the courts could not try the question whether or not the treaty pledge had been observed. An appeal was made upon purely technical grounds, and the Supreme Court affirmed the judgment of the Circuit Court. (*Taylor* v. *Morton*, 2 Curtis 454; 67 U. S. 481 (1862).)

Powers v. Comly (1879)—Distinction between place of origin and place of re-export not inconsistent with a favored-nation pledge to the country of origin.—By act of June 6, 1872, a surtax of 10 per cent ad valorem was imposed on goods (with specified exceptions) produced in countries east of the Cape of Good Hope, but imported from countries west of that point. The Supreme Court held that the charging of this surtax upon opium produced in Persia but imported to the United States from Liverpool was not inconsistent with the most-favored-nation provision in the treaty with Persia of 1856. The court said:

We see nothing in the act of Congress which is in conflict with the treaty with Persia. If the subjects of Persia import their products directly to the United States they are required to pay no more duties here than the "merchants and subjects of the most favored nation." It is only when their products are first exported to some place west of the Cape of Good Hope, and from there exported to the United States, that the additional duty is imposed. (*Powers* v. *Comly* (1879) 101 U. S., 789.)

North German Lloyd Steamship Co. v. Hedden (1890)—Distinction as to the places from which vessels sail allowable.—An act of Congress of 1884 imposed a duty of 3 cents per ton on vessels from any foreign port in "North America, Central America, the West India Islands, the Bahama Islands, the Bermuda Islands, all the Sandwich Islands, all Newfoundland," and a duty of 6 cents per ton on vessels from all other foreign ports. The Circuit Court for the District of New Jersey held that Germany was not entitled, by virtue of the most-favored-nation clause, to the lower rate, since the classification was merely geographical and the 3-cent rate applied to vessels of all nations coming from the specified ports. (*North German Lloyd Steamship Co.* v. *Hedden* (1890) 43 Fed., 17.)

United States, petitioner, v. M. H. Pulaski Co. et al.—"**Five per cent discount cases**" (1917)—**The 5 per cent discount provision in section 4 of the tariff act of 1913 is contingent and not yet in effect.**—In the tariff act of October 3, 1913, there appears a section declaring that a discount of 5 per cent shall be allowed on the duties on such goods as shall be imported in vessels admitted to registration under the laws of the United States. To this there is added the proviso " That nothing in this subsection shall be so construed as to abrogate or in any manner impair or affect the provisions of any treaty concluded between the United States and any foreign nation."[1]

The Court of Customs Appeals decided that the discount was to be applied, because of treaty provisions, to goods imported in vessels of Belgium, the Netherlands, Great Britain, Austria-Hungary, Germany, Italy, Spain, and Japan. The Government carried the case to the Supreme Court, contending that the statute relied upon future negotiations to make effective the change in policy which it implied, and that action must be suspended while present treaties remained in force. The case was decided in the Supreme Court on March 6, 1917. The Supreme Court followed the reasoning of the counsel for the Government. It took the view that Congress had indicated a policy to be pursued when possible.

It grants a discount only to goods imported in vessels registered under the laws of the United States, and conditions even that grant upon its not affecting treaties.

A grant in present terms subject to a condition precedent is familiar to the law and is not unknown in grants of the present kind.

The court concluded with the opinion that the provision actually granted the discount to no one, and ruled that judgments allowing the discount to the claimants be reversed. The 5 per cent discount provision in Section IV of the act of 1913 is, therefore, not in effect.[2]

---

[1] Sec. 4, par. J, subsec. 7, act of October 3, 1913.
[2] See Treas. Dec., Vol. 32, No. 37104.

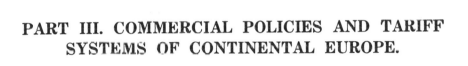

PART III. COMMERCIAL POLICIES AND TARIFF SYSTEMS OF CONTINENTAL EUROPE.

PART III. COMMERCIAL POLICIES AND TARIFF SYSTEMS OF CONTINENTAL EUROPE.

COMMERCIAL POLICIES AND TARIFF SYSTEMS OF CONTINENTAL EUROPE.

TARIFF SYSTEMS.

Tariff problems.—As international trade has developed in volume and commercial relations have increased in complexity, the differing circumstances and needs of the leading commercial countries have given rise to distinct tariff policies. This has led in turn to the adoption of several different tariff systems and to the use of a variety of instruments in these different systems.

Tariff policies and tariff systems.—In recent times most European States have framed their tariffs with a view not only to protecting domestic industry and trade against foreign imports, but also to the encouraging of export trade by securing, through tariff bargaining, concessions in duties from other countries. Although general, this has not been the universal practice.

Schedules of duties are established, generally speaking, either by law or by treaty. Schedules established by law are known as "statutory tariffs." Those established by treaty are known as "conventional tariffs." The complete tariff of a given country at a given time may contain schedules of either or of both types. A tariff system in which the schedules are statutory only—that is, produced by domestic legislation exclusively—may be described as "autonomous." By making up its schedules independently of treaties and conventions, a State preserves its freedom of action in relation to rates. This may or may not imply indifference to the attitude, the policies, or the measures of other countries. It does imply the conviction that it is inexpedient or that it would be unprofitable to fix rates of duty by pledges to foreign powers, thus surrendering for the time being the right to alter these rates. The terms "autonomous tariff" and "single (or single schedule) tariff," though frequently used interchangeably, should not be confused. "Autonomous" refers to source, "single schedule" refers to form. An autonomous tariff system may employ a single schedule, or it may employ two or more schedules. In the latter case, it becomes an "autonomous, multiple (schedule) tariff system."

Single (schedule) tariffs.—A single-schedule tariff, or "single tariff," is a tariff in which there is employed but one schedule of duties; it offers for any given article but one rate of duty—this applying equally to importations of that article from any and all countries. There may be exceptions, as, for instance, when some other rates are established in favor of a particular country by the conclusion of a special reciprocity agreement, but the establishing of these special rates does not amount to the creation of second or supplementary schedules.

A tariff system may employ a single schedule and yet not be autonomous. For example, Belgium, although it applies but one set

461

of duties to imports from all foreign countries, has made up its single schedule from rates established some by legislation and some by treaty. The Belgian tariff, therefore, is single but not autonomous. On the other hand, a tariff system may be, as stated above, autonomous and yet have more than one schedule; for instance, a country may establish, by legislation only, a general schedule and a preferential schedule or schedules. Thus, certain British self-governing dominions have autonomous tariff systems, but they employ, in addition to the general schedule, preferential schedules of duties in favor of British wares; France arranges autonomously her maximum and her minimum schedules.

Multiple (schedule) tariff systems.—In contrast with the single-schedule tariffs are the multiple tariffs now in force in the majority of the European States.

Multiple tariff systems assume various forms. All are marked, however, by one common characteristic—they involve the establishing of two schedules of duties or more, and to the imports from any particular country they apply rates from one or another of these distinct schedules according to circumstances. A State which employs two or more schedules may penalize another which pursues a policy unsatisfactory to it, by applying to that country's imports the rates of a higher schedule; it may favor another with whose policy it is satisfied, by extending to the latter's wares the benefit of the rates in a lower schedule.

As has been pointed out above, a State may both retain its tariff autonomy and establish more than one schedule of duties. A State which does this employs a multiple tariff which is statutory, entirely the product of its domestic legislation. A plurality of schedules thus produced may appear in either a " preferential " or in a " maximum-and-minimum " tariff system.

Multiple-schedule tariff systems appear in the following forms:

(*A*) *Preferential*.—A " preferential " tariff system takes as its starting point a general tariff, that is, a schedule of rates intended to apply to most countries ("in general"); and alongside of this it establishes special schedules consisting of lower (or higher) rates intended to apply to imports from one or more countries specifically designated by the legislature, or to countries which fulfill or may fulfill conditions laid down by the legislature. A conspicuous example is the system now in force in Canada.

(*B*) *Maximum and minimum*.—A " maximum-and-minimum " tariff system involves the establishing of two complete schedules, one containing maximum and the other minimum rates for every article in the tariff list. The rates of both schedules may be identical for some items. The application of the rates, one set or the other, to given commodities of individual countries or groups of countries is left to be determined sometimes by separate legislation, sometimes by executive action, sometimes by the operation of treaty pledges. But, whether the rates of the maximum or those of the minimum tariff be applied, there remains with the legislature freedom to alter the individual rates within the schedules. Thus not only is tariff autonomy retained, but the regulation of concessions is kept well within the control of the legislative authority. The leading example of the maximum-and-minimum tariff system is that of France.

(*C*) *General and conventional.*—It has become the policy of a number of States to make tariff agreements with other States wherein, by a process of bargaining, fixed rates of duty for certain commodities are pledged. A schedule comprising such rates derived from one or several treaties constitutes a " conventional tariff." Associating this with the regular or " general " tariff schedule which has been made by the legislature, the country becomes possessed of a " general-and-conventional " tariff system. If the agreement be one whose provisions are subject to the operation of the most-favored-nation clause, the benefit of these special rights accrues to other nations which are entitled to most-favored-nation treatment.

Under the operation of the most-favored-nation clause the benefit of the rates of the conventional tariff may or may not extend to third countries entitled to favored-nation treatment, this depending on the character of the favored-nation contract which they possess and the circumstances under which the rates, individually, have been fixed.

A country which subscribes to a conventional tariff necessarily sacrifices some part of its tariff autonomy; usually it binds itself to keep certain rates unaltered for a definite term of years. The system of maximum-and-minimum tariffs leaves room for greater freedom of action with regard to revision of rates. A State which employs the latter system will contract to extend to another its minimum rates, but it will not agree to a fixed figure for those rates for any long period.

(*D*) *Combinations and modifications.*—It is possible to combine in some degree the working features of the minimum tariff and those of the conventional tariff. In Germany, for example, the legislature has fixed by law minimum rates on specified wares, below which the Government may not go in negotiating commercial treaties. In France, on the other hand, the Government has found itself unable to maintain the ideal of complete autonomy. It has been forced, in dealing with other powers, to fix by negotiation, although for a short period, some rates below those contained in its minimum tariff.

Just as features of the maximum-and-minimum and of the general-and-conventional tariff systems may run together in practice, so either of these systems is capable of indefinite modification and complication when put into operation. Spain, for instance, developed and retained for a considerable period of time a highly complicated multiple tariff with four schedules. The " maximum " rates represented a punitive tariff, to be employed in commercial wars. The " minimum " rates, so-called, were in reality so high that Spain could not manage to induce other countries to accept them. They were applied only to two South American States. Below the " minimum " was another set of rates, resulting from commercial treaties and representing the normal level of rates on the basis of which Spain did business with most other countries. Finally, even below these rates, which were granted to the " most-favored " nations, was still another level, preferential rates granted to the neighboring country, Portugal.

Prevalence of multiple tariff system.—Five European States employ single-schedule tariffs—Great Britain, Belgium, Denmark, the

Netherlands, and Turkey.[1] Each of these also, as it happens, levies comparatively low rates of duty. The remaining States have adopted one or another of the multiple tariff systems, that favored by the majority in recent years being the general and conventional.

SKETCH OF RECENT TARIFF AND COMMERCIAL TREATY POLICIES.

A survey of the recent policies of European States calls for some reference to certain general tendencies which have been apparent in different periods. The same or like influences have affected in common large groups of States and have so shaped the development of policy in all of them that it is possible to distinguish, in reference to all, separate phases more or less well marked. Three distinct periods need to be considered.

Commercial Treaties and Lowering of Tariffs, 1860–1880.—In the first part of the nineteenth century there still prevailed in the commercial policies of European States that attitude of exclusion, with its high tariffs, which had come down as a legacy from preceding centuries. The most conspicuous single event in the commercial history of the nineteenth century was the negotiation and conclusion of the so-called Cobden Treaty of 1860 between England and France. The Cobden Treaty marked the full acceptance by the United Kingdom of the principle of free trade and involved the abrupt departure of France from the old system of high tariff and exclusion. In France, prohibitions of imports were removed and rates of duty on many wares were reduced from their former high level to 30 per cent ad valorem and shortly after to less. The contracting parties agreed to mutual and unconditional most-favored-nation treatment.

Almost at once England generalized the concessions which she had made. Gladstone's budget of 1860 retained only a few insignificant remnants of protection. France continued to apply her higher rates of duty to other States, but she was ready to negotiate to extend reductions to such States as would accept the new principle and reciprocate. Countries which desired to share at reduced rates the advantages of the rich French market had to make with her treaties similar to that into which she and England had entered. France was still almost at the head of the list of European States in population and in wealth; the market was tempting, the opportunity alluring. When the movement toward making treaties for tariff reductions had once begun, the probable penalty for failure to participate was speedily apparent. The result was a rapid succession of treaties, involving tariff concessions and including the most-favored-nation clause in its unconditional form between France and the continental countries; these included, between 1861 and 1866, Belgium, Prussia and the German Customs Union, Italy, Switzerland, Sweden-Norway, Spain, Holland, Portugal, and Austria. These countries made further treaties inter se involving a general lowering of duties and pledging favored-nation treatment. The principles of the movement toward lower duties, championed by advocates of free trade, were destined to dominate European commercial policy until about 1880.

---

[1] Turkey has special import tariffs, however, for Bulgarian and Greek products.

Comparing the tariffs in force at the end of the period with those of 1860, an English author found that in only 2 out of the 16 major European States was there any increase in duties.[1] The two exceptions were Italy and Greece, in which countries the level of duties had been raised for special reasons. In general, the duties had been lowered.

The Return to Protection, from 1878.—Protectionist sentiment had begun to reappear sporadically soon after the Franco-Prussian War; it gained strength after 1875; in 1878 Bismarck presented his plans for a new German tariff, with a raising of duties; and in 1879 the German Government committed itself to a protectionist program by adopting Bismarck's proposals. Austria and several other countries were likewise ready, for a variety of reasons, to revert to protection. New tariffs began to take the place of old. As old treaties expired they were renewed; but they differed from those of the seventies, since the new tariffs showed a marked tendency toward higher rates of duty. In 1882 France and England gave up the Cobden Treaty. The decade from 1881 to 1891 was one of readjustment. It was followed by the adoption by France and Germany, respectively, of new and distinct tariff policies, each devising a system which it thought best adapted to the protecting and the promoting of national interests.

In the period of readjustment many treaties were made; but these treaties terminated almost simultaneously in 1892, which made it possible then to put new tariff laws and systems into effect and to negotiate new treaties. The year 1892 may be said, therefore, to mark the beginning of the modern tariff and tariff-treaty era of Europe.

New and Actually Prevailing Systems, since 1890.—As a consequence of the readjustment, France departed in 1891 from her former conventional-tariff policy, and adopted the principles and practice of the maximum-and-minimum tariff. At almost the same time, Germany abandoned the employment of the (relatively) autonomous tariff (she had made some modifications by treaty) to which she had reverted after 1879, and made the principle of tariff bargaining—that is, of the conventional tariff—the basis of her policy. The rôles of France and Germany had been reversed.

Thenceforth and until the outbreak of the present war, there were distinguishable in Europe in respect to commercial policy three groups of States, representing three types of practice. One group, including Great Britain, the Netherlands, Belgium, and Denmark, retained the single tariff system. (Turkey, because her commerce is relatively small and because of her location, need not be included in the classification.) All of these had lowered or removed their duties to such extent that they may be called " free-trade " States. Peculiarly located in regard to transportation and peculiarly circumstanced in regard to production, these States had been in a position to let down the barriers to importation without fear of an adverse effect upon domestic industry and trade, and with expectation of advantage to their export trade. They contrived their tariff schedules more for purposes of revenue than as instruments of protection. With a system not adapted to bargaining and finding them-

---

[1] George Baden-Powell: State aid and state interference, London, 1882, pp. 215 ff. The estimates appear to be but rough approximations, measured with respect to British exports.

selves not discriminated against by other countries, for a variety of reasons, the States in this group have been relatively indifferent to the possibilities of bargaining by means of tariff treaties; they have made commercial treaties, but they have been neither eager nor reluctant to make or to gain concessions in the process.

The second group, which at first included only States in central Europe, but later States in eastern Europe also, enacted general tariffs, by legislation, to constitute their maximum schedules, but made bargaining by treaty and the construction of conventional schedules the guiding principle of their tariff policies.

The third group, consisting of France, Spain, and (for some time) Russia, employed the maximum-and-minimum system, displaying a readiness to give express recognition to export interests by conceding variations in the rates on imports, a determination not to go beyond certain points in conceding favors, and an inclination to be passive rather than active in treaty making.

This classification and association of States in groups is based on possession of common characteristics in commercial policy. It does not imply local contiguity or community of interests. In the second group all of these features were present. It consisted of Germany and the States with which Germany made treaties in 1891—Austria-Hungary, Italy, Switzerland, Belgium, and, later, the Balkan States and Russia. As France had been after 1860 the leader on the Continent in the making of the commercial treaties of the free-trade period, so now Germany took the initiative in determining the principle upon which treaties were negotiated, the new tariff policy being that of protection. It may be an exaggeration to say, as does an Austrian author, that the new course in commercial policy was "imposed by the powerful will of Germany,"[1] yet there is much in the evidence to support that conclusion. Germany had outdistanced France in commercial development; she used her newly achieved superiority to push her projects with characteristic vigor, sometimes approaching ruthlessness. The influence of the principles upon which the Cobden treaty was based and the example of France in the application of those principles had operated toward the diffusion of a liberal attitude, an approach in a measure to commercial internationalism, throughout the Continent of Europe. The tendency and the effect of the new German policy were to group and consolidate the interests of central European States with the German Empire as their point of focus.

Comparison of the earlier and the later tariff-treaty policies—Features of the latter—Most-favored-nation practice.—There are some differences of essential importance between the practice of the recent tariff-by-treaty policy and that of the era succeeding the Cobden treaty. Although the principle of most-favored-nation treatment has continued in force, the practical effect of favored-nation pledges has been limited very decidedly by increased specialization of tariff schedules. All the ingenuity of experts has been exerted so to construct the schedules which are to be the basis of concessions in tariff treaties that the reductions granted shall have a maximum value for the contracting parties and at the same time afford a minimum of advantage to other States

---

[1] " Ce régime et sa tendance ont été imposés par la puissante volonté de l'Allemagne." A. von Matlekovits. La Nouvelle ére de la politique douanière, Revue Econ. Internat., August, 1906, vol. 3, pt. 3, p. 245.

which are entitled, by the operation of the most-favored-nation clause, to enjoy the benefit of these concessions. Not only have the effects of tariff bargaining been more or less localized, but the importance of the bargaining process has been considerably increased. The treaties of the Cobden era effected changes in tariff schedules which were previously in force; these schedules had been framed with no reference to or thought of bargaining possibilities. In recent years, in contrast, the States of central Europe have realized that the working form of their tariff schedules is to be determined by their treaties, and they have framed their general schedules not with a view to their being made operative but with reference to the advantages which they may offer as a basis for negotiation. This being the case, when one State raises the rates in its general schedule, its act is equivalent in effect to serving notice upon other States that they must either follow suit or see their interests suffer when their representatives negotiate for tariff reductions. Thus the last German tariff, of 1902, gave rise to a general movement in central and eastern Europe in the direction of higher rates. Before it went into effect, in 1906, Russia, Austria-Hungary, Switzerland, Bulgaria, Roumania, and Serbia had all framed higher general schedules that they might be better able to negotiate for reductions. Along with the increasing of the rates in the general schedules appear reductions of rates in the conventional schedules, these reductions being greater in amount than would otherwise be the case. As a consequence, it becomes exceedingly difficult adequately to appraise the net effect of this policy among the factors which determine the prevailing levels of tariff rates.

THE COMMERCIAL POLICY AND TARIFF SYSTEM OF GERMANY.

Prussian and German policy before 1870.—A study of tariff developments among German States in the period immediately preceding the formation of the present Empire is highly instructive in showing how commercial policy may be subordinated and used as a means to a political end. In 1860 the German customs union embraced most of the territory which now lies within the boundary of the Empire. It had been built up by Prussian statesmen, and it had adopted the Prussian tariff. Although Austria's position in German affairs was recognized by an arrangement giving her special favors in trade across the boundary, Austria was outside the union and was treated as foreign territory. Trade with France was obstructed by special restrictions, the product of many years of commercial hostility.

In the period immediately following 1860, questions both of domestic and of foreign politics complicated the commercial policy of the customs union. In 1862 there was negotiated, in spite of the bitter opposition of Austria, a treaty with France which gave to that country a reduction of the German duties and gave to the customs union, through the operation of the most-favored-nation clause, all the advantages established in the European commercial treaty system. This went into effect in 1865.

The whole policy of the dominant German State, Prussia, had been directed with a view to the unification of Germany, and when the Empire was established in 1870, the new imperial State was able to continue with no abrupt break the commercial relations and the treaty arrangements which had previously been established. The war of 1870–71, however, necessitated a reconsideration of the relations with France. The conclusions reached in the negotiations by which the terms of the Franco-German commercial intercourse were settled became a highly important factor in European commercial relations and remained such until the outbreak of the present war.

Article XI of the treaty of Frankfort.—The business men of Germany proposed that they should realize from the success of the German armies a direct advantage for the promotion of their trade; and they would have required of France a pledge of special tariff concessions, binding for some definite period. Statesmen, however, who were responsible, on the German side, for the negotiation of terms, regarded this suggestion as impolitic. Bismarck declared that he could not offend a great nation by requiring from it as a part of the spoils of war a definite commercial agreement which would bind it for years to come; and it was further a question whether France, if seriously interfered with in the framing of her tariff schedules, could pay the war indemnity promptly. The German negotiators, therefore, proposed a renewal of the treaty of 1862 or the formulation of another containing like terms. Even this did not appear acceptable to the French, who demanded freedom of action in altering their customs duties to suit their fiscal needs and who, under the leadership of Thiers, were strongly inclined toward protection. A compromise, suggested from the French side, was finally agreed upon and was inserted among the peace terms as the now famous Article XI of the treaty of Frankfort.

The important portions of the text of that article read, in translation, as follows:

> The commercial treaties with the different States of Germany having been annulled by the war, the French Government and the German Government will take for a basis of their commercial relations the régime of reciprocal treatment on the footing of the most favored nation. * * * However, there shall be excepted from the above rule the favors which either of the contracting parties has accorded or shall accord to other States than the following: England, Belgium, the Netherlands, Switzerland, Austria, Russia.

The most remarkable feature of this arrangement, that which distinguished it from any others in the recent commercial agreements of the great powers, is the fact that it was made a part of a formal peace treaty, a political agreement intended to be permanent and not subject to modification by either party. The Germans accepted as a satisfactory amendment of the original proposition this permanent assurance that they would always be as favorably treated as might be six others of the most important European States. The French, on the other hand, were left free to frame their own tariff schedules, with a limitation that they might not discriminate against Germany; and they were not even bound to share with Germany the benefit of arrangements which they might make with their Latin neighbors, Spain, Portugal, and Italy. In its operation, both parties to the Frankfort agreement grew restive under its terms long before the treaty was dissolved by the outbreak of the present war. The French soon complained, and they have complained bitterly, of restrictions which they felt to have been imposed on them by force. The restriction became, in their view, particularly burdensome as the development of protectionist policy in France led them to estimate as increasingly valuable any favors granted to foreign powers. After the raising of her tariff in 1881, France made new commercial agreements with the important States of Europe, and she necessarily had to extend to Germany the concessions which she made to the co-contracting powers. When, on the other hand, Germany raised her rates of duty in the same period she refrained from making treaties which would entail important reductions, and it was not until the conclusion of the German-Swiss convention of 1888 that there accrued to France any advantage whatever from the operation of the treaty of Frankfort.

The Germans, on their side, began to realize the disadvantages of the treaty when, after 1890, they took the initiative in tariff bargaining and were compelled to share with France the concessions which they made to other States. As they developed the conception of a tariff union in central Europe, the favored-nation provision in the Frankfort treaty stood as a serious obstacle. Thus, the permanently binding character of Article XI became a political irritant both in France and in Germany. At the same time it operated with a beneficial effect to stabilize the commercial relations of European States in general, and it was of considerable importance in that it discouraged the elaboration of plans which might have led to the rupture of commercial intercourse on equal terms between different groups of States.

Antecedents to the protective tariff of 1879.—The tariff which the German Empire inherited from the customs union was marked by low rates, measured by the standards both of that time and of the present, and these rates were reduced still further in the early years of the Empire. It is estimated that, in 1877, 95 per cent of the imports entered duty free. All raw materials and iron were on the free list, while the protection granted to such industries as the textile and the chemical were very moderate. This was the result partly of political considerations, which had led Prussia to adopt low rates as a measure to exclude Austria from membership in the customs union, and partly of convictions with regard to the advantages of free trade.

The system was not subjected to criticism so long as the people prospered under it. But when a period of depression set in, about the middle of the seventies, when manufacturers began to complain of overproduction and hard times, and particularly when the landed proprietors found that they were losing their accustomed markets to competing producers in Russia and in the United States, the movement ripened for a change in the direction of protection. The circumstances gave Bismarck the opportunity which he desired—to effect a new grouping of parties and, incidentally, to alter the imperial tariff system, the revenues from which were proving inadequate to the needs of the central Government. When the active political elements—the officials, the great landowners, and the large-scale manufacturers—had been brought to agreement, the change was effected with but little opposition from the classes whose economic convictions or material interests were really best served by the low tariff which had hitherto been in force. A new tariff law was enacted in 1879 whereby the existing duties on manufactured articles were raised, many protective duties were revived, and an era of energetic protection for agriculture as well as industries was ushered in. By the act of 1879, the duty on wheat and rye, for example, was set at 1 mark per hundred kilograms; this was raised in 1883 to 3 marks, and in 1887 to 5 marks, such duties being equivalent to a substantial percentage of the selling price of the chief foodstuff of the people.

Commercial policy, 1871–1890.—In the two decades between the establishment of the German Empire and the accession to power of Count Caprivi, the treaty policy of Germany in commercial matters was negative in character. Germany became, it is true, a party to many commercial treaties, but most of these were with minor European countries or with non-European countries, and their terms showed that the German Government was disinclined to make any concessions. This may be accounted for in no small measure by the existence of the favored-nation provision of the Frankfort treaty. When the tariff law of 1879 was under consideration, the opinion was expressed that its increased rates would facilitate negotiations by extending the power of the Government to grant favors. It seems, however, to have been the inclination rather than the power which was lacking, for the establishment of the new tariff law made little difference in the course pursued. Germany continued to follow afterwards, as she had done before, an autonomous policy.

Treaties with important neighboring States—Austria, Switzerland, and Belgium—expired in this interval, and these were renewed merely on the basis of most-favored-nation treatment without the fixing of rates. Only in its relations with countries of southern Europe—Spain, Italy, and Greece—did Germany display a willingness to fix its own rates for like action by the other contracting parties. Moreover, in the concessions to these countries she restricted her granting of favors to raw materials, such as iron ore, or to noncompeting products, such as the fruits of Mediterranean countries, on which duties were levied for fiscal purposes. Some departures from this policy of autonomous protection occurred, notably in the convention concluded with Switzerland in 1888, but the interests of the large landowners and manufacturers were, in general, safeguarded. Furthermore, the feeling of the time, as expressed in a formal resolution of the manufacturing interests, was opposed to treaty obligations made binding for a considerable period of time. The treaty with Austria was made binding for but five years, with the provision that it might thereafter be denounced upon notice of one year. The treaty with Italy was made subject to denunciation at any time, allowing one year before the denunciation should take effect.

Adoption of the policy of the general and conventional tariff, 1891.—The disadvantages of the autonomous policy became increasingly evident as the year in which many of the European commercial treaties were to terminate (1892) approached. The chain of French treaties from which, by the operation of the treaty of Frankfort, Germany enjoyed many advantages, would be broken, and the treaties would be revised. Germany had been able, with her independent attitude, to drive good bargains with some smaller States, especially in the Balkans, but she had had to content herself with colorless arrangements, subject to rapid change, in her relations with the great powers. She suffered in 1890 from the exercise by another power of the privilege of autonomy such as she had insisted on reserving for herself. The McKinley tariff of the United States was a blow to a number of German industries. In relations with Russia, Germany did not even enjoy most-favored-nation treatment, and she had to submit not merely to increased duties on the wares which she sent into that market but even to a differential treatment in favor of those of her competitors whose commerce was sea borne.[1] In the period 1880 to 1889, Germany's exports to Russia actually declined.

Some evidence exists on which to base the surmise that the Government planned, before Bismarck's resignation (March, 1890), to face the situation by framing a new tariff with higher rates of duty as a weapon to force from other countries, by commercial treaties, the market opportunities desired for German exports. The new chancellor, Caprivi, was content to accept the existing tariff as the basis of negotiation, but he, too, resorted to the process of special bargains by treaties with particular countries as the guiding feature of German commercial policy. Negotiations were first opened with Germany's ally, Austria-Hungary, and were then extended to include Switzerland, Belgium, and Italy. The year 1891 was much taken up with conferences between representatives of the different States. In these deliberations the German Reichstag had no share. It was aware, indeed, that negotiations were in progress, but it knew little about the discussions until the treaties were presented to it for ratification, December 7, 1891. In spite of some opposition, to which Bismarck, then in retirement, contributed, the treaties were passed rapidly through the legislative stages. They were not even subjected to consideration in committee [2] and were definitely confirmed on December 19 by a vote of 243 to 48.

The four " great " treaties, with Austria-Hungary, Italy, Belgium, and Switzerland, were to be in force from February 1, 1892, to December 31, 1903, nearly twelve years, and subsequently until a year's notice had prepared the way for their abrogation. In many respects these treaties continued arrangements previously existing, guaranteeing most-favored-nation treatment on both sides and specifying terms with regard to certain matters of commercial intercourse (railroad traffic, frontier trade, etc.). The important change which they marked in commercial policy appeared in the extension of the policy of lowering and fixing duties. Italy conceded fixed rates on 254 items in place of the previous 8; Switzerland on 293 in place of 26; Germany, which had formerly refused, with slight exceptions, to grant and fix reductions on articles competing in the home market, now conceded the point not only in respect to many manufactured wares, but also in respect to grain, hitherto the most sacredly guarded object of agrarian-protectionist solicitude. The duty on wheat and rye imported into Germany, which had been 5 marks per 100 kilograms since 1887, was reduced for countries party to the treaty to $3\frac{1}{2}$ marks.

Considerations determining the change in policy.—In presenting the treaties to the German Reichstag for ratification the Government

---

[1] Lotz, Die Handelspolitik des deutschen Reiches unter Graf Caprivi und Fürst Hohenlohe (1890–1900. Schriften des Vereins für Socialpolitik, 92 : 64, Leipzig, 1901.
[2] Zimmermann, A. Die Handelspolitik des Deutschen Reichs von Frankfurter Frieden bis zur Legenwart, Berlin, 1901, p. 303 ff.

expressed frankly its concern over the future of German commercial relations. The official report contained such statements as the following:

A consideration of the whole present situation with respect to commercial policy leads to the conclusion that this present condition, which involves for Germany considerable advantages, will terminate on February 1, 1892, the date to which the French and most of the other European commercial treaties are binding, or at which time they may be abrogated; and at that time a complete transformation of the European commercial policy threatens to take place.

The conclusion of new international treaties with mere stipulation of most-favored-nation treatment, without binding of tariffs, would, indeed, leave Germany the opportunity of assuring the home market to domestic production by such a protective tariff as might be thought fitting, but would not afford the slightest guarantee that the foreign markets, which are indispensable to our export trade, would be kept open. In face of the competition of all economically progressive States, which has become constantly more acute with the increasing growth of production and of the means of production, an enduring commerce among them is conceivable only in the form of a reasonable exchange of wares, and this, again, assumes a certain reciprocal renunciation of freedom of action in tariff matters. Germany, particularly in view of the present ruling tendencies in commercial policy, could not count on maintaining its export trade if it did not, by such a limitation on its own side, assure to other countries the possibility of paying for the wares which they take in whole or in part, in their own products.[1]

The chancellor and other representatives of the Government professed still to be adherents of the policy of protection, but they declared that it must be modified to suit the conditions. With respect to the rapidly rising cost of living, the chancellor expressed his doubt whether the country could find food and employment for a growing population if the grain duties were not lowered. " Either we export wares or we export men." [2] Looking abroad he saw a danger of commercial war to the death if the country did not assure its position by treaties. Mere treatment on the footing of the most-favored nation meant little when other countries dissolved their treaties and raised their rates; and persistence in the former course of autonomy would mean to Germany the ruin not only of her industry and her labor but possibly also of the State itself. The chancellor urged further the political advantage of strengthening the commercial ties among the members of the Triple Alliance, and, at a time when the alliance between France and Russia was beginning to attract the attention of the public, he was able by this plea to move some hearers who would have been deaf to any economic arguments. The Reichstag accepted the proposals and ratified the treaties (Dec. 19, 1891), as seen above, with almost no opposition.

Three treaties in another group, known as " the little treaties "— with Spain, Serbia, and Roumania—were ratified in 1893, but only after a sharp struggle with the agrarian party, which feared the grain exports of Roumania and complained bitterly of the low prices in the home market.

Advantages derived from the new policy.—What judgment may be passed on the success of German policy in its new manifestation? Two questions present themselves: (1) How much of what they wanted did the Germans actually attain in the negotiations of the expert representatives by whom the treaties were prepared? (2) When the treaties were secured and put in force, what and how extensive were the advantages which actually accrued to the German nation? The mere statement of the questions suggests the difficulty of definite and conclusive answers.

The simple facts were that Germany had been assured of fixed rates on certain of her exports to certain countries for a period of twelve years; she had agreed to admit certain products from certain countries at fixed rates for the same period; she had secured and had accepted definite provisions with regard to veterinary arrangements, protection of patents and trade-marks, regulation of traffic at the frontiers, and regulation of railway traffic. The chief advantage which the treaties brought both to Germany and to the countries with which she had made the treaties lay in the fact that duties, satisfactory or unsatisfactory, could be counted on for a considerable and definite period. Business men knew where they stood; whether their position was or was not all that they would have liked to have it; they could at least make their plans with assurance of freedom from political interruption and complications. The effect of the treaties must be judged not only by what happened, but also by what did not happen, after they went into force. By fixing the duties among the parties to the agreements, they exercised a stabilizing effect on the schedules of duties in force on the products of other countries; and they must receive credit for having had a favorable influence on the conditions of German trade with countries to which no particular concessions were granted.[1]

The second point appears paradoxical. It suggests that the benefit of the treaties to Germany consisted not in what that country got in concessions from others, but in what it yielded in concessions to them. The type of evidence which leads to such a conclusion is strikingly illustrated by an incident which occurred in the period just before the treaties were framed. The German harvest had been bad, times were hard, and there was sore need of an increase in the supply of breadstuffs, but the high duties on grain prevented the importation of food in the quantities needed. The Government was urged from all sides, even by Count Kanitz, one of the leaders of the agrarian party, to reduce the grain duties for the relief of the people. It refused to make the reduction, because this action, desirable as it might be from the standpoint of the German consumer, was also desired by other countries which had a surplus of breadstuffs to export; and the Government would have lost an advantage in bargaining with foreign producers if it had framed its policy solely with respect to the immediate interest of domestic consumers.

Dr. Lotz, an economist whose contributions to the history of German commercial policy are an important guide, considers that the great benefit of the Caprivi treaties lay in the modification not of foreign tariff rates but of the German rates themselves:

If the only point in the framing of treaties of commerce were to maintain for oneself high protective duties, and to overreach the other party, the "great commercial treaties" of 1891 would represent but slight success. In reality more is not to be expected from shrewdly led, independent States, in their commercial treaties, than that they allow themselves a lowering of rates which they regard as beneficial in their own interest.[2]

---

[1] Cf. Lotz, Die Handelspolitik (1890–1900), p. 196.
[2] Ibid.

The lowering of the grain duties, that action which the Emperor called "a deed of rescue,"[1] must be accounted one of the great bene-fits to Germany of the Caprivi treaties.

Reductions of rates on industrial products were of less significance. The fact that most German manufacturers accepted without protest the reductions, in the treaties of 1891, on the wares in which they were interested shows that these were not seriously to their disadvan-tage. Only in the cases of paper and of fine yarns was there serious opposition in the press and in Parliament.[2]

Effects of the treaties of 1891.—One would expect to find the com-mercial effects of the treaties registered in the statistics of German trade, and the Government certainly held out hopes that the treaties would lead to a considerable development of German commerce in central Europe. The following table presents in summary form the conditions before and after the treaties were in effect.[3] The figures represent values, in millions of marks, of the trade in goods (precious metals not included), and are averages for three-year periods, 1889–1891 and 1896–1898.

Trade of Germany with—	Imports into Germany.		Exports from Germany.	
	Before.	After.	Before.	After.
	Average, 1889–1891.	Average, 1896–1898.	Average, 1889–1891.	Average, 1896–1898.
	Millions of marks.	*Millions of marks.*	*Millions of marks.*	*Millions of marks.*
Austria-Hungary	560	613	328	455
Italy	137	153	94	90
Switzerland	164	158	175	251
Belgium	299	187	147	182
Total	1,161	1,113	744	978
Percentage of total German imports	28.4	22.5		
Percentage of total German exports			23.1	25.4

These figures suggest at least one conclusion, which is confirmed by reference to more elaborate statistics which have been compiled— the effect of the treaties was far from decisive. In the play of forces to which the trade of each country was subject, the treaties were but one factor among many, and changes in the course, character, and volume of the trade show no uniform effect of the new treaty ar-rangements. In this connection it is possible to refer with emphasis to the relatively slight changes which the treaties of 1891 introduced.[4] The total imports of Germany (special trade) in each of the two years immediately preceding 1891 were, in round numbers, a little under 4,000,000,000 marks. The imports of those items on which rates were reduced by the treaties were valued at about 700,000,000 marks, about one-fifth of the whole. Of these wares about one-third, to the value of about 260,000,000 marks, were imported from the four States with which the treaties were later framed. On these, it

[1] Dawson, W. H., "The new German tariff," Economic Journal, 1902, 12 : 20.
[2] Cf. Sombart, W., Die neuen Handelsverträge, in besondere Deutschlands Jahrbuch für Gesetzgebung, 1892, vol. 16, p. 588.
[3] See figures compiled by Ernst Francke, "Zollpolitische Einigungsbestrebungen in Mitteleuropa," Schriften des Vereins für Socialpolitik, 90 : 202, Leipsig, 1900. Further discussion of the effect of the treaties will be found in Georg Gothein, Die Wirkung der Handelsverträge, Berlin, 1895.
[4] See the figures and references in Lotz, *op. cit.*, p. 83.

was estimated that the average duty on the basis of most-favored-nation treatment, before the treaties went into effect, was 14.4 per cent ad valorem, and that the duty was reduced by the treaties to 13.5 per cent.   When the figures are presented in this fashion the difficulty of tracing the influence of the treaties on German trade with the four co-contracting States becomes obvious.   Going further, one is inclined to ask what influence the treaties had on German trade as a whole, even assuming, as was the fact, that the tariff reductions, by virtue of most-favored-nation treatment, were conceded to most other countries.   Did the treaties really have the importance which has been implied by the active interest shown in them at the time of their negotiation and by the frequent reference to them in later commercial history?

To that last question the statistics above give no basis for a satisfactory answer; if used to that end they will certainly mislead.   The treaties unquestionably were, as the Germans then and later have thought them to be, of great importance.   They were important on the positive side in what they accomplished in certain respects, notably in relation to the reduction of the German grain duties; they were much more important in what they prevented, both in Germany and in other States.   The force of this assertion will appear in considering the relations of Germany and some of the other States, not partners to the treaties, in the period immediately following their negotiation.

Commercial relations with Russia.—Of Germany's European neighbors, Russia more than any other appeared to offer the greatest natural field for the extension of German trade.   But Russia, on the other hand, followed a tariff policy the most hostile to German commercial interests.   Both Russia and Germany had followed protective policies, but with this difference, that in Russia the protective duties were intended mainly to develop domestic manufacturing industries, while the German tariff system was highly protective on agricultural products.   The rates of the Russian tariff, already high, were considerably raised in the period immediately preceding 1891, the year in which Caprivi negotiated his first great treaties, and the increase affected particularly important branches of the German export industry chemicals, textiles, and metal wares.   Furthermore, in trade with Russia, Germany was not even given most-favored-nation treatment.   That Finland was bound to give to Russia preferential treatment in commercial matters is explicable on political grounds.   Russia's discrimination against wares entering by the land frontier in favor of those imported by sea was a more serious matter, for it gave England a distinct advantage over Germany in the trade in cotton, coal, and iron.

When the Caprivi treaties were in process of preparation Russia sought to win a share in the advantages which Germany offered in her new conventional tariff, but proposed in return merely to fix certain duties, refusing to lower her rates or to abolish discriminations.   This proposal was not acceptable to Germany.   At the time (1891–92) Russia was suffering from famine, and had put an embargo on the export of grain, so that the higher rate payable in Germany on Russian grain in comparison with that paid on grain from countries party to the Caprivi treaties (5 marks as against $3\frac{1}{2}$) was not for the moment inconvenient to Russia.   The return to normal

conditions (1892–93) made the question important. Russia adopted
an aggressive policy in support of her interests. This provoked
Germany to retaliation, and there ensued a brief but bitter tariff
war.

Tariff war with Russia, 1893.—In 1893 Russia framed a double-
schedule tariff, of which the minimum rates, based on concessions
made in a commercial treaty with France of that year, differed from
the maximum rates by variations running up to 20 and 30 per cent.
It was proposed to give the minimum rates to all countries granting
Russia the treatment of the most favored nation; the maximum rates
were designed for penalizing purposes.[1] Negotiations between representatives of Russia and Germany showed neither country willing
to recede from its position. Russia put into effect the punitive rates
(July, 1893), and gave the Minister of Finance power to raise these
rates still higher. Germany replied by raising by 50 per cent the
duties on the more important Russian exports, whereupon Russia not
only put in force an equal advance on the rates of its maximum
tariff, but also raised twentyfold the dues paid by German ships entering and leaving Russian harbors.

So injurious to both parties were the effects of this war of rates
that an agreement was effected, and a commercial treaty establishing a tolerable basis of relations was concluded within less than a
year, in March, 1894. Germany was the more inclined to make
terms, because, as intimated above, Russia had made a commercial
treaty with France (June 27, 1893) conceding most-favored-nation
treatment and the reduction of some duties, which caused concern to
the industrial interests in Germany. Also, on the other hand, there
was doubt whether Germany could control effectively the movement
of Russian wares on which the extra rates had been imposed. There
was nothing to prevent Russians from exporting their surplus grain
to Austria-Hungary, where it would release an equal quantity of
the native product which had a right to enter Germany under the
treaty rates; and there was no satisfactory way to control the milling
of Russian grain in Austria-Hungary and its sale in the German
market when its identity had been lost.

Results of the tariff war.—A brief statistical table will illustrate
the effect of the tariff war on commerce between Germany and Russia.[2] The figures give the value of merchandise exports and imports
in millions of German marks.

Year.	German imports from Russia.	Per cent of total German imports.	German exports to Russia.	Per cent of total German exports.
	Millions of marks.		*Millions of marks.*	
1890	522	12.3	183	5.5
1891	578	13.9	145	4.6
1892	381	9.5	129	4.4
1893	352	8.9	135	4.4
1894	439	11.2	170	5.8
1895	567	13.8	207	6.3

[1] Zweig, E., Die Russische Handelspolitik seit 1877—Staatsund sozialwissenschaftliche
Forschungen, Heft 122, pp. 38–39.
[2] Zweig, E., op. cit., p. 48. The figures are based on the official German statistics.
Zweig gives in parallel columns, for part of the period, figures from the Russian statistics,
which show a wide divergence. On materials of this kind it is evidently unsafe to base
any except the most general and obvious conclusions.

So serious are the economic losses proceeding from tariff wars that observers of these conflicts have always expressed surprise and regret that differences could not be settled in a peaceful and sensible manner. But States, like individuals, must learn by experience; and the two States which engaged in this particular tariff war seem to have needed the lesson which experience could teach them.

In a memorandum prepared by Mr. (later Sir Cecil) Spring-Rice, British secretary of embassy at St. Petersburg, the following opinion was advanced with regard to this conflict:

> But a review of the conditions under which the struggle was conducted, and especially of the points of view of the two antagonists, makes it appear doubtful whether ordinary negotiations, without the sanction of force, would ever have led to a satisfactory compromise, or whether the protective policy of the two nations would ever have been modified except after an experience of the results of protection in its extremest form.[1]

Commercial treaty with Russia, 1894.—The commercial treaty of 1894 between Germany and Russia was to be binding for ten years. It remained in force actually until 1906. Its most important feature was the pledge of most-favored treatment on both sides. This assured Russia the enjoyment of the lower rates which the Caprivi treaties had given the countries of central Europe. Germany in addition bound herself to fixed rates on some 27 items, but practically all of these had already been fixed by treaties with other States, and the only result of this action was to assure Russia a veto power during the life of the treaty, even though the other States consented to a modification of the rates.

In making definite concessions, Russia appears to have gone further than Germany. Russia reduced and fixed the rates on 71 items, including a number which had not figured in the treaty with France, abolished the preference formerly given to certain wares imported by sea, and pledged herself to introduce no differential duties during the life of the treaty.

German writers have made elaborate arguments to prove that Russia gained more than Germany from the operation of the treaty. The feeling among the German agrarians that their interests had been sacrificed by the lower rates granted to Russian foodstuffs remained alive and was an important political factor when the time came for the renewal of the treaty. However, the new arrangement brought to an end a period of commercial hostilities which had been intolerable between neighboring great States. It led to a rapid revival of the commercial relations that had been so seriously interrupted.[2]

Tariff war with Spain. In this period Germany displayed toward some other States the same aggressiveness in the negotiation of commercial bargains which marked her course in dealing with Russia, but without the same success.

Spain stood conspicuous among European States, throughout a large part of the nineteenth century, for the rigor of her tariff policy. A tendency toward more liberal measures, expressed in lower rates

---

[1] Reports on tariff wars between certain European States (Cd. 1938), Great Britain, Parliamentary Papers, Commercial, No 1, 1904, Vol. 95, p. 40.
[2] An excellent account of the commercial relations of Germany and Russia (Tariff Relations between Germany and Russia (1890-1914), by L. Domeratzky), has just been published by the Bureau of Foreign and Domestic Commerce of the U. S. Department of Commerce as Tariff Series No. 38.

and the negotiation of commercial treaties, was followed by a period of reaction to the old policy; and the Spanish legislation of 1892 raised the rates on important imports, both in the maximum or general tariff and in the minimum tariff which had been designed as a basis for the negotiation of commercial treaties. Germany was dissatisfied particularly by the higher duty placed on alcohol, the chief German export to Spain, and by the refusal of Spain to include in her general treaties the entrée to the Spanish colonies. A provisional arrangement continued trade between the two countries on the basis of most-favored-nation treatment; but the treaty negotiated in the interval, though it settled outstanding differences to the satisfaction of Germany and was confirmed by the Reichstag, proved unacceptable to the Spanish Cortes. When the provisional arrangement expired, May 15, 1894, each country enforced against the other the rates of its general or maximum tariff; and on May 25 Germany levied an additional duty of 50 per cent on the most important imports from Spain. If the volume and character of the trade between the two countries had been such as to make them commercially interdependent this condition would have been insufferable. The total exports of Spain in 1890 were valued at 937,000,000 pesetas; of these, only 11,800,000 pesetas went to Germany. The total imports into Spain in the same year amounted to 941,000,000 pesetas, and of these, 44,400,000 pesetas came from Germany. Thus, in the total Spanish foreign trade the German share was but 3 per cent. Between the two countries in question, which not only were separated by physical distance but were also relatively indifferent to the effects of the stoppage of trade on the domestic organization, and doubtless stimulated to opposition by national pride, the tariff warfare continued until an arrangement was made on July 25, 1896, by which each country granted to the other its lowest normal rates. Later, in 1899, they returned to the basis of most-favored-nation treatment. At that time Germany purchased from Spain the Caroline Islands, complicating the commercial bargain by the inclusion in it of an exchange the benefit of which to either party it is impossible to appraise.

Controversy with England and Canada regarding Canadian preference.—A controversy with Canada in this period led likewise to a tariff war, of which the result was even less to the satisfaction of Germany. Canada determined in 1897 to give a preference to the United Kingdom, reducing the rates of duty on imports from that country at first by one-eighth. Germany contended that the treaty of 1865 between the Zollverein and England entitled her in the British colonial markets to treatment equaling that given the mother country, whence she claimed for herself the advantage of this reduction. The German claim was conceded, but the English Government found itself, as Lord Salisbury said, " compelled to terminate a treaty which is no longer compatible with the general interests of the British Empire." [1]

In 1898 the Canadian preference was increased to one-fourth and confined to imports from the British Empire. The German Government was forced to make a decision of serious import in choosing the course which it would hereafter follow in its commercial relations with England herself and with the British colony in question.

---

[1] Barker, J. Ellis, Modern Germany, 5th edition, p. 153.

The German newspapers, including even the Hamburger Nachrichten, in an 'article credited to Prince Bismarck, demanded that England, if she desired the advantage of most-favored-nation treatment, should purchase the right by concessions of some kind, or at least by the exercise of such compulsion as would lead Canada to retrace this first step toward imperial preference and the establishment of a British customs union. The official correspondence of the German Government contained veiled threats, directed to the same end. Germany was in fact entirely unwilling to enter on a commercial war with a country which granted complete freedom to the German export trade, and to which Germany sold far more than to any other customer—about one-fifth of her total exports. There was not the slightest reason to suppose that the British Government would yield even if the German attitude led to tariff action. Actually the commercial relations between the two countries were left undisturbed. In the absence of a formal treaty, the German Government granted most-favored-nation treatment to the United Kingdom from year to year or for short periods of years.

Tariff war with Canada.—Toward Canada the German attitude was less indulgent. There can be little doubt that German statesmen at this time were seriously exercised over the possibility that the British Empire would approach a realization of the plan of imperial commercial union and were inclined to resist the progress of the movement for fear of the developments to which it might lead. German trade with Canada was in itself inconsiderable. The total of German exports (special trade) in 1898 amounted to 4,011,000,000 marks; German exports to all of British North America, to 23,900,000 marks, a little over 0.59 per cent. German imports from British North America amounted to only 5,900,000 marks. Canada's imports from Germany amounted to 4.10 per cent of her total imports; and Canada's exports to Germany were only 1.12 per cent of her total exports.[1]

Canadian exports were declared subject to the German general tariff in spite of protests from the English side that Germany had acquiesced in arrangements like the Canadian in reference to French, Spanish, and Portuguese colonies. Negotiations that were prolonged over several years proved fruitless, and Canada in 1903 inserted in her tariff law a clause providing that when any foreign country treated imports from Canada on less favorable terms than imports from other countries, a surtax amounting to one-third of the duty established in the general tariff might be imposed. This clause was put in force to penalize imports from Germany, which caused the latter to fall about one-half in value.[1] It is noteworthy that when other self-governing British dominions adopted the Canadian policy and introduced preferential duties in favor of the mother country or other British dominions, the German Government refrained from action. The German attempt by pressure to block this policy in Canada had injured Canada, it is true, but it had hurt Germany also without gaining for her any advantage. Finally, in 1910 the German Imperial Council approved an arrangement whereby

---

[1] See figures in Statistik des deutschen Reichs, Neue Folge, Bd. 122, Berlin, 1899, p. 6; and Statistical Yearbook of Canada for 1898, Ottawa, 1899, p. 183.
[1] See the figures in Trescher, Vorzugszölle, p. 60.

Canada was allowed most-favored-nation treatment of specified wares, the important items of the Canadian export trade, in return for a withdrawal of the surtax on imports originating in Germany.[1]

German policy with respect to the United States, to 1900.—Before Germany, in 1891, adopted the system of the general and conventional tariff, and began vigorously to employ this system to open foreign markets to her products, the Imperial Government had found grounds for dissatisfaction with the United States. In some respects the commercial position of the latter country in regard to Germany resembled that of Russia. The United States offered for export large quantities of the foodstuffs which the agrarian party in Germany desired to exclude; on the other hand, it protected its home market against the articles of export produced by German manufacturers, by a tariff which, complained of even before by European observers as inordinately high, was raised still higher by the tariff act of 1890.

If the German Government had heeded the wishes of the agrarians, and, indeed, if it had adhered rigidly to the principles on which some economists urged the adoption of the conventional tariff system, it would have applied to the United States the rates of its general tariff, and would have invited such measures of penalization as the act of 1890 empowered the President to apply. But, though it could be urged that it was illogical to establish the rates of the conventional tariff by tedious negotiations with the States of Europe and at the cost of considerable concessions to them and then to lavish all these favors on the United States without requiring equivalents, the German Government saw good reasons for adopting that course. By the Saratoga convention of 1891, Germany gave the United States the benefit of various reductions which she had conceded in the commercial treaty with Austria, and withdrew the prohibition against American pork, which had been established on alleged sanitary grounds, in return for merely the assurance that German exports, particularly sugar, would not be subjected to a surtax upon their entry into the United States.

The consideration which then, as later, caused the German Government to deviate from the aggressive policy which marked its attitude toward some other States, and to maintain tolerable relations even at the cost of considerable concessions, are obvious. The character of the trade between the two countries put Germany in a position of distinct disadvantage. The exports from Germany to the United States were mainly manufactured wares, which Americans could buy from other countries or manufacture for themselves if the German supply were cut off. On the other hand, the United States exported to Germany certain raw materials, notably cotton and copper, on which important branches of German industry were so dependent that an interruption in their supply would be distinctly inconvenient.

In the decade following the Saratoga convention, the exports of Germany to the United States remained relatively steady in value, but declined in proportional importance as the value of the total exports increased, while the imports into Germany from the United States doubled in value and increased by one-half in proportional

---

[1] U. S. Department of Commerce and Labor, Tariff Series No. 7, revised edition, 1911, p. 8.

importance. The growing dependence of Germany on its American imports was unwelcome but could not be avoided. New sanitary regulations imposed in Germany put difficulties in the way of the importation of American foodstuffs, and the obstacles which German trade encountered in higher tariff rates and in the administration of the regulations governing importations into the United States provoked protests from German exporters. Dr. Lotz is of the opinion that only the circumspection of the two Governments averted a tariff war.[1] The passage of the American tariff act of 1897 gave the opportunity to arrange, in form at least, for some return by the United States for the benefits of the German conventional rates. A convention was made on July 1, 1900, granting Germany the lower rates which had already been granted to France, Italy, and Portugal, on wines, paintings, and other articles.

Growth in power of the Agrarian Party.—The factor in domestic politics which most influenced the course of German commercial policy after the framing of the Caprivi treaties of 1891 was the growth in power of the Agrarian Party. A new period in the history of that party began in 1893, when the discontent over the low prices of farm products led to active organization and demonstration aimed against the lower duties of the Caprivi treaties. The Agrarians helped to bring about the downfall of Caprivi in 1894, and although they could not effect a change in the tariff rates, now fixed by treaties with other powers, they secured changes in administration of the import duties, which had important commercial effects. On the grounds of "sanitary" protection, strict rules were adopted regulating the importation of meats into Germany; the expenses and delays of inspection were equivalent in effect to heavy protective duties, and the importation of some classes of meat products was expressly or practically prohibited. The result of this reactionary policy was a sharp decline of meat imports into Germany, a rise of prices and restriction of consumption in that country, followed by a series of reprisals along similar lines by foreign countries like Russia and the United States whose export interests were affected.

Preparation of a new tariff.—The Caprivi treaties were to run to the end of 1903, but as early as January, 1897, responsible officials of the Government called to the attention of the Reichstag the need of amending the tariff which the treaties had established and the desirability of beginning early the preparations looking to that end. The Government established in 1897 a commission[2] similar to that which had been employed in 1894 when the Russian treaty was in preparation, composed of 30 members, of whom half were appointed by the Government and half were chosen to represent the specific interests of agriculture, industry, and trade. This committee conducted an elaborate investigation. It is said to have sent out 53,000 questionnaires to procure the information and suggestions desired. There was much difference of opinion as to the impartiality and reliability of the data on which it based its proposals. The composition of the committee, which included no representatives of consumers, of the laboring class, or of producers on a small scale, was sharply criticized by the opposition. The committee was accused

---

[1] Lotz, op. cit., p. 158.
[2] Economic committee for the preparation and consideration of measures of commercial policy.

of being biased in favor of high protection. Whatever ground there may have been for the assertions of the critics, it seems certain that the Government made more extensive and thorough investigation in determining the basis of its policy than had ever before been made.

After four years of preliminary work the Imperial Government was ready, in 1901, to discuss its proposals with representatives of the Governments of the separate German States; in November its proposals were approved by the Federal Council, after which they were laid before the Reichstag for consideration.

Opposition to the conventional tariff system.—In the meantime there had been an active discussion of the policy which Germany should pursue in bargaining with other States, and there were those who proposed that the Government should abandon the existing practice of a general tariff modified by the lower rates of the conventional tariff which extended to most countries by the operation of the most-favored-nation clause. The industrial and commercial interests were satisfied with the general-and-conventional tariff system. Under its operation they had seen an unparalled development of German manu-factures and commerce, and they hoped, with treaties based on cer-tain modifications of rates in the new tariff, not only to strengthen their hold on the home market, but also still further to extend their export trade in foreign territory.

The agitation for a change came principally from the side of the Agrarians, whose interests in defending themselves against imports overshadowed their desire to insure an open market for such agri-cultural products as sugar and alcohol, and who would have pre-ferred the absolute seclusion of Germany, with a policy of self-sufficiency, to a lowering of the tariff barrier.

The Agrarians had managed, in 1895, to secure from a committee of the Reichstag a report in favor of the denunciation of all the treaties which established general most-favored-nation treatment, and, although this radical proposal came to nothing, it evidenced their general attitude. They asserted that the operation of the most-favored-nation clause generalized favors which should be specific; that it made real reciprocity impossible; and that it actually ren-dered commercial relations insecure, since the relations between two originally contracting countries were made dependent on the ar-rangements which one of these countries might make with a third power. The Agrarians thought that their interests had been sacri-ficed in the Caprivi treaties, and proposed that the Government should be restricted in granting concessions. Some urged that Ger-many should adopt the French system of a maximum and a minimum tariff; some proposed the application, to certain articles at least, of an established minimum below which rates might not be lowered in the negotiation of treaties.

The passage of the Government proposals through the legislature was attended by a bitter partisan struggle. After modifications and compromises, which did not alter the general character of the measure, the new tariff law was passed by the Reichstag in December, 1902. After an interval of some three years, devoted to the negotia-tion of new commercial treaties based upon its provisions, the law went into effect on March 1, 1906.

Characteristics of the tariff law of 1902.—The German tariff had not been subjected to a thorough revision since 1879, and the tariff law of 1902 showed, as was to be expected, great changes in comparison with the older measure. Important in relation to treaty making were the following features:

Protection.—The rates, in general, gave evidence of an inclination to a stricter application of the policy of protection. This appears in the schedules on industrial products, but is most marked in the duties affecting agrarian interests.

Partial application of principle of minimum tariff.—While the previous policy of a general or maximum tariff, to be modified by commercial treaties, was retained, there was a partial application of the idea of a minimum tariff. One of the first paragraphs of the new law provided that "the duties on the following cereals shall not be reduced by treaty or agreement below the following: Rye, 5 marks per 100 kilos; wheat, 8 marks; spelt, 5.50 marks; malting barley, 4 marks; oats, 5." The Agrarians would have gone further, by voting into the bill minimum duties on live stock and meat, but the Government was able to resist their demands, and fixed the rates in the final act as follows: General rate, rye, 7 marks; wheat, 7.50 marks; conventional rate, rye, 5 marks; wheat, 5.50 marks.[1] It will be recalled that the Caprivi treaties of 1891 had set for both rye and wheat a general rate of 5 marks and a conventional rate of 3.50 marks. In two points, therefore, in fixing the absolute height of the duties and in establishing a bar to their reduction by treaty, the Agrarians had effected important changes.

Specialization.—The new act was framed so as to limit the scope of favors which might be conceded in treaties with other States. To meet the objections of those who asserted that the most-favored-nation clause distributed too widely the reductions of duties granted in treaties, the rates were specialized to an extent previously unknown. In comparison with the former tariff, 1,446 items were separately enumerated, as against 387. On cotton goods there were 48 rates instead of 6; on iron products 118 instead of 15; on silk and silk manufactures, 22 instead of 4.[2] In so devising its tariff the Government prepared a convenient basis for treaty negotiations; it could now balance concession against concession with all the nicety, if it desired, of minute distinctions. The treaties carried the process further. Thus, for example, the original tariff established a single rate, 40 marks, for a group of vegetables—artichokes, melons, mushrooms, rhubarb, asparagus, tomatoes, when dried or otherwise simply treated; by treaty provisions the rates on tomatoes were fixed at 4 marks; on melons and mushrooms at 8 marks; on the remainder of the group at 10 marks. The most striking example, often referred to, of the length to which this process of specialization may go appears in item No. 103 of the conventional tariff, which accords a special rate to "large dappled mountain cattle or brown cattle, reared at a spot at least 300 meters above sea level, and which have at least one month's grazing each year at a spot at least 800 meters above sea level." A note in the tariff schedule carries the specifica-

[1] See the text of the act in U. S. Tariff Series No. 7, p. 9.
[2] Matlekovits, A. von, "La Politique Douaniere" in Revue Econ. Internat., August, 1906, vol. 3, pt. 3, p. 251.

tion even further: "Brown cattle are those breeds which * * *
belonging to the long-headed variety, especially to the races of Al-
pine cattle * * * have a silver gray to dark or very dark brown
hide, with lead-colored muzzle, bordered with very light brown, almost white; black hoofs and horn tips, and dark tail tuft." Duties
on this particular variety of cattle could evidently be reduced to a
very low rate, in favor of the farmers and milk-cure establishments
of southwestern Germany and of imports from Switzerland, without fear of the general market being flooded, under operation of the
most-favored-nation clause, by imports from Russia, the Netherlands, or France.

Punitive measures provided.—Section 10, the "Kampfzoll" (tariff
war) paragraph of the tariff, put into the hands of the Government a weapon by which to force equality of treatment from States
which might show a tendency to partiality in the distribution of
their favors.

Dutiable goods proceeding from States that treat German ships or products
less favorably than those of other nations may, in addition to the duties provided for in the tariff, be subjected to a surtax not exceeding twice the amount
of the tariff rate imposed on such goods or even to a surtax equivalent to the
total value of the goods themselves. Goods free of duty according to the tariff
may, under those conditions, be taxed with a duty not exceeding 50 per cent
ad valorem.

In like manner, and save treaty stipulations to the contrary, foreign goods
may be subjected to the same duties and customs formalities as are applied to
German goods in the country of origin.[1]

Provision was made for putting these measures in force by imperial ordinance, after approval of the Federal Council and subject to
the confirmation of the Reichstag when assembled.

The section is remarkable not only because it authorized ad valorem duties for purposes of reprisal, while the regular rates were all
specific, but also because of the additional freedom of action which
it granted the Government in respect to the employment of penalizing
measures. The tariff act of 1879 had allowed a surtax of 50 per cent
for use in tariff wars; a law of 1895, enacted during the commercial
war with Spain, had raised the surtax to 100 per cent and provided
for imposing 20 per cent ad valorem duties on articles on the free
list; the new act of 1902 went as far as might be gone, short of authorizing, as in the French law, actual prohibition.

Commercial treaties based on the tariff of 1902.—On the basis of
the tariff act of 1902 the German Government framed commercial
treaties, in the years 1904–5, with eight States. In order of time
these were concluded with Belgium, Russia, Roumania, Switzerland,
Servia, Italy, Austria-Hungary, and Bulgaria. Treaties were later
negotiated with Greece, Sweden, and Portugal.

An indication of the effect on the tariff schedules of Germany and
of other States which entered into these treaties may be had from the
table following, which shows the number of items on which the
rates were fixed in the schedules of each of the countries.[2]

---

[1] Translation in U. S. Department of Commerce and Labor Tariff Series No. 7, p. 9.
[2] Matlekovits, in Revue Econ. Internat., August, 1906, vol. 3, pt. 3, pp. 248 and 249.

In the treaty between Germany and—	In the German schedule.	In the schedule of the contracting country.
Belgium	203	107 (Belgium).
Russia	48	182 (Russia).
Roumania	76	146 (Roumania).
Switzerland	196	790 (Switzerland).
Serbia	48	117 (Serbia).
Italy	232	202 (Italy).
Austria-Hungary	772	580 (Austria-Hungary).
Bulgaria	165	69 (Bulgaria).

An analysis of these figures by an Austrian authority, Matlekovits, shows that none of the concessions which Germany made appeared in all the treaties, and that few appeared in more than two, while most of them appeared in only one treaty. In the treaty with Austria-Hungary, for example, 345 rates were fixed, of which none were included in any other treaty. The specialization to which reference has been made above restricted the scope of these concessions. Only by a special study of the subject would it be possible to determine how generally their effect was diffused by the operation of the most-favored-nation clause. The net result was to fix the rates, for the ensuing twelve years, on a majority of the items in the German tariff actually applied. From among a total of 1,446 items in the schedules, the Government retained complete freedom of action in reference to but 664. It is to be noted, however, that Matlekovits counts an item as tied when any special class of ware under the general head of that item is regulated by treaty; in the counting, therefore, fractions of an item become integers, and the effect of the treaties is exaggerated.

Effects of the commercial treaties.—The considerations which rendered impossible an accurate appraisal of the success of German policy in connection with the Caprivi treaties [see supra] apply likewise to an inquiry with regard to the later developments. In the interval, however, a new element of difficulty had been injected. The rates in the statutory tariffs of other countries had ceased to be what they had once been, those thought best for purposes of revenue or protection. Under the compelling influence of the German policy they had become bargaining rates. They were made, not to be maintained, but for purposes of negotiation. The States of Europe were no longer following the business principle of a "fixed price." Each had now for favors to be granted its "asking price" and a "selling price," the latter more or less definite and considerably lower. Because of this fact, it is impossible to estimate in figures the success of German policy. An index is given neither by the number of rates agreed to by foreign States in response to German representations, nor by the number of rates reduced or the extent of the reductions. The success of a policy can not be estimated on the basis of its removal of obstacles which it has itself created.

Prince Bülow asserted before the Reichstag that as a result of the new tariff and of the treaties based upon it, Germany was assured of effective protection for her agriculture, and of the desired openings for her industry. On their face, the facts seem to bear out this confident assertion. German agriculture, long suffering from depression in some branches, entered upon a new period of prosperity; and German industry recovered from the depression which had marked the opening years of the century and went on with its amazing development. It is, however, impossible to determine to what extent the German commercial policy contributed to this outcome. An Austrian observer, writing as recently as 1914, was of the opinion that Germany would continue the same lines of commercial policy and much the same tariff when the expiration of the treaties in 1917 would call for a decision on these matters.[1]

Though the conclusion may not be susceptible of statistical proof, it appears that Germany had bargained more effectively than the other parties to the treaties. At the time when the treaties were framed, peculiar circumstances hampered the efforts of two States most important among those with whom Germany bargained. Russia, just emerging from the war with Japan, was already entering upon the period of revolution which followed. Austria-Hungary was suffering from one of her recurrent internal crises, and had been unable even to arrive definitely at satisfactory terms for commercial relations between the two units of the monarchy. Doubtless Russia and Austria-Hungary gained considerable advantages from the treaty arrangements to which they agreed, but it seems clear that they might have gained more if they had been politically as well organized and secure as were the Germans, and if their Governments had made equally patient and painstaking preparations for the negotiations.

Recent policy with respect to the United States.—The policy of Germany toward the United States continued after 1900 on much the same lines as those followed before. The German Government did not commit itself to any course of action that would be likely to lead to a tariff war, but it refused, on the other hand, to recognize the justice of conditions whereby the United States should enjoy, without a return, the benefit of the German conventional rates. Between the framing of the new tariff, in 1902, and the application of the new conventional rates, in 1906, much was heard on both sides of the Atlantic of the possibility that the German Government might subject the products of the United States to the increased rates of the general tariff. The German Government endeavored to obtain concessions from the United States, but when the new tariff went into effect, while negotiations were still in progress, it granted to American imports the temporary application of the new conventional rates. An agreement was reached in May, 1907, by which there was extended to Germany the benefit of the limited reciprocity offered under the American tariff act of 1897, and an assurance from the American side of an amendment of certain administrative regulations which were felt by German merchants to be oppressive. In return, Germany agreed to extend to the United States not all of the conventional rates, but those which went into effect on March 1, 1906, which did not include the reductions granted in a treaty concluded with Sweden shortly afterwards. The practical effect of the exception was not important, for it has been estimated that not more that 4 per cent of the American imports to Germany were subject to

---

[1] Schilder, Sigmund, in Weltwirtschaftliches Archiv., 1914, vol. 3, Chronik der internationalen Handelspolitik, p. 182.

the higher rates,[1] but it is significant as an illustration of the German attitude in this period.

So later, when the passage of the American tariff act of 1909 abrogated existing reciprocity arrangements, the German Government granted the United States the conventional rates "in the existing commercial treaties," in return for the minimum American rates in the new tariff; but as the United States would not extend to German paper and wood pulp the treatment accorded these products when they were of Canadian origin,[2] the German Government refused to grant this country the new conventional rates established by treaties with Japan and Sweden, made in 1911.[3] The enactment of a new tariff by the United States in 1913 opened the question of the commercial relations of the two countries, which had meanwhile been troubled by the controversy over the tax levied on the export of potash from Germany by Americans. Germany attempted again to negotiate a special agreement, and, when this proved impracticable, assented to a continuance of relations on the former basis, but with an evident sense of dissatisfaction.

---

[1] U. S. Department of Commerce, Bureau of Foreign and Domestic Commerce, Foreign tariff systems and industrial conditions, Washington, 1913, p. 17.

[2] As a consequence of the decision rendered by the Supreme Court in the case of *American Express Co. et al.* v. *U. S.*, and others, in 1913, the rates applied to imports of paper and wood pulp from Canada were extended to the same articles coming from Germany and other countries. See account in Part II of this report, The most-favored-nation clause, p. 383, infra.

[3] Foreign tariff systems, 1913, *cit. supra,* p. 17.

THE COMMERCIAL POLICY OF FRANCE.

The Cobden Treaty, 1860.—The Cobden Treaty of 1860, between France and England, notwithstanding its harmony with contemporary economic tendencies, would not have been concluded but for the peculiar conjuncture of political factors. France was at the time under the thinly disguised absolutist rule of Napoleon III. The Emperor had lived in England, had become'a convert to the classical doctrine of free trade, and had done much before 1860 to modify in detail the prohibitive characteristics of the old French tariff. These changes were effected by the personal power of the Emperor, against the opposition of business interests and the criticism of the legislative body. Under a republican form of Government such as later prevailed in France they could hardly have been brought about. Even the Emperor would probably not have forced the sweeping change involved in the Cobden treaty had he not been moved by political considerations. Cobden was of the opinion that he had finally decided in favor of the treaty because of representations made to him of the hostility toward and distrust of himself in England, and of his desire to win support in that country against Russia, Austria, and Prussia.[1] It was, again, the personal influence of the Emperor which led to a reduction of duties even beyond that promised by the treaty; and the Emperor took an active interest in the negotiation of the liberal treaties, with their rate reductions and most-favored-nation clauses, which followed.[2]

Protectionist opposition to commercial treaties.—The opposition to the imperial policy was real even when it was latent, and it became active before the war of 1870, which marked the end of the imperial régime. Business troubles which followed the commercial crisis of 1864 were ascribed to the low tariff fixed by the commercial treaties; and a group of parliamentary representatives hostile to the new course grew in numbers and importance. The war with Germany brought into power, under Thiers, a party of avowed protectionists, who carried well along toward final execution a project involving sharp increases of rates, which they were prevented from carrying into effect only by the existence of the commercial treaties. The treaties with the United Kingdom and Belgium were denounced; new treaties with these two powers permitted a part, at least, of the departures proposed from the policy of Napoleon III; but treaties with many other powers, some running for years to come, were still in force. The government of Thiers fell before it could establish its tariff policy; and the protectionist reaction lost its force for the time being. As treaties terminated they were extended by provisional arrangements, and the Government, apparently through inertia rather than by conviction, continued in the course that had been laid out by Napoleon III.

---

[1] Morley, J.: Life of Richard Cobden, London, 1896, II : pp. 255–256.
[2] For the details of these treaties see Amé, Étude sur les tarifs de douane et sur les traités de commerce, Paris, 1876, vol. 2.

Investigation of 1875.—In 1875–76 the Government was at length prepared to consider, without haste or distraction, the principles that should determine its action. The ministry addressed to the chambers of commerce and to the so-called auxiliary chambers of industry (chambres consultatives des arts-et-métiers) a circular inviting opinions on the operation of the French tariff and treaty policy, and asking whether France should continue the policy of the conventional tariff, with rates fixed by negotiation, or should abandon this for an autonomous (" Generaltarif ") tariff.[1] The answers were conflicting but showed a distinct preponderance of opinion in favor of the conventional tariff. Forty-seven chambers of commerce and 15 auxiliary chambers favored the renewal of treaties. These included representatives of the largest commercial cities and of the strongest French industries. Only 14 chambers expressed themselves in favor of the autonomous single tariff, and its is significant that these included the cities in which the less firmly established branches of the French textile industry, cotton and linen, were prominent—Rouen, Arras, Tourcoing, Roubaix, etc.

The Paris Chamber of Commerce advanced its argument for adherence to the system of the conventional tariff, as follows:

Treaties assure to trade and industry the stability which they need for undertaking and carrying out important business, without fear of hindrance in the course of their operations from the changes which may result from the frequent revision of tariffs fixed by a legislative act.

Another answer was to the effect that—

Trade needs a constitution which survives changes of personnel in the Government, even in the convulsion of a war, and it finds this constitution (charte) in treaties.[2]

The arguments advanced in favor of an autonomous tariff were drawn in part from the experience of the years immediately preceding. It was asserted that treaties bound the hands of the Government and prevented it from making the adjustment of rates which fiscal needs or industrial changes might require; and that the legislative power was deprived of a large share of its influence when the executive negotiated treaties and presented them to the legislature simply for acceptance or rejection. The advantage of stability was recognized, but it was suggested that this would be attained if the tariff were to be revised only at intervals of five years. Advocates of an autonomous tariff objected decidedly to the most-favored-nation clause, and in this matter were in agreement with a majority of the advocates of the conventional tariff.

It is clear that the representatives of French industry and trade were favorable to departure from the low rates which the Empire had imposed upon them, and which they had never cordially accepted. There was general agreement as to the need of a revision of the old tariff, which included survivals from earlier periods, dating back even to the eighteenth century. But in reference to individual rates and to the form of commercial policy to be adopted there was decided difference of opinion. Though the majority opinion ap-

---

[1] Ernest Rausch: Französische Handelspolitik von Frankfurter Frieden bis zur Tarifreform von 1882, Leipzig, 1900, Schmoller's Forschungen, 78 : 87 ; Devers, A.: " La politique commerciale de la France depuis, 1860," contained in " Schriften des Vereins für Socialpolitik," pamphlet 51 : p. 157.
[2] English translation from the German translation in Rausch, op. cit., p. 87.

proved the continuance of the conventional system, there was a demand even there that treaties be arranged to expire simultaneously, so as to facilitate the action of the Government if it should choose to alter the level of rates.

The tariff of 1881.—Five years passed before the final adoption, on May 7, 1881, of a new tariff. The interval was marked by essays and failures which testify to the division of opinion and the conflict of interests. In its treaty relations, the Government sought to prolong existing arrangements, without any radical changes, until the new tariff should be framed, and it assumed that conventions binding through 1879 would be sufficient for that purpose. It negotiated with most of the powers arrangements of this kind on the basis of most-favored-nation treatment (in the case of all except Portugal); and when the period approached its end, with the tariff still far from completion, it secured, against the opposition of the protectionists, authority to extend the application of these provisions still further.

Various policies proposed and considered.—In 1878 a proposal had been submitted to the legislature which involved the principle of a maximum-and-minimum tariff, and the question of the adoption of a system of this type to regulate commercial negotiations with other countries was often thereafter under discussion. The plan was favored by the protectionists, but it met with opposition on the ground that it neglected the interests of the export trade, and it was rejected in favor of the single-schedule tariff. The relative merits of the autonomous and the conventional tariff systems were also considered; and the arguments which had been advanced during the investigation of 1875–76 were presented and debated afresh. Ultimately both the claims to authority of the different branches of the Government and the needs of commercial policy were met by the compromise plan which was adopted: The establishment by legislative act of a general tariff which was to be modified in its practical operation by agreements with other powers. A proposal on the part of a group of Agrarian protectionists to establish and fix minimum rates beyond which the Government might make no concessions, a plan which was later adopted by the Germans in 1902, was rejected by the Government on constitutional grounds. The French tariff of 1881 raised the duties on most manufactured wares by about one-fourth (24 per cent), in comparison with the rates which had been granted the most favored nations on the basis of the former conventional tariff. Raw materials and foodstuffs as a rule remained on the free list or were made subject to low rates. The protectionists had to be satisfied with the assurance on the part of the Government that it would in its negotiations leave untouched the rates on cereals and live stock and would not in general yield to other countries more than the 24 per cent by which the rates of the new general tariff exceeded the level of the old conventional schedules.

On the basis of the new tariff, the Government framed treaties, which were to expire in all cases on February 1, 1892, with seven of the European powers. These reduced and fixed various rates, establishing thereby the new conventional schedule. The results corresponded in general to the promises of the Government and showed no sweeping change from the previous conditions; if later they were subjected to bitter criticism, it was because of economic developments which could not at that moment have been foreseen. To make a tariff treaty with England proved not practicable; that country had already given so much to all the world that it had little more to offer to any one power, and it was not willing to bind itself to any fixed rates. With that power, and with Germany, Austria-Hungary, and others, there were framed simple conventions granting most-favored-nation treatment.

Tariff war with Italy.—In the decade following the adoption of the tariff of 1881, the group which demanded the protection of the home market even at the expense of interests engaged in foreign trade grew steadily in numbers and in political importance. The financial crisis of 1882 introduced a period of depression in industry and trade. The agriculture of France shared with that of other countries of northwestern Europe the burdens of the general depression and had, in addition its peculiar difficulties, notably the ravages of phylloxera. In 1887 Italy promulgated a new tariff which introduced sharp increases in the rates, and she took advantage of the provision in her treaty with France which allowed denunciation upon one year's notice, to dissolve the existing arrangement and to demand concessions beyond those which she had already received. In the face of higher duties imposed by Italy on most French products, which were felt to be particularly injurious to the silk and woolen trades, the French showed no inclination to reduce their own rates; negotiations undertaken in Paris and in Rome led to no solution; and in March, 1888, open warfare, in the commercial sense, broke out. The French Government had proposed duties equal to the Italian, to be applied to wares of Italian origin, but these did not satisfy the French tariff commission, by whose influence they were raised still higher, Italy retaliated with differential duties.

The commerce of France was so large and varied that the tariff war with Italy had no great effect on its total volume. Although the decline in exports to Italy was serious, particularly in the case of textiles, which dropped to a little over one-third of the former figure, compensation was found in the growth of trade with other countries. Italy suffered more severely; the total values of her exports and imports showed a sharp decline. Exports to France fell to about one-third of their former amount, the silk trade declined to one-third, the wine trade to one-tenth. The total loss of trade between the two countries in the course of this tariff war has been estimated at three billions of lire, roughly $600,000,000.[1] This estimate appears, however, to cover the whole period to 1898, during which the general tariffs were applied.

In December, 1889, Italy withdrew the special surtaxes, applying thenceforth to imports from France the rates of her high general tariff. In 1892 France adopted, *mutatis mutandis*, a similar course.

The tariff of 1892.—The conflict with Italy was an additional factor strengthening the position of those who demanded a change in French commercial policy. The demand was met in the tariff law of 1892, which not only effected a considerable increase in the level of rates for purposes of protection, but also altered the whole basis of tariff relations by abandoning the general-and-conventional tariff system in favor of an autonomous "maximum-and-minimum" system.

---

[1] Great Britain, Parl. Papers. Reports on Tariff Wars between certain European States, Commercial No. 1. 1904 (Cd. 1938), pp. 15, 21.

The tariff law of 1892 established two sets of rates, those of the general or maximum tariff and those of the minimum tariff. The first article of the law provided that "the minimum tariff may be applied to goods the produce of countries where French goods enjoy equivalent concessions and are admitted at the lowest rates of duty.[1] This tariff, the autonomous act of the French legislature and subject to revision at its pleasure, was to take the place of the previous conventional tariff, which had resulted from bargains with other powers, and had been fixed for a definite period by treaties with them. The difference in level between the rates of the two tariffs, as originally proposed, was estimated by the French tariff commission as approximately 30 per cent; in the final form in which the measure was passed it averaged 25 per cent.

The general object of the measure, comparing it with the previous system, is evidenced by an extract from the report to the French Senate:

> The coexistence of the two tariffs implies the expectation and the desire to enter into tariff agreements. It stimulates them, it gives to foreign nations a picture of the concessions which can be granted them; it invites them to propose such concessions to us in their turn. On the other side, the fact of the establishment of a minimum tariff shows by the very name which is given it and the two words which make up this name, that the agreements will be merely applications of a tariff subject to modifications, and that they will not be able to lower duties below fixed limits. * * * The Chamber of Deputies and the Senate Committee agree in recognizing that the establishment of the minimum tariff is designed to rule out any agreement with a fixed term.[2]

Objections to the policy of a conventional tariff.—An inquiry which the ministry instituted in 1889, the results of which were compiled in 1891, showed a distinct change in opinion since 1875–76, when the system of tariff making by treaty had been acceptable to the majority. Ninety-five chambers of commerce voted for and one against terminating the existing treaties; 66 voted for and 35 voted against abandoning altogether the system of the conventional tariff.

The Government summarized as follows the arguments against the conventional system.[3]

1. Treaties do not respond to changes in conditions of modern industrial production.

2. The clause of the most-favored-nation disturbs the equilibrium established by a preceding treaty.

3. New negotiations and new concessions do not treat different industries impartially, but sacrifice some to others.

Of these criticisms the first, that freedom of action was unduly limited, and the second, that the operation of the most-favored-nation clause generalized favors, were emphasized in the later debates. In the discussion the question of treaty policy was subordinated to the general question of protection versus free trade. The stability of commercial relations under the system of the conventional tariff was called in question, and attention was directed to the frequent changes that treaties had made in the rates on wine and meat, while the periodic revision of a group of treaties was pictured as most disturbing to commerce.

---

[1] U. S. Department of Commerce and Labor, Tariff Series No. 25, p. 11.
[2] For the French text see Augier, C., La France et les traités de commerce, Paris, 1906, p. 66.
[3] Bajkic (Dr.) Wellimer J. " Die Französische Handelspolitik," p. 45.

On the other hand, advocates of the new plan promised that it would give the needed stability in commercial relations and at the same time provide a flexibility in the realm of policy such as was impossible under the conventional system. The government would be able to adjust the tariff rates to suit altering conditions. The critics who suggested that the high rates of the double tariff would stimulate reprisals were assured that their fears were groundless, and reasons were advanced why the different countries would accept the new rates without a contest. In the modern commercial world, it was said, discrimination was more objectionable than a high level of rates equal for all, and equality of treatment was one of the features of the maximum-and-minimum tariff.

Before the final adoption of the new tariff, the Government procured the passage of a law empowering it to prolong the expiring commercial treaties except in so far as they involved fixed rates of duty and to apply the rates of the minimum tariff, in whole or in part, to the wares of those countries which at that time enjoyed the benefit of the conventional tariff and would promise most-favored-nation treatment to France. These arrangements, however, were not to be made binding for more than one year. The debate attending the passage of the law brought from the Minister of Foreign Affairs an expression of doubt as to whether he would be able to maintain in their entirety the rates of the minimum tariff. Exception was taken to this by some among those who had hoped to secure full autonomy in rate making by the adoption of the new plan, and who in this very debate had listened to a depreciation of the German commercial treaties of 1891 as products of an inferior commercial policy; but the debate left still unsettled the question of the exact character of the minimum tariff and of the right or duty of the executive to negotiate departures from it.

Reception of the French tariff of 1892 by other countries.—France had treaties in which rates were fixed with six States—Sweden-Norway, Belgium, the Netherlands, Spain, Portugal, and Switzerland—and all of these treaties expired simultaneously on February 1, 1892. Only one of these States, the first named, was willing to make a treaty (terminable on one year's notice at any time) based on acceptance of the French minimum tariff. Belgium and the Netherlands refused to accept the minimum tariff as adequate compensation for any pledges on their part, but they granted France, on their own volition, most-favored-nation treatment, revocable at any time. Switzerland invited France to a conference looking toward the revision of the minimum rates and, pending its outcome, entered into an agreement for reciprocal most-favored-nation treatment, to be binding until 1893. Spain, like Switzerland, demanded concessions below the minimum tariff before it would grant France the benefit of its lowest scale of rates. Portugal had lately adopted a tariff which appeared to the French unduly high, and she was averse to making any promise of most-favored-nation treatment. Roumania, also, could not be brought to terms. Against these countries, therefore, as against Italy, the French put their general tariff into effect. To England most-favored-nation treatment was extended by law, and to the important States of the Continent, aside from those named above, the advantage of that treatment had been given by previous treaties.

The operation of the French double tariff can not be fairly judged until the full course and conclusion of the conflicts to which it gave rise has been considered. The conventional rates, on which even the supporters of the double tariff laid much stress, had been practically eliminated from the French system. France had indeed secured freedom of action for the time being, but at the cost of isolation. Some States refused to accept the minimum rates as a fair equivalent for the favors expected of them. Other states found no inducement to make specific promises, binding for any period of time, to a country which expressed so frankly its intention to emphasize certain national interests regardless of the reactions which its policy might provoke abroad.

Negotiations with Switzerland.—The Swiss Government announced that it was not disposed to enter into negotiations unless the French would consider some deviation from the rates established in the minimum tariff. The French Government accepted the condition, and agreed that a number of rates might be reduced, in return for the Swiss offer of their conventional tariff with certain rates amended to suit French interests.

This procedure would have meant, of course, a definite surrender of the plan of the minimum tariff almost immediately after its adoption, and it was vigorously opposed, both in the committee to which it was referred for consideration and in the Chamber of Deputies. The points made against it in committee were as follows:

1. The Government had solemnly promised to regard the rates of the minimum tariff as the lowest limit of concession.

2. The minimum tariff formed a whole, with the rates interdependent; and a change in specific items would disturb the balance.

3. The proposed reductions in rates would benefit other countries more than they would Switzerland.

With certain modifications, nevertheless, the proposal was accepted by the committee, only to be rejected by the Chamber as a whole. The Government urged the practical considerations which had moved it to the measure, minimized the scope of the changes, and pictured the evils of the alternative, a tariff war. The opposition of the protectionists was, however, too strong to be overcome, and the measure was defeated by a decisive vote in an early stage of its consideration.

Tariff war with Switzerland.—The Swiss Government maintained its position, defending it with extraordinarily severe measures. The Swiss general tariff was thought to be no effective equivalent for the French, which was termed prohibitive; hence, special punitive rates, many of them borrowed directly from the French general tariff, were applied against French wares. The increase of the rates above those of the Swiss conventional tariff is estimated at 190 per cent; that is, the rates were nearly tripled. "The same quantities, for example, which in 1892 paid duties amounting to 7,650,000 fr., in accordance with the Swiss conventional tariff, were taxed in 1894 at 22,222,000 fr., or an increase of 14,572,000 fr." [1] Silk ribbons which paid a duty of 60 francs per 100 kilos under the conventional tariff, and of 100 under the general tariff, were subjected to a rate of 300 francs if they were of French origin. Silk textiles, which were free

[1] Reports on tariff wars between certain European States (Cd. 1938), Great Britain, Parl. Papers, Commercial No. 1 (1904), p. 3.

under the conventional tariff and dutiable at 16 francs under the general tariff, were subjected to a rate of 400 if of French manufacture. This was the sole example, it is true, of such enormous disparity. On the other side, it is estimated that Swiss wares subject to the French general tariff paid rates higher by about 40 per cent than the minimum; but it must be remembered that the rates of the French general tariff ranged considerably higher than those of the Swiss general tariff, and were in some cases actually higher than those of the Swiss punitive tariff.[1]

Under these conditions there was inevitably a great shrinkage in the trade between the two countries. Comparing the years 1892 and 1894, " French exports for consumption in Switzerland fell from 227,885,000 to 129,871,000 francs, representing a decrease of 98,000,-000 francs, or 43 per cent; while the imports into France from Switzerland shrunk from 91,958,000 to 66,650,000 francs, a decrease of 25,-308,000 francs, or 27 per cent." [2]

Termination and effect of the tariff war.—The period of the tariff war was one of general depression, both in agriculture and in industry, and in Switzerland as in France vigorous protests were made against the continuance and aggravation of this abnormal situation. Conferences of representatives, at first unofficial, prepared the way for formal negotiations, and in June, 1895, a convention was signed to settle the questions at issue.

The arrangement of 1895 differed in nothing but the details from that which the French Government had proposed in 1892. Reductions were made in 29 instead of 62 items, and the French Government refused, as a rule, to reduce the rates on any product which was imported from other countries in greater quantities than from Switzerland. Yet it was undoubtedly the experience of the tariff war, rather than these alterations, which changed the spirit of the French legislature. The measure which, in its first form, had not even reached the stage of detailed discussion, was passed by the Chamber of Deputies by a vote of 513 to 11, and by the Senate without two negative votes.[3] In Switzerland the majority in favor of the compromise was similarly decisive, though the opposition vote was stronger than in France.

The conflict between the two neighboring States had forced both of them to seek elsewhere new markets and sources of supply. Other States, notably Germany and Belgium, profited by this.[4] Of the two contestants, Switzerland, with its relatively low tariff and with its foreign market assured by treaty agreements, appears to have been the more successful in effecting a satisfactory readjustment.[5] The convention of 1895, while it reestablished peaceful commercial relations, could not effect a return to the conditions preceding the tariff war. New habits of trade had established themselves, and the high French tariff still remained a barrier. Figures from the Swiss

---

[1] For the table of rates see Bajkic, " Die Französische Handelspolitik," pp. 155–157.

[2] Reports on tariff wars between certain European States (Cd. 1938), Great Britain, Parl. Papers, Commercial No. 1 (1904), p. 3.

[3] Figures as given by Eysoldt, Grete, " Der Follkrieg zwishen Frankreich und der Schweiz," p. 129. Figures for the votes given by Bajkic, op. cit., pp. 227–228 (vote 485 to 8), show slight differences. It should be noted that France already had reduced some of its " minimum " rates by the convention with Russia of Apr. 17, 1893.

[4] Eysoldt, G., op. cit., chap. 4, pp. 72–115, provides a detailed study of the effect of the tariff war on trade with other countries.

[5] Eyesoldt, op. cit., p. 132.

customs returns show that even in 1902 the trade relations between France and Switzerland had not yet recovered their former prosperity.[1]

Difficulties between France and other countries.—In the relations of France with other States which protested against the tariff of 1892, there were not such serious differences as marked the conflict with Switzerland. Portugal, it is true, was obdurate in refusing most-favored-nation treatment in return for the French minimum tariff, and against her the maximum French rates remained in force; but Portugal invited treatment of this kind at the hand of its neighbors on the Continent, and received it from other countries as well as from France. Spain desired a bettering of the French rates on wines, and refused to grant France the benefit of her lowest rates without some concessions beyond the French minimum rates. A war of punitive rates was threatened, but this was postponed by provisional agreements, and was finally averted by an exchange of notes in December, 1893, in which France and Spain reached an agreement on certain matters of tariff administration which did not involve the change of specific rates of duty. A short tariff war with Roumania, in which case it was France that demanded changes in the other country's rates, was brought to an end by an agreement on the basis of mutual most-favored-nation treatment.

In relations between France and Italy the most bitter period of commercial conflict had preceded the adoption of the French tariff of 1892, but the two countries continued thereafter to apply their high general tariffs in the trade with each other, and did not come finally to terms until 1898, ten years after the beginning of their differences. In the agreement France was able to except from the application of the minimum rates, which she now conceded, silk—a very important item; while Italy granted not only her conventional tariff but also some further reductions in rates.

A statistical survey of the commerce of France with other countries which had assumed, because of the tariff of 1892, an attitude of commercial hostility is presented in the following tables. Values are given in millions of francs, and refer to "special" trade, implying (with important exceptions, however) that the imports were for consumption and the exports were of domestic products.[2]

France—Imports and exports.

	1887	1892	1894	1900	1901
IMPORTS FROM—	*Millions of francs.*	*Millions of francs.*	*Millions of francs.*	*Millions of francs.*	*Millions of francs.*
Spain	356	278	174	220	157
Italy	307	132	121	148	140
Switzerland	104	91	66	107	104
Portugal	38	8	8	11	...
Roumania	35	36	29	26	...
EXPORTS TO—					
Spain	149	134	108	135	122
Italy	192	132	98	155	155
Switzerland	216	227	129	211	217
Portugal	22	13	12	22	20
Roumania	5	8	7	3	5

[1] Reports on tariff wars between certain European States (Cd. 1938), Great Britain, Parl. Papers, Commercial No. 1 (1904), p. 6.
[2] Bajkic, op. cit., p. 424; cf. Annuaire statistique de la France, Résumé rétrospectif, Tableau III.

The tariff law of 1910.—When the time came for the revision of the tariff, which was finally effected in 1910, the principles of autonomy and of the double schedule were accepted as "absolute dogma."[1] The object of the revision was to alter the rates—to increase their effectiveness as instruments of protection rather than to change the form in which the tariff was presented to foreign countries. In the general report to the Chamber of Deputies, the objects were stated to be:

1. To fill up gaps in the tariff made evident by changes in technique and the appearance of new industrial products.

2. To remove anomalies in the rates.

3. To systematize the assessment of wares, particularly in taking account of the amount of labor incorporated in them.

4. To apply with more justice the principle of protection.

The new schedules which were produced were considerably higher than those of the tariff of 1892, as regards both the minimum and the maximum rates. Some rates were reduced,[2] but in general the plan was adopted not only of raising minimum rates, but also of increasing the disparity between these and the maximum rates, making the difference almost systematically 50 per cent.

Maintenance and modification of the system of maximum-and-minimum tariff.—The leaders of French policy professed themselves unalterably opposed to a return to the system of the conventional tariff. Méline, who was at the head of the protectionist party, had said earlier, in reference to the experience of France with Switzerland and its outcome in the lowering of minimum rates, that if the French did not take care they would reach a condition in which they would have none of the advantages of commercial treaties, but would be subject to all their disadvantages.[3] Speaking in the Senate in 1910 he explained, "this time it is really a minimum tariff which we are making, it is not a bargaining tariff" (tarif à négociations).[4] The proposal of an intermediate tariff, of which the rates were to take a place between the minimum rates granted the most-favored nations and the maximum rates established for punitive treatment, was rejected;[5] but a departure in this direction was admitted by article 8 of the new law, as follows:

The Government may, under exceptional circumstances and as a temporary measure, apply the rates of the general tariff of the preceding law to all or some products originating in a country where French products are not discriminated against.

Measures taken to carry out the provisions of the preceding paragraph shall be submitted for ratification to the Chambers, immediately if they should be in session, or as soon as they shall have convened.[6]

Relations with the United States, 1892–1909.—These paragraphs of the new law, as well as certain exceptions made in the rates of the general tariff, were designed to ease relations with the United States, which had not been on the basis of complete most-favored-nation

---

[1] Sayous, André E.: Les modifications apportées au tarif douanier de la France par la loi du 29 Mars, 1910, Révue Econ. Internat., August, 1910, vol. 7, pt. 3, p. 237.

[2] See the list in Sayous, op. cit., pp. 241–242; most of the wares affected were of slight importance.

[3] Méline, J.: Traités de commerce et conventions commerciales, Révue Econ. Internat., January, 1917, vol. 4, pt. 1, p. 27.

[4] Sayous, op. cit., p. 238.

[5] The text of the proposal, its application limited to "exceptional circumstances," will be found in U. S. Department of Commerce and Labor, Tariff Series No. 6 E, p. 5.

[6] U. S. Department of Commerce and Labor, Tariff Series No. 25, 1910, p. 15.

treatment since the passage of the French act of 1892. Through this long interval of time France had never granted the minimum rates in their entirety to the United States. In 1893, to meet the threat contained in a provision of the McKinley Act of 1890, which empowered the President to impose duties on certain products if in his judgment the exporting country levied duties on American products "reciprocally unjust or unreasonable," the French Government had made some slight concessions. In return for the free admission to the United States of sugar, hides, and a few other products, France conceded the minimum rates on canned meats, fruit in various forms, hops, and some of the cruder forms of wood.[1] The concessions affected articles which amounted altogether to a little over one-fortieth (18 million out of 773 million) in the value of the trade between the two nations.[2] The list of concessions on the French side was extended later by the inclusion of mineral oils; and it was further amended in 1898, when a convention was arranged to take advantage of the reciprocity provisions of the Dingley Act. At that time mineral oils were dropped from the list, and sausages and lard were added. The French duties on these meat products had recently been raised considerably, but with a proviso in the act that the minimum rates applicable to them might be granted to countries not enjoying the full minimum tariff. France was opposed to any departure from autonomy in tariff making, but could evidently, by doling out piecemeal the favors of the minimum tariff, follow a method of bargaining not altogether unlike that involved in framing a conventional tariff. A convention signed July 25, 1899, would have given the United States most, though not all, of the rates of the minimum tariff, in return for certain reductions in the established rates on the American side; but this convention was not ratified by the United States, and it never went into effect. The fact that it was under consideration, however, secured for the United States the benefit of a curious provision in the French law of February 24, 1900, which increased the general rates on coffee and other semitropical or tropical products, but authorized the continuance of the minimum rates on these products to countries with which a treaty of commerce was pending at the time of the passage of the law. This concession was granted to the United States (in 1902 also to Porto Rico) by decrees which were renewed as they expired, in spite of the failure of the United States to ratify the convention of 1899.[3]

It has been estimated that these various concessions to the United States affected from one-third to one-half, in value, of all the dutiable American imports into France. They were all rendered void, however, by the passage of the American tariff of 1909, which terminated all reciprocity arrangements. For five months all imports from the United States were subjected in France to the rates of the maximum tariff.

Relations with the United States under the tariff law of 1910.—Thus matters stood immediately before the passage of the French tariff of 1910. The Governments of France and of the United States had been

[1] See Part I, p. 155, infra. Also see references and details in U. S., Tariff Series No. 6, p. 99 ; and No. 25, p. 8.
[2] Bajkic, op. cit., p. 163.
[3] See Part I, p. 211, infra.

in negotiation, and though a treaty between them for the amendment of conditions was not consistent with the French policy of the period, the French legislature passed, on the day on which the new tariff law was enacted, an act regulating commercial relations with the United States. This act authorized the Government to admit from the United States at the minimum rates the wares which had previously been privileged, numbering 25 according to the tariff classification, and 68 additional; and in accordance with the special provisions of the new tariff law quoted above, it allowed to be imported under the rates of the old general tariff certain other articles to the number of 45.[1]

More than two-thirds (67.1 per cent in 1908) of the American imports were already, and would remain, entitled to enter free of duty. Of the remainder, with the concessions made by or under the act of 1910, it was estimated that 29.3 per cent of the total imports would be admitted at the rates of the minimum tariff; 0.4 per cent would be admitted at the old general rates, now intermediate between the new general and the minimum; and 3.2 per cent of the total imports would be subjected to the rates of the new general tariff.[2]

Relations with European States under the tariff law of 1910.—The French tariff of 1910 was accepted by the other States of Europe without the conflicts which had followed the enactment of the law of 1892. Protests, it is true, were made by Germany and Belgium against rates of duty which were thought to be exorbitantly high, but only in the case of Belgium was the feeling sufficiently strong to lead to threats of commercial war. The committee on tariffs of the Belgian Superior Council of Industry and Commerce condemned the French tariff unanimously, expressed the hope that France might be induced to return to the treaty system of the former period, and suggested that an increase in Belgian rates on such French exports as wines would be a proper form of retaliation. A measure of reprisal was formulated by the Belgian Minister of Finance, which received the support of many representatives of industrial interests but was not adopted.

---

[1] U. S. Department of Commerce and Labor * * * Tariff Series No. 25, p. 9.
[2] Ibid, p. 10.

THE COMMERCIAL POLICY AND TARIFF SYSTEM OF RUSSIA.

Survey of Russian commercial policy.—Upon Russia, as upon the States of western Europe, the commercial liberalism of the third quarter of the nineteenth century had its effect. Between 1850 and 1875 the average rate of duties upon imports was reduced by about one-half. When Germany began the return to higher duties, Russia promptly followed. By 1884 the low average which had prevailed during the years 1869–1876 was raised by about 50 per cent; by 1890 it had been doubled; by the end of the century it had been almost tripled. On certain types of goods the rates were exceedingly high. It was estimated in 1904 that the average rate on British manufactures was 131 per cent ad valorem.[1] The import trade, it is interesting to note, had reached its highest figure during the period of the lowest duties; it had risen steadily as the rates were reduced; it declined thereafter steadily as the rates were increased, until 1890, after which there was some recovery in the last decade of the century. The following table shows how the rates of duty were reduced and raised and how the value of imports increased and decreased:[2]

	Percentage of duties levied in proportion to total value of imports.		Annual average value of imports (millions of pounds sterling).
1851–1856	24.0	1861–1865	22.0
1857–1868	17.6	1866–1870	33.8
1869–1876	12.8	1871–1875	60.4
1877–1880	16.1	1876–1880	55.2
1881–1884	18.7	1881–1885	52.8
1885–1890	28.3	1886–1890	41.9
1891–1900	33.0	1891–1895	49.5

The movement toward a higher level of rates, which marked the last quarter of the century, was due in part to influences which were common to other European countries, the development of nationalist feeling, and the pressure of industrial interests seeking protection. In part also it was directed against Germany in retaliation for the increases in the German tariffs of 1879, and 1887, of the rates of duty on important Russian export products. There was, however, in Russian commercial policy a fiscal factor which has in no other country shown equal force. Not only did the Russian treasury seek revenue from the tariff to provide for its military expenditures and the costs of internal development; it sought by means of the tariff to control the balance of trade and to protect the national currency from an outflow of specie. To reach these ends, duties were levied

---

[1] Schooling, John H., British Trade Book, London, 1911, p. 340, citing (Cd. 2337), 1904.
[2] Report on tariff wars between certain European States, Great Britain Parl. Papers, Commercial No. 1, 1904 (Cd. 1938), p. 41.

not only on manufactures but also on partly manufactured wares and even on raw materials, and on occasion these were raised abruptly by large amounts.

For her tariff purposes Russia employed the autonomous single-schedule system, which was, in all probability, the system best adapted to the stage of her development and the circumstances of her commerce. Russia was not yet fully within the current of European commercial influences. Though she had with various States commercial treaties stipulating unrestriced most-favored-nation treatment, she had in certain treaties limited the scope of favors and concessions by the use of the conditional form of the favored-nation clause; and, in her relations with two important neighbors, Austria and Germany, she had no claim of any kind to share in favored-nation treatment.

Departure from the system of single-schedule tariff, 1893.—The adoption by Germany in 1891 of the practices of the general-and-conventional tariff system forced Russia to depart from her established practice. In the single month of June, 1893, Russia adopted machinery both of the maximum-and-minimum and of the general-and-conventional systems. She began the month with a single schedule, with rates at the level to which they had been raised by legislation in 1891. On June 13, she established by law alongside this schedule another, of which the rates were higher by from 20 to 30 per cent, this being intended to serve as a weapon against Germany. On June 17, she acquired, through the coming into force of the commercial treaty with France, a conventional schedule of which some rates were 25 per cent below the general level. As the treaty with France was subject to abrogation on one year's notice, it involved only a limited cession of tariff autonomy on the part of Russia.

It was explained officially that the adoption of the higher schedule was intended to prevent the unjust and discriminatory treatment of Russian agricultural exports by some of the States in western Europe. The maximum schedule was undoubtedly framed for the specific purpose of forcing Germany to concede a more generous treatment of Russian exports. The rates were adjusted to the measure of the differential duties to which Russian exports were subjected in countries like Germany. Russians disclaimed any aggressive inclinations in commercial policy and in support of this were able to cite the reduction of rates to which they agreed in the French treaty.

Adoption of the general-and-conventional system.—The application of the maximum schedule led to a tariff war with Germany which was brought to an end by a commercial treaty which marked the definite acceptance by Russia of the general-and-conventional tariff system. The transition and this new conclusion in Russian policy were the products of political as well as economic considerations. The commercial treaty with France had been negotiated at a time when the two countries were drawing together in support of their international interests. Although the word "alliance" was first used officially in reference to their relationship in 1895, the Russian Government had contracted loans in Paris in 1889 and 1891, and there were various conspicuous evidences of the growing rapprochement during the years 1890–1895. At the same time the relations between Russia and Germany had been unsatisfactory in other respects than merely commercial for some years. Since 1887, when

German capitalists under Bismarck's influence had sold out their Russian investments, the German Reichsbank had refused to lend on Russian security. The commercial treaty of 1894, which brought to an end the tariff war between Russia and Germany, contained no provision regarding this matter. But the Berlin money market was again opened to Russian borrowers in 1894, and the resumption of normal commercial relations was attended by a more friendly attitude, both in business and in politics. Among the reasons advanced by the Russian State Council for concluding the treaty of 1894, the economic advantages of the opening afforded for Russian exports and of the assurance of settled conditions for a term of ten years were recognized, but the treaty was probably completed as much on political grounds as on the basis of economic interests.

The treaty of 1894 did not remove all causes of difference between the two countries, and in the years immediately following, measures on the part of each State gave rise to complaints from the other. Nevertheless, the trade between the two countries increased rapidly under the new conditions.

Commercial treaties with other States.—In her relations with other European countries, Russia employed the general-and-conventional tariff systems to which she had committed herself in the treaties with France and Germany. She concluded treaties with Austria, Serbia, Portugal, Denmark, Belgium, and Bulgaria, which followed in general the model of the German treaty and pledged, except in the case of Portugal, unrestricted most-favored-nation treatment on both sides. The number of the rates which were fixed by these new treaties was relatively small.

Use of penalty duties.—After the tariff war with Germany in 1893, Russia appears to have made no other general application of the rates of the maximum schedule. When, in 1901, the United States levied countervailing duties on Russian sugar which had been granted an export bounty, the Russian Government protested that this was a violation of rights arising under the most-favored-nation clause. Unsuccessful in the prosecution of this claim, it levied penalty duties, higher by from 30 to 50 per cent than the conventional rates, on various manufactures of iron and steel imported from the United States, and a few months later on some other articles. These special punitive rates were restricted to a relatively limited number of articles, and they were withdrawn in 1905.[1]

Tariff of 1903.—As the time drew near when the treaty with Germany was to expire, Russia anticipated new negotiations and prepared for them by the adoption, in 1903, of a new general tariff, designed for bargaining purposes. Rates were raised on many items, particularly on manufactured wares, by about 50 per cent as compared with the rates of 1891; on some articles the rates were more than doubled. The schedule was more sharply specialized than before and was made again to include the provision which had been, before 1894, so obnoxious to Germany; goods imported by land were to pay duties 20 per cent higher than those levied on goods imported by sea.[2]

---

[1] See Part I, p. 220, infra.
[2] The essential portions of the new tariff and comparison of the rates with those preceding are printed in Great Britain, Parliamentary Papers, 1903 (Cd. 1525), vol. 75.

Treaties after 1903.—Germany offered as a basis of negotiation the new general tariff of 1902, in which the duties on agricultural products had been raised and on the most important foodstuffs minimum rates were fixed below which the Government was forbidden to make concessions. The Russian representatives exerted themselves to obtain concessions in respect to these items and, as their demands were refused, held resolutely to the increased rates of their own tariff on industrial products. Some reductions were made on each side; Russia gave up the proposed surtax on goods imported by land, the surrender of which meant a benefit to other countries as well as to Germany; but the net result was an increase of rates on both sides. A German authority has suggested that Russia was brought to terms only when Germany threatened again to withdraw the privileges of the Berlin money market, at a time when Russia particularly needed financial support.[1]

The treaty with Germany was concluded in 1904. It was followed in the next year by a treaty with France, in which Russia pledged the continuance of the lower rates established in the treaty of 1893 on many articles, and conceded on some articles a reduction of rates below the previous level. Treaties following in general the lines laid down in the German treaty were made with several other States, including Austria-Hungary, Italy, and Portugal. The new tariff went into effect on March 1, 1906.

Before the period for which the treaties were to run had expired, the beginning of the European war had interrupted commercial relations between Russia and her Teutonic neighbors. In March, 1915, the Russian Government ordered by imperial decree a "temporary increase of the rates of the general customs tariff for Europe." The conventional rates established in the treaties with Germany and Austria-Hungary were abrogated; no change was made in reference to goods the duties on which were fixed by the treaties with France, Italy, and Portugal; the former rates on a small number of specified articles remained in force; the goods which were previously affected by the rates of the German and the Austro-Hungarian treaties were, together with all other goods, with the exception of certain specified articles, to pay the former general rates increased by 10 per cent. The differential duties established in the law of 1903 in respect to duties on various classes of goods imported over the European land frontier were restored to operation, the effect being in almost all cases a 20 per cent increase over the rates on imports by sea. It was understood that the measure was of a temporary nature due to existing circumstances, pending a complete revision and reissue of the general tariff at the conclusion of the war.

---

[1] Zweig, E.: Die Russische Handelspolitik, p. 54.

Countries employing the general-and-conventional system.—As Russia was affected by the influence of Germany, so, in varying degree, have been Austria-Hungary, Bulgaria, Greece, Italy, Portugal, Roumania, Serbia, Sweden, and Switzerland. All of these have adopted the general-and-conventional tariff system; all have made treaties involving, reciprocally, tariff concessions.

Sweden and Switzerland alone of this group, having remained neutrals, have suffered from the present war no interruption of their commercial treaty relations. The tariff treaties of Italy were affected by the fact of the war perhaps less than were those of any other of the major European belligerents. Italy had concluded between 1900 and 1914 some 10 treaties or agreements in which she had made tariff concessions. One was with Brazil; one with Japan; one only, that with Germany, was with a State which became, by the war, an enemy to Italy.[1] Most of these treaties were to expire at the end of 1917, and due notice was given by the Italian Government of its intention to regard the treaties as terminated at that time. On December 30, 1917, however, the Government announced that it would continue in force until December 31, 1918, the rates of duty fixed by the treaties (or agreements) with Brazil, France, Japan, Greece, Roumania, Servia, Spain, and Switzerland.

Systems in force in Spain.—Spain originated the maximum-and-minimum system; she is still classed as a maximum-and-minimum tariff country; but her practice has become essentially that of the general-and-conventional system. The Spanish tariff law of March 20, 1906, provided that the rates of import duties should be revised every five years. The revision was duly made in 1911, the new tariff going into effect on January 1, 1912. This law stands at present, the revision due in 1916 not having been made on account of the war. It establishes, in form, a two-schedule tariff. But Spain had earlier (and subsequent to her adoption of the maximum-and-minimum system) made with several European States treaties wherein she conceded rates lower than those in the minimum schedule of her statutory tariff; these treaties are still in force; and the benefit of the treaty rates accrues to all States entitled to most-favored-nation treatment. This means that there has been created and is in operation a third, a "conventional" schedule. Furthermore, special concessions have been made to Portugal, with respect to which it is expressly stated in Spain's treaties with other States that the operation of the most-favored-nation clause does not apply. The special treatment of Portugal was based on provisions of a treaty of March 27, 1893. This treaty was denounced on September 4, 1912, but a modus vivendi was arranged shortly thereafter, pending the adoption of a new commercial treaty. Portugal thus has the advantage of a special, essentially a fourth, set of rates. The net effect in the actual application of the Spanish tariff is this: Those States only which are not entitled to most-favored-nation treatment are subject to the maximum rates; two countries only, Colombia and Ecuador, pay the rates of the minimum (second) schedule; countries party to the tariff treaties, and

---

[1] For list of all Italian commercial treaties in force June 1, 1914, see Giretti, E.: Trattati di commercio e politica dogarale, 1914, Appendix III.

others entitled to most-favored-nation treatment pay the "conventional" rates; and Portugal pays "preferential" rates. It will thus be seen that the tariff plan actually in operation in Spain exhibits features of each of the systems distinguishable under the appellation "multiple tariff systems." The Spanish system, as it stands in actual operation, should be associated with, the general-and-conventional group rather than with the maximum-and-minimum group.

The maximum-and-minimum system in practice.—France and Norway employ the maximum-and-minimum system. Spain is usually thought of, as just indicated, as using this system, but her practice exhibits a combination in which the making of rates by treaty appears an accepted procedure. The theory of the maximum-and-minimum tariff is that there shall be two schedules of rates, made autonomously, below the lower of which the treaty-making authorities may not make concessions. The practice, however, does not always correspond to the theory. The Spanish minimum schedule did not continue to be the lowest rate applied. France also has found it necessary to grant certain reductions below the rates of the enacted minimum. This occurred, for instance, in bringing to a conclusion the tariff war with Switzerland. In the French tariff law of 1910 provision was made to facilitate the work of the treaty-making authorities, by the granting of authority to impose special duties to offset discriminations on the part of other countries against French products.

"Preferential" tariff system.—No State in Europe employs a tariff which can be designated as a "preferential" system. For purposes of comparison, however, it is desirable to refer again to features of that system. Like the general-and-conventional and the maximum-and-minimum systems, it requires at least two schedules; unlike the former, it is autonomous; unlike the latter, its minimum schedule is intended not for the most-favored nations, but for specially "preferred" nations. Under other systems it frequently happens that special treatment, excepted from the operation of the most-favored-nation clause, is established between countries in respect to whose relationship there are peculiar circumstances; but this is usually accomplished by agreement. In the case of Spain and Portugal, for instance, the preferential treatment is mutual and is based on a reciprocal agreement. But where a "preferential" tariff system, in the accepted sense of the term, is in use, one country establishes by its own legislation a régime of special treatment in favor of another or others.

The Canadian system affords the most conspicuous example of this. In the Canadian tariff there are three schedules of duties, all enacted by law—a general, an intermediate, and a British preferential schedule. The rates of the general schedule are applied to imports from all countries not entitled by law or by treaty to special treatment. The intermediate schedule is intended as an instrument for negotiation—its rates may be applied to the products of any country "in consideration of benefits satisfactory to the Governor in Council." Since 1897 Canada has given preference to imports from the United Kingdom. The preference consisted originally of a reduction of one-eighth from the general duties on almost all dutiable articles; in 1898 this reduction was made one-fourth; and in 1900 it was made one-third. In 1906 the uniform deduction was discontinued and specific rates were prescribed for British goods. By this change it became possible to adjust the preference to the individual requirements of trade in given articles; it also rendered simpler the calculations to be made by customs officials.

South Africa, Australia, and New Zealand have all followed the example of Canada in the establishment of a preferential schedule in favor of certain British articles. Between several continental European countries and their colonies, preferential practices in some form and degree are in force. Brazil enacts each year a preferential schedule on a limited list of American products.

The single-schedule system passing.—The countries of Europe which still adhere to the single-schedule system are either "free trade" countries, like the United Kingdom, Belgium, Denmark, and the Netherlands, or countries of minor commercial importance, such as Turkey. The characteristic feature of the system is the employment of but one schedule of duties, the same rates being applicable to the same goods from all countries. Even with a single schedule, however, it is possible to establish special rates for particular commodities from particular countries, as has been done, for instance, in the reciprocity experiences of the United States.

There has been a marked tendency toward the abandonment of the single-schedule system, especially among countries in whose tariff policies protection is a feature. Even the countries which have nominally retained the single schedule have found it to their advantage to adopt some of the expedients and methods of multiple tariff systems.

Advantages and disadvantages of the various systems.—No one of the systems is in all its features exclusive. Each has some of the features of some of the others. The peculiar characteristic of each must be sought not in its parts, but in its grouping of features. The virtues of each must be estimated in relation to the condition and circumstances of the country which practices it.

The single-schedule system has certain advantages in administration. A single schedule is, obviously, simpler in application than a multiple schedule. Where the unconditional interpretation of the most-favored-nation provision is in vogue, there is no difficulty as to most-favored-nation treatment—except as there may be deliberate attempts at evasion; all nations are presumably to be treated alike. As against this advantage, the single-schedule system lacks elasticity, and is not adapted to negotiations for promoting export trade. The country which has only one tariff schedule is at a disadvantage in negotiating with another which has two or more schedules. If it is a free-trade country, it can offer nothing in the way of tariff concessions. If it is a protectionist country, any concessions which it grants tend to make a breach in the wall of its protection and may necessitate some readjustment in its fiscal arrangements. The more its inclination to generalize such concessions, the more disturbingly is this the consequence. The less it is willing to generalize the concessions, the more and the greater the difficulties in which it is likely to find itself with countries which call for unconditional most-favored-nation treatment.

One unquestionable advantage the single-schedule system possesses; it is autonomous. This advantage the preferential system shares with it. The preferential system, on the other hand, though it is less simple, is superior in elasticity. Devised partly for bargaining, the characteristic feature of the preferential system is that its minimum schedule is established by law to apply, without negotiation, to imports from a given country or countries, with the deliberate intention of favoring these exclusively. This means, of course, that its application between independent nations would usually provoke objections and protest. Actually, preferential treatment among the British self-governing dominions and in favor of the United Kingdom has been the subject of no little amount of complaint on the part of States which consider this contrary to the requirements of their most-favored-nation agreements with Great Britain.

Among the advantages claimed for the maximum-and-minimum system the most conspicuous is the maintenance of "tariff autonomy." Though the theory of the system implies the retention of tariff autonomy, its working does not assure this, as shown in the experience of Spain. Though autonomy in rate making may be retained, this does not guarantee independence, as shown in the experiences of France.

A second advantage attributed to the maximum-and-minimum as compared with the general-and-conventional system is that it gives assurance to the home producer that the rates of duty will not within a given period be reduced below a given point. The reality of the assurance may be doubted and disputed; at best it is relative rather than absolute. The likelihood of stability in the minimum rates is, of course, increased when the change can be made only by the legislature and not by the executive.

A third advantage claimed for the system is that it makes bargaining possible and yet retains in the hands of the legislature the making of the schedules of duty, thus avoiding the transfer to the executive of a certain measure of authority in connection with the fiscal machinery. This feature it does not possess exclusively. Its value is susceptible of various estimates from differing points of view.

Among the disadvantages of the maximum-and-minimum system, as compared with the general-and-conventional, is the fact that the former has not the elasticity and does not allow, in general, the promptness of action and nicety of adjustment possible in the latter. With a general schedule carefully devised for purposes of bargaining, and with the bargaining process itself subsequently entrusted to experts, the granting of concessions may be accomplished with more logical reference to the needs of a given moment than in a system where the concessional rates are fixed and every considerable alteration must wait upon legislative action.

In attributing credit to the maximum-and-minimum system for keeping control of rate-making within the hands of the legislature, it must not be overlooked that there is nothing inherent in the general-and-conventional system requiring that the legislature surrender this control. If, as is generally the case, the treaty-making authority is required to submit the treaties, in which it has made concessions, to the legislature for approval, it remains that the actual fixing of the rates is the work of the legislature. Where this procedure is followed, it may even be contended that there has been no real surrender of tariff "autonomy." In agreeing to maintain certain rates, as fixed by treaty, a State is thus temporarily by the action of its own legislature placing a check upon its own freedom of action in case it be inclined within the period prescribed to change these rates.

The general-and-conventional system has perhaps the maximum of elasticity. In the use which it makes of experts, and in its dissociation of tariff problems from questions of domestic politics, it tends to promote continuity of policy and action. It has superior possibilities in the realm of promptness.

To appraise the claim made for the maximum-and-minimum system that it confers stability by insuring the maintenance of specified minimum rates, it must be taken into consideration that the alternative system also tends to foster stability. The general-and-conventional system by establishing rates in a series of treaties " fixes " them for a known, and often long, period of years, for such treaty rates are not likely to be altered during the treaty period.

In estimating the success of the general-and-conventional system in Germany, the fact should not be overlooked that the German Government has incorporated in its tariff system some of the features of the maximum-and-minimum system. It has adopted the plan of setting, by the action of the legislature, limits below which the treaty-making authority may not make reductions; otherwise leaving to the executive wide discretion in the negotiation of treaties, it has required that the treaties be ratified by the legislature. Several other factors, supplementary to, rather than inherent in the German tariff system, must be kept in mind: German " thoroughness " has been as conspicuously active in commercial as in some other fields; German economic enterprises have achieved a momentum bound to have an apparent effect at every point of commercial contact. In respect both to the promotion of production and to the solving of problems of distribution and consumption, as well as in connection with tariff rate-making and treaty negotiations, the government has taken particular pains to use the best expert talent and insure the best possible scientific investigation and determination.

If the treaty-making authority be entrusted entirely to the executive, the general-and-conventional tariff system may tend to diminish the relative importance of the legislative authority, and to throw rate-making and administration mainly into the hands of the executive. But these consequences are not necessary to the employment of the system.

The maximum-and-minimum feature in the United States tariff act of 1909.—In the approach to the maximum-and-minimum system which was made by the United States in the tariff act of 1909, the authority of the executive was severely restricted. Unlike the plan in the European systems, in this act it was prescribed that the general schedule, instead of being the maximum, should be the minimum. Its rates would be, therefore, those which would apply to the most-favored nations. Taking the general rates as the basic schedule, the maximum rates were to be determined by adding uniformly 25 per cent of the value of the import. The maximum rates were to be applied to imports from any country which discriminated against the exports of the United States. This was in fact a penalty duty provision. In actual operation the Government, after negotiations, in no case found itself in a position where it was deemed necessary for the President to apply the maximum rates.

Most-favored-nation practice in relation to the maximum-and-minimum and the general-and-conventional systems.—When a European country has granted, either by legislation or by treaty, a tariff concession in favor of one country, that concession becomes, through the operation of the most-favored-nation clause under the European interpretation, generalized in favor of other countries which are entitled to favored-nation treatment. This remains true whichever tariff system is employed. Commercial agreements either provide simply for most-favored-nation treatment, or specify rates of duty on certain articles and pledge in addition most-favored-nation treatment. The requirements of the maximum-and-minimum system are better met, apparently, by the former than by the latter type of agreement; the general-and-conventional system is best served by the latter type, in fact, requires it.

Germany concluded treaties with the important commercial countries, in which, regularly, tariff concessions were made reciprocally. In the negotiating of such treaties, concessions are sought by each State on the leading products which figure in its export trade to the other. It is obvious that, although the rates which are conceded become subsequently applicable to imports from all favored-nation States, nevertheless it may be expected that the bulk of the imports of the specified commodities will come from the State which has particularly sought and in original treaties obtained the concession.

The experience of the Japanese treaties of 1911 will illustrate this. In four of the 12 commercial treaties which Japan made during and soon after 1911—the treaties with Great Britain, Germany, France, and Italy—tariff concessions were made reciprocally. By virtue of the fact that Japan extended unconditional most-favored-nation treatment to practically all nations entitled to favored-nation treatment, the rates of the conventional schedules became applicable to the imports of all nations alike. The skill with which the bargaining States on the European side had chosen their concessions may be inferred from the exhibit in the following table:

Imports into Japan and benefits of the conventional rates, 1912, 1913, 1914.

Total imports into Japan from—					
Countries having conventions establishing rates—				Country not having such convention but whose exports to Japan resemble those of Germany.	Country not having such convention and whose exports to Japan were not within the classes specifically provided for.
Great Britain.	France.	Italy.	Germany.	Austria-Hungary.	United States.
Yen. 331,000,000	*Yen.* 15,500,000	*Yen.* 2,634,000	*Yen.* 174,000,000	*Yen.* 9,037,000	*Yen.* 346,000,000
Amount of the above benefiting by conventional rates.					
Yen. 77,224,000	*Yen.* 5,411,000	*Yen.* 1,163,000	*Yen.* 39,391,000	*Yen.* 4,375,000	*Yen.* 6,956,000
Percentage of the above benefited by the conventional rates.					
23.31	34.91	44.15	22.64	48.42	2.01

The tendency in framing tariff schedules is toward detailed specifications. It is possible by the use of minute descriptions, either in the treaty or in the tariff law, to limit the applicability of a reduction in rate to the commodities of the country with which a particular tariff bargain is made. In this manner similar but not identical products of other countries are excluded, and real discrimination established. The detailed specification in the German tariff with regard to certain sorts of cattle illustrates this practice in legislation. The definitions of " port wine " and " Madeira wine " in the treaty concluded between Germany and Portugal in 1910 show to what extent the particularization may be carried in treaty making. There it was agreed that—

The designation "port wine" shall be confined to grape wines produced in a wine region of the Portuguese district of Douro and shipped with the proper certificates of origin and purity through the port of Oporto. Similarly, "Madeira wine" shall be confined to grape wines produced in the island of Maderia and shipped * * * through the port of Funchal.

It is, then, by no means accurate to assert or to assume that the generalizing of concessions under the European construction of the most-favored-nation clause means the establishing of complete equality of treatment in a given market.

One thing tariff treaties do accomplish positively and effectively: They fix or "bind," rates of duty for a specified term, insuring that they will not be increased. In some cases the rates thus fixed are reduced rates; in others they are merely those of the general tariff. Tariff treaties take from the States which make them, the right during the treaty period, to increase the rates, regardless of changes which may occur in economic or political conditions; and they offer to all countries, for a definite period,[1] certainty that the rates on the articles thus provided for will not be raised.

---

[1] Tariff treaties are usually framed for a specified period, frequently ten years.

UNITED STATES RECIPROCITY TREATIES.

Treaties, conventions, agreements, etc.--Continued.

Wines:

    duties on. in act of 1897, 202.

    imports of, under argol agreements, 231, seq.

Witte, Count. 221.

Wood alcohol, exports to Germany, 253.

Wood, military governor of Cuba, urges tariff concessions to Cuba, 318.

Wood pulp and paper, duties on, Canadian, 37, 280, 411.

Wool:

    trade in, under Canadian reciprocity, 87.

    Hawaiian, 122, 123, 126.

    Latin American, 142.

    from Argentina and Chile, 142, 157.

    proposal for penalty duty on, 148.

    in act of 1890, 149.

    from Mexico, 157.

    concessions on Argentine wool in Kasson treaty, 220.

Wool clothing, imports of, into Cuba, 354.

Woolens, in treaty of 1899 with France, 216.

Worsted spinning in United States, and free admission of Canadian wool, 80.

Zanzibar, m. f. n. treaty with United States, 1833, 404; 1902, 404.

Zollverein, German treaty with, 1844, 59.

ADDITIONAL COPIES

OF THIS PUBLICATION MAY BE PROCURED FROM
THE SUPERINTENDENT OF DOCUMENTS
GOVERNMENT PRINTING OFFICE
WASHINGTON, D. C.
AT
50 CENTS PER COPY ·